B. H. ROBERTS

One of the earliest images of B. H. Roberts. It was probably taken around the time he graduated from the University of Deseret.

B. H. ROBERTS

A LIFE IN THE PUBLIC ARENA

JOHN SILLITO

SIGNATURE BOOKS | 2021 | SALT LAKE CITY

For Richard C. Roberts, 1932–2017,
good friend, valued colleague, and my link to the man himself

 Printed domestically on paper certified by the Sustainable Forestry Initiative.

The opinions expressed in this book are not necessarily those of the publisher. Photos courtesy of the author, except as noted.

Jacket design by Jason Francis

FIRST EDITION | 2021

LIBRARY OF CONGRESS CATALOGING-IN-PUBLICATION DATA

Names: Sillito, John R., author.

Title: B. H. Roberts : a life in the public arena / John Sillito.

Description: First edition. | Salt Lake City : Signature Books, 2021. | Includes bibliographical references and index. | Summary: "Without question, Mormonism's most influential scholar was during the first half of the twentieth century was B. H. Roberts (1857–1933), historian, theologian, public intellectual, and member of the First Council of Seventy of the Church of Jesus Christ of Latter-day Saints. Outside of his official church duties and his passion for research and writing, Roberts was an active figure in partisan politics, having run for Congress twice, elected once, but due to opposition from both political parties over polygamy, was never seated. This biography by prize-winning historian John Sillito, the fullest and most scholarly assessment to date of the controversial church leader, examines Roberts's entire life, with particular attention to the public figure who remains influential, even today. Born in England to LDS convert parents, Roberts served as a missionary and several years after his call as a general authority, at age sixty began serving as a chaplain during World War I. From 1922–27 he presided over the church's Eastern States Mission. Although a hero to many even today for his scholarly output—a feat still rare among those called to church leadership—modern assessments recognize antiquated views on race and women's suffrage. Yet Roberts remains a deeply compelling figure worthy of study"— Provided by publisher.

Identifiers: LCCN 2021023419 (print) | LCCN 2021023420 (ebook) | ISBN 9781560852940 (hardback) | ISBN 9781560854005 (ebook)

Subjects: LCSH: Roberts, B. H. (Brigham Henry), 1857–1933. | Mormon scholars—Biography. | Religion historians—United States—Biography. | Politicians—Utah—Biography. | LCGFT: Biographies.

Classification: LCC BX8695.R58 S55 2021 (print) | LCC BX8695.R58 (ebook) | DDC 289.3092 [B]—dc23

LC record available at https://lccn.loc.gov/2021023419
LC ebook record available at https://lccn.loc.gov/2021023420

CONTENTS

INTRODUCTION

It has been more than eighty years since Brigham Henry Roberts died—a period longer than his time on earth. During his adult lifetime, and since, Roberts was regarded by many as Mormonism's preeminent public intellectual. He was one of the LDS Church's seven presidents of the Seventy, and a prolific author of polemics, histories, biographies, and even fiction. His best known works—the two multi-volume studies, *History of the Church of Jesus Christ of Latter-day Saints* and *Comprehensive History of the Church*—along with his other histories, are still quoted by general readers and scholars alike, despite the more professional "New Mormon History" which has emerged in the last forty years. He produced hundreds of articles in newspapers and journals, and many more sermons and talks—exhorting the faithful from the pulpit of the Salt Lake Tabernacle as well as in LDS wards and stakes in this country and abroad.

Roberts embraced plural marriage; he married three women and spent a term in the Utah territorial prison because of his commitment. Compelling evidence suggests that his third marriage occurred after the Woodruff Manifesto despite his and his third wife's claim that it had taken place in spring 1890. Roberts struggled with accepting Woodruff's 1890 pronouncement, thinking it shortchanged his own commitment and that of others to the "Principle." While he would come to make his peace with that change, he maintained his decisions even to the point of personal sacrifice.

Simultaneously, he was active as a political figure, helping to build the "Sagebrush Democracy"—the nineteenth-century term for Utah's Democratic Party. Roberts served in the state's constitutional convention, campaigned for Congress twice, was elected once, and then was denied the seat he won because of his practice of plural marriage. As a partisan political figure, he made both friends and enemies—especially early on when he opposed adding a provision for woman suffrage into the Utah constitution. And even though his expulsion from Congress in effect ended his political career, at least as a candidate, Roberts always maintained an active interest in politics generally, and the Democratic Party specifically. As an "Elder Statesman," his voice was heard in party councils and on the hustings in support of various candidates. For example, at the 1916 Utah Democratic convention, his support played a major role in the 1916 nomination of Simon Bamberger, Utah's first—and so far only—Jewish governor

When he was at the height of his powers, Roberts may have been the best-known and most recognizable Mormon figure both within the church and throughout the nation, partly due to the notoriety he gained in the national campaign to deny him a seat in Congress. Roberts is also considered by many to be among the handful of significant intellectuals produced by Mormonism. Clearly, he was one of the most important thinkers of Mormonism's second generation—those who matured in the Utah period. Noted historian Leonard J. Arrington called Roberts "the intellectual leader of the Mormon people in the era of Mormonism's finest intellectual attainment."[1] Brigham D. Madsen, one of the most thoughtful and important students of Roberts, believed that he was marked by a "deeply imbedded integrity," and that he "had the capacity to change his views when confronted with new and persuasive evidence."[2] However, Roberts was a product of his times when it came to race. He was one of the earliest proponents of what became the priesthood ban for black males, writing, "That the Negro is markedly inferior to the Caucasian is proved both craniologically and by six thousand years of planet-wide experimentation; and that the commingling of inferior with superior must lower the higher is just as certain as the half-sum of two and six is only four."[3] This was not Roberts's finest hour as a religious or a political thinker.

Over the past thirty years, there has been an outpouring of scholarship on Roberts, including significant collections of his writings

1. Arrington, "Intellectual Tradition," 22.
2. Roberts, *Studies of the Book of Mormon*, 30.
3. Roberts, *Seventy's Course in Theology*, 1:166

such as *The Essential B. H. Roberts*, edited by Brigham D. Madsen,[4] and Lynn Pulsipher's two-volume *Scrapbooks*,[5] which contain previously hard-to-find excerpts of Roberts's work. The publication of Roberts's most long-lasting work, *The Truth, The Way, The Life*[6] (in two different editions), continues to attract the attention of those interested in theology. References to Roberts still grace the pages of scholarly Mormon publications, as well as in papers delivered at sessions of the Sunstone Symposium, the Mormon History Association, and other forums.

A number of valuable biographical studies have been produced about Roberts, including those by Truman Madsen,[7] Robert Malan,[8] and others, along with the publication of Roberts's own autobiography edited by Gary James Bergera.[9] My own edited collection of his diaries has added a better understanding of Roberts's life and times—especially his years as a missionary in the Southern States.[10]

While all of these studies were useful to me, I quote the most from Truman Madsen's biography. His book, while lacking complete footnotes and at times exhibiting a defensive tone, is one that any serious scholar of Roberts needs to read. Although he does not always indicate where some of his primary sources may be found, Madsen had access to people and documents that others, including me, did not. Moreover, as Madsen researched, he spoke at LDS firesides on Roberts and occasionally attracted former missionaries from the Eastern States who had served under Roberts, which in turn led to more interviews, sources, and information for the book. His papers, held privately by his family, were unavailable as I researched my own book, but hopefully someday scholars will have access and can sort through the details. In short, I trust readers will understand that I do not quote Madsen uncritically,

4. Madsen, *Essential B. H. Roberts.*

5. Pulsipher, *Scrap Book by B. H. Roberts.*

6. One edition was edited by Stan Larson, the other by John W. Welch. Each volume contains essays discussing the text and Roberts's process. An earlier volume of excerpts was edited by Brian Stuy.

7. Madsen, *Defender of the Faith*; Madsen, *B. H. Roberts, His Final Decade*; and Madsen, "B. H. Roberts and the Book of Mormon."

8. Malan, *B. H. Roberts.*

9. Roberts, *Autobiography of B. H. Roberts.*

10. Roberts, *History's Apprentice.*

nor am I unaware of his book's shortcomings, but where he offers details that are not found elsewhere, I believe it is important to include them.

So how does this book differ from previous studies? What it seeks to provide is a single-volume account of Roberts the public person: as a politician, writer, thinker, and, above all, exponent of Mormonism in word and print.

Because so much scholarship has been devoted to Roberts's ideas, this book focuses more on his actions and activities, and how that involvement made him such an important public figure. It traces his early life, missionary service, ascension to the ranks of church leadership as a member of the First Council of Seventy, his political life, and his service as a chaplain in World War I. Roberts led a busy and dedicated life "in the arena," and I emphasize his commitment to church, country, and party. Over the span of his life and service, Roberts was a "real person"—one who experienced doubts, disappointments, and defeats, along with many successes. Despite his elevated position in the Mormon pantheon, Roberts was no "saintly" Latter-day Saint. He could be overbearing, petty, and at times disagreeable. On occasion, he could be self-centered and self-important—even close colleagues such as J. Golden Kimball criticized him for it. And at various stages of his life, he struggled with alcohol. Because of the stress of maintaining three families, Roberts was constantly seeking to balance his need for financial resources with his commitment to church service. His struggles tell us a great deal about not just Roberts, but the times in which he lived and the personalities with whom he dealt.

On balance this is not a comprehensive study of Roberts. But I have sought to provide much new information on him and his public life. What I do not detail in this book is a thorough chronicling of his theological views and thought. I will not delve deeply into his widely debated views on the historicity of the Book of Mormon or the revelations of Joseph Smith. This book does not pretend to be a thorough and comprehensive account of his historical contributions. Nor is this a study of his extensive writings in other areas. Even though Roberts served on the First Council of Seventy for more than forty years, I do not attempt to consider the inner workings and development of that presiding quorum.[11] This is also not a "family history," detailing his home and personal life, though obviously those elements contributed to and shaped what Roberts did as a public figure. Much of that family information may be found in earlier studies—most recently in the late Richard Roberts's *A History of the B. H. Roberts Family*,[12] which, though written by a grandson, is neither hagiography nor uncritical. Finally, I do not intend for this to be a "psycho-historical" examination of Roberts—I lack both the data and the training to accomplish such a study. Still, one can sense many of the interior motivations in a life that began at the margins of society and traveled to an important and honored status.

I have tried to examine as widely as possible the sources—created by him and others—that document Roberts's life. One of the things I have learned is that Roberts always attracted notice—especially in the letters and diaries of those he came in to contact with, and in official records. My work has benefitted from the vast array of printed sources, many of which are now available through the internet. I have discovered that the vast number of newspapers now available electronically through a variety of sources has increased our knowledge of Roberts dramatically. For all of his public life, Roberts's actions and views were well chronicled in the press—both at home and elsewhere. This was especially true during the two years from his election to Congress and that body's decision not to seat him.

Moreover, I have been able to search, either in person or electronically, primary source documents from a wide variety of archival repositories, and archival personnel from around the country have responded quickly and generously to my requests for assistance. As one who practiced the archival craft for nearly forty years, I was not surprised at that response. At the same time, I was again reminded how dependent scholars are on those who keep and make available primary documents. At the risk of slighting any individual or repository that has provided assistance, three repositories stand out as absolutely indispensable to me—and to anyone else engaged in Mormon studies. First is the fine collection of Roberts-related

11. For background on the First Council of Seventy, see Quinn, *Extensions of Power*, 140–55.

12. Roberts, *History of the B. H. Roberts Family*.

materials—and the great people—at the L. Tom Perry Special Collections of the Harold B. Lee Library at Brigham Young University. Second is the superb staff and amazing holdings of the University of Utah's Marriott Library Western Americana collections. Finally, without the assistance of the LDS Church Historical Library in Salt Lake City and its helpful librarians and archivists, this study could not have been completed. Time after time, staff members of this department went out of their way to make materials available, allow me access to pertinent parts of closed holdings, and even copy or digitize items for my use. Their kindness made my task much, much easier. Rarely—with one crucial exception—did they deny me access to materials I requested. That exception was Roberts's voluminous correspondence, which no doubt would have added greatly to my understanding. Perhaps in the years ahead other scholars will gain access to this resource.

I want readers to hear Roberts's voice and the voices of his contemporaries. I quote liberally from sources and in doing so have silently corrected some of the more egregious spelling errors and added some punctuation. All sources are cited for readers who wish to seek out the originals. The bibliography includes call numbers for manuscript collections, and many sources at the LDS Church History Library are scanned and available online. To distinguish between sources, I use the past tense for sources contemporary to Roberts and the present tense for modern biographies or reminiscences. For example, Roberts "wrote" a letter to his mother or "recorded" in his journal, while Truman Madsen "writes" about Roberts.

Many years ago, I took a course on writing biography at the University of Utah taught by my friend and mentor F. Alan Coombs. In that course he told us that any biographer faced a basic challenge when trying to chronicle the life and times of another person: to decide how much life, and how much times, and then balance the two. At every juncture of this study I have had Alan's words in the back of my mind. I hope I have come close to achieving that important balance.

One of my first ideas for the title of this book, "A Hunger to Prove and Experience Life," came from an unsigned editorial in the *Deseret News* written at Roberts's death. When I first encountered it, the description seemed apt. It is the two halves of that equation—theory and experience, philosophy and action—that embody Roberts's earthly quest. When young "Harry," as he was generally known in his youth, arrived in Utah at age nine, he was in many ways just one more of the numerous Mormon converts who, in the nineteenth century, left their homelands and gathered to Zion in support of their newly acquired faith. Between then and his death nearly seventy years later, Roberts left an important legacy. As D. Craig Mikkelsen summarizes, Roberts

> was the church's most prolific writer, its leading historian, one of the most popular and exciting speakers, a missionary, theologian, journalist, and widely admired champion of Mormonism before the world; and ... many of the same qualities which equipped him to be a defender of the faith—his oratorical skill, polemical ability, and a total lack of aversion to controversy—suited him as well for public life.[13]

I believe my examination of Roberts's life and career supports that assertion. Davis Bitton noted in a review of Truman Madsen's *Defender of the Faith* that for the "next generation at least," it would "stand as the standard life of Mormonism's great warrior."[14] Implicit in that remark is a call for a future generation of scholars to produce a biographical reassessment of Roberts. I hope this present book, building on the earlier work of many others, may serve as a catalyst and provide a new reconsideration of Roberts's amazing—even inspiring—journey, as Mormonism approaches its third century.

13. Mikkelsen, "Politics of B. H. Roberts."

14. Davis Bitton, review of *Defender of the Faith*, by Truman Madsen, *Sunstone*, Nov.–Dec. 1980, 56, 58–59.

ACKNOWLEDGMENTS

As every writer knows, the process of writing history is at once solitary and collaborative. Solitary in the sense that you spend so many hours alone at the keyboard, or mining the important sources. Collaborative in the sense that you rely on the scholarship of others, and the work of librarians and archivists to make those sources available. This has been my experience on this book.

At the same time, I have benefitted from the advice and support of several key individuals. First and foremost is Gary Bergera who has patiently championed and supported this project. I owe him a great deal.

Early on, as I have said elsewhere, I had the good fortune to have two individuals, Garn Coombs at South High School, and Alan Coombs at the University of Utah (not related to each other), take an interest in me and my work. They taught me, guided me, encouraged me, and were good role models. I hope I have repaid their confidence through my writing and teaching, and perhaps I helped someone in a similar fashion in my years at Weber State.

My colleagues at Signature Books have watched my work on Roberts with interest and encouragement. The board—including Gary, Ron Priddis, Marti Bradley-Evans, Ken Cannon, Lavina Fielding Anderson, Lisa Bickmore, John Hatch and, most especially, George Smith—are not only longtime friends, but scholarly inspirations. Ken Cannon provided copies of important correspondence between Roberts and Isaac Russell, which made my job easier. John Hatch played a major role in shaping the final version of this book. And Jason Francis not only designed a beautiful book, but located important photographs which add greatly to the finished project.

Similarly, the history faculty at Weber State made the eight years I spent with them a pleasure. They not only showed an interest in my work, but understood how such a project takes over one's life. My colleagues during that period were Richard Sadler, Gene Sessions, Susan Matt, Sara Dant, Brady Brower, Jeff Richey, Stephen Francis, Vikki Deakin, Greg Lewis, Larae Larkin, Branden Little, Matthew Romaniello, Nathan Rives, Eric Swedin, and my friend since grad school days, Kathryn Mackay. Additionally, on more than one occasion, Jenna Daniels, Jenny Eckenbrecht, and Ryan Stephens rescued me from the black hole of technology! Truly, I couldn't have done it without you.

Greg Thompson and I have been friends and colleagues for longer than either of us can remember. As I have worked on this project, along with the previous Roberts diaries project, Greg has been a consistent champion. As is noted, the extensive holdings of the Marriott Library are an essential spot for students of Roberts to start, as they are for every aspect of Utah's social, political, economic, and cultural history. Future scholars will owe much to Greg's collecting efforts, as I do now.

Several others have provided important help as I finished this book. While slogging away at the Church History Library I reconnected with the late Mike Quinn. We were friends for over forty years—tracing back to when our paths crossed at the LDS Church archives in the 1970s. He listened to me as I tried to make sense of some of the aspects of Roberts's life, and provided answers to several questions. It was much appreciated. Sadly, his death in April 2021, deprives the Mormon historical community of an important voice, and me of a good friend. Jessie Embry has been a friend and colleague since the 1980s. Again, I have benefitted from that friendship along with her articles, books, and conference papers. Most recently she encouraged me to shape a part of this study into an article in the *Journal of Mormon History*. At the same time, Tom Alexander helped me better understand a particular question I had about Roberts and plural marriage. I appreciated his guidance on this point as much as I have gained over the years from his scholarship and friendship.

I was fortunate to have Lonna Rivera in my life during the writing of this book. She was always there – listening, encouraging me and telling me I really could pull it off. To her I say from the bottom of my heart, with love, thank you. To the future! Let's grow old together.

Finally, B. H. Roberts has been a part of my life for the past two decades. First as I edited his diaries which were published as *History's Apprentice*. Most recently as the subject of this biography. My goal in both cases was to produce an accurate account; one that Roberts himself would have found satisfactory, even if he disagreed with some of my conclusions. I sought to capture as best I could the importance of the man himself, and the times in which he lived. I hope I have met that mark.

And now for the obligatory disclaimer. Despite the guidance, assistance, support, encouragement, and interest provided from those above, and many others not mentioned, whatever errors and weaknesses in this text are the fault of the author, and the author alone.

John Sillito
Ogden, Utah
May 2021

ABBREVIATIONS

There are multiple B. H. Roberts collections held by various archives associated with Utah and the LDS Church. The LDS Church History Library, for example, has a B. H. Roberts Collection, a B. H. Roberts Papers, and a B. H. Roberts Scrapbook. To distinguish between which papers or collection is cited, I use the following abbreviations in footnotes and the bibliography.

BYU	L. Tom Perry Special Collections, Harold B. Lee Library, Brigham Young University, Provo, Utah.
CHL	Church History Library, the Church of Jesus Christ of Latter-day Saints, Salt Lake City.
UDSH	Utah Division of State History, Research Center, Salt Lake City.
UU	Special Collections, J. Willard Marriott Library, University of Utah, Salt Lake City.

ONE

THE EARLY YEARS, 1857-80

When Salt Lake City residents opened their newspapers on September 28, 1933, they were greeted with the news that B. H. Roberts, Mormon general authority, writer, and theologian, had passed away the previous day. Not surprisingly, the LDS Church-owned *Deseret News* announced the death in a full front-page, eight-column, banner headline, and a long obituary calling him "one of the premier exponents of Mormonism."[1]

The paper editorialized that he took part in "establishing the new society that arose here in the west, its members born in many lands," and, later, was a central figure in the "difficult adjustment" that pitted the American government against his church. Within him was a hunger to "prove and experience life," that allowed him neither to evade conflict nor to become complacent to "accepting things as they are." Roberts "was a foe of injustice, violence, compulsion, and any force that diverted man from his rights and opportunity."[2]

His death made front-page news in other Utah papers as well. Even the *Salt Lake Tribune*, whose pages had once called for his expulsion from Congress over his practice of plural marriage, noted his passing with respect, and even admiration,[3] calling his death an "irreparable loss." The "warmth of his friendship and his sympathy for the distressed elevated him in the admiration of his associates

1. "B. H. Roberts' Funeral Sunday," *Deseret News*, Sep. 28, 1933, 1. The paper noted that the "stalwart princely figure of President Roberts will be missed by his associates and the people of the Church generally … [who] honor and revere him as their friend. … Through his fearlessness and his staunch defense of the principles of the Gospel, President Roberts has won many outsiders to friendship for the Church."

2. "President Brigham H. Roberts," *Deseret News*, Sep. 28, 1933, 4.

3. "Noted LDS Leader Dies in Hospital," *Salt Lake Tribune*, Sep. 28, 1933, 1. See also "Funeral of LDS Leader Set Sunday," *Salt Lake Tribune*, Sep. 29, 1933, 25.

in his church, in the community, and in the wide field in which he toiled unselfishly and always with a fixed purpose."[4] The *Ogden Standard Examiner* editorialized that his life was marked by "years of intense living," and that from "boyhood on" Roberts was heroic: "He … never yielded to discouragement, for he fought on, ever achieving, and ever setting an example of courage and fortitude."[5]

A United Press International story, which ran in various major dailies, including the *New York Times,* referred to him as a "champion of common people," and that while he himself was gone, "the liberalism and courage characteristic of him prevailed." Many papers pointed to a recent trip he had made to "to demand fair play and justice for striking coal miners" in Utah's Carbon County.[6] The San Luis Obispo *Daily Telegram* called him "one of the last links between modern times and the polygamous days of Mormonism," and remembered how "he startled the world with a powerful and eloquent defense of polygamy, made on the floor of the United States house of representatives. That it was a brave stand and an able plea even his enemies—swayed by religious prejudice admitted."[7]

He was memorialized and eulogized to an extent that would have seemed unimaginable to those who, sixty-seven years earlier, saw the scruffy, nine-year-old immigrant trudge into Salt Lake City.[8] One longtime resident remembered Roberts when he was "a mere boy" in Bountiful, often seeing him pass by as he brought "his stepfather's horses from the field. … No one realized that he had the material in him to become such a marvelous man."[9]

When Roberts came into the world on March 13, 1857, his parents—Ann Everington and Benjamin Roberts—had been members of the LDS Church for about five years, and married for eleven. Family lore holds that Ann was on her way to deliver some sewing when she was "attracted by a huddle of people on a busy corner" and

4. "Brigham H. Roberts," *Salt Lake Tribune*, Sep. 29, 1933, 4.

5. "Death of B. H. Roberts," *Ogden Standard-Examiner*, Sep. 28, 1933, 4.

6. See "Brigham H. Roberts, Mormon Leader Dies," *New York Times*, Sep. 28, 1933, 21; and "Prominent Mormon B. H. Roberts, Dies," *Bakersfield Californian*, Sep. 28, 1933, 1.

7. "'Grand Old Man' of Mormon Utah Dead," *Daily Telegram* (San Luis Obispo), Sep. 29, 1933, 2.

8. For a full account, see Roberts, *Autobiography*.

9. "B. H. Roberts Son of This County Who Won Renown Dies," *Davis County Clipper*, Sep. 29, 1933, 1.

by the lilt of a beautiful, male tenor voice singing a hymn. A missionary told the crowd that not only had God brought forth a prophet, but had restored the gospel in its fullness. While there are few details, we know that Ann attended Mormon meetings, read their tracts, accepted the Restoration message, and, according to Truman Madsen's account, was baptized early one August morning in 1851 in the cold waves of "the Irish Sea … while a small group of Saints looked on."[10] According to her obituary, however, she was baptized at Woolwich, Kent, England, by "Elder Thomas Botterell."[11] To her husband's protests she reportedly replied that she had joined the "true Church."[12] Eventually Ben relented and was baptized himself in August 1857, but in his son's words "it was a perfunctory thing to him and of doubtful credibility."[13]

Benjamin Roberts was born on May 3, 1826, to William and Mary Roberts in Sussex, England, and moved frequently during his childhood. At one point his family lived in Woolwich, Kent, not far from where William and Elizabeth Reed Everington resided with their family, where he likely became acquainted with Ann. Ben was thought of as "jovial and good-natured," though he apparently lacked much of a sense of responsibility, and had little interest in religion. But he also possessed a "passionate drive for self-education,"[14] a trait that would characterize his son Brigham Henry as well. Ben Roberts, an itinerant blacksmith, eventually landed at the Woolwich Arsenal in Kent, where he became reacquainted with Ann Everington.[15]

---

10. Madsen, *Defender of the Faith*, 3.

11. "Dies at Eighty-three," *Davis County Clipper*, Jan. 14, 1910, 1. The paper misidentified the town as Wollich.

12. Madsen, *Defender of the Faith*, 3–4. Along with Roberts's own autobiography, and the family history by Richard Roberts, Madsen's work is essential to understand Roberts's early life. This chapter draws heavily on Madsen's work, and, despite its occasional errors and devotional tone, anyone interested in a full understanding of Roberts's life needs to reckon with the book. Similarly, on these early years, readers should carefully consult Adah Roberts Naylor, "An Immigrant Mother and Her Son," *Relief Society Magazine*, Jan. 1934, 3–8.

13. Roberts, *Autobiography*, 7.

14. Madsen, *Defender of the Faith*, 4. Even Roberts would recall his father's "pleasing character and genial good nature."

15. Malan, *B. H. Roberts*, 1. While not as fully researched as some later works, Malan's book, which represents the first full-length study of Roberts, is valuable for any reader of Roberts and his times. See also Roberts, *History of the B. H. Roberts Family*, 77–79.

In later years, Ann would describe her husband as a "sunny, genial, handsome man," and that she had been "swept away" by his charm.[16]

Ann Reed Everington, a "serene Anglo-Saxon girl"—was a few months younger than her husband.[17] She was born on December 18, 1826, in Norfolk, England, where her ancestors had lived for several generations, to William and Elizabeth Reed Everington.[18] The Everingtons were regarded as a "serious, thoughtful and studious family."[19] Ann, described by one scholar as "determined, resourceful and independent," supported herself from an early age as a seamstress.[20] Like many women of her time and class, she was largely self-educated, and Truman Madsen believes that her serious, thoughtful character—marked by spirituality, an "inclination to think deeply about the issues of life," and the love of books—was instilled in her young son.[21]

During the first twelve years of their marriage, Ann bore seven children: Mary Ann, called Polly (1849–1931); Annie (1851–1929); Benjamin Jr. (1853–58); twins Amy [Emma] and Sarah (1855) who survived only three days; Brigham Henry, who went by Harry or Henry (1857–1933); and Thomas (1860–62).[22] Only three of the children lived into adulthood.

Ben Roberts was "restless and inclined to wander," and while traveling was an economic necessity, he "freely chose" to move from place to place in search of work.[23] While travelling, Ben was not given to communicating with Ann and the children, or sending them the money they needed (much of it likely squandered on drink and gambling), forcing his wife to find her own ways to feed and shelter their family. But even when Ben was at home, family life

16. Madsen, *Defender of the Faith*, 4

17. Madsen, 2.

18. There is some confusion as to her birth year. Her Utah death certificate lists 1826. Her grave marker in the Bountiful cemetery, however, has 1827. Other sources say she was born in 1828. Richard Roberts's book indicates 1826. Because the bulk of evidence suggests 1826, I have accepted that date.

19. Madsen, *Defender of the Faith*, 2.

20. Malan, *B. H. Roberts*, 1. Truman Madsen writes that Ann was "orphaned at an early age." In fact, her father died when she was twenty-nine and her mother when she was thirty-eight. Madsen, *Defender of the Faith*, 2.

21. Madsen, *Defender of the Faith*, 3

22. Roberts, *History of the B. H. Roberts Family*, 76.

23. Madsen, *Defender of the Faith*, 4.

was marked by his frequent bursts of temper. One night, Ben came home, and finding "no supper prepared (perhaps there was no food in the house) ... stood in the pantry door impatiently hurling and twirling the plates across the room."[24]

Ben Roberts also proved to be anything but a devoted Latter-day Saint. While initially his baptism produced a time of "diminished wanderings," increased tithe payments, and meeting-going, he eventually came into conflict with local church officials. He once threw some of them out of his house, believing that they were there to collect tithes. Ultimately, he was summoned to a church court, which he refused to attend, and was excommunicated. In later years his daughter Mary would recall, "From then on Father began to grow indifferent—and to stay away from home for long periods—and once more our life was made miserable."[25]

Ann Roberts became "insatiable to go to America where her children would be numbered among the Chosen people,"[26] a decision not atypical of many other British converts of the time who saw emigrating to the United States as a way of freeing themselves from the grinding poverty of the mid-nineteenth century.[27] The growing United States seemed to offer economic opportunities, social mobility, and a standard of living that could never occur in their home country. Historian Richard O. Cowan has estimated that between 1840 and 1870 more than 90,000 British citizens converted to Mormonism, and roughly two thirds of them left for the United States. Estimates suggest that during the decade of the 1860s—when both Ann and her children emigrated—some 14,716 Mormon converts left Britain for the United States.[28]

Though Ben opposed the idea of the family going to the United States, he actually became the catalyst for Ann to make the journey. At one point in April 1862, he forwarded to Ann enough money

24. Madsen, 4.

25. Malan, *B. H. Roberts*, 6

26. Bartholomew, *Audacious Women*, 134.

27. Richard L. Jensen, "British Gathering to Zion," in Bloxham, Moss, and Porter, *Truth Will Prevail*, 165.

28. Taylor, *Expectations Westward*, 144–45. Two thousand of that number came in 1866, the year Roberts and his sister traveled to Utah.

for them to rejoin him; instead, she took the money to provide the initial funding for the trip to America.

Ann prepared for herself and two of the children, Annie and Thomas, to make the journey while leaving the older children, Mary and Harry, in England. Twelve-year-old Mary was left with some distant relatives and church members, Martin and Emma Pye. The couple, who were in their late twenties at the time, were not interested in also taking the five-year-old Harry, so Ann eventually turned to some recent Scottish converts, John Tovey and his wife. Though Ann knew little about them, their church membership allayed her concerns, and she left Harry in their care.[29] Mary wrote that her mother

> left Staffordshire in 1862. B. H. and I went to see them off. Mother climbed up the steps to the elevated train. As the train pulled out, B. H. and I stood looking after it with tears in our eyes. We dreamed of a promise—we looked forward to the time when our mother would be able to send us enough money for the tickets to the land across the sea. No one can imagine my feelings as I turned and slowly descended the platform with my small brother. We were to face a future which we could only hope was bright. I seemed alone and friendless.[30]

Ann Roberts sailed with her two children from Liverpool[31] on May 14, 1862, aboard the *William Tapscott*.[32] Estimates for the number of Saints on the ship range from 807 to 927. Ann wrote her husband "some three weeks" after she sailed, "having passed the point of no return." After receiving the letter, he reportedly visited Ann's sister in what she called "a fearful order," claiming that Ann had deceived him and he would never forgive her.[33] Indeed, there was no other contact between the two. Ann suggested dissolving the marriage and giving her husband his freedom, but his responses are lost to history.

---

29. As Malan observed, "Ann had complete faith in those numbered in the membership of the church." Malan, *B. H. Roberts*, 5.

30. "Memoirs of Mary Ann Martha Roberts Day," quoted in Madsen, *Defender of the Faith*, 9.

31. Obviously not all the emigrants leaving Liverpool were Mormon converts, but it was Europe's most important port of emigration. See Taylor, *Expectations Westward*, 163.

32. According to Conway B. Sonne, the *Tapscott*, weighing some 1575 tons, "carried more Mormons across the Atlantic than any other single sailing vessel." See Sonne, *Saints on the Seas*, 41, 49, 83.

33. Madsen, *Defender of the Faith*, 9. In his account, Madsen identifies the ship as the *John Bright*, but it was the *William Tapscott*.

The *William Tapscott* arrived in New York on June 26 where the Saints were met by church immigration agents, most notably William C. Staines.[34] From there the family likely traveled up the East Coast to Albany, New York; then west by train to Detroit; on to Chicago; and finally down the river to Quincy, Illinois, then west to Nebraska. In any event, a little less than two months after their arrival in New York, on August 10, the Roberts trio left Florence, Nebraska, as part of the Horton D. Haight Company.[35] The train, containing some 650 travelers, arrived in Salt Lake on October 19, 1862.[36] Unfortunately, young Thomas, who had first gotten "ship fever"[37] on the high seas, died on the trail on September 29, 1862, and was buried near Chimney Rock in a borrowed "bread box coffin"[38] Such deaths were common. A *Deseret News* account upon the arrival of the train in Salt Lake City reported that, "There were … thirty deaths in the company on the plains; most of whom were sick when they left the Missouri river, principally children."[39]

At the same time, all was not well for either of the other two Roberts children who stayed behind. They were separated from each other and living in difficult straits. Mary was required to earn her support by working in a kiln that Pye operated. Harry did not fare much better as he lived

> a Dickensian existence with Mr. and Mrs. Tovey. They fed him, clothed him, barely, and expected him to work in the same stone sawyer trade which Mr. Tovey followed. The boy learned to sift sand and then carry it and water to the sloping board in a bucket on his head. He also helped polish marble slabs for fireplace mantels. At the end of these tiring days, he went home to a scanty meal and bed on the bare floor with no blanket for cover.[40]

34. See Tiffany, *City Saints*, 29.

35. For an overview see Hulmston, "Mormon Immigration in the 1860s," 32–48.

36. "Liverpool to New York, 14 May 1862–25 June 1862," Saints By Sea, https://saintsbysea.lib.byu.edu.

37. This was a term used for epidemic typhus, which was common on crowded ships. For more, see Baker, "Illness and Mortality," 77–90.

38. Malan, *B. H. Roberts*, 9. Richard Roberts reports that the young boy had been sick since birth with "hydrocephalitis" which he believes caused his death. See Roberts, *History of the B. H. Roberts Family*, 76

39. "Arrival of Trains," *Deseret News*, Oct. 22, 1862, 4.

40. Madsen, *Essential B. H. Roberts*, x.

Indeed, the experience with the Toveys did little to provide any sense of family stability in the young boy's life. In biographer Robert Malan's words, the young man was "unloved, unfairly exploited and often unwanted."[41] Roberts himself later wrote, the Toveys, though church members, were "scarcely ideal people for honesty and right living," and he sensed that "shadowy references" to their past suggested "something was irregular."[42] Not only did they use more than one name, but Harry had the feeling that some of their relatives—perhaps even the couple themselves—had spent time in prison. Often the couple had no dwelling place at all, huddling together at night "under the hedges, in a stack of straw, or wherever else they might find something to serve as a bed."[43]

Alcohol was frequently present in Roberts's early life. There is evidence to suggest that his father was a heavy drinker, as were the Toveys.[44] Roberts later recalled that "notwithstanding their church membership, they were both addicted to periodical heavy drinking, and as I afterwards remembered, most of their evenings were spent in country taverns and saloons, they dragged me with them [while I] curled up under the tables where the drinking went on and slept.[45]

But the Toveys also played a part in introducing their young charge to literature and reading, beginning his lifelong love affair with the spoken and written word. In his autobiography, Roberts traced this in part to a summertime trek by foot "through a beautiful country side of England." While resting in the "shade of a hedgerow" Roberts saw a few pages of a newspaper and rushed out of the shade into the afternoon sun to gather them, begging "the old lady" to read them to him. "The old lady reading to me [became] something of a passion" for him. Through her, he was exposed to the *Latter-day Saints' Millennial Star* and even "Samuel Mosheim Schmucker's *History of the Mormons*. ... [It] is usually conceded to be the fairest anti-Mormon account ... up to that time. His discussion of the martyrdom of the prophet at Carthage, Illinois, was as vivid

41. Malan, *B. H. Roberts*, 7.

42. Roberts, *Autobiography*, 10.

43. Malan, 6.

44. Madsen quotes Roberts in later years as saying that if his father was "alive, he is drunk; if he is dead, he died drinking." Madsen, *Defender of the Faith*, 7.

45. Roberts, *Autobiography*, 10.

as also were the engravings illustrating it. This was a choice section of the book to me, and I pleaded frequently for it to be read to me. Old Mrs. Tovey was kind enough to do this."[46]

Despite his drinking, old man Tovey fancied himself quite a preacher. At times he would mount a chair to hold forth, and when the "threatening rabble" forced Tovey to make a quick exit from his pulpit, young Harry's task would be to save the chair for another day of preaching.[47] At times the Toveys sought to rid themselves of their young charge, and Roberts sensed that his presence had become "something of a bone of contention" between them. Sometimes he also sensed a struggle between the couple over which of them would be in charge of his fate. On more than one occasion they tried to apprentice him out. Roberts decided to run away. He told some friends later that he was gone three months, going through "a somewhat aimless, scrappy period of plodding through lanes and streets … [eating] discarded crusts and peelings."[48]

After a particularly bitter quarrel, the couple apparently decided to separate, and neither wished to care for the young boy anymore. They arranged to have him serve as a drummer boy in the army, going so far as to visit a local barracks where they received a shilling as B. H. was measured for a uniform. They were told to return in the morning, but, according to an account by Edwin Baird, Roberts awoke that night to hear a voice saying, "If you go to the army to be a drummer boy you will never be able to keep your promise and go to America and live with your mother."[49]

No doubt frightened and desperate, and with very little sense of where he was or where he was going, Roberts bolted. For some time, he wandered the streets begging for food, sleeping wherever he could, constantly looking for someone who could help reunite him with either his family or church members. Eventually he located "an old Scotchman who was a shoemaker and who sometimes had gone with John Tovey on his preaching exploits," and whom Roberts felt would help him find a solution to his plight. As it turned

46. Roberts, 15.

47. Malan, *B. H. Roberts*, 7.

48. Madsen, *Defender of the Faith*, 17.

49. Edwin Baird, "A Short History of the Life of Elder Brigham Henry Roberts," in Baird, *Autobiography*, 131.

out, however, the shoemaker "somehow ... got into communication with the Tovey's," and they reappeared to "take charge of me."[50] On another occasion Tovey told him it was his intent to apprentice the young boy to a saddle maker so that he could learn a trade. Again Roberts said he heard a voice telling him to flee or he would be unable to keep his promise, so he "slipped down the stairs and out into the night," and for another period subsisted on beating "the dogs to the garbage cans in order to sustain life."[51] Ultimately he returned to the Toveys, but one gets a sense that by this time Roberts had given up his hope of finding a way out of the situation, and his life "settled back into its now familiar routine struggle for an existence."[52]

Finally, his mother was able to raise sufficient funds, apparently calling on local Saints, and the Church's Perpetual Emigrating Fund Company, to bring her two children to Utah. Finding Mary was relatively easy, but it took time to locate her young son. When Roberts was reunited with Mary, they, along with 790 others left Liverpool for Utah on board the Union Line's *John Bright*[53] "at four o'clock on the afternoon of April 30, 1866."[54] B. H. Roberts was nine years old, and had spent the last four years alternating between homelessness and life with the Toveys.

Migration records indicate that Henry and his sister paid a deposit of five pounds ten shillings.[55] Later, Roberts remembered that his provisions, stored in several canvas bags, consisted of "fat-side

50. Roberts, *Autobiography*, 15.

51. Baird, "Short History," 131. Throughout his life and writings, Roberts would give accounts of these events with some minor differences. See Roberts, *Autobiography*, 13–16.

52. Malan writes that by this point the Toveys were so poor that their only possessions consisted of "a Bible, a violin and a small bundle of cast off clothing." Malan, *B. H. Roberts*, 6, 9.

53. The *John Bright* transported three separate companies of Mormon emigrants in 1858, 1866, and 1868, before sinking off the coast of Brazil in 1874. See Denbaugh and duBarry, *William H. Webb*, 197–98. See also Sonne, *Saints on the Seas*, 116–17 The vessel is named for John Bright (1811–89), a member of Parliament known as a great orator, supporter of free trade, and opponent of the Corn Laws.

54. See "Diary of Caroline Hopkins Clark," Apr. 30, 1866, Saints By Sea, https://saintsbysea.lib.byu.edu. Hereafter cited as Clark Diary. A variant format was published as Caroline Hopkins Clark, "Liverpool to Utah in 1866," in Holmes, *Covered Wagon Women*, 151–62.

55. See "Liverpool to New York, 30 Apr 1866–6 Jun 1866," Saints By Sea. The register lists Mary a "spinster"—being seventeen—and Henry as fifteen, six years older than his actual age.

bacon made greenish by the intense pickling of the pork to make it suitable for food" along with "some loaves of bread [and] hard tack," for the six-week voyage. He described his fellow passengers as a "motley crew of Mormon emigrants, drawn from the English working class."[56] The company was under the guidance of Elder Collins Moore Gillet, who had just completed a three year mission in England.[57]

One of those on board, Caroline Hopkins Clark, records that the first few days were cold, snowy, windy, and wet, and that many people suffered from seasickness. While noting on May 3 that it was a "grand sight to see the waves roll mountain high," Clark also recorded that a hailstorm had commenced and "the vessel is rocking very much at times. It is about time for prayers."[58] These conditions continued for the rest of the month. Still, all was not gloomy. In a letter published in the *Millennial Star*, Septimus W. Sears notes that there was "Good order, love and union in our midst, and things have more the appearance of a pleasure party, than a lot of people performing a long, tedious journey. … I can say truthfully I have never spent a more happy month in my life than the one on the *John Bright*."[59]

Gillet reported that after thirty-seven days the ship arrived safely on June 6.[60] He told the *Millennial Star*, "We got along first rate, and the officers of the ship seemed to think we were indeed a peculiar people, to be able to get along with the inconveniences existing on board ship, without swearing, quarreling or fighting."[61]

On that day Roberts found himself in Castle Garden inside

---

56. Roberts, *Autobiography*, 4. Malan says that while on the ocean voyage young Roberts got a small blue anchor tattoo. Malan, *B. H. Roberts*, 11.

57. Gillet (1837–66) served in various places and was president of the Sheffield District. He died from cholera on August 20, 1866, near Ft. Kearny while returning from his mission, and was buried on the plains. See "Obituary," *Deseret News*, Aug. 30, 1866, 4.

58. Clark Diary.

59. Septimus W. Sears, "Letter," *Millennial Star*, June 30, 1866, 413–14.

60. Conway Sonne notes "there were no deaths and only one storm. Three births and one marriage were recorded." Sonne, *Saints on the Seas*, 116–17.

61. C. M. Gillet, "Letter," *Millennial Star*, June 30, 1866, 411–12. Gillet notes that despite an outbreak of measles, which erupted five days after they left Liverpool, by the time the ship landed "All were enjoying good health." According to Clark, the ship actually arrived in New York harbor the day before.

Battery Park, at the southernmost tip of Manhattan, where most immigrants passing through New York City were processed.[62]

> I was a boy of no prepossessing appearance. In the first place I was clad in just a pair of barn-door trousers and jacket (made from the old trousers of an English policeman), a pair of iron-rimmed wooden clogs, and on my head was what was supposed to be a jaunty Scotch cap, faced with bright plaid around the rim and ending in two black streamers behind—a headgear I heartily despised. … On the whole I was stolid, and sober-faced. There was no joy in boyhood in my appearance, no disposition to mill round with the seven hundred other emigrants thronging the Old Castle Gardens. I seemed to be without companions and doubtless would have been repulsed by me if they manifested friendliness. I was a boy evidently accustomed to being alone—apart from the throng. I was not restless, but rather solemn and gloomy.[63]

His experience was probably typical of most Mormon immigrants once in New York. After landing at Castle Garden, they met a church immigration agent who "guided them through the immigration process and across the river to Newark, New Jersey, where they boarded trains for the West."[64] The trip itself began on June 8 when they boarded a train at "break of day," and the train went day and night through Canada.[65] On June 19, 1866, Henry, Mary, and their fellow passengers arrived in Wyoming, Nebraska, where the immigrants lived in tents. During this period they experienced hot weather and frequent thunderstorms.[66] One member of the party, William Grant, recorded that Wyoming, Nebraska, was "a frontier town, very small. … We got a few willows and made a tent with quilts and sheets to creep in at night and many hundreds of others do the same so we are only imitators."[67]

A month later, the pair joined William Henry Chipman's wagon train, which left on July 11. Some 416 immigrants made the

62. Castle Garden is today Castle Clinton, administered by the US National Park Service and where tickets to visit the Statue of Liberty and Ellis Island are distributed.

63. Roberts, *Autobiography*, 3.

64. Tiffany, *City Saints*, 29. "Some members who arrived without funds would stay in the New York area to earn train fare. The immigration agent would assist them in finding housing and work so they could eventually make the trip to Utah."

65. Clark Diary, June 8–11, 1866.

66. Clark Diary, June 20–21, 1866.

67. Grant, Autobiography and Diary, 19.

two-month trek in some sixty wagons. After the journey,[68] which Roberts recalled as full of "trials and hardships," the siblings arrived in the Great Salt Lake Valley.[69] Roberts remembered, "The train, falling into its old line, swung down the low foothills until they struck a well-defined road leading into the city." As Captain Chipman's immigrants traveled down "Emigration Street" (today 300 South) and turned onto Main Street, young B. H. found himself "at the head of the lead yoke in that team, walking up the principal street of the city, the rest of the team following." People in the city lined the street to welcome the new arrivals. It was then Roberts spotted "a bright-colored, dainty, charming little girl approaching me in the middle of the street. It was a strange meeting, we two."[70]

Though the "dainty little lady" was somewhat timid in approaching the young Roberts, who by his own admission was an "ugly duckling," unkempt in appearance, with ill-fitting clothes and a shock of "unmanageable" hair, she offered him a fruit basket of peaches, plums, and grapes. Roberts took what he supposed a "reasonable portion," shared them with his sister, then resumed his place at the front of the train and "marched on until the head of Main Street was reached."[71] One senses that for the first time in a long time, perhaps ever, Roberts felt welcome. That sense of belonging—geographically and spiritually—would mark Roberts for the rest of his life. Despite the conflicts, defeats, and occasional disappointments he experienced, B. H. Roberts was to his core both a Latter-day Saint and a Utahn—by adoption if not birth.

The two siblings reunited with their mother and accompanied her to her small, unfinished home in Bountiful, Utah, just to the north of Salt Lake City. During their absence she had married William John

68. Chipman records five deaths in his notebook. He also notes the presence of a party of two, headed by Mary Roberts. See Chipman Notebook. For more on the journey, see Roberts, *Autobiography*, 24–43.

69. Roberts made this comment at the funeral of his sister Mary. See "Mrs. Mary Day, Sister of B. H. Roberts, Died at Her Home, February 14th," *Davis County Clipper*, Feb. 20, 1931, 1. Apparently the hardships included falling into a barrel of molasses. See Roberts, *Autobiography*, 31.

70. Roberts, *Autobiography*, 40.

71. Roberts, 41.

Nichols[72] who had died two years later, and was raising their young daughter, Elizabeth Audrey.[73]

A year after he arrived in Utah, B. H., or "Henry," as he was increasingly known during this period, was baptized by Seth Dustin,[74] who would become his stepfather in April 1869.[75] With Dustin, Ann would bear her last child, Byrnina.[76] This third marriage, though not fated to last, had a great impact on Roberts—whether for good or ill depends on which account one reads. As Dustin family member Brenda Dustin Young writes:

> children in that generation began working at a very early age doing farm chores or working as hired hands. Seth was a hard working man and expected hard work from his children as well, desiring to pass this legacy on to them. His strict approach to teaching his children was not always appreciated by young Brigham Henry, who, at thirteen may have viewed his stepfather as stern. Yet, Seth worked patiently with young Brigham Henry, teaching him to drive an ox team. Seth ... paid B. H. for his labor, enabling B. H. to repay the Perpetual Emigration Fund that he owed the Church for his passage to America and for his journey to Utah.[77]

According to Young's account, by this time the couple was "experiencing some troubles in their marriage," possibly because of Seth's occupation as a miner and railroad grader which led to "his being away for a few weeks or a season." Family sources suggested that while Ann was dynamic and gifted, "she could also be "hell to live with." Even though "the couple did not get along," it was "to [Seth's]

72. Nichols (1821–65) was an English convert. A farmer, musician and painter by profession, he was killed accidentally while operating a horse-drawn threshing machine.

73. Elizabeth Audrey Nichols Barnard (1864–1917) later married Thomas Barnard, (1848–1925) a widower, on December 27, 1883. They were the parents eleven children. See "Mrs. Barnard of Blackfoot Dies in Logan," *Davis County Clipper*, Sep. 26, 1917, 1.

74. Dustin (1825–1903) married Hannah Loveland Dustin (1825–67) in 1846; they were the parents of eight sons and one daughter.

75. Roberts was known by many names during his lifetime. As indicated, he often went by "B. H." as well as "Henry." At other times he used "Harry" and "Brig" in signing his letters to his mother. See Roberts to Ann Dustin, Apr. 25, 1883 and Oct. 29, 1884, box 3, fds. 7 and 8, Roberts Papers (UU). See also Roberts, *History of the B. H. Roberts Family*, 91–92.

76. Byrnina Ann Dustin (1872–1951) married Jeremiah "Jed" Willey (1870–1944) in 1891. They had one child who lived to adulthood, also named Byrnina.

77. Young, *Seth Dustin*, 96.

credit that he worked as hard at the marriage as he did."[78] It is also possible that B. H. "never got over the loss of his father, finding no room in his heart for Seth, as his sisters did." Seth's move to Arizona, and Ann's decision to not join him, was taken by later family members as a sign of Ann's on-going affection for her first husband, Ben.[79]

In any event, while the couple was married, young Henry says he was uncomfortable with his extended family, especially Seth's "grown-up sons who were ignorant in their manners, [and] boisterous in their conduct."[80] Roberts, however, joined his stepfather, who had contracted with the railroad to work on the line between Salt Lake and Ogden, to handle the ox teams used in scraping the grade. Roberts proved adept at doing "the work of a man."[81] Shortly after, Roberts accompanied his stepfather as he searched for coal on the west side of the Wasatch Range, and to Dry Canyon, near Ophir, where Dustin took charge of a company organized by a group of "well-to-do farmers in Davis County" who believed they would get rich prospecting for silver.

Family biographer Richard Roberts paints a grimmer picture, saying that after "two or three years of marriage, Seth Dustin left home one day and was never heard from again. There never was a legal divorcement." Roberts family genealogical records show that the couple's sealing was cancelled on August 9, 1884.[82] According to a few letters to his mother, B. H. Roberts frequently saw his role as her defender in that marriage.[83]

In Dry Canyon, Roberts became acquainted with the dangers that marked a miner's life—accidents, fights, gunplay, profanity, gambling, and "the company of men … of very irregular habits."[84] Roberts also became acquainted with alcohol, a demon that had

78. Young, 98.

79. Young, 105.

80. Roberts, *Autobiography*, 48. Roberts does not specify which of the sons they were. The boys ranged in age from five to twenty-two at this time: Edwin S. (1847–1915); William Henry (1851–1932); Chauncey B. (1853–80); Chester Moroni (1854–1910); Hyrum N. (1855–1931); Chauncey L. (1863–1937); and, Levi J. (1864–1938). All but the last two were older than Roberts.

81. Roberts, *Autobiography,* 47.

82. Roberts, *History of the B. H. Roberts Family*, 91.

83. Roberts to Mother, Aug. 26, 1878, box 4, fd. 1, Roberts Papers (UU).

84. Roberts, *Autobiography*, 48.

trapped his father, the Toveys, and others in his early life. As he recalled, despite resisting many offers to imbibe, one day near sunset, he "yielded to the solicitation and drank a half tin cup full of the fiery liquor. Its effect upon me, unpracticed in that kind of beverage, can be imagined. I was soon in the swirl of intoxication, with a reckless dare-devil spirit that had been awakened."[85]

Drunk and losing control, Roberts was mounted on a "scarcely broken three year old colt," which he proceeded to put through its paces, all the while challenging anyone who was listening to a race. Finally, the horse bucked its hapless rider, and after quarreling with some of the men, Roberts was dumped into a wagon to sleep it off. In the morning, the miners urged the hung-over youth to try the "hair of the dog that bit him" (a shot of whiskey) as a cure. He declined.[86]

Over the next few months Roberts found himself not only laboring as a miner, but also "nearly betrayed into the gang of horse thieves ... associated with one Ben Tasker, a noted Utah outlaw."[87] Throughout the 1870s and 80s, Tasker made his living as a "horse thief, highway robber and murderer."[88] Tried for the latter offense, he escaped from jail in the mid-1880s and moved to Arizona where he became "chief devil to a gang of outlaws who lived in the mountains east of Phoenix." Tasker apparently met his end at the hand of his own gang. He was "shot and killed" in Arizona just over the Mexican boarder after a dispute when he refused to share profits from a recent cattle raid with other gang members.[89]

Roberts told a congregation in Ogden, Utah, in the early 1930s that "I joined up with a gang of horse thieves and for a while, I, with them, roamed the hills and back country. I took my whiskey straight and my coffee black. But it didn't last too long, as I could see

---

85. Roberts, 48.

86. Roberts, 48–49.

87. Roberts, 52–54.

88. For more information on Tasker, see a series of reminiscences in the *Millard County Chronicle*: Jan. 22, 28, Feb. 25, Mar. 17, 24, 31, Apr. 7, 14, 21, 1932, and July 7, 1938. Charles Kelly indicates that Tasker had once lived in Centerville, which may make the tie to Roberts more plausible. See Kelly, *Outlaw Trail*, 111. See also Palmer, "Early Day Trading," 367.

89. "Ben Tasker's Last," *Salt Lake Daily Tribune*, Feb. 12, 1880, 4; and "Ben Tasker," *Salt Lake Daily Tribune*, Nov. 14, 1883, 4.

no future in that. Then I got a chance to work with a blacksmith."[90] Indeed, in the midst of this unruly life, in 1874 Roberts was apprenticed for three years to James Hyrum Baird,[91] a Centerville blacksmith, replicating his father's profession.[92] Roberts "moved into the home and lived as one of the family," and became very close with them.[93] Baird's son Edwin said that when Roberts came to live with the family he was using the name "Henry Nichols,"[94] and that he was "still practicing some of his wild ways."[95] Although Roberts worked hard to learn the blacksmith trade, it became apparent to his sponsor that "his mind was on something else," forcing Baird to closely supervise his apprentice's work. It also became apparent that his "youthful habits were not changed and on weekends he was often in trouble."[96] Many of Roberts's youthful indiscretions seem relatively harmless in retrospect. On one occasion he was riding in a sleigh with a group of young people when, as they were crossing a stream, he disabled the sleigh and "dumped the whole group into the icy water." Another time, James Baird dispatched him to a Bountiful woman for some raspberry and currant starts. When she asked his name, he thought a minute then said it was B. H. Roberts. In response the woman said that a "gang of ruffians came" and pulled up her garden "in the middle of the night. She said that she had been told that a fellow by the name of Henry Nichols had been the leader of the gang." The woman handed over the starts to

90. Baird, "Short History," 131–32.

91. Baird (1848–1910) was born in Quincy, Illinois, and came to Utah with the Alvus H. Patterson company in 1863. He married Fanny E. Sessions (1855–1908) on March 7, 1870, and Margaret Ellen Randall (1858–1931) on July 8, 1880. He was well known as a blacksmith in Davis County, and also worked as a surveyor for the Denver and Rio Grande Railroad. See Baird, Cooper, and Baird, *Remembrances and Biographies*.

92. According to the local newspaper, this occurred in approximately 1874 when Roberts was seventeen. See "Hon. B. H. Roberts," *Davis County Clipper*, Oct. 10, 1895, 2.

93. In a letter to Melvin J. Ballard, Roberts referred to Fanny Sessions Baird as "the wife of the man with whom I served as the apprentice in the blacksmith trade, with whom I made my home for three years, and was a 'mother' to me." She died the day before Ballard's father, Henry Ballard. See B. H. Roberts to "My Dear Melvin," Feb. 28, 1908, box 1, fd. 1, Ballard Scrapbooks.

94. If this is the case, it is an interesting rejection of his stepfather, Seth Dustin, in favor of identifying with Ann's second husband, William John Nichols, a man he had never met.

95. Baird, "Short History," 132.

96. Madsen, *Defender of the Faith*, 16.

Roberts, "not knowing that he was the one who had pulled up the plants the night before."[97]

At times, Roberts's rough edges came in handy assisting James Baird, who, in addition to being a blacksmith, served as a Davis County deputy sheriff. On one occasion he learned that three brothers living in the area had stolen some horses and were heading to Montana with their ill-gotten gain. Baird deputized the rough-and-ready Roberts, and they trailed them northwest to Tremonton, catching up with them at daybreak while they were sleeping. At that point, Baird "held his gun on them while B. H., on hands and knees, crept up and removed their guns."[98] Roberts's life reached a turning point one day while Baird was working at the anvil. Obviously stressed, he went to Baird

> and excitedly said "I need five dollars. The sheriff is after me." James replied, "For the last several years I have sponsored you and gotten you out of scrapes. No, you can just face the music." B. H. stepped up to him and extended his hand across the anvil saying "Here is my hand and here is my honor. If you get me out of this scrape, I promise that you will never have to do it again." James put his hand in his pocket, pulled out the five dollar gold piece and gave it to him. B. H. was as good as his word. James never had to bail him out again."[99]

With his new commitment to clean living, education became extremely important to Roberts. He had arrived in Utah functionally illiterate, his only real training coming from Mrs. Tovey. Once he settled in Bountiful, his mother arranged to have him spend time in a private school run by Hannah Flint Holbrook. In his agreement with Baird, Roberts had arranged that he could attend the local school three months out of the year.[100] It also appears that at some point he was enrolled in Morgan Commercial College, which taught grammar, spelling, commercial law, and business correspondence. Roberts is included on a list of students covering the years 1867–74.[101]

---

97. Baird, "Short History," 132.

98. Baird, 133.

99. Baird, *Life of James Hyrum Baird*, 317–18.

100. Madsen, *Defender of the Faith*, 7.

101. Morgan Commercial College Collection. Others on the list included Heber J. Grant, Orson F. Whitney, James H. Moyle, Matthias F. Cowley, and J. Golden Kimball—all of whom would play a role in Roberts's later life. Roberts's possible attendance

Baird introduced his young apprentice to the Young Men's Club of Centerville, a forerunner of the LDS Church's Young Men's Mutual Improvement Association, and later persuaded Roberts to give a short talk. Gripped by stage fright, he was unable to utter a word, and, as laughter broke out, Baird led him back to his seat. The next morning at breakfast the two of them talked about the experience, and Roberts predicted to Baird that "The day will come when I will stand before the pulpit and they will listen to me preach."[102] Despite this difficult experience, the club soon provided better companions, fellowship, an opportunity for service, and a sizable library of historical and theological volumes.[103] By this point Roberts had "taken to books and would have a book in his hand reading while working the bellows at the forge." Eventually, such intellectual pursuits replaced his tendency toward a life on the rowdy margins of Utah society, and Roberts's "talents began to unfold, and he showed ability as a speaker."[104] But occasionally, his rough past was useful. When a boisterous local

> gang of ruffians had vowed to disrupt the [MIA] dances, James deputized B. H. to help him when he got word that the ruffians would be there. The dance had a good start when one of the troublemakers walked out onto the center of the floor and started jumping up and down, yelling, and making a general disturbance. James Baird walked out to where he was, took a good swing at him with his powerful blacksmith arm and the man measured his length on the floor. He and B. H. then carried him about a half block to the jail where he lay until morning, when they found he had a broken jaw. Needless to say, they had no more trouble at the dances.[105]

---

occurred after March 1869 since he is not listed as attending in a publication of that date. See *Morgan's Commercial College*, 3–4.

102. Baird, *Life of James Hyrum Baird*, 317–18.

103. While no record of that library seems to exist, its holding were probably similar to those of the Kaysville YMMIA library. Among the titles included were *Plutarch's Lives*, Mosheim's *Ecclesiastical History*, McCauley's *History of England*, Chambers's *Encyclopedia*, Gibbons's *Decline and Fall of Rome*, and biographies of US political figures like Franklin, Washington, and Lafayette. Many of these titles found their way into Roberts's writings from then on. See "Catalogue, YMMIA Library, Kaysville, Davis County, UT," CHL.

104. "B. H. Roberts, Son of This County Who Won Renown Dies," *Davis County Clipper*, Sep. 29, 1933, 1.

105. Baird, "A Short History," 133.

On March 8, 1877, five days before his twentieth birthday, Roberts was ordained to the Melchizedek Priesthood office of Seventy.[106] That same month, he fulfilled his contract with Baird and left to work on a ranch for the Centerville Dairy,[107] run by two of Baird's brothers-in-law. A dozen or so young people worked at the ranch. While working there he wrote a lengthy letter to his mother asking her to send him some clothes because the "girls are like so many sisters for they treat me as if I were their own brother, [and] … both wash and mend my clothes." He also told his mother,

> I have been to Porterville today and from our ranch it is a distance of some 20 miles & back. … I then got a fresh horse and rode ten miles further making 50 miles I have rode today, and I returned in time to milk 17 cows. I am getting to be quite an accomplished horseman, and it takes a long days ride to tire me. … I have read the Book of Mormon, P. P. Pratt's Key to Theology, a discussion between O. Pratt and J. G. Newman. Also a work on practical morality. I have renewed a course of English grammar, besides that I have kept a lively correspondence with my schoolmaster … on various points of doctrine. I also do my share of conversation and endeavor to cheer up my companions and make time pass as quickly as possible. …[108]

Among the young people on the ranch was Sara Louisa Smith (usually referred to as Louisa), the eldest daughter of Davis County Stake President William R. Smith, and his first wife Emeline Leavitt Smith. She and Roberts may have first met when Roberts

---

106. At that point, the office of seventy, which originated in the 1830s under LDS Church founder Joseph Smith, was being re-conceptualized. Essentially, Seventies quorums were organized at a local level—generally in wards and stakes—and given the task to preach and bear witness to non-Mormons. They were thought of as the church's missionary cadre. Over the next five decades Roberts would be a fierce defender of the importance of the Seventies within the church, and rise to be one of their leading figures. For an overview of the situation at this time, see Hartley, "Seventies in the 1880s," 62–88.

107. Baird allowed Roberts to stay with his family until his marriage. Edwin Baird notes that "many of the people of Centerville" sent their cows up to forage for food at the dairy, which was located in Weber Canyon at a place called Cottonwood. Baird says that despite the noisy hilarity between the boys and the girls as they tended the cows, Roberts "was always in a corner reading a book. He had developed such concentration that the noise never bothered him unless they mentioned his name." Baird, "A Short History," 132.

108. Roberts to Mother, June 27, 1877, box 4, fd. 1, Roberts Papers (UU). Roberts was a faithful correspondent with his mother over the years, and those letters are important sources of his activities and attitudes.

accompanied her father as they preached throughout the stake.[109] They were a very dissimilar couple, but Louisa discovered that Roberts "was poetic, full of life, and in his bearing and aspirations something of a Romeo." Roberts and Louisa were married on January 24, 1878, by Church President John Taylor in the Salt Lake Endowment House.[110] The couple acquired two small lots in Centerville, and a little over a year later their first child, Adah, was born on February 12, 1879.[111]

Roberts's attitudes toward this first marriage is telling. In his autobiography years later, Roberts questioned the wisdom of the marriage in dispassionate, unemotional words, saying that among the many

> foolish things done while attending school was to contract a marriage without any forethought or scheme looking to the maintenance of the relationship with dignity and reasonableness of successful negotiation with the consequences involved in such relation. I had been engaged before the opportunity for attendance at the university had come to me. It was an engagement that I could not reconcile myself to ignore after the opportunity to attend school had come to me. It therefore happened that I undertook to fulfill the engagement without proper preparation to meet the obligations. It was with a sense of being bound in honor to that obligation that I undertook to fulfill it. Of course, it resulted in multiplying my problems in life.[112]

This assessment contrasts markedly with views expressed at other times. For example, while serving his first mission in Tennessee, writing on his twenty-fifth birthday, Roberts noted that the autumn after finishing his apprenticeship to Baird without "money, property or sense,"

109. "B. H. Roberts Son of This County," 1. William R. Smith (1826–94) married Emeline Leavitt (1832–88) on March 3, 1853. At this point, Smith had four plural wives as well.

110. Taylor (1808–87) was called as an apostle in 1838, was close to Joseph Smith, and was imprisoned at Carthage Jail beside him. He became the third president of the church after the death of Brigham Young in 1877. Taylor was a major influence on Roberts.

111. Adah Roberts Naylor (1879–1946) was always close to her father. She accompanied him to Washington, DC, serving as his secretary when he was seeking to be seated in Congress. See "Roberts' Fight is On," *Morning Post* (Raleigh, North Carolina), Dec.10, 1899, 14. Truman Madsen calls Adah "bright and certainly the most literate of Louisa's children. In her mature years she became a tower of strength to her father." Madsen, *Defender of the Faith*, 105. See also "Adah Roberts Naylor, Native Centerville Woman Dies in California," *Davis County Clipper*, May 31, 1946, 5.

112. Roberts, *Autobiography*, 70

was married "having had the unparalleled audacity to ask a well-to do-farmer's daughter to come and walk the uncertain path of life with me." As a result, Louisa exchanged "a comfortable house" for none and leaving "the plenty she enjoyed [to] share my poverty." Roberts recorded that he "never regretted my choice of a wife, as I might look the world over and I never could find one who would better suit my temperament than she—my success in securing her, is the luckyest 'hit' I have ever made in life, but fear it will not prove that on her side."[113] For his part, young Roberts found Louisa as providing a "balance" and "steadiness" that he had always lacked in his family life.

In 1877, with the assistance of Baird, bishop of Centerville Nathan B. Cheney, and others, Roberts found himself at the University of Deseret enrolled in teacher training courses.[114] Roberts came to the university when its president, Dr. John R. Park, was seeking to improve the school's curricular and academic standing, aligning it with secular educational institutions.[115] Part of Roberts's education was paid for by a grant that required him to "teach one year as a district school teacher for each year of free tuition received."[116]

Among his fellow students were future political leaders James Henry Moyle,[117] Frank J. Cannon,[118] George M. Cannon,[119] and Martha Paul, who would become the first female state senator in the U.S., under her married name, Martha Hughes Cannon.[120]

113. Roberts, *History's Apprentice*, 85 (Mar. 13, 1882).

114. For general background, see Moffitt, *History of Public Education*, and Chamberlain, *University of Utah*.

115. See Jeppson, "Secularization of the University of Utah," 103.

116. See Moffitt, *History of Public Education*, 286.

117. Moyle (1858–1946) went from school to serve a mission in North Carolina, 1879–81, then to law school at the University of Michigan. He and Roberts would be lifelong friends and political allies. See Moyle, *Mormon Democrat*.

118. Cannon (1859–1933) went on to become an important journalist and politician, serving as US Senator from 1896 to 1899. Though the son of prominent church leader George Q. Cannon, he became a political gadfly and critic of Mormonism. He wrote, with Harvey J. O'Higgins, *Under the Prophet in Utah* (Boston: C. M. Clarke, 1911). For a good overview, see Cannon, "Modern Mormon Kingdom," 60–114.

119. Cannon (1861–1937), son of Angus M. Cannon and plural wife Sarah Maria Mousley, was a nephew of George Q. Cannon. He served as the first president of the Utah State Senate and was active in politics and business.

120. Cannon (1857–1932) was a medical doctor and suffragist. As the plural wife of Angus M. Cannon, she was George M. Cannon's stepmother. For more, see Lieber and Sillito, *Letters From Exile*.

Each day—by walking, riding on a mule, or hitching a ride with a farmer—Roberts would make his way to the university. Roberts was a dutiful, hardworking student, who seemed anxious to complete his studies, especially after the birth of Adah. Biographer Malan wrote the "desire for an education became a directing point in his life," and he graduated "at the head of his class."[121]

At the same time, as Truman Madsen observed, if Roberts's "intellectual gifts set him apart from the other students, so did his poverty." Roberts could no longer commute to school so he "made arrangements to bunk with three temple workmen in a little log house ... sustained by wages provided by the people of Centerville."[122]

Roberts was ashamed of his temporary living arrangements and kept them secret from his classmates. He was also ashamed of the "one ill-fitting suit" he wore daily to class during the year. But he doubtless took advantage of the school's 3,000-volume library, and Park became an important influence on him, as did Orson Pratt.[123] Roberts "was fascinated with Pratt's lectures on astronomy and mathematics," which he believed "had structure and symmetry, like a column of Roman soldiers marching by in stately, regular fashion."[124]

University records indicate that Roberts finished his course of study by attending all four terms from August 1877 to June 1878 without a break.[125] The academic year closed with commencement services on June 7, 1878. The *Deseret News* reported that after the certificates were awarded to the graduates, "an appropriate address was made by Mr. Roberts ... in which he expressed the good feelings of the pupils toward [t]he teachers, and evidenced in his own language and sentiment the excellence of the training received at their

121. Malan, *B. H. Roberts*, vii. See also "Hon. B. H. Roberts," *Davis County Clipper*, Oct. 10, 1895, 2.

122. Madsen. The above-mentioned General Register lists Roberts as living in Centerville during his first terms, but in Salt Lake City from November 1877 to June 1878. According to a later account, this temporary lodging was located in the Salt Lake 17th Ward, which was located between 200 North and South Temple, west from Main to 200 West. See "The Boyhood and Girlhood Days of Prominent Men and Women," *Deseret Evening News*, Dec.14, 1907, 7.

123. See Roberts to Mother, June 27, 1877.

124. Madsen, *Defender of the Faith*, 251.

125. See General Register of the University of Deseret, box 1. The records indicate that Roberts paid $10 per term.

hands." Roberts later noted that as he approached the talk, he realized that if "there ever was a time perhaps when an address should have been carefully written out it was then." But Roberts admitted he lacked the "disposition" to commit his thoughts to paper and that he "ventured into that rather august assembly" with the words in his head, not on paper. Roberts also admitted that he still felt limited by his inability to fully enjoy college life, and felt that his remarks were a failure, and he left quickly after delivering them. Yet, as he made his escape, a "ray of sunshine" came from LDS Apostle Joseph F. Smith who "laid his hand upon my arm and said with a twinkle of humor in his serious eyes, 'Them's my sentiments too.' That remark cheered my mind."[126]

While the local press commented on the "appropriate" remarks Roberts had made, initially there was some opposition to his being chosen to speak at all. Roberts was not present at a class meeting that Park had called to choose the speaker—perhaps "the good doctor [Park] had arranged it so I might not feel embarrassment." The meeting nominated some "popular and prosperous-born" young ladies, an action that was clearly seconded by the group. Park, however, suggested popularity was not the "usual method" of choosing the valedictorian and noted that Roberts "held the highest graduation marks and by all means should be made the one to deliver the graduating address." After some awkward silence—and criticism of Roberts's shabby attire—Park's motion carried. Roberts responded by replacing his worn brown suit with a more suitable one.[127]

Clearly the university experience was transformative. For the rest of his life, Roberts would place a high importance on the value of knowledge, intellectual challenge, and on-going improvement. Indeed, in some ways one almost senses that he stressed the life of the mind as a way of compensating for his humble beginnings and lack of formal education. He told his mother, "You have two sons in heaven that will rejoice with you." Roberts questioned his own worthiness to be in their presence someday. "It remains to be seen how I conduct myself in the future before it can be known whether I shall be worthy to mingle in. the society of my brothers Benny & Thomas;

126. Roberts, *Autobiography*, 69.

127. Roberts, 70.

but I hope to be worthy of meeting them." He also thought about the father he had not seen for many years, and about his own reputation. "[I] also wish to make the name that my father dishonored by his drunkenness honored and respected in the earth; and redeem that which he perhaps lost."[128]

After receiving his degree, Roberts taught school in Bountiful. He noted that "as my education is limited," he could only hope for "a middle place in that profession."[129] While teaching, Roberts was called on May 25, 1879, to serve as superintendent of the Davis County Stake YMMIA.[130] Roberts took his role in the MIA very seriously, and he was already writing for church publications. His article "Self Government" was published in the January 1880 issue of the *Contributor* (only the fourth month of the magazine's publication). It appears that this was Roberts's first published article.[131]

Just as Roberts's life seemed to be settling into a rhythm, it took another turn on February 29, 1880, when President John Taylor wrote to him asking if he would consider a mission in the United States. Roberts responded three days later with a lengthy, semi-autobiographical account:

> I am a young man, just started in life and therefor have little property. In fact, I have not paid much attention to acquiring property, as my endeavors so far in life have been to obtain an education. In this I have succeeded so far as to graduate in the Normal Department of the University of Salt Lake City; and as I have had neither the assistance of parents or friends it has taken pretty much all my time. I have, however, two city lots, a cow and a few other domestic animals. I also have money enough on hand to release me from my obligations, and perhaps pay my traveling expenses to my field of labor. My family, however, consisting of a wife and child I cannot leave in independent circumstances during my absence.[132]

---

128. Roberts to Mother, undated, ca. 1878, box 4, fd. 1, Roberts Papers (UU).

129. Roberts, *History's Apprentice*, 85 (Mar. 13, 1882). For an overview of conditions in the schools in Davis County at that period, see "Correspondence," *Deseret News*, Aug. 27, 1879, 2.

130. Davis Stake Young Men's Mutual Improvement Association, "Minutes and Records." See also "Quarterly Conferences," *Contributor*, Oct. 1879, 23.

131. The *Salt Lake Herald* called the issue "unusually interesting." In addition to Roberts it includes articles by Moses Thatcher, Orson F. Whitney, and B. F. Cummings Jr. See "The Contributor," *Salt Lake Herald*, Jan. 1, 1880, 3.

132. Roberts to Taylor, Mar. 3, 1880.

Roberts told Taylor he did not "offer these statements as excuse or obstacle, but that you may know my conditions, and knowing that, if you present my name at the conference I shall cheerfully and willing respond to the call; leaving the care of my family in the hands of the Lord and my brethren."[133] Taylor did present Roberts's name. He was set apart by Apostle Charles C. Rich on April 9, along with eleven others, to serve as missionaries in the United States. In total, some sixty-eight missionaries were sustained,[134] with the bulk going to Great Britain and Europe.

Numbering some fifty strong, the group of missionaries left Ogden on Friday, April 13. There "was quite a lively scene at the U[nion] P[acific] ticket office, and owing to the great pressure, the regular train, which was an unusually long one, was about forty-five minutes late in leaving the depot." It is not hard to imagine Roberts and other missionaries saying farewell to their families. "Many were the touching scenes witnessed by those present as the train started—husbands parting from their wives and children, and parents from their sons, [which] called forth and touched the deepest feelings of the human heart."[135] For the first time since his arrival in the Great Salt Lake Valley, Roberts was leaving home.

---

133. Roberts to Taylor.

134. Ironically, another missionary sustained that day was Milford Bard Shipp. His ex-wife, Margaret, would become Roberts's plural wife. For a list of the missionaries, see Historian's Office, Journal History, Apr. 7, 1880, 2.

135. "Missionaries Gone," *Ogden Junction*, Apr. 17, 1880, 2.

TWO

FIRST MISSION TO IOWA

William M. Palmer, who was called to preside over the Wisconsin–Michigan conference of the LDS Church, became Roberts's seatmate on the train journey east.[1] Roberts recorded that the elders were assigned to a "special car," and that he was surprised when some of the passengers in the Pullman car requested that one of the missionaries come and "present to them the message of the Mormon company." Because Palmer had served a previous mission in Michigan, and was "a man of some experience," he was chosen to speak for the group. Roberts bristled that "Lightning seemed to be striking close to me, and I wondered how I would have felt or appeared had the choice been delegated to me. There was an awful feeling of blankness when that thought asserted itself, and I made a hasty movement for a Bible to find out some text that I could use for such an occasion."[2]

After leaving Ogden, one of Roberts's missionary colleagues, John William Jackson, wrote, "When night came we found ourselves many miles away from home. ... After prayers ... we slept in the seats we sat in during the day ... which was very disagreeable ... but it is all for Zion so who cares?"[3] Palmer, feeling that Roberts was "very young and utterly inexperienced in missionary work," decided that he "should accompany me for a few days in missionary service" in the Sioux City, Iowa, area before leaving for his own assignment.[4]

The train arrived in Omaha at 3:00 p.m. on April 15, and the

1. Palmer would take over as president of the Northwestern States Mission, serving off and on until 1889 in that capacity

2. Roberts, *Autobiography*, 77.

3. Jackson Diary, Apr. 13, 1880.

4. Sioux City is the Woodbury County seat and is located near the headwaters of the Missouri River. In 1880, the town had a population of 7,366. Roberts would frequently stay in the various county seats, using them as a base and traveling to smaller communities.

missionaries paid twenty-five cents each to cross the river to Council Bluffs.[5] The next morning, Roberts, Hyrum Jensen, and Jens Mortensen set out for Sioux City, some ninety-five miles north, traveling along the Missouri River on the Chicago & North Western Railway. Palmer, who had stayed in Council Bluffs to take care of some business, rejoined the others later in the day. The missionaries located a church member named Samuel O. Gibbs,[6] who, as it turned out, was preparing his family to go to Utah. Despite that, in Palmer's words, Gibbs "welcomed us to his home." The next morning Jensen and Mortensen left for Minnesota.[7]

For Roberts, the return to the banks of the Missouri River brought back his journey across the plains some fifteen years earlier. On April 21, he wrote in a long poem, "Can it be that I again stand upon thy banks, that I when a mere child watched thy troubled waters. … I was then a child; leaving my native land to seek another. I was then a poor, bare-footed, ill clad, immigrant boy formed to suffer perils that I knew not of." Roberts recalled his experiences of crossing the plains, and that he now returned "for a season" to preach the gospel. He concluded, "And so it is that I stand again upon thy banks, Oh Mighty River, watching thy troubled waters. … And when I think of the mighty change since last I looked upon thee, my heart is filled with gratitude to him who has so prospered and blest me."[8]

In consultation with Gibbs, Palmer and Roberts decided that a public meeting should be held on Sunday, April 18, a day prior to Gibbs's departure for Utah. Gibbs supplied them with the funds to rent a hall for future meetings.[9] Palmer and Roberts put a notice

5. Jackson Diary, Apr. 15, 1880.

6. Gibbs (1825–1908) was born in New York and came to Sioux City in 1869. At the time that Roberts and Palmer arrived in Iowa, Gibbs was working as a carpenter, and also owned a meat market. According to one source, he "visited Salt Lake City in 1880," but returned to become the proprietor of the American House hotel. He is listed in the 1880 census as living in Salt Lake City. Gibbs, a Republican, served in the Union Army during the Civil War, and was later treasurer of Concord Iowa Township. See *History of Western Iowa*, 225–26. In his autobiography, Roberts mistakenly says that Gibbs lived in Omaha.

7. Palmer Diary, Apr. 16, 1880. See also Northern States Mission Manuscript History, Apr. 16, 1880. As we will see, Jensen joined Roberts later, and his presence proved to be very problematic.

8. B. H. Roberts, poem, Apr. 21, 1880, box 6, fd. 3, Roberts Papers (BYU).

9. See Historian's Office, Journal History, July 23, 1880, 7. Roberts may have his facts confused since the *Sioux City Daily Journal* reported that Gibbs, his wife, some of

in the local paper announcing, "Two Elders of the church of Jesus Christ of Latter Day Saints will hold a meeting on Sunday afternoon … in the house of S. O. Gibbs in the vicinity of the machine shops. If there be not room to accommodate all who come we will preach in the open air at that place."[10] While the numbers at the meeting were small, Gibbs recorded that those in attendance were "very much interested."[11]

Roberts and Palmer traveled back and forth across the Missouri River over the next few days looking "in vain" for a hall to rent in Covington, Nebraska.[12] Instead, the pair held several small meetings at the Gibbs residence after Gibbs apparently postponed his trip west. Each time the numbers at the meetings grew. The pair finally secured a hall in Sioux City and a school house on the other side of the river. They spruced up the rented hall and found "goodly numbers" in attendance. They were also able to rent a "small hall" on the Nebraska side, at the cost of "$5 per week."[13]

Roberts and Palmer decided to attempt another Sunday evening meeting. They distributed a handbill: "Mormons—Two elders of the Mormon church will deliver lectures … Sunday 22nd."[14] Roberts recalled that "with a bucket of paste and an armful of notices of the meeting, we placarded the town, giving notice of the meeting. It was a new feature of missionary work to me, and it was something of a trial."[15] The work stung Roberts's ego. "I must confess that it was a little galling to my sense of pride to become a bill poster, and it was only a strong sense of duty that induced me to do it."[16] Once the placards

---

their children, and his married daughters left for Utah on May 20. The paper also noted that Frank Mattox and Charles L. Oliver had "started by team two weeks" earlier. See "Mere Mentions," *Sioux City Daily Journal*, May 23, 1880, 5.

10. "Notice," *Sioux City Daily Journal*, Apr. 18, 1880, 3. They signed the notice, "Respectfully, Wm. M. Palmer and B. H. Roberts."

11. Palmer Diary, Apr. 18. Palmer also noted that after their meeting they attended local Baptist services.

12. See Northern States Mission Manuscript History, Apr. 20, 1880.

13. Palmer Diary, Apr. 21, 1880. The pair also rented a schoolhouse where they held meetings later in the month.

14. Palmer Diary, Apr. 23, 1880.

15. Roberts, *Autobiography*, 78. See also Palmer Diary, Apr. 24.

16. B. H. Roberts, "An Inspired Prayer," *Juvenile Instructor*, May 1, 1884, 130–31. Hereafter cited as "Inspired Prayer."

were in place, Palmer notes that they worked "cleaning up the hall" before holding a night meeting with a "goodly number" present.[17]

Palmer and Roberts, in conversation with Gibbs, were startled to find out that while Gibbs had been a member of the church in Nauvoo, he had, in Roberts's words, been "led away by the sophistry" of James J. Strang.[18] Further, while Gibbs had been baptized, most of the party heading for Utah were not church members, though several were "interested and sympathetic."[19] As the conversation continued, Gibbs "launched [into] some of the ideas of Strang having to do with Genesis 49:24," which refers to the stone of Israel.[20] According to Gibbs, the "stone" mentioned in the passage could be interpreted to mean the "stone box" that contained the gold plates. Roberts commented that from his perspective, Gibbs's "elaboration" was "given an importance which in no way could I be led to understand." Palmer on the other hand "seized upon it as a wonderful new thought," and announced that he would use it as his text at the Sunday meeting. Roberts asked his colleague if "he was not jumping at a conclusion rather suddenly." But Palmer assured Roberts he was being prompted by the Holy Ghost and that the matter was settled.[21]

When the Sunday night meeting of April 22 arrived, Palmer indeed brought up the scriptural reference, but, according to Roberts, quickly ran "into confusion," and after "about ten minutes of floundering and making nothing of what he was trying to say, he suddenly stopped." The remaining time was left to be occupied "by me, his younger and less experienced companion." Roberts admitted that his mind "seemed all confusion" when he rose to speak, but he collected his thoughts and then related "in the most simple manner" Joseph Smith's story of the Restoration. This decision, he reported, "gave me

17. Palmer Diary, Apr. 24, 1880.

18. James J. Strang (1813–56) joined the LDS Church in Nauvoo in early 1844 and was close to Joseph Smith. After Smith's martyrdom, he was one of several claimants to replace Smith as church leader. Initially he had a large following, including prominent citizens of Nauvoo. Ultimately he relocated to Voree, Wisconsin. For more, see William D. Russell, "King James Strang: Joseph Smith's Successor," in Sillito and Staker, *Mormon Mavericks*, 131–57, or Speek, *"God Has Made Us a Kingdom."*

19. Madsen, *Defender of the Faith*, 107.

20. "But his bow abode in strength, and the arms of his hands were made strong by the hands of the mighty God of Jacob; (from thence is the shepherd, the stone of Israel)."

21. Roberts, *Autobiography*, 78–79.

confidence to feel that I had struck the right line of approach, and the people listened with rapt attention." After the meeting formally concluded, Roberts recalled that "there was a long line lingering of the people asking questions concerning this subject, and considerable time was spent in answering these questions. I elaborated some portion of the great events which Joseph Smith's first vision introduced and the consequences growing out of it." For Roberts, the experience confirmed his belief that not only did he possess the talent and ability to be a good missionary, but, more importantly, convinced him that his task was to stay close to the basics of the Mormon message. This meeting marked the first time that Roberts had faced a large, almost exclusively non-Mormon crowd. Palmer apparently suffered greatly from his failure to connect with his audience, "and as soon as the house was cleared," Roberts found him "lying full length face down on the bank of the river ... in an agony of spirit."[22] For Roberts, his belief that he had made the right choice of topic was confirmed the next morning when four members of the Gibbs company "who had not been members of the church, offered themselves for baptism. They were the first fruits of my missionary services. They were baptized in the Mississippi River, and in the afternoon" departed for the West.[23]

During his stay with the Gibbs family, Roberts had a very "vivid" dream in which he had returned "to Utah without a proper release." In the dream, Roberts was reunited with his wife; she threw her arms around his neck and proclaimed, "I am so glad to see you, but O I do wish you had stayed and finished your mission." Roberts was thinking about all the practical questions of how he had gotten back to Utah and what he would say in explanation to President John Taylor for "leaving his post" when he woke with a start. He got up and, to make sure it had only been a dream, crossed the room to find Palmer "not only sleeping but snoring." The dream impacted Roberts for the

22. Roberts, 79–80.

23. Roberts, 80. In his autobiography, Roberts does not identify all four members of the Gibbs family who joined, but mentions a 'Mr. and Mrs. Oliver" as two of the individuals who were baptized. See Historian's Office, Journal History, July 23, 1880, 7. This was Gibbs's son-in-law Charles L. Oliver (1851–1909) and Gibbs's daughter Estella May Oliver Gibbs, (1857–1939). The other two family members baptized were Elizabeth Gibbs and William Burton Gibbs. See Palmer Diary, May 3–4, 1880.

rest of his mission. He prayed and "thanked God [for] this experience of what would probably happen should I desert my post. ... So acute had been my suffering and so real a counterfeit presentment to my mind that it stood as a permanent lesson." From that moment on, any temptation Roberts might have felt to shirk his duty was abandoned. "It was only necessary to recall the suffering endured in this dream to put any such thoughts from my mind thereafter."[24]

The missionary pair held "fifteen public discourses, eight of them in the same hall," though attendance steadily diminished to the point that "at the last meeting" only one man arrived.[25] One newspaper joked that the "numerous friends of Perseverance Williams are anxious to know how it was that he mistook the Mormon meeting for a barber shop the other day."[26] It also reported that the "two Mormon missionaries who are laboring in this town have not met with brilliant success so far."[27]

Around that time Roberts wrote to his mother about his experiences. He told her that he was "very busy and am not yet settled. ... I have met with no accident or mishaps of any kind since leaving home, but to the contrary I have enjoyed the blessings of God at every time. All I desire is that I may order my life so that I can claim his holy spirit." Roberts wrote his mother about the Gibbs family, telling her that "some of them were rather weak when we came but they have taken new courage and are more believing. ... I have held nine meetings since leaving home and have as many more opportunities."[28]

After trying, and failing, to get permission to hold a meeting in the First Baptist Church, Roberts arranged for a meeting to be held in the "vacant storeroom" under the Hubbard Hotel, one of the largest buildings in town. He used an empty box for a pulpit and formed pews out of planks stored near the building.[29] A few "genuinely

24. Roberts, *Autobiography*, 82.

25. Palmer Diary, Apr. 27–30, 1880.

26. "Mere Mentions," *Sioux City Daily Journal*, May 6, 1880, 3.

27. The paper followed the progress of the church. It reported that "a carload of these missionaries were sent out," and that the Mormons had enjoyed their "greatest success" recently in "the South, particularly in Missouri and among the poor whites in the back counties of Georgia and South Carolina." "Mere Mentions," *Sioux City Daily Journal*, Apr. 27, 1880, 3.

28. Roberts to Mother, Apr. 26, 1880, box 4, fd. 1, Roberts Papers (UU).

29. "Inspired Prayer."

responsible, interested persons" attended the meeting, but some hecklers came as well, turning their fury on Roberts. "There came a furious assault upon [me]," Roberts recalled. "Brick bats and what not were hurled … and the door stood likely to be crashed through. My patience was too short for this kind of treatment, and I was emphatic in my denunciations."[30] Once the meeting had concluded, the hecklers assembled in front of the building itself, shattered the windows, and seemed "intent upon manhandling" them. Palmer noted in his journal that "mobbing commenced, outside a gang … kept throwing missiles at the front door which generally confused the people & especially the women. One of the sisters was so unnerved that she could not sleep. They throwed several [things] at the front of the door, then came to the back door near the stand and throwed at it. It sounded as if they would break it down."[31] Roberts later recalled that the Sioux City police eventually intervened, but the missionaries were "encouraged" to move elsewhere.[32]

Over the next few days, they held a few meetings that were ill attended. On May 2, the only attendee at their meeting was one "unbeliever," so the missionaries bore their testimonies, "sang a hymn and dismissed."[33] Recognizing the limited opportunities there, Roberts and Palmer moved eastward.

Truman Madsen observes that initially Roberts "devised a strategy to determine which directions his preaching would take him: he would spread out the map of Iowa, pray for direction, then run his fingers along the map until he felt a sense of peace and assurance."[34] At other times, Roberts would simply respond to an internal sense of where he should go next.[35] Eventually, the pair traveled by train to

30. Madsen, *Defender of the Faith*, 112. See also "Inspired Prayer."

31. Palmer Diary, Apr. 26, 1880.

32. Madsen, *Defender of the Faith*, 112. Although the local newspaper reported on several incidents that required police intervention, there was no mention of any involvement such as Roberts describes.

33. Palmer Diary, May 2, 1880. Palmer and Roberts attended a Catholic meeting, which Palmer said consisted of "perfect nonsense." See also "Inspired Prayer."

34. Madsen, *Defender of the Faith*, 112.

35. It is difficult to ascertain Roberts's exact movements in Iowa. We know that between mid-April and late-December he was in Sioux City, Rockford, and Eldora for significant periods of time. During that time, he also traveled to many smaller communities. I have tried to keep track of his fluid movements throughout the state, but Roberts's later memories and Truman Madsen's chronology are imperfect. While there

Alden, Iowa, where Palmer had a second cousin (though they apparently never actually met).[36] After resting in a grove, the "weary and tired" missionaries made the thirty-mile trek on foot to Belmond, Iowa,[37] where Palmer also had relatives, who received them "kindly."[38] Roberts and Palmer had traveled some two hundred miles from Sioux City. Roberts recalled that they preached in Belmond on their first Sunday in town to "a large and interested audience." A second meeting was held the next day, with a "full house and good order," and among those in attendance was a Congregationalist minister who seemed "much interested" and invited the pair to come to his small community of Fryeberg.[39] But Palmer left on May 10 for his assignment in Michigan,[40] leaving Roberts, at least temporarily, to "carry on the work we had begun" alone.[41] "I was truly without purse and scrip," Roberts recalled, "all the money I had brought with me having been expended. But occasionally the way was marvelously opened, and I began the missionary experience of an elder in my church. The means came in to my hands through a gift, and I was

---

are indications that Roberts kept some sort of journal during his first few months in Iowa, the earliest journal that is extant covers the period from December 25, 1880, through December 1881.

36. Alden had an 1880 population of 495. Hardin County's population at the same time was 17,807. It appears Palmer's relatives may have been named "Farrell," with many residents in Hardin County having that name. The same is true for Alden, Iowa, as well.

37. Belmond was a small community in Wright County, with a population of 5062.

38. Palmer Diary, May 8, 1880. See also Northern States Mission Manuscript History, May 4, 1880.

39. Palmer Diary, May 9, 1880.

40. Roberts reports that prior to leaving, Palmer had written a letter "advising Elder [Hyrum] Jensen to come and labor with me" as soon as possible. See Historian's Office, Journal History, July 23, 1880, 7; and Madsen, *Defender of the Faith*, 111. Jensen would not arrive until early July. See also Northern States Mission Manuscript History, May 10, 1880.

41. Palmer Diary, May 10, 1880, and Historian's Office, Journal History, July 23, 1880, 7. Palmer continued to encounter considerable opposition over the issue of polygamy. Palmer had one wife at the time, though he would marry into polygamy sometime in 1881. The *Kalamazoo Gazette* reported that "William Palmer, a Mormon preacher laboring in Montcalm County, publicly charges that a prominent Methodist preacher whom he does not name, hired a certain woman in Grand Rapids to register with him as his wife at the Ionia Hotel and then talked to Palmer on the exceeding wickedness of polygamy, all the way from Grand Rapids to Ionia, the virtuous woman sitting by and apparently helping along the argument." "State News," *Kalamazoo Gazette,* May 6, 1881, 1. See also, "Missionaries in Michigan and Minnesota," *Deseret News,* Oct. 5, 1881, 569, and Palmer Diary, May 10, 1880.

able to hire halls, print notices in the newspaper and was excessively active through all this region of the country."[42]

Roberts was effectively alone, preaching in the Belmond area, as well as in Franklin, Cerro Gordo, Floyd, and Butler Counties.[43] He labored without a companion and had no direct supervisor. As a result, he sent written reports "directly to President Taylor," his long-time role model and hero, who personally provided instructions on how he should proceed.[44]

While he was in Floyd County, a group of ministers pledged to attend Roberts's next public meeting with the goal of "exposing and stamping out Mormonism." Roberts wrote that he rose to the occasion because the

> spirit of the Lord was with me, it loosened my tongue, and the ministers soon became tired of taking notes. It was proved from holy writ that God had always called men by prophecy, inspiration and revelation to preach the Gospel and administer the ordinances of salvation ... and I then proclaimed to them that God had again spoken again from Heaven ... [and] that I was sent to them by that authority to call upon them to repent of their sins and turn unto the Lord.[45]

Roberts said that his remarks left the ministers at the meeting silent, and it was only when they returned to their own congregations that they could again attack Mormon claims. However, a contemporary newspaper account derided his efforts, saying that "Their audiences are largely ladies, as are a majority of their converts."[46]

In June 1880, Roberts traveled to Cerro Gordo County, where he spent time in Rockwell, which had approximately 250 residents. "My past experience had taught me that it was almost useless to apply [to preach at] those sectarian church houses, so I applied to

---

42. Roberts, *Autobiography*, 82.

43. All four counties are located in north central Iowa. None of them exceeded 15,000 in population.

44. Madsen, *Defender of the Faith*, 111. More than a decade later, Roberts would author a biography of Taylor in which he said he "loved" the Mormon leader because he "was the embodiment of those qualities of mind and heart which most become a man." See Roberts, *Life of John Taylor*, iii–iv.

45. Madsen, *Defender of the Faith*, 114.

46. [Untitled], *Alden Times*, July 30, 1880, 1.

Mr. Howard,[47] the director of the school house, for the use of that building. After explaining my business, he willingly gave his consent, but stated that he would not attend the meeting as he was not a religious character, and did not care to attend religious meetings."[48]

After advertising the meeting throughout the town, Roberts arrived at the building to find it locked. He learned that the school's teacher "was a Methodist [who] had taken the key with him as he did not want a 'Mormon' to preach in *his* school house." A group of "young men" was gathered at the door to "hear the 'Mormon'" and asked if they could take the door off the hinges to gain entrance. Ultimately, Howard was able to locate another key, the door was unlocked, and the meeting commenced. Roberts recalled that the "room was crowded, and I had good liberty of the Spirit." He announced that he would hold another meeting the next night, and that since he was there "without purse or scrip," he would "regard it as a great kindness if some one present would give me food and lodging." But no one offered, so, after the meeting ended, Roberts "blew out the lights; and after committing myself to God made my valise a pillow, and laid down to pleasant dreams."[49]

The next morning Roberts resolved to find better sleeping arrangements to continue his mission in Rockwell. So "at early dawn I left the school house, and … asked the Lord to open the way before me, and direct me to a place where I could obtain lodging during my stay in the neighborhood. I noticed a large, white house, nearly surrounded by poplar trees. The Spirit said that was the place." A man who identified himself as Trapp[50] said he was the owner. Roberts explained who he was and what he was doing in Rockwell and asked if he could provide him with "food and lodging for about two weeks." Roberts was astonished when Trapp, who had at first seemed taken aback, quickly agreed to his request. "He bid me welcome, and he lodged and fed me throughout the time, and never wavered. …

47. This was likely George W. Howard (1842–1913), a store clerk who lived in Rockwell.

48. B. H. Roberts, "A Fair Infidel," *Juvenile Instructor,* May 15, 1884, 148–49.

49. Roberts, "Fair Infidel."

50. This was likely David S. Trapp (1826–91) who was a farmer living with his wife Margaret L. Trapp (1832–94) and five of their eight children—Frank, Ida, Charles, Minnie and Lilly. Trapp was a Union veteran of the Civil War who enlisted in 1862.

He had a very beautiful and intelligent daughter, and it was darkly hinted that he would regret his folly in keeping that 'Mormon' around when he found his daughter ruined by running off with me to Utah, etc. But none of these things appeared to move him."[51] Roberts admitted that while he had talked with many of the people in Rockwell, he did not make "many friends," and Trapp's home was the "only place where I could get a meal or a bed at night."[52]

Not long after holding his first meeting at the school house, the local Methodist minister, a Rev. Coleman, along with a group of members of his church, called upon Howard and asked him to prevent any future meetings in the school. Howard denied the request, saying, "If you preachers can't meet the boy's arguments, and show the people he is wrong, and get rid of him in that way, he can remain and use the house so long as I am director of it." After Roberts's second meeting, a similar delegation came from the local Baptist church and met with the same response from Howard. The local Congregationalists likewise challenged Howard after a third meeting with the same result.

After holding two more meetings, it became apparent to Roberts that the people of Rockwell seemed "determined not to hear the truth," so he left. Roberts regretted leaving the Trapps, but he also appreciated the "brave stand" Howard had taken in allowing him to use the school house in the face of determined opposition. "It [w]as not because he believed our doctrine," Roberts noted, "but he believed the time had come in the history of the world, when all parties desiring a hearing on any subject should be granted it."[53]

From Rockwell, Roberts went south to the small community of West Fork, in Franklin County, where he held several meetings at the local school house. These meetings attracted great attention in the community. Here again he encountered the opposition of local ministers. "I had adopted the plan of giving my hearers an opportunity of propounding questions to me at the close of each meeting, on the subjects treated of in the discourse; and these ministers hearing

51. Roberts, "Fair Infidel." The reference was probably to Ida Trapp (ca. 1863–1946).
52. Roberts.
53. Roberts.

of this, said that would be their opportunity." They would question [me] ...and 'expose Mormonism' generally."[54]

The meeting that night "was crowded—not even standing room for all that came," and the three ministers were seated in the front row facing Roberts who was seated in "the teacher's desk which served ... as a pulpit." As he began, the ministers "were ready with their pencils to take notes," and he stepped from behind the desk and stood in front of them "addressing them as a lawyer would a jury." Roberts recalled that the "Spirit of the Lord was with me," and the ministers soon "became tired of taking notes." As a result, while the ministers "moved uneasily in their seats," Roberts said it was now their turn to ask questions. After ten minutes of "perfect silence," someone in the rear of the hall said, "I guess we can go home now?" Roberts responded, "Yes I am through for the evening," and "the people filed slowly out of the house—the ministers being among the first. They had changed their mind about 'Tying up the young Mormon.'" Roberts said the next day the ministers were "visiting the members of their respective flocks, advising them not to encourage the 'Mormon' meetings by their presence," and suggesting that by listening to Roberts, they ran the risk of becoming "unsettled in their faith." Roberts felt vindicated.[55]

By June, Roberts was in Rockford, Iowa,[56] near where, some months before, Ann Eliza Webb,[57] plural wife of Brigham Young, "had poisoned the minds of the people" in lectures held in "sectarian churches."[58] Webb had spent considerable time in the Midwest in

54. B. H. Roberts, "Tying Up a 'Mormon' Elder," *Juvenile Instructor,* June 19, 1884, 171–72.

55. Roberts, "Tying Up."

56. The town, located in Floyd County, had a population of 739 in 1880. The county itself had a population of 14,677.

57. Ann Eliza Webb Young was born in Nauvoo in 1844 to Chauncey and Eliza Jane Webb. After a marriage to James Dee ended in divorce, she married Brigham Young in 1868. She divorced him in 1873, was excommunicated in 1874, and caused a stir with her book *Wife No. 19*. She died in Sparks, Nevada, in 1917.

58. It is not clear when Webb was in the area. Copies of the *Rockford Reveille* for 1879 and 1880 are no longer extant. Roberts identifies her as Webb, though often in the press she was identified as Young. Roberts also refers to her as the reported "nineteenth wife" of the Mormon leader. See "Local News," *Atlantic (Iowa) Telegraph*, Apr. 7, 1880, 4, which noted regarding Mormonism that "Few could listen to her without feeling that our government has been entirely too lenient in its dealings with this moral and social evil."

1879–80 as part of her national anti-polygamy tour lecturing on the topic of "In and Out of Utah." Because of national legislative efforts, it was a good time for critics of Mormonism. She said her "sole desire" was to "arouse the people of the country against the shameful evil" of polygamy, which was "openly practiced in Utah."[59] As a result, Roberts states, "only a very limited hearing could be obtained in the city."[60]

On July 9, while in Rockford, Floyd County, Roberts was rejoined by Hyrum Jensen, who had originally been sent to Minnesota.[61] Roberts secured a hall and placed ads in the local paper with the understanding that Jensen was coming with sufficient funds to pay for these obligations. But though his new companion had left Utah "with several hundred dollars," he was as broke as Roberts. Nonetheless, Roberts and Jensen held "several meetings," and despite it being "a very busy time of the year, our meetings have been very well attended." Over time, however, they found the people in Floyd County "so busy ... that it was very difficult to get hearers. This being the case we worked awhile in the harvest field, and procuring some money we [rented] halls in the towns of this and other counties as long as we had means."[62]

It may seem that Roberts met all these challenges undaunted, but in an early-August letter to his mother, Roberts admits that he had been "sad at times," being unwell both physically and psychologically, though he had overcome any depression to "a great extent since

---

59. Typical accounts may be found in "Ann Eliza Young," *Davenport Daily Gazette*, Mar. 25, 1879; "Utah's Social Scourge," *Daily Inter-Ocean* (Chicago, IL), Nov. 26, 1879, 2; and "Ann Eliza Young," *Wisconsin State Journal*, June 1, 1880, 8. Many of her lectures were held in churches or sponsored by denominational women's home missionary societies.

60. Roberts, *Autobiography*, 82–88.

61. Jens Hyrum Jensen (1859–1909), who went by his middle name, was born in Brigham City, Utah. He was set apart for his mission on April 9, 1880, by Apostle Charles C. Rich, and released on February 22, 1881. He apparently stayed in Iowa until October 1883. Roberts told his wife, Louisa, that while Jensen was later upset by his release he had been "negligent" in his duties. Apparently, Jensen had grown weary of proselytizing without purse or scrip and took a job with Allen Hughes to finance his mission. Roberts cautioned Louisa not to discuss his comments about his companion "as it might make his relatives in Davis County" feel bad. See Roberts to Louisa, Dec. 20, 1880, box 4, fd. 13, Roberts Papers (UU); and Roberts, *Autobiography*, 110–11.

62. Historian's Office, Journal History, July 23, 1880, 7, and Nov. 6, 1880, 3.

I have been absent from home. I hope eventually to control myself altogether in this thing."[63]

He did not even consider the possibility of returning home. "I would rather that my bones bleach on the plains and never see those I love than return home without the approbation of God, the Priesthood and my own conscience. It is a poor contemptible coward that will desert his post whatever the trials or difficulties he may be called to pass through. I am going to stay until the Twelve say 'It is enough, come home.'"[64] In September 1880, while working in Bremer County, *The Contributor*, an LDS magazine published for young members, printed an article by Roberts titled "The Warfare Then and Now." He told his readers that humanity would always struggle with the eternal contest between "the hosts of heaven and the legions of Lucifer."

After a time, Roberts and Jensen moved on, first working in Marshalltown,[65] then journeying some seventy-five miles toward the smaller settlement of Guttenberg,[66] not far from the Iowa–Wisconsin border. The journey was "rough, attended with hunger and sleeping out of doors," and was combined with "unfriendly" reactions along the way. Because he was suffering from malaria, Jensen's strength eventually "gave out," and he "could travel no further." Roberts left him near Elkader,[67] and traveled another twenty-five miles to Guttenberg where he pawned a watch for a few dollars and returned for his companion.[68] Once the duo was reunited, they went to Guttenberg where Roberts took Jensen "to a hotel and nursed him for two or three days with quinine and hot lemonades to fight off the malaria." Despite their initial optimism, Guttenberg "did not yield much encouragement for finding places of labor for the winter season." Instead they settled in

63. Roberts to Mother, Aug. 12, 1880, box 4, fd. 1, Roberts Papers (UU).

64. Roberts to Mother.

65. Marshalltown was the Marshall County Seat. It had a population of 6,240 in 1880. The county itself was one of the larger ones that Roberts and Jensen labored in with a population at the time of 23,572.

66. At the time, Guttenberg had a population of 1,076, and a large percentage of its residents were of German origin. Considered "one of the most conservative towns" in Clayton County, it had a strong, long-standing Lutheran presence, which may have made it less than hospitable to Roberts and Jensen's efforts. See Pierce, *History of Clayton County*, 259, 344.

67. Elkader was the Clayton County seat. In 1880, it had a population of 851. The county population was 28,829.

68. Roberts, *Autobiography*, 102.

Elkader, where Joseph Smith's youngest brother, William B. Smith,[69] lived in a "humble log and frame house in the hill two or three miles west" of town.[70] Smith biographer Kyle Walker wrote that Roberts, who "had never met an immediate family member of the founder of the Church he espoused," was excited and uneasy at the same time as he went in search of the prophet's mercurial brother.[71]

Roberts stated that initially Smith's wife took the pair to be missionaries from the Reorganized Church of Jesus Christ of Latter Day Saints[72] and received them with a "hearty welcome." But when she discovered that they were from Utah, the reception "became frigid." Roberts assured her that their intent was not to convert Smith, but that they "merely wanted to see the brother of the Prophet" and converse with him.[73] This "quieted things," and when the prophet's brother "expressed a desire for such a visit," it was arranged. After several years of spiritual wanderings, Smith had affiliated with the Reorganization led by his nephew Joseph Smith III.[74] As a result, William Smith had again returned to missionary work and had "preached both Christian and Mormon sermons near his home in Elkader.[75] Kyle Walker notes that the "various denominations in the area not only trusted William to teach and preach, but also assigned him to fill out their "Report of Sunday Schools' to send to the Iowa State Sunday School Association."[76]

Roberts described Smith in vivid detail, noting that at the time he was

> very advanced in age. He was an unusually tall man and, though emaciated, disclosed a symmetrical and splendid skeleton of what must have

69. Roberts states that Smith was using the initial "B," which he had taken during the Civil War to "distinguish himself from the many William Smith's that were among the enlisted men." Roberts, *Autobiography*, 102. See Walker, *William B. Smith*, 447, 449, and Bates, "William Smith," 11–23.

70. Roberts, *Autobiography*, 103.

71. Walker, *William B. Smith*, 1.

72. Today the church goes by the Community of Christ. Throughout this book I use Reorganized Church or RLDS, since that was its name throughout Roberts's lifetime.

73. Roberts, *Autobiography*, 103.

74. See Walker, "William B. Smith and 'The Josephites.'"

75. Smith told his nephew Joseph Smith III that during the time Roberts had visited he had delivered some forty-five sermons. See Walker, *William B. Smith*, 109–10, 549–50.

76. Walker, 549; "Independence Day," *Elkader Register*, July 8, 1880, 3.

> been a man of about 215–30 pounds, erect, full of form, with aggressive appearance and boldness that would well nigh surpass understanding. Now, emaciated as he was, his head appeared unusually large. The features, however, were strong and fine. He was slow of speech, owing perhaps to being so subdued by the members of his household. The eyes were soft but deep blue, easily converted by the depth of them to almost dark eyes which animated or stirred with emotion. He expressed at this table conversation complete faith in the divine calling of his brother and the ultimate triumph of the work he had introduced to the world.[77]

Roberts recalled that as he and Jensen conversed with Smith, they discovered that the wife "dominated the household and William, once the proud, rebellious, pugnacious and dominant spirit in both his father's house and likewise in the church was now tame and submissive … to his arrogant and dominating wife."[78] Roberts and Jensen also witnessed that the couple's children were harsh toward their father.[79] A daughter was "disobedient and even impudent" toward Smith about the prophet Joseph Smith. One son had run away from home; another "was lying sick supposedly of malaria." When Smith asked Roberts and Jensen to administer to the son, the wife "spurned" the request with "all the contempt her nature was capable of."[80] Still, albeit grudgingly on the wife's part, it was agreed that the two missionaries would stay the night.

After the supper table was cleared, Smith showed the two missionaries photographs and manuscripts concerning the early days of Mormonism, which Roberts said were "of great interest," admitting that at the time he was "not very well informed as to the Nauvoo period history of the Church." Smith also gave them his view of the "difficulties" the Saints had suffered in Nauvoo, and showed Roberts copies of the church's official Nauvoo periodical, *Times and Seasons*. This first-hand exposure to the character of Joseph Smith and the

---

77. Roberts, *Autobiography*, 104.

78. Roberts, 103–04. Roberts frequently used the term "dominating" to describe both William Smith and his wife.

79. Apostle Anthon H. Lund wrote that Roberts reminisced that William Smith had "received him kindly but his wife would not let him pray or administer to his dying boy. The old man dared not say his soul was his own and even a daughter seventeen years old was very disobedient. If he asked her to do something she would tell him to do it himself." See Lund, *Danish Apostle*, 33.

80. Roberts, *Autobiography*, 103.

complexity of the Nauvoo years had an impact on Roberts, and set in motion an interest that would lead to his many historical studies in the years ahead. The visit also made Roberts aware of the value of primary documents and first-hand accounts. At the same time, Roberts did not accept Smith or his views uncritically.

The next morning, after an unpleasant breakfast with Smith's wife, it was clear she would not welcome them for another night, so William proposed to accompany Roberts and Jensen to Elkader. Upon arriving in town, Smith took them to a drug store owned by a friend and arranged for them to stay there. Roberts discovered that Smith was well regarded in the town, and even those who had no desire to affiliate with any branch of Mormonism viewed Smith as an honest and decent man, and certainly a persuasive defender of his brother Joseph. Smith then announced that he would return to his home. As they walked with him to the place where he would turn and go another direction, Smith extended his hands to Roberts and Jensen and "burst" into "a flood of tears." Roberts mused on what might have moved the elderly man into such a show of emotion. "Was it the recollection of his own youth when he too under the favor of God had been an itinerant missionary going from house to house to present the great message of the New Dispensation. The question could not be determined, nor all the dramatic experiences of William Smith in the church at Nauvoo, Kirtland, and in New York." After walking a "short distance," Roberts and Jensen stopped to look at the "retreating form of the prophet's brother" and discovered that he had stopped as well. As he walked up the hill, on three occasions Smith stopped, looked directly at them, and waved farewell until finally he was out of view. And so ended what Roberts called his personal "contact with the nearest relative of the prophet Joseph Smith" that he had ever made.[81] Throughout the rest of his life, Roberts would continue to be fascinated with Joseph Smith and wrote many studies of him and his times.[82]

81. Roberts, 105. For more details on William Smith, see *Autobiography*, 105–07.

82. In addition to his multi-volume chronological studies, Roberts was the author of *The Rise and Fall of Nauvoo* (Salt Lake City: Deseret News Press, 1900), and *Joseph Smith: Prophet–Teacher* (Salt Lake City: Deseret News, 1908).

By this time Roberts noted they had traveled 550 miles, held ninety-five meetings, and listed sixteen houses that had "closed their doors against us."[83] Roberts and Jensen stayed in Elkader for about two weeks, but found "no very promising hopes of a permanent field of labor."[84] They returned to their original plan and went on to Guttenberg which "did not yield much encouragement for finding a place of labor for the winter season, and so unfriendly was the population through which we traveled that we had to sleep out [in the open] several nights."

They moved on to Eldora, Hardin County.[85] Part of their decision came because Roberts had discovered that "a Mr. Thomas, who for some years had lived in Utah and worked in the mines … and who had married a daughter" of his stepfather Seth Dustin was living there.[86] When they made contact, they discovered that Thomas and his family were "living in very humble circumstances and scarce could give an abiding place for more than a few days."[87] Over time, they made the acquaintance of several people, including a farmer of some means named Allen B. Hughes, who "invited us to make his house our home, which we did to quite an extent during the time we remained in Hardin County."[88] The two missionaries were able to preach in four separate school houses, rotating among them "for

83. "Correspondence," *Deseret News*, Nov. 24, 1880, 679.

84. Roberts, *Autobiography*, 107.

85. Eldora was the county seat of Hardin County. The total population of the county in 1880 was 17,807. The three most populated towns were Eldora, 1,584; Ackley, 1,517; and Iowa Falls, 955.

86. Roberts is referring to William Thomas (1842–1918) and his wife Hannah Sophia Dustin (1849–1904), a daughter of Seth Dustin and his first wife, Hannah Loveland Dustin. The couple was married on November 8, 1874, and had lived in the Eldora area since 1876. At the time Roberts visited them, they were the parents of two sons. "Death Notice," *Semi-Weekly Herald* (Eldora, Iowa), Apr. 6, 1904; and "Obituary," *Semi-Weekly Herald*, Apr. 9, 1904. Sophia, who had previously been married to Jerome W. Kinney, was described as "a good wife, a loving mother and a neighbor who will be sadly missed in the community." Several of Sophia's daughters from her marriage to Kinney also lived in the Eldora area.

87. Roberts, *Autobiography*, 107.

88. Hughes (1824–1914), his wife, Laura (1826–85), and their son Rollin (1859–1949), were longtime residents of Hardin County, having arrived in 1859. Hughes and Roberts kept in touch over the years. At his death, the *Hardin County Ledger* called Hughes "a man of excellent reputation . . . held in high esteem by all who knew him ("Old Resident Passes Away," *Hardin County Ledger*, July 16, 1914, 1); Sillito, *History's Apprentice*, 4, 14 (Dec. 25, 1880, Feb. 4, 1881).

some length of time." Hughes continued to care for them and "furnished an excellent young team and a carriage and placed it at our disposal that we might go from one to the other of the schoolhouses." Hughes was "deeply interested in our message and professed much faith in many of the things we were proclaiming."[89]

Roberts and Jensen repaid their benefactor by helping him to finish his threshing. This effort was the "talk of the neighborhood" and did "much to establish our welcome throughout this district."[90] The young Mormons were also "hired about the neighborhood to different farmers" as a way of earning the funds they needed to "meet the obligations of life."[91] The local populace was so fond of Roberts that he was "offered a written contract" for a sum of $1,600 to stay in the area as their minister. Roberts declined.[92]

Later newspaper accounts of Roberts's activity in Iowa give a picture of his approach as a missionary. The

> young fellow advertized by word of mouth among the neighboring farmers that he would, on a certain night, address the citizens of the

---

89. Roberts later wrote that he and Jensen had held more than thirty "generally well attended" meetings in these four schoolhouses." *Autobiography*, 108–09. See also Historian's Office, Journal History, Feb. 14, 1881, 4.

90. Roberts, *Autobiography*, 109.

91. Roberts's Iowa connections would re-emerge some nineteen years later when efforts were undertaken to deny him a seat in the US Congress. See "B. H. Roberts in Iowa," *Omaha World Herald*, Apr. 14, 1899. The paper reported that Roberts had contacted Hughes during the congressional efforts to deny him a seat, and told of his "wandering ... from the time of his departure from Hardin County 'till the present time." The paper further editorialized that Roberts made no mention of "being the husband of three wives" in disregard of the law, but asserted his "implicit belief" that Congress would not deny him the seat in the legislature "vouchsafed to him by the constitution." The article was widely reprinted. See also "Was Once an Iowa Man," *Opinion-Tribune* (Glenwood, Iowa), Apr. 13, 1899, 4; and, "He Does Not Fear," *Daily Iowa Capitol* (Des Moines, Iowa), Oct. 11, 1899, 8. While copies of the petition seeking to prevent Roberts from being seated in Congress were circulated by women at the First Presbyterian Church in Sioux City, there is no mention that he had once been a missionary in the area. See "Seeking to Expel Roberts," *Sioux City Journal*, Feb. 12, 1899, 5.

92. Madsen, *Defender of the Faith*, 123. Roberts confirms this offer. There is also evidence that Jensen, "who was offered a stock management job," stayed in the area but not as a missionary. See Roberts, *Autobiography*, 108–10. At the time Roberts told his wife, Louisa, that while Jensen had grown weary of proselytizing without purse and scrip, he initially took the job to support his mission. This may have been how Jensen became "negligent" in his duties and had been released (see above). Jensen was formally released on February 22, 1881, after Roberts had left for Tennessee. See Roberts to Louisa Roberts, Dec. 20, 1880, box 3, fd. 3, Roberts Papers (UU).

> community upon the subject of Mormonism. A large crowd gathered at the little school house on the night of the advertized lecture, and so electrified were those who heard him that he was repeatedly urged to talk upon the subject extensively. The young man would accept no collection taken among the populace, looking toward the defraying of current expenses. … He was hired about the neighborhood to different farmers; and it was thus he met the obligations of life.

Some local residents "frequently went from one schoolhouse to another" to hear the young missionaries and their message.[93]

But "health problems intervened."[94] Roberts suffered from severe nasal allergies, which were aggravated by the weather and climate. As he traveled throughout the state, Roberts, "especially when he worked in the grain fields, was in eye-itching, stuffed-nose misery." As a consequence, his "sermons became a mixture of nasal twang, sneezes and handkerchiefs." In late November Roberts "was taken sick and remained so for some time."[95] Roberts, realizing that his "health was failing rapidly," informed President John Taylor of the situation, and requested a transfer.[96]

Roberts announced his decision to his friends in Hardin County and prepared to leave. Allen Hughes insisted that Roberts spend Christmas with the Hughes family. As other visitors came to the home, Roberts decided it would make sense to relocate to Mr. Severson's who had urged him to make more frequent visits, and began to pack his things. Once Hughes discovered that Roberts intended to leave, he "came to the bedroom that had been assigned to me in the home and with mock severity demanded to know what the occasion was of the packing." Roberts said that it was not right that he should keep "this beautiful bedroom" when others could use it. Hughes dumped out Roberts luggage and said "Mr. Roberts, if the Queen of England should come to the Hughes residence she would

93. "B. H. Roberts in Iowa."

94. Madsen, *Defender of the Faith*, 123–24.

95. "Correspondence," *Deseret Evening News*, Feb. 24, 1881, 4.

96. See Roberts to Louisa Roberts, Dec. 20, 1880. Roberts records that he requested the transfer because "the severe coldness of the oncoming winter was seriously affecting my ailment of a head trouble from swollen membranes of the sinus cavity." See also Roberts, *Autobiography*, 111.

not be permitted to disturb your lodgings here."[97] Hughes asked Roberts to stay, visit with his guests, and "teach them your faith." As a result, Roberts made "proper excuses" to Severson, and remained with the Hughes family. Over the course of the next few days, he held his final meetings "in the four schoolhouses enclosing the square" and engaged in "extended conversations and explanations" to the other visitors, including "three ladies from Chicago, who became intensely interested in the message I had to deliver."[98]

A few days later in December, upon Taylor's recommendation, Roberts received word from President John Morgan[99] of the Southern States Mission that he was being "transferred to the more congenial climate of Tennessee."[100]

97. Roberts, *Autobiography*, 112.

98. Roberts, 112.

99. John H. Morgan (1842–94) served in the Union army during the Civil War, came to Utah as a non-Mormon to establish Morgan Commercial College, and was baptized into the LDS Church in 1867. He was a missionary and then Southern States mission president from 1875 to 1884 when he returned to Utah to become a member of the First Council of the Seventy. Roberts and Morgan became close friends. See Richardson, *Life and Ministry of John Morgan*.

100. Madsen, *Defender of the Faith*, 123–24. Roberts later reported that he received a "sufficient" amount of money from the church to "meet the railroad and other expenses" involved. He was also given support in funds and clothing from the local residents. By this time there is very little mention of the missionary efforts of Hyrum Jensen. Roberts notes that while he was receiving this tangible aid from local residents in preparation for the move to Tennessee, Jensen was still working for Hughes, and makes it clear that he never received "any part of Elder Jensen's remuneration." Roberts received an overcoat from Hughes and a "fine pair of handmade boots" from Severson. Roberts, *Autobiography*, 110–11.

THREE

MISSIONARY SERVICE IN TENNESSEE, 1881-82

Roberts spent two days saying goodbye to his friends, Severson and Hughes, then left Iowa for Tennessee on December 27, 1880.[1] His companion, Hyrum Jensen, took him to Eldora where, after waiting for seven hours, he caught what he called the "Iron Mountain Railroad"[2] south, the route paralleling the frozen Mississippi River.[3] It was the beginning of a long journey that included layovers in Ottumwa, Iowa,[4] and St. Louis, where it was "intensely cold,"[5] before making his way via the Memphis and Chattanooga railroad line through Kentucky. While in Columbus, Kentucky, Roberts made friends with "a young Kentuckian," and they sought a "place of stopping." In response, the railroad conductor "told us to go to the waiting room [of the depot]. Doing so we found the floor and benches covered with woolly haired Negroes and tramps. They were rather rough looking so we concluded to seek other quarters." Told there was a hotel "further up the river," Roberts and the Kentuckian knocked on the door and "presently a Negro crawled out of his nest & opened the door. There was a good fire." Eventually, the "little negro" went to a larger room occupied by "three niggers" and asked

1. A useful resource for understanding the mission is the Southern States Mission Manuscript History.

2. Roberts seems to be referring to the St. Louis, Iron Mountain and Southern Railway.

3. Roberts later made a comparison of the Mississippi River's conditions with those of 1846, when the frozen river "marked off the beginning of the exodus of the saints from Nauvoo." Roberts, *Autobiography*, 113.

4. A small town in southeast Iowa approximately forty miles from the Missouri border.

5. Roberts remembered the journey as uncomfortable, noting that the "weather was so severe" that when he left the St. James Hotel in St. Louis "to catch a streetcar for the depot to resume the journey, my ears were frozen white and stiff, both hands being engaged in carrying my valises, books and clothing. From this little incident I suffered quite sharply for several days." See Roberts, *Autobiography*, 113; and, "Correspondence," *Deseret Evening News*, Feb. 24, 1881, 4.

since there was only one bed what they should do to accommodate the two white men. Roberts says that he and his Kentucky friend assessed the situation and "told him we would sit by the fire until morning."[6] In many ways this was Roberts's introduction to issues of race, and the start of his attitudes toward it.

Roberts arrived in Nashville on December 29.[7] After visiting the state capitol and the grave of US President James K. Polk, Roberts traveled via the train to Tullahoma, and then on to Manchester, in Coffee County.[8] He expected two missionaries, George H. Carver[9] and Joseph Ford,[10] to meet him at the train station, but they were nowhere to be found. He believed the two missionaries to be staying with a church member named Richard T. Fagan,[11] and tried to find the way to his house. After crossing a partly frozen stream three times to try and find them, he "prayed to the Lord and he showed me the way to a house where a man by the name of Anderson lived."[12]

Truman Madsen records that Roberts told Anderson "rather pitifully" that he was "wet, tired and hungry. I would like the privilege of sitting by your fire till morning." Anderson was "famed as an anti-Mormon, and had announced publicly that no Mormon elder would be safe in his 'clearin.'"[13] He must have been unaware that

6. Roberts to Mother, Jan. 10, 1881, box 4, fd. 1, Roberts Papers (UU).

7. For more on the journey, see Roberts, *History's Apprentice*, 4–5 (Dec. 27–28, 1880).

8. Manchester, the Coffee County seat, is approximately sixty-five miles southeast of Nashville, and twenty miles northeast of Tullahoma. The county had a population of 12,894, and Tullahoma, 1,083. Roberts was in this area for the next two weeks.

9. George H. Carver (1854–1922) was born in Kaysville, Utah. He was set apart for his mission on June 14, 1879, by Joseph Young Sr., and released on February 1, 1881. Carver noted that in 1880 there were sixty three baptisms, while eighty-two converts "bid adieu to their Tennessee homes and emigrated to Colorado, where prosperity has crowned their existing labors in building new homes and thereby strengthening the Stakes of Zion." Such reports encouraged Roberts in his efforts to baptize and relocate local residents. See "Correspondence," *Deseret News*, Feb. 23, 1881, 59.

10. Joseph Ford (1852–1948) was born in England. Ford was set apart on September 4, 1880, for his mission by Apostle Joseph F. Smith, and returned on May 1, 1882. Ford had moved to Centerville with his family when he was three, and he lived there the rest of his life. He was a stock raiser, farmer, and fruit grower. Ford survived Roberts by fifteen years; they remained good friends.

11. Richard Thomas Fagan (1830–1895) was a farmer living in Coffee County with his wife Lydia Ann Ward Fagan (1840–1893) and their nine children. A few months later, Fagan became the leader of the LDS branch in Manchester, Tennessee.

12. Roberts, *History's Apprentice*, 5 (Jan. 1, 1881); Madsen, *Defender of the Faith*, 124–25.

13. Madsen, *Defender of the Faith*, 124.

Roberts was a Mormon missionary, for he was "miraculously hospitable" towards him. The next morning Anderson's son assisted him with a boat, and he crossed the river and made his way to the Fagan home, but the two missionaries were not there. Roberts finally located them on January 3, and settled in to tract with them in the area. Roberts wrote to his mother that the change in climate had worked and his "health is better; not being at all troubled by my headaches."[14]

The next few days Roberts, Carver, and Ford spent most of their time traveling and tracting around Coffee County, holding small meetings and staying with locals. Roberts's arrival was the signal to Carver that he could return home, and they separated from him on January 10, continuing on to Wilson County,[15] some fifty miles north. There, Roberts met J. I. Sanders, a wealthy Wilson County magistrate and farmer who, though he never joined the church, provided support and accommodations to the young missionaries on several occasions.[16] J. Golden Kimball, who would become acquainted with Sanders two years later, remarked

> although he is a perfect libertine and immoral as he can be, yet he has done a great deal of good. He is one of those eccentric fellows and is the owner of 1500 acres of land. Three year ago he could not read, but becoming interested in the Bible, he soon learned to read and is now able to wind up any of the ministers. I heard him go after one man. He said "My God man, where are your prophets? Your Apostles and anything like the kingdom? You haven't got it and you will all go to hell before your ears get cold." He serves all that visit him with the same dose.[17]

---

14. Roberts to Mother, Jan. 10, 1881, box 4, fd. 1, Roberts Papers (UU). As we will see, Roberts experienced frequent and, at times, debilitating headaches throughout his life.

15. Located in north central Tennessee, the county had a population of 28,747 in 1880. See Drake, *Historical Sketch of Wilson County*.

16. J. I. Sanders (1824–?) was a widowed farmer living in Wilson County with his five children and two grandchildren. Apparently, his middle name was Irving, and Roberts refers to him by that name as well as on other occasions "Irve" and "Erve," and described him as a "popular man in Wilson County" because of his charity in lean times. Roberts notes that while "wealthy and engaged in large enterprises [he] could not read or write," and was a man "loose in his relations with women, and in addition to his own large family by legal marriage, he was the father of many children to whom he sustained an attitude of great kindness." Roberts and Ford held several meetings in his "spacious but ill furnished home." See Roberts, *Autobiography*, 118–19; and Madsen, *Defender of the Faith*, 124–25. Both sources refer to him as "Saunders," which is incorrect.

17. Kimball Journal, June 27, 1884.

While staying with Sanders, Roberts and Ford held meetings "nearly every night."[18] But these meetings met with little success. It probably did not help that the local press seems to have taken an interest in Mormonism. On February 25, the *Hickman Pioneer* reported that "accusations of dishonesty" were now made by some Mormons against the money received as tithing. The paper asserted that the church received "a million dollars annually" from tithing.[19] These were other issues, including polygamy, that Roberts would have to deal with.

He continued to have headaches, likely tied to the sinus problems he had experienced in Iowa.[20] Apparently he drank some whisky to relieve the pain, but this self-medicating made him feel "bad because my old weakness is still not overcome."[21] A few months later he prayed "for strength to master my weakness."[22] Roberts also suffered frequently from melancholy—what we would probably today call clinical depression. It could be that his headaches and occasional use of alcohol as a remedy were related to the depression.[23]

By this time Roberts and Ford were residing in Baird's Mill[24] with J. R. Baird and his family.[25] LDS missionaries had been active in the area for two years. On Saturday, January 22, they obtained permission to hold a meeting at the courthouse in nearby Lebanon, where they found themselves in front of a "good congregation."

18. "Correspondence," *Deseret Evening News*, Feb. 24, 1881, 4.

19. "Peery County," *Hickman Pioneer*, Feb. 25, 1881, 4.

20. Such sinus headaches would continue for the rest of his life. For example, see Lund, *Danish Apostle*, 226.

21. Roberts, *History's Apprentice*, 13 (Jan. 28, 1881).

22. Roberts, *History's Apprentice*, 25 (Mar. 25, 1881).

23. Roberts would continue to think about the Word of Wisdom generally, and the effects of alcohol and tobacco specifically. For example, George F. Richards recorded that he attended a lecture by Roberts on January 21, 1884, where he told his listeners, "Tobacco oil is as poisonous as strychnine. Tobacco juice will kill a dog, hence we are in danger when we chew tobacco. Smoking brings on consumption. Liquor does not unite with the blood. One part of the body governs muscular faculties and when liquor enters it cannot do its duty and the muscles relax." See Richards, *A Family of Faith*, 215–16.

24. Organized around 1874, it was named for the Baird family, which was prominent in the area. See "Baird's Mill Branch of Wilson County, Tenn., 1881–88," *Amateur Mormon Historian*, Dec. 29, 2014, amateurmormonhistorian.blogspot.com.

25. Likely this refers to Jerome Ridley Baird (1848–1936), a farmer in Wilson County living with his wife Sarah (1848–1930) and their four children. Baird is a common surname in Wilson County, and includes both white and black residents.

Despite the attendance of some representatives from Cumberland University,[26] a Presbyterian institution with a significant law school and theological school, Roberts noted that the "spirit of God rested upon us and we were enabled to bear a faithful testimony." They also held a meeting the next evening and afterward received a petition signed "by many citizens" asking them to speak the following night on the subject of polygamy. Roberts and Ford agreed, and arrived to find "a greater number than ever assembled." The interest among the audience well exceeded the two hours that had been set aside for the discussion. Roberts noted that "the divinity students expressed their surprise that so much could be found in the scriptures and in the nature of things for the Mormon system of marriage." As a result, he stated, "the way was cleared in Lebanon for respectful deference for Mormon elders whenever we visited the place."[27]

After returning to Baird's Mill, they learned their lectures had spurred another petition to circulate upon local ministers[28] "to come and investigate our doctrine with us and test it with the scriptures." When Roberts and Ford arrived in Lebanon, they discovered that the minister who would "test" them was "a Mr. Alsup of the Campbellite or Christian faith,[29] who had "a reputation of never having engaged in public debate without driving his opponent from the platform."[30] Prior to the debate, Roberts and Ford had agreed that Roberts would speak for them. The topic was listed as "The doctrines of the 'Mormons' contradicts the teachings of the King James translation of the Bible."[31]

Alsup began, in what Roberts later conceded was a "skillfully arranged" effort, by attacking the Book of Mormon, "claiming that if he could prove it to be false or in conflict with the bible he would

---

26. Founded in 1842, the school added the law school ten years later, and the theological school two years after that. Almost destroyed during the Civil War, the school re-emerged and was operating at various locations in the town by 1866.

27. Roberts, *Autobiography*, 121–22.

28. At times it appears this number may have been as high as nine.

29. This is the Restorationist Christian movement tied to the writings of Alexander Campbell (1788–1866) and his father Thomas Campbell (1763–1854) whose followers organized a non-denominational Christian church known under several names. Most often it is called the Christian Church or the Disciples of Christ.

30. Madsen, *Defender of the Faith*, 127.

31. "Correspondence," *Deseret Evening News*, Feb. 24, 1881, 4.

have established his point." He went on to argue that "the Book of Mormon claimed to be a history of the descendants of *Joseph* who was sold in to" Egypt, and that "said descendants kept the law of Moses." But he noted an account of Nephi making two individuals priests while the Bible said that this priesthood was given to the tribe of Levi. Because this contradicted the Bible, Alsup charged, it made the "Book of Mormon as worthless as an almanac."[32]

Roberts responded to Alsup, agreeing that in fact the Bible did have an account "of the Lord taking the tribe of Levi for priests instead of the firstborn which were at first chosen, but it was nowhere said that the *Levites and the Levites alone* should minister before the Lord." To the contrary, Roberts argued, other parts of the Bible provided accounts of "others than Levites being called to minister before the Lord," and pointed specifically to the book of Samuel.[33]

In his next presentation, Alsup charged that the Book of Mormon "contained an account of the gospel of Christ being preached upon this land of America several hundred years before there was such a being." Roberts responded that Mormons held that the "gospel was preached in America before the birth of Christ at Bethlehem, but certainly not before he had an existence, as he existed before the world was … [a]nd by him the world was created." In response, Alsup mentioned the "old Spaulding" story, saying that the Book of Mormon "must have been the work of *one man* because there was a *sameness* throughout the whole book." Alsup also claimed that the "Mormon Bible" contradicted the Bible because it held that "that in the book of Luke 23, it was stated that there was darkness from the sixth to the ninth hour, but the Book of Mormon says that the darkness covered the land for three days."

At that point, Roberts offered an admission that might have startled his listeners. He told the group that while Alsup was correct in his assertion that the Book of Mormon was the work of one man, but not as he held, the creation of Joseph Smith. He told his listeners that the Book of Mormon is indeed the "*work of one man* with the exception of the last few chapters. It is an abridgement made by one, Mormon, from the more voluminous histories that had been

32. "Correspondence."

33. The case of Samuel was cited, 1 Sam. 1 and 2, also 16:1–6.

written." Roberts skillfully turned Alsup's argument against him. The "*sameness* complained of is an evidence in its favor." Roberts also rebutted the argument taken from Luke, and insisted that the Book of Mormon's account of darkness covering the land need not be the same event discussed in the Bible. "Seeing then that no reference is had to the *same event*, that it occurred at *different times*, and on *nearly opposite* sides of the world, there can certainly be no contradiction to the Bible."

Alsup turned his attack on Joseph Smith, producing a number of contemporary accounts concerning "the character of Joseph Smith, and of the whole Smith family," saying that these accounts were signed by more than eighty "respectable" men, and asserted they must be true because "eighty men would not combine to destroy the character of any man." Roberts retorted that Smith was tried forty nine times "before the tribunals of man, and if he was the kind of character he was represented to be by our opponent he would certainly have been convicted on some one of these numerous charges, but like those who tried the Savior, they were compelled to say we find no guile in this man." Roberts again turned Alsup's argument against him, saying that "if 150 or 200 men can be found who will blacken their faces and perpetrate such a hellish crime as to murder an innocent man as Joseph Smith was, it will not be difficult to find 80 men who will traduce his character."[34]

At one point on the third day, in what Roberts described as a "rapid verbal exchange," Alsup "ridiculed" a particular passage in the Book of Mormon, and Roberts denied there was such a passage. Almost immediately he realized he was in error, but rather than risk the "audience's sympathy" for his argument, he chose not to bring it up. During the lunch break, Roberts and Ford prayed that "the whole matter" would be taken from the minds of their opponents. Roberts and his companion believed that their prayers were immediately answered. Not only did Alsup "not mention the passage, but he announced that he was finished and closed the debate." But, despite this seemingly miraculous turn of events, Roberts was dismayed at

34. The account of Roberts's debate is from "Correspondence," *Deseret Evening News*, Feb. 24, 1881, 4.

his own sloppiness and he never forgot it, forcing him to hone his debate skills for future encounters.[35]

Truman Madsen wrote that Roberts was "permanently influenced" by Alsup's charge that "unlike the Bible which is rich in proverbs, aphorisms and wisdom-literature, the Book of Mormon had not a single redeeming verse." At the time Roberts replied meekly by quoting from the Book of Mormon in Ether 12:26: "Fools mock, but they shall mourn; and my grace is sufficient for the meek." This exchange was the reason that Roberts dedicated much of the rest of his life to searching the Book of Mormon for passages that would debunk Alsup's charges.[36]

Roberts reported three baptisms resulting directly from the debate. Within a month and a half, the elders had "baptized enough people when added to the few who had already been baptized to make up a branch of over sixty" members.[37] Alphonso H. Snow,[38] Roberts's former classmate at the University of Deseret, and soon his missionary colleague, wrote that as a result of the "widespread" notoriety of the debate itself, as well as the "sensational newspaper reports," the missionaries found "no difficulty in getting schools to use and large congregations."[39]

Many years later, Roberts encountered the writings of Alexander Campbell and discovered in them the basic arguments, "point for point," that Alsup had used in the debate. He felt at this time that

35. Madsen, *Defender of the Faith*, 128.

36. Madsen said Roberts had a "lifetime preoccupation" with the Book of Mormon, noting that he "continued to revise, supplement, and expand his … scholarship, eventually publishing more than fifteen hundred pages on the Book of Mormon." See Madsen, 128–29. For additional perspective, see Roberts, *Autobiography*, 123–25.

37. Roberts, *Autobiography*, 126. In LDS parlance, a "branch" is a smaller, less fully organized administrative unit than a "ward," which is considered the rough equivalent of a Catholic parish. See also "History of the Southern States Mission," which called the debates "far reaching" in their long-term importance."

38. Alphonso Houtz Snow (1858–1933) was the son of Apostle Lorenzo Snow and his plural wife Eleanor Houtz Snow. He was set apart for his mission on April 7, 1881, by Apostle John Henry Smith, and returned on April 3, 1883. Roberts noted that he had enjoyed becoming reacquainted with Snow after their school years together and "enjoyed his society very much." Roberts described him as possessing "a good disposition, is refined in his manner and chaste in his conversation; intelligent, witty and [withal] has a liberal education." Roberts, *History's Apprentice*, 73. The two men will continue their association in the years ahead.

39. "Interesting Missionary Letter from Tennessee," *Logan Leader*, Sep. 23, 1881, 4.

he had not only bested Alsup, but by extension, Campbell himself.[40] Once the debate was over, Roberts and Ford returned to their missionary routine. "Friends appear to spring up all around me," Roberts wrote to his mother. "The people want me to send for my wife and settle among them promising to give me a good salary if I will preach for them all the time." He also reported that these same individuals would build him "a new church etc.," if he stayed."[41]

By the end of April, he and Ford had traveled to Nashville[42] to meet with mission president John Morgan and Alphonso H. Snow.[43] Roberts noted that he, Snow, and Ford had spent the "day visiting places of interest and listening to the counsels of Bro. Morgan." That night, the four of them witnessed the opening of the Nashville Centennial Exposition, which featured a grand display of electric light and fireworks.[44]

After this April meeting, Morgan, Roberts, and some of the others left for Shady Grove[45] in Hickman County, where they were joined by several newly arriving elders and held a missionary conference.[46] The meetings in Shady Grove occurred near the residence

---

40. Madsen, *Defender of the Faith*, 127.

41. Roberts to Ann Roberts Dustin, Feb. 21, 1881, box 4, fd. 1, Roberts Papers (UU). In the letter Roberts commented on the fact that his stepfather, Seth Dustin, has just deserted his mother. He told her that she had "not lost much, and I should feel like congratulating you on your freedom." In that vein he also tells his mother that because he has not "heard from Louisa for one month" he has concluded that she has been as negligent to him as "Seth has you."

42. Morgan had rented a small room in Nashville in 1877 that doubled as an office. The mission headquarters would remain there until it moved to Chattanooga in October 1882. Seferovich, "History of the LDS Southern States Mission," 68.

43. They had also visited in Nashville a month earlier, staying at the Nicholson House. See "Personals," *Daily American*, Mar. 29, 1881, 4; and, "Hotels," *The Tennessean*, Mar. 29, 1881, 4.

44. Roberts, *History's Apprentice*, 29 (Apr. 27, 1881).

45. Shady Grove is "located on Dunlop Creek, about a mile from Duck River. The name was given by Henry (Harry) Nichols, an early merchant in the 1840s, noting that the spot was located under a shady grove of trees." Both the Chickasaw Trace and later the Natchez Trace ran through the area. It was an early location for the Church of Christ as well as a later location for the Latter-day Saints. Primarily a farming community, the area also was the source for phosphate mining. See *Patchwork History of Hickman County*, 111.

46. Roberts, *History's Apprentice*, 30–31 (Apr. 28–May 1, 1881). Some of the other missionaries mentioned above departed for assignments farther south.

of one of the most important early Latter-day Saints in Tennessee, Isaac Emmons Church.[47]

Roberts was proselytizing primarily in Baird's Mill, along with Elders Ford and Hammond. As Roberts told his mother, "The mission is looking up. Last winter Bro. Ford and myself were the only ones in this part of the state, now there are six and we expect two more … and all will find plenty to do." Roberts also says that, despite their efforts, they were not baptizing many, though about "fifty people in this neighborhood do believe, and have believed our teachings for the past few months, but have not found it to the water's edge."[48] By the middle of September, however, Roberts's calling changed. On September 12 he received a letter from John Morgan telling him that he was appointing Roberts to preside over the Tennessee Conference[49] and requesting that Roberts come to Nashville for further instruction.[50] Before leaving, Roberts baptized a number of individuals, organized the Baird's Mill branch, and set apart William Gwyn to preside over it.

The missionaries began to encounter an undercurrent of hostility toward the Mormons, especially over the issue of polygamy. Roberts recorded that on Saturday, September 3, Daniel R. Bateman[51] and Thomas H. Merrill[52] were staying in the small community of Spring

47. Isaac Emmons Church (1820–96) was a longtime Saint living in Shady Grove with his wife, Mary (1825–98), and two of their teenage children. He is an older brother of Robert R. Church.

48. Roberts to Mother, Aug. 29, 1881, box 4, fd. 1, Roberts Papers (UU).

49. This change in leadership was reported in the *Deseret News*, noting that Belnap was "succeeded in his position as president of the Tennessee Conference by Elder B. H. Roberts of Centerville." Belnap had left in June 1879, and "labored the whole of his time in Tennessee," where he held 323 meetings and baptized twenty-three. The paper also reported that Belnap "was threatened with violence at the hands of the oppositionists, but never suffered any." See "Local and Other Matters," *Deseret News* Oct. 12, 1881, 1. See also Belnap Autobiography, 163, in Hyrum Belnap Papers; and Southern States Mission Manuscript History, Sep. 1881.

50. Belnap Autobiography, 163.

51. Daniel R. Bateman (1857–1942) was set apart for his mission on October 11, 1880, by Apostle Charles C. Rich and returned home on November 22, 1882.

52. Thomas Hazen Merrill (1859–1935) was the son of Apostle Marriner W. Merrill, and was set apart for his mission on July 6, 1881, by Apostle Franklin D. Richards. He was released on June 6, 1883. After his return, he was active in church callings and became a teacher, farmer, dairyman, and stockman in Richmond, Utah. He also served on the city council and was a member of the Utah House of Representatives, 1903–05.

Creek with Walter Weems and his family.[53] Around midnight a group of ten to twelve men surrounded the Weems house "endeavoring to get to the Elders, threatening their lives and cursing bitterly the while." Unable to gain entry, the group left, "warning" them that if they continued to preach in the area, they would "never preach again." The two missionaries disregarded the warning, held a meeting on Sunday, and baptized two individuals. From there, Bateman and others went to Wayne County to preach where a member's home had been burned. Returning to Spring Creek, they received more threats and, to "escape pending trouble," spent the night sleeping in the woods. On Sunday, September 25, Roberts records that "a company of men some 12 or 15 in number took possession of the school-house. Five of them were armed with double barreled shot guns, and others with pistols and swore the Elders should not preach that day. The brethren to avoid bloodshed and bringing trouble on our friends and the Saints remained."[54]

The next week Alphonso H. Snow went to the Baird's Mill post office where he found a notice addressed to "Roberts, Snow and Ford" which read, "Most infamous Scoundrels: you are warned to leave this country in one week. If you remain it will be at the cost of your lives. This is no empty talk. It is solid truth. We have measured the ground. Scud! Or We will hang you like dogs." It was signed "Indignant Citizens."[55] Roberts conferred with Morgan and the other missionaries at Love's Branch, a small town in northwest Maury County.[56] Based on their experiences and reports from other places in the South, they concluded to proceed in their usual fashion but with caution.[57]

---

53. Likely G. W. Weems, a thirty-four-year-old merchant living in Hickman County with his twenty-four-year-old wife, Rebecca, and their four children.

54. Roberts noted that the five armed men were Rowe J. Strickland, Max Strickland, Frank Twilly, John Smith, and Hart Weems, "once a friend but now a traitor." *History's Apprentice*, 55 (Sep. 30, 1881). Weems is probably Hartwell Weems (1859–) who was working on the farm of his father, August Weems, in Perry County. It is not known what, if any, relationship he had to Walter Weems.

55. "Scud" is a colloquial expression meaning to leave quickly without preparation. Roberts, *History's Apprentice*, 56 (Oct. 8, 1881).

56. Southeast of Hickman County, with a population of 39,904 in 1880.

57. As an example of their resolve, Morgan, Roberts, and the others organized a small branch of the church in the community. See Roberts, *History's Apprentice*, 56 (Oct. 8, 1881).

Approximately two weeks later, Roberts, travelled to Spring Creek where he was joined by several other elders including James W. Eardley,[58] who informed him that "mobs were still raging" in Benton County[59] and they had given "Bro. Henderson Conder ten days notice to leave the county."[60]

Roberts, along with Daniel Bateman, concluded that they should return to Spring Creek to stay with Walter Weems. While there, he learned that the Ku Klux Klan was active in the area, and that "for three Sundays men had been guarding the school-house with shot guns and that they had concluded the 'Mormons' should hold no more meetings there." Roberts wrote that Weems "appeared to be much alarmed for our safety" and believed that "nothing but buck shot can save you fellows now."[61] Weems encouraged them to leave; the two missionaries did just that and made their way to the Henderson Conder residence.

Upon his arrival at the Conders, Roberts decided that he and Bateman were no safer there. Perhaps recalling the rowdiness of his youth a decade earlier, he decided that the chances of their being attacked "were good." The house they stayed in "was a single log room with two doors but no window. The chinking was out nearly all around so that men from without could shoot us all to pieces" and, in addition, "Bro C[onder] had no fire-arms of any description, so our chances for a shot gun argument would not be called good."[62]

58. Eardley (1854–1937) was set apart for his mission on October 11, 1880, by Orson Pratt and returned home on November 20, 1882. He and Roberts would become close in Tennessee, and remained lifelong friends. Eardley relocated to Baker, Oregon, in 1897, where he served as bishop of the Baker Ward from 1921 until his death.

59. Located in northwestern Tennessee, just north of Peery County, and thirty miles south of Kentucky, the county had a population of 9,780. It borders the western fork of the Tennessee River.

60. George Henderson "Henry" Conder (1838–1915), who was born in Hickman County, lived in the area with his wife, Harriet Brattlefield Conder (1855–1953), whom he married on November 30, 1872, and their three children. He was a veteran of the Confederate Army and served in the 3rd Tennessee Infantry from May 1861 until he was captured during the battle of Fort Donelson in February 1862. As a prisoner of war, he was taken to Camp Douglas in Chicago until he was released in a prisoner exchange on September 23, 1862. He was recaptured in May 1863 and escaped two months later. Conder and his wife joined the LDS Church in 1880 or 1881. They left for Colorado in 1887 and eventually settled in northwest New Mexico.

61. Roberts, *History's Apprentice*, 59 (Oct. 18, 1881).

62. Roberts.

Roberts and Bateman "started out to the woods to have prayer," but were interrupted by the shouts of Conder who told them that Eardley had just escaped from a mob of "some 12 to 15 men [who] had surrounded him armed with shot guns, and with bitter oaths would take our lives." The missionaries concluded that it would be safer to spend the night in the woods. The next morning they awoke "still stiff and sore from [the] night's exposure" and decided to seek out all the other missionaries in the area and find a more secure place.[63]

Over time, the threats dissipated and the missionaries returned to their work. But Roberts and James Eardley stumbled across earlier violence when they stayed with Wesley Hunt in Spring Creek, Perry County. Roberts learned that "five of those parties who had disturbed us in our meetings had been arrested ... but if the court punishes these men for disturbing a 'Mormon' meeting we shall record it as an anomaly in American jurisprudence."

Roberts, as was his wont, kept records in his diary of how far he had walked or traveled, how many meetings he had attended, and other details. At the end of the year, he noted that he had "rode horseback and in wagon 299 miles, on R[ail] R[oad] 404 miles; have walked 1846 miles making a total of 2,549 miles that I have traveled in this year to preach the everlasting gospel." He also records that he "held or attended rather, 152 meetings, at which I have occupied the whole or part of the time with a very few exceptions." Finally, he wrote that he had "assisted in the organization of three branches of the Church, and the reorganization of one more. Have baptized seven persons, and have assisted in the baptism of five others."[64]

As the new year arrived, Roberts was still staying with Robert R. Church and his family in Shady Grove, and though the "day was bitter cold," he and Eardley "rode twenty miles to fill an appointment at Totty's Bend.[65] Only a few were present, and as the house was very uncomfortable, we only held meeting for half an hour." Not long

63. Roberts, 60.

64. Roberts, 73–74.

65. A small town in Hickman County, approximately five-and-a-half miles east of Centerville. Roberts consistently misspelled Totty, which I have silently corrected. The original settler, Robert Totty, for whom the area was named, settled on a bend on the Duck River in 1810. During the time Roberts was there, Totty's Bend had a school, general store, and post office. See *Patchwork History*, 125.

into the new year he wrote to his mother recounting his activities in 1881 and telling her of his holiday celebrations:

> Spent a Merry Christmas with Saints at Shady Grove. Preached twice that day, taking dinner at Sister Nicholas' Monday following we entirely spoiled the looks of a huge fat turkey at Sister Laura Churches; to say nothing of dinner.... If Christmas had lasted much longer we should have had a fit of indigestion; but we are all right now, have got back to our hot cakes and bacon. ... I am an ardent admirer of the Southern people. They are so generous, open hearted, and when you secure their friendship it is lasting.[66]

He signed the letter "Parson B. H. Roberts."

Roberts remained in Shady Grove and the surrounding area for the next three weeks. He suffered regularly from headaches, perhaps migraines, and while he held several meetings, they were sparsely attended because of the unpredictable weather, especially the "prodigious" rain, which caused the creeks to run high. "It inundated a good portion of Nashville," Roberts wrote. But he and his colleague continued preaching in schoolhouses and private homes, holding many meetings. During his spare time, Roberts read "several of Shakespeare's plays through. Also some of [William] Cowper's and Thompson's works; from which I made some valuable extracts."[67] Roberts also kept up with Utah politics. In January 1882 a petition signed by Roberts and 193 others was introduced into the Utah territorial house of representatives, calling on the legislature to "guard the sanctity of the nomination franchise" in county elections, and urging that territorial law be clarified on this matter.[68]

As February neared, Roberts and Alphonso Snow started for Rutherford County to fill a variety of appointments. Roberts and Snow had grown close, and he records they "had a fine day, and [we] enjoyed ourselves in an agreeable conversation during the whole of the long walk—the distance was twenty miles." That evening they

---

66. Roberts to Mother, Jan. 7, 1882, box 4, fd. 1, Roberts Papers (UU). He also told his mother that he had received a letter from Allen Hughes who invited him to return to Iowa in the summer, commenting, "But I don't know how that will be."

67. Roberts is apparently referring to the English writer William Cowper (1731–1800), and his contemporary James Thomson (1700–48), a Scottish poet whose best known work is the epic poem "The Seasons."

68. "Legislative Assembly," *Salt Lake Herald*, Jan. 31, 1882, 5.

held a meeting where Roberts discussed the "internal evidence of the Book of Mormon." Two days later they held a morning meeting, which attracted "some "fifteen or twenty" who gathered to hear Snow "on the subject of Revelation." As a result, several of those in attendance asked to be baptized, "so we repaired to the river close by where I administered the ordinance of baptism to them." The next morning Roberts and Snow returned to Baird's Mill.

Two days later, Roberts and Snow took the afternoon train to Nashville, and "after putting up our grip-sacks at the boarding house, we strolled about the streets. Step[p]ed into the church where the Evangelist Dr. Hammond was holding forth.[69] Spent the eve. at the [Masonic] theatre saw Miss Fanny Davenport[70] in 'School for Scandal': play was well rendered." The next morning Roberts took leave of Snow and headed for Shady Grove and the residence of Robert R. Church.[71] He stayed in the area for most of the rest of the month and spent some of his "time reading Dr. Mosheim's Church History, principally that part that pertains to the Reformation."[72]

On Saturday, February 26, Roberts left Shady Grove for the small community of Leatherwood for a preaching meeting at the local school. He noted that the "house was filled in the afternoon, and I preached on 'Faith.' Several of the Shady Grove saints came over to [the] meeting." But he reflected on his return that "the last two days I have manifest much lightness of mind, and that decorum

69. Edward Payson Hammond (1831–1910) was a prominent evangelist and author. A graduate of Williams College in 1858, he was ordained an evangelist by the New York Presbytery five years later. Hammond became an associate of Dwight L. Moody.

70. Fanny Davenport (1850–98) was an actress and producer. She was born in London but came to the United States as a child, settling in Boston. She first appeared on the New York stage at age twelve. Over the next three decades she became extremely successful because she often produced the performances she starred in.

71. Robert Robbins Church (1826–84) and his wife, Laura (1838–1929) were married in 1874 and were longtime Latter-day Saints.

72. Johann Lorenz Mosheim (1694–1755) was an eighteenth-century Lutheran scholar. Roberts is probably referring to his two-volume work *Ecclesiastical History, Ancient and Modern*. The book went through many printings in the nineteenth century. It was also published in four volumes as *Institutes of Ecclesiastical History, Ancient and Modern*. On February 25, Roberts noted that when he reviewed his "own labor's in God's Kingdom, and then compare it with the exertions of some of these faithful men, I am almost put to shame. Still the most of my period of man hood is before me and I hope to accomplish much good in the cause of truth." See Roberts, *History's Apprentice*, 82 (Feb. 25, 1882).

which should characterize a Servant of God, I have not observed. I wonder when I shall get through making Blunders?"[73]

The next month, Roberts baptized Totty and George Holderfield in Totty's Bend,[74] and the "whole neighborhood came out to witness the baptism." There were "twenty Elders in this state," he wrote, and "the work in this state is in a prosperous condition: we have baptized sixty within the last six months, and the outlook for the future is still more flattering. We expect to accomplish a good work in this conference this summer."[75]

However, beneath that wave of optimism ran an equally strong undercurrent of self-doubt and regret. On his twenty-fifth birthday, Roberts lamented that perhaps one half of his life had already "passed away."

> [A]nd what have I done? But little of anything, either of good or evil: my misdeeds are like my talents—on the small order. I have made attempts to accomplish something in various directions, but "*miserable failure*" is written across the face of each of them. When about fourteen I had arranged to leave home and go to the sea-coast determined to spend my life upon the sea, but this fell through; at sixteen determined to join the army and a friend of mine made application for me to the officers but I was too young to enter the service—so this project *failed*: I am satisfied that either of the above occupations would have suited my restless disposition better than anything else I could have engaged in. When seventeen, more out or respect for my mother's wishes than any taste I had for the occupation, I was bound out to a man for three years as an apprentice to the blacksmith trade; having but little ambition to excel as a tradesman I made but little headway in the shop—another thing which contributed to my failure here, was the fact that my employer had

73. Roberts, *History's Apprentice*, 82–83 (Feb. 27–28, 1882). Roberts is apparently paraphrasing from Montaigne's *Essays*.

74. Roberts likely refers to Frank Totty (1857–1935), a farmer living in Hickman County with his wife, Molly Springer Totty (1858–1904), whom he married on September 2, 1880, and his daughter, Lena (1882–1953); and to George Holderfield, (1854–1939), also a farmer and living with his wife, Isabella Moore Holderfield (1855–1927), whom he married on February 26, 1874, and their children, Lilly (1875–?), Horace (1877–1965), and Mary Leona (1881–1931), in Hickman County.

75. Roberts to Mother, Mar. 6, 1882, box 4, fd. 1, Roberts Papers (UU). He again referred to his friends in Iowa, saying he wrote occasionally "as I desire to keep open that field for there are quite a number of honest in heart there who may some day embrace the truth. They are anxious I should return and preach to them."

> me out in the garden considerably—an occupation I always detested. I managed to stay the time out, as my employer was kind to me. The Autumn after finishing my apprentice-ship, like many another young "greeny" without money, property, or sense, I got married; having had the unparalleled audacity to ask a well-to-do farmer's daughter to come and walk the uncertain path of life with me,—to change a comfortable house for none! to leave the plenty she enjoyed and share my poverty—to leave the meadows, and batten on a dreary moor.[76]

He calls Louisa "the luckyest 'hit' I ever made in life, but fear it will not prove that on her side." In terms of his two years of missionary service, he notes that what he might "accomplish in that line nothing but the future will unfold." Observing that he could not "but choose to regret the past when looking over it, but as I cannot call it back to amend it, or straighten out the crooks which appear in the path I have trod, I will look to the present and future, trying to profit by the experience of the past: and maybe after all 'There's a divinity that shapes our ends, Rough-hew them as we may.'"[77]

A week later, John Morgan requested that Roberts meet with him in Nashville. While there, Roberts wrote a letter to his longtime companion Joseph Ford giving him an honorable release from his mission. Roberts told him he had filled his mission "satisfactorily to the Priesthood of God—you have done a good work, go take thy well earned rest."[78] The events of the next few months of Roberts's mission suggest that Roberts was perhaps in need of such "rest" himself.

He returned to Shady Grove where he says he remained "with the Saints … reading, writing, and I cannot deny but some of our time was wasted pitching horse-shoes, boatriding [et]c, [et]c." Again, he noted his feeling that he was not properly fulfilling his assignments. On March 26, he remarked that he preached at the school house but felt badly because he had made "some unwise remarks, and in my

76. Roberts, *History's Apprentice*, 85–86 (Mar. 13, 1882). He had said similar things to his mother in a letter dated a week before his birthday: "I shall soon be … twenty-five years old. Think of that and weep! Perhaps half my life is gone and but very little accomplished." Roberts to Mother, Mar. 6, 1882.

77. Shakespeare, *Hamlet*, 5.2.10–11.

78. Roberts, *History's Apprentice*, 88 (Mar. 21, 1882). Apparently Ford had some health issues, including a "bad sore leg." See Ford and Nelson, "History of Joseph Ford," 3, and Roberts to Hyrum Belnap, Aug. 25, 1881, Belnap Papers. Roberts assured Belnap that Ford was "healing rapidly and we think will soon be well."

tone displaying considerable egotism." He struggled with feelings of unworthiness. "As a general thing in speaking I truly enjoy the Spirit of God, and feel well in my endeavors to instruct the people; but occasionally I appear to be left to myself, or nearly so, and for what purpose I know not unless it be to show my weakness and dependence upon the Holy Spirit."[79]

Along with Eardley and Charles C. Brown, he started studying the book of Revelation beginning "at the 4th chapter and read all the way through, reading a chapter at a time and then stopping to ask questions, make remarks, and exchange views on whatever subject the matter we read might bring up"[80] He also started work on an essay entitled the "Mission of Joseph Smith."[81] He wrote that these activities made him feel "more alive" to his missionary duties and noted that he had held six meetings that month, assisted in two baptisms, and traveled a total of 197 miles: thirty-seven on foot, sixty on horseback, and one hundred by rail.[82]

During April, an abortive meeting in Clifton loomed large over Roberts's missionary efforts.[83] In a letter to Morgan, he noted that the hall they were preaching at was "pretty well lighted up." There was a pulpit and "a pitcher of water and glass" and chairs ready. "But seven o'clock came and found no occupants upon them. Half past seven—the scene had not changed." Finally at 8:00 p.m., "a curly head and dusky face over which is spread a ghastly grin is thrust through the half open door to see if we are all here." But even after the owner rang "the supper bell to call the people in," only a few more wandered over. After the abysmal attendance and "such little interest was manifest by the people we … ended our efforts in Clifton." The missionaries discovered "that the good parsons of the place had visited the people at their homes and used their influence to keep the people away."[84]

Roberts retreated to Shady Grove where he spent time with the

79. Roberts, *History's Apprentice*, 88 (Mar. 26, 1882).

80. Roberts, 89 (Mar. 27–28, 1882).

81. Roberts is likely referring to what was later published as "Joseph Smith's Mission," *Journal of Discourses* 25, Jan. 28, 1884, 130–43.

82. Roberts, *History's Apprentice*, 90 (Mar. 31, 1882).

83. A small community in Wayne County.

84. Roberts to Morgan, Apr. 18, 1882, box 70, fd. 12, Smith Family Papers.

newly released Joseph Ford, with whom he talked "over old times." He also met with Robert C. Camp, James Eardley, and others, insisting that, despite setbacks, the work was "progressing." A few days later, Roberts and Ford preached their final sermon together at Pennington's Peak schoolhouse. On April 14, the pair set out for Columbia where they had their "photographs taken together[,] Bro. Ford sitting[,] my self standing. At three o'clock I took leave of Bro. F[ord]. He was now to go to his friends and family, I must return to my labors of preaching the Gospel."[85]

A week later, Roberts and the missionaries left for Cedar Creek, Perry County, to hold a district conference with John Morgan, where Roberts was asked to preside.[86] After a morning session and lunch, Roberts wrote, "Before meeting this afternoon Pres. Morgan took me aside, and informed me that I had filled an honorable mission, and would be released to return to my home. I will not attempt to describe my feelings at this announcement—suffice it to say my heart gave a big throb of joy to learn that my labors had been performed satisfactorily."[87] Though he spent part of April readying to leave, Roberts still held seventeen meetings, blessed four children, and traveled a total of 320 miles: fifty-four on foot and 266 on horseback.

The first three weeks of May would be busy ones for Roberts as he finished his missionary efforts. On May 3 he noted that he received $3 from Robert Church "to help me along," and that he "felt truly bad in leaving these my friends to whom I had become warmly attached, and who I believe reciprocated my feelings of friendship. It was nearly as bad as leaving home, and I saw the tear of regret standing ready to fall from the eyes of those whose hands I shook for the last time perhaps."[88] Roberts specifically mentions here the "kindness of Sister Phoebe Church[89] to me, and all the rest of the Elders. She was ever ready to administer comforting words

85. Roberts, *History's Apprentice*, 92 (Apr. 14, 1882).

86. Morgan notes that he met Roberts at Columbia, and "hiring a hack of Mays and Goodson went together to Shady Grove where we met Elders Brown and Martineau and the Saints." Morgan Journal.

87. Roberts, *History's Apprentice*, 95 (Apr. 29, 1882).

88. Roberts, 97 (May 3, 1882).

89. Phoebe Church (1861–1929) was the daughter of Isaac Emmons and Mary Ann Church. She was baptized in November 1879 by Hyrum Belnap.

or actions to the Elders—would smile when they smiled; would weep when they had cause to weep." Roberts wrote that during a during a "spell of sickness I passed through at the house of her father, she was ever anxiously watching for a chance to do something to relieve my pain."[90]

Roberts's reference to Phoebe Church is interesting, and perhaps suggests a romantic interest in her, even if from afar. She would not be the first woman Roberts became infatuated with. Apart from Phoebe, however, throughout his diaries Roberts is careful not to speak of women, nor even suggest that he is spending time in the company of women—especially young, unmarried ones. No doubt this is in part because of the attacks on the missionaries from local residents over polygamy, and the purported proclivities of the Mormons to seduce local women. While Roberts does not specifically address this situation in his journals, he was probably warned of such associations when he was called on his mission. The experience of John B. Fairbanks,[91] who also served a mission in the South, is probably typical. In his diary, Fairbanks mentions that when he was set apart a number of church authorities gave him advice on avoiding romantic temptations. Wilford Woodruff[92] told the missionaries that they would "have many temptations," and specifically encouraged them to avoid "wine and women." Apostle Moses Thatcher[93] told the missionaries directly that they "must not hug or kiss any woman or allow them to hug or kiss us." At the same time, Apostle Francis M.

90. Roberts, *History's Apprentice*, 97 (May 3, 1882).

91. Fairbanks (1855–1940) was set apart for his mission on October 10, 1881, by Apostle Moses Thatcher, and released on September 26, 1883. After his service in the southern states, Fairbanks studied at the Julien Art Academy in Paris. He became an important Utah artist, particularly known for his murals in the St. George, Salt Lake, and Mesa temples.

92. Woodruff (1807–98) was ordained an apostle in 1839 by Joseph Smith. He became the fourth church president in 1889 and served until his death. Married to at least seven—and possibly nine—women, he is best known for the 1890 Manifesto, which began the slow process of weaning the church off of plural marriage.

93. Moses Thatcher (1842–1909) served as an apostle from 1879 until his death, though he was dropped from the Quorum of the Twelve in 1896. He was a prominent and successful businessman in Logan, serving as president of the Utah Northern Railway. He was Cache Stake president, 1877–79, and a trustee at Brigham Young College, 1877–97. Thatcher would become one of the founders of the Utah Democratic Party, and he and Roberts would become close friends and political allies in the years ahead.

Lyman[94] "spoke very pointedly on the woman subject" saying that he knew of some missionaries who had "played with the girls, throwing pillows, pinching and nearly every one has apostatized."[95]

Soon Roberts left for Nashville, recording that he arrived there "at five P. M. Attended service at the Christian Church. Bought a suit of clothes for which I paid $16.50. Wrote to my wife informing her of my release." The next morning he took the train to Lebanon where he would reside for another week.[96] On May 12, Roberts met with other missionaries for a final three-day conference with John Morgan presiding.[97] In the morning, the missionaries met as a group where the "brethren all expressed their willingness to continue their labor," and they received "good instructions on their duties as workmen in the Kingdom of God. Mostly on how to approach people with the Gospel—what to teach &c. &c."[98]

The missionary conference re-assembled in the afternoon at a private residence where they made some administrative changes.[99] The next morning the meetings continued, and Roberts observed that the "room was crowded, and the spirit of the Lord was with us. Most of the people remained at dinner with the saints who had provided for them as on the day before."[100]

After that, Roberts spent several days "visiting among the saints

94. Francis M. Lyman (1840–1916) was a member of the Quorum of the Twelve Apostles from 1880 until his death. Lyman served a mission to England in 1860–62, and after his return was active in church, civic, and political affairs in Fillmore and Tooele. He served several terms in the Territorial Legislature, and was president of the European Mission, 1901–04.

95. Fairbanks Diary, Oct. 10, 1881. Woodruff also encouraged the missionaries to maintain the Word of Wisdom, keep a journal, and report briefly to the Historian's Office on their activities when they returned. Apostle Lorenzo Snow counseled that the missionaries would be "warned of coming dangers by visions and dreams." Roberts, whether he received that advice specifically or not, clearly accepted its importance.

96. As Morgan noted, "At 7:30 Bro. Roberts left for Wilson County." Morgan Journals, May 4, 1882.

97. On May 11, Morgan noted that he left "for Lebanon on the 7:30 a.m. train. Arrived at Lebanon and put up at the Jackson House where I met Elder Roberts, and in the p. m. accompanied Mr. Huddleston and Bro. Roberts to the home of the former." The next day he "met in council with all the Elders in the East Tennessee Conference and spent a couple of hours quite pleasantly, and again in the p. m. ... A good spirit prevailing." Morgan Journals, May 11, 12, 1882.

98. Roberts, *History's Apprentice*, 98 (May 12, 1882).

99. Roberts, 99 (May 13, 1882).

100. Roberts, 99 (May 14, 1882).

and friends in this locality." He also learned that his Centerville Seventies quorum had responded "most promptly" to a request from Morgan and provided $70 for his return home.[101] Roberts departed for Nashville, and then, two days later, "bid the brethren farewell and started for *home*. I shall not try to record my feelings only those who have been absent from their loved ones over two years can appreciate it."[102] From Nashville, Roberts went to St. Louis where he met Elders Matthias F. Cowley[103] and George E. Howe[104] who were on their way south. The next afternoon, Roberts met with local Mormons, and spoke to them about their duties, advising them "how to obtain the Spirit and then how to retain it."[105] By nightfall he continued on his journey home.[106]

He arrived in Utah on May 26, 1882. The scene may have been even more joyous for Roberts than had been the case when he had first arrived as a young boy in 1866. Clearly he had grown much as an individual during those sixteen years. He recorded in his journal, in a somewhat dramatic literary style, that

> this eve[ning] the West bound train over the U[nion] P[acific] R[ail] R[oad] dashed into Ogden and I was aboard, and soon on the S[outh] bound U[tah] C[entral] R[ail] R[oad] for Centerville, I need not try to tell my feelings in thus coming to the home of the Saints. I had been absent for two years and two months or nearly that, I had filled my mission and my sky was without a cloud. The train steamed into Kaysville and on the plat-form was my wife, my little girl Adah, my mother and Father in law. … Let the curtain fall until we reach Centerville Station,

101. "At 8:40 Elder Roberts left me for home." Morgan Journals, May 19, 1882.

102. Roberts, *History's Apprentice*, 100 (May 20, 1882). See also Morgan Journals, May 19, 1882.

103. Matthias F. Cowley (1858–1940) served two missions in the Southern States from 1878 to 1882. Cowley was ordained an apostle on October 7, 1897, and resigned on October 28, 1905, over his support for unauthorized plural marriages. He married Abigail Hyde (1863–1931) in 1884; Luella Smart Parkinson (1870–1962) in 1889; Harriett Bennion Harker (1858–1923) in 1899; and Lenora Mary Taylor (1885–1971) in 1905. See Quinn, *Extensions of Power*, 62–63, 182, 652–54.

104. George Edward Howe (1858–1949) was living in Salt Lake City when he was set apart for his mission on October 14, 1881, by Apostle George Q. Cannon. He returned on October 10, 1882. He lived much of his life in Richfield, Utah, where he was a machinist.

105. Roberts, *History's Apprentice*, 100 (May 21, 1882).

106. For a complete list of missionaries called to the Southern States during 1882, see "Fifty-Second Semi-Annual Conference," *Millennial Star*, Nov. 20, 1882, 737–38.

> where quite a number of my friends had turned out to meet me, among them my old traveling companion, Joseph Ford, who had been so kind to me in a strange land.[107]

Roberts was driven to the home of his father-in-law for a "good supper," and then the evening "up to a late hour was spent in pleasant conversation."[108] The next day, Roberts traveled to Salt Lake City where he met with President Wilford Woodruff[109] who "listened to my report and told me much of his experience in the early days."[110] Also in attendance were Apostles Franklin D. Richards[111] and Joseph F. Smith.[112] Roberts recorded in his journal that the three church leaders "gave me a hearty welcome home accompanied with a wish that God would bless me. After thus winding up my missionary labors so far as this mission was concerned went to my home where I had other duties to attend to."[113] However, it would not be long before he would return to missionary service, not just in Tennessee, but throughout the South.

---

107. Roberts, *History's Apprentice*, 100–01 (May 26, 1882).

108. Roberts.

109. Woodruff was president of the Quorum of the Twelve.

110. Madsen, *Defender of the Faith*, 133.

111. Franklin D. Richards (1821–99) had been an apostle since February 1849, and would succeed Wilford Woodruff as president of the Quorum of the Twelve in 1889 when Woodruff became church president. At this time, Richards was dealing with the recently passed Edmunds Act which had just been signed into law. Richards said the legislation would punish the Saints for practicing polygamy and "turn the Territory of Utah over into the control of our enemies." See Richards, *Family of Faith*, 207. Roberts was likely unaware at this time of the impact this law and others would ultimately have over his own life in the years ahead.

112. At this time, Joseph F. Smith (1838–1918) was serving as second counselor in the First Presidency. He was a member of the Quorum of Twelve Apostles beginning in 1866. Smith became the sixth president of the LDS Church in 1901. As the son of Hyrum Smith, and nephew of Joseph Smith, he provided a direct link to the church's earliest days. Smith and Roberts would have a complicated relationship in the next decade as Roberts became more politically active and identified with the Utah Democratic Party.

113. Roberts, *History's Apprentice*, 101 (May 27, 1882).

FOUR

RETURNING TO THE SOUTH, 1883-84

Back at home, Roberts turned his attention to earning money to support his family. He worked for a time with brother-in-law Henry Rampton[1] in his blacksmith shop (owned by his mentor, James H. Baird), and then in the spring worked shearing sheep at Goose Creek with former missionary companion Joseph Ford. Roberts notes that going "from preaching to sheep shearing was a radical change in work,"[2] but while he was "out in this country," he took the opportunity to preach "several times to the people in Goose Creek Valley." He returned to Centerville on July 4 and began "the erection of a house 18 x 32, making two rooms."[3] Then he became a US citizen on September 6, 1882,[4] and began teaching school in Bountiful.

That fall Roberts had one of his first tastes of local politics when he became involved in the race for territorial delegate in Congress between the Liberal Party's candidate Philip T. Van Zile,[5] supported by the gentiles, and the Mormon-backed People's Party nominee, John T. Caine.[6] On September 27, Roberts attended the Davis

1. Henry Rampton (1855–1927) was married to Louisa's sister Luna Smith Rampton (1860–1922). He and Roberts were close friends throughout their lives though Rampton was not especially active in the LDS Church for much of his life. See also Harris, "Pioneer Blacksmiths."

2. Roberts, *Autobiography*, 136.

3. Roberts, *History's Apprentice*, 102 (undated 1882).

4. A copy of his certificate of citizenship is found in box 6, fd. 3, Roberts Papers (BYU).

5. Philip T. Van Zile (1843–1919) served in the Civil War and was a judge and politician in Michigan. In 1878 he was appointed by President Rutherford B. Hayes to serve as US District Attorney for Utah Territory. In that role he was instrumental in enforcing the various anti-Mormon laws passed by Congress. After his defeat, he returned to Michigan and resumed his activity in the Republican Party.

6. John T. Caine (1829–1911) came to Utah as a schoolteacher, and later became involved in territorial politics. He served as Utah's territorial delegate for a decade from

County party convention where he spoke at several rallies supporting Caine.[7] On the eve of the election, Roberts was the main speaker at a "rousing" rally in Kaysville, where "amid tremendous applause" he frequently "brought down the house."[8] When the votes were counted, Caine scored a resounding victory over Van Zile, garnering 23,039 votes to 4,884.

By this time Roberts was frequently in the company of some of the church's leading figures. In December he attended the Davis Stake Conference in Kaysville where his old friend and colleague John Morgan spoke. Also in attendance were Apostles Wilford Woodruff, Joseph F. Smith, Franklin D. Richards, and President John Taylor.[9]

After the Christmas holidays, Morgan approached Roberts and suggested that he was "confining" his efforts within four walls and "thought the sphere was too limited." Morgan had been released from being the full-time LDS mission president in November and had asked the First Presidency to choose Roberts as his successor. The next September, Morgan wrote to John Taylor, saying that Roberts had informed him that "he is preparing himself to respond to the call, expected to be made upon him at the October conference."[10] That call did not occur, however, and Morgan again wrote Taylor, asking if the should send forward the "name of some other elder?"[11] The First Presidency decided that Morgan should remain in Utah, exercising a kind of executive authority over the mission, while Roberts served as a "field man," running the day-to-day operations of the mission, which encompassed eleven states.[12]

Roberts was eager for this new challenge, but he also knew that the assignment would constitute a "severe trial" for Louisa and his mother. Still, he recognized his youth and imperfections and wrote

---

1882 until 1892. He was also one of the founders of the *Salt Lake Herald.* After his service in Congress, he was an unsuccessful candidate for the Democratic nomination for governor in 1895, and served a term in the Utah state senate. For an overview, see "John T. Caine," *Biographical Dictionary of the U. S. Congress, 1774 to Present* at bioguide.congress.gov. See also Haslam, "Utah's Delegates to Congress," 178–227.

7. Roberts, *History's Apprentice*, 102 (undated 1882).

8. See "Ratification at Kaysville," *Deseret News*, Nov. 8, 1882, 1; and, "People's Rally at Kaysville, *Salt Lake Herald*, Nov. 2, 1882, 8.

9. "Davis Stake Conference," *Deseret News*, Dec. 27, 1882, 2.

10. Morgan to Taylor, Sep. 29, 1882, box 2, fd. 6, Morgan Papers.

11. Morgan to Taylor, Oct. 19, 1882, box 2, fd. 6, Morgan Papers.

12. Madsen, *Defender of the Faith*, 136.

that during his short time at home he had "done many things that were wrong which were not becoming a servant of God, I frequently gave way to passion in my family, which was not proper; I met with many temptations, that nearly overcame me; and often grieved the spirit of God." He expected to "be chastened and reproved, as I did not sin unto death, and the stripes may be many, but I will try to bear them."[13]

In his letter accepting the mission call, Roberts stated that he would need to rely on "the assistance of my brethren at home."[14] Several of his neighbors in Centerville, led by John Ford[15] and Melvin Randall,[16] "laid the floor, put on the roof, put in the windows and did the carpentry and the plaster work" on Roberts's new home. Other local residents assisted in absorbing some of his debts and provided tangible financial assistance to leave with his family, while the Centerville Mutual Improvement Association "gave a complimentary benefit" to support his call to the Southern States.[17]

Two days later Roberts was set apart by John Taylor to serve in his new calling as assistant president of the Southern States Mission.[18] Taylor promised Roberts that God would bless him "with the spirit of revelation to guide you in your labors," and that he would become "an instrument in the hands of God in bringing many to the knowledge of the truth and in … leading them to Zion."[19] Clearly, Taylor was referring to the ongoing efforts to relocate church members to Utah or, in some cases, the Mormon communities in Colorado,[20]

---

13. Roberts, *History's Apprentice*, 102–03 (undated 1882).

14. Roberts to Taylor, Feb. 18, 1883, box 2, fd. 2, First Presidency, Missionary Calls.

15. Ford (1843–1928) was the older brother of Roberts's missionary companion Joseph Ford. A longtime resident of Centerville, Ford was active in church and civic affairs. At this time he was second counselor in the Centerville bishopric. See "Joseph Ford Called by Death at Eighty-Five," *Davis County Clipper*, Oct. 26, 1928, 1.

16. Randall was another counselor in the Centerville bishopric at the time.

17. "Local and Other Matters," *Deseret News*, Apr. 11, 1883, 4; and Roberts, *History's Apprentice*, 106 (Apr. 2, 1883).

18. See Historian's Office, Journal History, Mar. 29, 1883, 2; "Local and Other Matters," *Deseret News*, Apr. 4, 1883, 8; and Southern States Mission Manuscript History, Mar. 29, 1883. See also Cannon Journal, Mar. 29, 1883.

19. Roberts, *History's Apprentice*, 105–06 (Apr. 1, 1883); and Madsen, *Defender of the Faith*, 136–37.

20. Indeed, by that time, Morgan had returned to Tennessee and was in Chattanooga "with a company of Saints from the Southern States bound for Manassa, Colorado."

which John Morgan had played an important role in creating.[21] As Morgan told Joseph F. Smith, "Almost the entire Southern emigration goes to Colo[rado]."[22]

Roberts boarded a Union Pacific train on April 2. In a scene reminiscent of three years before, Louisa, Adah, his father-in-law, and several friends gathered at the station as he left. The train was bound for Cheyenne, Wyoming, with a transfer to Denver, Colorado. He arrived in Denver, spent the day touring, then left the next day. His route took him through territory in Colorado that would soon prove important—LaJara, Richfield, and Manassa,[23] where he was met by Morgan and former missionary companion Charles C. Brown.[24] He reacquainted himself with several of the families he had baptized in Tennessee and assisted in emigrating west. He toured the various settlements in the San Luis Valley and received instruction from Morgan before leaving for Tennessee. He arrived in Chattanooga,[25] which had replaced Nashville as the mission headquarters,[26] bringing "twenty four new elders from Utah"[27] along with him.

---

21. See Stewart Memorandum. Stewart noted that Morgan had been counseled that it was "thought best not to bring them to Utah, but to locate them in the Western front of Colorado, or in Eastern Utah." An early account of the settlement by W. Christenson of Manassa is found in "Correspondence," *Deseret News*, Nov. 24, 1880, 7.

22. Morgan to Joseph F. Smith, Feb. 28, 1882, box 8, fd. 20, First Presidency Correspondence. Morgan included a clipping of a letter from Bishop William L. Ball that had been published in the *Deseret News*. Ball extolled the virtues of the San Luis Valley and the prosperity of the settlements, and encouraged "all good Latter-day Saints who desire to emigrate from their present locations" to come to the valley where there was "room for all." Interestingly, a few years later he will identify Ball as an apostate. See Historian's Office, Journal History, Mar. 29, 1883, 2. See also "The Colorado Mormons," *Deseret News*, Nov. 24, 1880, 678. The paper assured readers that the "people who are settling in Conejos County are ... principally from the Southern states, and ... they are industrious, thrifty, peaceable, orderly and temperate."

23. The Mormons had established a settlement in the San Luis Valley in southern Colorado. Many converts from Tennessee and the South relocated to this area. It would be a place Roberts frequently visited in the next few years, even relocating Celia and her family there for a time. LaJara, Richfield, and Manassa were three of the most important settlements in the colony. For background, see Bird, *Century of Saints*; Flower Jr., "Mormon Colonization"; and Anderson, Shawcroft, and Compton, *Mormons*. See also Stewart Memorandum.

24. Morgan Journal, Apr. 11, 1883, in Morgan Papers.

25. "Missionary Messages," *Ogden Herald*, Apr. 24, 1883, 2.

26. Historian's Office, Journal History, Oct. 10, 1882.

27. Roberts, *Autobiography*, 136. See also Southern States Mission Manuscript History, Apr. 9, 14, 1883, for a list of the missionaries.

Roberts found himself in a very different position on his return to the South. Even though he had been given leadership responsibilities in the past, he was now primarily responsible for the day-to-day operations of a mission that was geographically large and significant in the role it played in Mormon missionary plans. He took these new responsibilities seriously, using every opportunity to make sure that the missionaries were well-prepared. For example, James Roskelley[28] noted in his diary that before he was sent to his assigned field, Roberts met with him and others and "told us to take our time and not hurry too much in walking or speaking, and in speaking to speak more on the subject and to be careful and not get angry." According to Roskelley, Roberts also advised the missionaries that if they were asked questions they did not understand to leave them "open."[29]

The missionaries ranged from age twenty to fifty, including single, married, and polygamous men. There was a large contingent from Davis County who were known to Roberts. Several, like Roberts, were immigrants, though a few could trace their time in the church back a generation to the Missouri and Nauvoo periods. No doubt their knowledge of the Mormon story was useful to the always inquisitive and historically minded Roberts.

One of Roberts's young missionaries was J. Golden Kimball,[30] son of church leader Heber C. Kimball.[31] Kimball recollected that he had left Salt Lake City with a group of twenty-seven missionaries:

28. Roskelley (1865–1919) was set apart for his mission on May 26, 1884, by Wilford Woodruff. He was released on September 16, 1886. He also served a mission in the Northwestern States from November 1913 until May 1914. In later years Roskelley was a Smithfield farmer active in local government and the Republican Party. He married Frances Anne Emery (1867–1941) on September 18, 1890.

29. Roskelley Journal, June 4, 1884, in Roskelley Collection.

30. Kimball (1854–1938) had been set apart a few days earlier on April 9, 1883, by Moses Thatcher. He returned in April 1885. Inactive in the church for many years before his mission, Kimball pursued business and political affairs after that and was active in the Democratic Party. He was called to the First Council of Seventy in April 1892 and served until his death in an automobile accident near Reno, Nevada. He and Roberts would have a friendly, competitive, and occasionally contentious relationship.

31. Heber C. Kimball (1801–68) was chosen in 1835 as a member of the original Quorum of the Twelve Apostles, then served as first counselor in the First Presidency from 1847 until his death. He led early Mormon missionary efforts in England, serving there in 1837–38 and 1839–41. Kimball married forty-five women, including his first wife, Vilate Murray (1806–67), and had sixty-six children from seventeen of his wives. He

> There were all kinds of elders in the company—farmers, cowboys, few educated—a pretty hard looking crowd and I was one of that kind. The elders preached and talked, and sang and advertized loudly their calling as preachers. I kept still for once in my life. I saw a gentleman get on the train. … He knew we were a band of Mormon elders. The elders soon commenced a discussion with the stranger and before he got through they were in grave doubt about their message of salvation. He gave them a training that they never forgot. That man proved to be President B. H. Roberts.[32]

As historian Mary Stovall Richards observed, the missionaries were most successful in the countryside, with converts drawn largely from "small farmers and mechanics" and their families; they were especially successful among those who had never "been members of any denomination." There is little mention of African Americans in journals, and when there is, they seem to reflect prevailing stereotypes. Robert S. Spence's views are typical: "After supper we held a meeting for a few negroes that had assembled. Bro. Bateman spoke after which the negroes sang some real old camp meeting songs and it was a treat—such singing, oh dear—I do not think a negro minstrel troupe, even is extravagant enough to represent them. I would not have believed it if I had not seen it."[33]

Roberts noted that one of his "first activities" was to renew his ties with the Saints in Shady Grove, which had been so central to his activities when he first arrived in Tennessee. He "crossed the Duck River on a flatboat and climbed the steep bluff cutting across the lawn to the spacious log plantation home of Uncle Robert Church." They spotted Roberts as he crossed the river "and were standing on the crown of the lawn bluff of the river with outstretched hands to welcome me, and an informal social greeting took place on the lawn."[34]

As they stood as a group, Roberts was reunited with another old

---

led one of the trains into the Salt Lake Valley in July 1847. During the next two decades he was one of the most important ecclesiastical, political, and business figures in Utah.

32. J. Golden Kimball, *Conference Report*, Oct. 6, 1933, 42. Kimball mistakenly suggests in his retrospective account that the meeting had taken place "either in Cincinnati or St. Louis."

33. Spence Diary, Nov. 15, 1881.

34. Roberts, *Autobiography*, 137.

friend, Church's horse Old Traveler, who was "an institution in the Southern States," as he claimed his place with the other well-wishers. After that visit, Roberts returned to Chattanooga, settled in, then began his travels throughout the mission, eventually making his way to Lebanon where he "spent the next few days … visiting among the Saints." Roberts had been here before and was delighted to greet the people again: "This was my old field of labor on my first mission. I had labored diligently among them preaching the Gospel for months; had baptized quite a number of them, and now I was receiving my reward: for who would witness the affection of these people and not feel that he was paid for all the labor required to convince them of the truth?" He expressed "they love me, and I am proud of their love. He who fails to win the love of his fellow man, in my opinion has lived in vain."[35]

From there Roberts journeyed on to a missionary conference in Baird's Mill, also familiar territory. Roberts's mind turned to redeeming his family. He told his mother, "I have no time to get rich. In the first place I desire to see my father's name made honorable among the people of God. I wish to redeem it from its fallen position and I admit that I am ambitious to do so." He even imagined a day when "I shall have an opportunity of visiting England and looking up our genealogies, and then, when temples are completed near us, we can attend to ordinances for our dead." Roberts felt "sustained by a power that I know is of God. I desire to ever be faithful and humble in my sprit, that I may not become puffed up in pride, and make a shipwreck of my faith."[36]

At the end of the month he was in Wayne County, Tennessee,[37] for the West Tennessee Conference[38] where he became reacquainted with John H. Gibbs. Seventeen years earlier, while on board the ship that brought him to Utah, Roberts had an encounter with an older boy over the ownership of some marbles,

35. Roberts, *History's Apprentice*, 115 (Apr. 28, 1883).

36. Roberts to Mother, May 10, 1882, box 4, fd. 3; and Roberts to Mother, Sep. 1, 1883, box 4, fd. 3, Roberts Papers (UU).

37. Wayne County is located in southwestern Tennessee, adjacent to the Alabama border. It had a population of 11,301 in 1880.

38. Historian's Office, Journal History, June 5, 1883, 3. The report was provided by Gibbs, who was secretary.

and a scuffle had ensued. He was stunned to learn the older boy was Gibbs. When they realized the connection, Truman Madsen noted, "both recalled with amazement this shipboard experience, faded but not forgotten," and it "proved to enhance the bond of missionary brotherhood they felt."[39]

Roberts had attracted the attention of his missionaries both for his concern for their welfare and his oratorical skills. One of those in attendance at the West Tennessee Conference was Willis E. Robison,[40] who noted, "Bro. Roberts occupied the entire time and preached the most able discourse it has ever been my good fortune to hear. He employed the spirit of the Lord in a most marked manner, and his sermon had the effect of turning the best wishes of many toward us."[41]

While in Decatur, Alabama,[42] preparing for an Alabama mission conference, Roberts saw two unsuspecting missionaries—Andrew M. Israelsen[43] and Otto L. Mayhew[44]—on a train and sat next to

39. Madsen, *Defender of the Faith*, 27.

40. Robison (1854–1937) was born in Illinois and came to Utah in the Peregrine Sessions Company, 1854. He was baptized in October 1862 and married Sarah Ann Ellet (1855–1907) on July 8, 1874. Robison was living and farming in Scipio at the time of his mission call. He was set apart on October 9, 1882, by John Henry Smith and returned on December 22, 1884. He would later be involved in the aftermath of the Cane Creek Massacre. After his return from the mission, he settled in Wayne County where he was active in church affairs, serving as Wayne Stake president, 1893–95. Robison and Roberts would reunite as members of the Utah constitutional convention. After the death of his first wife, he married Mary Elizabeth Reeve (1868–1914) on February 12, 1908, and Mary Louisa Ellet Young (1866–1939) on February 21, 1918.

41. Robison Diary, May 27, 1883, in Robison Papers.

42. Decatur is located along the Tennessee River in northern Alabama. It was an important rail and river stop.

43. Israelsen (1857–1939), a Norwegian immigrant, came to Utah in 1864 with his parents and three siblings. He married Boletta Wilson (1863–1952) on November 23, 1882. Israelsen was involved with the Young Men's Mutual Improvement Association and living in Hyrum, Cache Valley, when he was set apart for his mission by Joseph F. Smith on February 22, 1883. He was released on December 25, 1884. He returned to Hyrum where he spent the rest of his life as a farmer. He was also active in various church callings, including a counselor in the Hyrum Stake presidency, and was an unsuccessful Republican candidate for local office.

44. Mayhew (1836–1917) came to Utah in 1853 and settled in Pleasant Grove. That same year he served for two weeks as a member of the Pleasant Grove home guard during the Indian Wars. Mayhew was set apart on May 29, 1882, by Brigham Young Jr., and returned home on November 20, 1883. He spent the rest of his life in Pleasant Grove, where he was active in church callings, worked for the post office, and never married.

them. Roberts repeated his act of pretending to be a curious inquirer. "It was not long before I was engaged in conversation with them passing myself off as a disciple of R. G. Ingersoll."[45] Roberts tried to stump the missionaries as he "struck points with which they were not familiar. They explained Mormonism to me gave me tracts etc, etc. After riding 85 miles we arrived at B[irmingham] where I introduced myself to the brethren. Imagine their confusion."[46]

While in Mississippi, Roberts encountered a shadow of the antagonism that would soon explode in the Southern States Mission. A Mormon convert named Isaac T. Hamilton had died in May, but his funeral service was not held until June 10. Even though Hamilton was an "old citizen and respected neighbor," those in charge of the local church would not allow Roberts to preach a sermon inside because they were unwilling "that the sound of a 'Mormon Elders' voice should be heard within its sacred portals."[47]

Missionary Leo A. Bean's daughter later wrote of her father's experiences, and it is representative of what happened regularly:

> Even though buildings were burned that they planned to use as meeting places, and threats were posted along their way telling them to leave the country, the work went on. Many meetings were held under the trees and in the homes of the converts, who many times feared for their own safety in harboring the elders. Conducting meetings with an ominous mob surrounding the building took courage and faith and much stubborn determination to the work they were sent to do.[48]

In April 1884, Charles L. Flake and his companion "had some trouble … after baptizing a family we were attacked by a mob with shot guns. They seemed determined to have 'A Mormon on their dish' as they said. We refused to leave the state, which they said was the only salvation for us, but God delivered us out of their hands and we continued our labor."[49] Indeed during this period a

45. Robert G. Ingersoll (1833–99) was a noted writer who was thought to be an opponent of organized religion. For his part, Ingersoll believed he was an advocate of science and reason. He was also an early popularizer of the views of Charles Darwin.

46. Roberts, *History's Apprentice*, 119–20 (June 13, 1883).

47. "The Sunny South," *Deseret News*, July 18, 1883, 3.

48. Russell, "Biography of Leo Albert Bean," 2. The account is based on Bean's diary and family interviews.

49. Charles L. Flake to John Taylor, Feb. 28, 1885, in Missionary Reports.

missionary named John T. Alexander[50] had been "tied to a tree and shot at" by a mob. He survived but made his way to Chattanooga and ultimately back to Utah.[51] As Roberts noted, the experience "had so shattered [Alexander's] nerves that it was felt necessary to return him to his home."[52]

While in Georgia, Roberts and the missionaries discovered one morning that a horse belonging to one of the local members had been taken from its stable and the perpetrators had "cut or rather hacked off his mane and tail."[53] Later they discovered that the local Ku Klux Klan had stuck a large note on a tree warning the missionaries to leave the area.[54] While they did not leave, and indeed held several meetings, they took precautions to gather arms and sleep in the woods while being guarded by various members and missionaries.[55]

By the time Roberts was back in Tennessee, historian Patrick Mason notes that "virtually every segment of Southern society"—governmental leaders and politicians, the press, business interests, women's groups, law enforcement, preachers, and even ordinary citizens—"had mobilized against the Mormon threat" and had created "a regional anti-Mormon rhetoric" that led John Morgan to state that in the South "the 'Mormon' iron is red hot."[56] John Gibbs wrote that most of the criticism he received from "locals" was primarily over polygamy, noting that he had been accused of "debauchery, fornication

50. Alexander (1861–1930) was an English convert. He was set apart on his mission on April 9, 1883, by Seymour B. Young, and returned to Salt Lake City on June 28, 1883. The missionary register says his mission "was shortened due to injuries suffered from a mob attack." Single at the time he went on his mission, he married Camilla Josephine Schoenfeld (1860–1942) the same day he arrived in Salt Lake City. Alexander was a stock raiser in Salt Lake County.

51. See Seferovich, "History of LDS Southern States Mission," x. For a contemporary account, see "Our Injured Missionary," *Juvenile Instructor*, July 1883, 207.

52. Roberts, *Autobiography*, 156. Samuel J. Parrish (see below). who accompanied Alexander back home, reported that more than a year later Alexander had been "injured so severely" that he still suffered from the effects of the incident. See "An Elder From Tennessee," *Deseret News*, Oct. 1, 1884, 1.

53. Roberts, *History's Apprentice*, 122 (July 1, 1883).

54. This was a very prevalent tactic during this time. In addition to written notices, missionaries also were victim to verbal and physical abuse. Seferovich, "History of Southern States Mission," 100.

55. Roberts, *History's Apprentice*, 122–23 (July 1, 1883).

56. Mason, *Mormon Menace*, 14.

and what have you." After that, Gibbs noted, the most important topic for opponents was the Mountain Meadows Massacre.[57]

Mason, who has written extensively on violence against Latter-day Saints in the South, notes that the

> most violent forms of southern anti-Mormonism targeted LDS missionaries, who personified Mormonism's unorthodox religious beliefs and social customs. The fact that most of these missionaries were born in the North, West or abroad did not ease their position among white southerners who ... railed against the evils of non-native political, military, business and religious intruders in the region. More seriously, however, southerners saw missionaries not just as religious carpetbaggers but as seducers intent on wrecking homes and enticing women to join them in the West, where they would become veritable slaves in the Mormons' degraded polygamous society.[58]

Mason argues that the rhetoric about Mormons as seducers paralleled that of the "contemporary" fear of Southern white men against Black men as rapists. Clearly Morgan, Roberts, and the other missionaries in the South sensed they were "situated at the intersection of gender, religion and violence in the South."[59] Mary Stovall Richards writes that by the late 1880s, "as the national consciousness of polygamy and [the] concurrent agitation against it grew," so did the editorials, sermons, and even violence.[60]

An editorial in the *Deseret News* addressed the subject of what it called the "Shotgun Policy," noting that in some places in the South the success of the missionaries had convinced some that "a few doses of shotgun at short range would soon stampede those who were able to flee, and those unable to go could be 'boxed up.'" But Mormonism "cannot be shot out of existence," the *Deseret News* stated, "nor out of the hearts of its votaries. The more you shout the [stronger] will be

---

57. Gibbs to Morrell, Jan. 10, 1884, Morrell Correspondence. In September 1857, Mormons and local Paiutes attacked a wagon train and massacred its members. For more, see Walker, Turley, and Leonard, *Massacre at Mountain Meadows*.

58. Mason, *Mormon Menace*, 14–15.

59. Mason, 15.

60. Stovall, "Orthodoxy Vs. Conformity," 4–5. For a different view, an untitled observation in the *Wilkes-Barre Telephone* noted, "This howling about Polygamy among the Mormons appears like a great farce, coming as it does from a Nation full of uncleanness and crowded with divorced men and women." [Untitled], *Wilkes-Barre Telephone*, Mar. 1, 1884, 2.

their conviction, and the brighter the zeal of the devoted missionaries who bear its message of truth, peace and salvation to the world." The *News* reminded readers that violence in the Mormon past only encouraged the Saints to work harder: "The blood of Joseph and Hyrum still smokes to heaven, not only as a witness of the guilt of a State whose honor was pledged for the protection of those men of God, but as a token that the shotgun policy produces the very opposite of the intended effect."[61]

During July 27–29, Roberts presided over meetings of the North Carolina Conference, where William H. Clayton[62] reported that his "field of labor [was] not in a very flourishing condition" because local residents were "poisoning the minds of the people" by spreading "inaccurate reports." Roberts concurred, saying that when he had been in the area "prospects were not favorable, the people seemingly did not care to hear" the gospel message. In such situations, he told the elders, he felt it was "his duty to offer the Gospel to [the people] and leave the results with the Lord."

"Our work in the South goes steadily on," Roberts wrote to his mother, "and I believe we shall yet accomplish a greater amount of good than we have yet accomplished." Roberts "had the opportunity of addressing" what was "a large turnout" in one area. "Oh such a variety of opinions about what was said. Some rejoice at the glad tidings we brought them, others were cold and indifferent, and still others were boiling with rage." Roberts saw their fury, but he remained committed: "I could plainly see that some would like to roast the preacher. We however bore our testimony to them, and, having cleaned our garments of their blood, we leave them in the hands of God."[63]

As Roberts traveled throughout the South, it became clear to him that the efforts of the missionaries were attracting negative views

61. "Shotgun Policy," *Deseret Evening News*, June 27, 1883, 2. The paper further noted that the "blood of the martyrs is the seed of the Church."

62. Clayton (1843–1913) was born in Nauvoo, the son of Joseph Smith's scribe, William Clayton. He came to Utah in 1848 in the Heber C. Kimball company with his father, mother, two other plural wives, and eight relatives. Clayton was living in Kanab when he was set apart on his mission October 10, 1881, by Wilford Woodruff. He returned on September 30, 1883. He later resided in Garland, Box Elder County, where he was a carpenter.

63. Roberts to Mother, July 24, 1883, box 4, fd. 3, Roberts Papers (UU). The letter was written on stationery from the Greensboro, North Carolina hotel, The McAdoo.

from both the locals and the press. After his visit to Georgia, for example, a Savannah newspaper reported that the "agents of Mormonism" were "actively at work" in several counties throughout the state, their methods "so stealthy that intelligent people are seldom aware of their presence." The Mormons' alleged plan was to "make nocturnal calls, and when enough subjects are brought over to their views, to hold a lonely meeting at lonely places where converts can be instructed and in time depart … for Utah." The Mormon's sinister plan could trick "a great many ignorant people with no church relationships" who "are easily approached by the Mormon bishops, and are so secretive that it is impossible to get a revelation from them."[64]

The *Franklin News* reported that not only were there "Mormon emissaries" in the county, but "what is worse, they find fools who will listen to their foul discourse." While the paper was sure such views were not given much consideration by "respectable families," it considered the Mormon presence troubling, and encouraged its readers to "keep cool and leave 'Mormonism' to take care of itself. It's a hard thing to kill. In fact, it will not die."[65]

This report may have been prompted by a Mormon missionary conference the week before in Burke's Garden, Virginia, where, "under the direction of President Roberts we dedicated a spot of ground for secret prayer, adopting nearly the form of prayer used in sacred places of the Saints."[66] J. Golden Kimball referred to it as a "circle prayer."[67] After that, according to Levi J. Taylor, Roberts "spoke for 2 1/4 hours delivering one of the most instructive discourses that I ever listened to showing the difference between the Church of God and the churches of men."[68] As Taylor reported, the party was so large it "caused the people to stare to see so many 'Mormon' elders."[69] The next day, Roberts, Kimball, and several other missionaries traveled toward Jeffersonville to baptize William Jamison and his wife,

64. As quoted in "Mormonism in Georgia," *Ogden Daily Herald*, Aug. 16, 1883, 2.

65. "Mormonism in Georgia."

66. Levi Taylor Diary, Aug. 11, 1883, in Levi Taylor Papers. Hereafter cited as Taylor Diary.

67. Kimball Journal, Aug. 11, 1883.

68. Taylor Diary, Aug. 11, 1883.

69. Taylor Diary, Aug. 12, 1883.

who had "entertained the Elders for years and have heard the Gospel for years, but Roberts's "sermon overpowered them."[70]

Roberts continued to suffer from some of the same health problems that had plagued him for the past few years. On September 20 he had "been very sick all day with my old complaint-headache." The next day he traveled to Knoxville where again the headache returned, and he noted that he suffered so much that he "took a dram of Rye whiskey—the first I ever took while on a mission."[71] The whiskey deadened the pain for a time, but the next "morning I find my self sick. About as ill as ever I was in my life. I suffered extreme pain in my head, and nothing would relieve me." He called for some missionaries who "administered to me and again in about half an hour." He slept and awoke feeling well enough that "in the afternoon I dictated five letters [but for] several days I remained quite unwell, and only attended to writing the letters which of necessity had to be attended to."[72]

No doubt the stress tied to the demands of the mission were contributing to these conditions. Shortly after this headache attack, he had the additional burden of receiving the news that Charles E. Robison, presiding in South Carolina, had died. The responsibility to ship the body home fell to him.[73] Roberts told his mother that a "cloud of sorrow" was passing over the Elders as a result of Robinson's death, and stated, "No one could ask a nobler place to die at than the post of duty."[74]

While Morgan was in Utah, Roberts not only ran the day-to-day activities of the mission, but in effect was its public spokesman. The *Deseret Evening News* reported in September 1883 that the *Chattanooga Times* had recently published some "very bitter and antagonistic" editorials on Mormonism, and that Roberts had replied

70. Kimball Journal, Aug. 11–13, 1883. Indeed, Roberts and others had stayed with the couple during the conference.

71. Roberts, *History's Apprentice*, 142 (Sep. 20, 1883).

72. Roberts, 142–43.

73. Roberts to John Taylor, Sep. 26, 1883, Incoming Telegrams, First Presidency Correspondence. George Q. Cannon noted that "This intelligence has shocked us, because Bro. Robeson [*sic*] was … comparatively young when he a sent out as a missionary." Efforts were being made to contact his widow and his father, and Daniel H. Wells would "call upon his mother who resides in this city and inform her of the sad news." See Cannon Journal, Sep. 26, 1883. Roberts also informed John Morgan of the death.

74. Roberts to Mother, Sep. 27, 1883, box 4, fd. 3, Roberts Papers (UU).

to them, though the paper's editor "ungraciously refused to publish it, showing that he was unwilling for both sides to be heard."[75] Instead the *Deseret Evening News* published Roberts's response and, reflecting the fact that he was still less known in Utah, described "Elder Roberts" as the assistant to Morgan. "We like to encourage the young men of our people, and we are pleased to see how well Brother Roberts understands and is able to defend the position taken by the Church of which he is a member, on many of the important questions which have for some time been agitated in this country."[76]

Morgan returned to the mission in November 1883.[77] By that time the mission consisted of some 832 members, divided into twenty-five branches, with eighty-seven traveling elders laboring there.[78] Later in the month, he and Roberts "conducted an emigration of seventy-three Saints to Zion."[79] Roberts, and a "small company of saints and Elders," met up with Morgan in Cincinnati and made their trek west, stopping first in Colorado where they arrived on November 18.[80]

Roberts reached home on November 26, joining Morgan in a meeting with the First Presidency.[81] After that he remained primarily in Centerville. On December 8 Roberts attended the Davis Stake Conference in Kaysville. His service in the Southern States Mission was noted, and he participated along with several general authorities and church leaders, including Joseph F. Smith, Charles W. Penrose,[82]

---

75. This is interesting in light of the fact that the paper's editor, Adolph Oaks, was later described by the *Salt Lake Herald* as a friend of Morgan and sympathetic to the church.

76. "Reply to the Chattanooga 'Times,'" *Deseret Evening News*, Sep. 24, 1883, 2.

77. Morgan Journal, Nov. 13, 1883.

78. "History of the Southern States Mission," *Latter-day Saints Southern Star*, Apr. 15, 1899, 153–54. See also Southern States Mission typescript in Morgan Papers, Nov. 1883, which says they were "accompanied by 7 elders, 5 of whom have been released, the other two transferred to Colorado to labor among the Saints there."

79. Morgan Journal, Nov. 14, 1883.

80. Morgan Journal, Nov. 15, 18, 1883.

81. Morgan Journal, Nov. 26, 1883.

82. Penrose (1832–1925) was an English convert then serving as editor of the *Deseret News*. He had previously been active in church and civic affairs in Logan and Ogden where he was associated with the *Daily Junction*. He served as an Assistant Church Historian, 1896–99, and as an apostle (1904) and counselor (1911) in the First Presidency until his death.

and John Taylor.[83] Roberts had come a long way since leaving for his first mission in the spring of 1880. The young, inexperienced elder was now a confident man, sharing the stand with general authorities, including the church president, and having gained their trust in executing an important assignment in the South.

Roberts spent the holidays in Davis County with his family, speaking occasionally to wards on one of two topics: "The Divine Mission of Joseph Smith"[84] and the "Improvement of the Youth of Zion." The *Deseret Evening News* reported that whenever "he appears on the platform, he is greeted by large and appreciative audiences."[85] On January 28, Roberts, along with Morgan, visited George Q. Cannon and Joseph F. Smith to discuss matters pertaining to the Southern States Mission.[86] The next day, accompanied by Harvey H. Perkins,[87] a recently called missionary to Missouri, Roberts left on the Denver & Rio Grande train to return to Tennessee,[88] unaware that 1884 would be the most fateful year during his time in the South.

Roberts spent a few days in the Mormon colonies in Colorado, then arrived in Kansas City on February 3.[89] He stopped in St. Louis and Independence, Missouri, where he toured many of the local sites, including the Temple Lot.[90] He wrote to his mother that his visit had put the area, and that chapter in church history, "in a new light." The Temple Lot was "surrounded by a good wire fence,

83. Morgan had met the group on the train while heading to Logan. See Morgan Journal, Dec. 8, 1883.

84. See "Lecture," *Salt Lake Herald*, Jan. 27, 1884, 12. This lecture would become a Roberts staple, and was delivered many times in many places over the years.

85. Historian's Office, Journal History, Jan. 16, 1884, 2.

86. Morgan wrote, "In company with Elder B. H. Roberts called at the President's Office and had a talk with Presidents Cannon and Smith relative to missionary matters. … Attended a lecture at the 14th Ward Assembly Hall at 7 p. m. by Elder B H Roberts, President W. R. Smith … Elder Roberts stayed all night." Morgan Journal, Jan. 28, 1884.

87. Perkins (1840–1920) came to Utah in 1848 where he was soon orphaned. He moved to Bountiful in 1863 and was active in church affairs and was a stock raiser. He was set apart for his mission on January 22, 1884, by Apostle Wilford Woodruff but returned two months later. See "Harvey H. Perkins Suddenly Called," *Davis County Clipper*, Dec. 31, 1920, 1.

88. See Historian's Office, Journal History, Jan. 28, 1884, 14–17; and Jan. 29, 1884, 3. John Morgan recorded, "Looked after a pass for Bro. Roberts this a. m. and at 9 a. m. bid him goodby." Morgan Journal, Jan. 29, 1884.

89. Historian's Office, Journal History, Feb. 3, 1884, 3.

90. The Temple Lot was dedicated by Joseph Smith in 1831. Smith said a temple would be built there as part of what he envisioned as the city of Zion in the last days.

and not a thing on it. No unhallowed hand has been permitted to desecrate it, and I pray that it may remain in that condition until the time has come for the Saints to build the Temple."

He arrived in Chattanooga on February 6[91] and on February 14 headed back west again with "a company of emigrants numbering 33 souls."[92] In a long article to the *Denver Tribune,* Roberts said that because the Southern Saints were so poverty stricken, Utah land was out of reach, but in Colorado they could "obtain land at a government price." They left the South to better their conditions and found that in the San Luis Valley there was food, plenty of work, and good wages.[93] In February 1884, for example, John Gibbs, then tracting in Centerville, Tennessee, wrote, "There is a young man here by the name of John Westbrook.[94] Bro. Roberts is well acquainted with him." Westbrook had been "assisting us in the ministry for a short time. Now he wants to emigrate to Colorado." But Westbrook and his family could not afford the thirty-eight-dollar cost to travel with the company. "He is a good, faithful young man and can do nothing in country by way of getting means etc."[95] Gibbs also mentioned to mission secretary Nathaniel W. Haws that "a company of ten or more" Saints from Lewis County were "preparing to leave" for Colorado in April or May.[96]

After spending several weeks in the mission headquarters, Roberts presided over a meeting of the East Tennessee Conference on April 19 and 20 in Baird's Mill, speaking specifically about Southern Saints relocating in the West. Roberts said it was "well known that it is part of our belief that the people who embrace the Gospel should

---

91. The mission history noted Roberts had been in Utah "visiting his family and friends." "History of the Southern States Mission," Feb. 1884.

92. "History of the Southern States Mission," Feb. 1884.

93. See "Colorado Mormons," *Denver Tribune,* Mar. 3, 1884, 3. Roberts also took this as an opportunity to address charges that the Mormons practiced Blood Atonement. He stated that the church's position was based on biblical teachings, and that "when a murderer is to be executed, having been found guilty and condemned by the laws of the land, the manner of the execution should be such as to shed his blood."

94. This is likely John Henry Westbrook (b. 1869), who was living with his widowed mother, Susan (1846 1904), and several of his siblings in the area. Westbrook married Jennie Nunger on December 5, 1887, in Weakley, Tennessee.

95. Gibbs to Haws, Feb. 6, 1884, box 4, fd. 3, in Gibbs, Southern States Mission Letters. There seems to be no record of Gibbs going to Colorado.

96. Gibbs to Haws.

gather to the valleys of the mountains." Such a policy was necessary because those who embraced the gospel were automatically persecuted and thus "almost compelled to emigrate." Those choosing to relocate were following longstanding precepts and covenants they had made when joining the church, and were to be gathered to the "tops of the mountains" because it was there that they "might be taught the ways of the Lord and walk in his paths, that they might not partake of the sins of the world nor receive its plagues." Roberts turned to the persecution the missionaries felt from the locals. "Mark the path of the cyclones which have devastated the land and you will find them to be … in that region where the Elders have labored and their testimony has been rejected." Moving westward was the will of the Almighty as "God has declared that he would gather his people and take them to the wilderness and there purge out the rebels from amongst them. In Colorado some of this purging has taken place." Roberts described Colorado as a place "where by hard work and plenty of it, a man can live." None of the people there have starved, and the church would see to it that none would. He also encouraged his listeners that if any of them went there "for the love of the gospel, and if that is not sufficient reason, by all means stay where you are."[97]

In March 1884, Roberts informed J. Golden Kimball that he and Morgan wanted him to come to Chattanooga "and assist us in the labors of the mission at this office." Kimball did not want to leave day-to-day missionary work for a role in the office, but he accepted the summons, saying "I grumbled, kicked and felt grieved, but … I concluded to go and do my level best. Obedience is better than sacrifice and to my opinion it takes in both of them."[98] Describing the relationship Kimball and Roberts developed over the next several months, Kimball wrote, "He trusted me, and I never betrayed him. He confided in me, the only time in his life, about his own affairs, his family etc." Kimball acted as secretary, and the men shared one room for an office and a bedroom for "$25.00 a month for rent and board. It was hotter than hades most of the time. He walked the floor and dictated, and I wrote long hand volumes and stored away a fund of

97. Historian's Office, Journal History, Apr. 21, 1884, 4.

98. Kimball Journal, Apr. 14, 1884.

information."[99] The two would, despite occasional differences, become lifelong friends and serve together in the First Council of the Seventy. In later years, Kimball said he did not believe there was a living person who "knew Elder Roberts any better than I did. There was an affection, a friendship, formed in the missionary field that exceeds any love I have ever known outside of my own family."[100]

On April 26 and 27, Roberts organized and presided over the Northwestern Tennessee Conference in McEwen, Humphreys County,[101] where John Gibbs was sustained as president of the northwest division, which included seven branches, seventy members, and seven elders. Additionally, Gibbs and William S. Jones were appointed to "take a roving mission to lecture in the principal towns … of the South in vindication of our people's rights and integrity of character and profession and to represent truthfully the historic moral, social and political phase of the 'Mormon Problem.'"[102] Gibbs seems to have relished the opportunity, telling his friend Joseph Morrell that while he would have "preferred to have stayed in my field," the assignment would give him a chance to "bind up the law and seal up the testimony," among the larger community.[103]

Some sources have suggested that Jones was a good public speaker and "a talented debater [which] caught the attention" of Roberts.[104] Gibbs described Jones as a "refined young man of good education and qualifications. … His deportment is good, his expression is adequate and in all I have a good partner."[105] John Morgan wrote to John Taylor saying that they were having "good success" and were speaking to "fair sized audiences and in some instances large attendance to hear what they have to say on the *political situation in Utah*" (emphasis in original). Morgan told Taylor that he was convinced

99. J. Golden Kimball, *Conference Report*, Oct. 1933, 43. One wonders if one of the confidences he shared was his marriage to Celia Dibble.

100. Kimball, 42.

101. See Robison Diary, Apr. 25–28, 1884.

102. Historian's Office, Journal History, Apr. 27, 1884, 2.

103. Gibbs to Morrell, Apr. 22, 1884, Morrell Letters Received.

104. Crow, *Land of Strangers*, 46–47.

105. As late as August 2, 1884, only a few days before his murder, Gibbs mentions the work he and Jones were doing. See Gibbs Journal, May 8, 1884, Aug. 2, 1884.

Jones and Gibbs were making "headway" with those "who wield extensive influence in Society."[106]

Later reminiscences from the family of William S. Berry[107] suggest he may have undertaken a similar assignment. Berry "traveled considerably over the state … serving as an ambassador for the Church among state and city officials and prominent businessmen. This was part of his missionary assignment, to break down the prejudices against the … Church. In this he had a large measure of success."[108]

But there was a foreshadowing of violence. As they were meeting in Humphreys County, Gibbs received a letter, simply signed "Boston," stating that "a mob already made up" from Hickman, Dixon, Humphreys, or Perry Counties intended to give the missionaries thirty days "to collect your band and skip."[109] Gibbs recorded on July 28, 1884, another notice, full of misspellings, ordering the Mormon elders to "Get away from our country and stay away and never show yourselves in here any more."[110] But such threats were not new to Gibbs. He had told his friend Joseph Morrell that he had been "threatened the hickory, tar & feathers, and even death," though "none of the above have ever come in to effect."[111] In early May, Gibbs returned from Chattanooga to Lewis County to discover that a newly built log chapel had been burned. He received another note threatening him with violence and suggesting the missionaries leave before "hickory switches" were used freely.[112]

William S. Berry was experiencing a taste of threats as well. He

106. Morgan to Taylor, July 22, 1884, box 2, fd. 7, Morgan Papers.

107. William S. Berry (1838–84) was born in Tennessee and moved with family to Nauvoo, Illinois. He was living in Kanarraville when he was set apart for his mission by Wilford Woodruff in April 1884. The Missionary Register notes, "Shot by a mob on 10th day of August 1884." His diaries are held at the Church History Library.

108. This same source also commented that "Berry blood is martyr's blood. More of it, perhaps, has been shed for the Church of Jesus Christ than of any other family. … But as for the guilty ones, they still are in the hands of God and mercy shall never rob justice." See "Men You Should Know," fd. 1, Berry Family Autobiographies.

109. Historian's Office, Journal History, May 17, 1884, 8. See also Gibbs Journal, May 1, 1884. Another glimpse of these threats comes from a letter of Joshua Hawkes published in "West Tennessee Conference," *Deseret News*, May 7, 1884, 3.

110. Gibbs Journal, July 28, 1884.

111. Gibbs to Morrell, August 18, 1883. Morrell Letters Received. As Gibbs stated, "Through all the threats we have managed to get just enough hold for our toes."

112. As quoted in Linam, "Our Sorrows They've Seen," 25. Linam's study has a great deal of useful information about Lewis County.

noted in his diary on May 13, 1884—while in the company of Willis E. Robison and Willard H. Robinson—that he "had a notice from 40 men that if the missionaries came back," they would be lynched. He also noted that he had received a letter from Gibbs worrying that if he and his colleagues did not leave their area, the anti-Mormons would "tar and feather and burn them. He said for us ... to be prayerful and tend to our duties."[113]

Despite these and other threats, Roberts continued to travel widely, holding conferences in many states where he preached and organized mission affairs and the local church branches, which, he wrote, were growing "with marvelous rapidity."[114] Roberts wrote to his mother on May 20, commenting on the recent birth of a girl to his sister Annie, "we have more boys than girls in Utah anyway, and with our peculiar faith respecting marriage, we have need for plenty of the fairer sex." Then he commented on the conference: "Not so much interest manifest in this state, but it is on the increase." Elders who had met him when he arrived at the conference "had a bucket of tar thrown over them, and a mob made some threats, but nothing more serious happened." Roberts, oblivious to the depth of the threats, concluded, "We are getting along very quietly so far this year—very few instances of mob violence."

Charles Shumway reported that while he and A. M. Israelsen were staying with a member family in Alabama, they felt a premonition that they should leave the house. Shortly after they hid in a cornfield, a mob, "cursing and swearing," surrounded the house "and demanded that the two missionaries show themselves." When the family assured them that there were no Mormons inside, the mob went looking. Shumway and Israelsen made their way to a river, hid under a ledge bank, then waded to a small island in the middle where they hid until the group had left. By morning the local members had located the embattled missionaries, fed them, and assisted them on their way. Leo Bean's daughter remembered

> there was much persecution of the elders at that time and much danger of mob violence in the areas where there was hostility to the Church.

113. Berry Journal, May 13, 1884.

114. Historian's Office, Journal History, May 21, 1884, 3. See also "Proselyting in the South," *Deseret News*, Mar. 10, 1886, 14.

> Floggings and tar and feathering were not uncommon. … One incident that my mother recalled to us was when a mob surrounded the house he and his companion were in and began clamoring for a "sign," Father walked out and faced them, slowly and deliberately taking off his coat and rolling up his sleeves. He then stepped up to one of the men, collared him, and said "Step back now all of you: I am going to strike this man blind for a sign." The crowd melted away and they were unmolested during the remainder of their stay in that locality.[115]

By the end of July, Roberts had finished his extensive tour, not only of the mission itself but also of Chicago and Nauvoo.[116] Upon arriving in Chattanooga, he found J. Golden Kimball "in a precarious state of health, jaundice and malaria had fastened upon him, and it was quite evident that he needed a respite from the strenuous work … at the mission headquarters."[117] Roberts directed him to go to stay with the Church family in Duck River where he could "recuperate for a few weeks." This decision left Roberts without headquarters staff.[118] In early August, Roberts wrote a long letter to his friend John M. Whitaker[119] speculating that the anti-Mormon violence seemed to be tied to the temperature, but that the missionaries were meeting with "much less violence from mobs than we expected."[120] His optimism was misguided.

---

115. Russell, "Biography of Leo Albert Bean," 2.

116. Kimball Journal, July 9, 1884.

117. Kimball noted that for some time he "had not felt very well, my system being out of order, but hope to be better soon." Kimball Journal, July 8, July 31, 1884. Kimball's biographer, Claude Richards, notes that the bout with malaria "left him with its effects for the years to come." See Richards, *J. Golden Kimball*, 41.

118. Roberts, *Autobiography*, 138. Roberts generally uses the spelling of "Kane."

119. Whitaker (1863–1960) was born in Centerville. He graduated from the University of Deseret and was engaged in various capacities in railroading, including as secretary to John W. Young. Whitaker organized the Salt Lake Stake Free Library and Reading Room. He married Ida Oakley Taylor (1860–1946), daughter of John Taylor, on September 22, 1886. Whitaker was set apart on December 1, 1897, by Seymour B. Young to serve in the Eastern States, and returned on January 25, 1900. A stenographer who also taught shorthand, he was secretary to the First Council of Seventy and to the Deseret Sunday School. In that role and others, he would grow close to Roberts.

120. Roberts to John Mills Whitaker, Aug. 4, 1884, box 10, fd. 37, Whitaker Papers.

FIVE

THE CANE CREEK MASSACRE

On August 10, 1884,[1] B. H. Roberts was in Chattanooga, "attending to ... secretarial duties, answering correspondence," and finishing an article for the *Juvenile Instructor* when he fell into a "restless sleep." The next morning, he dressed and, as was his custom, set out for his usual breakfast at the Hotel Florentine. As he entered the hotel's foyer, he found "the inmates regarding me unusually but none spoke," then he was given a copy of the paper which "in flaring headlines [contained] an account of Mormon elders being massacred on Kane Creek in Lewis County."[2] Roberts recoiled, finding the report of the death of John Gibbs and William Berry in the home of Jim and Malinda Conder "too horrible to believe as true."[3]

The press dubbed the incident "Tennessee's Mormon Massacre." The Conder home "is said to be the bloodiest house imaginable after the affair was over; the blood being spattered over everything and standing nearly an inch deep on the floor."[4] The *Nashville Banner* called it "one of the most horrible butcheries ever enacted in this state."[5] Nathan Tanner Jr.[6] recorded, "I see from the Nashville American that some troubles have occurred between a mob and the

1. The date is mistakenly listed as August 20 in Roberts, *Autobiography*.

2. The *Chattanooga Daily Commercial* was not published on Mondays. The *Chattanooga Daily Times* carried a small story on August 12. See "Mormons Murdered," *Chattanooga Daily Times*, Aug. 12, 1884, 1. See also "Horrible Butchery," *Nashville Weekly American*, Aug. 14, 1884, 1.

3. J. Golden Kimball wrote, "The report of the massacre was all over the country on Monday and we did not hear of it until Tuesday." See Kimball Journal, Aug. 10, 1884.

4. "Terrible Tragedy," *Hickman Pioneer*, Aug. 15, 1884, 2.

5. "Murder of Mormons," *Nashville Banner*, Aug. 12, 1884, 4.

6. Tanner (1845–1919) was born in Iowa and came to Utah in 1848 in the Amasa M. Lyman company. Tanner was living in Ogden when he was set apart for his mission on April 7, 1884, by Francis M. Lyman and returned on May 17, 1886. Tanner served in the 1882 constitutional convention and was active in Ogden politics.

Elders in Wilson, Co, but I cannot credit it because I know the paper to be unreliable and second from the way the story is told it does not look plausible. I hope it is not so."[7]

J. Golden Kimball was already close to the incident because on August 9, while staying at Emmons Church's home, still "feeling miserable as malaria can make a person," he

> heard the voice of Elder Jones and looked anxiously for Elder Gibbs as they were companions. Elder Jones then related how he had been captured by a mob, and abused, but finally through the providence of God, his guard who appeared to be more friendly allowed him to escape. This caused us great uneasiness on account of the other brethren, but never dreaming that anything of a serious nature would happen to them, we waited patiently for their return, knowing if they left Monday [August 11] they would not arrive here until about Tuesday at 12 a.m.[8]

However, they received the news the next day. They hoped it was "too horrible to contemplate," but obtained horses and traveled to Cane Creek. When they got within twelve miles of their destination, they encountered Henry Thompson[9] and William Garrett. Since Thompson was said to be among those killed, Kimball's "heart leapt for joy," thinking the reports were untrue. But they soon discovered the reports were true, that the elders' bodies had been buried, and that if they proceeded, it was to certain death. Kimball "acknowledged the hand of the Lord in preventing our going down there." They returned to the Church home intent on going to Columbia, but decided, since the telegraph would be closed, to spend the night and leave at 3:00 a.m., on August 11. Once there they telegraphed Roberts, "put up at a second class hotel," and waited.[10]

The missionaries' initial contact in the Cane Creek area had taken place in 1879, and then increased when Hyrum Belnap began

7. Tanner Jr. Diary, Aug. 19, 1884. Tanner was likely referring to "Horrible Butchery," *Nashville Weekly American*, Aug. 14, 1884, 1.

8. Kimball Journal, Aug. 9, 1884.

9. Henry Bronson Thompson (1859–1941) was born in central Utah and spent the first half of his life there. After returning home following the Cane Creek Massacre, he married Elizabeth Yates (1865–1938) in December 1884. He served a second mission to Scotland, 1898–1900. He later moved his family to northern Utah, where he was a sheep and cattle rancher until his death in 1941.

10. Kimball Journal, Aug. 10–11, 1884.

proselyting in January 1881. As one historian observed, there "were few places in Tennessee more remote than Lewis County," and in that county there was "no place quite so remote as the east fork of Cane Creek."[11] Belnap gave George Henderson Conder a copy of the Book of Mormon, and the family said they "desired us to keep coming." Belnap was successful in baptizing several members of the Conder family, including George Henderson Conder, but in the process had displeased Green Ledbetter[12] who owned the farm Conder was renting. He accused the Conders of "sheltering the Mormons."[13]

In May 1884, John Gibbs, who served as president of the West Tennessee Conference, arrived in Cane Creek to set up a branch. Gibbs discovered that the "recently constructed log meeting house" he anticipated was, in fact, a "pile of ashes."[14] Gibbs also found an anonymous note threatening the Mormons with violence if they did not cease preaching in Hickman, Perry, or Lewis counties. Gibbs wrote to John Morrell that "during May … we received more persecution threats and abuse from our opponents than any previous month since I have been out. … The same reports came from nearly all the other elders in this conference."[15] The threats did not deter him, and he gathered a group together and began preaching. In the crowd were some of the men behind the burning of the church, and they saw Gibbs baptize several local residents. After that Gibbs, along with William Jones,[16] travelled around the Southern States Mission giving the series of lectures Roberts had tasked them with. Gibbs and Jones returned to

---

11. Wingfield, "Tennessee's Mormon Massacre," argues that bitterness toward the Mormons extended to the very beginning of the church's work in the area.

12. Ledbetter (1824–1901) married Elizabeth Harp (1820–99) on September 26, 1848. He was a Confederate 2nd Lieutenant in the 42nd Regiment of the Tennessee Infantry. He was a farmer who lived his entire life in Peery County.

13. See Belnap Autobiography, 113–20, in Hyrum Belnap Papers.

14. There is an abundant literature on this seminal event. For the purposes of this biography, I have chosen to examine primarily the basic facts, and the way in which Roberts responded. It is my contention that his actions led to his increasing prominence in the church from this point onward. At the same time, anyone looking for a detailed overview should consult Crow, *Land of Strangers*.

15. See Gibbs to Morrell, June 5 and 10, 1884, Morrell Letters Received.

16. William Jones (1858–1918) was living in Brigham City when he was set apart by Lorenzo Snow for his mission in April 1883. He also served a mission in the Eastern States, November 1885–November 1887, to attend Cornell University. Jones, who was employed as a teacher, was apparently not active in the LDS Church in later years.

Cane Creek in early August where they met with other missionaries, including the recently arrived William S. Berry and Henry Thompson, and scheduled a meeting at the home of James and Malinda Conder[17] for August 10. According to a later account, local residents "were keeping pretty close tab on the movements of the Mormons, for news of the meeting was noised about, and a band of citizens who were determined to put an end to Mormon preaching in that section, made plans to give the elders and their followers a scare."[18]

Accounts of the massacre are many and varied, but a general description suggests that about an hour before the services were to begin on Sunday morning, Jones was "seized by a band of masked men armed with pistols and shotguns" near the ford on Cane Creek. The men—perhaps fifteen in number—demanded to know the whereabouts of Gibbs. Leaving one man to guard Jones, the rest of the group set out for the Conder home. Jones's guard, Ruben "Rube" Mathis,[19] told Jones that he intended to let him go, but that the others were intent on doing harm to the missionaries and church members. Later local sources insist that most in the mob were intent on administering "thrashings to the elders and request they leave." When they reached their destination, the elder Conder was outside and alerted the others inside to the imminent danger. After an initial scuffle, shots broke out and Gibbs was instantly killed, then the mob killed Berry and James's son Martin. At that point, Martin's stepbrother John R. Hudson came down from the loft, armed with a shotgun, and killed a member of the mob named David Hinson.[20] The mob then killed Hudson, and as they left fired one last shot

17. Malinda Carroll Conder (1833–1916) was married to John R. Hudson (1831–56) and William James Conder (1832–1911) whom she married in 1862. She was the mother of both Martin Conder and John R. Hudson.

18. "Bloody 'Mormon' Massacre on Cane Creek, Significant Event in Tennessee History, *Nashville Banner*, June 30, 1931, 16. Hereafter cited as "Bloody Mormon Massacre."

19. Mathis (1851–ca.1935) was a farmer in Lewis County. He married Elizabeth Williams (1850–1932) on September 27, 1868.

20. Hinson (1843–84) served in the Confederate army as a member of the Tennessee 3rd infantry from 1861–65. At one point he was a prisoner of war at Chicago's Camp Douglas. He married Rebecca "Caroline" Curry (b 1844) in 1860, and they had four children, three living with them at the time of the massacre, ages fifteen to twenty-one. Later, Lorenzo Hunsaker, who had served a mission in Tennessee, said that Hinson was "a Methodist preacher, a man people looked up to for the word of God. . . . It is nine times out of ten it is Christian ministers that raise mobs against our people." See "Memorial Services," *Utah Journal*, Sep. 13, 1884, and Historian's Office, Journal History, Sep. 2, 1884, 7.

into Berry's lifeless body, some of the buckshot lodging in the hip of James's wife, Malinda, who survived "but for the rest of her life walked with pain and a serious limp." Taking Hinson's body with them, the group retreated. The "entire melee" had lasted only "a matter of minutes."[21] True to his word, Jones's guard let him escape.

In late August, the *Indianapolis News* carried a "graphic" account of the events based on eyewitness John F. Henschen.[22] The paper reported that Henschen was riding near Conder's house where he met the band headed by David Hinson. They "halted him at the muzzle of a revolver," making him a "quiet spectator" to what followed. In Henschen's account,

> The band numbered fifteen or twenty, wearing masks, and were armed heavily, and with them was a wagon in which were a number of whips, a kettle of tar and supply of feathers. As they neared the house Gibbs was seen at the window reading from a book and he was shot dead without warning. The fire was returned from the house, and for a few moments the fusillade reminded Henschen of his army experiences. The Mormons finally fled, but not until Cond[e]r, Hudson, Gibbs and his associate [Berry] had been shot dead, and Mrs. Conder badly wounded. The attacking force lost one man, Hinson, who was killed in the first fire from the house. Henschen was one of the judges at the inquest, and in his certificate to the Governor he made return of death at the hands of unknown parties.[23]

Henschen reported that in the days after the shooting several of the local Mormons had left the area. He said that one of them, "an old resident" named Elisha Talley,[24] had sold him "his farm of 264 acres together with the crops, farming utensils, live stock etc ... in order to

21. A later account suggests that Hinson was "badly wounded" when he left the Conder cabin and carried by "old Kudge Sisco, a Negro who had followed the masked men. One of Hinson's companions it is said cried 'I'll have a revenge!' and shot Hudson killing him immediately. Death came to Hinson laying under a nearby tree a few minutes later." "Bloody Mormon Massacre."

22. Henschen (1841–1919) lived in the area with his wife, Dena C. Hamann Henschen (1843–1908), whom he married in 1866. Both were German immigrants. Henschen served 1862–65 in company G. 60th Indiana Infantry. It appears they left the area around 1890.

23. "Killing of the Mormon Elders," *Indianapolis News*, Aug. 21, 1884, 1. The paper had spelled some of the names incorrectly and they have been corrected here. The article was reprinted as "The Mormon Tragedy," *Nashville American*, Aug. 28, 1884, 1.

24. Talley (1837–1902) married Barbara E. Hutson Talley (1835–1912) in March 1859. Talley served as a Confederate soldier in the 42nd Regiment of the Tennessee Infantry. Both were baptized on September 20, 1879, and were mainstays of the Cane

leave at once." The *Indianapolis News* commented that "further trouble is anticipated, as the Mormons have a large church, known as Shady Grove, about thirty miles distant, and they will not let the occasion pass without an effort to regain their former footing" in the area.[25]

In 1938, one of the participants in the event, Henry B. Thompson, provided an interesting retrospective on the event to his great-grandson Harold M. Thompson. Thompson recalled that "the living room of the Cond[e]r home was filled to capacity." There was a small church service being held and "they had concluded the signing and had called upon Elder Gibbs to speak [when] suddenly the front door was thrown open and a mob of masked, armed men charged into the room, shooting their guns as they came." The mob "shot Elder Gibbs and young Martin Cond[e]r." When one of the mob aimed his gun at Thompson, "Elder Berry knocked the gun aside as it was discharged. The mobber in a rage, turned his gun on elder Berry and shot him down."[26]

Thompson told his grandson that he believed he was the one "they were after" and that if he could "get out of the house, perhaps the terrible shooting would stop." At first he thought to "turn and run out the back," then changed his mind and "walked slowly through the front door to escape." Resisting his first impulse to hide in the cornfield, Thompson opted to "squat down behind a small bush near the front door" instead. Shouting that Thompson had escaped, the mob "ran out the front door, cursing and swearing," and searched the cornfield "row by row while [Thompson] listened in terror behind the bush." After their failure to locate him, the mob "scattered through the woods to the west in order to cover a wider area," forcing him to spend two days and nights in "the thick forest to the east" without "food and shelter" until he made his way to Brother Garrett's where they sheltered him that evening.[27] The next morning, hidden in a load of hay, he escaped.[28]

Creek Branch. Apparently, Barbara was related to John Riley Hutson. Despite what Henschen states, they seem to have lived the rest of their lives in Lewis County.

25. "Killing of the Mormon Elders," *Indianapolis News*, Aug. 21, 1884, 1.

26. Thompson, "Account of the Gibbs and Berry Massacre."

27. While not part of this interview, the grandson reports that Thompson told his son Merwyn that on the day after the massacre "the mob used bloodhounds to track him down," but that he was able to hide behind the beams and decking of a bridge, and while the dogs did not find him, "he could feel their breath on his face." Thompson Account.

28. Thompson Account. The chronology of this account is at odds with the diary

Willis E. Robison had been scheduled, along with Willard Robinson,[29] to meet Gibbs, Jones, and Berry on August 12 in McEwen. The two missionaries "waited all day and then, the Brethren not having arrived," they concluded something had detained them, and feeling they could wait no longer went to the McEwen post office. It was there they saw the newspapers. Despite "protests from local folks," they decided to head the next morning for Cane Creek via Centerville. They took the precaution of putting on different clothes.[30]

Meanwhile, Roberts wired reports to Salt Lake and requested $1,000 to cover the costs he would accrue in retrieving the bodies and returning them to Utah. But, knowing the funds would take time to arrive, he went to "Bernard Moses and his brothers,"[31] who had some previous contact with the missionaries, to say he needed "steel caskets in which the bodies could be hermetically sealed, as the railroad would accept no other." Moses not only guaranteed payment at the undertakers, but also "withdrew several hundred dollars from his own bank account and loaned it without security or even a note certifying such a loan."[32] Roberts arranged for the caskets to be sent to a church member named Samuel Hoover[33] who lived near Cane

accounts of J. Golden Kimball, which suggests that they encountered Thompson and Garrett earlier.

29. Robinson (1861–1934) was single and living in Salina when he was set apart for his mission on April 7, 1884, by Francis M. Lyman. He returned on September 14, 1886, and soon married Mary Jane Crane (1866–90). After her death he married Lorette Neilson (1871–1958) on January 20, 1892. Robinson was a farmer and accountant at various times in his later life.

30. "Tennessee Mission Events," fd. 4, Robison Journal.

31. Moses (1863–1950) was a Chattanooga clothier born in Baltimore. He and Roberts would stay in contact over the years. Roberts mentions his brothers, and a clerk named David Moses is listed in the Chattanooga City Directory for 1884–85 as residing at 113 Oak Street, a downtown location. Perhaps he was the other brother. Roberts may well have meant fellow Jews by the term "brothers." At the same time, Roberts might have meant Simon and Sigmund Levi who were partners with Moses in the Excelsior Clothing House. Sigmund, for example, resided in the Hotel Florentine where Roberts stated he frequently had his breakfast. The Florentine was at 9th and Broadway, while the clothing house was at 8th and Market. Moses lived close by in the Read House, on West 9th Street near the depot. There is no listing for Morgan, Roberts, or the Mission itself. See *Chattanooga Directory* for 1883 and 1884. See also "Bernard Moses," *Baltimore Sun*, July 29, 1950, 12.

32. Roberts, *Autobiography*, 2. For a later reminiscence see "Lent Money to Roberts," *Baltimore Sun*, Dec. 9, 1899, 9.

33. Roberts had met Hoover over three years earlier when he had held a meeting near his home. Hoover was a young farmer living in Hickman County with his wife

Creek.[34] Roberts's efforts to "procure coffins" in Chattanooga were reported in the local press, as was his assertion that the missionaries had made no "provocations," but were only "teaching the gospel as they understood it." When asked if the missionaries would continue to proselytize in the area, Roberts responded that "most assuredly" they would.[35] Roberts left Chattanooga for Columbia in search of Kimball and the missionaries he had gathered there. He found his colleagues safe, but housed in a "fourth rate rooming house on the south edge of the city." The owner of the house understandably was terrified that a mob might track the Mormons and "drag them from their rooms to do them violence." Roberts acted quickly to have "the elders transferred to the principal hotel of the town, where I myself had registered, and while the elders, including Elder Kimball, slept, I wrote the authorities in Utah statement of what had happened."[36]

Kimball and the other missionaries had a difficult night as they "counseled and talked over this sad occurrence until 2 AM." The next day they obtained horses at the livery stable, dispatched Jones to Shady Grove "to acquaint the Churches of our movements," and returned to Nashville.[37] The *Nashville Banner* reported their arrival, and Roberts told a reporter that he was there to "make arrangements for securing the bodies of their brethren," so they could be returned to Utah. But he could not resist a shot at the press, noting "it may be true that the ignorant only engage in actual mob violence," but the southern press "has frequently published sensational reports of nude baptisms and other unreasonable acts which never have occurred and which decent people would not for a moment contemplate." He

---

and son. Roberts frequently stayed in the Hoover home. Roberts was near the Hoover residence when violence was threatened in Spring Creek at the home of Walter Weems.

34. Roberts, *Autobiography*, 141–43.

35. Historian's Office, Journal History, Aug. 10, 1884, 21.

36. Roberts, *Autobiography*, 143. The *Deseret News* indicated that it had received a "private dispatch" from Roberts which gave the details of the killings and the burial of Gibbs and Jones. He also reported that "we are making efforts to get the bodies and get the Elders out of the adjacent neighborhood. There is much excitement, and the Elders are in danger. We came here [Columbia] to see the Governor. He is out of town and I fear we shall get no help. Let the friends be assured we shall get the bodies." See "The Murdered Elders," *Deseret News*, Aug. 20, 1884, 1. See also Kimball Journal, Aug. 11, 1884, which confirms this account, noting that it was "the Bethel House, one of the finest of hotels I had been in."

37. Kimball Journal, Aug. 12, 1884.

laid part of the blame directly at the newspapers' feet and said they "cannot be entirely exonerated as the ignorant have taken license from these reports and remarks regarding them."[38]

Once he finished speaking to the press, Roberts began making preparations to go to the site of the massacre, hiring a buggy to go as far as Shady Grove. While it was being secured, Roberts noted that a "company of rough looking men gathered near the entry of the livery stable" and were engaging in an "animated conversation" in which the word Mormon was frequently used. Roberts unobtrusively eavesdropped. At this point the owner of the livery stable called Roberts to his side, informed him that this group had been trying to arouse hostility toward the Mormons in the town, and cautioned him that if he went to Lewis County the same men who had killed the others would try to kill him as well.[39]

Roberts set out for Columbia via Shady Grove, arriving at the Church residence near dusk. During the night he was able to obtain two wagons and assemble a team to make the journey. He gained the support of a Mr. Harlow, who, while not Mormon, was a friend, and along with Church would drive one wagon. Roberts had resolved that he would drive the other because, while journeying to Columbia "sitting alone on the train" he had heard the whisper of God tell him, "You will go to secure those bodies and all will be well with you, but you must go." From that moment, Roberts "had no other intention than to go myself on this expedition."[40]

Roberts thought of a young man named Rufus Coleman to assist him, and Phoebe Church set out to find him some distance away. While waiting for Coleman to arrive, Roberts went "up into the loft" and "donned an old suit of clothes, a hat, and rough cowhide boots belonging to one of Robert Church's hired help." But Roberts, working so often in an office alongside Kimball, did not look like hired help. He needed to "hide the indoor complexion of my face," so he turned to the "soot and grease accumulated on the walls, for the loft room had been used as a smokehouse by the family."[41]

38. "The Mormon Murder," *Nashville Banner*, Aug. 14, 1884, 4.

39. Roberts, *Autobiography*, 144.

40. Roberts, 144.

41. Roberts, 145. As we will see, photographs in this attire were taken and remain to this day one of the most frequently shown representations of Roberts. His secretary Elsie

When Coleman arrived, Roberts said, "Rufy I am going down to Kane Creek with two teams to secure the bodies of the elders who have been murdered," and asked him to drive the other wagon. Standing relaxed and with his hands in his pockets, Coleman straightened and told Roberts in a "delightful" southern drawl, "Why yes Mr. Roberts I'll go anywhere with you, sir." Roberts was deeply moved by this expression of trust and fidelity.[42]

With the teams assembled, and carrying a lunch prepared by Laura Church, Roberts met "the teams some distance out on the road," so that he would not be recognized, and the group set out for Hoover's residence[43] where the caskets had "been delivered safely."[44] Roberts stopped at the depot clad in his disguise and interacted with individuals to see if he would be recognized. No one seemed to, and it was a good thing, as Roberts soon heard that roads leading toward Cane Creek the east and north "were being watched by members of the mob who had done the killing." The party proceeded south to the home of Thomas Garrett, a friend of the Mormons who lived near the Conder residence.[45] The disguised Roberts handed Garrett a note signed "President B. H. Roberts," which said that he had been "employed by the president to come and get the bodies in his behalf." Roberts asked Garrett in the note to "render this stranger all the assistance he could in taking the bodies from the graves and preparing them for shipment over the railroad." The ruse worked; Garrett read the letter carefully but did not recognize the man who had handed it to him. Garrett "said he would render the stranger all the help he could and asked what he could do."[46]

The two men went ahead of the others toward the Conder residence. Roberts, now confident that his disguise was effective, dropped

Cook reported that Roberts kept a copy of the photograph in his office in a frame given to him by Bernard Moses. See Cook to Truman Madsen, undated, Aiwohi Collection.

42. Roberts, *Autobiography*, 145.

43. Kimball Journal, Aug. 14, 1884.

44. Roberts, *Autobiography*, 145.

45. As noted previously, Garrett's assistance led to his being forced out of the area. Roberts recorded that "because of threats of violence made against him and destruction of his property," Garrett and his family settled in Bond County, Illinois. He also received assistance from the church in "surviving his forced departure." See Roberts, *Autobiography*, 155. See also Historians Office, Journal History, Jan. 12, 1885, 6.

46. Roberts, *Autobiography*, 147.

his southern accent when he spoke to Garrett. But Garrett still did not recognize him until Roberts revealed himself. When they reached the Conder residence, a number of people were on the scene, including some whom Garrett identified as part of the mob who had done the killing. Nine in total, they were "armed and ... on the alert," suspecting Roberts was coming. They stood about twenty yards from where the work of exhuming the bodies was proceeding. The mobbers offered no help, and the church members were reluctant "to give much assistance" fearing retribution. Finally, the coffins were "drawn up and each placed by the open grave." Roberts remembered the grisly scene:

> With an ax the plain board coffins and sides were pried open, and the bodies lifted into the caskets ... with two clean white sheets, and these were now spread over the bodies and carefully tucked under the shoulders and hips and feet and head so that they had the appearance of being completely swathed in the pure white sheets. The bodies having been in the warm earth for several days had become much swollen, and the face of Elder Gibbs had pressed up against the cover of the coffin in a manner to ... disfigure the face.[47]

The ranks of the mob grew. Roberts secured the casket lids as Garrett "followed with a burning rag in which tobacco was wrapped and kept it burning in my nostrils to disguise the odor arising from the dead bodies." A physician arrived who certified that the men had not died from disease. By sundown, the caskets were loaded into the wagons and the party started its return to the Garrett residence. As the group gathered for supper, Garrett revealed the true identity of the rough stranger by asking Elder Roberts to say grace. Roberts was sent to sleep in the loft, while Garrett and the others stood guard over the bodies. A later report indicated that "a week after the fatal event the only visible signs of the violent struggle were three newly heaped mounds in weedy burying grounds and two open graves."[48]

After getting a night's sleep, each one alternating with the other "to guard against danger," Roberts, Coleman, and the others cautiously made the long trek toward Mount Pleasant where they could

47. Roberts, 148–49.
48. "Bloody Mormon Massacre."

put the caskets on the train.[49] Still in his disguise, Roberts saw that he had time before Kimball's arrival and "wandered out to the outskirts of Nashville and walked about on the heights overlooking the river."[50] While there, he made a spur-of-the-moment decision that would link him to the Lewis County tragedy for the rest of his life. He

> chanced to pass a colored man's tin type photograph gallery and thought perhaps it might be a family interest if I could show them the outfit in which I made the trip. Accordingly I walked inside and … took a seat on an imitation stump in front of a scene of an outdoor scene and waited until the photographer … asked if I wanted my photograph taken and was answered in the affirmative … and told him to get his machine ready and shoot. … This photograph without my wish was reproduced widely and published in Utah.[51]

Roberts met Kimball at 9:00 that evening and they obtained rooms at the Gilchrist Hotel. The funds from Utah had not arrived, so Kimball had borrowed an additional three hundred dollars from Moses, who gave it, as he recalled, "without hesitation and without security."[52] The *Deseret News* commented that Roberts believed "it was a case of Judah helping Ephraim, and an act of generosity of so rare occurrence in the heartless days of cold business transactions that it is at once conspicuous and likely to be long remembered."[53] Kimball brought with him a suit of clothing, and Roberts changed out of his disguise. He met with members of the press, one of whom described him as "a medium sized man … has brown hair, gray eyes and a rather impressive manner. He is very earnest in his talk, and is apparently a highly educated man. He wore a black suit and a black felt hat." Roberts told another reporter that "he was not aware that any of the elders engaged in proselyting in the South had more than one wife, though they might have for all he knew." Clearly that

49. Roberts told a reporter, "I wish you would mention that at Mount Pleasant we found a kindly influence and received some little assistance." See "The Mormon Trouble," *Nashville American*, Aug. 21, 1884, 1.

50. Roberts, *Autobiography*, 153.

51. Roberts, 153–54.

52. Kimball to Bernard Moses, Jan. 11, 1930, Moses Papers. John Morgan telegraphed Roberts on August 13, 1884, that five hundred dollars had been wired from the Deseret National Bank to the Third National Bank in Chattanooga.

53. As quoted in "Helped by a Hebrew," *Ogden Daily Herald*, Aug. 27, 1884, 3.

was a disingenuous answer. Roberts put blame for the massacre on the people of Lewis County, who, he asserted, had done "absolutely nothing," to "cleanse" Tennessee from the "foul, dark stain that disfigures it" in the form of the murders.[54] But another account reported that Roberts believed "the people of Lewis County would do all they could to bring the violators to justice."[55] He particularly sought to discount the assertions of Tennessee governor William B. Bate[56] who alleged that the killings were in retribution over "improper relations in the families of the people where [the missionaries] labored."[57]

John Morgan said that, in terms of bringing the killers to justice, he did "not think much will be done." He believed that the friends of the two murdered members, if they discovered the perpetrators, "will probably get revenge in the manner customary in many districts thereabouts–i.e., by taking the drop on the murderers when the opportunity presents itself."[58]

One unidentified individual in Palestine, Tennessee, reported in a front-page article in the Nashville *Daily American* that Gibbs persuaded "one of his converts, a young woman, that as a prerequisite to baptism, God had revealed it to him to sleep with her, which she did." The paper also claimed that Gibbs tried to seduce "another young woman, and as she escaped from him he tore from her person a part of her clothing." Finally, after all of this, Gibbs was found with yet another young girl convert, "one arm around her waist and the other in her bosom." The newspaper insisted that "no attempt is here made to vindicate the Hinson party, but the facts as given should go in mitigation of its action." How could decent people be expected to let these "outrageous reports" go unanswered "in a county heretofore peaceful and quite and noted for its law-abiding people."[59]

Katie Cooper,[60] fifteen at the time of the massacre, wrote that the

54. Historian's Office, Journal History, Aug. 27, 1884, 8. See that date for a reprint of article from *Nashville Banner.*

55. "More About the Mormon Massacres," *Muscatine Daily Journal,* Aug. 15, 1884, 3.

56. William B. Bate (1826–1905) served as governor of Tennessee from 1883 to 1887. A former Confederate officer, he later served in the United State Senate.

57. "The Mormon Trouble," *Daily American,* Aug. 19, 1884, 1.

58. "Morgan's Reaction to the Shooting of an Elder," box 3, fd. 20, Morgan Papers.

59. "The Mormon Trouble," *Daily American,* Aug. 19, 1884, 1.

60. Cooper (1869–1950) lived in Lewis County her entire life where she worked as a domestic servant.

mobbers were not "a band of ruffians ... united for the purpose of ruthlessly murdering the Mormon elders." The real reason for their actions was to "forever put a stop to ... Mormon preaching," especially on the subject of polygamy. By 1884, she remembered, it had become "generally known" that the Mormons held regular church services on Cane Creek, with some "thirty five or forty" members. As the baptisms multiplied, Cooper said it became clear that the missionaries were paying particular attention to female converts who were singled out for sexual exploitation. Cooper contrasted the way the men were baptized and confirmed with that of women "who were carried to some near house in order that she could receive the Holy Ghost." She accused the Elders of promoting the view that female converts were as much their wives as they were their husbands'. She also claimed that several young women were lured into leaving the area for Utah. "Can hellish reasons not be inferred" from such examples?[61]

As for the men who attacked the Conder cabin, she concluded, "Brave men who loved their wives and daughters avowed their readiness to shed their lives last blood for the protection against the evil teachings of polygamy."[62] This was apparently a typical version of the event as told in the area. However, William W. Pollock,[63] publisher of the *Lewis County Herald*, observed a half century later that based on "years of close study of this tragedy and conversations with many who were present at the time of the killings," he was convinced that "there was not the slightest intention of murdering these elders

61. Katie Cooper, "The Mormon Massacre, 1884," copied by Lillie L. Skelton, in WPA Historical Records Project, 465-44-3-115, Lewis County, Tennessee, 1938. Copy in vertical files, "Lewis County," Tennessee State Library and Archives, Nashville. Hereafter cited as Cooper Account. Interestingly, Cooper's article was published in its entirety as the work of W. L. Pinkerton, "The Mormon Massacre," *Lewis County Herald*, Oct. 21, 1943, and Nov. 4, 1943. Copy in vertical files, "Lewis County," Tennessee State Library and Archives, Nashville. Hereafter cited as Pinkerton.

62. Cooper Account.

63. Pollock (1886–1970) married Maggie Allison (1882–1950) on January 30, 1910, and later Maggie Snyder (1898–1977). He purchased the *Lewis County Herald* "from a local bank that had taken ownership through bankruptcy proceedings." This seems to have occurred in the 1920s. Additionally, he farmed and was employed in a family-owned gravestone business. It was Pollock who delivered the stone erected by the LDS Church over the graves of John Riley Hutson and William M. Conder in 1934.

when the mob went to the Cond[e]r home," but that some members of the mob "were intoxicated."[64]

In the immediate aftermath of the murders, the *Nashville Banner* warned readers of imposters pretending to be LDS missionaries. "Many crimes are committed in this state by bogus Mormon elders." These "scoundrels with glib tongues" roam the state to "draw innocent and ignorant women into their neatly-woven web." The fake missionaries vanish after "the ruin of these women is accomplished," and the church and its real elders cannot be blamed for these actions.[65]

Such sympathetic views, however, were not frequently expressed. Indeed, generally arguments were being made in the press that while the specific acts in Cane Creek were "lawless and murderous," the response to the threat of Mormonism to the sanctity of the home and family was understandable. One newspaper account stated that missionaries were seen as agitators seeking to encourage men to join a conspiracy to support plural marriage, a "crime against civilization itself," and that they were "endeavoring to seduce women to lives of degradation and shame." Naturally, all American males would "bitterly resent this invasion of their homes." Thus, while carefully avoiding "all illegal methods," the paper asserted, the threat of Mormonism "sooner or later" must be stopped.[66] The *Atlanta Constitution* labeled the killings "a terrible affair," suggesting that the death of anyone, even "some one engaged in … the prostitution of men, women and girls to the doctrine of polygamy," was wrong. Still, the killings were "neither unexpected nor uninvited," because many voices in the South had warned the "Mormon Elders" that the "people would not submit to their vile teachings," that "Mormonism in Georgia and the South must go."[67]

The killings forced many missionaries to curtail their activities in various places in the South. Ransom M. Stevens, for example, noted in a letter to First Presidency secretary L. John Nuttall after he returned home that he and his companion's "preaching was suspended

64. As quoted in Pinkerton.

65. "Mormon Elders," *Nashville Banner*, Aug. 13, 1884, 4.

66. Historian's Office, Journal History, Aug. 10, 1884, 21.

67. "Mormon Massacre," *Atlanta Constitution*, Aug. 14, 1884, 5; and, "The Mormon Killing," *Atlanta Constitution*, Aug. 15, 1884, 4.

for a season." Stevens, who was then in Alabama, was sent to explore fresh territory in Louisiana.[68] The shock of losing the missionaries permeated the air for the elders and Saints in Tennessee.

The bodies of Gibbs and Berry left Nashville on the evening of August 18, and mourning services were planned for their arrival in Utah.[69] The first was held in Salt Lake City, where the leading brethren celebrated the "fidelity of these recent martyrs to the cause of the New Dispensation." Memorial services were also held in Logan, Ogden, Brigham City, Provo, and American Fork.[70] Resolutions of respect were issued by many stakes, wards, and quorums. Typically, the meeting houses were draped "with the emblems of sorrow," and in American Fork a large banner over the stand proclaimed "the martyrs, Berry and Gibbs, God will avenge." One of the largest meetings was held in Logan where remarks were offered by Joseph Hall of Ogden,[71] who called the killings "one of the darkest deeds that ever disgraced a nation," and said that someday their murderers will "tremble with fear and horror" as they contemplate the judgment of God for "those whose blood they shed."[72]

If Utah Saints saw the event as a martyrdom in the defense of God's restored gospel, residents of the Cane Creek area continued to see it as an attack against an unpopular and unchristian presence. As an account written nearly fifty years later noted,

> intense feeling was aroused throughout the community as a result of the killings, [and] the masked participants ... always remained more or less unknown. Individuals who had aligned themselves with the local Mormon church were forced, either to leave their teachings, or leave the

68. Ransom M. Stevens to L. John Nuttall, Feb. 28, 1886, Missionary Reports.

69. For important details, see Morgan Journal, Aug. 20–24, 1884.

70. For a good overview, see Historian's Office, Journal History, Aug. 26, 1884, Aug. 27, 1884, 7–10; and, "The Martyrs," *Salt Lake Herald*, Aug. 23, 1884, 9. Interestingly, Adolph Ochs, editor of the *Chattanooga Times,* happened to be in town. Ochs would later become the owner of the *New York Times*. Ochs and John Morgan were acquainted, and Morgan speaks of the "many kindnesses he and other elders have received at the hands of Mr. Ochs." See "A Tennessee Editor Here," *Salt Lake Herald*, Aug. 24, 1884, 9.

71. Hall (1825–1906) was a British convert baptized in 1841 who served as a missionary in various places in the British Mission. He was an early newspaper reporter and editor with the *Ogden Herald* and other papers. Hall served in the Echo Canyon War as an officer of the Nauvoo Legion, as well as a schoolteacher, postmaster, justice of the peace, notary public, and coroner. He was a longtime member of the Weber Stake High Council.

72. Historian's Office, Journal History, Aug. 27, 1884, 9.

> country. To this day, the individuals of the region speak with deep bitterness of the Mormons who left the scars of theirs upon the secluded community of forty years ago. Old men and women who remember that day have told and retold the story and the advancing generations listen with bated breath to the tale of the death blow which their ancestors dealt to polygamy on Cane Creek.[73]

However, the event helped in raising funds to aid the church members in the Cane Creek area to resettle in Utah and Colorado. Not all left Tennessee; many in the Conder family, while "they removed from the scene of their sorrow," elected to relocate to other areas in western Tennessee.[74]

Roberts returned to Chattanooga rather than accompany the bodies of Berry and Gibbs because he believed his presence was "necessary to meet the violence that was still rife in the South." On August 20, Roberts drafted a petition to Governor Bate, explaining the facts of the case and seeking his assistance in bringing the guilty parties to justice.[75] Once the petition had been notarized, Roberts and several of the missionaries met with Bate. Among them was Jones who commented that the governor "was surly. He stated 'Yes, he would give a reward—some reward though the treasury was low just now.'" Jones thought he "never observed a man more unconcerned … than the governor was in this matter."[76] Governor Bate did offer a $1000 reward "for the capture of any or all of the parties engaged in the Massacre of Mormon Elders in Lewis County."[77]

That evening Roberts suggested that Jones, Thompson, and Willard Robinson return to Shady Grove. The trio, accompanied by Roberts and Kimball, went to the Nashville depot where they were warned by many people they would be killed if they returned to Lewis County. Jones admitted that he and Thompson must have appeared "pale and

73. "Bloody Mormon Massacre."

74. Roberts, *Autobiography*, 155.

75. See "Petition to Governor Bate," *Latter-day Saints' Millennial Star*, Sep. 22, 1884. The petition was signed by Roberts along with J. Golden Kimball, William H. Jones, Henry Thompson, and Willis E. Robison. For a complete text, see "The Mormon Elders," *Nashville Banner*, Aug. 20, 1884, 4. The *Daily American* mistakenly referred to Roberts as "B. H. Sullivan." See "The Mormons," *Daily American*, Nov. 21, 1884, 5.

76. Jones Diary, Aug. 20, 1884, Jones Reminiscences.

77. "Still Another Outrage," *Salt Lake Herald*, Aug. 23, 1884, 9. Roberts had asked for such a reward in his petition to the governor.

terrified."[78] After a complicated journey, the trio arrived at Duck River where they found Robert Robbins Church "sick with a fever," and the branch "in much excitement in consequence of threats made about in the immediate neighborhood."[79] Many of the local Saints believed that Church's health had been compromised by the turmoil surrounding the murders.[80] Jones administered to the elderly man and reported the distinct impression that he would not recover. Indeed, Church died the next day. Shortly thereafter Jones and the others discovered there were rumors of a mob coming from Hinson's settlement, and they were convinced that their goal was to kill the missionaries and get them "out of the way." After spending their last Sabbath in Hickman County, they returned to the relative safety of Nashville.[81]

Even there, however, a certain level of hostility, if not outright violence, existed. Not long after the massacre, Rev. William Henry Strickland[82] delivered a sermon on Mormonism at the Edgefield Baptist Church, which was "filled to overflowing." Strickland discussed the recent "tragedy," saying he had no opinion "as to the right or wrong in the case," but, while deploring the violence, stated that "law abiding citizens charge these Mormon missionaries ... under the guise of religion" of "attempting to seduce their wives and daughters from the paths of virtue." Moreover, he lashed out at the marital practices of the Mormons who rejected the "true idea of marriage" which was the "union of one man and one woman for life." After a lengthy recital of Mormon history and the role of plural marriage in it, he said that if Mormonism prevailed it would "sap the very foundations of society and wipe out the Christian home." Strickland ended by saying that while he did not "excuse" the men who carried out the attack in Cane Creek, he believed that those "outraged men in Lewis County did what you would have done, what any of us

78. Jones Diary, Aug. 20, 1884.

79. Jones.

80. "Mormonism," *Daily American*, Aug. 25, 1884, 1.

81. Jones Diary, Aug. 20, 1884. At Roberts's instruction, Willard Robinson was sent to Murfreesboro where it was believed he would be safe, and "among friends." See Roberts to Jones, Aug. 28, 1884, Jones Reminiscences.

82. Strickland began his ministerial career in South Carolina. Strickland served as pastor of Edgefield Baptist Church from September 1883 until February 1886. He later served as pastor of Nashville's Spruce Street Northern Methodist Episcopal Church until his death in a streetcar accident on March 3, 1906.

would have done under the circumstances" to stop anyone who came "into our homes to destroy the chastity of our wives and daughters and sisters."[83] In early September, the *Daily American* reported from Hickman County that "while there are a few who think that the masked party were in the wrong, there is a great mass of people, and our best citizens, who openly advocate the act, but many seem to think that the mob only went there to administer to the elders a severe flogging and the act of Condor and others provoked them to do what they did."[84]

In response, Roberts wrote a lengthy letter to John Tanner:

> What think you when hundreds seek to excuse the crime, and defend and sympathize with the murderers? The tone of the press is generally "We don't believe in mob violence, but in what other way can the people get rid of the Mormons," and "This is but the beginning of the fierce protest that the people of this country are prepared to make in defense of their family alters," and on the back of such expressions, demand more radical measures enacted by Congress. While there are many who sincerely deplore the occurrence, there are more than any one would believe, unless he had moved among them and heard their remarks, that rejoice in the accursed act.[85]

There were a few sympathetic expressions. An editorial in the *Milan Exchange* a few days after the murders called the event a "terrible outrage." The paper said that while they had "no patience with the Mormon nastiness," there was no "excuse … for this murderous way of eradicating the evil from the state." The editorial called on law enforcement to "promptly arrest every man connected with this terrible tragedy, and the courts will promptly punish them."[86] Similarly, the *Memphis Daily Appeal* said the killings represented an act of "ignorance" with unexpected results. Moreover, the paper said that the "ignorant, unwise and blundering as well as guilty Tennesseans" who had committed this murder "ought to meet with the fate the law awards to their crimes," but also should realize they had

83. "Mormonism," *Daily American*, Aug. 25, 1884, 1. See also "A Sermon on Mormonism," *Nashville Banner*, Aug. 25, 1884, 1.

84. "Warner," *Daily American*, Sep. 3, 1884, 6.

85. Roberts to Tanner, Aug. 29, 1884, box 1 fd. 27, Tanner Collection.

86. *Milan Exchange*, Aug. 16, 1884, 4.

"supplied the Mormon Church with martyrs."[87] The *Southern Standard* printed that while they had "no sympathy whatever with the Mormons, we have less with any mob of men who mask their faces and commit such crimes as these." The paper said that "mob violence is never a proper remedy for any wrong," and unless the perpetrators were punished, the "dignity of the State of Tennessee … and its peace will be very seriously jeopardized."[88]

Over the next few weeks, several other missionaries either came to Chattanooga seeking refuge or reported threats made against them. Roberts told Joseph F. Smith that while matters were "more quiet," a "mobbing had taken place recently in Lawrence County."[89] Jones notes in his journal that at one point he "handed Roberts a postal card containing a threat against his own life." Jones confided that he believed "there is no safety anywhere."[90] Roberts answered that "unless an overruling providence intervened in our behalf we would all be taken out of Tenn[essee] dead men."[91] During this period, Roberts and Kimball concluded it was "thought best" to honorably release Jones and Thompson, and they did so. Roberts told the pair that he was "troubled" by the possibility of a threat to their safety. At the same time, no doubt reflecting the mission's financial situation, he told them that they were short of funds "and all we can do is let you have enough money to pay your way home."[92]

The atmosphere remained tense. Jones feared for the safety of those in the mission office, noting that Kimball "doesn't go out at night."[93] Samuel J. Parrish, then laboring in Wilson County, described the

87. "Tennesseans, Mormons and Martyrs," *Memphis Daily Appeal*, Aug. 20, 1884, 2.

88. "Mob Violence," *Southern Standard*, Aug. 16, 1884, 4.

89. Roberts to Smith, Aug. 23, 1884, First Presidency Correspondence. See also "Still Another Outrage," *Salt Lake Herald*, Aug. 23, 1884, 9, which states Roberts had also telegraphed John Morgan. The paper reported the victim was "Elder J. J. Roberts," though it was more likely J. J. Fuller. Moreover, the paper asserted the telegram to Morgan "shows to what outrageous excesses the animosity of the Tennesseans to the Mormon elders is carrying them."

90. The day before, however, Jones recorded that Roberts had telegraphed James Jack telling him that "Elders in counties surrounding Lewis" were housed in "tolerable safe quarters." William Jones, Diary, Aug. 18, 1884, Jones Reminiscences.

91. Jones Diary, Aug. 19, 1884.

92. Roberts to Jones, Aug. 28, 1884; Aug. 31, 1884, Jones Reminiscences The pair left on September 7, 1884.

93. Jones Diary, Sep. 5, 1884.

atmosphere in the area as "very bitter," and reported that Thomas Huddleston, who had long been friendly with the Saints, had received a letter written in red ink, apparently to signify blood, to be delivered to the missionaries. The letter, which is full of typographical and grammatical errors, was addressed to "the Mormon Elders that operate in Wilson County." It states that the doctrines being taught by them were "very obnoxious to an enlightened and virtuous people and cannot be tolerated by the virtuous class of citizens in Wilson County. We cannot endure the idea of our little sons and daughters being taught that prostitution is of divine origin." The letter gave the missionaries ten days to leave Tennessee or else they "will share the same JUST FATE that the notorious seducing imposters—Gibbs and Berry JUSTLY received." It was signed "Citizens of Wilson County" and included the author's deep regret at the "death of the noble gallant and brave Dave Hinson," who made the "first strike against the polygamists in Tennessee."[94] Similar notices were posted "in conspicuous places" in Mt. Pleasant and other communities in Lewis County; they all made references to the killing of Gibbs and Berry, and gave the Mormons thirty days to leave. As one handbill announced, "Go peaceably if you will, but go you must."[95]

At the same time, Elders Jesse J. Fuller and George J. Woodbury faced serious opposition while proselytizing in Lauderdale County, Alabama. Late one evening while sleeping they were "set upon" by an armed mob of "nine or ten men" who ordered them to "arise, dress themselves and accompany them to the woods." They complied but asked what they had done to "be thus disturbed." The mob replied that their crime was that they had "preached old Joe Smith's doctrines." Ultimately Woodbury escaped, but Fuller "was taken by his captors to the woods and given 100 lashes with persimmon sprouts ... about the thickness of ones finger," before being freed with a warning

94. "An Elder From Tennessee," *Deseret Evening News*, Oct. 1, 1884, 1. The article contains the full text of the note because Parrish brought the original home with him for safekeeping. A reference in the *Cincinnati Post* indicates "Roberts received in the mail a note postmarked Chattanooga saying: 'You are hereby warned to leave the state within twenty-four hours on penalty of going like the other two Mormon elders.'" See "Those Dead Mormon Elders," *Cincinnati Post*, Aug. 19, 1884, 1.

95. "The Mormons Must Go," *Daily American*, Sep. 9, 1884, 4.

to "leave the county and never return."[96] The missionaries remained in spite of the threat but managed to avoid further harassment. Fuller told Roberts that some of the local church members had informed him that "there is a mob of 60 persons that intend to give the Elders one more final warning setting date for them to leave."[97]

What caused this conflagration that culminated in the murders of two LDS missionaries? As the local newspapers made clear, locals were appalled at the Mormons in their midst. Polygamy was abhorrent to them, and it may have reminded them of the mixed-race relationships they feared. The missionaries, for their part, may have "provoked their own misfortune with feelings of invincibility, unwise proselyting activities, bravado, and the foolishness of youth," writes historian Gene A. Sessions.[98] John Gibbs and William Berry were not the only missionaries killed. Other historians have demonstrated that throughout the Southern States Mission "between 1879 and 1898, five missionaries were killed and hundreds of others were beaten or physically abused by mobs."[99]

Church leaders and members were understandably interested in all the news they could get about the massacre. In late August, Roberts received a letter from church president John Taylor suggesting that he "had better take a brief vacation" from his labors and return to Colorado to meet with Joseph F. Smith, Erastus Snow, and John Morgan who all would be attending stake conference in Manassa.[100] Accordingly, Roberts departed on August 31, leaving Kimball as acting president.[101] After he finished his work in the San Luis Valley, Roberts continued westward to spend "a few weeks with my family and friends in Utah." On September 12, George Q. Cannon had "a most interesting interview this morning (though in some respects

96. See "Proselyting in the South," *Deseret News*, Mar. 10, 1886, 14.

97. Fuller to Roberts, Sep. 1, 1884, box 70, fd. 12, Smith Family Papers. See also Joseph F. Smith to John Taylor, Aug. 23, 1884, First Presidency Correspondence. Fuller and Woodbury had served together for several months. See "Missionary Experience," *Deseret News*, Feb. 6, 1884, 41.

98. Sessions, "Myth, Murder, and Mormonism," 218.

99. Seferovich, "Hospitality and Hostility."

100. Roberts, *Autobiography*, 157. See also "For Colorado," *Salt Lake Herald*, Aug. 27, 1884, 8, which noted that these three men would set out for Colorado and might be joined at some point by John Taylor as well.

101. See Morgan Journal, Sep. 5–7, 1884. See also Kimball Journal, Aug. 31, 1884.

painful) with Elders B. H. Roberts, Henry Thompson, W. H. Jones and John T. Heninger, missionaries from the Southern States." Since Thompson was in the home during the massacre at Cane Creek, and Jones was besieged by the mob, Cannon "requested them to go to the [*Deseret*] *News* Office and give them a statement."[102] Two days later, John Nicholson presented a lecture on "The Tennessee Massacre: Causes and Consequences."[103] The *Deseret News* noted that the lecture came before "the most densely packed audience" ever found "within the walls of the Salt Lake Theater." Not only were the audience seats filled, but the stage was packed with dignitaries.

On October 4, Roberts participated in a semi-annual conference of the combined Mutual Associations, and then, a few days later, attended sessions of the church's October general conference. On October 9, he and Morgan met with church officials "and prepared statements respecting the Southern Mission and present[ed] the propriety of the Church assisting the Saints on Cane Creek to gather to Colorado." Roberts and Morgan reported to President Taylor, his counselor George Q. Cannon, and several members of the Council of the Twelve that there were approximately "seventy five Elders in the field," and that they were baptizing "nearly thirty a month."[104]

As if the massacre had steeled Roberts's resolve and commitment to his faith, he was often contemplating the question of plural marriage. He and several others had visited with Thomas Howells where they "spent a pleasant evening in instructing our wives on the principles of Celestial Marriage. And I believe our remarks will do good."[105] Roberts later wrote that he "had obeyed the whole law of god except that which required the full entrance into the marriage system of

---

102. Cannon Journal, Sep. 12, 1884.

103. Later published as Nicholson, *Tennessee Massacre and its Causes*. The *Deseret Evening News* noted that Nicholson's lecture was "already in the hands of the printer and will be ready before the end of next week." The paper also said that because of the "great interest created by the lecture, and ... the subject it is likely to have an extensively large sale." See "To Be Published," *Deseret Evening News,* Sep. 27, 1884, 5. Notice of the lecture was picked up by Western Union and carried in Tennessee as well. See "A Mormon Lecture," *Daily American*, Sep. 16, 1884, 1.

104. Roberts, *History's Apprentice*, 148 (Oct. 9, 1884).

105. Roberts is using another term for plural marriage. In the 1840s Joseph Smith taught that the "new and everlasting covenant" of marriage was required to attain the highest degree of the Celestial Kingdom.

the church ... including plural marriage." But the experience he had with Erastus Snow and his plural wife Elizabeth while in Colorado affected him deeply. Through "the example of this apostle," Roberts was "much instructed" in how a man might treat a plural wife. Snow "was accompanied by" his fifty-three-year-old plural wife Elizabeth Ashby Snow, "now well beyond the heyday of youth and even middle life." But Snow's "gallant attitude towards her," Roberts wrote, "had quite a remarkable influence upon me." It was "the beautiful spirit" between Snow and his wife that "had a tremendous significance" as he made his decision to enter into plural marriage.[106] In observing Snow, Roberts felt that Mormonism's curious institution

> left him in an exalted state of mind, kindness, a beautiful appreciation of a wife, calling forth the tenderest emotions and care for the other at every turn. Nothing within him had been brutalized or perverted. Gentleness, kindness and love unfeigned had possessed him. The corruption of promiscuity had not entered into his life or nature. His love was purified and exalted, and if the plural wife associations under such sentiments in which he had practiced it was the symbol of the effect of such associations upon men, the principle of plural marriage stood vindicated, and one not need be in doubt on that score.[107]

He resolved that this example would give him sufficient strength to "honor this principle of religious faith" if the opportunity to take a second wife came his way.[108] But he was motivated to move quickly because he had a premonition that he would not survive his second trip to Tennessee. So he laid the matter "before my wife Louisa and she had consented thereto."[109]

Roberts and Louisa decided he should approach Celia Dibble and ask her to join their family as a plural wife. Seven years his junior, Celia was a "splendid reader," "shy, reserved, temperate, kindly, [and] highly cultured."[110] Truman Madsen's account of the proposal includes details not available elsewhere, and reports that Louisa had already approached Celia to prepare her for Roberts's proposal of

106. Roberts, *Autobiography*, 158–59.
107. Roberts, 159.
108. Roberts.
109. Roberts.
110. Madsen, *Defender of the Faith*, 157.

marriage. Roberts "walked around the Dibble home several times before he knocked at the door." He warned Celia, who sat with her parents, that he was often away as a missionary and that things would not always be easy. Regardless, Celia agreed to marry him.[111]

That Roberts had recently been thrust into the public eye because of the Gibbs and Berry murders may have spurred Celia's consent to the marriage. She was also likely aware of his recent article published in the *Contributor* about the case.[112] Whatever her reasons for consenting to become a plural wife to Roberts, the two married on October 2, 1884, in the Salt Lake City Endowment House.[113]

Roberts was also making plans for his return to the South. Along with Morgan, he visited the offices of the *Juvenile Instructor* to make "arrangements for getting tracts to the Southern Mission." Much of the rest of his time was spent visiting with Louisa, Celia, his mother, and other close friends. Then, on October 15, he "once more bid my family good-by and left for the Southern Mission."[114]

On October 16, Roberts met with Morgan and traveled to Ogden where they met "with a number of the Saints who had come from San Luis Stake Colo[rado] to go through the temple at Logan and were now enroute for their homes in Col." Roberts journeyed with these Colorado Saints until they reached Pueblo. He reached Kansas City on the October 20, then took a train to St. Louis, and from there to Cincinnati. He arrived in Chattanooga on October 24[115] where he was met by J. Golden Kimball: "On my return from breakfast who should I meet but Elder Roberts; words fail me in

111. Madsen, 157. Madsen provides no source for this information. He states that the marriage was not consummated. He also notes that Roberts wrote his new wife "honest, emotional letters from the mission field, and their relationship blossomed." If Roberts did write, those letters do not seem to still be extant.

112. See B. H. Roberts, "The Tennessee Massacre," *Contributor*, Oct. 1884, 16–23.

113. While this is the commonly held date for the marriage, there is some evidence—including Roberts's own recollection—to suggest that it took place in 1883.

114. Roberts, *History's Apprentice*, 151 (Oct. 15, 1884).

115. "While in Cincinnati I bought the Library of Universal Knowledge in fifteen volumes for $7.50. Spent part of the afternoon in the reading room; towards night I took a stroll through some of the principal streets. At 8.50 P.M. took train for Chattanooga." Roberts, *History's Apprentice*, 153 (Oct. 23, 1884). Roberts likely refers to *Library of Universal Knowledge: A Reprint of the Last (1880) Edinburgh and London Edition of Chamber's Encyclopedia with Copious Additions by American Editors*, 15 vols. (New York: S. W. Green's Sons, 1882).

describing my feelings at this moment, but to say the least it was a pleasure indeed."[116]

Roberts spent the next few days "reading letters striving to get hold of the run of matters in the mission. I find a good feeling generally among the Elders though there is an idea in their minds of some of the brethren that the mission will be abandoned because of the late tragedy on Cane Creek. But of course the work of the Lord cannot be stayed because of the opposition of a mob: the Gospel must be taught to the nations." Roberts was also very busy communicating with the church members intending to emigrate with the next company.[117] He received a letter from James A. Eldredge, who was at Bairds Mill, reporting that the "mobs are beginning to make their appearance in that locality." Roberts, who kept detailed notes on these events in his diary, wrote that a "company of masked men rode up to brother Linard Burk[e']s[118] in the night and asked if he knew where any Mormons lived, he replied that he was one—they told him that all Mormons would be compelled to leave in twenty days. This brother answered with a laugh and they rode on."[119]

On Sunday the elders and members held a testimony meeting and all seemed calm. Later that night, however, "they were aroused by the tramping of horses and we[re] called to come out." One of the men asked if there were any Mormon elders in the house, and when they replied in the affirmative, they demanded that they "bring him out here we wish to see him and be quick about it and come with uplifted hands." Eldredge complied with this request, and was "confronted by five armed and masked men who presented their pistols in his face and asked if he really believed in the obnoxious principles taught by the L.D.S. and if so didn't he expect to deny them. He replied that he hoped he never would deny them." At that point the individuals told him that he would not be hurt if he "would agree to leave the state in a given time. He told them to bring some of their wise men and ministers, [and] if they would confute the doctrine

116. Kimball Journal, Oct. 18, 23, and 24, 1884.

117. Roberts, *History's Apprentice*, 153 (Oct. 29, 1884). Ultimately the branch at Cane Creek would be dissolved.

118. Linard Burke was a twenty-nine-year-old farmer living in Wilson County with his twenty-eight-year-old wife, Emma, and their young daughter, Maud.

119. See Roberts, *History's Apprentice*, 153–54 (Oct. 29, 1884).

he advocated he would leave." Eldredge's defiance only enraged the mob further, and they insisted that the locals would support them. They were "determined that he should leave" and gave "him ten days" or else "death would be the result. Elder Eldredge made no reply would not promise."[120] Roberts wrote to Eldredge to "use every caution—staying only at those places where he would least likely to be attacked by mobs; to keep a shot gun handy and if needs be use it, and never again place himself in the hands of those wretches."[121]

After dispatching a new batch of missionaries to their various fields, Roberts "felt sad all day long, and felt like I wanted to burst into tears though just what the matter is I can't say. O, dear what strange beings we Mortals are!"[122] In late October, he wrote his mother about efforts to move the Tennessee Saints to Colorado: "We are making every effort to get our brethren and sisters off Cane Creek, though it is questionable whether Sister Condor will be able to stand the trip or not. Still we hope so, and are exercising our faith for her."[123] Among the Saints who were emigrating were "23 Saints from the Cane Creek branch"; another fifty-two from Tennessee, Alabama, Georgia, Mississippi, and Virginia; and, among that number, "eight colored people who belonged to the Church." In addition to the seventy-five members planning to leave, another twelve elders would go as well. All of them gathered at a railroad depot where hundreds of people "gazed in wonderment and surprise." Roberts met with reporters and answered questions while J. Golden Kimball "collected about $1800 from the Saints to pay for R[ailwa]y tickets." The mission borrowed a few hundred dollars from the Perpetual Emigration Fund to pay the way for others. Kimball "was going all day" and finally collapsed in bed sometime after 1:00 a.m. "tired and weary."[124]

One of the reporters who questioned Roberts wrote about the "queer crowd … stretched prone upon the floor" worried about the "simple kindly folk" on their way west to the "most potent and powerful religious despotism existing." He opined that the females in the

120. Roberts, 154 (Oct. 29, 1884).

121. Roberts, 154 (Oct. 30, 1884).

122. Roberts, 156 (Nov. 2, 1884).

123. Roberts to Mother, Oct. 29, 1884, box 4, fd. 3, Roberts Papers (UU). Mrs. Conder did not make the journey and remained in Tennessee for the rest of her life.

124. Kimball Journal, Nov. 12, 1884.

group would not be "tempting" to any Mormon Elder "who hankers [for] more wives." As for Roberts, the reporter admitted that he had expected "to see a long-haired crazy devotee, half making up in equal portions of demagogue and zealot," and was surprised to discover that "Elder Roberts was none of these." He identified Roberts as looking like a businessman who "was a gentleman in his ways, an educated man by his speech and evidently sincere in his religious belief."[125] If the reporter expected Roberts to be secretive, he was surprised when he "submitted gracefully to the pumping process and replied freely and with apparent candor to inquiries propounded." Roberts took the time to explain some of the church's beliefs about the Bible, the Book of Mormon, the ever-present topic of polygamy. Roberts apparently told him that "not more than seven, certainly not more than ten percent of the men possess a plurality of wives."[126] When asked directly whether Roberts practiced polygamy, he replied, "Not literally and personally." It was a strange and dishonest answer, especially considering Roberts's second marriage only the month before. Finally the reporter from the *Daily Commercial* editorialized, in views that were widely held, that these "poor illiterate pilgrims are to be pitied. They have abjured the faith of their fathers to accept strange gods; have turned their backs upon the cabins in which they were born to follow a semi-idolatrous ignis fatuus to a new home under new skies ... what is to become of them?"

Finally, at 5:00 a.m. on November 13, 1884, the company started the journey west.[127] Roberts recorded that "nearly all were feeling well except some children who had the hooping cough," and that in fact he "was quite poorly myself, having a severe headache and about seven o'clock had a chill followed by a high fever." The group arrived in Cincinnati at 5:00 p.m. where they changed trains and, according to Roberts, discovered that there were several thousand people "in and about the Depot, and learning that we were 'Mor-

125. "More Mormons," *The Daily Commercial*, Nov. 18, 1884, 2.

126. The reporter wrote that "Roberts has charge of the missionary work in the Southern States, and has preached in them for four years, never having been placed in bodily danger, although he has seen some singular experiences." "More Mormons," *The Daily Commercial*, Nov. 18, 1884, 2.

127. Apparently, some church members had begun to leave earlier. See "Mormon Converts Immigrating," *Daily American*, Sep. 27, 1884, 4.

mons' considerable curiosity was excited. Their mocking, scorn, and pointing of fingers put me in mind of the vision of Lehi as recorded in the Book of Mormon" (1 Ne. 8).[128] There was no mention of the arrival of the Mormons or response to it in the local paper.[129] However, a few days before, the *Enquirer*, a Democratic paper, reported that a "large number of free passes on the 'Salt Lake Railroad' have been printed and given out, gratuitously. They read 'Republican free passes from all points in the United States to Salt Lake to stay. Good on all railroads in the north and south. Trains will leave November 29, 1884. No stop over allowed. Second class passage. Board and lodging free."[130]

Kimball and Roberts "unloaded our company, bunched them up," and then Roberts led the front and Kimball "followed up the rear and herded them into the waiting room." Kimball confirmed Roberts's account of staring spectators as "hundreds of people both rich and poor gave way and stood with abhorrence depicted on their countenances at the strange sight" of the Saints marching through the depot. "It was repugnant to their lofty ideas of respectability–but I thought O, what a change will be wrought hereafter."[131]

After "a run up town," the immigrants were taken to the cars for the next leg of the journey. Kimball said that it was "a terrible job, but thanks to the Lord it all worked out in our favor." At 7:00 p.m., "the engine 'roared like a lion, yea like young lions,' and they took hold of its prey and sped with it swiftly while all around was darkness, at least that was my idea of the matter."[132] Kimball would leave the group early the next morning at Flora, Illinois, headed for Shawneetown, Illinois, where he would shepherd another group west.[133]

Roberts and his party arrived at Pueblo on the evening of November 15, and the group staying in Colorado separated from those headed for Utah. Those remaining went on to LaJara Station where

128. "Nothing of particular importance occurred. Enroute I continued to be unwell and therefore unable to look after the welfare of the Saints so closely as I desired." Roberts, *History's Apprentice*, 159 (Nov. 13, 1884).

129. See *Cincinnati Enquirer*, Nov. 14, 15, 1884.

130. "Local Brevities," *Cincinnati Enquirer*, Nov. 9, 1884, 4.

131. Kimball Journal, Nov. 13, 1884.

132. Kimball.

133. See Kimball Journal, Nov. 14–21, 1884. Shawneetown was the county seat of Gallatin County in southeast Illinois.

they arrived the next morning "and were met by a large company of Saints from adjacent settlements of our people." Roberts recorded that the luggage was gathered "and loaded into wagons and the new comers distributed among the Saints in the various settlements for a season until they could secure homes of their own." Kimball arrived at La Jara Station a week later, bringing with him "three families of Saints from the South."[134]

Once this new group of immigrants was settled, Roberts and Kimball returned to Manassa where they took supper with Silas S. Smith. After dinner Roberts spent the night with Jens Martin Christensen who was superintendent of the Sunday school.[135] The next morning Roberts was so ill that he could not get up. He was still suffering because the "pain in my head which has troubled me ever since I left Chattanooga became so severe that I was nearly wild. About eleven o clock it became much easier and I arose." That afternoon and evening he joined with Kimball in speaking to different gatherings.

On November 26 Roberts and Kimball parted company; Kimball returned to Chattanooga[136] and Roberts went "west to my home." Roberts arrived in Salt Lake City the next day and spent the night with John Morgan, bringing him up to date on his activities. Morgan "appeared well satisfied with all" Roberts had done, and his approval delighted Roberts. He compared Morgan's happiness to what it must be like to "return to our Father in heaven and shall find

---

134. Roberts, *History's Apprentice*, 160 (Nov. 22, 1884). Kimball recorded there were "eight grown persons and eleven children" in the group along with himself and Elder Jesse J. Fuller in the party. See Kimball Journal, Nov. 18, 1884.

135. Christensen (1843–1908) was superintendent of the Sunday schools in Manassa from 1883 through 1894. Jensen came to Utah in 1866 in the Abner Lowry Company. He married Maren Johannah Rasmussen (1838–1923), who also came in the Lowry Company, on October 28, 1866. Christensen served a mission in Scandinavia from April 1886 until May 1887.

136. Initially, Morgan had some concerns that because of Kimball's ill health he should return home as well. According to Kimball, Morgan told him: "The mission is very hard-run for money. It will cost twenty-four dollars to send you home alive, but it will cost three hundred dollars to send you home dead." Kimball wrote that "it was a matter of business in that office; they had no money. I think maybe that was all I was worth." Kimball protested and convinced Morgan he should remain. See Richards, *J. Golden Kimball*, 46. For a description of his activities after his return to Chattanooga, see Kimball Journal, Nov. 30– Dec. 30, 1884.

their course of life approved of Him! and hear it said unto them well done good and faithful Servant enter into the joy of thy Lord."[137]

From there he returned home to Davis County to be reunited with his two families, and, after a few days of rest, returned to his typical pattern of writing and lecturing. But, apparently, he and Morgan were also working with church leaders to decide the fate of the Southern States Mission. Earlier in the month, Roberts had received a letter from Morgan saying that "the people by considerable majority and some of the brethren of the Authorities were in favor of sending no more Elders to the Southern Mission." Apparently President John Taylor and George Q. Cannon agreed with Roberts and Morgan that "the work of preaching the Gospel should go on," but they were in a minority. If missionary work continued, according to Morgan, he and Roberts "would be held responsible for the lives of the Elders."[138] That was too much for Roberts to shoulder. He replied that, as far as he was concerned, he did not wish to "take any such responsibility." Roberts, skirting the boundary of criticizing church leaders, said that if "Pres. Taylor would not take the responsibility of sending them don't let *us* assume the responsibility of doing so" (emphasis in original). Roberts felt the wisest course would be to inform every elder called to the South that they came to the mission "at the risk of losing his life," and communicate this concern with every missionary then in the South and let them know that the responsibility to remain rested "where it belonged—upon each Elder."[139]

During this uncertain time, rumors flourished, and Kimball wrote, "There had been an impression that the mission was about to be closed. Several of the Apostles felt that way and the people in general considered that sufficient preaching had been done in the Southern States." But after much discussion with various general authorities, on December 30, "it was decided that the labors should

137. Roberts, *History's Apprentice*, 162 (Nov. 27, 1884). See also Kimball Journal, Nov. 26, 1884.

138. Roberts, *History's Apprentice*, 157 (Nov. 6, 1884).

139. Roberts, *History's Apprentice*, 158 (Nov. 6, 1884). See also Roberts, *Autobiography*, 157.

continue on as heretofore and the Elders carry their message to all that would listen."[140]

Roberts, however, did not return to Chattanooga. He had been released from his missionary service. His time in the Southern States Mission was a formative experience. He grew and developed as a writer, speaker, and administrator. He met and worked with a number of young men who would cross his path in the years ahead. He dealt with the aftermath of the horrible murder of two missionaries and two members. The impact of the "Tennessee Massacre" would continue to hold the attention of the Saints in the years ahead, and Roberts's bravery would be associated with it.[141] His actions attracted press attention throughout the country. And he demonstrated his allegiance by entering in to the principle of plural marriage. All of this had been noticed by the church hierarchy. Clearly, B. H. Roberts would be looked to for leadership positions in the years ahead.

140. Kimball Journal, Dec. 30, 1884.

141. In 1895, Willard Bean, half-brother of Roberts's missionary colleague Leo A. Bean, visited the area and spoke with many of the residents who remembered the event. His lengthy account was placed retrospectively in Historian's Office, Journal History, Aug. 10, 1884, 9–20. See also Bean Autobiography, 64–71, typescript in fd. 3, Bean Collection. At the same time, an account from a local perspective may be found in Garrett, *Historical Sketches of Hickman*, 79–86; and in Donald M. Axelrod, "Cane Creek Violence Took Four Lives in 1884," *Daily Herald* (Columbia, TN), Mar. 26, 1964.

SIX

ESCAPE TO ENGLAND

B. H. Roberts chose a difficult time to join the ranks of polygamy. The years after he came home from the Southern States Mission are called the "Raid," an attempt by the federal government to use anti-polygamy legislation not only to destroy polygamy but to cripple the church itself. Roberts's colleague John Morgan was "under fire" for entering into plural marriages, "and the federal marshals were dogging his footsteps."[1] J. Golden Kimball received a letter from Roberts informing him that polygamist "D. H. Wells had gone to England, that Joseph F. Smith absented himself—going to the Sandwich [today Hawai'ian] Islands. Pres. Morgan was forced to secret himself and they were endeavoring to implicate Pres. [John] Taylor and [George Q.] Cannon. All this is done simply because they have obeyed the commandments of God."[2] Two weeks later, Morgan let Kimball know that after being "forced to leave home on account of their belief and practicing it," he would return to Chattanooga.[3] Roberts's father-in-law William Smith "had to keep out of the way," because federal marshals "were after him for unlawful cohabitation."[4]

As part of the Raid, federally appointed judicial officials embarked on a "grinding process" designed to put the fate of Mormon polygamists in the hands of gentile (non-Mormon) grand juries and other legal proceedings. At first, many LDS officials attempted to comply with the harsh measures of the Edmunds Act by living with

1. Roberts, *Autobiography*, 163. See also "John Morgan," *Salt Lake Herald*, May 21, 1885, 8, which quotes the *Atlanta Constitution* on the efforts of the "notorious Mormon elder," and his "infamous sect," in bringing converts west.

2. Kimball Journal, Jan. 13, 1885.

3. Kimball Journal, Jan. 30, 1885.

4. Roberts, *History's Apprentice*, 169 (Feb. 6, 1885).

only one of their wives, thus they could hardly be accused of "cohabitating." But it soon became clear, as historian Edward Leo Lyman has written, that "harsh judicial treatment was intended for all," so most polygamists went into hiding. The Mormon underground "was a rather elaborate network of hiding places, escape routes, warning systems, and support from much of the Mormon community in an effort to avoid capture."[5]

Roberts saw the government's efforts as a direct, illegitimate, and unwarranted attack on the civil and political rights of the Saints. On January 11, 1885, he addressed an audience in the Salt Lake Tabernacle asserting that religious liberty means "not only the right to believe but to practice a religion."[6] Roberts was often bothered that "federal officials are very active in hunting for those whom they suspect of being guilty of obeying this one of God's laws while the libertine and whore-monger are unmolested." He saw LDS polygamists as "honorable men" whose footsteps were dogged by spies and traitors.[7]

Between the end of January and the middle of March 1885, Roberts visited "nearly every settlement in the Utah corridor" to take subscriptions to the *Contributor* and help build the Young Men's Mutual Improvement Association (YMMIA).[8] He frequently took these opportunities to attack the federal government's handling of Mormon polygamy, and he turned these talks into articles for the *Contributor*. His arguments focused particularly on the role of the federal government and the anti-polygamy legislation that had been adopted. He asserted that the Morrill Anti-Bigamy act, passed in 1862, "which defined the plural marriage of the Latter-day Saints to be a crime, and made it punishable by fines and imprisonment was passed in violation to the first amendment of the Constitution."[9]

5. Lyman, *Political Deliverance*, 25. See also Lyman, *Finally Statehood!* No doubt Roberts was also aware, as Lyman makes clear, that the church "not only aided in supporting the family" of anyone apprehended in these raids, but "also provided legal counsel," as well.

6. Historian's Office, Journal History, Jan. 11, 1885, 12.

7. Roberts, *History's Apprentice*, 169.

8. Roberts, 163–83.

9. See B. H. Roberts's series "Celestial Marriage and the Acts of Congress," appearing in the *Contributor* between November 1884 and April 1885. Hereafter cited as "Celestial Marriage."

He further argued that all who respected the Constitution and its guarantees of freedom and liberty should note that a violation of the rights of one group threatened the rights of others. He said the Saints believed that so long as men "in practicing their religion, do no violation to the rights of others, government cannot rightfully interfere with there religion." He quoted from the first amendment that federal officials "cannot prohibit the free exercise thereof," and believed someday "when the correctness of this interpretation of the Constitution regarding is recognized, the Celestial Marriage of the Latter-day Saints will no longer be punishable by fines and imprisonment." Roberts added, though undoubtedly the US Congress would disagree, that polygamy was "not injurious even to those who may not believe it."[10]

The level of suspicion among the Saints was so high that Roberts himself was "taken for a Marshall" when he enquired of the residence of a local bishop in American Fork.[11] As he continued on his canvass of Utah County towns, he found himself in Pleasant Grove where a young woman

> stepped off the train with a babe—very young—in her arms. Her trunk was put off the train, and I could see that she was distressed. I stepped up to her and she asked me if I knew where an acquaintance of hers lived. ... I am assured that this ... sister ... was one of those who have to flee because she dared obey the commandment of the Lord—these are hunted as the hart on the mountain for becoming the wife of an honorable man who had more than one wife, and a virtuous mother while the strumpet can unmolested and unblushingly walk the streets and not excite ire of these zealous executors of the law.[12]

Roberts during this time showed his defiance. He composed a song titled "Have Courage My Girl to Say Yes," which encouraged

---

10. Celestial Marriage," Apr. 1885, 216. See also the editorial "The Crusade Against the Mormons," *Contributor*, Apr. 1885, 274–76. While this does not appear to be written by Roberts himself, it was clearly influenced by the series of articles he had published in the journal's pages.

11. Roberts, *History's Apprentice*, 169 (Feb. 7, 1885). Roberts also records that he had attended a meeting in the Tabernacle where he found the "seats usually occupied by the [General] Authorities were vacant, and I have seldom experienced such a feeling of gloom and sadness."

12. *History's Apprentice*, 171 (Feb. 10, 1885).

"the daughters of Zion," as outside forces "menace the Saints," to enter into plural marriage.[13] Similarly, a few days later he discovered a poem which he had composed "some ten days ago when having the blues," and thought was lost, that was "meant for a lady friend of mine." It seems to have been written for Kate Chase.[14]

In April, he was made a member of the subcommittee to draft the "Declaration of Grievances and Protest" to US President Grover Cleveland.[15] A month later, he participated in a mass meeting held in Salt Lake City to ratify it.[16] Similar meetings were held in Ogden, Logan, Provo, and Farmington.[17] Roberts spoke briefly, saying that whenever oppression occurred it "became the duty of every freeman to resist the hand of tyranny. We cannot afford to sit idly by while one class of citizens [are] being assailed."[18] LDS women "had entered into the marriage relation, believing they were doing God's will." They had started families and created homes that were "centers where Christian principles were taught and revered" and now federal agents were breaking down the doors of those homes and stomping in to drag their husbands away. "Is it not time we protested against such … proceedings? … We are contending for our homes, privileges, and rights guaranteed to all citizens of the United States and we are willing to grant the same to all mankind."[19]

Roberts's remarks were greeted by "loud and continuous applause," and the declaration of grievances was "ratified and adopted amid the most unbounded enthusiasm."[20] James Moyle said of Roberts, "Education has not made an Infidel of him but has enabled him to become a powerful champion of the people."[21]

---

13. For full text, see *History's Apprentice*, 177 (Feb. 23, 1885).

14. *History's Apprentice*, 179–80 (Feb. 28, 1885). It was rumored by some in Davis County that Chase was indeed a plural wife of Roberts, though no evidence of such a marriage has been uncovered.

15. Whitney, *Through Memory's Halls*, 186. The text is found on 186–89.

16. "The Mass Meeting," *Deseret Weekly News*, May 6, 1885, 4.

17. See "The Mass Meeting," *Salt Lake Herald*, May 6, 1885, 7; and "At Provo," *Salt Lake Herald*, May 8, 1885, 7.

18. "A People's Wrongs," *Salt Lake Herald*, May 3, 1885, 2.

19. "A People's Wrongs."

20. "The Mass Meeting," *Deseret Weekly News*, May 6, 1885, 5.

21. Gene A. Sessions, ed., *Biographical and Reminiscences from the James Henry Moyle Collection* (Salt Lake City: N. P., 1974), 190–91.

On May 17, 1885, Roberts joined the staff of the *Salt Lake Herald*,[22] which was owned by Apostle Heber J. Grant,[23] and where he worked with editor Byron Groo[24] and business manager Horace G. Whitney.[25] He was hired primarily to travel and solicit subscriptions and receive payments for the paper, but he was soon working as an associate editor.[26] Beyond helping to deal with his dwindling finances, Roberts found that the editorial stance of the Democratic paper "was agreeable to the methods of thought which I had acquired." Exactly when Roberts had begun to think of himself as a Democrat is unclear, but there were movements within the state toward building support for the two national parties during this period.[27] His association with Groo was pleasant, that he "respected my faith and I his doubts. Many a night we sat and discussed Mormonism until the wee small hours, and he … appeared at times greatly interested." Roberts came to feel that journalism constituted "responsible, educative involvement," and he fell "in love with that kind of work," along with how it allowed him to stay close to his two families.[28]

That summer, the twenty-eight-year-old Roberts undertook an assignment sponsored by the *Contributor* to take photographs

22. The paper was published each morning except Monday, and also featured a semi-weekly published on Wednesday and Saturday, and a weekly on Thursday.

23. Grant (1856–1945) was called as an apostle in 1882. At the time he was married to Lucy Stringham (1858–93), but two years later on successive days he married Augusta Winters (1856–1952) and Emily H. Wells (1851–1908). Grant became the last polygamist president of the Church upon the death of Joseph F. Smith in 1918. By then two of his three wives had passed away. Grant and Roberts were close over the years.

24. Byron Groo (1849–1915) came to Utah with his family in 1854. After graduating from the University of Deseret, he taught school for several years. In 1873 he joined the *Salt Lake Herald* and rose from reporter to editor before he resigned in 1892. An active Democrat, Groo was appointed registrar of the US Land Commission by President Grover Cleveland and served in that position until 1897. After that he was active in business and banking.

25. Whitney (1858–1920) was active in literary and dramatic affairs. He was the business manager of the *Herald* for many years then left to hold a similar position at the *Deseret News*, 1899–1920. During these years he was active in many church callings and in business, most importantly as the longtime secretary-treasurer of the Utah–Idaho Sugar Co. "Horace G. Whitney," *Salt Lake Telegram*, Oct. 26, 1920, 7.

26. "B. H. Roberts," *Salt Lake Herald*, May 17, 1885, 12; and "Personal," *Salt Lake Herald*, May 19, 1885, 8. Precisely when Roberts became associate editor is unclear. He suggests that it was sometime in the spring of 1886, a fact held by Truman Madsen as well. When he was arrested the next year, the paper refers to him as "one of the staff."

27. See "Democratic Club of Utah," *Deseret News*, Dec. 3, 1884, 4.

28. Madsen, *Defender of the Faith*, 161.

of church history sites in Missouri and Illinois.[29] The trip seems to have been somewhat secret.[30] Writing from Richmond, Missouri, Roberts told his mother there was "little I can say about my business or my visit to this land but when I return, or shortly thereafter I shall be able to relate it all in detail." He does mention that he was surrounded by "many interesting events in the history of the Church and this nation."[31] In September the *Contributor* announced that a forthcoming issue would contain these photos and solicited anyone who lived there during those years "to forward their names & a brief account of their experiences."[32]

Toward the end of the year, Roberts traveled throughout Utah again on behalf of the Mutual Improvement Association and the *Contributor.*[33] He told his mother, "I am absent from home so much that it is a great trial to Lou & I feel sorrowful for her at times & yet I can't see how I can help it unless I take her with me … when it is possible for me to do so."[34] Roberts also was involved with groups like the University of Deseret, and was part of creating a Normal Alumni Association at the school.[35] Roberts was chosen as the association's first vice president on the recommendation of George M. Cannon who told the gathering that Roberts "could even make dry bones talk."[36]

In January 1886 Roberts became more closely tied with the *Contributor* as a stockholder, secretary-treasurer, and member of the board as the periodical moved from "a private concern to a corporation."

29. See "B. H. Roberts Will Write the Descriptions," *Deseret News*, Sep. 30, 1885, 16.

30. Indeed, the *Salt Lake Herald* simply announced that Roberts had "returned from a trip east in the interests of the *Contributor.*" See "Personals," *Salt Lake Herald*, Aug. 27, 1885, 5.

31. Roberts to Mother, July 25, 1885, box 4, fd. 3, Roberts Papers (UU).

32. "The Contributor Announcement," *Deseret News*, Sep. 30, 1885, 12.

33. "Provo Points," *Salt Lake Herald*, Nov. 6, 1885. While there, the paper reported that Roberts also delivered the "most entertaining lecture this season … on his experiences as a missionary." See also "Local Briefs," *Salt Lake Herald*, Dec. 12, 1885, 8.

34. Roberts to Mother, Oct. 19, 1885, box 4, fd. 3, Roberts Papers (UU).

35. See "Normal Alumni Association," *Deseret News*, June 2, 1886, 305. Three of those in attendance were from his class: Roberts, George M. Cannon, and James H. Moyle.

36. Ralph V. Chamberlin, *Memories of John R. Park* (Salt Lake City: Deseret News Press, 1949), 137.

Out of two hundred shares, valued at $100 each, Roberts held five, with Junius Wells holding the most at forty-five.

On July 24, 1886, Roberts spoke at the celebration of the thirty-ninth anniversary of the Mormon arrival in the Salt Lake Valley. The First Presidency did not attend, because, as a banner hung over the podium read, they were "In Exile for Conscience Sake." Referring to the banner, Roberts said the "silver haired patriots" of that trek found themselves imprisoned for their belief in God's laws, and not until these patriots "shall be able to take their place in our midst ... shall the voice of rejoicing be heard on Pioneer Day." Roberts echoed a common theme among Latter-day Saints: It was not the United States that was the problem, but its current leaders, perverting and subverting the rights of polygamists. The Saints would not only fight for their rights, but they "believe it to be our destiny yet to rescue that sacred document, the Constitution, from the hands of those who would destroy it. We will remain true to those principles that have been bequeathed to us by the fathers of the Republic. But we will not surrender the convictions of our hearts, or be untrue to our parents, or untrue to our God—we refuse to make that sacrifice."[37] Roberts, already a naturally gifted speaker, had become a captivating orator.

His defiant speeches and writing aside, Roberts's marital status caught up with him, and he "seemed as much amazed" by this turn of events as anyone.[38] In early December 1886, while busily "engaged in preparing the daily dispatches" of the *Salt Lake Herald*, two deputy marshals, Arthur Pratt[39] (ironically a son of Roberts's early hero Orson Pratt and his plural wife Sarah Marinda Pratt) and Oscar Vandercook,[40] came into the office at 4:30 p.m. and arrested Roberts

37. "In Solemn Assembly," *Deseret News*, July 28, 1886, 8; and "Pioneer Day," *Ogden Herald*, July 26, 1886, 4.

38. "B. H. Roberts Arrested," *Salt Lake Herald*, Dec. 3, 1886, 8. The report states that "one" Celia Dibble was the "young lady named as the second wife " and that she is a "resident of Kaysville." As noted, the paper refers to Roberts only as "one of the staff of this paper."

39. Pratt (1852–1919) later served as warden of the Utah State Prison.

40. Vandercook (1846–1939) himself was arrested on moral charges, in November 1885 by the Salt Lake City police in a sting conducted by B. Y. Hampton to entrap anti-Mormon officials. He was charged with "lewd and lascivious conduct" with Mrs. A. J. Fields, a police decoy. See Nichols, *Prostitution, Polygamy and Power*, 1, 33–34.

on a bench warrant for unlawful cohabitation naming both Louisa and Celia in the complaint.[41] Roberts went with the marshals to appear before Commissioner William McKay[42] and entered into a $1,000 bond with the promise to appear the next day. The *Herald* said that the two deputies "threw something of a bombshell—if that term be taken as the synonym for the tallest amusement," into the office when they arrested him.

The charges against Roberts were brought to the authorities on September 11, 1886, by Daniel W. Rench,[43] who alleged that Roberts had cohabited with Celia Dibble over the period between October 1, 1883 and September 1, 1886.[44] With formal charges filed, several witnesses were subpoenaed including Louisa, Celia's parents Philo and Antoinette Dibble, Edwin C. Sidney, and Celia's thirteen-year-old brother, George E. Dibble.[45] Deputy John Wesley Greenman[46] indicated that, while she had been subpoenaed, "the alleged wife Celia Dibble could not be found."[47]

41. Truman Madsen reports that Ann Roberts had been in the *Herald* offices; she stepped out of the office so she would not be recognized and arrested as well. Madsen, *Defender of the Faith*, 162.

42. The term "commissioner" here referred to a federal appointee who handled routine court business.

43. Rench (1838–1893) came to the territory in the late 1860s, married Emily Sophia Foote (1846–1926), and served as a deputy marshal. Later he was active as a tax collector and selectman in Tooele. He was active in pursuing possible unlawful cohabitation cases during that period. The *Deseret Evening News* called him a "well known character," and said he was engaged in mining and stock raising. See "D. W. Rench Dead," *Deseret Evening News*, Dec. 4, 1893, 1; and, "Obituary," *Salt Lake Tribune*, Dec. 4, 1893, 8.

44. The nature of the charge was interesting in that Rench stated the ceremony was performed in 1883, while most other sources suggest that the marriage to Celia took place in 1884. According to the *Salt Lake Herald*, Roberts testified in 1889, when he was sentenced for unlawful cohabitation, that the marriage took place in 1883. See "B. H. Roberts's Case," *Salt Lake Herald*, May 2, 1889, 5. See also previous chapter.

45. George Elliot Dibble (1873–1955) lived his entire life in Davis County, where he was involved in agricultural and educational activities. Like Roberts, Dibble was a Democrat. See "Funeral Services Held Tuesday at Layton for George E. Dibble," *Davis County Clipper*, Jan. 28, 1955, 4.

46. Greenman (1840–1917) was born in Illinois and served in the 8th Regiment, Wisconsin Infantry, in the Civil War, rising to captain. After holding political office in Vernon County, Wisconsin, he came to Utah as a Deputy US Marshal in 1876 and served in that capacity until 1887. He was a US Commissioner, 1889–95, and during his time in Utah, he was active as a Mason and Odd Fellow.

47. "B. H. Roberts Arrested," *Deseret News*, Dec. 8, 1886, 4. Hereafter cited as "B. H. Roberts Arrested." See also "B. H. Roberts Disappears," *Territorial Enquirer*, Dec. 7, 1886, 3. John Morgan noted in his journal, "The papers brought the news of the Arrest of B H

Roberts failed to appear at the scheduled hour. The anti-Mormon *Salt Lake Tribune* said that Roberts, the "loud mouthed carrot eater of Israel" who had said he would go to jail rather than submit to federal authority, chose "when his lechery was about to be exposed" to skip out to the underground. In fact, the paper reported, "Brother Roberts" had not been seen all day at the *Herald*'s offices or by his attorney.

Roberts emerged from hiding later that evening and met with Apostles John Henry Smith[48] and Heber J. Grant to discuss the situation. If Roberts were convicted, he would face five years in jail and a fine of $500—and the fact that Roberts had taken Celia as a plural wife would be disclosed publicly.[49] The men decided that Roberts would take the pseudonym "James Reed" and escape to England where his editorial talents could be used by the church's *Millennial Star*. Smith wrote, "B. H. Roberts skipped by the light of the moon. He has gone to England. I set him apart for a mission."[50] Truman Madsen reports that later

> that evening Roberts rushed to Centerville and managed to throw a few clothes in a satchel. He abruptly kissed his wife, Louisa, Adah, and three-month old child Ben, good-bye. Then behind a team of horses obtained from Heber J. Grant's livery stable, he started up the canyon toward Peterson, Utah. It was bitterly cold and he was not warmly dressed. The wind chill forced him into a deserted house to get "thawed out." By traveling all night, he managed to arrive at a railroad junction, by 10:00 a. m. to catch a [train] to Evanston, [Wyoming].[51]

Roberts at Salt Lake for unlawful cohabitation." Morgan Journal, Dec. 8, 1886, in Morgan Papers.

48. Smith (1848–1911) was bishop of the Seventeenth Ward, 1875–80, then served as a member of the Quorum of Twelve Apostles from 1880 until his death. He served in the territorial legislature in 1881, and as president of the European Mission, 1882–85. Smith was an active Republican and friend, yet political opponent, of Roberts's in the period before statehood. They served together at the constitutional convention where Smith was the president.

49. John Henry Smith noted in his diary that, upon returning from a conference visit in Provo, he "learned that B. H. Roberts had been arrested. Grant, Wells and myself talked the matter over." See Smith, *Church, State, and Politics*, 159.

50. Smith, *Church, State, and Politics*, 159. Clearly LDS leaders thought Roberts would perform missionary work as well as editorial assistance. A copy of his missionary appointment letter and missionary certificate signed by John Taylor and George Q. Cannon is found in box 1, fd. 11, Roberts Papers (BYU).

51. According to Madsen, Celia was living in Logan under the name of "Mrs. E." She was staying with Roberts's former missionary colleague Joseph Morrell and his family. See

From there he made for Denver where his journey almost ended. In Evanston, he "observed two men, evidently on the look out for possible escaping … violators of the Utah law." Roberts felt they might know of his pseudonym so he did not pick up a first-class ticket that had been bought for him under the name of Reed, but purchased a second-class ticket to Denver instead. While on board the conductor came through announcing he had a telegram for James Reed. Thinking it might be a trap, Roberts did not respond. To further disguise himself, Roberts wore "a second best suit of clothing and a slouched hat, and … took passage in the smoking car."[52] When he got to Denver, he had another impression that he might be discovered and changed his destination to Kansas City where he arranged direct passage to New York. A few days later he was on board a ship bound for England.[53]

While on board he wrote a lengthy letter to his mother pledging that he would repay the bondsmen, but that "having freedom rather than several years of imprisonment was well worth a thousand dollars."[54] He told her that he was aware of, but not frightened by the danger the move entailed, and would "endure it cheerfully," though he admitted to be filled with "anxiety and dread" for the impact it might have on his family. In the end, he simply hoped "to be useful in preaching the Gospel of Christ in England & other parts of Europe, which may accomplish more good than spending a number of years in prison." Calling himself her "devoted but unworthy son," he instructed her to write him at church headquarters at 42 Islington Street in Liverpool, but suggested she "post your letter from S. L. C."[55] Oddly, he did not suggest she use the pseudonym James Reed

---

chapter four. A few days later a visitor to the home mentioned that there was a rumor that Roberts "had decided to jump bond and go to England." Madsen says these individuals deduced, based on the expression on her face, that Celia was Roberts's wife. Madsen, *Defender of the Faith*, 162. See also, Roberts, *History of the B. H. Roberts Family*, 133.

52. Roberts, *Autobiography*, 164.

53. Madsen says that apparently "those who saw him sign his ticket 'James Reed' had … learned that this was his assigned pseudonym, and planned to identify him and apprehend him in Denver." Madsen, *Defender of the Faith*, 162.

54. As quoted in Madsen, *Defender of the Faith*, 163.

55. Roberts to Ann Roberts, Dec. 16, 1886, box 4, fd. 6, Roberts Papers (UU). John Morgan noted that he had "received a letter from brother B. H. Roberts who was on a vessel off the coast of Ireland to Liverpool." Morgan Journal, Jan. 10, 1887.

until several months later. Perhaps he still worried that the name was known to federal authorities.[56]

Roberts wrote another revealing letter from Kansas City as well. It was addressed to Joseph Morrell. Writing in the third person, he said that he supposed "hells a poppin' in Utah and that people have lost all faith in B. H. because of his departure and leaving the bonds men." Noting that he hoped Morrell "was not among that number," he told him

> You may be assured that I took no such step unadvised and that I made such arrangements that my bondsmen will in me lose nothing. That is all I can say about that now, and whatever of censure the uniformed will heap upon me I shall have to bear until that day when all can be known. … You may well believe that I am pressed with many cares and much anxiety … [and] all my affairs will have to be arranged by letter. And now my dear Joseph if any of my former friends are inclined to judge harshly of B. H., tell them to judge nothing before its time.[57]

Roberts also indicated that he had written Celia: "She will tell you what I wish her to do until I can find out how matters stand, then I can advise her further." Clearly with Celia in mind, he told Morrell that he was not "unmindful of my obligations to you, and as soon as I can make some will make an effort to discharge them."[58]

Roberts had taken pains to make sure that none of his friends and family, nor his attorney, James H. Moyle, could be accused of abetting his flight from the law. Saying that Roberts had missed an appointment with him, Moyle reported

> that in his conversation with Mr. Roberts after the arrest, no intimation was given other than he would be on hand. … The disappearance of Mr. Roberts caused the utmost amazement wherever he was known. He did not return to the *Herald* office the evening after the arrest and he has not been seen there since. … Messrs. Burton and Wells stated that they have never received a hint of an intention not to appear and they were

56. Roberts to Mother, July 6, 1887, box 4, fd. 6, Roberts Papers (UU). He noted, "It would have been alright to have given my address to Matty Cowley, for I think half of Utah by this time knows where I am."

57. Roberts to Joseph Morrell, Dec. 6, 1886, Morrell Letters Received. He signed the letter "B. H. R." See also Morrell Correspondence.

58. Roberts to Morrell.

> as much surprised as anyone to hear the news. Both … have entire confidence in Mr. Roberts, and if he has really gone they feel no doubt of him indemnifying them. … Mr. Roberts' sister called at the *Herald* office yesterday … and was very much surprised not to find him at his post. … [H]is mother … too was astonished that her son was missing. His departure, therefore was taken in a hurry and apparently on his own.[59]

According to the British Mission manuscript history, Roberts arrived on December 23, 1886, on the National Lines's *S. S. Egypt.*[60] Roberts clearly enjoyed his time aboard ship. A dozen or so of his fellow passengers were Canadians, the younger sons of titled British families who had homesteaded in western Canada, and were now returning to visit their relatives. Roberts described them as a "care free crowd" and full of the fast-approaching Christmas spirit. He and his fellow passengers participated in a sort of mock parliament that discussed Gladstone's bill[61] for Irish home rule that was being debated in the actual Parliament. Because he had studied the bill closely and had definite views on it, he was dubbed the "Parnell" of the debates.[62] It made him a "noted character and general favorite" on the ship, and he "formed some very cordial friendships by the time the ship arrived."[63]

Church leaders' decision to commit so much time, energy, and money to moving Roberts out of Utah is curious—and telling. He was not quite thirty years old and held no major ecclesiastical office. But he had attracted a great deal of attention over his activities in the Southern States and was rapidly becoming a well-known speaker. Church leaders seem to have thought that his writing and speaking skills might be useful in furthering the work of the church in Great Britain.

---

59. "By the Great Route," *Salt Lake Herald*, Dec. 4, 1886, 8.

60. British Mission, Manuscript History, vol. 1, part 2. Other polygamists made their way to England. According to the same source, Henry Ballard arrived on November 17 on board the *Alaska* and Apostle George Teasdale arrived on the *City of Berlin*, November 30.

61. William Gladstone (1809–92) was a fixture in Victorian England government for some fifty years. He was a member of Parliament and chancellor of the exchequer. He served as prime minister four times as head of the Liberal Party.

62. Charles Stewart Parnell (1846–1891) was a member of Parliament from Ireland and a strong supporter of home rule. Interestingly, Roberts became familiar with Parnell and Irish home rule through articles in both the local papers and the *Contributor.*

63. See Roberts, *Autobiography*, 164–65.

Apostle George Teasdale,[64] who had recently taken over as editor of the *Millennial Star*, met Roberts at the dock, and Roberts began to explore the local area, attend the theater, become familiar with the subway system, and begin his work with the *Millennial Star*.[65] Over time, however, the cold and foggy weather brought back the sinus headaches that had plagued him in the Midwest. Teasdale noted that Roberts's head was "very bad," and that he had administered to him on several occasions. "Bro Roberts is troubled with a curious headache that starts in the morning and leaves in the evening. It is a most singular thing."[66] As they had in the past, the headaches subsided and soon Roberts was back at work on the paper as well as speaking various church meetings, including a new hall they located on Bittern Street.[67]

While there is no mention in the *Millennial Star* of Roberts's arrival, he was deeply involved with the publication, at first writing under pseudonyms or initials. For example, an article titled "The Lord Has Spoken," with the byline "B H" appeared in early January.[68] After that, there were a series of articles with the listed author as "R."[69] Roberts confirmed to his mother that he was both "B H"

64. Teasdale (1831–1907) was an English convert to Mormonism in 1852 and immigrated to Utah in 1861. He married six women; the last two marriages took place after the 1890 Manifesto and were apparently performed at sea off the California coast. After serving missions to England in 1868–69, and the Southern States in 1875, Teasdale was Juab Stake president, 1877–82. He was president of the European Mission, 1887–90, and served as a member of the Council of the Twelve from 1882 until his death.

65. See Teasdale Journal, Dec. 23–31, 1886, in Teasdale Papers (CHL). Hereafter cited as Teasdale Journal.

66. See Teasdale Journal, Jan. 10, 1887. See also entries between Jan. 1 and Jan. 12.

67. Teasdale Journal, Jan. 6 and 16, 1887. Interestingly, another missionary at that same meeting was Milford B. Shipp, the husband of Roberts's future plural wife, Margaret. For more on his activities, see "Correspondence," *Millennial Star*, Mar. 11, 1887, 172–75.

68. B. H., "The Lord Hath Spoken," *Millennial Star*, Jan. 10, 1887, 24–27.

69. See R, *Millennial Star*, "New Wine in Old Bottles," Jan. 17, 1887, 40–42; "The Disturbances at Swansea," Sep. 19, 1887, 603; "The Swansea Disturbance," Sep. 26, 1887, 616–19; "The Word of Wisdom," Oct. 3, 1887, 832–33; and "The Close of the Volume," Dec. 26, 1887, 820–21. In this last article Roberts wrote, "The year 1887 will in future ages display a bright record for the Saints, and one correspondingly discreditable to the foes of the Kingdom of God." See also R, *Millennial Star*, "The Gospel and the Jews," Feb. 6, 1888, 88–91; "The Book of Mormon," Aug. 27, 1888, 552–54; "Suggestions to the Readers of the Book of Mormon," Aug. 27, 1888, 554–58; and "Prosecutions Under the Edmunds Act," Sep. 3, 1888, 568–70.

and "R."[70] Even without that admission, Roberts's style and interests become evident. There is the article "Reported Outrages," which discusses the attacks on the morals and actions of "the Elders in the South."[71] Then there is "Missionaries and Their Treatment" that says missionaries "have been shot down in cold blood; so that when one leaves his home on a mission it is understood that he takes his life in his hand."[72] And, finally, "A Word of Counsel to the Emigrating Saints."[73] One of the articles signed R, "The Character of the Mormon People,"[74] was later published as a pamphlet under Roberts's name.[75] In March, the paper published "Celestial Marriage," by Elder B. H. Roberts, which was originally published in the *Contributor*. This was the first and only mention of Roberts during the first three months of 1887. There was nothing about him fleeing Utah or being in England.[76] Instead, the paper lists "James Reed of the Liverpool office" as attending several missionary conferences.

As 1888 progressed, newspapers grew increasingly comfortable with acknowledging Roberts's presence. The *Deseret News* said that Roberts was "using his pen in vigorous style in Great Britain in defense of the Latter-day saints. Some of the English papers are liberal enough to pen their columns to him in repelling scandalous assaults made through the public journals upon the 'Mormon' people."[77] The *Millennial Star* reported that Roberts's tract *The Second Coming of the Messiah and the Events to Precede It* had recently been released and called it an "excellent assistant to the Elders in introducing the

70. Roberts to Mother, July 6, 1887, box 4, fd. 5, Roberts Papers (UU).

71. R, "Reported Outrages," *Millennial Star*, Dec. 19, 1887, 808–09.

72. R, "Missionaries and Their Treatment," *Millennial Star*, Feb. 13, 1888, 104–07.

73. R, "A Word of Counsel to the Emigrating Saints," *Millennial Star*, Apr. 30, 1888, 283–86.

74. R, "The Character of the Mormon People" *Millennial Star*, 49 Aug. 1, 1887, 488–92. The *Millennial Star* noted that "The Character of the Mormon People," a sixteen-page pamphlet, "has just been issued from the office," and said it "appeared necessary, because of the misrepresentations, lies and slanders that continue to be uttered regarding the Latter-day Saints." The editors hoped the Saints "will assist us in our efforts to place [this pamphlet] in the hands of those who are disposed to investigate the principles of the Gospel." See "Untitled," *Millennial Star*, Oct. 31, 1887, 699.

75. Roberts had reviewed the tract with Teasdale and others on several occasions. See Teasdale Journal, Sep. 20 and Sep. 28, 1887.

76. B. H. Roberts, "Celestial Marriage," *Millennial Star*, Mar. 28, 1887, 193–97.

77. "General Items," *Deseret News*, Apr. 4, 1888, 5.

Gospel" to non-Mormons.[78] He also contributed an article under the name "R" on "The Gospel and the Jews," in which he argued that the Book of Mormon would eventually become a "powerful agent in converting many ... Jews to a belief in Jesus as the promised Messiah ... leading them to receive the Gospel in its fullness."[79]

In March and April, Roberts spoke at the Welsh Conference, the Norwich Conference, the Leeds Conference, and in the Bristol Conference, though he seemed to be working mostly in the office during much of the rest of the spring. He told his mother that office work did not provide much to write about: "I am O. K., putting in good solid work at my desk & all the time writing, as in addition to my work on the Star I am keeping up on my articles in the Contributor and it takes nearly—aye, more than all my spare time & sometimes I feel as if I would like to run away from myself & go where pens, paper & ink were unknown for a while."[80]

While he was speaking and working in the office, he also began work on "A New Witness for God" which was published in ten monthly installments in the *Millennial Star* between May and July.[81] In it, Roberts demonstrated his growing commitment to evangelization and dialogue with the Christian community, which characterized the rest of his ministry. These ten installments were the early forms of what became a long project for Roberts that would result in the publication of one of his classic works under the same title several years later.

Roberts, doing missionary work, was not paid for these publications, and about this time he wrote a lengthy letter to his mother noting that the exile had come just as he hoped he would be making more money. He was concerned with his family's survival since he was unable to provide for them. "I have borne with these continued separations from home & friends & the buffets of fortune without ever before complaining, but just now the clouds look so lowering that it is a struggle to keep serene amidst it all." Wearied by constant

78. "New Tract," *Millennial Star*, Feb. 6, 1888, 91.

79. R, "The Gospel and the Jews," *Millennial Star*, Feb. 6, 1888, 89.

80. Roberts to Mother, May 14, 1887, box 4, fd. 5, Roberts Papers (UU).

81. See B. H. Roberts, "A New Witness for God," *Millennial Star*, 1888, May 14, 313–15; May 21, 330–35; May 28, 344–47; June 4, 360–63; June 11, 376–80; June 18, 392–97; June 25, 408–13; July 2, 424–28; July 9, 440–44; and, July 16, 456–61.

correspondence, editing, and proofreading, he also confessed that he had lost interest in writing:

> It never occurred to me that any of my friends would be interested in anything I might or could write, so have never sent the Star to anyone but Brother John Morgan. I confess at one time I felt a little ambitious in the matter of writing, but lately I have lost nearly all interests and it becomes irksome to me & it is all unlovely in my own eyes & I look at most of my productions like a mother does upon a deformed child, they give me no pleasure. ... The most of the time is taken up on the paper as I have no help whatever in preparing the articles or in proof reading. And to get the correspondence and articles of others in some shape costs one much more labor than it would to write the whole thing. My Contributor articles make me considerable labor since I am separated from many of my notes and books.[82]

As if all these responsibilities were not enough, Roberts had his hands full dealing with apostate Mormon William Jarman, who had embarked on a long-term speaking tour of England to promote his anti-Mormon book *Uncle Sam's Abscess or Hell Upon Earth*.[83] In his book, which was sensational, digressive, and long-winded, he wrote that he spent twelve years in the "Sodom and Gomorrah" of Mormonism,[84] but over time, his wives, children, property were stolen, and he was "reduced to beggary and want." So he returned to New York "and started my little tongue wagging against the Mormons. It will continue so to wag until silenced by death or Mormonism pegs out."[85] His first attack on the LDS Church took place November 19, 1880, in the Brooklyn Tabernacle and continued in the United States during the next few years. Lecture tours by former Mormons were not uncommon, but Jarman was particularly sensational. In 1882, for example, he insisted that Brigham Young, who had died in August 1877, was still alive, saying that he had seen the Mormon

82. Roberts to Mother, July 6, 1887, box 4, fd. 5, Roberts Papers (UU).

83. See Sillito, "Goliath of Their Cause."

84. Jarman, *Uncle Sam's Abscess*, 14. See also "Who Is Mr. Jarman?" *Southern Utonian*, Aug. 24, 1888, 1, in which his ex-wife, Maria B. Ford, whom he married in 1862, accused him of a variety of crimes, stated he was married in polygamy, and added that his ridicule of the Mormon Church led her to divorce him on August 21, 1869. Ford said the couple "embraced Mormonism, and we were baptized in the sea at Exmouth ... and soon after emigrated to the United States."

85. Jarman, *Uncle Sam's Abscess*, 24.

leader "a few days before his supposed demise," and that he appeared to be in excellent health. Jarman said many "thousands of Utahns" believed the prophet's death had been faked because he was facing legal action.[86] He also charged that the Mormons had engineered the murder of his son Albert; a very much alive Albert and Jarman's ex-wife, Maria B. Ford, swore out affidavits to the contrary.[87]

After returning to England in the mid-1880s, Jarman became an instant sensation through his lecture, "Mormonism Exposed."[88] While gathering more material for his attacks, he contacted the *Millennial Star* requesting a copy of the June 27, 1887, issue, and inquired how much it would cost to secure a yearly subscription. Jarman also enclosed a copy of one of his recent anti-Mormon tracts. An outraged Teasdale wrote that he had "returned his filthy leaflets," while writing on them a quotation from Proverbs 19:9: "A false witness shall not be unpunished, and he that speaketh lies shall not escape."[89]

Nephi Y. Schofield, a British native who had immigrated to Utah then returned to serve a mission in November 1885, paints a colorful picture of Jarman and his approach. A few minutes before a lecture was to begin, Jarman would step from a hired taxi

> a short distance away and then, garbed in his Temple robes,[90] he walks quickly through busy streets and back to the hall. There is method in his madness. By the time he arrives the spacious hall is wholly inadequate to hold even a third of the noisy motley crew collected on the way. Now there is a wild scramble to get in as they are eager to her more about the "Hell on Earth" as blazoned forth on the illuminated banners, held aloft by his deluded serfs. Never for a moment does Jarman loiter on this trip. He knows better. When parading the streets in this grotesque costume he shrewdly remains silent and hastily proceeds to the hall so as to accomplish his advertising stunt, and yet keep with in the law to avoid arrest. Once inside the building he is master and supreme for the

86. See "Untitled," *Lowell Weekly Sun*, Mar. 18, 1882, 4. Jarman asserted that "one thing is very certain, the Mormon leaders are very tricky, and this trick would be only in keeping with many other … tricks … whereby the people were deceived." See also "Brigham's Resurrection," *Boston Herald*, Mar. 16, 1882, 4.

87. See "Jarman's 'Murdered' Son," *Millennial Star*, Jan. 21, 1889, 45–47.

88. See "Malodorous Jarman," *Salt Lake Herald*, Dec. 28, 1884, 12.

89. Teasdale Journal, June 27, 1887, 678.

90. Latter-day Saints wear ceremonial clothing in their temples; Jarman's use of it outside the temple as part of his lecture was especially flagrant to Mormons.

> hall has been hired and pro-tem it belongs to him. Mounting the platform in a storm of yells from the turbulent crowd, Jarman menacingly flourishes a glistening dagger, displays a couple of revolvers in his belt, and announces "with these weapons" he is ready to preach Mormonism. Then he dares any Latter-Day Devil from Utah, any Elder from Hell, to come to the stand and refute his statements. In defiant attitude he pauses for a response and this seems to please the rabble who yell still louder. It was a tense situation and one could sniff danger in the air.[91]

Jarman divided his lectures into two parts. At the beginning he took the stage "in what he alleged to be the robes used in connection with the sacred mysteries of Mormon Temple rituals." After that, while Jarman changed into regular attire, his assistants distributed leaflets which Roberts said made "outrageous charges" against both polygamy and the character of the Mormon people themselves. This was followed by a challenge to any Mormons who happened to be in attendance to meet him in public debate.[92] Some missionaries and local Saints then confronted Jarman—usually unsuccessfully. Several of them wrote to Teasdale to see if Roberts would take on their foe. Based on his experiences in the South and the notoriety he had gained, he seemed a logical choice. Roberts expressed a willingness to accept the task, but requested that he have a "free hand" in devising his course of action. As he proceeded, he realized that Jarman "had been permitted to lead mobs against the headquarters of the elders in the respective conference districts, to break down the doors, to scuttle the rooms, and to strew the contents of valises up and own the streets. My view was that the opposition should be taken to him and his debates instead of allowing the conference meetings of the Saints to be disturbed."[93]

91. Schofield, Autobiographical Reminiscence.

92. Roberts, *Autobiography*, 166. Jarman distributed flyers that read in part: "I … challenge all the Mormon missionaries from Utah to meet me upon a public platform, to discuss the doctrines and practices of the so called 'Latter-day Saints' in Utah, or refute my statements if they can, or dare. I defy them to do so." See "The Notorious Jarman," *Deseret News,* Dec. 14, 1887, 16.

93. Roberts, *Autobiography*, 166. At the same time, Roberts was approached by local papers. Teasdale noted that he had been asked by one reporter who "promised him the columns for an article if Bro Roberts wished to reply to Jarman's Trash." Ultimately, Teasdale noted that "Bro Roberts wrote a piece for the Barnsbury Independent which we have a chance of publishing." See Teasdale Journal, June 26 and June 28, 1887, 678.

In July, Roberts debated Jarman at Hoyland Common in Yorkshire, denying "the existence of the Danites, the doctrine of blood atonement or Mormon complicity in the Mountain Meadows Massacre." Those anxious to attend Jarman's lectures were not predisposed to be friendly to the Mormons. According to an account in the *Salt Lake Tribune*, after the two had debated, a vote was held to see who had won, and "five put up their hands for Roberts and 800 for Jarman."[94] Another encounter occurred at a large meeting of Jarman's held on Sunday, October 30, at the recently constructed Burmondsey Town Hall.[95] Schofield noted that this part of town was "heavily inhabited by a rather degenerate class who may be described as human derelicts." These people were mostly a "poor, illiterate order with a liberal sprinkling of the criminal element." This, thought Schofield, explained Jarman's success; he was convinced Jarman could not make "headway in any respectable, intelligent community where the people travel, read and reason for themselves." Jarman had also added a "cheap magic lantern"—a predecessor of kinetoscopes and nickelodeons—to project flickering images "alleging scenes in Utah among the Mormons."[96]

As Jarman began to close the second part of this particular show, Roberts stood up, identified himself, and stated he was quite willing to take up his customary challenge and debate him.[97] Taken somewhat aback, Jarman said that if Roberts would come to his lecture the next evening, he would give him fifteen minutes to respond. Roberts challenged Jarman saying that it seemed like a small amount of time to answer over two hours of "outrageous misrepresentation," but he accepted. Roberts later recalled that when he did this, "pandemonium broke loose" in the hall, and the crowd turned against him and his colleagues,[98] making their escape from the second floor of the

94. "Troubles of the Saints," *Salt Lake Tribune*, Sep. 18, 1887, 4.

95. See James J. Chandler, "Correspondence," *Millennial Star*, Nov. 2, 1887, 748–51. Hereafter cited as Chandler, "Correspondence."

96. Schofield, Autobiographical Reminiscences.

97. See Chandler, "Correspondence."

98. See "Correspondence," *Millennial Star*, Oct. 17, 1887, 666–69. Ballard noted that whatever effect Jarman's activities "may have had on the minds of the Elders and Saints in other parts of the Mission, it is quite certain that we who have witnessed and passed through them have been intensely interested." He also stated that because of Jarman's activities many people "are investigating and [we] are kept very busy visiting

auditorium to the street almost impossible. Once outside, as the mob crowded around them, tearing at their clothes and spewing epithets, they hopped into a cab where "the cabby ... cracked his whip ... and the horse forced its way through the crowd."[99]

Schofield remembered the escape differently: "fortunately the police took charge. Using their clubs with terrific effect right and left they cleared a passage for getting to us and defied the mob." Instead of hopping into a cab, Schofield said that four policemen "walked us to London Bridge—a distance of two miles." But these same police who initially protected them from physical harm, "being residents of the district, were equally as hostile, and verbally just as abusive as the screeching mob from whom they had delivered us."[100]

Roberts's debate with Jarman was eventually held on November 2. A "large number of police were on the outside" to prevent harm to either speaker from "1500 persons gathered in the hall." It was chaired by John W. Cripps,[101] a resident of Rotherhithe some two miles east of Burmondsey. One of those in attendance, Elder James J. Chandler,[102] who had known Roberts in Centerville a decade earlier, commented that Roberts did so well in taking on Jarman that

---

them," and says that Jarman continues in his efforts in an attempt to "gather in any coppers and keep out of the asylum." His biographer, Douglas Crookston, observes that Ballard "never felt comfortable speaking at a street meeting and avoided it if possible," but "felt perfectly at ease" speaking in halls. See Crookston, *Henry Ballard*, 147.

99. Roberts, *Autobiography*, 167.

100. Schofield, Autobiographical Reminiscence.

101. Cripps (1834–1917) was employed as an engine driver at Fisher's Sufferance Wharf, which was located in the Port of London on the south bank of the Thames near Rotherhithe Street. He had previously been a laborer and had come to his present employment in 1884. While a religious freethinker, he seems also to have been opposed to trade unions. See Royal Commission on Labor, *Digest of the Evidence*, 46, and *Minutes of Evidence*, 380–82. Roberts refers to him as "John Cripps, a locomotive engineer who had relatives in Utah, the Haywards." *Autobiography*, 167. This was Elizabeth Ann Cripps Hayward (1830–1932), and her husband, Gammon Hayward (1828–79), whom she had married in 1850. The couple came to Utah in 1853. See John W. Cripps Family Papers, in possession of the author.

102. James Jarvis Chandler (1849–1922) was born in England and arrived in Utah on October 15, 1866, with his parents and two sisters. He taught school in Willard, Utah. He married Harriett Eliza Cordon (1858–1936) in 1874 and Mary Ann Williams (1866–93) in 1884. Chandler was set apart on April 13, 1886, by Heber J. Grant, and released June 6, 1888. He served as president of the Norwich Conference. At one point Chandler had taught school in Centerville where he seems to have known Roberts as a pupil. Davis, "James Jarvis Chandler," 26, 110–117.

Jarman "feigned illness" as a way of ending the debate. Roberts later received a letter from Cripps stating that he came to the debate with "a rather unfavorable opinion" of Jarman, and that the debate had "confirmed my first impression of [his] character." He commended Roberts for showing "a great deal of courage" in facing "the lion in his den." Moreover, he told Roberts that he had been offered literature to study by some of the missionaries,[103] and wished to obtain copies "of the sermons" which Jarman quoted from. Roberts responded, "The very greatest blessing that would overtake you in this life would be the conviction of the truth of what the world calls 'Mormonism.'" But if that did not happen, then "let us be friends and brethren" committed to the larger goal of "the universal brotherhood of man." What Cripps apparently did not tell him was that his parents—Charles and Elizabeth Cripps—had joined the church in the early 1850s, as had his two sisters, Elizabeth and Mary, and that the family had emigrated to Utah at various times between 1856 and 1864.[104]

Roberts also engaged in a series of encounters with Jarman in Swansea, Wales. One of these encounters in June 1888 was published in a local paper called the *Western Mail*.[105] Roberts and Jarman met "on the same platform, before an audience of over 3000 people," most of whom were "antagonistic to the Mormon religion." While "Elder Roberts did his best to disprove the charges by quoting their tenets of religion and placing the opinions of the United States authorities before the audience … he was received with such enthusiastic demonstrations of unpopularity belonging rather to the class than to the individual, that he was compelled to desist for five minutes at a time."[106]

103. The missionary probably was James Chandler. See Davis, "James Jarvis Chandler," 116.

104. Records indicate that Charles Cripps (1795–1879) had been baptized on May 25, 1850, by David Shorten. Charles Cripps sailed on the *Amazon*, June 4, 1864; his wife, Elizabeth (1801–1901), came three years earlier aboard the *Underwriter*, on April 18, 1861. Cripps Papers.

105. See "Discussion of Mormonism at Swansea," *Millennial Star*, July 16, 1888, 455, hereafter cited as "Discussion of Mormonism." See also "Lectures in Wales," *Deseret News*, Apr. 11, 1888, 7. The paper noted he had "a large audience who listened with close attention, the only exception being an attempt on the part of a number of rowdy youths to create a disturbance."

106. "Discussion of Mormonism," 455.

According to the *Cambria Daily Leader*,[107] Roberts traced the history of the church, its migration to Utah, and the efforts of the federal government to oppose his people. As voices were raised protesting polygamy, Roberts said his noisy critics were "paid" agents of Jarman's and quoted Episcopal Bishop Daniel S. Tuttle, "an honorable opponent of Mormonism," that the Mormons were patriotic people. Then, "in deference to the repeated requests of a noisy mob at the back of the hall," Roberts talked about the Mountain Meadows Massacre. Roberts told the audience, inaccurately, that Brigham Young "and those who stood by him" were exonerated by the government from involvement, and said John D. Lee had "for the sake of booty induced the Indians to attack the party," while appealing to a group of local residents to "defend the travelers from the Indians." Roberts then stated that some "of the people went out upon this misrepresentation, but when they found the true state of affairs they returned to their homes, and fearing they would be implicated, they resolved to keep the matter quiet." But Lee was tried "at the hands of a Mormon jury" and executed. The paper reported that the "interruption at this juncture became so great" that Roberts was forced to simply restate his main points. Only when it was announced that the money raised by admission fees was to be given to the Cambrian Institution for the Blind was order restored.

After a debate the next night, a "large crowd followed the Elders to their lodgings at my house, and there was some shouting and hissing, but nothing further was attempted, and neither shouting nor hissing break bones." In a letter to the editor of the *Daily Leader*, Roberts noted that he was "deeply grateful to Captain Barrett of the Sailors' Home," who "insisted, notwithstanding my protests, upon taking my arm and accompanying me to my lodgings, that the weight of his character and respect for his grey hairs might be to me a shield from the insults and prospective violence of the crowd which had gathered in the streets and followed me to my house."[108] He reported that in addition to the "insults and prospective violence"

107. See "Reply to Mr. Jarman," *Millennial Star*, July 23, 1888, 468–70. See also "Mormons In Wales," *Utah Enquirer*, July 27, 1888, 1.

108. B. H. Roberts, "Elder Roberts's Letter to the Editor of the Leader," *Millennial Star*, July 23, 1888, 475–76. Hereafter cited as "Elder Roberts's Letter."

a large number of young men "called upon me to express their regret at my not having a better opportunity of defending myself."

Roberts used Jarman's crusade to advance the church's public image. In July 1888, for example, the *Herald of Wales* published a long interview with Roberts that not only dealt with Jarman, but covered other topics including reasons behind the immigration to Utah. Describing Roberts as open and pleasant, the reporter asked Roberts if he had known Jarman in Utah to which he replied he had never met him until their initial debate in London the previous year. Roberts told the reporter that Jarman "admitted in his book that he had escaped from a lunatic asylum," and that he had contacted the staff at the Exminster Asylum, who had confirmed that Jarman had indeed been housed there. Such information, Roberts indicated, was "a new revelation to me; it afforded an explanation to the pretended horrors he details" about Mormonism. Roberts continued that if he had known about Jarman's time in the asylum, instead of debating him, he would have published it in "the papers, and then, if people wished to fall in with the ravings of a madman all well and good until they learned better." Roberts concluded that it understood now that Jarman's "blood-curdling stories" about Utah and the Mormons were "merely the coinage of a mind diseased."[109]

Schofield later remembered the efforts against Jarman as a "campaign that required two solid years before the enemy was finally subdued." He said it was "exceedingly doubtful" that anyone other than Roberts could "have successfully waged this fight because Jarman had all the cunning, all the craftiness and showmanship and all the oratorical ability of the devil himself."[110] However, Jarman continued to lecture and write on Mormonism until his death nearly thirty years later.[111]

109. "Interviewing Elder Roberts, The Mormon," *Millennial Star*, July 23, 1888, 485. Hereafter cited as "Interviewing Elder Roberts."

110. Schofield, Autobiographical Reminiscence.

111. "W. Jarman, Apostate Dies in England," *Salt Lake Telegram*, July 29, 1917, 39. The paper notes that in addition to his anti-Mormon crusades, Jarman had done much for "the poor people of the city in which he lived," was "very generous," and held "several high positions of honor." Moreover, Jarman came to Utah several times in later years. See "City and Neighborhood," *Salt Lake Tribune*, July 20, 1899, 4, which notes that Jarman was in the city "seeking title to several millions of dollars of Salt Lake property." See also "Jarman to Begin Suit," *Salt Lake Tribune*, Sep. 13, 1899, 5.

Beyond the campaign against Jarman specifically, Schofield noted that "hundreds of times," he and Roberts used London's Hyde Park corner as their pulpit. Under "the brilliant lights one may find a dozen or score of groups listening to some embryonic Demosthenes regaling his audience on religion, politics, labor unions or what have you."[112] Roberts's eloquence soon became known and frequently the crowds, deserting other speakers, would flock in a body to hear him. Lorenzo J. Haddock heard Roberts speak in Hyde Park frequently, later recalling that the young Roberts was "the nemesis of various open-air orators" regardless of their ideology and they were left to combine forces "to drive him from the place for such meetings because their followers deserted them whenever 'that Mormon' began to speak."[113] Roberts later said that while it was difficult to "preach the gospel at Hyde Park," he was "desperately in love with London," and if he were a "man of the world," he would live there.[114]

As "in love" with London as he was, Roberts would occasionally get tired. Sometimes he would find his task so difficult that he wished he could turn away from "humanity with all its pride" and simply "play the hermit" instead. He labeled missionary work at times a "thankless task," marked by hardship and heartache, and said that if anyone thought it was "pleasant" work to go "into the world and combat the terrible prejudice existing against faith he by all means ought to try it."[115] Most of the time, however, he relished the challenge. He wrote to apostle Joseph F. Smith that he knew "that the Gospel is true; and that behind us and sustaining us is the God of heaven and however many blunders are made He will at last in His own way and time come to our deliverance." Roberts was committed to his faith, and until God brought the deliverance he awaited, or "until death shall put a period to my labors in this life, I hope to be faithful and do nothing that will forfeit my right to the blessings promised under the new and everlasting covenant."[116]

Many times, because of his love of literature, Roberts took the opportunity to visit the homes and important places associated with

112. Schofield, Autobiographical Reminiscence.
113. Madsen, *Defender of the Faith*, 113.
114. Madsen, 165.
115. Madsen.
116. As quoted in Madsen, 178–79.

writers like Byron, Scott, Shakespeare, and others. Roberts also had a fascination for English history and politics. Upon returning from one of these trips, he reflected in his diary that he was grateful for the chance to tour the countryside, noting that he believed that "the grandeur of the scenery through which I have passed will have the effect of ennobling my nature, & making me thirst after the beautiful, virtuous & grand." He felt that he was "sorely in need of such influences" and wrote "shame upon him who has such opportunities if they do not increase his love for the virtuous, the beautiful, & the god-like."[117]

In January 1888, Roberts received a letter from his friend and mentor John Morgan, written after returning to Utah from Colorado. Morgan discussed his release from the Southern States Mission, saying that he felt "a great load had lifted off my shoulders and felt myself suddenly grow many years younger." He also noted that he was "walking the streets of Salt Lake in broad daylight, coming and going at my very own sweet pleasure" since he felt the statute of limitations had expired "at least until the next offense." He then told Roberts that "prior to my leaving," he had read an "account of your bout with Jarman in London and trust you have, at least, succeeded in temporarily stopping his devilment. It was possibly the only thing that could be done, but it is so humiliating to an Elder to have to stoop to contend with such degraded spirits. I have often thought that Satan was a gentleman besides such vermin."[118]

The next month Roberts wrote an article titled "The Growth and Stability of Mormonism," which appeared in the March 3 issue of the *Herald of Wales*, and was later reprinted in both the *North Gazette* and the *Cambria Daily Leader*.[119] By this point, Roberts was seen as a positive public face of Mormonism, one whose articulate discourses could be used to counter opposition. In the lengthy article, Roberts quoted the words of Henry Ward Beecher, after returning from a trip to Utah, who counseled that Mormonism's "ignoble origin must not lead you to despise it," and suggested that observers of the faith look at it in terms of its accomplishments and actions. Mormons

117. Roberts, *History's Apprentice*, 199 (Aug. 8, 1887).

118. Morgan to Roberts, Jan. 15, 1888, box 3, fd. 1. Roberts Papers (BYU).

119. B. H. Roberts, "The Growth and Stability of Mormonism," *Millennial Star*, Mar. 12, 1888, 163–66. Hereafter cited as "Growth."

"may be pardoned if they conclude that their church has outgrown its infancy, and has developed into a sturdy, promising youth, and is rapidly approaching within sight of a glorious manhood." Roberts reports that, as of April 1887, the church was seeing a "steady increase" in its membership with some 162,383 members in Utah alone.[120] He then asserted that the church's strength "consists not so much in their numbers, as in the character of the community." Roberts extolled the practices and beliefs of the Saints that "requires them to abstain from the use of intoxicants, tea, coffee, tobacco, and only to indulge in a temperate use of meat. It also teaches them industry, cleanliness, frugality and honesty." Mormonism taught its adherence "reverence for God, and faith in future existence, the degree of happiness which depends upon their faith, devotion, and righteousness in this life."[121]

In an article on the prophecies of Joseph Smith published in the *Millennial Star,* Roberts, still signing as "R," noted that "it has become proverbial that the more 'Mormonism' is opposed the better it thrives." He quoted former Confederate vice president Alexander Stephens that "when asked what would be the result of … the United States Congress to crush out 'Mormonism' by legislative enactments, his laconic, yet wise reply was, 'The result will be to make more 'Mormons.'"[122] Anticipating the attacks on the church over polygamy, Roberts wrote that Mormonism "enjoins" on its adherents a "strictly chaste life" and said it held that "chastity" was equally expected for men and women, and, in Victorian terms, asserted that "any violation of it is as reprehensible in man, and even more so, than in woman." Mormonism believed marriage was honorable, children were a "heritage from the Lord," and as a result, its adherents "are not recruited from the lower strata of society," but rather from the "most energetic, vigorous and desirable portion of it."[123] Roberts went on to sketch the Joseph Smith story, describe Mormonism's spread from New York to Ohio to Illinois to Utah, and offer a brief overview of the Book of Mormon's origin and message. Contemporary

120. Roberts explained that this number does not include "Australia, New Zealand, the European countries not the Eastern nor Southern States of America."

121. "Growth," 163–64.

122. R, "Was He a Prophet?" *Millennial Star,* June 27, 1887, 410.

123. "Growth," 164.

efforts in Congress to destroy the church via the Edmunds–Tucker Act, Roberts wrote, were not new, and that through its inception Mormonism

> has been assailed by powerful foes from without, and frequently betrayed by false friends from within; though the course it has trod has led the Saints through floods of affliction and … the blood of their leaders and many of their brethren stains the free soil of the United States, and their trail across the dreary plains from the Missouri to the Rocky Mountains could at one time be traced by their graves, still Mormonism survives … and today it is beginning to be respected and recognized as a permanent institution.[124]

Roberts later realized that as a result of his many editorial efforts, he "formulated quite an extended treatment of the gospel,"[125] which later became the foundation of his first book, published in 1888 as *The Gospel: An Exposition of its First Principles.*[126] John Morgan would say of the book that it was "very minute in all of its details and contains a large amount of information."[127]

Roberts remained deeply involved in the editorial and production work of the *Millennial Star*, a task he found very satisfying. He later recalled that the publication's offices at "42 Islington [Street] was about five minutes walk from the very celebrated Liverpool Picton Library … at which I spent my leisure time, making an immense collection of notes about evidences of American antiquities and archeological works which provided external evidences for the Book of Mormon."[128] Beyond the library, the neighborhood itself seemed friendly to the Saints as they labored there. A small lodging house, known as Stewart's Hotel, adjoined the *Millennial Star's* office on the south. The hotel, which was likely where Roberts resided, was run by William Andrew Stewart; he was remembered as one

124. "Growth," 166.

125. Roberts, *Autobiography*, 165. See also Teasdale Journal, Jan. 16, 1887.

126. The book was later revised and published as *The Gospel: An Exposition of its First Principles and Man's Relation to Deity* (Salt Lake City: George Q. Cannon, 1893). It represented one of Roberts's most important contributions to Mormon thought. In referring to the "revised and enlarged edition" of the book, the *Deseret Weekly* believed that "the work … in its new dress will prove to be a valuable addition on the library of all interested in theological topics." See "A Good Book," *Deseret Weekly*, Mar. 11, 1893, 862.

127. Morgan Journal, Feb. 4, 1889.

128. Roberts, *Autobiography*, 173.

who provided "many acts of kindness to the Elders and their friends while under his roof."[129]

Roberts's time in England was also marked by the death of three individuals who had played a significant role in his life. The first was his friend and mentor, church president John Taylor, who died on July 25, 1887, at Kaysville. While Roberts lost an ally, Taylor's death opened up an opportunity to write a significant biography of Mormonism's third president, something he would undertake in a few years. Erastus Snow passed away on May 27, 1888. He had provided Roberts with a positive view of plural marriage during the time both were in Colorado.[130] The third death was that of Horace S. Eldredge,[131] whose demise would make room for Roberts to join the Seven Presidents of Seventy. These deaths must have given him pause not only for the loss personally and the impact they had on the church, but also because he was unable to attend the funeral services. He must have felt that despite all his opportunities he was a long way from home.

Roberts wrote to Apostle Joseph F. Smith about the anxieties he felt concerning his families after nearly two years of absence from them. While he had been able to communicate with Louisa, he could not write Celia, who was living in Logan under the name "Mrs. Ellison." He admitted that he found the situation draining; he also worried about providing for his family and told Smith he "would prefer to go home, plead guilty to the charge, go to prison for six months," then he could live as a monogamist while still working for "both families … for they have need of my doing so, since I have no income but what my labor can secure, and the reflection that my family is upon the charity of others breaks my spirit."[132] George Q. Cannon wrote that the First Presidency was helping the "Family of B. H. Roberts" during his absence. On January 26, 1888, there was an appropriation

129. "Untitled," *Millennial Star* Jan. 9, 1893, 37.

130. See previous chapter.

131. Horace S. Eldredge (1816–88) was a member of the Seven Presidents of the Seventy from October 1854 until his death. He was an important figure in territorial Utah, and among other things, served in the legislature and as superintendent of ZCMI. Roberts had worked with his son James in the Southern States Mission.

132. As quoted in Madsen, *Defender of the Faith*, 179.

of $200.[133] Two weeks later Cannon said that "Bro. B. H. Roberts's family was assisted by an appropriation of $40.00 per month, to be divided between his families, and $100.00 to defray overdrafts that may have been made by them at the Tithing Office."[134]

Despite being thousands of miles away, Roberts kept in touch with many friends and was aware of the situation many faced because of their commitment to plural marriage. In light of this Roberts must have been worried about his own fate, as well as that of his wives and families. John Morgan, for example, went out of his way to visit Louisa when he was in Centerville attending to Seventies assignments.[135] In August he noted that he had visited Louisa and "stayed the day" with her in Centerville while federal deputies were in pursuit.[136] Roberts realized how hard his absence was on his first wife:

> I have a great deal of sympathy for Louisa; on the whole she is having a hard time of it. ... It has been the dream of Lou's life to have a quiet home and a husband with her always. I guess I suit her & all that if it was not for the fact that I am such a flyaway & all the time on the wing, & have been unsettled for which, of course, I am not to blame. I suppose I was born to be so. But then I have not always been as wise and considerate as I should have been, or might have been—who is? But at any rate I love Lou dearly and though I have reproved sharply at times, and do so now & expect to do so whenever occasion requires, yet she is very dear to me & I love her more than she thinks I do, & have it in my heart to do good and will too.[137]

At the end of the summer of 1888, Roberts received a cable from church president Wilford Woodruff indicating that he had been released and should return home. Roberts noted in his autobiography that he did not understand exactly what had prompted this "unexpected call" but goes on to say that it became "a settled conviction with me that ... the ... call to return home had something to do with the settlement of the $1000 bond note that was to hold me to appear in court on the charges of unlawful cohabitation." Regardless

133. Cannon Journal, Jan. 26, 1888.
134. Cannon Journal, Feb. 10, 1888.
135. Morgan Journal, Jan. 29 and Mar. 4, 1888.
136. Morgan Journal, Aug. 3, 1887.
137. Roberts to Mother, Feb. 5, 1888, box 4, fd 5, Roberts Papers (UU).

of the reasons, Roberts "prepared to leave the British Isles in response to the release."[138]

George Teasdale met with Roberts and "had an interview with him on finances etc. Bro. D. M McAllister and myself laid hands upon him. I was mouth in blessing. Bro Roberts was afflicted by neuralgia pains.[139] We are all sorry to be separated. We have had so pleasant a time together working in such harmony and good feeling that it makes the separation far more painful." Later that day Teasdale accompanied Roberts and a group of departing missionaries to the dock: "Here we parted. I to go to Wales and Bro. Brigham to Zion. God bless him, heal him of all his pains and restore him in peace and safety to his family and friends and preserve him from his enemies."[140] There is nothing in the *Millennial Star* after September 1 announcing the departure, though the publication's pages are typically full of the comings and goings of missionaries. The mission history states simply that Roberts left on September 1, 1888, aboard the *Wyoming*.[141] Roberts is not listed among the passengers of the ship, suggesting he was still being cautious as a man wanted on cohabitation charges.[142]

Roberts's group arrived in New York on September 11.[143] Willard Hansen, another missionary who, unlike Roberts, was listed as a passenger, noted that they had enjoyed "good weather across the ocean," and that after their arrival in New York, he spent several days seeing the sights with Roberts and "had a very good time"[144] Roberts wrote almost nothing about his journey home, except to say in his autobiography that of "the account of my journey across the Atlantic, and the continent to Utah we shall pass."[145]

Once he was back in Utah, Roberts's "whereabouts were known only by the intimate circle of his family and friends."[146] With the

138. Roberts, *Autobiography*, 173.

139. Neuralgia is often characterized by a shooting pain in the face.

140. Teasdale Diary, Sep. 1, 1888, in Teasdale Papers (UU).

141. Built in 1870, the ship made numerous voyages from Liverpool to New York until it was scrapped in 1893.

142. British Mission Manuscript History. Nor is there any mention of Reed.

143. British Mission Manuscript History.

144. Hansen Diary, Sep. 1888, in Hansen Papers.

145. Roberts, *Autobiography*, 173.

146. See Malan, *B. H. Roberts*, 41.

death of Eldredge, the surviving members of the First Council of Seventy had been requested to recommend ordained Seventies to fill the vacancy. George Reynolds's name was first but he was vetoed by George Q. Cannon because he was thought to be too valuable as secretary. Others on the list included Roberts, Job Pingree, and Joseph W. Summerhays.[147] On October 7, Heber J. Grant presented Roberts's name at general conference to act as one of the First Seven Presidents of Seventy to replace Horace S. Eldredge.[148] Roberts was formally sustained to the office, and received his ordination two days later at the hands of Lorenzo Snow[149] in the Church Historian's office.[150]

Roberts's selection to a church body that supervised missionary work was a logical choice in light of his experiences over the past few years.[151] As he noted in his autobiography, the Seven Presidents of Seventy "have a double office. First they preside directly over the First Quorum of Seventy ... [but it] is also the third general presiding council of the church, the other two being the ... first presidency and ... the Council of the Twelve Apostles. The First seven presidents also preside indirectly over all the Seventy in the church."[152]

However, this new lifetime assignment came without financial compensation, and Roberts's family situation required paid work. During the next few months, still in hiding from federal marshals, Roberts took over the editorship of the *Contributor* and "wrote

147. Van Orden, *Prisoner for Conscience Sake*, 161. John Morgan recorded that these four names were "chosen out of quite a number submitted" to the authorities. See Morgan Journal, Oct. 3, 1888.

148. See "The Closing Day," *Salt Lake Herald*, Oct. 9, 1888, 2; and "General Conference," *Deseret News*, Oct. 8, 1888, 2. Interestingly at an overflow meeting that day held in the Assembly Hall those in attendance heard from Roberts's friend John Morgan and first missionary companion, William M. Palmer. See "The Overflow Meeting," *Deseret News*, Oct. 8, 1888, 2. See also Morgan Journal, Oct. 7, 1888.

149. Smith, *Church, State and Politics*, 209.

150. Truman Madsen found "no record" of the text "of his ordination blessing." See Madsen, *Defender of the Faith*, 180.

151. As he explains, the Seventies "are a group of men organized into quorums of seventy members in each quorum and presided over locally by seven presidents chosen from among the number of the quorum." Roberts would hold this lifetime calling until his death in 1933. During that nearly fifty-year period, he would routinely visit and encourage individual quorums of Seventy, which at the time of his death constituted 234 separate quorums. See Roberts, *Autobiography*, 174.

152. Roberts.

nearly all of the ... editorials" that appeared in the publication "under the nom de plume of Horatio and Gratiano,"[153] though, oddly enough, the name of B. H. Roberts was also prominently featured in the pages of the *Contributor* after he returned to Utah.

By April 1889 Roberts had concluded that "the time arrived ... to surrender to the federal authorities." He had been assured there would be no attempt to collect the bond that had been initially posted and "that a severe sentence would not be urged by the prosecuting attorney." Aware that these events had put his mother under "mental distress," he went to see her and told her that "this was an opportunity to get the penalty, whatever it might be" behind him.[154]

His attorney, LeGrand Young, attempted to postpone the case for two weeks by arguing that Roberts needed time to take care of his families, but was denied.[155] Roberts admitted marriage to Celia, told the court he had fathered one child with her, and that he had no statement to make to the court.[156] At the sentencing, Judge Sandford[157] scolded Roberts, saying that he had "deliberately, in full knowledge of the law, married another wife, and lived with her and she had one child. You make no statement of regret for what you have done, nor do you make any promise as to your future conduct."

153. These names—Horatio from *Hamlet* and Gratiano from the *Merchant of Venice*—reflect Roberts's recent experiences in England as well as his love of Shakespeare. Roberts's writing had appeared in the *Contributor* under Horatio and Gratiano as early as December 1887. See Horatio, "A Visit to Newstead Abbey," *Contributor*, Dec. 1887, 49–56. Roberts's other works under this name and published in the *Contributor* include: "The Religion of Robert Burns," Nov. 1, 1888, 30–33, and Dec. 1888, 66–68; "A Story of Zarahemla," Jan., 1889, 94–101; "Legitimate Fiction," Feb. 1889, 133–36; "The Demon of Socrates," Mar. 1889, 164–67; and "Why Christianity Lives," Apr. 1889, 218–20. The pseudonym Gratiano seems not to appear.

154. Roberts, *Autobiography*, 175.

155. See "Judicial and Criminal," *Salt Lake Tribune*, Apr. 30, 1889, 6; "The Jurors Hang," *Salt Lake Herald*, Apr. 30, 1889, 8; and "B. H. Roberts Surrenders," *Utah Enquirer*, Apr. 30, 1889, 2.

156. "B. H. Roberts's Case," *Salt Lake Herald*, May 2, 1889, 5. Roberts gave the year of his marriage to Celia as 1883. According to court records, some 498 individuals were convicted of unlawful cohabitation between 1884 and 1888, which, when added to the convictions for polygamy, amounted to a total of 514 convictions. During that same period, more than $44,000 in fines were collected as well. See "Prosecutions for Polygamy," *Millennial Star*, Oct. 8, 1888, 659.

157. In his autobiography, Roberts misidentifies the Judge as Ogden Hiles. In fact, Hiles was an assistant US Attorney. The US Attorney who led the effort in court against Roberts was George Peters.

Saying that because Roberts was a first-time offender, he was not "disposed to be severe," but added that not only did he not see any regret or remorse, it appeared that Roberts had no intention to obey the law in the future. In his autobiography Roberts writes that the judge implied that he did "not need to go to jail at all if he will only promise to obey the law for the future." To this, he said he replied *sotto voce*, "Judge, you know that would be a promise impossible for me to make."[158] However, nothing of this conversation is reflected in the press accounts. Roberts was sentenced to four months in the Utah penitentiary with a fine of $200 and court costs.[159]

The penitentiary was run by Arthur Pratt, one of the marshals who had arrested Roberts in the *Herald* office in 1886.[160] Roberts noticed tension between those imprisoned for violating polygamy or unlawful cohabitation laws and the "toughs" who were sentenced as a result of committing crimes like burglary, robbery, or murder. During Roberts's period of incarceration, some one hundred different individuals served all or part of that time for either polygamy or unlawful cohabitation.[161] Built originally in 1855, the prison consisted of two bunkhouses and was located in Sugar House some six miles southeast of downtown Salt Lake City. A twenty-foot-high adobe wall surrounded the facility, and on the outside were various outbuildings, including the warden's office and residence. In May 1888, officials built a third bunkhouse out of "two-by-sixes laid flat and spiked together for walls, floor and ceiling."[162] They proved to be a good breeding ground for bed bugs. The new addition was not large but had room for some fifty inmates who slept in bunkbeds surrounded a small heating stove, and a few "windows and ventilating shafts in the roof relieved the stuffiness." Outside the barracks were several other buildings including an infirmary, bathrooms, washrooms, and a dining hall where "several large tables" stood in

158. Roberts, *Autobiography*, 175. Roberts defends his action, noting that there were still points in the definition of the law before the Supreme Court of the United States that had not been settled. "Hence to be true to my conviction and the contention then going on, as to the rightfulness of the position of the Church, I was under the stress of moral obligation to uphold the position of the church, which I did."

159. "Current Events," *Deseret Weekly*, Sep. 21, 1889, 16.

160. See Van Wagoner and Van Wagoner, "Arthur Pratt," 22–35.

161. See Larson, *Prisoner for Polygamy*.

162. See Jenson, *Church Chronology*, 162.

the middle of a roughly constructed Spartan structure that could accommodate one hundred diners at a time.[163]

Roberts's life in prison was "monotonous," broken up by people who wanted to "gratify their curiosity at seeing Mormons in prison." While there, Roberts, perhaps remembering his own wayward youth, was able to befriend some of the "toughs," noting that he "had the patience and broadness to listen to the stories of the worst prisoners, and they often confided to me the adventures which brought them to their present place of conflict with society and the laws." He was clear that he did not approve of their behavior or "sympathize with their lawlessness and warfare upon society but because I had a habit, while their crimes were hateful to me, of considering the criminal apart from the crime and holding out hopeful possibilities for them."[164]

Roberts received many gifts from the outside, ranging from cigars to wholesome food and preserved fruit which he distributed to his "fellow prisoners," both cohabs and toughs, which tended to give him "standing" among the inmates while improving the "monotony of prison food."[165] John Morgan visited Roberts a few times, noting that he "had a pleasant visit" with Roberts "who was looking and feeling well."[166] The time there broadened him, and opened his eyes to the plight of many men who otherwise he would have never known, while strengthening his disposition to "aid the under-dog in strife or those under the wheels of society's juggernaut." Roberts soon came to the attention of prison officials who proposed that he become a trustee, an offer he declined because he viewed himself "as a prisoner of honor" who would "fulfill my term as proscribed without favors."[167]

Roberts was released on September 10, 1889. In addition to the four-month sentence, he apparently served an extra thirty days to cover the fine and court costs.[168] The recently appointed warden,

163. Hedges and Holzapfel, *Within These Prison Walls*, xli. The book also contains a drawing of the ground plan of the bunkhouse. See also Bashore, "Life Behind Bars," 22.

164. Roberts, *Autobiography*, 177.

165. Roberts.

166. Morgan Journal, July 10, 1889.

167. For a good overview of these experiences, see Roberts, *Autobiography*, 175–80. See also Madsen, *Defender of the Faith*, 186–98.

168. Historian's Office, Journal History, Sep. 10, 1889, 2.

Joseph Amos,[169] admonished Roberts to "abide by the law in the future," and expressed a hope, with which Roberts "heartily" concurred, that he would "not be seen again within prison walls." Roberts later wrote that he was not "abandoning the plural family I had established. … On the contrary, I resolved that there should be no sacrifice or abandonment but contrived to … establish my family in the settlement of Colorado."[170] So, though Louisa and her five children would continue to live in Davis County, Celia, pregnant with their second child (a son named Harold Dibble Roberts, born January 17, 1890) along with their daughter, Lena, relocated to Manassa.[171] Celia would find herself both pleased and pained by the move. On the one hand, she developed close relationships with the other general authorities' wives, especially Emily Wells Grant, wife of Heber J. Grant—but these plural wives and their children "constituted less than 10 percent of Manassa." Historian Ronald W. Walker summed up the plight of polygamous wives in this era: "Many women longed for something more than occasional marital companionship. They saw themselves as second-class wives, living outside the law and subject to arrest."[172]

Free from jail, Roberts lectured about his prison experiences. On September 29, Roberts "spoke for one hour upon his imprisonment" in the Salt Lake Tabernacle.[173] He said that "rather than cast aside those dearer than life, men have unhesitatingly gone to prison … and women and children have been exiled." There had been a "great deal" of suffering—both physical and mental—especially "for those least able to endure it," women and children. The "object of

169. Amos, who came from the Ohio State Penitentiary, had replaced Arthur Pratt on July 27, 1889. A local paper reported that Pratt was seen by most prisoners as providing "kind treatment" and enforced "strict discipline by firm yet gentle means." It appears he was Joseph Amos (1838–1909) who had served as a member of Co. H, 46th Ohio Volunteers in the Civil War. The local papers referred to him as "Captain Amos," but he had mustered out as a lieutenant. See Van Wagoner and Van Wagoner, "Arthur Pratt," 22. See also "A New Warden," *Deseret Weekly*, Aug. 3, 1889, 4.

170. Roberts, *Autobiography*, 180.

171. See Roberts, *History's Apprentice*, 203–18 (Nov. 3–Dec. 11, 1890).

172. See Walker, "Mormon 'Widow.'"

173. Woodruff, *Wilford Woodruff's Journal*, 9:55 Woodruff reported that Roberts not only talked about polygamy and persecution, but he also gave an overview of the organization of the US government, and gave his views on conditions in Europe, and the possibility of European wars.

our enemies," Roberts said, "has been neither more nor less than the destruction of the Church of Christ … [b]ut the church is still here. The Church has stood unmoved in the midst of hate." Prison had not tamed Roberts; he exhorted the faithful to "adhere firmly to the divine principles entrusted to their care," and God would "bring them deliverance, and protect them in the path of duty."[174]

On November 10 he was in Ogden speaking on "agnosticism" at the Weber Stake's semi-annual conference. He noted that after a "four year absence," he found himself back in Ogden and wanted to see what changes had taken place in the city. "I passed up a street I once knew. It was Main street, now metamorphosed into Washington avenue. I saw a building I had not seen before. On it was written 'Agnostic Hall—Let it Shine!' What a paradox! It would have been better 'Darkness, let it shine.'" Roberts said that this sign got him to think about agnosticism, and from there he "studied in order to give you the result of my investigation." Since his listeners were mainly priesthood-holding men, it was incumbent upon them of "not only knowing the truth but to teach it to your fellow men. You must then be intelligently informed on the errors taught as well as the truth received."[175] Roberts traced the development of agnosticism, linking it to the writings of Aldous Huxley, who in mid-life began to wonder if he was an "infidel Christian or a free thinker." Over time, he chose the term "agnostic" to differentiate himself from the "nostic of church history who professed to know so much." Ultimately, he said, Huxley came to believe agnosticism was a middle ground between atheism and belief. As a result, Roberts concluded that "agnosticism is by far more dangerous" than atheism

> for it comes to us in a less offensive form. The old style, 'there is no God,' so shocks us that we shun the speaker and his views. The agnostic comes smoothly, slyly winning the respect of his victims and then … in the nicety of difference between the two … one is the bold criminal the other the sly seducer. By other definitions we learn that agnosticism is not a creed but a method in which you should follow your own judgement and intellect. … We are told that one who accepts this method can

174. "Sunday Services," *Deseret Evening News*, Sep. 30, 1889, 2; and "Religious Services, *Deseret Weekly*, Oct. 12, 1889, 13.

175. "Sunday and Monday," (Ogden) *Semi-Weekly Standard,* Nov. 13, 1889, 7.

> look the universe in the face and without fear look to the future. … We can here judge the results of this philosophy. There is nothing in it but uncertainty except its disbelief in God. … Agnosticism is sapping the vitals of Christianity today.[176]

Roberts exhorted his listeners that there was no excuse for any Latter-day Saint to "believe that there is no God." The Saints, he said, had seen, and would continue to see, the fulfillment of God's prophecies; that they knew there was "sufficient data" to demonstrate that God's word, through Joseph Smith, was coming to pass.[177]

Roberts was called to join the "Defense Fund," a committee that included two sons of John Taylor's—Apostle John W. Taylor and Frank Y. Taylor—to raise resources for those "hailed before the courts" charged with violating federal polygamy laws and who lacked sufficient resources to defend themselves. Roberts was also on the lookout for gainful employment and soon took to writing for church publications, including the *Semi-Weekly Herald*. And, throughout it all, he continued to serve in his capacity as a member of the First Council of Seventy.

176. "Sunday and Monday."
177. "Sunday and Monday."

SEVEN

POLITICAL TENSIONS AND THE WORLD'S FAIR

As a new year and a new decade began, Roberts returned to his usual routine—writing and ecclesiastical duties—but his time was increasingly occupied with partisan political activity. The latter role was not new; as early as 1882, he spoke throughout Davis County in support of John T. Caine's campaign for territorial delegate.

On January 1, 1890, the First Presidency called Roberts, along with his old friend John Morgan, to speak out in public against attitudes—in the words of Heber J. Grant—"engendered by the late decision of Judge Anderson."[1] Government attorneys had charged the Mormons with disloyalty to the federal government, and though the church had called a large group of leaders and lay members to testify, Judge Thomas Anderson[2] of the Third District Court ruled against the church, "issuing a sweeping indictment of church doctrine and practice."[3] Anderson's ruling condemned the Saints' belief that it saw itself above the law of the land as the kingdom of God, and, as historian Thomas Alexander, wrote, it "would eventually overthrow the United States and all other governments."[4] Anderson's decision effectively ended citizenship for future Mormon immigrants.[5]

In response, the First Presidency concluded in December 1889 that Roberts and Morgan should "go east and labor as opportunity

1. Grant Journal, Jan. 1, 1890, as quoted in Alexander, *Things in Heaven and Earth*, 411.

2. Anderson (1837–1910) was from Iowa. An active Democrat, he was involved in local politics serving as Marion County Surveyor, 1858–60 and editor of the *Democratic Standard*. Admitted to the Iowa Bar in 1860, he entered military service in 1862 and was a lieutenant in Company A, 40th Iowa Infantry until 1865. After a defeat for Iowa governor as a Democrat in 1887, he was appointed Assistant Commissioner of the General Land Office, which led to the Utah judicial appointment.

3. Alexander, *Things in Heaven and Earth*, 256.

4. Alexander.

5. See Alexander, "Odyssey of a Latter-day Prophet," and Alexander, "Charles S. Zane."

offered with the press, in endeavoring to correct the false rumors and statements that were afloat, and to create, if possible, a public opinion more favorable to the truth on our question."[6] George Q. Cannon met with the two men and "explained to them the character of the duties that they were expected to perform on their mission east."[7]

On Sunday, January 5, 1890, Roberts spoke at the Salt Lake Tabernacle about the political intentions of the Saints after they had arrived in Salt Lake Valley and their commitment to the US Constitution. He denied that it had "been the purpose of the Latter-day Saints to establish an independent kingdom in the land, their opportunity was when they first entered this valley. They were removed a thousand miles from the frontiers of the United States." The Saints were isolated at the time, and no rapid communication existed, yet "as soon as practicable" the Saints "applied for admission into the Union. They could not forget … that their destiny was intertwined with the destiny of the nation whose Constitution God had inspired." Thus, when the Civil War broke out, the Saints were not tempted to join the Confederacy though overtures were made. Despite the anti-polygamy legislation and the "unjust laws" of the present day, the Mormon people would "hug hard those principles of liberty which are intertwined with the rest of the country." The *Salt Lake Tribune* commented that this was the first time that they had ever heard about the South approaching the Saints at the beginning of the Civil War. "It is hardly probable that if such a thing occurred the Mormons leaders would have kept quite about it all these years." While Roberts spoke, "an old man wearing a long silk robe … and carrying a banner" stood and announced that he was Christ. The man "created a great commotion," and while many "arose to get a look at him," Roberts told them to sit and pay attention to his discourse.[8]

Roberts began to take an active partisan role, supporting the successful candidacy of John T. Caine in 1890, and two years later that of Joseph L. Rawlins, both elected territorial delegates as Democrats.[9]

6. Cannon Journal, Dec. 17, 1889.
7. Cannon Journal, Dec. 28, 1889.
8. "Elder B. H. Roberts's Fictions," *Salt Lake Tribune*, Jan. 9, 1890, 4.
9. See Haslam, "Utah's Delegates to Congress," 228–55.

As a result of his support for them, Roberts realized that his "reputation as a political advocate received immense impetus. Without my being conscious of it, I was rising as one of the political factors to be accounted for in the future."[10] Indeed, as a result of his growing visibility, Roberts became known as a forceful advocate of the territorial Democratic Party, and he solidified the label he had previously earned of the "Blacksmith Orator." He would later be remembered as "[l]ogical in mind, eloquent of speech, majestically emotional in expression," and, as a result, no one who had ever seen

> his leonine mane, his handsome, magnificently sculptured face, his flashing eyes, his powerful figure, has ever remained unmoved during one of his masterful speeches. To say that B. H. Roberts was to be the speaker upon any occasion—patriotic, political, social, or religious—was to draw to the meeting place all those who could by any means be there. His tongue had the power to cut like the sword of the Lord or to soothe or to buoy up like the whisper of angels.[11]

Roberts left on January 7 for his speaking tour. He met Morgan "at the Union Depot in Denver," and the two arrived in New York City on the morning of January 13. They met with John W. Young to "have a long talk with him over the situation,"[12] and the next day, "after a long search," secured a permanent residence "at 110 W. 29th Street at $7 per week." Initially, they drafted an article for the *New York Herald* "in hopes they would accept the facts we presented as their own." However, as Roberts said of many newspapers, they "refused to do anything with this matter on the merits of the case; but if our situation would [affect] the political issues of the Country, they were willing we should have a hearing."[13] So Roberts and Morgan found a way to link their views to "the fortunes of the Democratic

10. Roberts, *Autobiography*, 182. Caine served from 1882, when he replaced George Q. Cannon, who was not seated by Congress, until 1893, when Rawlins was elected. Caine was an unsuccessful candidate for governor as a Democrat in 1895, but was elected to the Utah State Senate a year later. On Cannon, see Haslam, "Utah's Delegates to Congress," 132–77. See also Roderick, "Historical Study."

11. "Brigham H. Roberts," *Springville Herald*, Oct. 5, 1933, 2.

12. Morgan Journal, Jan. 13, 1890. Apparently Young and other Mormons in the city had offices at 57 Broadway, where many of the meetings took place.

13. First Council of Seventy, Minutes, Mar. 5, 1890, typed copy in possession of author, hereafter First Council Minutes.

Party," and were thus able to interest Charles A. Dana[14] of the *New York Sun*, who consented to an interview with Morgan "and expressed his willingness to pen its columns for the presentation of our views on those lines." This did not occur, however, because George Q. Cannon had written them suggesting such an approach "might not be wise" if it turned the effort into a partisan issue.

Roberts and Morgan continued to seek out anyone whom they felt could facilitate a positive hearing in the press.[15] They worked with Spencer Clawson, who suggested an interview with the editor of the *New York World*, and set one up for the next day.[16] But when they arrived, the editor was "home unwell," and rescheduled their meeting for January 20.[17] In the meantime, they left their rooming house and moved to the Lincoln Hotel on Broadway and 52nd Street where they paid $10.50 per week. The next morning, they returned to the *World* office and again found that the editor was ill.[18] They spent the next three days trying to meet when they finally made contact with "Mr. Graham, associate editor of the *World*," and spoke with him on January 25. After a "talk of some length," Graham promised "to do something in a day or two."[19] The next day, Roberts and Morgan met with David H. Cannon and others of the local Mormon community, and in the evening "met with Mr. Eakins of the *World* and submitted a statement of the situation in Utah."

Their persistence bore fruit. On January 27, they were the subject of a lengthy article in the *New York World*, which presented the arguments Roberts and Morgan had originally written for the *New York Sun*. The duo accused Republicans in Idaho, Utah, and Arizona territories—with the "active and unscrupulous aid" of the government—of attempting to disenfranchise 300,000 citizens, create

14. Dana (1819–97) controlled the paper from 1868 until his death. By this time, the paper was staunchly opposed to President Benjamin Harrison. The paper also supported conservative Democratic policies.

15. Morgan Journal, Jan. 15–16, 1890.

16. Morgan Journal, Jan. 17, 1890. Coincidentally, while Roberts was occupied that day, Celia delivered her second child and first son, Harold.

17. Morgan Journal, Jan. 18, 1890. In his journal, George Q. Cannon notes his visit but does not mention Roberts or Morgan. Cannon Journal, Jan. 18, 1890.

18. Morgan Journal, Jan. 20, 1890.

19. Morgan Journal, Jan. 25, 1890.

three new states out of those territories, and then use them to swing the 1892 election to the Republican Party.[20]

Indeed, in a lengthy written statement, Roberts and Morgan said legislation by Senator William M. Stewart of Nevada "proposes the wholesale disenfranchisement of the Mormon people thus leaving the political control in these three important territories in the hands of the political wire pullers of the Republican party." If that were to occur, they said, it would deliver the people of these states "into the hands of a crowd of carpet bagger plunderers." Morgan and Roberts noted that part of this effort was predicated on the fact that Idaho already had a clause in its territorial constitution preventing Mormons from voting or serving. They also pointed to recent efforts to remove Utah Territorial Chief Justice Elliot Sandford and A. B. Carlton from the Utah Commission because these Democrats "were out of harmony with the President." The statement went on to say that "step by step, these political conspirators have moved forward to the accomplishment of these nefarious schemes under cover of popular prejudice on the Mormon question." Finally, they assured readers of the *New York World* that polygamy was "a dead issue," pointing to the fact that an 1888 constitutional convention produced a document "with a clause forever excluding polygamy and affixing penalties thereto and relegating to congress alone the power to repeal the clause." This was done, they asserted, by Mormon delegates, and secured the "almost unanimous vote of the people of the territory."[21]

Morgan commented in his journal that the paper had "contained our article this a.m. with big head lines. I am in a quandary as to whether we have made a mistake or not, and can only say we have done for the best—right or wrong."[22] He and Roberts were doubtless spurred on by the upcoming municipal election in Salt Lake City where the gentile-supported Liberal Party was pitted against the Mormon-supported People's Party. *Salt Lake Tribune* owner P.

20. "A Dark Plot Revealed," *New York World*, Jan. 27, 1890, 1. The paper described "B. N." Roberts and Morgan as "well educated and look like shrewd, successful men of affairs. Mr. Morgan bears a striking resemblance to [Thomas C.] Platt, which is borne out in his manner of speaking."

21. "A Dark Plot." For more on the politics of Utah statehood, see Lyman, *Finally Statehood!*

22. Morgan Journal, Jan. 27, 1890.

H. Lannan observed that a Liberal victory would place "the city in harmony with national law and authority," and since the city has "a great influence" on the territory itself, a Liberal victory "will mean the redemption of Utah is slowly but surely being accomplished."[23]

Roberts and Morgan approached James McKnight, managing editor of the *New York Press*, who told them the paper had made arrangements for a Liberal Party view of the forthcoming Utah municipal elections, suggesting that a People's Party response would be welcome. Roberts learned that the Liberal article, authored by O. J. Hollister—which Roberts labeled "one of the most villainous articles ever written against the Latter Day Saints"—was scheduled for publication on February 9. But in the interim McKnight had left the paper and been replaced; so Morgan met with the new editor and convinced him not to run Hollister's article. Instead, Roberts and Morgan "together made up an article that took its place, presenting a disinterested view of the situation."[24]

The Liberal Party won the election and ushered in non-Mormon control of Salt Lake City for the first time since its founding in 1847. The victory brought about what the *New York Times* called the "Mormon Waterloo."[25] The *Evening World* argued that the LDS Church was no longer a "political power," and quoted *Salt Lake Tribune* editor C. C. Goodwin that the victory would "Americanize Utah" and take the "kingdom … out of saintly control."[26]

On January 27, Roberts purchased a ticket "and left for Chicago to see what could be done there," which left Morgan "here alone to meet the issue and fight through it."[27] Roberts's presence in the city was noted by the *Chicago Daily Tribune,* describing him as "an intelligent appearing man … born and reared in the faith … [and] a monogamist in profession and practice" (which, of course, he was not). Roberts accused the "carpet-baggers who have lately drifted into Utah and are now leaders of the Gentile party, or 'Liberals' as they are called" of having seized "control of the telegraphic

23. "Today's Election in Utah," *Evening Post*, Feb. 10, 1890, 1. See also "Salt Lake City's Election," *New York Sun*, Feb. 10, 1890, 1.

24. First Council Minutes, Mar. 5, 1890.

25. "The Mormon Waterloo," *New York Times*, Feb. 12, 1890, 1.

26. "Down Goes the Temple," *Evening World*, Feb. 11, 1890, 4.

27. Morgan Journal, Jan. 27, 1890.

correspondence, and the attitude of the Mormon church is being persistently misrepresented." He repeated what he had told the *World*, that plural marriage was no longer an issue. "The Mormon Church has given up polygamy once and for all time," and therefore members were being "disenfranchised because they are members of the Mormon Church."[28]

In a later report, Roberts said that he drafted an article and presented it to the editor of the *Chicago Tribune* who said they "had no room for it." Despite that, he reported that the paper was printing daily "the worst trash and the most bitter misrepresentations, furnished by the Liberal ring in Utah." He also says that a hostile "conversation I had with their reporter appeared … the next day in which I was grossly misrepresented."[29]

On the other hand, Roberts said that Martin J. Russell,[30] the chief editorial writer for the *Chicago Times*, "received me very kindly," and as a result of this conversation, the paper published several fair articles and editorials. Apparently, Russell opposed the US Supreme Court's recent decision in the Idaho test oath case,[31] and "gave me his word that he would fight the disenfranchisement of the Mormon people."[32]

Beyond that, Roberts reported that while he got a hearing from the *Chicago Daily News*, he found himself "cramped in every way," because there was a "determination on every hand to destroy Mormonism." Roberts told his mother that he had written many articles for various newspapers, most of which had not been published, and those that were published had "been so changed that I am made to say things that I did not say."[33]

28. "Visitors at the Hotels," *Chicago Daily Tribune*, Feb. 6, 1890, 8. The paper noted that Roberts was staying at the Hotel Grace.

29. First Council Minutes, Mar. 5, 1890.

30. Russell (1845–1900) was active in Chicago newspapers circles from 1870 forward. He married Celia C. Walsh (1847–1938) in 1873. Russell was also involved with various civic, educational, and political matters. In 1895, along with Horatio Seymour he formed the *Chicago Chronicle*, a daily Democratic paper.

31. Idaho's test oath required Mormons to avow that they were not polygamists in order to register to vote. The Supreme Court ruled in *Davis v. Beason* that the oath did not violate the first amendment. For more, see Lyman, *Finally Statehood!*, 233.

32. First Council Minutes, Mar. 5, 1890.

33. Roberts to Ann Roberts, Feb. 17, 1890, box 4, fd. 7, Roberts Papers (UU).

A few weeks later, Morgan wrote to Roberts that George Q. Cannon had passed through New York and told Morgan "that we were to act on our own judgement, and if there was nothing further ... that we could do ... we were considered at liberty, and could consider ourselves released." By February 19, Morgan gave up his efforts and "took the N[ew] Y[ork], O[ntario] & W[estern] R[ailwa]y for home," stopping for a time in Chicago.[34] He arrived there on February 21, met Roberts at the depot, then "accompanied him to his room at the Hotel Grace and had a lengthy talk over affairs."[35] They left that afternoon for Colorado where Morgan stayed for some time, while Roberts went on to Salt Lake City.[36] On March 5, Roberts gave a lengthy, detailed report of the mission to his colleagues on the First Council of Seventy, whose minutes noted: "Report accepted, Labors approved."[37]

That August, Roberts and other Mormon Democrats were disturbed to learn that Idaho Democrats had passed a party platform calling for the enactment of any and all laws "necessary for the suppression of Mormonism and the protection of the purity of the ballot."[38] Meanwhile, Wilford Woodruff was in California meeting with various luminaries, including businessman Isaac Trumbo.[39] The actions of the federal government toward the church and its holdings "weighed heavily" on his mind[40] as the government's efforts to suppress polygamy threatened to destroy the church's financial standing. But since it was a longtime Mormon stance that plural

34. Morgan Journal, Feb. 19, 20, 1890.

35. Morgan Journal, Feb. 21, 1890.

36. Morgan Journal, Feb. 24, 26, 1890.

37. First Council Minutes, Mar. 5, 1890.

38. See "Idaho's Republican Ticket," *Philadelphia Inquirer*, Aug. 23, 1890, 2; and "Victory Assured," *Idaho Statesman*, Aug. 22, 1890, 1.

39. Trumbo (1858–1912) was a California businessman close to church leaders, especially Wilford Woodruff. He lived in the Gardo House in Salt Lake City where he was active as a Free Silver Republican and supporter of statehood. Trumbo believed he would be selected as one of Utah's first US Senators. When that did not occur, he returned to San Francisco. He maintained close relations with Woodruff who later died in Trumbo's home. For an overview of his political activity, see Lyman, "Isaac Trumbo."

40. In his journal of September 25, Woodruff wrote: "I have arrived at the point ... where I am in the necessity of acting for the Temporal Salvation of the Church. The United State government has taken a stand and passed laws to destroy the Latter-day Saints .... And after praying to the Lord and feeling inspired by his spirit I have issued ... [the] proclamation." Woodruff, *Wilford Woodruff's Journal*, 9:113–14.

marriage had come through revelation, any change to that practice would require revelation as well. Woodruff met with the Quorum of the Twelve on September 24 and informed them that he had sought God's will on the matter, and that it had been revealed to him that the church must end its practice of plural marriage. This stunning announcement was met with a unanimous vote that it was, in fact, a revelation.[41] Later that same day, the Manifesto was released to the press. In it Woodruff addressed press reports that the Utah Commission had alleged that "forty or more" plural marriages had been performed in the past year, and that the church was continuing to teach and urge "the continuance of the practice of polygamy." Woodruff's response read in part that:

> I, therefore, as President of the Church of Jesus Christ of Latter-day Saints do hereby, in the most solemn manner declare that these charges are false. We are not teaching polygamy or plural marriage, nor permitting any person to enter into its practice. ... Inasmuch as laws have been enacted by Congress forbidding plural marriages, which laws have been pronounced constitutional in the court of last resort, I hereby declare my intention to submit to these laws, and to use my influence with the members of the church over which I preside to have them do likewise. ... And now I publicly declare that my advice to the Latter-day Saints is to refrain from contracting any marriage forbidden by the law of the land.[42]

Few had been more forceful in defending the principle of plural marriage than Roberts. We have no contemporaneous account of Roberts's feelings on the issue since a diary for that period does not exist. What we do have is a reminiscence written on February 10, 1893,[43] that said he was returning by train from an extended

41. While Woodruff wrote that he felt "inspired" and the apostles agreed that ceasing the practice of polygamy came via revelation, the Manifesto was not the text of that revelation. It functioned instead as a political and public relations statement. See Lyman, *Finally Statehood!*, 252–58.

42. Wilford Woodruff, "Official Declaration," *Deseret Evening News*, Sep. 25, 1890, 2. The *News* reported that the statement had been sent to the Associated Press, but they had distributed it in a "condensed" form "which poorly conveys the sentiments of the writer." Despite that assertion, many of the accounts published throughout the country, while not verbatim, seem fairly accurate in reporting Woodruff's points. See, for example, "Denies the Report," *Norwalk Daily Reflector*, Sep. 25, 1890, 1.

43. Roberts later wrote that "for more than t[w]o years I have neglected my journal, and I shall fill up the gap between Dec[ember] 11, 1890 to Jan[uary] 5, 1893—when

tour in behalf of the church in Southern Utah with apostles Francis M. Lyman, John Henry Smith, John W. Taylor, and Abraham H. Cannon[44] when he discovered a newspaper with the account of Woodruff's announcement. His initial reaction was one of astonishment, but then "the Spirit said—'That is all right,' so it passed." He considered the pressures facing Woodruff, noting that in 1890 "the persecutions of our enemies threatened to be greater than ever. The prospect was that all the temples and the personal property of the Saints would be confiscated." He stated that he believed that Woodruff, "being inspired of the Lord," did what he thought best.[45] But, almost as quickly, acceptance turned to anger. As he "began to reflect on the matter," he thought of

> all the Saints had suffered to sustain that doctrine; I remembered my own exile, my own imprisonment; I thought of that of others, I remembered what sacrifices my wives had made for it; what others had made for it. We had preached it, sustained its divinity from the pulpit, in the press from the lecture platform. Our community had endured every kind of reproach from the world for the sake of it—and was this to be the end? I had learned to expect that God would sustain both that [principle] and his Saints who carried it out, and to lay down like this was a kind of cowardly proceeding [so] that the more I thought of it the less I liked it.[46]

Both John W. Taylor and John Henry Smith seemed to share his views, which by then had left Roberts "in quite an exasperated mood, and [he] felt crushed and humiliated."[47] Feeling a need for

---

I again commenced journalizing—from memory. I may not get matters in their proper sequence but the chief things I can doubtless remember very accurately." As far as can be determined, there are no diaries extant covering the period from August 31, 1887, to November 3, 1890, and the only diary we have for that year covers up to, as Roberts noted, December 11, 1893. See Roberts, *History's Apprentice*, 219 (1891–92).

44. Cannon (1859–96) was the son of George Q. Cannon. He married four wives before the Manifesto: Sarah A. Jenkins (1861–1940) in 1878; Wilhelmina Mousley (1859–1941) in 1879; Mary Elizabeth Croxell Young (1866–1955) in 1887; and Lilian Hamlin (1871–1920) in 1896. Cannon was the first editor of the *Juvenile Instructor*, and later the *Contributor*, and knew Roberts through these and other activities. He served as a member of the First Council of the Seventy from 1882–89 when he was called to the Quorum of the Twelve Apostles, serving from then until his death.

45. Roberts, *History's Apprentice*, 224–25 (1891–92).

46. Roberts, *History's Apprentice*, 225 (1891–92).

47. Ronald W. Walker notes that when the apostles met a few days later, Smith and Taylor still had their doubts, and neither at that time felt "quite right about it." See

solitude, Roberts retreated, leaving "the car in which the brethren were riding" and took a seat by himself to have full freedom to reflect on the matter. Lyman came to where he was seated and brought up "the subject of the Manifesto," but his reasoning was in vain, and Roberts felt that for every supportive reason Lyman could produce for the decision, he could counter with ten sufficient reasons "why we should hold to the principle even though it cost the very annihilation of the church." The question continued to disturb him as general conference approached.[48] By then he had concluded that because Woodruff had signed the document by himself, he was determined to carry alone the responsibility for it, and so he had become somewhat "reconciled to the Manifesto on that ground."[49] But it soon became evident that there were to be efforts during conference "to have the whole people" endorse it; a decision Roberts said he "viewed with alarm." When the "crisis came I felt heart-broken but remained silent. It seemed to me to be the awfulest moment in my life, my arm was like lead when the motion was put; I could not vote for it, and did not." The question "plagued me much, but I said but little about it."[50]

At some point, Roberts married Dr. Margaret Curtis Shipp as a plural wife. Born in St. Louis in 1849, Shipp was more than seven years older than Roberts. She graduated from the Women's Medical College of Pennsylvania in 1882, and had previously been married in 1867 to Milford Bard Shipp as the second of his four plural wives, which included fellow doctor Ellis Reynolds Shipp.[51] Exactly when and where the marriage between Roberts and Margaret took place is unclear,[52] but the specific date has tantalized historians: Did it occur

---

Walker, "B. H. Roberts and the Woodruff Manifesto," 363–65. Taylor would later resign from the Quorum of the Twelve and eventually be excommunicated for his continued support of plural marriage.

48. Roberts was not alone in his feelings. Abraham H. Cannon noted that when he returned to Salt Lake City he discovered that there was "considerable comment and fault-finding among some of the Saints," on account of the Manifesto. See Cannon, *Candid Insights*, 135 (Sep. 26, 1890).

49. Roberts, *History's Apprentice*, 226 (1891–92).

50. Roberts.

51. For a basic overview, see Priscilla P. Jennings, "Dr. Margaret Curtis Shipp Roberts," in Carter, *Our Pioneer Heritage*, 6:373–78.

52. Also important is the date of her divorce from Milford B. Shipp. One group of historians says that the divorce took place in either 1888 or 1892, and that the marriage

before or after the issuance of the Woodruff Manifesto? If it occurred before, was it one of the "forty or more" marriages Woodruff had denied taking place? If it was after, did it suggest that Roberts refused to accept Woodruff's counsel, or was it, like other marriages that would come, secretly approved by Woodruff? Many historians who have looked at the issue have given 1890 as the marriage date, while others disagree.[53]

Truman Madsen says, without giving a specific date, and without any citation, that "Official records place the marriage as about six months prior to the Manifesto."[54] Similarly, and again without source, Robert Malan says the marriage took place in April 1890.[55] Both biographers are probably relying on Roberts's testimony in the Smoot hearings. One account seems to attempt to sanitize the marriage saying, "Margaret married B. H. Roberts after the death of Milford Shipp and it was as Dr. Roberts that she traveled throughout ... the church."[56] This is clearly impossible since Shipp lived until 1918, though the writer may mean the civil ceremony that Roberts and Shipp had in 1923 after the death of Louisa. Henry D. Taylor, a future general authority who served under Roberts in the Eastern States Mission, says, based on his conversations with Roberts, that the marriage took place in April 1890, and that it was performed by Daniel H. Wells. Because Wells died on March 24, 1891, he could have performed the marriage either before or after the Manifesto. On the other hand, D. Michael Quinn, also without providing a specific source, says flatly that Roberts "married polygamously in violation of federal law, 1891."[57] Historian B. Carmon Hardy also explored the Roberts–Shipp marriage and

to Roberts occurred "circa 1890–1894." See Derr et al., *First Fifty Years of Relief Society*, 672. Margaret's entry in International Society Daughters of Utah Pioneers, *Pioneer Women of Faith and Fortitude*, 3:2607, suggests the sealing cancellation was "granted by Wilford Woodruff on June 15, 1888," and repeats the marriage date of April 1890.

53. Given their closeness, one wishes there was some clue in John Morgan's detailed diaries kept during 1890 and 1891.

54. Madsen, *Defender of the Faith*, 199, 416. The assertion that Madsen had access to "official" records seems at variance with what Roberts said during the Smoot hearings.

55. Malan, *B. H. Roberts*, 42.

56. See "Margaret C. Shipp Roberts," in Daughters of Utah Pioneers, *Museum Memories*, 2:55.

57. Quinn, *Extensions of Power*, 686.

concluded that it likely did not take place until 1894, since Shipp was still "living with her first husband until at least 1892."[58] Hardy says this seems plausible based on listings in the city directories for the period, and because Reed Smoot had told his assistant, Carl A. Badger, during the hearings that he was "reliably informed this was true." Finally, Hardy quotes a noted anti-Mormon figure of the time—Charles Mostyn Owen[59]—who "concluded that the marriage occurred in the Spring of 1894."[60]

Grandson Richard C. Roberts summarizes much of what we know about this third marriage. Sources from Margaret Shipp's family suggest that Roberts met his future wife after his release from prison when he was forced to live in a Centerville boarding house (by law he was prohibited from living with his plural wives), which was apparently run by a friend of Shipp's who visited her often and as a result was introduced to Roberts. Shipp enjoyed listening to Roberts and had heard him speak at conferences and lectures. Richard Roberts quotes at length from a letter dated December 5, 2007, from Elaine B. Hasleton, then-manager of Library Public Affairs at the LDS Church Historical Department, which says that based on research into existing records, it appears that Shipp was not divorced or separated from her first husband "until about 1892." Moreover, Hasleton suggests that Roberts's 1906 testimony, which says he was married by Daniel H. Wells, was given because

> we believe he used the name of a deceased but plausible man in authority who could have performed the ceremony. He gave this story to protect the identity of the person who really did perform the ceremony and gave the date to make it appear the two married plurally before the Manifesto. In actuality, they were probably married sometime between

58. Hardy, *Solemn Covenant*, 247.

59. A civil engineer, Owen was one of the most notorious enemies of polygamous Mormons. He moved to Las Vegas in 1926. The *Deseret News* editorialized that "Charles Mostyn Owen has for years sold his worthless services to anyone who would pay him for hunting up transgressions of law, real or alleged, among members of the Church." See Historian's Office, Journal History, Dec. 21, 1904, 1.

60. Hardy, *Solemn Covenant*, 247. In 1900, when Roberts was on trial for unlawful cohabitation, his attorney James H. Moyle admitted in court proceedings only that his client "married Dr. Margaret Shipp Roberts a number of years ago." See "Roberts Found Guilty," *Salt Lake Tribune*, Jan. 22, 1900, 8. Roberts was in California from early February until late March 1894.

late 1892 and 1894. The marriage was post-Manifesto and there is probably no existing paperwork to prove the marriage.[61]

Despite the lack of documentation as to the marriage date, Richard Roberts writes, "B. H. Roberts lived most of the rest of his life with her [Margaret], and the legitimacy of this marriage was not contested by local authorities." This marriage was "apparently more fulfilling," due to the fact that "Margaret was more culturally and intellectually attuned to the life B. H. was living at that time." Still, this fact came "at the expense of his other two families," and it was a major reason they "developed such disappointed feelings about the whole situation." These feelings worsened when, after Louisa died, Roberts took the step to marry Margaret in a civil ceremony designed to assure its legitimacy.[62] The decision caused hard feelings in Celia's family; it seemed they "had been overlooked, as B. H. skipped over the second wife to marry the third."[63]

In February 1893, while fulfilling a church assignment in Colonia Diaz, Mexico, where Roberts was explaining the "new position" of the church on celestial marriage, he felt "anxious" about Margaret:

> Dreamed in the ni[gh]t that I was within a house where I could look out and see her among a number of other sisters engaged in some pursuit of pleasures, the nature of which I could not understand. She was dressed superbly and looked … beautiful. She did not know I was near or that I was watching her. I was anxious that she should come into the house to me which she presently did, not yet knowing that I was there. Upon seeing me seated in a chair she was dumbfounded and turned deathly pale. She looked so white and wan, so care worn and sorrowful, so faded and exhausted, so different to what she looked with the sisters that I became much alarmed about her, and with an exclaim of mingled pity and alarm I sprang forward to catch her—for she seemed to be falling—and with this I awoke.[64]

---

61. Hasleton to Roberts, Dec. 5, 2007, qtd. in Roberts, *History of the B. H. Roberts Family*, 143.

62. See "B. H. Roberts to Wed Again," *New York Times*, Nov. 10, 1923, 2; and "Mormon Chief and His Plural Wife Wed Anew," *San Francisco Chronicle*, Nov. 15, 1923, 9. According to the *Chronicle*, Roberts reiterated that all three marriages had preceded the Woodruff Manifesto.

63. Roberts, *History of the B. H Roberts Family*, 145–46.

64. Roberts, *History's Apprentice*, 257–58 (Feb. 19, 1893).

Roberts says that after this he was "restless all night and slept but little," and wrote, "Bless and preserve to me my Margaret." She seemed to dominate his affections, and the two would share a loving, even passionate relationship until her death in 1926, even as Roberts "continued to express his love for his younger wives in letters."[65]

Roberts remained active in politics. In addition to his work with the Democratic Party, he also supported the People's Party and was one of its most popular speakers. He spoke at rallies (many of which were held in church-owned buildings) in Juab County, Salina, East Bountiful, Farmington, Layton, Kaysville, and Centerville, where he closed with a prayer: "My Father in Heaven, grant that thy people may tomorrow win a glorious victory over those who would politically disinherit them; and may they long enjoy the liberties, and have them enlarged, that are guaranteed to them in the institutions of their country, Amen."[66] When the votes were counted, John Caine defeated Liberal Party nominee C. C. Goodwin by a vote of 16,353 to 6,912, to retain his seat as territorial delegate.

Despite his success in the political arena, Roberts was having difficulty supporting his families since he received no income from his church duties. He was writing a history of John Taylor[67] as well as editing the *Semi-Weekly Herald* to bring in money,[68] but he needed more. Roberts, like several of his colleagues on the First Council, "was perpetually poor," and he worked to support "his plural families as best he could from royalties from lecturing and writing."[69] So he wrote to the First Presidency "telling them of my labors during the past six months and asking them to make an appropriation of six hundred dollars to aid me in my straightened financial circumstances."[70]

65. Quinn, *Extensions of Power*, 186.

66. Roberts, *History's Apprentice*, 203–04 (Nov. 3, 1890).

67. Roberts, *History's Apprentice,* 207 (Nov. 10, 1890). Roberts had access to Taylor family materials as he prepared his study. Some of these documents, with Roberts's notations, may be found in the LDS Church History Library. See John Taylor Collection.

68. An advertisement in the paper listing Roberts as editor said the *Semi-Weekly Herald* contained "all the cream of the daily edition with other matter specially edited for the issue." Published on Wednesday and Saturday, the paper said it was "larger than the regular daily, and is in all respects a model country newspaper. Its circulation is the best attestation of its popularity." See "Advertisement," *Salt Lake Herald*, Nov. 21, 1890, 4. Apparently this continued until November 1892. See [no title] *Ogden Standard*, Nov. 29, 1892, 4.

69. Van Orden, *Prisoner For Conscience Sake*, 174.

70. Roberts, *History's Apprentice*, 208 (Nov. 11, 1890).

Previously, he had suggested providing a fixed income to his calling, but George Q. Cannon strongly objected to "fixed salaries being attached to the offices of the Priesthood," though he also believed that general authorities should not "be expected to labor continuously in poverty." Cannon said to Roberts that a man's "first duty was to his family—a remark evidently made without reflection and on the spur of the moment." Roberts recorded, "I have often sacrificed my family, and its interests to labor in the interests of the Kingdom of God, believing in the scriptures: 'Seek first the Kingdom of God and its righteousness and all other things shall be added unto you.'"[71]

Roberts had also inquired from the First Presidency "whether he could have permission to employ himself at other work, if his support could not be furnished by the Church." As a result, "it was decided that he should be given permission to secure employment to sustain himself and family, and devote what time he could spare to his ministerial duties."[72] Cannon also noted that Roberts was "allowed $400 in cash and $200 in produce." Later, Roberts attended the First Council of Seventy meeting in Salt Lake City where he noted that his colleagues "seemed worked up about my being released from ministry— regretted it very much and think complications will grow out of it."[73]

Not long after that, Roberts sought advice from George Q. Cannon, saying that he wanted to go to Ann Arbor to study law for a year, "with a view to adopting the legal profession as a means of making a living." Roberts wanted to know if this would be "compatible" with his service on the First Council of Seventy. None of the members of the First Presidency seemed keen on the idea. Cannon recorded that "if he adopted the practice of the law as a profession, it would naturally engross his time and prevent him from attending to the duties of his calling." Apparently Joseph F. Smith thought Roberts might be less busy if he studied "surgery or medicine, which he thought a man might follow as a profession without interfering so seriously with his duties as a minster of the gospel."[74] Roberts indi-

71. Roberts, 209 (Nov. 11, 1890).
72. Cannon Journal, Nov. 11, 1890.
73. Roberts, *History's Apprentice*, 218 (Dec. 11, 1890).
74. Cannon Journal, July 23, 1891.

cated that "he had not taste" for either of those alternatives; the heart of the matter was how he would make a living if he did not practice law. Cannon wrote later that there seemed to be a disposition on Roberts's part "to either throw himself on the Church for it to sustain him, or to leave the ministry and devote himself to some profession."[75] Cannon, however, did intervene on Roberts's behalf when James E. Talmage was considering releasing a book that Roberts felt would "spoil" a book he had been working on. "It was suggested that it would be well to withhold the book until Brother Roberts could put his book on the market and dispose of it," Cannon reported.[76]

During this period, Roberts "became reconciled to" the Woodruff Manifesto, though he continued to believe that plural marriage was an eternal principle. In his 1893 journal retrospective, he wrote that he had allowed his own "prejudices, and my own shortsighted human reason to stand against the inspiration of God." As he received a "testimony … that the manifesto was alright," he

> repented of my wrong and courted most earnestly the spirit of God. … I did not understand the purposes for which [it] was issued (I do not to this day, Feb 10, '93) but sure I am that it is all right; that God has a purpose in it I feel assured, and in due time it will be manifest. The principle of plurality of wives is true … and in connection with all other truth will eventually prevail and be established on the earth; but I do not pretend to say what God's purpose is or what is to be accomplished by it. It is a matter in which I trust the divine wisdom implicit. God must be his own interpreter and in time will make it plain.[77]

Roberts also witnessed political changes in the church in 1891, as the Saints moved from supporting the church-controlled People's Party and affiliated with either the Republican or Democratic Party. Roberts believed that for a period of time it had been necessary for the church to "band together" to defend themselves and their religion "against their assailants." Federal officials, sectarian ministers, and others, he held, had joined with gentiles to "destroy the Church of Christ & the people of God." Church members were divided along Democratic or Republican Party lines, first in Ogden then

75. Cannon Journal, Sep. 21, 1891.
76. Cannon Journal, Sep. 14, 1891.
77. Roberts, *History's Apprentice*, 226–27 (1891–92).

in Salt Lake City. It gained the support of church leaders and a realignment began.[78] For his part, while clearly oriented toward the Democrats, Roberts realized, as leaders like John Henry Smith and others became Republicans, that this would not be a smooth transition. He criticized Smith particularly who, at a Republican meeting, "announced himself a Republican and declared his intention to work in the interest of that party. He did so … with much more zeal than wisdom; for everywhere he went he devoted himself to proselytizing for the Republican party both in season and out." Roberts felt that such public partisanship was a mistake, "not because he had declared himself a Republican," but too often he unwisely advocated his "doctrines at improper places, times and manner." For his part, Roberts noted that as political efforts in the territory "were gradually growing hotter" he "received many invitations to speak at political gatherings but [refused] to accept them." He was especially pressed to speak in Utah County, where the "division movement" to align along parties was strong. "Some appointments were made for me for Utah County, but the Spirit whispered to me to keep out of it & I cancelled them the very afternoon I was to start to fill them."[79] Roberts's political reluctance would not last.

Roberts continued to travel back and forth to Colorado, finding it difficult to balance his public demands with his family obligations, and tensions developed. Celia, as the second wife, was frequently left out. In November, she wrote to her grandmother that she had "high hopes" that "Henry" would be there for Thanksgiving. But apparently, he spent the holiday in Utah. Celia told her grandmother she was "disappointed, as I never had the pleasure of attending anything nice with him. I have never attended one party with him, but live in hopes that it won't always be so."[80] After the first of the year, she again wrote to her grandmother that while Roberts had spent part of December in Colorado, "when he is here it seems impossible to get anything but housework done," and while she had a "pleasant visit with Henry," a visit of two weeks seemed short after a "four months absence." Recognizing her ambiguous status, she concluded, "But

78. Roberts, 227–29.

79. Roberts, 230.

80. Celia to "Dear Grandma," Nov. 22, 1891, box 3, fd. 3, Roberts Papers (UU).

I suppose we must endure these things and hope for better times which for my part is not too distant. Henry has given me the chance to come home in the spring and stay all summer, but obey the law of course. How do you think I will stand it? I think I shall try it at any rate. If I could keep out of sight I think I would get along all right."[81]

Throughout 1892, Roberts continued his activity on the First Council of Seventy, in the YMMIA, at the *Semi-Weekly Herald*, and on the speakers' rostrum. He also completed and delivered to church authorities a manuscript that would eventually be published as *Outlines of Ecclesiastical History*.[82]

Roberts's activity in the Democratic Party was also increasing, and he was "without question one of the foremost orators in Utah and thoroughly familiar with the principles of the great party." Whenever he spoke, he "cast the light of truth upon … doubtful minds."[83] But political tensions in the ecclesiastical ranks also began manifesting themselves.

In May, Roberts was invited by Apostle Moses Thatcher to attend a Utah Territorial Democratic state convention, but his schedule would not permit it. Roberts later learned that Thatcher had spoken at the meeting, and that he held the convention "spellbound" with an "able speech against centralization of power in government."[84] Shortly thereafter, Thatcher came under criticism from Joseph F. Smith and John Henry Smith who identified as Republicans, and said Thatcher had profaned the name of Jesus in his speech, "and accused the Democratic Party with being the cause and instigators of all the wrongs heaped upon the Saints." Roberts responded in an unsigned editorial for the *Herald* in which he accused some "of our Mormon Republican friends" for attempting to win support for their party by appealing to the "prejudices

81. Celia to "Dear Grandma," Jan. 4, 1892, box 3, fd. 3, Roberts Papers (UU). Interestingly, she signed the name "Lena" which apparently was a code name she often used. The handwriting, however, is clearly Celia's. At that point, their daughter Lena was only six. Indeed, Roberts sometimes referred to her by that name in correspondence.

82. Roberts, *Outlines*.

83. "Democratic Rally," *Salt Lake Herald*, Jan. 17, 1892, 5.

84. See "Utah Shouts Democracy," *Salt Lake Herald*, May 5, 1892, 1; "Mr. Thatcher's Address," *Salt Lake Herald*, May 18, 1892, 4; and "Issues of the Times," *Salt Lake Herald*, May 18, 1892, 6.

and the passions" of citizens. Their charges, Roberts stated, were based on a misreading of history.[85]

The next month, Roberts took a more active political role, speaking at a "pretty good sized" rally held in the Knutsford Hotel in Salt Lake City where the Democratic presidential and vice presidential nominees—Grover Cleveland and Adlai Stevenson—were endorsed by Utah Democrats.[86] A few weeks later, along with his friend J. H. Paul, Roberts spoke at an outdoor Democratic ratification meeting in Farmington where he called on his audience to endorse the Cleveland–Stevenson ticket.[87] Between then and the end of July, Roberts attended several Democratic "ratification meetings in Davis County, Utah County," saying that "the Democratic party of the nation was working for the welfare and freedom of Utah" and that Utahns would not forget it.[88]

While Roberts may have believed that leaders like John Henry Smith and Joseph F. Smith were too active in promoting the Republican Party, they felt that he was too active in promoting the Democrats. A few days after Roberts spoke, Joseph F. Smith stated at a San Luis Stake conference, with Thatcher in attendance, that there were

> brethren in the Church who were going contrary to the counsel of the First Presidency. He stated it was not a serious matter as yet but there was danger. He stated he had no reference to political matters, but notwithstanding his disclaimer there were plenty who understood him and continued after his disclaimer to insist that he had reference to myself and Bro. Thatcher. If he did—which I cannot believe after his disclaimer—then it was a very unjust accusation so far as I am concerned as they never said anything to me on the subject of politics and I esteemed myself perfectly free in the matter according to the public declarations of the brethren. … But in the minds of many we … were marked men.[89]

85. [B. H. Roberts], "Some Bits of History," *Salt Lake Herald*, May 29, 1892, 4.

86. See "Cleve and Steve," *Salt Lake Herald*, June 30, 1892, 8; and "Great Democratic Lights," *Salt Lake Tribune*, June 30, 1892, 5. Neither account mentions Roberts by name, though Roberts wrote in his diary that he spoke at the meeting. See Roberts, *History's Apprentice*, 233 (1891–92). Stevenson was the grandfather of Illinois governor Adlai E. Stevenson, who was the Democratic presidential nominee in 1952 and 1956.

87. "Farmington Facts," *Salt Lake Herald*, July 15, 1892, 3.

88. "Davis County Ratification Meetings," *Salt Lake Herald*, July 9, 1892, 8; "Provo Democrats," *Salt Lake Herald*, July 16, 1892, 1.

89. Roberts, *History's Apprentice*, 233 (1891–92).

Seymour B. Young confirmed that there was also concern in the First Council of Seventy over Roberts's political activity. On August 4, Young had "quite a long talk with Bro. Roberts he holding different views & teaching a different policy in Politics" from that of the church authorities. A week later, he records that, along with George Reynolds and Christian Fjeldsted,[90] he "spent some time with Woodruff and Cannon," all agreeing that "Roberts seems determined that we shall all be democrats which we must not all be."[91]

Despite these tensions, Roberts continued to write on political questions for the *Herald* and spoke at political meetings throughout the state.[92] He was nominated at the Davis County Democratic convention to be a delegate to the state nominating convention.[93] His activity at the Territorial Democratic convention where he spoke on the issue of the tariff[94] met with further displeasure from some ecclesiastical colleagues.[95] Indeed, it is clear that his role in the election had been problematic, and it presaged future developments. Historian D. Michael Quinn has explained, "Although general authorities had the freedom to speak and publish on behalf of the Republican party throughout most of 1892, the First Presidency and Quorum of the Twelve decided on 4 October that no general authorities 'should take the Stump to make political speeches.' … Democrats Moses Thatcher and Brigham H. Roberts, felt that this ruling was designed to aid Republicans. The two continued their political activity."[96]

90. Fjeldsted (1829–1905) served as a member of the First Council of the Seventy from 1884 until his death. As such he was a longtime colleague of Roberts's.

91. Seymour B. Young, Journals, Aug. 4 and Aug. 11, 1892, copies in possession of author. Hereafter cited as Young Journals.

92. See "Centerville Comments," *Davis County Clipper*, Nov. 3, 1892, 2. As would be his custom over the next few years, Roberts combined his political activity with church service. The Sunday after the election, for example, he spoke in the Centerville Ward on the life and example of Jesus. See also "Centerville Comments," *Davis County Clipper*, Nov. 10, 1892, 3.

93. "Democratic County Convention Nominates Candidates and Delegates," *Salt Lake Herald*, Oct. 5, 1892, 3; and "J. L. Rawlins for Delegate," *Salt Lake Herald*, Oct. 6, 1892, 1.

94. "Work of the Utah Democracy," *Salt Lake Times*, Oct. 6, 1892, 4.

95. See Roberts, *History's Apprentice*, 234–40 (1891–92). See also Lyman, *Political Deliverance*, 207–08.

96. Quinn, *Extensions of Power*, 350. See also Woodruff, *Wilford Woodruff's Journal*, 9:221. Woodruff frequently referred to Roberts as H. B, and I have silently corrected it back to B. H. Woodruff wrote that on October 10 Joseph F. Smith and George Q. Cannon spoke "very Plain on the Political Situation of Utah." The next day, Woodruff met with Roberts and Thatcher and "talked politics." Woodruff, 9:222.

As a result of Thatcher's and Roberts's actions, the authorities "punished the two renegades" along with Charles W. Penrose, forbidding the trio from attending the dedicatory services of the Salt Lake Temple in April 1893 unless they "acknowledged their error." The three men held out until the night before the dedication and "confessed" that they had been in error, but it would not be the end of political problems for Thatcher and Roberts. [97]

Roberts continued to campaign throughout the territory, frequently with Joseph Rawlins. On October 22, he spoke at the Grand Opera House in Provo.[98] Then, on October 29, Roberts appeared at "a large and enthusiastic" rally in Spanish Fork. Other campaign appearances included Sugar House, Payson (where Roberts helped the local Democrats carry their city ticket with a large majority),[99] Brigham City (where he criticized both Joseph F. Smith and John Henry Smith for inappropriately trying to tie the Republican Party to the church), and the Salt Lake Theater. He continued to draw the attention of church leaders, who disapproved of his actions.

On the afternoon of January 21, he left for a church assignment in Franklin, Idaho. Apostle Moses Thatcher was on the train who told him that "both himself and me were somewhat under the ban for part we had taken in political affairs." Thatcher confided to Roberts that the First Presidency had "approved a letter of Jos[eph] F. Smith and J[ohn] Henry Smith against his Ogden speech."[100]

Between the end of January and the end of March, Roberts was touring on church business in Colorado, Mexico, Arizona, and California before returning home.[101] On April 25, he traveled to Ogden, accompanied by Margaret, to lecture on Spiritualism, and it is clear that he—if not both of them—spent the night at the home

97. Quinn, *Extensions of Power*, 350.

98. "Notes on the Side," *Salt Lake Herald*, Oct. 21, 1892, 3.

99. "Payson Patriots," *Salt Lake Herald*, Nov. 10, 1892, 8.

100. Roberts, *History's Apprentice*, 242 (Jan. 21, 1893).

101. For details, see Roberts, 241–78 (1893). See also "Personal," *Arizona Republic*, Mar. 18, 1893, 8. "Tempe Echoes," *Arizona Republic*, Mar. 22, 1893, 2; "St. Johns Stake Conference," *Deseret Weekly*, Apr. 1, 1893, 450; and "Maricopa Stake Conference," *Deseret Weekly*, Apr. 1, 1893, 462.

of Moroni F. Brown,[102] then returned the next morning.[103] The unanswerable question is whether Roberts and Margaret were living as man and wife by now, or if they considered themselves as "married" even if a ceremony had not yet taken place. Roberts mentioned in his diary that he had been spending time with Margaret, and inviting friends, like his missionary colleague James Eardley and his wife, for dinner at her home. Margaret also accompanied him to the Salt Lake Temple, and he had taken her "through" the building during the open visiting sessions. At the same time, he suggests that she is still occupying her own space, and that he is spending his evenings in Centerville.[104]

In May he busied himself with a course on church history and doctrine at LDS College (Salt Lake City), delivering seven lectures between May 18 and June 1. At his last lecture, he told the students, "Doubt all things until you prove all things was a maxim of one of the leading schools, but the gospel teaches to believe all things that you may know all things."[105] He also went to Logan to speak at the commencement of Brigham Young College. Oddly, for him, he wrote that his remarks were "a great failure—had no liberty. … Felt as if I never wanted to speak again,"[106] but the *Logan Journal* reported that the address "could not fail to impress his auditors with a sense of the responsibilities they were about to assume, and inspire them with a desire to perform a labor that would be a credit to themselves and to the institution from which they had just graduated."[107]

Later he met with his friend Henry Ballard, with whom he had labored in England, and Moses Thatcher, who had been ill. Roberts noted that Thatcher had been in attendance at the commencement

102. Brown (1857–97), grandson of Ogden founder James Brown, was bishop of Ogden's First Ward from 1890 until his death. He served a mission to Great Britain in 1880–82. Brown married Elizabeth "Lizzie" Weaver (1863–1955) on November 29, 1883.

103. Roberts, *History's Apprentice*, 286 (Apr. 26, 1893). Roberts notes concerning the lecture that "Large audience tho[ugh] the Trans-Mississippi conference was in session. Several of its members came to the meeting."

104. For an overview, see Roberts, *History's Apprentice*, chapter nine.

105. Transcripts of the lectures are found in the student magazine *The Idea*, June 1893, 98–102.

106. Roberts, *History's Apprentice*, 297 (May 26, 1897).

107. "The Commencement Exercises," *Logan Journal*, May 27, 1893, 8. See also "The Graduates," *Logan Journal*, May 27, 1893, 8; and "Affairs in Cache's Capital," *Salt Lake Tribune*, May 29, 1893, 3.

exercises, and he was glad to see him because he was afraid he was going to "pass from among us." But instead Roberts discovered that Thatcher "was much better than I expected to find him." The two friends "spent a pleasant afternoon" and they "talked of our being called before the brethren and the difficulties explained away." Thatcher was proud to have "preserved his honor," while Roberts explained that he had spoken with some of the church leaders. Thatcher asked him if the rumors of a divide among the apostles were true, and Roberts told him "I heard no such thing but I did hear the brethren say the unity was complete & they rejoiced in it & so did I and prayed that it might never be broken."[108]

Roberts also spent time with J. H. Paul, engaging in what proved to be an important discussion of Roberts's future activities. Paul told him that when it appeared that Joseph L. Rawlins was going to step aside, "the determination was formed in the north to nominate me [Roberts] for the office." Roberts told Paul that the idea was "absurd." For one thing, as a result of his term in the territorial prison, he had lost the right to vote. Paul told him that this had all been considered, and the view was that "these difficulties" could be overcome should Roberts choose to run in the future. Paul reminded Roberts that another election would soon be at hand and asked him "to consider the propriety of my becoming a candidate, as all the leaders in the north desired it." Roberts replied that he "did not look upon myself as having any political future & that to my thinking the difficulties in the way of it were insurmountable." Paul strongly disagreed, saying that eventually Utah would "need my services in that capacity."[109]

In July 1891, Roberts wrote an editorial for the *Salt Lake Herald* encouraging church leaders to seek to be included in the upcoming Chicago World's Fair. He proposed participation in the Parliament of World Religions as a way of exposing the church's "history, theology, and cultural contributions" to the general public. The World's Fair of 1893, sometimes called the Pan-American or Columbian Exposition, was one of the major events of the United States in

108. Roberts, *History's Apprentice*, 297–98 (May 26, 1897).
109. Roberts.

the last decade of the nineteenth century. More than two hundred buildings were erected in Jackson Park near the Lake Michigan waterfront. Dubbed the "White City," the exposition "marked for many the end of an era."[110]

Part of the World's Fair was the Parliament of World Religions, "a seventeen-day-long assembly" whose stated goal was "to unite all religions against irreligion" and to seek to secure the "coming unity" of humankind in the "service on Man and God."[111] But, as historian Konden Rich Smith has written, while parliament organizers proclaimed their goal to bring together all those who "are groping, however blindly, after God," it was clear that the parliament "was an attempt by white evangelicals to clarify and reestablish what they understood to be a proper understanding of American Christianity." In the process, "what it ultimately produced was an awareness of the religious insecurities and prejudices many Americans carried with them."[112]

Roberts wanted very much for Mormonism to be a part of the parliament. He wrote that the opportunity "reminds us that Mormonism is an American product, one of which all the inhabitants of the earth have heard, and about which they will have a curiosity if not an interest."[113] He renewed his call for participation at the priesthood session of October 1891 general conference but noted there was "no enthusiasm" for the idea. He made a similar request in April 1892, and this time a committee was selected to consider the idea, but "nothing ever happened."[114] The attitude of the LDS hierarchy could only be described as "lukewarm," at best.[115] While there seemed to be no interest among the hierarchy, the church's newspaper, the *Deseret News*, published several editorials about the

110. Bradley and Woodward, *Four Zinas*, 356.

111. See Seager, *World's Parliament of Religions*, xv–xvii; and Seager, *Dawn of Religious Pluralism*, 6.

112. Smith, "Appropriating the Secular," 155. See also Hansen, *Frontier Religion*, esp. chapters 4 and 5.

113. B. H. Roberts, "A Religious Congress," *Salt Lake Herald*, July 15, 1891. As quoted in Neilson, *Exhibiting Mormonism*, 147. See also Bitton, "B. H. Roberts at the World Parliament."

114. Neilson, *Exhibiting Mormonism*, 149.

115. Bitton, "B. H. Roberts at the World Parliament."

parliament.[116] Moreover, both the fair and the parliament were covered in the pages of the *Deseret Weekly*.[117]

Utah state officials prepared for the World's Fair by starting the Utah World's Fair Commission (UWFC) "for the express purpose of removing the prejudice that existed against" Utah Territory, in the words of historian Reid L. Neilson. The committee oversaw the creation of the Utah Building to showcase the state, its people, industry, and accomplishments. The building opened in September 1892—ahead of the fair, which opened on May 1, 1893—and ran until October of that year. Many notable non-Mormon Utah leaders supported the enterprise.

Once the decision had been made for Utah to participate as a territory, church leaders moved toward involvement as well. As Neilson notes, after "decades of geographical isolation and theological separation," the fair offered the Latter-day Saints a chance to "be as American as their neighbors," and "to remake their image and refresh their appearance … on the world's largest stage."[118] Their plans included visits by church leaders, an appearance by the Tabernacle Choir, and participation in the Woman's Religious Auxiliary Conference. The church's decision to participate brought "over two million non-Mormon visitors" to the Utah Building and the other "major and minor Utah exhibits scattered throughout Jackson Park."[119]

Utah governor Caleb West spoke on Utah Day and emphasized the agreements of the present rather than the "struggles and differences" of the past, which, he said, had been "buried." West assured his listeners that the Mormon pioneers were loyal patriots who wanted to move Mormonism into the mainstream.[120] All of this caused the Chicago *Sunday Herald* to conclude, "Mormons and gentiles came

116. See "A World's Parliament of Religion," *Deseret News*, Apr. 8, 1892, 4; and "A Congress of Thinkers," *Deseret News*, Apr. 25, 1891, 5.

117. See J.M.S., "Religious Conference," *Deseret Weekly*, Nov. 19, 1892, 694–96. The initials likely stand for Janne M. Sjodahl, a writer and translator for the church. See also "Utah and the World's Fair," *Deseret Weekly*, Apr. 16, 1892, 542; and "The World Parliament of Religion," *Deseret Weekly*, Apr. 16, 1892, 544.

118. Neilson, *Exhibiting Mormonism*, 73.

119. Neilson, 74.

120. "Mormon and Gentile," *Sunday Herald*, Sep. 10, 1893, 8.

together as friends."[121] Indeed, Konden Smith called it a "tipping point in Mormonism's modernization"[122]

As historian Andrea Radke-Moss has summarized, the fair "marked a major crossroads for Mormon women poised exactly mid-point" between the passage of the Woodruff Manifesto [1890] and "the achievement of statehood [1896]."[123] Indeed, it was a unique opportunity for women of the church, and a chance to "tear down suspicion among their fellow American and foreign sisters."[124] The Mormon women were given a full day on May 19 to present the views of leaders of the Relief Society and the Young Women's Mutual Improvement Association. Those in attendance read like a Who's Who of Mormon feminists: Zina D. Young, Jane S. Richards, Bathsheba W. Smith, Sarah M. Kimball, Emmeline B. Wells, Mary Isabella Horne, Zina Y. Card, and others. Talks were given by Martha Hughes Cannon and Electa Bullock.[125] Emily S. Richards delivered a paper authored by Roberts, at the request of the First Presidency, on the "Legal and Political Status of Utah Women."[126] Through the efforts of these and other LDS women, anti-Mormon bias over polygamy was blunted, and Mormon women were often

121. "Mormon and Gentile."

122. Smith, "Appropriating the Secular," 178.

123. See Radke-Moss, "Mormon Women, Suffrage, and Citizenship," 97–112.

124. "Editor's Department," *Young Woman's Journal*, Apr. 1893, 326.

125. Zina D. Young (1821–1901) was president of the Relief Society from 1888 until her death; Jane S. Richards (1823–1912) was a counselor to Young; Bathsheba W. Smith (1822–1910) succeeded Zina Young as president of the Relief Society in 1901 and served until her death; Sarah M. Kimball (1818–98) was president of the Fifteenth Ward Relief Society from 1857 until her death. She was active in the General Relief Society as well; Mary Isabella Horne (1818–1905) was president of the Salt Lake Stake Relief Society; Zina Y. Card (1850–1931) was active in the Primary Association, serving as a member of the general board and as Utah Stake Primary president; Electa Bullock (1834–1911) was president of the Utah Woman Suffrage Association, a delegate to the National Woman Suffrage meetings in 1891, and chair of the Woman's Department of the Utah Building at the fair.

126. Emily S. Richards (1850–1929) was a leading LDS feminist. She played an important role in the Young Ladies' Mutual Improvement Association and the Relief Society, and represented those organizations at the first International Women's Council meetings in Washington, DC, in 1888. Richards was a Democrat and a founder of the Utah Woman's Suffrage Association. She would cross swords with Roberts over his opposition to the vote for women. See Radke-Moss, "Truly Her Soul Rejoiced."

invited to participate in organizations like the National Council of Women and the International Council of Women.[127]

Compared to the women, the experience of B. H. Roberts at the World's Fair was very different. The men who organized the parliament had no intention of seeking LDS participation at the event. As Reid L. Neilson has written, the parliament's organizing committee had "posted over three thousand copies of its preliminary invitation to representatives of all religions around the globe," but "made certain that no invitation was mailed" to the LDS Church.[128] On July 10, 1893, with the parliament scheduled to open in two months, the First Presidency sent a letter to one of the organizers, Charles C. Bonney, saying, "We are given to understand that an invitation is extended to all denominations of Christians and to all religions of the earth" to come to Chicago and explain their beliefs. They argued that because the church had gained "success in the face of the stupendous opposition it has encountered gives it the right to be heard in such an assembly by its own accredited representatives." The asked that a delegation from the church be included and begged "pardon our lack of information on the subject since none of the literature treating of the movement has been forwarded to us."[129]

Knowing "full well they had been slighted," the First Presidency waited for ten days, then sent Roberts to Chicago "to meet face-to-face with exposition and Parliament officials." Roberts arrived July 25 carrying a letter on behalf of the Mormon people that said they desired to participate "in a friendly conference ... not for debate, but to speak of what are to them the supreme truths, to show the relation of these truths to the practical problems of modern life." He also brought letters of introduction from several prominent Utahns including Moses Thatcher, whose relative Solomon Thatcher Jr. and his wife, Clara E. Thatcher,[130] were members of the fair's organizing

127. See, for example, Madsen, "Power of Combination," and Radke-Moss, "Mormon Women, Suffrage, and Citizenship," 97–98.

128. Neilson, "Mormonism's Blacksmith Orator," 53–84.

129. Clark, *Messages of the First Presidency*, 3:248–50.

130. Thatcher (1833–99) married Clara Elsie Thatcher (1844–99) in 1864. Despite having the same last name, they were not related. Both were active in the Methodist Church in Chicago. See "Close of a Busy Life," *Chicago Tribune*, Mar. 18, 1894, 6; and "Mrs. Solomon Thatcher Dies," *Chicago Tribune*, July 14, 1899, 12. As a member of the Woman's Department of the World's Fair, Clara Thatcher spoke at a YMMIA General

committee.[131] Once there, Roberts tried to secure a Mormon Bureau of Information and an exhibit in the Hall of Religions.[132] Drawing on Solomon Thatcher's help, he met with George R. Davis, director general of the exposition, who told him that all the space for such a bureau had been taken. Roberts was upset because, despite his efforts, "the church had missed out on the opportunity to represent itself in the greater exhibition, just as Roberts had feared."[133]

While Roberts was disappointed, "he was undaunted by the news," and turned to the second objective of gaining "Mormon representation at the Parliament." It is clear that his "insistence in Chicago for Mormon inclusion was unrelenting, as it had been in Utah."[134] After much effort, Roberts arranged a meeting with Bonney who treated him more coldly than had Davis, and who told him he had not replied to the First Presidency's letter because conference officials were "conflicted about the proper response to the undesirable Mormons." Bonney told Roberts that there was a "very general opinion" that the Mormons should not be admitted because their presence might be disruptive, and many felt little "good" would come from Mormon participation. The opposition stemmed largely from "Protestant outrage over the Mormon principle of plural marriage," but he conceded "common fairness" necessitated Mormon participation in some fashion.[135] Ultimately Bonney agreed to bring the matter back to the parliament's organizing committee, and told Roberts that while he could not take part in the deliberations, he should draft a memo on (a) why the Mormons should be allowed to participate, and (b) what he proposed to say. Roberts drafted the memo and waited for an answer.

Roberts wrote to his mother and gave her his assessment of the World's Fair itself: "Oh, it is splendid of course. Fairyland realized.

Conference in Salt Lake City on June 5, 1892. See "Women and the World's Fair," *Contributor*, June 1892, 362–65.

131. Neilson, "Blacksmith Orator," 61.

132. Roberts later published a series of four articles in the *Improvement Era* recounting the entire history of his efforts. See *Improvement Era*, June, July, Aug., and Sep. 1899.

133. Neilson, *Exhibiting Mormonism*, 151.

134. Smith, "Mormonism at the World's Fair," 364.

135. Indeed, Solomon Thatcher agreed that "the Latter-day Saints deserved a hearing on this point." See Neilson, "Blacksmith Orator," 62.

A triumph for architecture, taste, skill, and American energy. It has the glory of ancient Babylon—it is justly the pride of the nations. But I do not enjoy it over much because of the constant anxiety concerning my work and the slowness of my progress. I hope soon to have my uncertainties cleared up."[136] After ten days of "fruitless waiting," he returned to Utah "having failed to achieve either of the First Presidency's objectives." Before leaving, he provided Bonney with contact information.[137]

A few weeks later, on August 28, Roberts received a conciliatory letter saying he would be allowed to make a presentation in the main assembly room of the congress. Since the First Presidency was in Chicago with the Tabernacle Choir, he turned to Lorenzo Snow for direction. Snow told him to prepare the paper and hand deliver it to Bonney and Barrows, lest they simply "pigeon hole" the document.

Roberts was "excited by the renewed opportunity," and set out, arriving back in Chicago on September 8, three days before the parliament was scheduled to open. After several attempts to meet with Bonney, he was finally told that he would be "allowed" to deliver his address. The meetings, which the *Chicago Daily News* called the "New Jerusalem Congress," opened on September 11 with great fanfare.[138] Over the course of the next few days Roberts attended several of the sessions. Roberts said the "gentlemen of the Parliament were surprised to see me ... and they did all they could to discourage my hope of getting a hearing." He was not surprised because many of these men had supported federal efforts against the Mormons. He finally told the chair that "Mormonism was morally entitled to a hearing," but he realized the parliament officials were "afraid of public sentiment."[139]

Roberts was in attendance when Alexander Russell Webb, a convert to Islam, made a presentation on "The Spirit of Islam," in which he "offhandedly broached the Muslim practice of polygamy." Though he did not advocate polygamy, Webb said that "polygamy is no curse. A man can be a good Christian and yet be a polygamist."

136. Roberts to Ann Roberts, Aug. 13, 1893, box 4, folder 7, Roberts Papers (UU).
137. Neilson, *Exhibiting Mormonism*, 151–53.
138. "Meeting of Many Sects," *Chicago Daily News*, Sep. 16, 1893, 1.
139. Roberts to Mother, Sept. 18, 1893 box 4, folder 7, Roberts Papers (UU).

Such views were inimical to Victorian America's sensibilities, and they set off a firestorm.[140] Barrows, who may have urged Webb to discuss polygamy since he chaired the session in which the paper was delivered, "hoped to use the incident to disqualify Roberts and his pending presentation on the church. Ultimately the committee decided not to allow Roberts to present his remarks in the main hall, but move it to a side room."[141] Roberts, who made no mention of polygamy in his remarks, saw the move, probably correctly, as a slight and protested "over the way he and his church had been treated by supposedly open-minded Parliament organizers."[142] Roberts told Barrow that he would withdraw his paper if he were not allowed to present it in the larger hall, seeking only to have the privilege of speaking "from the same platform from which the great religious faiths had spoken, so that the LDS "position and principles could be compared and contrasted with the viewpoint and doctrines of other religions, by the enlightened thought of the age."[143]

On September 25, 1893, the *Chicago Herald* reported that Roberts was told he could speak only in Hall 3 before a "select assemblage of people particularly interested in his doctrines." After the audience "waited patiently," Roberts sent word that "he would not enter the congress at all unless he could appear before the representatives of all faiths."[144] When the appointed time came, Merwin-Marie Snell, president of the Scientific Section of the Parliament, who had become a friend of Roberts's, called the meeting to order and said that Roberts's decision not to give his remarks under these new circumstances was "right." Snell said that snubbing Roberts was a "blemish upon the name and future history of the great parliament of religions" and criticized officials that "such an insult should be heaped upon the Mormon Church." Snell condemned the reversals to which Roberts had been subjected, noting that he was "granted the privilege once of holding a presentation ..., but it was afterward revoked. I do not blame the elder for refusing to read a paper before a mere adjunct of

140. See Neilson, "Blacksmith Orator," 71–73.
141. Neilson, *Exhibiting Mormonism*, 166–68.
142. Neilson, 169.
143. The paper was later published in Roberts, *Defense of the Faith*, 1:5–22.
144. "Happenings of a Day," *Chicago Herald*, Sep. 25, 1893, 5.

the parliament."[145] The *Chicago Record,* said that "what the meeting lacked in numbers it made up in spice."[146] The events were picked up in the *Millennial Star,* which also quoted from the *Chicago Herald*, noting that Roberts had "good grounds" for his complaint since "the gathering … was a parliament of religions—not a parliament of Christian, or a parliament of monogamist religion. The people in attendance knew what they might expect when they accepted invitations to the congress. If they decided to hear only what was entirely agreeable to them they might better have stayed away."[147]

The remarks Roberts prepared—simply titled "Mormonism"—were published a decade later in volume one of his two-volume collection *Defense of the Faith and the Saints.* Roberts began by asserting that Mormonism was one of the "most instructive " and "important religious movements of the nineteenth century," because it appeared in an age "which believed that God's voice would no more be heard giving revelation; that said the volume of scripture was completed and forever closed; that declared angels could no more visit the earth to communicate the divine will; and that sedulously taught that all miracles had ceased." Because their teachings were so different, Roberts argued, the Latter-day Saints had met with much opposition and many obstacles in the church's sixty-three years of existence. Despite ridicule, satire, bigotry, hatred, misunderstanding, mob violence and persecution from individuals, churches and the federal government, Mormonism had become recognized as a "potent religious force," which is why he believed it had the "right to be heard in this Parliament, in giving expression to its faith and distinguishing characteristics." Roberts also contrasted Mormonism with what he called "new religions," which

> when struggling for existence in the face of adversity, with few followers and no influence, may expect to be treated with silent contempt by the supposedly orthodox; but when a religion has fought its way through all opposition to a position of influence, and counts within its pale hundreds of thousands of sincere and intelligent followers, it gives proof that its

145. "Happenings of a Day."

146. "Spoke for Mormonism," *Chicago Record*, Sep. 25, 1893, as cited in Neilson, *Exhibiting Mormonism*, 172.

147. *Millennial Star*, Nov. 27, 1893, 774–75.

> doctrines contain some measure of truth at least, and by reason of that fact, has a claim upon the respect and thoughtful consideration of mankind.[148]

He strongly endorsed the Book of Mormon, which he called "a volume equal in bulk and equal in importance to the New Testament." He defended the traditional view of its origins saying it was "revealed to the Prophet Joseph Smith by the ministry of an angel, and translated by him into the English language by means of the Urim and Thummin hidden with the golden plates upon which the record was engraven." He compared Mormonism with what he had learned in his brief attendance at the religious gathering, stating that while delegates had heard "voices from all nations and races" from throughout the world, these voices were "united in saying that in all these lands and in all ages God has not left himself without witnesses."[149] The Book of Mormon should be understood within that context. The Book of Mormon, he said, should be seen as further evidence "of the authorship of the Jewish scripture" at a time when it was challenged by the modern concept known as "Higher Criticism" because it constituted a record "of a colony of Israelites that left Palestine six hundred years before Christ" who had "preserved with great care" and handed down generation after generation, these teachings so that the volume was indeed a "New Witness for God."[150] Roberts argued that Mormonism is "progressive" and

> destined to become the religion of the age. Within it is scope for all the intelligence that shall flow unto it. Within its atmosphere is room for every intellectual wing. It does not, as some have supposed, thrive best where ignorance is profound, nor does it depend upon superstition and ignorance for its existence and perpetuity. It possesses within itself principles of native strength that will enable it to weather every storm, outlive all hatred born of ignorance and prejudice, and it will yet prove itself to be what indeed it is, the gospel of Jesus Christ, the power of God unto Salvation to all those who obey and believe it, the Church of Jesus Christ.[151]

After the Parliament of Religions ended, Roberts addressed a letter to Bonney, as president of the World's Congress Auxiliary, and

148. Roberts, *Defense of the Faith*, 1:7.
149. Roberts, 1:11–13.
150. Roberts, 1:19–20.
151. Roberts, 1:21–22.

Barrows, as chair of the General Committee Religious Parliament, complimenting them on the event, saying that the parliament would "take its place in the history of the nineteenth century as one of the most important events connected with the most important century since the one in which the Messiah was born." He said that in general the Parliament has "established a reputation for broad-minded fairness, toleration of differences in religious thought and even-handed and high-minded justice to all men of all religious faiths." This representation would have been more "fairly achieved" had parliament organizers not allowed a "spirit of narrow bigotry" to deny him the right to speak. Roberts then provided a long recitation of the history of the church and the successes and persecutions the Mormons had experienced. "Were you afraid," Roberts asked rhetorically, "I would speak of these things if given an opportunity to speak?" His proposal, he stated, "made the slightest reference to these things ... for we were more anxious to tell you about the great truths of our religion than to relate our sufferings."[152]

The experience of LDS women and of the Tabernacle Choir was at odds with Roberts shabby treatment by the World Parliament of Religions. "Nevertheless," Reid Neilson comments, "the Mormon successes—and struggles—at the Chicago World's Fair pushed church leaders to seek to escape the imposed confines and to exhibit thereafter their ecclesiastical institution as embodying a culturally advanced society."[153]

Ironically, while Roberts was seeking a hearing, RLDS president Joseph Smith III, Apostle W. W. Blair, and several associates attended the parliament's meetings and held RLDS services at Lincoln Hall without controversy. On September 17, Smith addressed the group on "The Signs of the Times."[154] Smith praised the gather-

152. B. H. Roberts, "An Open Letter," (Chicago) *Daily Inter Ocean*, Sep. 28, 1893, 4. The *Deseret News* agreed with Roberts and called the Parliament of Religions "a fairly harmonious assembly in the true spirit of evangelical alliance, on a broader scale than ever before. That the deliberations will be productive of much good can hardly be denied." See "The Religious Congress," *Deseret News*, Sep. 29, 1893, 4.

153. Neilson, *Exhibiting Mormonism*, 175.

154. See "Miscellaneous," *Chicago Tribune*, Sep. 17, 1893, 13; and "Services Today," *Inter-Ocean*, Sep. 17, 1893, 3. See also Ron Romig to Newell G. Bringhurst, July 10, 1996, box 12, fd. 1, Accn. 1341, Bringhurst Papers, Marriott Library, Special Collections, University of Utah.

ing, and some conference proceedings were published in the *Saints' Herald*. Smith later told a friend, "What a wonderful thing it was. Would the time come when all the world were akin in faith."[155]

The *Millennial Star*, however, saw it differently, editorializing that another "chapter has been added to the world's history of religious movements, but in that chapter is again found a page sullied by intolerance and marred by cowardice, prejudice and injustice." The "gathering has [not] accomplished anything except to make the East a little more acquainted with the West," and perhaps secure more tolerance and protection in "Oriental countries for the missionaries who shall be sent to teach [them] … a perverted gospel … without the power to save." Certainly it had not brought representatives of the various religions "nearer to each other."[156]

At the Utah Stake conference in Provo, held October 16–17, 1893, the *Deseret Evening News* reported that Roberts "referred to the Parliament of Religion held in Chicago. The contrast between the religious beliefs there expounded and Mormonism was so great that he was more grateful than ever for the Gospel. The religionists in Chicago reminded him of children playing at keeping house with broken dishes. They had only fragments of truth; but the Latter-day Saints had the fulness of truth."[157]

155. See Launius, *Joseph Smith III*, 296, 314.
156. "Parliament of Religions," *Millennial Star*, Oct. 30, 1893, 708–10.
157. "Stake Conference," *Deseret Evening* News, Oct. 16, 1893, 6.

EIGHT

WOMEN'S SUFFRAGE

At the conclusion of the World Parliament of Religions, Roberts returned his attention to politics. On October 22, 1893, he addressed a crowd of some nine hundred people at a rally sponsored by the Young Men's Democratic Club where he held forth for more than two hours. Most of his remarks centered on the tariff and his criticism of Republican policies. Noting that while the Republicans believed high tariffs protected American industries, Roberts argued that it was a defective approach because it was Americans, not foreigners, who imported goods, and "the great burden falls upon the poor man with large family instead of upon the rich." Democrats, on the other hand, believed workers, not manufacturers, should be protected, and taxes and duties should be used solely to raise revenue. At the same time, he argued this difference was typical of the basic split between the two parties—Republicans favored the wealthy, Democrats the working class. Under Republican rule "the people are being taxed until they are getting poorer and poorer," while the few wealthy are "growing wealthier." Roberts concluded by endorsing Joseph L. Rawlins, and making his standard call for Utahns to vote Democratic, not so they could influence the presidential race, but by positioning Utah, with Democratic support, for gaining statehood.[1]

On January 28, Roberts left Centerville to serve what was announced as a six-month mission to California.[2] For some of that time he traveled in company with apostles Francis M. Lyman and Moses Thatcher, who had gone partly for health reasons. After spending time in the Bay Area, Lyman and Roberts gave public addresses up and down the state as part of efforts to strengthen

1. "A Great Democratic Lecture," *Ogden Standard*, Oct. 23, 1892, 1.

2. "Centerville Chats," *Davis County Clipper*, Feb. 2, 1894, 1.

the California Mission, which was being led by Karl G. Maeser.[3] On March 10, the *Los Angeles Times* reported that Roberts was "the advance agent of the Mormon elders," who were currently "engaged in a proselytizing expedition" in that city.[4] A few days later while in San Bernardino, Roberts wrote a letter to his mother, telling her that he and Lyman "came to southern California on a preaching tour among the Josephites [RLDS] and the old Mormons who have drifted here." Even though he delivered twelve lectures, "which by the way were fairly well attended," Roberts struggled "to make any impression on these who have once known the way of truth and then have turned away from it.[5]

Roberts assured his mother he was "in the best of health and spirits," and that while as "busy as I can be … attending to my ministry," he was working on his forthcoming book "on New Witnesses."[6] He also told her that the schedule was to go to San Diego, then back to Los Angeles, and return home via San Francisco, "arriving around conference time in April.[7]

As was often the case, Roberts's activities attracted notice in the local press. Toward the end of his tour, the *San Francisco Examiner* published on his efforts in the Bay Area, reporting that Roberts, whom they called a "traveling preacher," spoke to a small gathering as part of organizing church branches there and in Oakland. As the paper summarized Roberts's argument:

> Generally it is supposed that Mormonism is a new religion. It is not. It does not ask you to worship a new God, but it asks you to worship God in action more than in word. It has no new gospel. A new gospel could not be true. But the gospel had become perverted, the spirit had changed, the laws had been transgressed. It had become necessary to restore the old religion and that is what Mormonism is doing.[8]

---

3. See Roberts to John Whitaker, Feb. 8 to Mar. 10, 1894, Whitaker Papers.

4. "City Briefs," *Los Angeles Times*, Mar. 10, 1894, 12; and "Personal," *Los Angeles Herald*, Mar. 10, 1894, 4.

5. Roberts to Mother, Feb. 23, 1894, box 4, fd. 7, Roberts Papers (UU).

6. Roberts, *New Witness For God.* The first of a trilogy, this volume dealt with Joseph Smith. Two later volumes were published in 1909, dealing with the Book of Mormon. They were a reprint of three YMMIA manuals used between 1903 and 1906.

7. Roberts to Mother.

8. "A Mormon Church," *San Francisco Examiner*, Mar. 27, 1893, 3. The paper commented, "There were four ladies in the congregation, but they were merely spectators."

Roberts enjoyed the trip, but as he told his friend Susa Young Gates, "the weather is delightful in this place—green grass and roses instead of Utah harsh winds and snow—but then give me Utah; for even sunshine and flowers will not make up for the separation from one's friends."[9] Roberts returned to Utah in late March.

While he traveled, a series of meetings was being held by LDS leadership to address Roberts's political activities as well as those of Moses Thatcher and Charles W. Penrose. On March 23, the First Presidency and the Quorum of the Twelve considered the actions of the three men. Specifically they asked the First Council of Seventy to work with Roberts.[10] Four days later, three apostles—Joseph F. Smith, Brigham Young Jr.,[11] and Francis M. Lyman—joined Seymour B. Young,[12] J. Golden Kimball, and George Reynolds[13] of the Seventies, along with Salt Lake Stake president Angus M. Cannon[14] and his counselor Joseph E. Taylor,[15] to discuss Penrose and Roberts.[16] Roberts began to learn about these meetings on March 30, when he attended a meeting of the First Council of Seventy.[17] Roberts wrote that "perhaps a misapprehension had existed as to the course I had taken." Roberts seemed to believe it was all a misunderstanding,

9. See Roberts to Susa Young Gates, Feb. 24, 1894, Gates Papers. Roberts ended the letter stating "for ever let us be friends."

10. Alexander, *Things in Heaven and Earth*, 295.

11. Brigham Young Jr. (1836–1903) served as a member of the Quorum of the Twelve from 1877 until his death. He married seven women, including one in 1901. Young was involved in a variety of church and civic activities. At one point a Democrat, he became a Republican toward the end of his life.

12. Seymour B. Young (1837–1924) was a member of the First Council of Seventy from 1882 until his death. Young was a medical doctor educated at the University of Deseret and University Medical College of New York. He was a Republican and was involved in a number of church, civic, and political activities.

13. George Reynolds (1842–1909) was a secretary to the First Presidency and a member of the First Council of Seventy from 1890 until his death. He had three wives, and is best known as the plaintiff in the US Supreme Court case *Reynolds vs. United States*, which upheld the anti-polygamy legislation of the 1880s.

14. Angus M. Cannon (1834–1915) was the younger brother of George Q. Cannon. He served as Salt Lake Stake president, 1877–1904.

15. Taylor (1830–1913) was an undertaker and businessperson who served as a counselor in the Salt Lake Stake presidency from 1876 to 1904. Taylor married four women before the 1890 Manifesto. He was a Democratic member of the Utah House of Representatives, 1897–98.

16. Alexander, *Things in Heaven and Earth*, 295.

17. At this point, there was an unfilled vacancy in the First Council caused by the death of Susa Young Gates's father-in-law, Jacob Gates, on April 14, 1892.

because he felt he had "called upon the Presidency during the course of the campaign and had submitted myself to their counsel offering to withdraw entirely fr[om] the campaign." But when he was done speaking, Seymour Young "desired that I should call upon the presidency and acknowledge my errors in regard to my political operations and also to express to Bro. [Francis M.] Lyman my present feelings on the subject of Pres. Woodruff's Manifesto in respect to Plural Marriage. I agreed to do so."[18]

The next morning, he met with President Woodruff. In addition to the First Presidency, Francis M. Lyman, Franklin D. Richards, John Henry Smith, George Teasdale, George Reynolds, and Brigham Young Jr. also attended. Woodruff began the discussion "remarking that I [Roberts] had come in to have some talk with them as to the course I had pursued in political affairs."[19] Roberts wrote that he was asked if he recognized the "right of the First Presidency to counsel the members of the church in all matters temporal or spiritual," or if he believed "they were limited as to the subjects upon which they should give council?" Roberts replied that he recognized the "right of the Almighty to give revelations to his children on all subjects temporal or spiritual" and that there were no limits that could be fixed. Moreover, he reassured the assembled authorities that, "as the President of the church is God's mouthpiece to the people he too was free to reveal to the people whatever God revealed to him & they were under the same obligations to obey … as when God himself spoke."[20] Roberts also acknowledged his "wrong" in regards to "the course I had taken on the Manifesto," and stated that this was then "accepted by the brethren & the Presidency" who extended their hand of fellowship to him.[21]

After this humbling before the First Presidency and other leaders,

18. Roberts, *History's Apprentice*, 278–79 (Mar. 30, 1893). Roberts also noted that later in the afternoon he "called upon Margaret; found herself & family well" though she had passed through "bitter experiences during my absence." He does not elaborate on the nature of those experiences.

19. Roberts, *History's Apprentice*, 280 (Mar. 31, 1893). Most church leaders were in the city for the Salt Lake Temple dedication, which began on April 6 and spanned nineteen days with thirty-one dedication ceremonies. This was done to accommodate all who wanted to attend.

20. Roberts, 280–81.

21. Roberts, 281.

Roberts for the next few days busied himself at home in Centerville, worked at the Seventy's office, attended general conference where he spoke on the importance of the temple, and made preparation for the temple dedication. After that, much of his activity centered around various church meetings, including engagements at the Davis Stake conference, a joint YMMIA and YLMIA conference in the Provo Tabernacle, and commencement services at Latter-day Saints University. He also participated in a series of debates with Rev. Samuel E. Wishard,[22] held in Nephi. Wishard was there for the Utah Presbyterian Church's annual conference. Over the course of the debate, which Charles Penrose also participated in, Roberts argued that the Bible itself was "not sufficient" for salvation, and rebutted Wishard's claim that Mormonism was "split" into factions, saying that the Josephites, Morrisites, and Godbeites "were not at all part of Mormonism." He also criticized Wishard's admission that the Presbyterians had spent $65,000 in support of missionary work in Utah, comparing that with the Mormon approach of going without purse or scrip. Moreover, he asserted that he could prove that Mormon missionaries "have been whipped with hickory whips, Elders have been shot down, and [that] Presbyterians were among some of the murderers." The *Deseret News* noted that the meetings "have caused considerable comment and by both Saints and non-Saints [and] it is conceded that Elders Penrose and Roberts were too much for their reverend opponent."[23]

A few months later, Roberts lost his good friend and mentor John Morgan, who died on August 14, 1894, after being seriously ill for more than a month, suffering from typhoid-malaria.[24] Roberts told the mourners who filled the hall—in what the *Tribune* called a "funeral panegyric"[25]—that he had first met Morgan when he was a

22. Samuel Ellis Wishard (1825–1915) was ordained a Presbyterian minister in 1857, the same year he married Sarah Evarts (1834–1912). Wishard first came to Utah in 1886. After a short stint in Des Moines, Iowa, he returned to the state in 1888 where he served as Synodical Secretary and supervised missionary work until 1915. Much of that time he lived in Ogden. He wrote a number of books and articles on Mormonism based on his first-hand experience. Among them is *The Mormons* (New York: Presbyterian Home Missions, 1904). See "Dr. S. E. Wishard," *Ogden Standard*, Nov. 13, 1915, 14.

23. See Cannon Journal, Aug. 28, 1894.

24. "Elder John Morgan Dead," *Deseret Weekly*, Aug. 18, 1894, 265.

25. "Funeral of John Morgan," *Salt Lake Tribune*, Aug. 19, 1894, 7.

student at his school in Salt Lake City, and that "he had learned to love and admire him as a teacher." He talked of the times they had spent together in the Southern States Mission where he and the other missionaries "learned to rely on his good judgement and how great the confidence they had in following his leadership." He closed by pointing to Morgan's coffin which was draped with a tattered Union battle flag, and reminded those in attendance that he was also a man who had served his country in the Union army fighting "through all the years of the great rebellion."[26] As he would later tell Susa Young Gates, Morgan was "the man who stood nearest to me, and one whose companionship was like the companionship of a brother."[27]

On September 10, Davis County Democrats met in a convention held in Farmington where they selected Roberts to run for delegate to the state constitutional convention.[28] Roberts was not present when he was nominated because he was filling a church assignment in Wyoming. When he became aware that he had been nominated for delegate, based on his belief that "prominent church officers would not stand for election to the convention," he called on the First Presidency. Roberts "learned from this consultation that the previous conclusions had been modified to permit prominent brethren of the church to be elected." Apparently church leaders realized that forbidding LDS authorities from political "consideration would deprive the state of some of the best service that could be given in the convention."[29]

Roberts says that based on "this understanding," he made preparations if elected for the convention and its duties.[30] Moreover, even though he had not been at the convention that nominated him, he must have known that the Utah Democratic Party had taken a firm

26. "Elder John Morgan," *Deseret Weekly*, Aug. 25, 1894, 32; "The Last Sad Rites," *Salt Lake Herald*, Aug. 19, 1894, 6; and "Elder John Morgan," *Deseret Evening News*, Aug. 18, 1894, 5. J Golden Kimball also spoke and told the mourners that the *Chattanooga Times* has said in 1884 that "to grasp his hand was to become his friend." Kimball would repeat that story many times in the future.

27. Roberts to Gates, Sep. 30, 1898, Gates Papers.

28. "Are Swinging Into Line," *Salt Lake Herald*, Sep. 11, 1894, 3.

29. Roberts, *Autobiography*, 183–84. See also "Roberts Makes a Statement," *Salt Lake Herald*, Oct. 14, 1895, 1.

30. Roberts, *Autobiography*, 184. Unfortunately, no diary seems extant for this important period of Roberts's political career.

stand in favor of woman suffrage. At the party's territorial convention in September 1894, the platform said that the "Democrats of Utah are unequivocally in favor of woman suffrage, and the political rights and privileges of women equal with those of men, including eligibility to office; and we demand that such guarantees shall be provided in the Constitution of the State of Utah as will secure to the women of Utah these inestimable rights."[31]

Beginning in early October, Roberts campaigned throughout the state. On October 8, he and Joseph L. Rawlins spoke at a "great rally" in Spanish Fork,[32] the Provo *Evening Dispatch* commenting that Rawlins and Roberts would "wipe all trace of Frank Cannon and [Hiram] Booth," the Republican candidates, "from the face of the earth."[33] From Utah County, they worked south into Juab County. The *Salt Lake Herald* reported that at a meeting in Minersville, Rawlins and Roberts "made the ground so slippery that several Republican have fallen on the right side."[34] As the election drew to a close, Roberts spoke along with Rawlins at a rally in Payson where "the meeting house was packed to a jam." According to press accounts, the rally was marked by four bands and "shouting, marching, music, fireworks" in a torch-light parade, and that the "grand speech of B. H. Roberts had its telling effect." According to the *Evening Dispatch*, "Many doubtfuls were won over and the Republicans are sadly rattled."[35]

Toward the end of October, Roberts spoke at a "Grand Rally" in the Continental Market Hall[36] to explore the "fundamental differences between the two parties," and to dispute the "misstatements and wild assertions of the Republican candidate for Delegate to Congress." The *Salt Lake Herald* called the rally "the political event of the season," and said Roberts's speech was "to say the least, superb."

31. Quoted in "What the Platform Demands," *Salt Lake Herald* Apr. 7, 1895, 4.

32. "Political Notes," *Salt Lake Herald*, Oct. 9, 1894, 8.

33. "Local Notes, *Evening Dispatch*, Oct. 11, 1894, 2.

34. "Rawlins and Roberts," *Salt Lake Herald*, Oct. 13, 1894, 3.

35. "The Tribune and Rawlins," *Evening Dispatch*, Oct. 25, 1894, 2. The paper noted that the team of Rawlins and Roberts had Republicans "wishing that it wasn't this party which is on the other side of the fight."

36. According to the *Herald*, "The place will be well warmed and every convenience offered. Ladies are specially invited, reserved seats being provided for them." "Rally Monday Night," *Salt Lake Herald*, Oct. 21, 1894, 8.

As the paper reported, "The house was packed so full that every seat was occupied, the aisles full of standing spectators, while so many were denied admission that an overflow meeting was necessary" for several hundred people. Among those in attendance were the leading lights of the Democratic Party, including Brigham Young Jr., Heber J. Grant, C. S. Varian, Joseph L. Rawlins and many others. Moreover, the paper noted that "campaign orators in advancing party arguments are too often prone to allow themselves to get in a rut, but not so with Mr. Roberts. He was most refreshingly bright and sparkling, clothing every thought advanced with language captivating and convincing."[37] Two days later, the *Salt Lake Herald* reported that Rawlins's prospects "grew brighter, as the days go by, while Frankie's [Frank Cannon] sun is on the decline and … disappearing beneath the snow crowned hills of the mountain range of defeat. … He is doing a world of good for Rawlins."[38] The event received a very different slant in the *Salt Lake Tribune*, which reported that the audience consisted of "fully 500 women and children, and about 400 men and 200 boys," and that while it was advertised as a speech in behalf of the Democrats, it "in truth, will make if correctly reported in full one of the best Republican campaign documents."[39]

In Ephraim, Roberts argued that Republican protectionist policies were designed "to crush the Lehi sugar factory and destroy the sugar industry in this territory." He advocated a resolution written by James P. Christensen, the local Democratic chair, that it was the "mission of the Democratic party to strike down trusts, combines and monopolies," and called on the introduction of similar petitions at every rally until election day, and to "continue the fight … so long as the infamous trust threatens our home industry," by pledging only to buy from "merchants handling the Lehi sugar."[40] The local correspondent for the *Herald* said, "Mr. Roberts made it so hot for the g.o.p. that the kingpin of the local Republicans, who was occupying one of the front seats had to get up and leave. His retirement was greeted with roars of

37. "A Magnificent Rally," *Salt Lake Herald*, Oct. 25, 1894, 3. The paper included a lengthy record of the speech itself. It also noted that "there must have been 2,000 people inside, at a conservative estimate, many of whom were ladies."

38. "The Local Situation," *Salt Lake Herald*, Oct. 26, 1894, 5.

39. "Entertained the Old Ladies," *Salt Lake Tribune*, Oct. 25, 1894, 6.

40. "Boycotting the Trust," *Salt Lake Herald*, Nov. 3, 1894, 5.

laughter from the enthusiastic Democrats.[41] Roberts closed the campaign with a well-attended rally in Ogden's Grand Opera House. The *Salt Lake Herald* warned Democrats "To look out for bogus tickets tomorrow. The Republicans are preparing them."[42]

Despite Democratic efforts, when the votes were counted, Frank Cannon was elected over Rawlins 21,343 to 19,523.[43] With the exception of Davis County, most of the places where Roberts campaigned intensely went to Cannon. When the votes in Davis County for convention delegates were tabulated, Roberts led the Democratic slate with 629 votes, while Barnes and Call each received 618 votes, and all three were elected as delegates to the Constitutional Convention. The Democrats out-polled the Republican ticket—E. P. Ellison, H. W. Haight, and John W. Hess—by about a margin of 140 votes. Roberts carried every voting precinct in Davis County except South Bountiful, Syracuse, and Kaysville.[44] Taking into account Roberts's election to the convention, the 1894 campaign had been a significant one for Roberts. He had toured the state, gained considerable press coverage, and established himself as a leading figure—at age thirty-three—in the Democratic Party.

Once the campaign was over, Roberts, along with sixty other prominent Democrats, participated in a "farewell banquet" for Rawlins held in the Knutsford Hotel on November 24. The *Salt Lake Herald* reported that "the tables were arranged in the form of a letter 'H,' and the menu was equal to Delmonico's[45] choicest." Rawlins asked his "Fellow Democrats and Friends in disappointment," to take heart, and that while the "case for which we have so valiantly fought has gone down temporarily … it requires only a little effort to bring it back to fruition. … Our principles will cause us to regain power and our party will be crowned with glories unending." Saying he believed the new state would soon be in the Democratic column,

41. "Tariff Is a Tax," *Salt Lake Herald*, Nov. 5, 1894, 3.

42. [Untitled], *Salt Lake Herald*, Nov. 5, 1894, 8.

43. Utah Commission, *Report*, 70.

44. Canvass of Special Election, Nov. 6, 1894, Utah Commission Election Returns Register, Book 4, p. 21. Interestingly, Roberts listed his occupation in the official record as "author." See Utah Commission, *Report*, 42.

45. Delmonico's was a famous New York City gourmet restaurant, and was probably the first restaurant in the U.S. to offer patrons menus instead of a single fixed meal. See Burrows and Wallace, *Gotham*, 437, 1154.

Roberts responded, "I for one am sure Utah will be redeemed from the disgrace that has come upon it. It will be written that Utah is for Democracy, and I pledge it in the blood of the braze."[46]

Between his election as a delegate and the beginning of the constitutional convention, Roberts continued his regular activity as a member of the First Council of Seventy and in his capacity with the YMMIA.[47] He also remained a featured speaker at the regular service held at the Salt Lake Tabernacle,[48] speaking on topics including "Why I Am a Mormon" and "Sin and its Consequences: Repentance and its Effects."[49]

Roberts was also at work on his book, *A New Witness for God.* On February 21, George Q. Cannon recorded, Roberts had met with him expressing "the desire that the work might be endorsed as authentic and orthodox by the council of apostles and the Seventies, and left me to infer that he wanted the endorsement of the First Presidency." Cannon said he told Roberts previously that he, and by extension the First Presidency, felt on the question of endorsing such works "that we thought it was a bad practice for us to indulge in … leaving each work to be sold on its own merits." Roberts told Cannon that the A. R. Barnes publishing company—a non-Mormon publisher—had told him that "the endorsement of the leading authorities" would result in better sales. So Cannon took Roberts's request to the First Presidency, who turned it down. The book was published locally by George Q. Cannon & Sons.[50]

Roberts was appointed by territorial governor Caleb West to be a member of the board of trustees of Utah Agricultural College,[51] and Celia delivered their fourth child, Naola. But once the constitutional convention began, Roberts's lectures, family duties, church assignments, and political meetings took a backseat.[52] Initially, as

46. "In Honor of Rawlins," *Salt Lake Herald,* Nov. 25, 1894, 8; "Big Consolation Blowout," *Salt Lake Tribune,* Nov. 25, 1894, 5.

47. "B. H. Roberts to Speak," *Brigham City Bugler,* Feb. 2, 1895, 1.

48. See for example "At The Tabernacle," *Salt Lake Herald,* Jan. 28, 1895, 8.

49. "Centerville Chats," *Davis County Clipper,* Feb. 7, 1895, 1; "Lecture by B. H. Roberts, *Deseret Evening News,* Feb. 9, 1895, 1.

50. Roberts, *New Witness for God.*

51. "Local and Other Matters," *Deseret Weekly,* Mar. 2, 1895, 16.

52. For example, he lectured to the Brigham Young Academy Polysophical Society on Mar. 22, 1895. See "Provo Paragraphs," *Salt Lake Herald,* Mar. 20, 1895.

the delegates organized, his name was mentioned as a possibility for convention president, although the fact that the Republicans would control the proceedings made such talk speculative.[53] At the same time, the *Salt Lake Herald* noted his presence, saying he was part of a "notable group" seated to the right of the president's desk, including Karl G. Maeser, Anthony W. Ivins, S. R. Thurman, David Evans, and Orson F. Whitney.[54]

Roberts came to the convention with definite opinions on the proper role and composition of government, and on limits on its powers. As historian D. Craig Mikkelsen has written, Roberts was "deeply concerned" about the attitude of state government toward private business. He saw corporate power as "the one great evil … which promises to overthrow the institutions of our country more than any other danger." He observed that corporations "have no bodies that you can kick, and they have no souls that you can tempt, and they are the most difficult things to contend with that ever confronted our civilization." He also opposed state subsidies for private business, even Utah's developing sugar industry. "I am not willing even that this enterprise laudable as … it is, should be sustained and supported by the expense of the people because … other projects will be inaugurated which will not be so laudable."[55]

At the same time, he had interesting views on the issue of statewide prohibition. On the one hand, he agreed with church leaders that placing prohibition into the state constitution was unwise and might well alienate gentiles and endanger ratification. On the other hand, he disagreed with them on efforts to outlaw the sale and manufacture of alcohol. For Roberts "prohibition was a species of laws governments had no business making and he opposed it—on moral grounds." He argued that "notwithstanding all the array of blood

53. "Plans of the Delegates," *Salt Lake Tribune*, Mar. 4, 1895, 8.

54. Whitney (1855–1931) was active in politics, theater, and literary efforts in the territory, including on the Salt Lake City Council, 1880–81, and as city treasurer 1884–88. After the convention, he taught at Brigham Young College in Logan, 1896–97. A Democrat, he served in the Utah State Senate, 1899–1901. His most important publication is his four-volume *History of Utah*. Whitney was an active Mormon who served several missions and was the longtime bishop of the Eighteenth Ward. He became a member of the Quorum of the Twelve in 1906 and served until his death. Prior to that he was associated with Roberts as an assistant church historian.

55. Mikkelsen, "Politics of B. H. Roberts," 30.

curdling incidents that may be related as growing out of the acts of men under the influence ... so dear is to me the liberty of the individual that I would pay the price for it, and if I could, I would not destroy the liberty and agency of man."[56]

But it soon became clear that the dominating issue for Roberts himself, and the constitution as a whole, was women's suffrage.[57] Indeed, on the eve of the convention, it was obvious to most observers that there was considerable support among Roberts's fellow Democrats for including a suffrage plank. As one historian of women at the convention has noted, "while the woman suffrage plank was placed near the end of the [Democratic] party platform," it received "a much stronger endorsement than it had from the Republicans," who simply said they favored "the granting of equal suffrage to women."[58] Emboldened, suffrage forces set out to consolidate their strength. Dr. Ellen B. Ferguson,[59] president of the Women's Suffrage Association of Salt Lake City, "urged members to visit the newly elected convention delegates to see if they intended to put Suffrage in the Constitution." She said some delegates were "wavering," while others were "inclined to hang back saying wait till we are a state and then we will give women suffrage." Additionally, Emmeline B. Wells warned that some women opposed it, and said they should think about that because they "might someday need political rights" for themselves or their children." Despite these concerns, by the time the convention opened, giving women the right to vote appeared to be a sure thing. Suffrage associations which had organized nineteen of Utah's twenty-seven counties "had done their work well," in the words of historian Jean Bickmore White. Women had already had the right to vote in Utah since 1870, until it was stripped away by

56. Mikkelsen.

57. Several historians have written on women's suffrage at the state convention, and I rely on their work, as well as contemporary accounts, to understand Roberts's opposition. See White, "Woman's Place"; Bradley and Woodward, *Four Zinas*; Madsen, *Advocate for Women*; Van Wagenen, *Sister Wives and Suffragists*; and Derr, Cannon, and Beecher, *Women of the Covenant*.

58. White "Woman's Place."

59. Ferguson (1844–1920) was a local physician affiliated with the Deseret Hospital. She was a delegate to the 1896 Democratic National Convention. Ferguson was excommunicated in 1898 for her advocacy of theosophy, and a few years later relocated to the East, where she died.

anti-polygamy legislation. Most suffrage advocates in Utah saw putting the right to vote into the constitution as a restoration of rights, not a new policy.[60] At the same time, it is important to note that Utah women—both Mormon and gentile—were not unanimous on the question of putting a suffrage section in the state constitution.

Roberts, along with all the other delegates, received their official certificates as delegates to the constitutional convention from the Utah Commission in January 1895.[61] The convention formally opened on March 4, 1895, in the largest room on the third floor of the Salt Lake City and County building.[62] While the delegates met in these rooms, the Utah Woman Suffrage Association, with representatives from across the state, gathered in the nearby probate court room to keep an eye on the proceedings. They were led by Emmeline B. Wells, and among their number were Jane S. Richards, Augusta W. Grant,[63] Zina D. H. Young, and Emily S. Richards. The group "produced a memorial to be read by Franklin S. Richards" at the convention which called on the delegates to place in the constitution a guarantee that "the rights of the citizens of the State of Utah vote and hold office shall not be denied nor abridged on account of sex, [and] that male and female citizens of the state shall equally enjoy all civil, political and religious rights and privileges."[64]

Very quickly it was clear that Roberts would have a major role in the deliberations over the question of whether women's suffrage should be a part of the final document passed by the body. The suffrage issue became a heated point of contention at the convention, and many suffragists felt betrayed when Roberts emerged as one of the fiercest opponents of a woman's right to vote. As one historian wrote, "The opposition was led by one of their own." Roberts's actions were apparently a surprise. He had told the First Presidency not to object to the suffrage clause, but then struck out on his own to fight it.[65] The roots of his opposition are not entirely clear, but at

60. White, "Woman's Place," 348.

61. "The Commission Meets," *Salt Lake Herald*, Jan. 29, 1895, 5.

62. See White, *Charter for Statehood*.

63. Grant (1856–1952) was a teacher and active in both the YWMIA and Relief Society, and the plural wife of apostle Heber J. Grant.

64. Bradley and Woodward, *Four Zinas*, 357–58.

65. White, "Woman's Place"; 349, Madsen, *Advocate for Women*, 283; and Van Wagenen, *Sister Wives and Suffragists*, 148.

the convention he said he feared that, if suffrage was included, the US Congress would not grant statehood to Utah.

The Committee on Elections and Suffrage produced a resolution that stated, "The rights of citizens of the State of Utah to vote shall not be denied nor abridged on account of sex" and that both men and women "shall equally enjoy all civil, political and religious rights and privileges."[66] On the afternoon of March 27, the full convention moved toward final action on the matter, starting a long, and at times, heated debate. Soon Roberts rose to deliver a "lengthy speech before a rapt audience."[67] Roberts said that while he recognized that an "overwhelming majority" in favor of woman suffrage existed, he worried that including it as part of the constitution might diminish support by some in Congress for statehood.[68] Moreover, Roberts said that while he had heard the calls to be true to his party and its platform, "My appeal to you is to do your duty in first securing statehood for the people of Utah, and then let these questions take what course they may after that. Vote woman's suffrage up or down afterwards, I care not, although I have no sympathy with the arguments by which the doctrine is supported."[69]

He said that he knew that the press argued that such a move was political suicide, but he did not fear his own political demise,

> after the first flush of displeasure shall have passed way, the people among whom my boyhood and manhood were spent will not impute to me improper motives. They will know, if nobody else knows, that however faulty in my judgement I may be, there is a deep conviction in my heart that the line of duty demanded that I should take this ground, that [it] is my duty as I conceived it. ... They cannot say that I played the part of a demagogue or that, like a scurvy politician, I pretended that which I could not see. All considerations of interest drew me in the opposite direction of the course I have traveled. ... If I had ... political aspirations, every consideration of interest would have required me to accept and adopt this idea of suffrage[70]

66. "Among the Committees," *Salt Lake Tribune*, Mar. 12, 1895, 3. *Official Reports of the Proceedings and Debates of the Convention*, 1:407–08. Hereafter cited as *Proceedings*.

67. White, "Woman's Place," 355.

68. *Proceedings*, 1:425.

69. *Proceedings*, 1:427.

70. *Proceedings*, 1:427–28. Roberts had denied that he had political aspirations on

Roberts told the convention that he placed "the values of women upon a higher principle, and there is not a suffragist among you that has a higher opinion" of women than he did, but "that the influence of woman as it operates upon me never came from the rostrum, it never came from the pulpit with a woman in it, never came from the lecturers platform with woman speaking; it came from the fireside, it comes from the blessed association with mothers, of sisters, of wives, of daughters not as democrats or republicans."[71]

The *Salt Lake Herald*, while disagreeing with Roberts's opposition to woman suffrage, painted a vivid, first-hand account of his performance.

> He spoke to an audience composed of the leading women suffragists of this city, the delegates of the convention and the packed lobby, in which there was not an inch of standing room. From the beginning of his speech until the last word was uttered ... the interest never flagged. All eyes were fixed on the orator as he stood in front of the desk, towering over those who were ready to oppose him the most, as he one moment rose to a climax thrilling in its intensity, and the next checked himself and allowed his voice to become slow and pleading. It took him sometime to gather himself, but once he did he was an oratorical avalanche. A stream of language, potent and pleasing, flowed from his lips and caught his listeners until even those who were most bitterly opposed to him were compelled to pay compliment to his power with rapturous applause. As he stood alone ... fully recognizing the consequences of his action, the suffragists themselves could not but admire his courage, and when he had finished they crowded around him and shook his hand enthusiastically.[72]

Still, the *Herald* concluded that the proponents of woman suffrage have "reason," while the opponents have only "rhetoric."[73]

On March 30, Roberts ominously told his colleagues that he feared "that there is a great probability ... that this ... speech of mine will be the last that I shall make upon the floor of this convention."

---

several occasions. For example, he had spoken forcefully to J. H. Paul on the difficulties he would face as a candidate because of his conviction on unlawful cohabitation. See Roberts, *History's Apprentice*, 298.

71. *Proceedings*, 1:469.

72. "Suffrage Is the Theme," *Salt Lake Herald*, Mar. 29, 1895, 1. See also White, "Woman's Place," 325.

73. "The Equal Suffrage Contest," *Salt Lake Herald*, Mar. 29, 1895, 2.

He had "received a dispatch signed by the democratic committee of Davis County this morning, saying 'We must ask you to cease opposing woman suffrage or resign. Party pledges are sacred and must be kept.'" Roberts replied that he had no intention to "change my course" but that the party could "do what you think proper."[74]

John R. Barnes said the Democrats of Davis County had taken their stand "because they feel that Mr. Roberts has taken a stand diametrically opposed to their views and to their request made upon their delegates." The letter said that if "your convictions will not permit you to vote in favor of it, then you might at least remain inactive in the matter, and thus save our party the humiliation of having their pledges broken." In his own speech, Orson F. Whitney said that he "could not but admire the courage" Roberts showed as "he faced a frowning multitude." Whitney, with a touch of hyperbole, said the he was initially reminded of "Horatius ... standing single handed and alone, beating back the Tuscan legions advancing to attack the Eternal City." But he could not compare "my friend to that hero," because while "Horatius was fighting for freedom," Roberts, his "mistaken friend was fighting against it."[75] Whitney said Roberts should realize that "because a man 'stands alone,' in the midst of 'the crash of worlds,' that of itself is no sure sign that he is right."[76] To the contrary, Whitney argued, some times "majorities are right," and the majority on the floor of the convention is right to "put woman suffrage in the Constitution; we will strike the fetters from the wrists of our wives, mothers, sisters and daughters." Whitney compared women's suffrage to civil rights for African Americans, and said that if the right to vote was "granted to the black man under the pledge of the declaration that 'all men are created equal,'" the next logical step "in the mighty march of human liberty" was to give those same

74. *Proceedings*, 1:517. See also "Hon B. H. Roberts," *Logan Journal*, Apr. 2, 1895, 4. The paper stated it believed "the Davis County Democracy has a grave mistake in calling for his resignation. B. H. Roberts is an able, honest, contentious man—he can afford to retire from politics better than the party can lose him. He stands head and shoulders above any man in the convention. ... Utah must still be proud of him though Davis County Democracy casts him off."

75. *Proceedings*, 1:505.

76. *Proceedings*, 1:506–07.

rights to women. Roberts and other opponents, he insisted, were "not in tune with the march of human advancement."[77]

Whitney recorded that there were many comments about his speech. Heber M. Wells[78] told him through his brother that "Orson took Roberts by the scruff of the neck and the seat of his pants, swished him three times around his head, mopped the floor with him, and then took him up to a third story window and dropped him out."[79] Whitney also wrote that his statements on woman suffrage would be published as a pamphlet by the Utah Woman Suffrage Association, which they were.[80]

Eventually, the "body failed to pass a motion for separate submission of the issue with only 28 votes in favor."[81] The Logan-based *Utah Journal* commented on the differences between Roberts and Whitney, noting that Roberts was like a "hurricane" who swept all before him, while Whitney "bites like a winter wind." In that sense, Roberts is a "popular orator [who] talks from the heart," while his opponent is a "classical orator whose appeals clearly to the mind." The *Journal* mused that "Roberts arouses men to action; Whitney causes them to pause and think." And while "Roberts is a natural orator, Whitney has acquired the gift." These comparisons went on for some time: Roberts was a lion, Whitney a panther; Roberts a man of action, Whitney a man of thought; Roberts a man of men, Whitney a man of books.[82]

Roberts said that he would give a summation on April 2. With this advance notice, there was a threat of crowding so great that the convention considered moving up the street to the Salt Lake Theater to manage the swarm of people.[83] The gathering remained in the Salt Lake City and County building, but "the hall and lobby … was fairly packed and some very prominent ladies even stood on the tables in the cloak room in order to see and hear."[84] As early as 8:00

77. *Proceedings*, 1:508.
78. Wells (1859–1938) was Republican governor of Utah, 1896–1905.
79. Horne, *Life of Orson F. Whitney*, 167.
80. See Whitney, *Speeches*.
81. White, "Woman's Place," 361.
82. "Roberts and Whitney," *Utah Journal*, Apr. 2, 1895, 4.
83. White, "Woman's Place."
84. "Roberts Ends the Debate," *Salt Lake Herald*, Apr. 3, 1895, 1.

a.m., a "number of enthusiastic persons found their way to the hall," and by the time the delegates started to arrive, police had to be called so that they could get through the crowd.[85]

Roberts stood to speak. He reminded the body that he had not been at the Democratic Party convention where he was nominated "when the territorial convention assembled and put in its platform the plank on woman suffrage, I felt myself so opposed to it that I had serious thoughts of declining the honor tendered to me by the people of Davis County." But because suffrage had, according to Roberts, not arisen in the minutes of the convention, he took it "as their united opinion that I could not be bound to support woman suffrage."[86]

Roberts said he had tried to add seven distinct questions to the debate which he felt had not been answered nor countered. These seven issues had little to do with Utah acquiring statehood, and showed Roberts's concern over shifting gender roles and expectations. First, he argued that the franchise ought to be confined to those who are capable of acting independently, and asserted that "such was the relationship of woman in the family that she was not capable of acting thus independently without the dictation or the suspicion of dictation from her husband."[87] Second, he proposed "that the elective franchise was a privilege … not a right," and this view had not been sufficiently challenged to discredit his assertion. Third, there had not been a successful argument raised to his assertion that "the great mass of women of voting age" was already sufficiently represented in political matters by "husbands, fathers, sons [and] brothers." Fourth, his opponents had not disproved his assertion that there was no discrimination against women—married and unmarried—in the matter of taxation. Fifth, he held that his opponents had not proven that "the principle upon which the franchise has been hitherto extended" to women was for protection as opposed to intellectual equality. Such protection was not needed because "men and women are not natural enemies, on needing protection against the other but that they are on the best of terms. The fact that they marry proves it."[88] Sixth, his

85. "Roberts Ends the Debate."
86. *Proceedings*, 1:583.
87. *Proceedings*, 1:591.
88. *Proceedings*.

opponents had not proven that the "steady refusal ... to grant women the elective franchise ... was unwise." Asserting that all change was not progress, Roberts said that customs "bequeathed to us by antiquity" should not necessarily be struck down. Indeed, Roberts argued, "some of these customs ... are monuments that bespeak the wisdom of our ancestors, and we ought to have a decent respect for them."[89] Finally, he contended that proponents of suffrage had failed to show how extending the vote to women in and of itself would bring about major reforms in contemporary society, nor had they shown "what laws women would change, or what law is desirable to change."[90]

Roberts also raised the question of the role suffrage might play if it were granted to women in terms of domestic happiness. It was one of his most ill-considered and intemperate remarks, and yet was also one of the most honest and revealing. He asked his colleagues to imagine a man who came home from "struggling" to elect the candidate which "he believes will serve the interests of the people, coming home from the sweat and heat of a campaign meeting ... tired and weary of the world," only to be met at the door by a wife "opposed" to him politically, thus forcing him to either "go over the fight" on the issues of the day or else "observe a sullen silence because of the impropriety of engaging in a discussion along these lines." How long might it be, Roberts wondered, after a man's wife had sapped him of his energy, before "the brow be cleared of the frown and the heart lose some of its bitterness, so that when the man leaves his home and again enters the arena with his foes, he may have some milk of human kindness running in his veins?" Roberts urged the men at the convention to "leave the home alone. Keep political strife out of it." He said that the "women of Utah be content to reign over the empire of domestic life, and it will bring more joy to your hearts than all the success you could have in casting your ballots at the polls."[91]

Roberts pivoted back to his "statehood for Utah first of all"

89. *Proceedings*, 1:592.

90. *Proceedings*. In looking back on these events later in his life, Roberts summarized his approach: "The summary of the chief points in argument was made at the conclusion of my third speech. The first speech ... as on the inexpediency of suffrage. The second speech entered into the merits of the question, and the third speech was made in answer to my opponents." Roberts, *Autobiography*, 189.

91. *Proceedings*, 1:588.

argument, and opposed those who said, "If we cannot have statehood with suffrage, they prefer territorial vassalage to statehood." He responded to Whitney, claiming that "though his arrows were pointed," there was nothing that hurt Roberts as much as "the charge that I was not sincere in that which I have done upon the floor of this convention." He thundered that he was "in earnest. My God! Don't you see that I am terribly in earnest? It is a question of liberties of my people among whom I have been reared."[92] These remarks in particular brought "prolonged applause."[93]

Roberts closed his lengthy remarks by saying he realized he could not change the outcome in the convention, and was aware that his views on woman suffrage would be "buried by your votes." As a consequence, he made "one more appeal to the women of this Territory" to take the lead in stopping what he believed was a mistake. He said to Utah women that it was within their power "to avert the dangers that threaten us." Putting suffrage into the state constitution would in the long run mean "bitterness, intense strife, it means ebullitions of wrath, it means unsettled conditions in this Territory, whether it defeats statehood immediately or not." He lamented the overt turn to politics, without noting his own role in it, and said that the state was doing well "before we began playing tricks of politicians to gain power and votes." Roberts painted a rosy view: "People were coming together and the old struggle was being given up. Good feeling was being engendered, and now this must needs come in to disturb our peace and threaten the stability of the State whose foundations we are supposed to be laying."[94]

Moreover, Roberts insisted that suffrage did not have the widespread support that its proponents claimed. Instead, "whips and spurs have been used to drag women into these women's suffrage meetings" and the existence of petitions proved nothing, since "we all know how petitions may be brought in and piled up—such a thing is easy enough." Five hundred names, Roberts continued, was nothing when the population of a county was forty thousand. He begged the women to "release these men from their obligations" to

92. *Proceedings*, 1:597.
93. *Proceedings*.
94. *Proceedings*.

vote for suffrage, since their support only existed out of political fear. "Release them I say, and save us from this impending danger."[95]

Much of the opposition to women's suffrage came from non-Mormon women who believed that giving women the vote was a ploy to expand LDS power and influence. As three historians of LDS women's history noted, these opponents "assumed that a Mormon woman's vote would, in effect, simply double her husband's." In their efforts, "they gathered 15,366 signatures opposing inclusion." At the same time, the efforts largely of Latter-day Saint women garnered 24,801 signatures in favor of inclusion.[96] Writing in the pages of the *Woman's Exponent*, suffragist Ruby Lamont[97] mocked Roberts's stand saying, "Begging pardon of the great Roberts," he "does not deny our right to education, our moral superiority, or our influence for purity and goodness. Well that was kind. But really education makes us feel, more and more, the falling bonds of political bondage; moral superiority, it seems can never compensate our first unfortunate mistake in the Garden of Eden."[98]

Before sitting down, Roberts also said many others shared his fears but were reluctant to take a public stand. He argued that the convention should defer action on the question of woman's suffrage until statehood was achieved and conditions were stable—"who knows but what if [suffrage advocates] will do proper missionary work ... possibly I too might be converted and help work for the enfranchisement of women."[99]

Roberts held his audience's attention and had "met" the expectations of those who had gathered to hear him speak. "Hardly anyone stirred from the uncomfortable position in which most of

---

95. *Proceedings*, 1:598.

96. Derr, Cannon, and Beecher, *Women of the Covenant*, 149.

97. Lamont was the pen name of Marie Miller Johnson (1863–1939). Johnson spent her early years in Richfield, Utah, where she married William Johnson (1855–1924) ca. 1881, and they later divorced. She moved to Salt Lake City where she was an active suffragist and author whose works appeared in various publications including the *Deseret Weekly*, *Contributor*, and *Woman's Exponent*. She was also an active socialist and theosophist. She left Utah and settled in California in 1915. Today she is best known as the author of *The Soul's Language* (Jamaica, NY: Beach Printing, 1925), published under the name Ruby Lamont.

98. Ruby Lamont, "Woman Suffrage," *Woman's Exponent*, June 1, 1895.

99. *Proceedings*, 1:598.

the listeners had to stand or sit. He was applauded frequently, notwithstanding the admissions of the chair and seemed to carry his audience with him."[100] Once the debate was over, Whitney recalled that "one of the first to congratulate me was Roberts himself. We had always been friends, and continued to be in spite of this rather sharp encounter—sharp though good natured throughout."

Not all people were so understanding. Roberts received a pointed letter from Lillie T. Freeze, one of Margaret's close friends, telling him that while many wealthy individuals would congratulate him on his stand, "in the name of thousands of defenseless women—the tax payers—the unmarried wage earners and widows with orphans of both sexes to support I appeal to the kindliest impulses of your heart to cease your gigantic efforts against their interests."[101] A flyer called *The Convention Alphabet* was distributed which contained witty couplets about members of the convention. Roberts's read: "R stands for Roberts, the greatest of all; A man who is not afraid of his grave in the fall."[102]

Despite this prediction, a petition signed by Matthew Arnold and seventy-five others lauded his stand on the question.[103] A number of prominent Salt Lake City women also invited Roberts to attend a mass meeting in the Grand Opera House to oppose the inclusion of suffrage in the Constitution. They indicated that their intent was to put the question to a "popular vote."[104] His friend David H. Peery Jr. sent him a telegram offering congratulations to "the noblest Roman of them all for being a man and not a political toady."[105] Ezra C. Rich assured Roberts that because "you are on the side of right," he trusted that "you will not resign."[106] Calling him "Respected Friend and Brother," David Candland,[107] who described himself as a

100. "Roberts Ends the Debate."

101. Copy in Roberts Scrapbook, fd. 364, Roberts Collection.

102. A copy may be found in Mowry Scrapbook, item #5.

103. See copy in fd. 674, Roberts Collection.

104. See fd. 674, Roberts Collection. The letter was signed by Mrs W. S. McCornick, Mrs. Cornelia Paddock, Mrs. Jennie A. Froiseth, Mrs. S. O. Cummings, and Mrs. J. M. Easton.

105. Peery to Roberts, Mar. 29, 1895, fd. 674, Roberts Collection.

106. Rich to Roberts, Mar. 31, 1895, fd. 674, Roberts Collection.

107. Candland (1819–1902) was born in England, emigrated to Nauvoo in 1842, and later lived in Mount Pleasant, Utah, at the time. He married a total of seven wives, divorced two, and was active in various political offices in Sanpete County.

"humble voter," said that while some thought Roberts had delivered his "political funeral sermon," he thanked Roberts for his "manly, conscientious and consistent arguments," and encouraged Roberts to be "patient, you will have a glorious vindication."[108] W. S. McCornick[109] sent Roberts a "magnificent bouquet" and a note that said, "Accept my heartiest congratulations on your masterly effort to save us from woman suffrage."[110] Writing on Brigham Young Academy letterhead, Benjamin Cluff Jr.[111] also lauded Roberts's "noble stand" and said he feared the question of woman suffrage was "very inopportune at present," and "that the old difficulties are going to return." Because of that, he wished Roberts "every success in your efforts to avert this evil."[112]

Of all the communications Roberts received, one of the most interesting came from his friend and fellow delegate to the convention Moses Thatcher. Noting that while he did not agree with Roberts's stand on suffrage, he condemned the "feeling of profound intolerance ... which must have activated those requesting your resignation. Political heat and the acrimonious sentiment arising therefrom sometimes destroy the judgement of otherwise excellent citizens."[113]

In addition to these private expressions of support, Roberts's voice was not the only one raised in opposition in the convention to women's suffrage. For example, Republican Anthony C. Lund,[114] despite their party differences, held similar views with Roberts. Similarly, C. C. Goodwin,[115] editor of the *Salt Lake Tribune,* asserted that he be-

108. Candland to Roberts, Apr. 5, 1895, fd. 674, Roberts Collection. Candland also told Roberts that he feared "suffrage and prohibition are the death notes of our otherwise brilliant prospects." Similar letters of support came from John E. Dooly, R. J. Taylor, and Amasa S. Condon.

109. McCornick (1837–1921) was an important banker and businessman in Salt Lake City.

110. "Brief and Breezy," *Salt Lake Herald*, Mar. 31, 1895, 8.

111. Cluff (1858–1948) served as president of Brigham Young Academy, later University, from 1892 to 1903.

112. Cluff to Roberts, Apr. 1, 1895, fd. 674, Roberts Collection.

113. Thatcher to Roberts, Mar. 1, 1895, fd. 674, Roberts Collection.

114. Lund (1871–1935) was the son of Apostle Anthon H. Lund, a teacher and musician living in Ephraim, Sanpete County. He was unmarried, and the youngest delegate at the convention. Lund later was conductor of the Mormon Tabernacle Choir from 1916 until his death.

115. Goodwin (1832–1917) had a colorful journalistic career in Nevada where he was associated with Mark Twain and Bret Harte. He married Alice Bertha Maynard (1851–1917) in 1877. Goodwin came to Utah in 1880 to serve as editor of the *Salt Lake*

lieved a woman's sphere was in the home and with her family, not in the public arena, but admitted that his stand was "pretty well known by those who read my newspaper, which, I take, will include all the intelligent people in this part of the country." Then he reached out to Roberts and said, "When his party shall have dropped him, it is not going to be so bad as he thinks."

In the political era of the 1890s, when oratory could sway voters, Roberts's speeches made an impact. Historian Lola Van Wagenen writes that his "arguments breathed new life into the moribund anti-woman suffrage camp." Groups such as the chamber of commerce mobilized to push for separate suffrage referendums. Many non-LDS women did the same, promoting Roberts's argument that statehood was more important than suffrage, and that even the most fervent suffragists could afford to be patient and wait until after statehood was granted.[116]

Ultimately, the equal suffrage section giving women the right to vote was adopted, seventy-five to fourteen with twelve absent and five excused "who would have likely opposed the motion.[117] At that point, the convention adjourned for several days to mark Arbor Day and allow attendance at the LDS general conference. On April 8, the article containing the woman suffrage section passed seventy-five to sixteen with thirteen absent and two paired.[118] But it was agreed at the time that by a simple majority they could move to reconsider.[119] Ten days later, such an effort failed by a vote of thirty-two for, sixty-nine against, three absent, and two paired.[120] Once that vote had been cast, Emmeline B. Wells telegraphed feminist leader Susan B.

Tribune. In the pages of his paper, Goodwin was critical of what he felt was the Mormon domination of political and economic life of the territory. After the Woodruff Manifesto, however, he urged amnesty for those who had practiced plural marriage and championed statehood. He sold the *Tribune* in 1901 and established another paper called *Goodwin's Weekly*. As a Republican, Goodwin would be a vociferous opponent of Roberts's congressional bids in 1895 and 1898, and supported efforts to deny him a seat in Congress.

116. Van Wagenen, *Sister Wives*, 148.

117. For a full account, see "Suffrage War Is Finished," *Salt Lake Herald*, Apr. 6, 1895, 1, 3. See also White, "Woman's Place," 362.

118. Pairing happens when two members of opposition parties agree to abstain from voting, so as to not affect the outcome.

119. White, "Woman's Place," 363.

120. "Victory Was Bloodless," *Salt Lake Herald*, Apr. 19, 1895, 1.

Anthony the good news.[121] Finally, on May 8, the entire section was agreed to and the convention moved on to other matters.

Roberts received a telegraph from "a score of leading republicans and democrats" of Beaver, Utah, offering "sincere congratulations" on his "Patrick Henry independence on the woman suffrage question." Anticipating a future electoral bid on Roberts's part, the telegram proclaimed that his "threatened political sarcophagus will be your senatorial vestment."[122] Roberts later said he received "personal expressions supporting" his stand on suffrage "through letters, telegrams, and petitions from mass meetings signed by hundreds of people."[123]

Of all these messages of support, however, it appears that the one that pleased Roberts the most came from William McKay, ironically the man who had been commissioner when Roberts was arrested for unlawful cohabitation. McKay told him "though you and I differ in national politics I see in that fact all the more reason why I should say to you that in the discussion of the question thus far you are in my opinion the only man with the possible exception of Lund who has approached the subject entirely free from the speech and the art of the demagogue."[124]

Roberts's fellow Democrats were not the only people caught off guard by his opposition to suffrage. LDS Church leaders were also surprised, and they were not all in agreement with Roberts.[125] Wilford Woodruff feared that without suffrage the constitution would be defeated and advised Roberts not to oppose it.[126] Later, Woodruff would say, repeating the words of Joseph F. Smith, that Roberts "had done more harm in his Speeches in the Convention" than had the Liberal Party in its political efforts.[127] A considerable amount

121. Emmeline B. Wells, Diary, Apr. 18, 1895.

122. "Utah's Patrick Henry," *Evening Dispatch*, Apr. 2, 1895, 4.

123. Roberts, *Autobiography*, 193–94. He also notes that he was extended the privilege for a month to use the Alta Club, Salt Lake City's premier gentile gathering place, from O. G. Sharp and Robert MacIntosh, both convention delegates, in recognition of his efforts. A copy of the invitation signed by Secretary C. L. Robertson is found in Roberts' Scrapbook, fd. 674, Roberts Collection.

124. A copy of this letter is found in Roberts' Scrapbook, fd. 674. McKay also returned the bond that he had forfeited when he had left for Great Britain. See also Roberts, *Autobiography*, 193–94.

125. Van Wagenen, *Sister Wives*, 148.

126. Lyman, *Political Deliverance*, 261.

127. As quoted in Alexander, *Things in Heaven and Earth*, 311.

of time was spent at the regular Thursday meeting of the Quorum of the Twelve, April 4, 1895, discussing Roberts's actions.[128] Heber J. Grant said, "I cannot sustain Bro. Roberts in the course he has taken."[129] Joseph F. Smith strongly supported women's suffrage, and told his colleagues that he would rather Utah remain a territory than see if become a state without "Woman Suffrage being part of the Constitution."[130] Smith also indicated that Roberts "had done more to injure us in the last two weeks than any ten Liberals have done in the last fifteen years. I consider him an assassin of the liberties of the people."[131] Roberts's good friend John W. Taylor, "a nominal Democrat," apparently believed that church general authorities had "no right to join any political party, or do anything else of a grave character, without first consulting the Presidency." He was disappointed that "the Gentiles in this city are glad at the conduct of Roberts, for he has betrayed the Church in what he has said and done." Taylor believed that leaders needed to "be united in politics so far as to seek and follow counsel, or we will be driven out of this country." He was so angry that he said "Roberts has broken his covenants, and should be called to an account."[132]

However, John Henry Smith noted that many Latter-day Saints opposed suffrage, and "that all the Gentiles in the Constitutional Convention were united in their opposition to the Woman's Suffrage provision of the Constitution. A great many of our people are in the same condition of opposition. Geo. R. Emery[133] went around [the Sixteenth Ward] and found that 100 out of 150 were opposed."[134] Another apostle, George Teasdale, stated he was "strongly in favor"

128. Cannon, *Candid Insights*, 627–30.

129. Cannon, 628.

130. Van Wagenen, *Sister Wives*, 148.

131. Cannon, *Candid Insights*, 628.

132. Cannon, 627– 29.

133. Emery was born in Salt Lake City where he resided his entire life. He married Rosilpha Wilding (1857–1934) in 1874 and Mary King Pierpont (1868–1953) in 1887. Emery served as a missionary to Great Britain, 1878–80. After that, he was a member of the presidency of the twenty-fourth Quorum of Seventy where he likely worked with Roberts. He became bishop of the Sixteenth Ward in 1899 and served until 1904 when he became first counselor to president Nephi L. Morris of the Salt Lake Stake. Emery was a merchant and accountant in Salt Lake City.

134. Cannon seems to agree with Joseph F. Smith, noting that "I am told that John Henry Smith has done more than any other man to injure the cause of Woman's

of omitting it from the constitution or, at least, submitting the question to a vote of the people.[135]

When the votes were tabulated in November, statehood carried decisively. The total vote was 31,305 in favor and 7,687 against.[136] The opposition was strongest in Weber, Salt Lake, and Summit Counties. As White summarized, an all-male electorate "found it possible to accept the new Constitution with political equality in it."[137] It was an important turning point that transferred the primarily Mormon-dominated Utah to the more politically integrated Utah of the coming century. And central to that effort was the experience of women—before the constitution, during the debates, and after. The issuance of the Woodruff Manifesto had "let the air out of gentile opposition to the Saints, though the balloon was slow to deflate."[138] Utah had statehood, and Mormons had proven their loyalty to the country. The inclusion of women's suffrage was a shock to many who continued to believe that LDS women were victims of polygamy.[139]

B. H. Roberts had been—at least initially—on the wrong side of both these transformative issues. His opposition to female suffrage would continue to be a factor as he pursued his political career.

Suffrage, from his having spoken enthusiastically of the ability and courage of Roberts in doing as he has done." Cannon, *Candid Insights*, 628.

135. Cannon, *Candid Insights*, 629.

136. Utah Commission, Minute Book G, p. 413.

137. White, "Woman's Place," 364. White gives several reasons why woman suffrage succeeded. First, it was not seen as radical in Utah because it had the support of many respectable people. Second, it had been tried in Utah Territory successfully in the past. Third, there was careful cultivation of grass roots support. Finally, there was a solid core of supporters at the convention itself.

138. Derr, Cannon, and Beecher, *Women of Covenant*, 139.

139. Radke-Moss, "Mormon Women, Suffrage, and Citizenship," 98.

NINE

A CONGRESSIONAL CONTEST

The 1895 elections in Utah revolved around accepting or rejecting a new state constitution, choosing the first state officeholders, selecting two US senators, and electing a representative to the Fifty-fourth Congress. Some party members speculated that Roberts might be a good candidate for either governor or congress.[1] In part, Roberts had appeal because he was not from Salt Lake City, though his stand on suffrage was problematic.

An initial step toward his run for Congress came during the summer of 1895. The "United Democracy of Utah" held a mass convention to organize with the goal of achieving statehood; building a successful team for the election; and, specifically, reaching out to women in recognition that they had "helped to make the territory what it is," and that they were part of the Democratic coalition. The *Salt Lake Herald* observed that "no woman who attended the convention could feel that her true womanhood had been lowered in the slightest degree by her participation," and that truly they were accepted by the male delegates as a "new and steadying element" of the party.[2] Attracting over a thousand individuals, about one-third of whom were women, from "the far distant parts of the territory," the convention demonstrated its commitment to women by naming Zina D. H Young and Eurithe K. La Barthe as vice presidents, and Electa Bullock as treasurer, while expanding the executive committee to "give the women full representation." Young, La Barthe, and Isabelle Horne were among the speakers.[3] Other important leaders

1. "Candidates For Positions," *Salt Lake Tribune*, June 30, 1895, 2.

2. "It Was Democracy's Day," *Salt Lake Herald*, July 14, 1895. 1; hereafter cited as "Democracy's Day."

3. "Democracy's Day." Horne's pointed remarks may have been dismissive of Roberts.

such as Jane S. Richards, Bathsheba W. Smith, Martha Hughes Cannon, Augusta W. Grant and Amelia F. Young attended, along with "many other prominent Democratic women … from Salt Lake … and outside counties."[4] Young probably spoke for many of the other women when she said, "I have been with you ever since the founding of Utah and I congratulate myself on the family this old grandmother sees," and believed that Utah women "would prove a credit to the party."[5] Also attending as delegates from Centerville were Roberts's daughter Adah and his old friend Kate Chase.[6]

At the convention, the delegates called for Roberts, and he "was brought forward on the stage and received a hearty round of cheers and applause." He acknowledged the women in the audience, realized that some were looking for him to make amends, and calmly told them that the "right to hold individual opinions and give utterance to them without regard to others is … the essence of Democracy." He then told the audience that, without "regrets for the past," he pledged to work to maintain the harmony that he saw around him who now had the challenge of "moving on the enemy." He said that in the past "Democrats were surrounded with gloom" as people found themselves out of work and the "hum of industry [was] well nigh hushed" in the wake of the Panic of 1893.[7] But, Roberts noted hopefully, "conditions have changed and are still changing," and Democrats "will win."[8]

Roberts encouraged Democrats to face the "leading question before the American people" which he said was the need to create an economy that would work for all, not just the rich. Clearly, he felt the key to that effort rested in the "remonetization of silver," which he said would bring "the return of our prosperity." In words that sounded much like a future campaign theme, he proclaimed there was a

---

She noted that "Men say that if women go into politics they will not be at home to wait on their husbands. … But the women can take care of their homes and go into politics also. Women will elevate politics. There will be no bribery of them."

4. "Democracy's Day."

5. "Democracy's Day."

6. "The Political Arena," *Salt Lake Herald*, July 13, 1895, 8.

7. Until the 1930s brought an even greater calamity, the Panic of 1893 was known as the Great Depression, so deep was the economic distress across the globe. See White, *Republic for Which It Stands*,

8. "B. H. Roberts' Address," *Salt Lake Herald*, July 14, 1895, 1.

> better hope of free coinage of silver at the ratio of 16 to 1 in the Democratic party than in the Republican party. Republicans … claim that they have wealthy and well educated people with them. No doubt they have. The Republican party is the party of the classes. The Democratic party is the party of the people. Gold is the money of the rich, and highly educated men. Silver is the money of the people. The party that boasts of the wealth and intelligence of its members will be true to the money classes. The party that proudly boasts that it is the party of the people will be true to the money of the people until it opens up the mints of the country to the free and unlimited coinage of silver.[9]

No doubt many of those in the hall were roused by Roberts's rhetoric and saw him playing an important role in that predicted victory. On the other hand, J. Golden Kimball, who was a delegate from Cache County, groused that the meeting "required all day to attend."[10]

In late summer of 1895, Roberts noted that he was responding to an "urgent request … by many friends" to consider running for either the US House of Representatives or the Senate; he ultimately settled on the former.[11] He immediately became a target for the *Salt Lake Tribune,* which painted him as a "weak" candidate, especially on the question of the tariff.[12] In early September, the paper noted that William H. King had been in Salt Lake City to "boom his congressional candidacy" with the goal of forcing Roberts to get out of his way and become a candidate for governor instead. The *Tribune* reported that King's friends "claimed … that Roberts will not have a walkover" to the congressional nomination, believing that King had over 250 votes from Weber, Sevier, Utah, Sanpete and Salt Lake Counties.[13] When approached by the paper on whether he would accept a gubernatorial nomination, Roberts "replied firmly in the negative, and said that he … is out for Congress and nothing else." Derisively, the paper said that Roberts's stand typified that of several leading Democrats who

9. "B. H. Roberts' Address."

10. Kimball Journal, July 13, 1895.

11. Roberts, *Autobiography*, 199. Any diary for 1895, if one was kept, seems no longer extant.

12. See "Mr. Roberts and the Tariff," *Salt Lake Tribune*, Aug. 30, 1895, 3.

13. "Worth Fighting For," *Salt Lake Tribune*, Sep. 4, 1895, 8.

only wanted nomination for national office and were "willing to let the state honors go by the board."[14]

The Democratic state nominating convention took place at Ogden's Grand Opera House on September 5, 1895. A "special train" arrived that morning at 9:15 a.m., bringing delegates from Provo, Salt Lake City, and "intermediate points" to the deliberations.[15] The *Ogden Standard*[16] predicted that a "battle royal" would "rage," but Roberts was soon nominated by John F. Tolton[17] of Beaver County who called him "one of the worthy sons of Utah," and a man who was a "lion who would make the 'lily of the valley' on the Republican ticket think a cyclone had struck him."[18] A "loud outburst of applause" broke out when the nomination was made unanimous.[19] The *Standard* labeled Roberts's selection "a poor one in view of the fact that [William H.] King could have been induced to accept the nomination," and would have been a stronger candidate. King's name was not even put into nomination because "when B. H. Roberts's name was presented for Congress it went through like a cyclone, and before King's supporters knew where they were at," Roberts was nominated by acclamation.[20]

Roberts thanked the delegates, telling them that he would never "forget" that he had "lived today" when he received the honor of the nomination. "I will win for you in November if I can,"[21] he pledged.

---

14. "Democrats in a Quandary," *Salt Lake Tribune*, Sep. 5, 1895, 8.

15. "Political Bee," *Ogden Standard*, Sep. 4, 1895, 4. According to the *Salt Lake Tribune*, the delegates left at 8:20 p.m. for a forty-five-minute trip on a Union Pacific train that was "appropriately and elaborately decorated." The fare was $1.50 for a round-trip ticket. See "Attention Democrats," *Salt Lake Tribune*, Sep. 2, 1895, 8.

16. The paper's name changed from time to time. For consistency, the title *Ogden Standard* has been used, and often the paper is simply called the *Standard*.

17. Tolton (1861–1950) lived his entire life in Beaver, Utah. He was a missionary to Great Britain in 1884–85 and married Caroline Olivia Hales (1861–1941) a year later. After service in the territorial legislature, he was a Deputy US Marshal, 1894–95. A staunch Democrat, Tolton served in the House from 1905 to 1907. After an unsuccessful campaign for governor in 1912, he returned to the House in 1917, and served as speaker. Tolton was Beaver Stake president, 1908–16.

18. "The Victims," *Salt Lake Tribune*, Sep. 6, 1895, 1.

19. "Nominations Made," *Deseret Evening News*, Sep. 6, 1895, 1.

20. "A Weak Ticket," *Ogden Standard*, Sep. 6, 1895, 4.

21. "Convention Clips," *Salt Lake Tribune*, Sep. 6, 1895, 3. The *New York Times* followed the convention, and later the campaign itself. On the conventions, see "Candidate for Senate," *New York Times*, Sep. 6, 1895, 5.

On the day after the convention, Roberts wrote to his mother with obvious pride: "If elected—and the prospect is bright and the assurances of my friends strong for my election—the position is equivalent to that of a member of parliament. ... Tell me mother of mine if in the days of some trial and sorrow in the wildest pitch of your fancy you thought such a thing would ever happen to your son?"[22]

The Republicans had nominated Clarence E. Allen as their candidate for Congress at a state convention held on August 28 in the Salt Lake Theater.[23] Allen, who was five years older than Roberts, had spent most of his life in Ohio. He moved to Utah in 1881 and was an instructor at the Salt Lake Academy until 1886. In the next decade he was active in politics, serving three terms in the territorial legislature and one term as Salt Lake County Clerk from 1890 to 1892. In that year he was an unsuccessful Liberal candidate for Utah's congressional delegate. A year later he switched his allegiance to the Republican Party and was admitted to the Utah bar. Clearly, Allen's selection was part of an effort to "balance the ticket between Mormons and non-Mormons."[24]

Allen, who chaired the convention's resolutions committee, supported the Utah Republican Party platform which championed women's suffrage, called for the "free and unlimited coinage of silver," a strong protective tariff, economy in governmental expenditures, a demand that LDS Church property still being held by the federal government be returned to the church, and support for the state constitution. The *Tribune* was filled with praise for the Republican efforts, saying that Allen represented "in his own person what can be done with pluck and ability," and concluded that his nomination for Congress "was a perfectly natural result" of the record he had compiled. Moreover, the paper called the party platform a "beauty" which would be "impossible for Democratic Orators to knock into splinters."

Utah Populists met in Salt Lake City on September 14 to nominate state and congressional candidates as well. Like their Republican and Democratic counterparts, Utah Populists endorsed women's

22. Roberts to Mother, Sep. 6, 1895, box 4, fd. 7, Roberts Papers (UU).

23. "Republican Ticket," *Deseret Evening News*, Aug. 29, 1895, 8.

24. White, "Utah State Elections," 39. The convention nominated three non-Mormons—Charles S. Zane, James A. Mine, and George W. Bartch—for the Utah Supreme Court.

suffrage, supported with some reservations the new state constitution, and advocated for broad support not only for free silver, but to "end the reign of monopolies and corruption, which have brought our once happy and prosperous people to the verge of ruin."[25]

The Populists nominated James Hogan[26] as their candidate for Congress. While Hogan was not likely to win the congressional seat, his strong support of silver and his deliberate appeals to organized labor forced Roberts to be mindful to his own support among workers. In an effort to shore up support with labor, Roberts responded to a series of questions posed to him by A. E. Graham and Stephen Tyne of the Utah Board of Labor, and P. O. Hagan and H. I. Barrett of the local branch of the Knights of Labor, telling them that he and the Democratic Party supported the cause of free silver. He also assured his questioners that he was in favor of the eight-hour day as the legal standard for the work week.[27]

Obviously, Republican Clarence Allen was much more of a threat to Roberts than was Hogan, and the Republicans, with the enthusiastic backing of the *Tribune*, set out on an ambitious effort to take Allen throughout the state. The *Tribune* carried on a campaign against Roberts on both the editorial page and the news columns of the paper, arguing that the Democrats nominated Roberts because they "counted on getting more votes as a president of the Seventies than for any other reason."[28] At one point, the *Tribune* accused Roberts of "acquiring the habits of certain politicians," by changing his views to fit particular audiences.[29] Even in his hometown, the paper asserted, Roberts was seen by many as someone who was distancing himself from his party and platform. At the rallies, a local music

---

25. "Third Party Convention," *Salt Lake Tribune*, Sep. 15, 1895, 1.

26. James Hogan (born ca.1867) was born in Ireland and came to the United States in 1890. A friend of Eugene V. Debs, he was imprisoned with him in Woodstock Jail. Hogan was one of the national officers of the American Railway Union (ARU), and had assisted Debs in organizing a branch of the ARU in Utah. He and his wife, Annie, entertained Debs in their Ogden home. See "American Railway Union," *Ogden Standard*, Sep. 8, 1893, 1. After leaving the Populists, Hogan affiliated with the Socialist Party.

27. "Organized Labor Queries," *Salt Lake Tribune*, Oct. 22, 1895, 3.

28. "A Host of Time," *Salt Lake Tribune*, Nov. 4, 1895, 4.

29. "Mr. Roberts Talks Through His Hat," *Salt Lake Tribune*, Sep. 4, 1895, 4.

group known as the Provo Quartet made the Republican faithful go "completely wild" when they sang "Who Killed Roberts."[30]

Conversely, the *Salt Lake Herald* was very supportive of Roberts, and what emerged in the midst of the campaign was a partisan newspaper war typical of the era. Instead of a "completely wild" Republican rally as described by the *Tribune*, the *Herald* reported a "discouraging" meeting, and that those who attended were "sadly disappointed."[31] Meanwhile, the *Herald* reported that enthusiasm for Roberts was growing everywhere he spoke, and said that a "B. H. Roberts drum corps" had been organized with a membership of twenty-five and another two dozen "applications for membership" pending.[32] This divergent pattern of reporting between the *Tribune* and the *Herald* continued throughout the campaign.

The *Tribune* asserted that the Roberts campaign was built on falsehoods, and when he "runs out of [them] he is well nigh bankrupt." It argued that Roberts—"because he holds a high office in his creed"—is in "one sense" a clergyman who preaches his beliefs "to the people," and should be "more particular about stating anything but the facts than the common ordinary Democratic politician." [33]The *Salt Lake Herald* responded to these and other attacks by saying that "a number of the most prominent Republican speakers are indulging in the disgraceful practice of mud-slinging," spreading "libels, insinuations and covert charges" that had originated in the pages of the *Tribune*. The real question, the paper concluded, was whether the Republican Party would disavow these falsehoods and tactics.[34]

The Provo *Evening Dispatch*, whose masthead read, "This is a Democratic Year," accused Allen of being allied with the *Tribune* in "fighting the Mormon people to the last," when they were associated with the Liberal Party. After that, the paper asserted, "both yielded when they discovered the [Republican] party to which they belonged had become converted to the sincerity of the Mormon

30. "Davis County Meetings," *Salt Lake Tribune*, Oct. 3, 1895, 2.
31. "Straight Talk From Powers," *Salt Lake Herald*, Oct. 3, 1895, 1.
32. "Local Briefs," *Salt Lake Herald*, Oct. 1, 1895, 7.
33. "Mr. Roberts's Vagaries, No. 3, *Salt Lake Tribune*, Oct. 12, 1895, 4.
34. "Is There to be a Clean Campaign?" *Salt Lake Herald*, Oct. 3, 1895, 4.

people."[35] At the same time, the paper attacked Allen for being a weak candidate, in part, because he was not a Mormon.

Roberts attracted big, enthusiastic audiences, and his efforts were noticed by the *New York Times* who called him a "most thoroughly respected and able man. Few men in the West have greater talents and attainments as a campaign speaker … and his personality cannot help but attract support to the ticket on which he is running."[36]

Meanwhile, it had become evident from his various engagements that Allen was not an oratorical match for Roberts. George M. Cannon, chair of the Republican State Central Committee, wrote to his Democratic counterpart, Orlando W. Powers,[37] indicating that because Allen's itinerary had been set "for the entire campaign," there was no room for a debate "throughout the entire territory." The paper called Cannon's remarks "a far fetched excuse," saying the hasty arrangements were designed solely to "refuse a joint discussion."[38] Allen and Roberts never engaged in a formal debate during the campaign.

One of Roberts's most important speeches occurred in Salt Lake City in early September when he spoke to a "large crowd" that packed a hall at 100 North and 500 West. Roberts charged the Republicans with exploiting the "hard times" facing the American people and asserted that when the Democratic Party had taken over nationally in 1893, the country's "finances were in a deplorable condition." The Democratic administration, he stated, had to meet that "crisis" and they did. He told the rally that the "Republican prophesies of the last two years have foreshadowed a period of great calamities. But these forebodings are met by the hum of awakening industries and the dawning of a brighter day for the Republic." Another significant

35. "To Defeat Statehood," (Provo) *Evening Dispatch*, Oct. 21, 1895, 2.

36. "Utah's State Campaign," *New York Times*, Sep. 24, 1895, 16.

37. Powers (1851–1914) was active in Democratic politics in Michigan until he came to Utah in 1885. He was appointed associate justice of the Utah Territorial Supreme Court, but left the next year. Powers married Anna W. Whipple (1860–1934) in 1887. He returned to the state in 1889 and was active in the Liberal Party, serving as chair and as a legislative candidate. By 1895 he was state chair of the Democratic Party, and one of the important non-Mormons in bridging the political gap in the state. Powers was an unsuccessful Democratic candidate for US Senate in 1898, and for the US House of Representatives in 1904 and 1906. He was one of the most prominent lawyers in the state, representing among other parties the *Salt Lake Tribune*. See "Judge O. W. Powers Suddenly Dies in Salt Lake," *Ogden Standard*, Jan. 2, 1914, 6.

38. "Republicans Are Afraid," (Provo) *Evening Dispatch*, Sep. 27, 1895, 1.

appearance took place in early October, when Roberts was the chief speaker at a "packed house" rally in the Lyceum Theater in Salt Lake City where he reached out to the working class by recalling his own humble background: "When I thought of a man who was born to hard-working parents, when I thought I had served my apprenticeship at one of the most honorable of businesses, and when I had a chance to read and travel a little, and have now still hard work to do, I think it just that I should be claimed as one of you."[39]

The biggest complication of the campaign, reaching far beyond it, came during a priesthood session at the October general conference. Apostle Joseph F. Smith, without mentioning Roberts and Thatcher by name, said,

> We have oracles in the Church, and their counsel must be sought. The moment a man in authority decides to do as he pleases, he steps on dangerous ground. One of the Twelve and one of the Seven Presidents of Seventy have done wrong in accepting obligations without first consulting and obtaining the consent of those who presided over them. No man surrenders his manhood by seeking the advice of his superiors.[40]

Apostle John Henry Smith noted in his journal that "by their silence" the First Presidency clearly endorsed these views.[41] J. Golden Kimball recorded that "the Republicans took it that the Pres. of the Church did not want Thatcher or Roberts ... and of course were very much pleased. ... the Democrats took it as church influence and thus 'Hell Fire' was thrown."

A few days later, Joseph F. Smith, in a meeting with the First Presidency and the Quorum of the Twelve Apostles, "forcefully denied that he had any intention of his statements being used for political purposes"[42] and defended his actions as being consistent with what had been said by apostles Francis M. Lyman and Abraham H. Cannon on "living oracles and the right of such to advise ecclesiastical brethren as to their duties."[43] Wilford Woodruff also issued a public statement deny-

39. "Roberts at the Lyceum," *Salt Lake Tribune,* Oct. 9, 1895, 8. See also "Speech to Workingmen," *Salt Lake Herald,* Oct. 9, 1895, 1.

40. See Cannon, *Candid Insights*, 741.

41. Smith also stated that George Q. Cannon said he "would not have dared to have said" what Apostle Smith said, "but it was true." Smith, *Church, State, and Politics*, 335.

42. Cannon, *Candid Insights*, 741.

43. "Political Situation," *Ogden Standard*, Oct. 14, 1895, 1.

ing any "political influence" on the part of the church. He denied ever trying to influence anyone toward a partisan position and stated that "part of my own family are Republicans and part are Democrats."[44]

Despite these assurances, the message and the intended targets were clear to all. It was reminiscent of what had happened in 1892 when the First Presidency had "reserved the right to impose rather strict restraints on the political activities of other general authorities." And, obviously, Thatcher and Roberts were "involved in both situations." Each had "recanted their views favoring political independence—at least for a time."[45]

Democratic chair Orlando W. Powers issued a lengthy response attacking Republican efforts to convince active Mormons that the church "desires the defeat of the Democratic ticket." The Utah Democrats had "no quarrel" with any church, but would oppose any group or individual who was "ready and willing to drag the Cross of Christ in the mud and dust and filth of politics to advance selfish ends." Focusing specifically on Thatcher and Roberts, Powers said if church officials believed they were "entitled to their time," they "should have been called before their particular quorum and there called to account."[46] Powers said that the Democrats had "seized the opportunity to show to … the nation that there is no dictation in politics by the church, and that the faith of the American people in the dominant church in Utah is safe."[47] He suggested a "reconvened convention," and, at the end of a nine-hour meeting, Democratic state committee members unanimously voted to reconvene the state convention.[48]

In a lengthy interview with the *Herald*, Roberts said that he had always communicated with church leaders when necessary, and that he had submitted all of "the manuscripts of tracts and books … written in advocacy or defense of the Mormon faith" to the inspection of the First Presidency. He noted that at "one point when considering a long standing intention" to study law, he sought advice from church leaders, and that while he "never received from them any direct

44. "Political Situation."

45. As Lyman says, "The controversy centering on the two during the ensuing … campaign was not an isolated incident." See Lyman, *Political Deliverance,* 207–08, 263.

46. "Political Situation."

47. "Democratic Night at Ogden," *Salt Lake Tribune*, Oct. 20, 1895, 7.

48. "State Convention Recalled," *Salt Lake Tribune*, Oct. 15, 1895, 1.

decision as to what in their judgement I ought to do," he learned "indirectly" that they opposed this course. So he gave up what had become a "life purpose."[49]

When the reporter asked if Roberts had been similarly attentive to church leaders in political matters, he pointed to the fact that some two years before "it was stated that it was thought wise for members of the Quorum of the Twelve, the first seven presidents of the Seventies, presidents of stakes and bishops" to avoid political affairs which might bring them into conflict with "their ecclesiastical relations with their people." He had disagreed but accepted what he came to see as a "general order." Yet, very soon after, he saw an apostle and a member of his own quorum "actively engaged in politics in the interests of the Republican party."[50] There were so many exceptions that it seemed to him that it had "destroyed the force of the rule." He said that after his nomination for Congress at the Ogden convention there "had been no word of warning given me by the First Presidency." He even recounted that immediately following the convention he "met one of the Presidency as we were both leaving the train. In his presence, a number of Brethren … congratulated me on my nomination but he was silent." Roberts seemed to take this silence for assent, since the First Presidency member "did not take me aside and reprove me for any breach of Church regulations." Then, a few days after this chance encounter, Roberts had been summoned to meet with all three members of the First Presidency. After some fifteen or twenty minutes, Roberts stated that "no complaint" was made about accepting the congressional nomination, and that the First Presidency clearly had the opportunity "to correct me if I had made an error."[51]

When asked if he believed the Republicans would use Smith's comments against him, he responded: "You might as well ask me if water will run down hill, or fire leap upward. Of course they will use it. They are already using it. The day after the Priesthood meeting … it was being rumored that I had been given so many days to resign my nomination or lose my standing in the church." Similarly,

49. "Roberts Makes a Statement," *Salt Lake Herald*, Oct. 14, 1895, 1.
50. He likely referred to John Henry Smith and Seymour B. Young.
51. "Roberts Makes a Statement."

Roberts said he had heard such accusations while campaigning recently in Willard, Utah, where he "confronted" a rumor that he was "out of favor with the Presidency of the church, likely to be disfellowshipped, and therefore must be defeated in the election." As further evidence, he pointed to a letter Democratic chair O. W. Powers had received from an unnamed Mormon Democrat in Willard who said that "Republicans approach Democrats with an exulting smile and ask how they enjoyed the priesthood meeting."[52]

Roberts believed that Smith's conference address had hurt his political chances and claimed that "a bishop's counselor told me that he had heard Republicans say … that had it not been for what had been said at the [priesthood] meeting their votes would have been cast for Roberts; but now they were in doubt." Roberts admitted there was "no denying" that these remarks had not hurt him so much among Democrats, but with "doubtful voters and favorable Republicans." Roberts believed there was "no middle ground" between church leaders forbidding participation in politics or allowing it. If they speak out, then it "would place the control of the respective parties under church officials and would give up political affairs entirely into their hands." The only answer, according to Roberts, was "trusting in the individual's own discretion and judgement." He brought the lengthy interview to a close noting that while he appreciated the "gravity of the crisis," he truly believed that church leaders "in good faith" did not want to interfere with members' political rights or dominate the state politically. While his position "in the Church of Christ is dearer to me than life itself," he concluded by saying he was "ready to risk my all in this cause."[53]

After touring throughout Box Elder and Weber Counties with Caine,[54] Roberts spoke in Ogden on October 19 as part of a large Democratic rally, complete with marchers, music, and mounted cavalry gathered outside the Ogden Opera House. Responding to the church issue, supporters marched outside holding several large banners reading "'B. H. Roberts—We Honor your Manly Courage,' and

52. "Roberts Makes a Statement."

53. "Roberts Makes a Statement."

54. "Caine, Roberts and Young," *Salt Lake Herald*, Oct. 19, 1895, 5. The candidates had visited in various locations, including West Weber, Hooper, North Ogden, Huntsville, and Plain City, before coming to Ogden.

'Our Candidates Don't Need Bishops Recommends.'" In addition, both the B. H. Roberts Drum Corps, dressed in its red uniforms, and the B. H. Roberts Quartet participated.[55] Outside the opera house hundreds were turned away, while inside "every inch of standing room" was taken. The *Salt Lake Herald* reported that Roberts's appearance was met "with a great burst of cheering and applause that was renewed again and again." The young candidate told the crowd that he had "heard that Demosthenes used to speak against the roaring of the audience but even he could not have spoken against you."[56]

Calling the Democratic Party the party of the people, especially young people, Roberts contrasted the era of Republican rule with what he labeled the "golden era of American prosperity" between 1846 and 1860 largely under Democratic rule. Without any mention of the divisions that led to the Civil War, Roberts used the opportunity to deliver a Jeffersonian states-rights appeal. Then he said he had heard through the "grapevine" that some individuals were attempting to win support for his candidacy by urging voters to support "Brother" Roberts over "Mr." Allen. "I do not want to be elected by any such method," he asserted. He contended that as the constitutional convention had avoided "the mingling of church and state," so should the election campaign. He closed by alluding to his stand on woman suffrage, noting he would support the majority, and encouraged women to help make it "a Democratic year."[57]

The *New York Times* turned its attention to the political situation in Utah. Referring to the forthcoming second convention, the paper identified George Q. Cannon and Joseph F. Smith as the main forces behind the Republican attacks. The paper commented that the two men wanted to induce Mormon Democrats to desert their party in the hope of preventing a Republican loss. "If the reassembled convention decides to stand by its candidates and go on with the fight it will be taken as an indication that the desperate experiment of Smith and Cannon has helped rather than hindered the cause of the Democrats of Utah."[58]

55. "Ogden Will Go Democratic," *Salt Lake Herald*, Oct. 20, 1895, 1.
56. "Ogden Will Go Democratic."
57. "Ogden Will Go Democratic."
58. "Utah Republicans Play with Fire," *New York Times*, Oct. 22, 1895, 4.

The reconvened Democratic convention met in Salt Lakc on October 22. Emmeline B. Wells observed that it was "a very unusual proceeding," and that it was "a cold dreary day—not at all favorable to good feeling."[59] Despite Wells's views, the meeting was large and boisterous.[60] A festive air came when the "B. H. Roberts Glee Club" rendered two numbers: "God Bless the Land of Washington" and "Democracy's Big Four." Eventually the delegates got down to business when P. J. Daly introduced a two-fold resolution calling for defeating statehood and the constitution and taking the current Democratic ticket out of running. Roberts opposed the resolution. He said that he had believed "the party this year was marching toward a glorious victory when, as if an earthquake had rolled under his feet we came to a stand-still and began to wonder if again it would be true that the unwelcome influence of the church was to rob us of a victory."[61] But he reminded the audience that despite the "adverse influence" of some Republicans in 1894, "19,000 good Democrats ... mostly of the Mormon faith" had voted for the party. Roberts urged his listeners not to support the resolution to defeat statehood and, in so doing, return to the bondage of territorial days. He assured them, as signer of the state constitution, that he favored its adoption by the voters and supported its principle of the separation of church and state.[62] The *New York Times* noted that "at the conclusion of his speech the excitement was intense, and the house rang with cheers."[63] Finally, the delegates voted down Daly's resolution. But they also adopted a lengthy statement outlining the history of the relations between the Democratic Party and the church over the past years. As part of this statement the delegates drafted a nine-part "Declaration of Truths" that, among other things, asserts "no

59. Wells Diary, Oct. 22, 1895.

60. Wilford Woodruff was critical of the meeting itself and the controversy that had erupted. In his diary he commented that "The Democrats are having a great Convention in the Theater today. The Salt Lake Herald is publishing Lies against the Presidency of the Church. And Republicans who are Presidents & Bishops are made to say in their Publick speaking things which are false. This done for Political effect." Woodruff, *Waiting For World's End*, 404.

61. "Roberts Takes The Floor," *Salt Lake Tribune*, Oct. 23, 1895, 2.

62. "Roberts Takes the Floor."

63. "Utah Democratic Protest," *New York Times*, Oct. 24, 1895, 1.

church, ecclesiastical body nor spiritual adviser should encroach upon the political rights of individuals."[64]

Roberts received some important help on the editorial pages of the LDS Church-owned *Deseret News,* which lauded the "enthusiasm and unanimity" of the delegates, and said the meeting should prove once and for all that church and state are separate in Utah, and that the church "does not desire the political serfdom or subserviency of its members." Such charges, the paper said, were the work of "scheming politicians," who deliberately assailed church authorities to advance their own partisan cause. As the paper concluded, "Both parties … and all their honorable leaders" should seek to promote the same "purity in politics" that the church "has done and is willing to do." If that happens, the *News* concluded, "Utah will be a model and not a hotbed for politics."[65]

As the campaign progressed, Roberts captured the attention of the recently created *Broad Ax*, edited by Julius Taylor, a black journalist, who said its goal was to "uphold the Democracy."[66] The paper reported that at a Democratic rally Roberts had delivered a speech that was "a feast of reason and a flow of the soul."[67] Labeling Roberts the "Cicero of Utah," because of his oratorical skills, the paper reported "as wide a difference" between Roberts and his opponent, Clarence E. Allen, as "between a sweet potato ridge and the Wasatch Range." Reflecting the paper's commitment to Free Silver, and using a play on words, it commented that Allen was "16 parts Republicanism to 1 of silver." Allen "possessed no fitness for the honorable position except noise and cheek." Allen, the *Ax* charged, was a racist who had "an unbroken record of hate for our people, and who, until the last moment opposed the admission of Utah as a state."[68]

---

64. See "The Mighty Voice of Democracy," *Salt Lake Herald*, Oct. 23, 1895, 1.

65. "Church and State," *Deseret News*, Oct. 23, 1895, 4.

66. The paper would be published from September 1895 until June 1899 when Taylor left Salt Lake City and relocated in Chicago. During that period the *Broad Ax* not only covered local matters, but paid attention to national issues affecting African Americans. At times the title is listed as *BroadAx*, but I have separated the two words. See Sweeney, "Julius F. Taylor." Roberts is listed among the "regular readers" of the paper along with many other local figures. Interestingly, also listed is Dr. Maggie Shipp. See "Some of Our Friends and Readers," *Broad Ax*, Nov. 23, 1895, 1.

67. "Chips," *Broad Ax,* Oct. 12, 1895, 2.

68. "Chips," *Broad Ax*, Sep. 7, 1895, 2.

While typically supporting the Republican ticket, and obviously representing the views of the church in general, the *Deseret News* featured less coverage of the campaign, and considerably less "editorializing" in the news columns. Such was not the case for the *Tribune,* which consistently reported on large, enthusiastic,[69] and successful Republican rallies throughout the state, with a Democratic Party disheartened and in disarray. In general the *Herald* was a Democratic paper, and not hostile to the LDS Church. It tended to cast Roberts's campaign in a positive light while attacking the *Tribune* and defending the Democratic Party.[70]

On November 1, Roberts and Caine were the main speakers at a large rally held in the Salt Lake Theater. The *Salt Lake Herald* said the large, enthusiastic crowd gave the Democratic stalwarts a "splendid reception" in the hall that was packed from "pit to dome." The paper noted that the pair had been brought to the theater by a parade headed by the B. H. Roberts Drum Corps, and the Business Men's Marching Club. Also in attendance was the B. H. Roberts glee club, a four-man male quartet which serenaded those in attendance with renditions of "Marching for Mileage" and "Sally in the Alley."[71]

Roberts attacked those "high ecclesiastical personages"—in obvious reference to Republican Joseph F. Smith and others—who had sought to disturb the harmony of recent years by introducing the "unwelcome" subject of church influence. He told the crowd that "when the people of Utah decided to divide on party lines according to their political convictions it was their intention to act in good

69. For general information on these three papers during this period, see Alter, *Early Utah Journalism*; Ashton, *Voice in the West*; and Malmquist, *First 100 Years.*

70. The paper had an interesting fifty-year history, existing from 1870 to 1920. For the last decade of its publication it had merged with the *Inter-Mountain Republican* to become the *Herald-Republican.* As Malmquist writes, "During its life … the *Herald* passed through numerous ownerships. Generally it defended the Mormon Church and its leaders, but it sometimes expressed disagreement with particular actions or policies. … While at times it sounded, as the *Tribune* put it, like 'the minor voice of the church' it certainly did not adopt *Deseret News* positions. It was a well-written and competently edited newspaper." See Malmquist, *First 100 Years,* 215.

71. For the lyrics, see "Speech to Workingmen," *Salt Lake Herald,* Oct. 9, 1895, 1. Another of the group's songs was "Ode to Trumbo," which made fun of Isaac Trumbo's failed efforts to become US Senator. Its lyrics went: "Just before the battle Trumbo, I am thinking most of you. Thinking of your perfect boomlet, Wondering where and when it flew." See "Church Officials Assailed," *Salt Lake Tribune* Nov. 2, 1895, 4.

faith" and LDS leaders had concurred by saying that "the church does not claim or exercise the right to interfere in the social and political rights of its members. Church and state were then declared to be separate and distinct; the one from the other."[72] But now, he argued, the Republicans "charge the Democrats with having nominated two prominent Church men ... in the hope that their standing in the church would help make the ticket win." Thatcher was chosen because he was superintendent of the YMMIA, and "I was named because I had written some church books." In fact, he said, Thatcher was nominated because of his "ability and fitness" and was seen as "the man whom Gold could not tempt." Roberts said he thought he himself was nominated "in spite of being a Mormon."[73]

Roberts insisted that he held no bitterness, and he understood the political motivations behind the charge. He urged those in attendance to look to the future. The *Salt Lake Herald* reported that when he finished, Roberts took his seat to "a cyclone of applause... and deafening cheers for Caine and Roberts."[74] But Roberts's words did not go over well with everyone. His friend and fellow Seventy J. Golden Kimball picked up on Roberts's criticism of Republican church leaders: "Roberts delivered a fine speech but spoiled it by denouncing some of the Brethren for using Church influence and capped the climax where he said that any man that used church influence should be branded as an enemy of the church and a traitor to the state." Despite what the *Herald* had reported, Kimball noted that he left the meeting "disgusted."[75]

On election eve, Roberts held a big rally at the Bountiful Opera house which the *Davis County Clipper* called the "grandest political event of the season." Roberts was met at the Woods Cross depot by a "brass band, banners and boomers," and taken to Bountiful in a "grand procession." In addition to the speeches, the rally featured

72. "Masterful Roberts," *Salt Lake Herald*, Nov. 2, 1895, 5.

73. For his part, George M. Cannon responded that he had received a message from Logan claiming that Cache County Democrats were telling people openly "that church authorities had instructed the people, irrespective of party to support Roberts." Cannon said he believed this message was a hoax to deceive Republicans. See "Democratic Canard," *Salt Lake Tribune*, Nov. 5, 1895, 5.

74. "Masterful Roberts."

75. Kimball Journal, Oct. 30, Nov. 1, 4, 5, 1985.

"illuminations, torch light processions and the firing of cannons." It was obvious, the paper commented, that local residents were "pleased to have the great Democratic orator … with them the night before the election."[76] The *Salt Lake Herald* editorialized that Davis County was a Democratic stronghold, and "on this occasion … the general opinion is that the great logician of the West will go far ahead of his ticket in this county."[77]

Election day was, in the words of George Q. Cannon, "quite lively."[78] But despite conducting a strenuous campaign throughout the state, when the votes were tallied, Roberts lost a close race to Clarence E. Allen by fewer than nine hundred votes out of 41,000 cast.[79] But while suffering defeat, Roberts ran well ahead of all the other statewide Democratic candidates and, despite what the *Tribune* had earlier suggested, out-polled Democratic gubernatorial nominee John T. Caine in Davis County.[80]

While disappointed by the outcome, Roberts took comfort from the fact that his personal popularity had been a major factor in running "well ahead of his ticket" in a losing race.[81] He was also pleased that his marital status had not been raised.[82] Even the *Salt Lake Tribune* had avoided the issue. (This would change in a few years.) Moreover, Roberts recognized that his stance on suffrage had hurt him politically, and he took steps to reach out to those who had

76. "Local News," *Davis County Clipper*, Nov. 7, 1895, 4.

77. "To Close the Campaign," *Salt Lake Herald*, Nov. 3, 1895, 3. These projections would be proven correct when the votes were tallied.

78. Cannon Journal, Nov. 5, 1895.

79. Republicans dominated not only the state and congressional offices, but "acquired a comfortable two-thirds majority in both houses of the legislature, virtually assuring the election of two Republican [US] senators." Democrats had done well in one area: electing six of the nine judges in Utah's seven judicial districts. Moreover, the strong Republican showing reflected "both national and regional trends—as well as a steady trend toward Republicanism in Utah's last years as a territory." See White, "Utah State Elections," 20, 29–32.

80. Utah Commission Minute Book G, 413. Hogan garnered 1,150 votes and had a strong showing in Salt Lake and Weber Counties.

81. Roberts's difficulties were not all at the ballot box. The *Davis County Clipper* reported on election eve that someone had entered the Roberts "granary and relieved him of several sacks of flour and also broke the lock from his hen coop stealing thirty of his best fowls." In an attempt at levity, the paper noted the thief must have been a Democrat, because a Republican would have taken all of the chickens. See "Centerville Chats," *Davis County Clipper*, Oct. 31, 1895, 1.

82. White, "Utah State Elections," 175.

opposed him. In December, for example, he wrote to Susa Young Gates and included information on some of his recently published books. Roberts told "Aunt Susa" that he did so to demonstrate the "esteem which I hold you notwithstanding the rather hard opinion you entertain of me." Beyond that, as we have seen, Margaret seems to have tried to help in the outreach as well with her friendly letters to Gates signed "Dr. Maggie."[83]

Roberts continued to deal with some of the other after effects of the election, especially the conflict he had stirred up among church leaders. Roberts, according to Apostle Abraham H. Cannon, was feeling "somewhat humble since his political defeat," and decided to find some "remunerative employment to sustain his family." Furthermore, it was clear that Roberts

> justifies himself for the course he has taken in politics by reason of advice given him by Pres. Jos. F. Smith, which was in substance that all the brethren were at liberty to engage in politics, with the full approval of the Presidency. He presents a very plausible side of the story, but in some things he is not right in my opinion, especially in his view as to the rights of the Priesthood. I advised him to see the Presidency and set himself right with them, but he did not feel that he could do it yet.[84]

At a meeting of the First Presidency and Quorum of the Twelve on December 12, 1895, according to George Q. Cannon, Wilford Woodruff told his colleagues that

> there must be some investigation of the conduct of Moses Thatcher and B. H. Roberts before they can be allowed to actively engage in the work of the ministry. Roberts has accepted the editorship of the [Salt Lake] Herald without consulting the brethren which is a bad sign, as it is bound to occupy his attention to the neglect of ecclesiastical duties. His appointment displaces Chas. W. Penrose, for whom it was thought some place might be found in the Historian's Office in the writing of Church History, which is very much needed. Pres. Snow felt that we

83. Roberts to Gates, Dec. 11, 1895. Roberts was close to Gates's father-in-law Jacob Gates, having served with him for four years on the First Council of Seventy. He remarked at the latter's funeral that his closeness was partially due to the fact that Gates was part of a diminishing group "who were acquainted with the Prophet [Joseph Smith] and figured in the early history of this church." See Historian's Office, Journal History, Apr. 17, 1892, 5. See also Shipps to Gates, Nov. 2, Nov. 13, 1895.

84. Cannon, *Candid Insights*, 761.

> will not be justified in presenting Moses Thatcher and B. H. Roberts for the votes of the Saints at our next April Conference unless they repent and seek the forgiveness of their brethren.[85]

Roberts was supposed to speak at the Mutual Improvement Association of the church, but Woodruff said that "the engagement should be cancelled."[86] After this cancellation, Roberts, perhaps realizing the seriousness of the trouble he had caused for himself, wrote the First Presidency and told them he had canceled all his speaking engagements. Roberts's decision placated Woodruff somewhat, who said he was "gratified with this action, as he thought it was very proper under the circumstances."[87]

On February 13, Roberts was brought before a "Meeting of the presidents of Seventies & 12 Apostles." One of the best accounts of this meeting is found in J. Golden Kimball's journal. President of the Quorum of the Twelve Lorenzo Snow explained that Roberts "had made statements in public gatherings and had taken positions in political matters that the Apostles felt it their duty to investigate." Brigham Young Jr. read short accounts from the *Salt Lake Herald* of statements Roberts had made during the campaign, particularly his interview with the *Herald* the day after the October priesthood meeting, and the course he had "taken at the convention regarding woman suffrage." After that, Francis M. Lyman "spoke exceedingly plain, and I thought very evenly," about how he felt these statements had been used to turn "the people against the Brethren of the authorities," arguing that Roberts had done "an almost irreparable injury," and "called him to repentance." Beyond that, each of those present spoke "and each one … stated they could not sustain Bro Roberts in the course pursued and advised him that he fall into line."[88] Roberts took it all in and then, according to Kimball,

> spoke upon each point brought against him and explained why he had said it, and the causes of his going into the political arena, and the fight in the convention … against woman suffrage. He was sorry that the brethren took the view of the course that they did, yet he had no regrets

85. Cannon, 771.
86. Cannon Journal, Feb. 14, 1896.
87. Cannon Journal, Feb. 18, 1896.
88. Kimball Journal, Feb. 13, 1896.

> for what he had said and had no apologies to make and if he continued he would justify his course. Elder Roberts … said he could not change his views, but would resign his place among the seventies if they desired, and fall back into the ranks. He thought he had climbed his little hill, and performed all that there was to do in this direction. [89]

Kimball recorded, "Lyman, Grant, Seymour B. Young and others cried like little children and begged and pled, but to no avail." Lyman asked for more time, which was "moved and voted for unanimously. The meeting was dismissed and Elder Roberts left at once." Another meeting was set to be held in the temple on March 5. Kimball was clearly mystified by his friend's actions, writing, "During the meeting he shed no tears, neither did he humble himself, but sat there like he was of stone." Despite Kimball's belief that "Roberts is a noble spirit, intelligent, brave, valiant and true," he was convinced that, in this case, Roberts was "in darkness." He never again wanted to witness "the weighing of so great a man in the balance." He prayed that Roberts's "heart may be softened, and the time speedily come when he can see his mistake and continue his great work."[90] The next day Wilford Woodruff noted that Roberts was taking "an independent Course against the Authorities," and there seemed little chance that he would "be reconciled to his quorum."[91]

On February 19, a council meeting was held in the Salt Lake Temple. Roberts did not attend but sent a letter to his colleagues via Seymour B. Young stating that he "would cancel all appointments and not meet with the council again" until the matter had been decided. But Young noted that Roberts also told him that "he hoped that the brethren would not consider him shut out from preaching the gospel as he had a desire to still be a preacher of the truth."[92] Kimball says that he spoke with colleagues Rulon S. Wells and Christian D. Fjeldsted "about Roberts's case and wondered if we could do him any good."[93] The next day at 7:00 p.m., Kimball and Wells went to the *Salt Lake Herald* office to have a "friendly talk"

89. Kimball Journal.
90. Kimball Journal.
91. Woodruff, *Wilford Woodruff's Journal*, 9:390-91.
92. Young Journal, Feb. 19, 1896.
93. Kimball Journal, Feb. 19, 1896.

with Roberts but found that he was not there. They ran into Roberts on the street, however, and he invited them to dine with him, which they did. They then went to the office of the Seventies "and talked freely regarding the previous meeting with the twelve apostles, and what had been said." Roberts was unmoved. "We both kindly labored with Bro Roberts but of no avail. He said he had no feelings of bitterness in his heart against anyone, but could not change his opinions."[94] Roberts was not at the council meeting a week later. Young noted simply, "Bro R seems to have taken his farewell of his brethren among whom he has labored so faithfully for lo these many years."[95]

On March 5, Woodruff reported that the First Presidency, the Quorum of Twelve, and the First Council of Seventy had met the "whole Day" in the temple "laboring" with Roberts "to get him to repent of his wrong" in his words and actions against the general authorities on political principles. Woodruff felt that Roberts was "going to Destruction."[96] John Henry Smith believed that "if he refused to meet the wishes of the Brethren," Roberts would be suspended for three weeks and after that if he still did not change, he would "be dropped from his calling."[97] Kimball wrote that Roberts justified his decision to run as a Democrat for Congress "without consulting the authorities" because he had presumed as a result of previous conversations with them that he had their permission. Interestingly, at the same time he believed "he was wrong" in accepting the position with the *Salt Lake Herald* "without their consent." Kimball states that Roberts appealed to his colleagues' sense of American individualism, insisting that it was "improper to ask counsel regarding political matters from men who were Republicans, and that it was ill becoming to an American citizen." Roberts continued to say that "he thought he was right" to move forward without the approval of church leaders. They tried to reason with him by reminding him that he had once "rebelled against the issuance of the Manifesto" and asked that if he was "wrong then, could it not be possible you were wrong again?" But

94. Kimball Journal, Feb. 20, 1896.

95. Young Journal, Feb. 26, 1896.

96. Woodruff, *Wilford Woodruff's Journal*, 9:394 (Mar. 5, 1896).

97. Smith, *Church, State, and Politics*, 343. Smith noted without elaboration: "I am not quite satisfied with our action in the Roberts matter."

after eight hours in the previous meeting, then six at this meeting, Roberts was not persuaded. Kimball concluded, "His mind was darkened and he desired the matter to be settled at once."[98]

Brigham Young Jr. moved that Roberts be dropped from the First Council, and that "he be suspended from all action in the functions of the Priesthood." Kimball said that this meant "that even if he repented at some future time he loses his place" on the council. Clearly this caused concern, and Heber J. Grant moved that Young's motion be tabled for three weeks. Grant said that if after that time had passed Roberts "could not humble himself before the Quorum," then Young's motion should pass. According to Seymour B. Young, Roberts "would not yield," and Grant's motion received a unanimous vote.[99] Kimball called the meeting "a most solemn occasion and one I will never forget."[100]

Lyman and Grant met with Roberts for several hours over March 12 and 13—Roberts's thirty-ninth birthday—and after Roberts initially told them to report to church leaders that he would not change his mind, they were finally able to move him. Grant wrote, "I noticed that tears came into [Roberts's] eyes ... and brother Lyman and I seemed to [be] blessed with ability in our talk to impress Roberts."[101] Roberts instead asked for another day to ponder his way forward. The next day he wrote the two apostles a letter and said he could not "think of anything in which I have not acted in all good conscience out of an honest heart," but since church leaders felt he was "in the wrong I will bow to them, and place myself in their hands as the servants of God." He thanked them for "your goodness to me."[102] Seymour Young was relieved that "Roberts is coming to his senses thank the Lord."[103] Grant wrote that he was "indeed a happy man tonight. I felt greater sorrow over the prospect of losing brother Roberts from the labors which he is able to perform in

98. Kimball Journal, Mar. 5, 1896. Interestingly, Cannon's diaries are silent during this period on the Roberts matter.

99. Young Journal, Mar. 30, 1896.

100. Kimball Journal, Mar. 5, 1896.

101. Grant, *Diaries*, Mar. 12, 1896.

102. Grant, Mar. 13, 1896.

103. Young Journal, Mar. 13, 1896.

building up of the work of God than any other sorrow that had ever come into my life."[104]

The next day, the First Presidency, eight of the Quorum of the Twelve, and the First Council of Seventy all met with Roberts. George Q. Cannon, presiding over the meeting because Woodruff felt unwell, stated, "That all his Brethren wanted of him was to show a broken heart and contrite spirit, which Bro. Roberts did. We took him into our fellowship. He with the others present shed tears of joy at the change in his spirit."[105] Cannon told Roberts that he would "need to change his views regarding church and state as much injury had been done in many of the stakes of Zion." He asked Roberts to write a full explanation of his views for publication, and have it signed by the presiding brethren. At the same time, Cannon made it clear that it was not so much what Roberts had said "as it was the spirit he manifested," but that they felt "very forgiving" at the present. Roberts went farther than he had in his letter and

> made one of the humblest and most perfect confessions I have ever listened to. He was willing to do more than asked … write the confession and publish it, make it before the whole world if necessary, and lay everything at their feet. Bro. Roberts broke down and sobbed as if his heart would break. It was a complete exemplification of a "broken heart and a contrite spirit." it was acceptable to us all, as all present wept. I never saw such rejoicing from our aged president, his two counselors, the apostles—each went to Bro. Roberts, shook his hand & blessed him. Some embraced him. It was a grand display of brotherly love.[106]

The issue was brought to the church at April's general conference where a "political manifesto" was announced. Prior to the session, the First Presidency, those members of the Twelve who were present, the First Council of Seventy, and the Presiding Bishopric met and signed the document. It "reaffirmed that before accepting any position that would interfere with the discharge of

104. Grant, Mar. 13, 1896.

105. John Henry Smith, Journal, Mar. 5, Mar. 19, Mar. 26, 1896, in Smith Family Papers.

106. Kimball Journal, Mar. 26, 1896. Kimball noted that "instead of Bro Roberts losing influence, he is a greater man in my estimation than ever, and is a giant in strength. He has been tested and tried and I pray God … that he may prove true and faithful until the end and gain Eternal Life."

his ecclesiastical duties, a leading church official should apply to the proper authorities to determine whether he could function adequately in both positions."[107]

Roberts spoke at the morning session, and his friend Kimball wrote that his remarks were "entirely satisfactory to the authorities and very pleasing to the people. If he always feels as he did on this day, he will be all right." Kimball also noted that "it caused a sensation" when Grant presented the political manifesto and it "was found that Apostle Moses Thatcher had not signed it." It was a greater sensation when Thatcher's name was "not presented to be sustained." Kimball believed that "it seems that Apostle Lorenzo Snow and Brigham Young visited Apostle Thatcher, who is dangerously sick, and presented the document. After giving him some time to consider it, he refused to sign it. This was the cause of his name not being presented."[108]

Over the next few days, Kimball recorded public reactions to these events. On April 8, he noted that there "seems to be considerable talk among the people regarding the suspension of Apostle Thatcher. Some cannot understand why they could not extend patience until Bro Thatcher got better, or died, as he is dangerously sick."[109] Kimball visited the ailing Thatcher, who told him in great detail of the political manifesto, the short time he had been given to read and comprehend it, and of the suspension itself. Echoing what Roberts had initially argued, Thatcher stated his belief that he thought it improper to seek "council from men of a different political faith, that it could not be done and receive justice." He told Kimball he believed the brethren had "blanketed their conscience" when they signed the political manifesto; that they had taken "advantage of him;" and that they "were afraid." Kimball sympathized with Thatcher, considered him still an apostle and "not guilty of anything" before the church until "has an impartial trial, for a man cannot be guilty until it is so proven by two or more witnesses." Kimball believed this was part of entering the political fray: "To say anything against Moses is to

107. For the full text, see "Minutes of the General Conference of the Church of Jesus Christ of Latter-day Saints," *Deseret Weekly News*, Apr. 11, 1898, 95–98. See also Craner, "Influence of the LDS Church," 117.

108. Kimball Journal, Apr. 6, 1896.

109. Kimball Journal, Apr. 8, 1896.

do him an injustice. All who have indulged in politics have got in trouble of some kind."[110]

Once news of the process was public, there was tremendous interest, and reporting of the circumstances proved complicated and contradictory. According to an explosive account in the *Salt Lake Tribune*, Heber J. Grant told a Cache Stake High Council meeting that "the brethren ... worked with B. H. Roberts for nine weeks before they brought him around." Eventually, Roberts had appeared at the church offices one morning and, according to Grant, said that "his dead relatives ... those who had died outside the Church had appeared to him in a vision and had asked him to bow to the will of the authorities and return to his standing in the church in order to temple work for their salvation."[111] The *Salt Lake Herald* printed Roberts's response to the *Tribune*'s story, saying that Grant must have been "misrepresented." When asked if his ancestors had played a role, Roberts smiled broadly and said, so far as he knew, his ancestors "have not been excited about the matter and have not appeared to me either to protest against my course or give me information as to what I should do."[112]

The *Logan Journal* took particular aim at Roberts for aiding in the effort against Thatcher. After reproducing the church's statement, it wrote that "it is hard to understand how men like B. H. Roberts and others who made, endorsed, upheld and defended the action of the reconvened convention, can endorse and sign a denial or retraction without vouchsafing one word of explanation to the party or apology to the people."[113] The *Springville Independent* said it was sorry for the "humiliation which came to Thatcher in his hour of suffering and pain." The *Sandy Independent* said it did not believe this "new" manifesto would bring about "peace, tranquility or good will."[114] Finally the *Park Record*, a Republican paper, argued that the church had made "the mistake of its existence," noting, "Apostle Thatcher

110. Kimball Journal, Apr. 12, 1896.

111. "A Hot Time," *Salt Lake Tribune,* May 10, 1896, 1. Grant also indicated that he and Francis M. Lyman had "been appointed a committee to persuade Roberts that he was in error."

112. "High Council Meeting," *Salt Lake Herald,* May 11, 1896, 8.

113. "The Objectionable Part," *Logan Journal,* Apr. 4, 1896, 4.

114. As quoted in "Spirit of the Press," *Logan Journal,* Apr. 18, 1896, 2.

... in refusing to sign the document greatly strengthened the esteem and regard in which he was held by both Mormons and Gentiles, while B. H. Roberts in rescinding the bold stand he took last fall and meekly bowing down has stultified himself in the eyes of heretofore staunch friends and admirers."[115]

An editorial in the *New York Times* on April 17, 1896, called the political manifesto a "worthless ... useless repetition" of previous statements, listing many efforts on the part of numerous general authorities—Wilford Woodruff, George Q. Cannon, Francis M. Lyman, and Joseph F. Smith—in "attacking" the Democratic Party and Democratic candidates from the pulpit and in various church meetings. The *Times* concluded, "The refusal of Moses Thatcher, the Democratic leader, to sign such a manifesto in his character of Apostle is gratifying," but it lamented "the course of B. H. Roberts."[116]

Roberts would refer to this whole series of events in the third person in his *Comprehensive History of the Church* written many years later, arguing that the church leaders were "right in reproving these brethren for their dereliction of duty." Still, he defended himself even decades later, insisting such dereliction occurred not "through wanton disregard of their superior officers of disrespect for the church, but through the confusion which at the time prevailed in regard as to what was to be the attitude of high ecclesiastics of the church respecting political office holding."[117]

By May 6, Roberts was again attending and participating in First Council of Seventy meetings.

115. "Local News," *Park Record*, Apr. 11, 1896, 2.

116. "The Mormon Manifesto," *New York Times*, Apr. 17, 1896, 4.

117. Roberts, *Comprehensive History*, 6:331. For more on Thatcher, see Lyman, "Alienation of an Apostle."

TEN

A PUBLIC RELATIONS MISSION AND A ROMANCE

On May 10, 1896, the *Salt Lake Herald*, where Roberts was the editor, announced that because the ownership of the paper had recently changed hands, it was proper for the paper to state its current editorial view. The paper would "consistently advocate" the principles which led to the "organization of the Democratic party" in Utah, and that they "would not concede to any church or its leaders thereof in this free state … that it or they may dictate or advise who of all of its members may or may not engage in politics or become a candidate for office." To do so would make Utah "a tool of the church and in the end turn it in to an instrument of its propaganda."[1]

In response, Roberts sent a lengthy letter to the paper resigning as editor,[2] saying that he feared that if he remained in his position, "misunderstandings and unpleasantness would grow out of the rather complicated state of affairs which this announced policy would likely force upon me." Roberts's friend Willard Done[3] argued that Roberts had been "practically forced out of that position by R. C. Chambers,[4] who now owns nearly all of the stock of the paper." The problem, Done explained, was "Roberts, in coming out

1. "The Herald," *Salt Lake Herald*, May 10, 1896, 3.

2. "Herald."

3. Done (1865–1931) was a prominent educator and a graduate of Brigham Young Academy, where he also taught from 1883 to 1886. He went on to be president of the Salt Lake Stake Academy, 1886–88, and returned in 1892 as principal. After leaving there in 1899, Done wrote *Women of the Bible* (Salt Lake City: by the author, 1900) and was active in the Republican Party as secretary to Utah governor John C. Cutler. He was a member of the legislature, 1903–05, and State Insurance Commissioner, 1910–14. Despite his Republican affiliation, he and Roberts were close.

4. On Robert C. Chambers, see "Senator R. C. Chambers Stricken Down," *Salt Lake Herald*, Apr. 12, 1901, 1; "R. C. Chambers Dead," *New York Times*, Apr. 12, 1901; and Don Maguire, "R. C. Chambers, President of the Ontario Silver Mining Company," *Colliery Engineer*, June 1901, 504.

in favor of the recent address of the authorities has displeased some of his Democratic friends, and as a consequence has resigned his position as editor of the Herald."[5]

A month later, Roberts and J. Golden Kimball, by appointment of the First Council of the Seventy, participated in services in Logan where a monument was erected honoring John H. Gibbs who had been killed in the Cane Creek Massacre while Roberts was presiding over the Southern States Mission.[6] The town's businesses all closed and "the people generally made it a holiday." Roberts delivered an address of some ninety minutes relating several instances where he and Gibbs "narrowly escaped mob violence." The day reminded Kimball "of old times."[7]

When finances dictated, Roberts seems to have spoken to various groups which used his book *Outlines of Ecclesiastical History* as a text. For example, he met with a large class in the Sixteenth Ward engaged in Bible study, which was described as numbering eighty-five and "constantly growing."[8] Apparently aware of his personal situation, church leaders looked to Roberts to perform another important assignment. On June 4, the First Presidency and Council of Twelve "decided that the First Presidency should interview Brother Roberts with a view to him taking a mission to the Eastern States, accompanied by some male members of the Tabernacle Choir as singers." President of the Twelve Lorenzo Snow motioned and "it was agreed to draw in equitable tithes for the support of his family, not to exceed $2000."[9]

Roberts called on the First Presidency the next morning to report that he had seen George D. Pyper[10] concerning the mission call, and that Pyper had "signified his willingness to go."[11] The First

5. Done Journal, May 10, 1896.

6. Kimball Journal, May 20, 1896.

7. Kimball Journal.

8. "Town Talk," *Salt Lake Herald*, June 23, 1896, 7.

9. Historian's Office, Journal History, June 4, 1896, 2.

10. Pyper had recently stepped down as associate editor of the *Contributor*. He was set apart for this mission by Brigham Young Jr. Pyper would go on to edit other church periodicals and serve as general superintendent of the Sunday Schools. Willard Done noted that Roberts and Pyper were "an excellent combination. The stand B. H. Roberts is taking on church matters, and the work he is doing for his people will sure to place his name on the roll of honor." See Done Journal, June 14, 1896.

11. Historian's Office, Journal History, June 12, 1896, 2. Just prior to this, Roberts

Presidency approved both him and Melvin J. Ballard, "he also being a good singer and player on the organ."[12] A week later, Roberts was given "a letter of appointment to labor as a missionary in the states lying east of Utah extending to the coast." He was sent to assess the condition and organization of the Northern States Mission, reinvigorate or create local units, encourage baptisms, and bolster the faith of missionaries and members alike.

On the eve of his departure, Roberts delivered a speech entitled "Mormonism: The Force Which Unites and Blends All Truth." Mormonism, he stated, "draws so to speak, through all time a golden thread which links together every truth under the sun. It is the one great ocean into which all the streams of truth flow." He told his audience that this awareness had come to him while he was visiting a mining camp and went through the stamping mills where ore in its "rudest form" is refined into a finished mass. "As I stood watching the process, the thought came to me that … what men call 'Mormonism' occupies [a similar place] in relation to the great mass of truth that is to be found in the world." Mormonism, Roberts said, was "cast into the confused truth of the world, unites and explains it, in fact, and shows it to be consistent from the beginning of time to the end of time." Roberts talked about his experiences at the Parliament of Religions where he was afforded "an opportunity day after day to an exposition of the faith of nearly all the religions of the world." He said he "was very much astonished … to discover so many truths in what … [are] called heathen religions that were facsimiles of the truths in Christianity." The various Christian churches had "but fragments of the truth," and it was necessary for Mormonism to unite "into one consistent whole" all the truths possessed by both heathen and early Christian alike.[13]

It was in this spirit that Roberts, Pyper, and Ballard left the evening

---

had ended his term as president of the University of Utah Alumni Association. See "Alumni Association," *Salt Lake Herald*, June 10, 1896, 2

12. Cannon Journal, June 12, 1896. Pyper noted that he had received a form letter from Wilford Woodruff, calling him to "labor in conjunction with Brother B. H. Roberts. Two days later he wrote a letter to First Presidency accepting "the call." On June 28, 1896, he gave a "farewell" address to the members of the Eighteenth Ward, noting that several people gave him money. George D. Pyper, Scrapbook, 1896–97, in Pyper Papers.

13. Roberts's address is in Stuy, *Collected Discourses*, 5:154–60.

of July 7, 1896.[14] The *Ogden Standard* reported that a "number of people assembled at the depot to bid them Godspeed on their journey."[15] They arrived in Kansas City two days later, a testament to how much rail travel had improved. The three men began an intense two weeks of activity. The *Kansas City Times* commented that "Elder Roberts is the great 'Mormon' preacher and author. It is generally conceded that he is one of the most eloquent expounders of Bible doctrine that not only Utah, but the great west affords."[16] Roberts told another paper, "It may be of interest ... to say that the place we call Zion for the final gathering is in Jackson County: in fact we might say is in Kansas City. We won't abandon Salt Lake, but the headquarters of the Church will be on the soil of Missouri."[17]

The group's first meetings were held at the Academy of Music on July 12 where Roberts spoke in the afternoon on "The Relationship of Mormonism to the Christian World," and in the evening on "The Mission of Joseph Smith." According to the mission history, some "twenty-five thousand bills were distributed announcing these meetings, and notices were published in all of the leading newspapers, but the meetings were rather poorly attended." Ballard recorded that there were 150 people present, while Pyper estimates it at one hundred. William F. Butt wrote to his wife, "It will take $12.50 to pay for the hall & advertizing will run up to about $20, so you can see it is going to be quite an expensive mission." As a means of comparison, Butt was paying $12.50 per month for rent.[18]

Two days later Roberts, Ballard, Pyper, mission president Samuel G. Spencer, and six other elders sought to escape the stifling heat with an excursion to Washington Park. After some recreation, as Pyper recalls, "dusk fell" and the group "found a spot a half mile

---

14. Pyper Scrapbook, July 7, 1896. Prior to that, he attended his last First Council meeting on July 1. As Kimball noted, "Saw Elder B. H. Roberts for the last time before his mission to the Eastern states." Kimball Journal, July 1, 1896.

15. "Random References," *Ogden Standard*, July 9, 1896, 8.

16. As cited in "Town Talk," *Salt Lake Herald*, July 6, 1896, 8. The paper described the group as "Mormon evangelists," and said that they invited "all lovers of the gospel and classical singing to attend." The account was also picked up by the *Logan Journal*, which described the paper as a Democratic paper. See [no title] *Logan Journal*, July 7, 1896, 1.

17. "Their Zion in Kansas City," *Kansas City Daily Journal*, July 12, 1896, 1.

18. Butt to Laura Butt, July 11, 1896, Butt Papers.

away at the top of the hill" in the woods where they held a prayer circle, Roberts asking "that the Lord would open the hearts of the people and assist us especially at out labors in Independence." Pyper remembered it as "a prayer filled with love for humanity and concern for the redemption of Zion & the welfare of the people."[19]

Their next stop was Independence. Ballard noted, "I shall never forget the feeling I had when entering that city, realizing that our people were but a short time before driven out by a mob."[20] Again the group blanketed the city with handbills advertising the meetings.

On July 15, Roberts spoke to a total of 120 people in afternoon and evening meetings held again at the Academy of Music. The next day he spoke to a crowd of 200—many of whom were members of the Reorganized Church of Jesus Christ of Latter Day Saints (RLDS)—lecturing on "Succession in the Presidency" and "Salvation for the Dead."[21] Pyper noted that the "house was better filled than the night previous."[22]

The RLDS newspaper *Zion's Advocate* took note of Roberts's lectures, criticizing him for asserting that the Mormon church was "better understood now," and that it was only a "matter of time until they would be crowned instead of rejected." It commented on how "complacently" Roberts and his colleagues take credit for their favorable reception in town, when the RLDS Church had worked hard to fight and live "down the prejudices engendered by the abominations in Utah, and have made the name of Saint ... honorable." It was their work, now taken for granted by the LDS missionaries, that "has made it possible for men like Elder Roberts and his brethren to come as representatives of a hierarchy ... as despotic and terrible in its rule as the Czar of Russia." That hyperbole aside, the newspaper thought that "personally they are fine appearing men," but they opposed the LDS mission because "they are polygamists at heart now;

19. Pyper Scrapbook, July 14, 1896.

20. Hinckley, *Sermons and Missionary Services*, 38.

21. The RLDS Church is today the Community of Christ. Throughout this book I use RLDS, since that was its name throughout Roberts's lifetime.

22. Pyper Scrapbook, July 16, 1896. Pyper states he was "greatly surprised" when Roberts asked him to be the opening speaker. He bore his testimony and felt that he did not do very well.

they still believe in the Adam–God doctrine.[23] How can any Saint strike hands with them on this basis?"[24]

After a break in public meetings, Roberts and Pyper decided to relax. They went to Independence not to proselytize, but "on a pleasure trip.' Pyper noted that they took a "Bull's Eye Camera with us" and "had a delightful time."[25] After that, they returned to Kansas City where they hired a boat "for 15 cents per hour" at the Big Blue River, and then "rowed to the Missouri River."[26] In the evening, along with Ballard, they went to Troost Park[27] and "shot the chutes." Pyper said it was "wonderfully exciting & consists of a 200 foot slide down a 45 degree track into a small lake of water. It makes ones hair stand on end, but it was fun."[28]

The Northern States Mission[29]—technically Roberts's first mission supervisory assignment—was in the midst of changing leaders. The mission headquarters had also been moved from Chicago to Kansas City in March. Louis A. Kelsch, who had known Roberts in the Southern States Mission in 1881–82 and who was to be the new mission president, arrived in July 1896, and would serve until 1901. Roberts worked with him and Spencer during the transition. On July 20, Roberts wrote to the First Presidency, "giving a report of his labors" and outlining the suggestion he had made to Kelsch "that it would be well to divide up that mission into more conferences" and that he visit the elders in those conferences instead of their coming to meet him. He believed such a move would not only reduce expenses but "accomplish more good."[30]

---

23. Brigham Young had taught that Adam and God were the same person. See Buerger, "Adam–God Doctrine."

24. "Utah Missionaries," *Zion's Advocate*, July 25, 1896, 1.

25. This camera, introduced in 1892 by the Boston Camera Manufacturing company, was the first roll-film camera with a red window as the exposure number indicator.

26. The Big Blue is a tributary of the Missouri and the site of a battle between Mormons and other Missouri settlers on November 4, 1833.

27. Troost Park was built by the Kansas City Cable Line Company in 1888. The "Shoot the Chute" was a common ride at many amusement parks of the day.

28. Pyper Scrapbook, July 19, 1896.

29. The Northern States Mission was created in 1889 and was originally part of the Northwestern States Mission, where Roberts labored in 1880. At this point, it was one of the largest church missions in terms of geography. Several changes were instituted after Roberts's visit. See "Northern States Mission," in Jenson, *Encyclopedic History*, 593–94.

30. Historian's Office, Journal History, July 20, 1896, 2.

Louisa wrote to Roberts on July 22, and told him that Apostle Abraham H. Cannon had died. Cannon, who was thirty-seven years old, died after he contracted an ear infection. Louisa told her husband that it "seems a very sad thing for a man of his age to pass away," probably thinking that Cannon was two years younger than her absent husband.[31]

Roberts wrote the First Presidency to ask that someone be sent who was more competent in musical accompaniment than Ballard, suggesting Edward P. Midgley.[32] After consultation with his father, Midgley told the First Presidency that "he would be ready in a few days," and he joined Roberts and Pyper on August 21.[33] Prior to Midgley's arrival, Elder Alvin A. Beesley[34] occasionally filled in as an accompanist. Beesley notes that at the July 18 meeting they had to hire an accompanist and "had to pay $4 … & they don't want that to occur again."[35] He said that the missionaries and the members held a social where "refreshments were served to fully one hundred fifty to see Bros R[oberts] & P[yper] off. … Surely his coming here has been a great benefit to all & [the] elders will reap the reward for his work as well as their own very soon."[36] Ballard was less optimistic: "There were but few who seemed interested and asked us to call upon them."[37]

Roberts and Pyper left Kansas City for St. John, Kansas,[38] visiting part of what was known as the Indian Territory Mission, which

31. Louisa to Roberts, July 22, 1896, box 4, fd. 3, Roberts Papers (UU).

32. Midgley (1872–1968) was set apart on August 1, 1896, by Joseph F. Smith, and returned on December 9, 1898. See Historian's Office, Journal History, Dec. 9, 1898, 2, 8. He was a musician and later a self-employed sign painter in Salt Lake City.

33. Historian's Office, Journal History, Aug. 1, 1896, 3. In a letter to Joseph F. Smith, Roberts called Midgley "a very valuable addition to our party and his skill as an accompanist renders our singing an assured success." See "Elder Roberts in St. Louis," *Deseret Evening News*, Sep. 1, 1896, 3.

34. Beesley (1873–1940) was a talented musician and the son of Ebenezer Beesley, a composer and director of the Tabernacle Choir, 1870–85. Beesley was set apart on August 31, 1894, by Heber J. Grant, and returned on July 29, 1896. A Seventy, he was active in church affairs, serving in the mutual and Sunday School at the ward and stake level. He was bishop of the Twenty-Second Ward from 1904 to 1930. In later years, he was active as an officer and organizer of the local Salt Lake chapter of the American Federation of Musicians. Beesley also served as a Salt Lake County Commissioner, 1933–35.

35. Beesley Journal, July 24, 1896.

36. Beesley Journal, July 26–27, 1896.

37. Hinckley, *Sermons and Missionary Services*, 38.

38. Beesley indicated Roberts "regretted that I could not go with them," since they were still without an accompanist. See Beesley Journal, July 27, 1896.

then contained Kansas, Arkansas, Oklahoma, and Indian territories.[39] While in the area, Roberts, as he had often done in the past, took the opportunity to explore part of the Mormon past when he visited with William Bickerton, who led a schismatic group colloquially known as the Bickertonites, located in St. John, Kansas.[40] The group called themselves the Church of Jesus Christ. Roberts called Bickerton a "man of much force of character but without education." Bickerton was a disciple of Sidney Rigdon, who had led his own group after Joseph Smith's death, and while a number of people in Pennsylvania and Kansas accepted Bickerton's teachings, the group, Roberts said, "amounted to nothing."[41] Years later he would tell one of his missionaries in the Eastern States that he "personally knew" Bickerton, then dismissively added that his group "has long been broken up, and even at the time of his death was of no importance as an organization at all." Roberts said that Bickerton had no "authority beyond the fact that he once was an elder in the church and doubtless was a very well meaning; but very greatly mistaken man in relation to the constitutions of the church and the succession of authority in it." As of this writing, the Bickertonites are the third-largest Restoration church.[42]

Next, the party headed to St. Louis, Missouri, and arrived during a period of stifling heat. Pyper recorded that it "was so intense that I was quite overcome and had considerable difficulty in breathing. ... It was unanimously decided to wait until the weather became

39. The mission was organized in 1855, closed in 1860, and reopened briefly in 1877. It was reorganized on April 20, 1883, and renamed the Southwestern States Mission on March 29, 1898. Six years later it became the Central States Mission. See "Indian Territory Mission," in Jenson, *Encyclopedic History,* 359–61. For additional background, see "Indian Territory Mission," *Deseret Weekly*, Apr. 11, 1896, 26. The headquarters was in St. John. The mission president at this time was Andrew Kimball.

40. See Entz, "Bickertonites," and Entz, "Mormon Origins of St. John." See also Stone, *William Bickerton.*

41. Roberts, *Autobiography*, 206. Roberts told the First Presidency that Bickerton "presides over his few remaining followers and was ... engaged in making a desperate struggle to keep the members of his church together, numbering all told 16 members." See Historian's Office, Journal History, Dec. 7, 1896, 3. Pyper wrote that Bickerton called the area "Zion Valley," and prophesied that the church he built "would stand forever." Instead, Pyper observed, a "gentle Kansas zephyr came along, toppled it, and many of his people left because of this prophetic failure." Pyper Scrapbook, July 24, 1896.

42. Roberts to Eva Lewis, June 21, 1924, in Lewis Collection; Stone, *William Bickerton.*

cooler before engaging a hall. … To begin now would be to throw money away."[43] As they ventured out a bit, they visited the area near the riverfront. Pyper records they were shocked by what they found, especially the black residents:

> Poverty, squalor, Filth. What a disgrace to St. Louis these quarters are! What a mixture of Jews, negro, Italian and every other nation on the earth. We saw the people gambling, drinking and in debauchery. I think this must be the worst city in the Union. There are 47,000 negroes here, and by the picaninies one sees they must be prolific while the whites are the opposite. Never long will it be at this rate before the negroes will rule the south.[44]

The missionaries were also offended by the open display of prostitution. As Pyper notes, while on an evening stroll for exercise, Roberts and he "passed along some street which seemed to be lined with houses of ill repute. We were horrified to see in the windows of nearly every house some female wretch who made appeals to the passers by, and advertized their degrading business. Oh St. Louis is a pure (!) Christian city. Nit!"[45]

In contrast to the poor of the city that the missionaries derided, Roberts took notice of the majesty of the Mississippi River, later remembering that he "watched the beautiful river as it flowed clear and pure, rippling and glinting in the sunlight." Below where he had stood, the "muddy, murky waters of the Missouri pour into" the Mississippi. "The two streams, the pure and the impure, run side by side for a little while and then they mingle in a dark stream. The muddy stream is not as muddy as it was. I grant you that. But the pure stream that has glittered in the sunlight, is never pure again."[46]

In early August, Roberts and Pyper visited the local RLDS congregation. Their presence in town apparently created some discord as the group was divided over whether to invite Roberts to speak.[47] On August 9, they attended morning services where they found

43. Pyper Scrapbook, July 29, 1896.
44. Pyper Scrapbook, Aug. 8, 1896.
45. Pyper Scrapbook, Aug. 10, 1896.
46. As quoted in "Roberts in New York," *Salt Lake Herald*, Feb. 17, 1897, 6.
47. Pyper Scrapbook, Aug. 8, 1896.

Reverend Myron H. Bond[48] presiding. Pyper wrote, "Pastor Bond ... quoted II Timothy, Chapter 3, Verses 1–9 and claimed it referred to the Utah Apostates." Among other things, these passages say "that in the last days perilous times shall come"; that men will become "lovers of their own selves, covetous, boasters, proud, blasphemers ... unholy ... despisers of those that are good ... lovers of pleasure more than lovers of God," and "never able to come to the knowledge of truth." Pyper said that he found it "queer" to be "called an apostate by the Josephites." That evening they again returned to Reorganized services, held in "a tent at Garrison & St. Louis streets." At this meeting Bond was replaced by Elder Russell Archibald Jr.[49] Pyper observed that Archibald "bore a testimony to the truth of his work and to seeing the sick healed, hearing speaking in tongues etc. Strange that an apostate church can have these signs."[50] Roberts and Pyper also visited several other churches, including the Pilgrim church and the Catholic Church. Such visits were typical of Roberts throughout his life.[51]

Roberts called his colleagues, especially Pyper and Midgley, "the pleasantest companions in the world, and I think it would be impossible to find men more united than we are."[52] On August 12 they "contracted for 20,000 dodgers and 200 streamers for meetings" at the cost of twenty-two dollars. The dodger was a pocket-sized pamphlet with the topics to be discussed by Roberts listed by week.

48. Bond (1843–1920) spent thirty-five years as an RLDS clergyman and writer. He was active as a missionary in Massachusetts, Illinois, Pennsylvania, and Missouri. He served in St. Louis from 1895 to 1901. Bond was a member of the Reorganized Church's First Council of Seventy, and later the Independence, Missouri, stake presidency, 1906–16.

49. Archibald (1869–1935) was born in St. Clair County, Illinois. He was an active pastor in the RLDS Church at various locations. Archibald was a member of Second Quorum of Priests; the Quorum of High Priests, 1911–12; and treasurer of the General Sunday School Association. In addition to his pastoral duties, he worked for several railroads much of his adult life.

50. Pyper Scrapbook, Aug. 9, 1896.

51. Pyper Scrapbook, Aug. 16, 1896. Pyper is likely referring to the Pilgrim Congregational Church, founded in 1866. They may have visited St. Mary's Catholic Church which was located in their neighborhood. Pyper commented, "What a lot of paganism is in the Catholic church. The original simplicity of the Gospel has been swallowed up in form and ceremony."

52. Roberts to Mother, Aug. 25, 1896, box 4, fd. 7, Roberts Papers (UU).

The streamer read in blue on white "Mormonism: B H Roberts the Noted Mormon Orator. Admission Free."[53]

But the group was strapped for cash. William F. Butt told his wife on August 19 that Roberts "was in sore need of $100 so us elders made up the amount. I loaned $60. It was for hall rent in St. Louis." Three days later he wondered if or when he would ever get the money back.[54] They had "engaged a hall [Chatsworth Hall] in the heart of the city for about one month for which we paid ... one hundred fifty dollars. You may depend it is a fine one."[55] Pyper noted, "We walked over this city until our limbs refused to carry us. We distributed 15,000 bills."[56]

Roberts attracted a great deal of press attention with this series of lectures, in which he discussed head-on church doctrines and the objections posed to Mormonism by contemporary critics. The *St. Louis Republic* mentioned his lectures on page one,[57] calling him a "celebrity," and a "Noted Mormon Orator."[58]

Roberts's first lecture was on the "Rise and Progress of Mormonism."[59] He would follow it with the "Relationship of Mormonism to the Christian World," the "Book of Mormon as a New Witness," and "Is Modern Christendom Justified in Believing Revelation has Ceased?" The *St. Louis Republic* said that the initial presentation was "remarkable for the distinct intentness with which the audience listened to everything that was said. Most of the seats were occupied with an intelligent array of people." Pyper happily noted, "Everything has come our way so far. The newspapers have been fair; have given us plenty of advertizing. ... The Post-Dispatch copied our articles of faith, a nice little article was written by the Republic and the articles of faith included therein. Altogether, it

53. Pyper Scrapbook, Aug. 12, 1896. Copies of each are included with the scrapbook.

54. Butt to Laura, Aug. 19 and 22, 1896, Butt Papers.

55. Roberts to Mother, Aug. 25, 1896.

56. Pyper Scrapbook, Aug. 20–22, 1896.

57. "Leading Events Reported in To-Day's Republic," *St. Louis Republic,* Aug. 21, 1896; and "To-Day's News in Brief," *St. Louis Republic*, Aug. 21, 1896, 2.

58. "A Mormon Elder Will Lecture Here for Thirty Days," *St Louis Republic*, Aug. 21, 1896, 12. The paper also published the letter signed by the First Presidency appointing Roberts to undertake the mission.

59. "News of the Churches," *St. Louis Post Dispatch*, Aug. 23, 1896, 16.

is a circulation of our articles amongst 100,000—a pretty good presentation of our faith."[60]

The *St. Louis Republic* followed Roberts's lectures closely. At one point they referred to him as "the Mormon Moody," referring to evangelist Dwight Moody,[61] describing him as a "powerful man ... in more than one sense," possessed of "sturdy frame and ... features." His face is "impassive except when the passion of oratory is upon him," and he becomes a "power on the platform." They commented on his "singularly pleasant voice, sort as a woman's in conversation and with some distinctly musical notes in it. He conveys an impression of sincerity the most prejudiced cannot fail to appreciate." Roberts told them:

> When our church began its existence its enemies said it was held together by the forceful personality of Joseph Smith and that when he died it would go to pieces. When he departed Brigham Young was raised up as a worthy successor. Then the world said 'He will hold them together, but wait till he is gone.' He has gone, but the church waxes stronger. The charge that polygamy, a system which they said pandered to the baser passions of men, gave the church its numerical strength, followed these. That tenet has been forsworn, and we believe that the public is ready to give us a hearing.[62]

Pyper again wrote of positive press coverage: "The newspaper this morning gave good accounts of our meeting last night. ... It makes one feel good to hear a favorable word said concerning the Gospel of Christ."[63]

By then Ballard had left the group; he was transferred to the Northern States Mission headquarters. The transfer was a difficult decision, and Ballard was disappointed.[64] Pyper wrote that Midgley

60. Pyper Scrapbook, Aug. 23, 1896. Pyper mentions that Midgley joined them on August 21, "and we are now prepared to sing our best music."

61. "The Mormon Moody," *St. Louis Republic*, Aug. 16, 1896, III:21.

62. "Latter Day Saints," *St. Louis Republic*, Aug. 24, 1896, 5; and "The Latter-Day Saints," *St. Louis Globe Democrat*, Aug. 24, 1896, 7.

63. Pyper Scrapbook, Aug. 23, 24, 1896. Pyper was likely referring to articles in the *Republic* and *Globe Democrat*. Pyper also noted they had traded a mention of Estey and Co. in their handbills for a loan of an "elegant organ."

64. Hinckley, *Sermons and Missionary Services*, 41–51.

had been sent to assist them, noting: "As he plays accompaniment pretty well it is a great relief to me."[65]

Roberts and local Mormons were also "engaged in a controversial battle with the St. Louis Church of God." A local pastor named William R. Covert[66] threatened Roberts and his colleagues "with prosecution and has advised them to desist" their preaching under "penalty of something dreadful he doesn't say what."[67] Another account in the *St. Louis Republic* reported that Covert[68] wrote a letter to Roberts challenging him, as the head of his "determined little band of Mormon missionaries," to a debate. Covert told the paper that the Roberts party was "trying to gain a foothold here, and I have made up my mind to put a stop to it if possible." He said the missionaries were attending his church services and staying after to "try to make converts," but that their success was due "to their great zeal and earnestness. They are the most zealous men that I have ever met." The paper reported that "Elder Covert purposes to meet this zeal with cold logic."[69] The next day Roberts declined the debate, telling Covert that because of the "coarseness, vulgarity and intemperance" of Covert's language, he could not conceive of the pastor "as a proper person with whom to engage in a public debate."

At the conclusion of their time in St. Louis, the Roberts group

65. Pyper Scrapbook, Aug. 25, 1896.

66. Covert (1853–1922) was raised in Pennsylvania and attended Edinboro State Normal school. He was ordained a minister at Harmony, Iowa, in 1874. Over the next few years, he served congregations in various states. In 1886 he became pastor of the Church of God at Stoners, Pennsylvania. While there, he was active in the Prohibition Party, and also became known as an opponent of Spiritualism.

67. Clipping, *St. Louis Chronicle*, Sep. 1, 1896, in Roberts Scrapbook. This scrapbook (MS 8616), not to be confused with another in Roberts's papers at the LDS Church History Library, exclusively covers Roberts's mission.

68. While the two men did not agree on religion, they seemed to share political beliefs. The *St. Louis Republic* noted that Covert was a supporter of William Jennings Bryan and Free Silver and reported on his remarks as the "principal speaker" at a meeting of the Missouri National Bimetallic Party. The paper described him as "a big man with a phenomenally developed fondness for fun. He expounded free silver doctrines in an original vein, interspersing knock-down argument with side splitting stories and with homelike illustrations that were often singularly effective. He has a powerful voice and at time was really eloquent in his withering denunciation of the sophistries of 'the gold bugs.'" At the conclusion of the speech, Covert was elected president of a newly formed independent silver club. See "Bimetallic Party," *St. Louis Republic*, Aug. 30, 1896, 3; and "Silver Party Club Organized," *St. Louis Republic*, Sep. 3, 1896, 9.

69. "Covert on the Warpath," *St. Louis Republic*, Sep. 1, 1896, 9.

met at Bowman Hall and organized a "small branch."[70] The *St. Louis Republic* gave an overview of local Mormon conditions, noting that there were twelve members: "This is the tangible result of the missionary labors of Hon. B. H. Roberts, George D. Pyper, Melvin J. Ballard ... who have been holding meetings at Chatsworth Hall, and who leave this week for Cincinnati, where they will engage in similar work for a month or more, afterwards continuing their meetings in other large cities in the East and North."[71]

Roberts wrote to Wilford Woodruff from Cincinnati that he had secured lodgings, but that "the rest of the little company had to be left behind for want of means to pay the expenses of transportation." He was "greatly in need of funds" and at "most times we had a balance of less than $5."[72] Then he wrote to Pyper and Midgley to suggest they might need to remain in St. Louis "two weeks longer."[73] On October 18 he notified Pyper and Midgley that they should plan on coming to Cincinnati in two days. Funds arrived within a few days and so did Roberts's colleagues. Pyper wrote a summary of their activities in Missouri, noting that collectively they had held forty-three meetings in St. Louis—thirty-one at Chatsworth Hall, eight at Bowman's Hall, and four in private homes.

On October 23, Roberts left for Chicago where he attended meetings of the Northern Illinois conference of the Northern States Mission. A local newspaper wrote that there were approximately fifty members in Chicago.[74] Conference President John N. Davis[75] sent a report that was published in the *Deseret Weekly*: "While it can be said that in a city like Chicago there is much wickedness and sin,

70. Roberts to Young, Oct. 5, 1896, Roberts Scrapbook; and St. Louis Branch Minutes, Oct. 4, 1896. See also "News of the Churches," *St. Louis Post Dispatch*, Sep. 27, 1896, 8.

71. "A New and Humble Church," *St. Louis Republic*, Sep. 27, 1897, 20.

72. Roberts to Woodruff, Oct. 19, 1896, in Roberts Collection

73. Pyper Scrapbook, Oct. 17, 1896.

74. While in Chicago, he delivered five lectures on various topics to the missionaries. See "Illinois–Chicago Manuscript History," in Northern States Mission Manuscript History; and "Latter Day Saints: Conference of Northern States Mission Comes to an End," *Chicago Daily Inter-Ocean*, Oct. 26, 1896, 7.

75. Davis (1864–1931) was a Seventy living in Vernal, Utah, when he was set apart for his mission by Abraham H. Cannon on June 28, 1895. He returned on July 6, 1897. He later served another short mission in the Southern States from November 1925 to May 1926. Davis was also a bishop of the Vernal Ward, and Uintah Stake patriarch. He was a member of the Utah House of Representatives, 1907–09.

and many bad people, there is one thing sure, and that is there are many good and honorable people. The Elders have been treated with kindness and respect."[76]

On October 27, Pyper wrote that they had received a letter from Roberts "who warmed us up with the good news" that he had received $150 from the First Presidency to assist in the work in Cincinnati, which he believed could start after election day.[77] In early November, Roberts began to look for a hall. He made an offer to the First English Evangelical Church,[78] but "after much whispering, we were informed that they 'would not entertain the proposition to rent from us as some of their members were sensitive about the use of the place.' And so we were refused ... because we were Mormons."[79] Eventually, they found another location, Academy Hall, on the corner of 15th and Elm Streets only a half block away from their "boarding house," at $12 per day.[80] Shortly thereafter, the group was part of a "wild ... city full of excitement" as they witnessed the election returns and William McKinley's 1896 election victory. Pyper notes he was "heart sick over the defeat of [William Jennings] Bryan," and that Roberts was so broken up "he said [he] could not stand it without oysters, so we enjoyed the feast and then went home to our rooms."[81]

The next morning the trio "prepared and sent notices to the papers for our Sunday meetings." Ultimately, Roberts held meetings each Sunday between November 8 and the end of the year, still accompanied by Pyper and Midgley. Only a handful of papers ran the notices of the first meeting,[82] but the *Cincinnati Enquirer* noted that he was greeted "with a large audience."[83]

Roberts and his colleagues spent the next week studying both

76. "Conference in Chicago," *Deseret Weekly*, Dec. 12, 1896, 18. The missionaries faced the difficulty of proselytizing not only to English speakers, but also the large German and Scandinavian population in the city.

77. Pyper Scrapbook, Oct. 27, 1896.

78. The property Pyper is referring to was located on Elm Street between Ninth and Court. The church had moved to the 1200 block on Race Street, and still stands at that location.

79. Pyper Scrapbook, Nov. 2, 1896.

80. Pyper Scrapbook, Nov. 3, 1896.

81. Pyper Scrapbook, Nov. 3 and 4, 1896.

82. See "Mormon Meeting," *Cincinnati Post*, Nov. 7, 1896; and Pyper Scrapbook.

83. "In Defense of Mormonism," *Cincinnati Enquirer*, Nov. 9, 1896, 8.

in their rooms and in the public library, which contained a large collection on Mormonism, both pro- and anti-Mormon titles. The papers printed notices of the next meeting, which was held on Sunday, November 15. In the morning Roberts addressed "Is Modern Christendom Justified in Believing Revelation has Ceased?" The evening's topic was "The Mission of Joseph Smith," which Pyper said was presented in a "masterly manner." Within a week, Roberts was looking for a "more suitable" hall to hold future meetings.[84]

While Roberts was in Cincinnati, the *Commercial Tribune* ran an editorial on the successful efforts of his friend, and occasional Democratic critic, Martha Hughes Cannon in being elected to the Utah State Senate in her "at large" race that also featured her husband, Angus M. Cannon, running as a Republican. The paper noted that her husband "lingered at home among the sister wives," while she ran a "vigorous campaign" and won "by a handsome majority."[85] Pyper said the race was "a subject of great sport here."[86]

Roberts, perhaps motivated by the political excitement, but also aware of ecclesiastical matters in Utah, wrote a lengthy letter to Moses Thatcher. He admitted his wrongdoing in the difficulties the pair had had with the other general authorities over their own political activities. He told Thatcher:

> I think we were both mistaken in the course we pursued in that matter. We took an extreme view of the action of our brethren, in relation to political affairs, and by denouncing their action in some things, and what was supposed to be their action in others, the effect of what we said and did—however upright our intentions, or honest our motives—the effect, I say, of what we said and did, was to represent our brethren as conspiring against the liberties of the people and trifling with their rights as American citizens. In a manner we brought them into contempt before the people of God, the Church, and even before the world.[87]

A "dispassionate view of the whole affair," Roberts believed, clearly demonstrated that church authorities were correct in their demand

84. Pyper Scrapbook, Nov. 14–15, 1896.
85. "Mormon Wife," *Cincinnati Enquirer*, Nov. 8, 1896, 17.
86. Pyper Scrapbook, Nov. 7, Nov. 8, 1896.
87. Roberts to Thatcher, Nov. 6, 1896, MS 2829, CHL. Hereafter cited as Roberts Letter.

"that we make this matter right, and it is for them to determine what is necessary to make it right." He then encouraged "dear Moses" to take the same course as he had done and acknowledge his errors, sign the political manifesto, and get into proper fellowship with church authorities. Admitting that he was blind, stubborn, proud, unyielding, and defiant, he commented in a very personal tone that

> I well nigh lost my place among them, but at last the spirit of the Lord came. I learned that it was my duty to yield completely to God's authority on earth and it was not for me to set up my judgement against the combined and united judgment of His servants. I was obedient, thank the Lord, to the promptings of the voice of that spirit. I did not reject its counsels as I did those of the brethren; and though following its instructions cost me the good opinion and Friendship of many of our 'gentile' friends, whose good opinion and friendship I prized; and though it has cause me to sacrifice many worldly ambitions and put a period to my political aspirations there has not been a day that I have regretted my obedience. ... And as my experience has been so, too, I am sure, yours will be if you take the same course.[88]

Roberts cautioned Thatcher to be aware that his church membership, priesthood, and holy apostleship were "at stake." He "earnestly" hoped "that the Spirit of God will bear record to your spirit that this is the right thing for you to do."[89]

But two weeks later, on November 19, 1896, when all members of the Twelve except Thatcher met in the Historian's Office "for the purpose of considering and taking action" on the case, it was too late. Thatcher was made aware of the meeting, but evidence suggests he was not invited to attend. Perhaps he would not have attended anyway. At the conclusion, quorum president Lorenzo Snow announced that "after a full consideration of all the circumstances of the case, and after each Apostle present had expressed himself upon the subject it was unanimously decided that Moses Thatcher be severed from the Council of the Twelve, and that he be deprived of his Apostleship, and other offices of the Priesthood."[90] In Cincinnati,

88. Roberts Letter.
89. Roberts Letter.
90. "Deposed," *Salt Lake Tribune*, Nov. 20, 1896, 1. For Thatcher's response, see "Stands Firm," *Salt Lake Tribune*, Dec. 13, 1896, 1.

Pyper reported that the action "causes us much pain and our prayers are that [Thatcher] may put himself in harmony with his brethren before it is too late."[91]

The *Salt Lake Tribune* speculated that if Thatcher "continues to be contumacious," Roberts would be the "logical candidate" against him for the Senate because "no good Mormon in the [state] legislature will refuse to vote for him." But another newspaper wrote that Roberts's going "back on the principles he so ably advocated at the reconvened convention" meant that "he who only two short years ago was Democracy's idol, is now looked upon as a traitor by every true Democrat in the state."[92]

Roberts's mind, however, was on different issues, particularly his dire financial situation. On November 17, he wrote to Heber J. Grant that he had borrowed $1,000 from a "gentile friend" and that the unsecured note was due on December 13. In an attempt to pay off that debt he proposed conducting a "Roberts Benefit Lecture" tour to various cities in the state—Nephi, Payson, Provo, American Fork, Salt Lake City, Ogden, Hyrum, Richmond, and Logan—where he would discuss "The Morning of Our Civilization." Roberts's plan was to use meeting houses free of charge, obtain copies of his book *New Witness of God* at wholesale, and offer it to anyone who paid $1.50 to attend his lecture at the retail price of the book. He believed he could attract "full houses" throughout the tour, clear one hundred dollars at each stop, and thus ensure his ability to pay off the debt. He noted that once the lecture tour was completed, he would "be content to become a missionary for the next five years," if that is what the authorities wanted.[93]

Roberts departed Cincinnati on November 27,[94] leaving Pyper and Midgley to continue their efforts there.[95] He arrived in Utah on December 3 and went to Centerville where he stayed for a few days, speaking at his local ward on his experiences.[96] Apparently the

91. Pyper Scrapbook, Nov. 23, 1896.

92. Both accounts quoted in "Etc., Etc.," *Salt Lake Herald*, Jan. 25, 1897, 5.

93. Roberts to Heber J. Grant, Nov. 17, 1896 copy in box 4, fd. 10, Kenney Collection.

94. See Pyper Scrapbook, Nov. 27, 1896. Pyper notes that as a result "Ed and I were left alone with this city on our hands."

95. For details, see Pyper Scrapbook, Nov. 28–Dec. 19, 1896.

96. "Centerville Chats," *Davis County Clipper*, Dec. 11, 1896, 8.

issue of the loan had been dealt with in another manner since the proposed tour did not materialize.

On December 7 he called on Wilford Woodruff and Joseph F. Smith of the First Presidency, and gave them a detailed account of his time in the mission.[97] The First Presidency believed that "the favorable notices which … Elder Roberts received have undoubtedly produced a good effect," and such favorable publicity "greatly assisted the missionaries generally in their various fields." Roberts told his brethren that he found it "almost impossible to receive any [financial] support from the people," and that after deducting the money given him from the First Presidency, and the small amount raised at meetings, "it had cost him personally about $200 and his fellow laborers $100 each." He told the First Presidency that to complete his assignment "as had been mapped out," he would need $250 per month.[98]

He attended a First Council of the Seventy meeting on December 9, where he gave his colleagues "all the information regarding his missionary labor in the Eastern cities." He met the next day with J. Golden Kimball, Joseph F. Smith, Francis M. Lyman, Thomas Hull, and Orson F. Whitney, "talking over the editing of a new magazine," which became the *Improvement Era*. He also attended the initial unveiling of a portrait by John Hafen at the exhibition of the Society of Utah Artists.[99] He seems to have spent considerable time in Centerville with Louisa. Reflecting his status, Wilford Woodruff recorded that "Brother & Sister Roberts and others" went with him to the Salt Lake Theater to attend the play "The Old Homestead."[100]

Ultimately the First Presidency agreed with Roberts's financial assessment, and he wrote about the details to his colleagues. Pyper recorded that "of course the news of Bro Roberts's return to us was most pleasant and our joy was manifested by dancing and shouting, not a very dignified, but surely a very expressive way of expressing our satisfaction."[101] In late December Roberts returned to the East,

97. Woodruff, *Wilford Woodruff's Journal*, 9:437.

98. Historian's Office, Journal History, Dec. 7, 1896, 3–5.

99. "The Art Exhibit," *Salt Lake Herald*, Dec. 7, 1896, 2; "In the Social Realm," *Salt Lake Herald*, Dec. 9, 1896, 5.

100. Woodruff, *Wilford Woodruff's Journals*, 9:438.

101. Pyper Scrapbook, Dec. 20 and 23, 1896. Roberts notified them that the tour would continue another two months, but that plans to go into the South had been

reuniting with Pyper and Midgley in Cincinnati to continue their missionary and public relations tour.[102]

At the beginning of the new year, Roberts, Pyper, and Midgley arranged for railroad tickets "on the Pennsylvania Road for Pittsburgh.[103] Before leaving they held two public meetings on January 3 in the familiar Academy of Music Hall.[104] The next morning, they left for Pittsburgh, and the following day, "amid a blowing snow storm," they secured lodgings and sought a hall for their first meeting on January 10. The *Pittsburgh Daily Post* mentioned that Pyper and Midgley "will sing sacred songs and Mormon hymns," and introduced Roberts to readers by quoting the late Kate Field: "Mr. Roberts has an excellent voice, is a natural orator, and is called the Douglas of the West. Having traveled in Europe and the United States as a Mormon missionary, he has rubbed against the crowd and acquired unusual polish for this territory. Fluent in speech and magnetic in person, Elder Roberts is popular with the Saints."[105]

A week later on January 17, the group attended RLDS services in the morning. Reorganized Elder G. H. Holmes distributed a leaflet pointing out the differences between the two churches, and they discussed them with him after the services "in a friendly way then left."[106] But Holmes let it be known that he was "decidedly opposed" to Roberts and his colleagues who were "now in this city for the purpose of making converts. The *Pittsburgh Daily Post* told readers that the Reorganites had been in the city for some thirty years, was a strong organization, and included "some wealthy and influential people" among its 170 members.[107]

The trio left on January 18 to begin their meetings in Philadelphia where the *Philadelphia Evening Bulletin* said they had determined to invade "the enemy's country." After staying the first night in the

abandoned. He told them he hoped to be in Cincinnati on January 1, and that they would leave for Pittsburgh on January 4.

102. See History of the Northern States Mission, Dec. 20, 1896.

103. Pyper Scrapbook, Dec. 31, 1896–Jan. 3, 1897. Pyper means the Cleveland, Cincinnati, Chicago and St. Louis railroad (CCC&S), which was called the "Big Four."

104. "Latter Day Saints," *Cincinnati Enquirer*, Dec. 30, 1896, 10.

105. "Campaign of Mormons," *Pittsburgh Daily Post*, Jan. 8, 1897, 2. See also "Kate Field's Ashes," *Pittsburgh Press*, Jan. 18, 1897, 4.

106. Pyper Scrapbook, Jan. 17, 1896.

107. "Are Different Peoples," *Pittsburgh Daily-Post*, Jan. 19, 1897, 2.

European Hotel on Chestnut Street, the group began their customary activities to secure more permanent lodgings, rent a hall (Market Hall for five meetings at thirty-five dollars), contact newspapers, put up signs, and do some sightseeing. Roberts updated his activities in a letter to his mother: "Philadelphia is a most beautiful city. Everywhere you see evidence of the elegance and wealth and education." Roberts confided that shortly after he arrived, he "felt very depressed and dreaded the task of speaking in such a place" since his own "education is far from finished." All the previous newspaper accounts calling Roberts a spectacular orator had not quelled his insecurities: "I am not a polished man, and while it may be well for me to speak in the county precincts of Utah & elsewhere—to speak here in Philadelphia is quite another thing." Still, he rated his performance as "the best I could" do and said that the meeting was good and "well attended & through the blessings of the Lord, the people were attentive & all came out right."[108]

Pyper noted that at Roberts's first lecture on January 24, they met William T. Cannon,[109] "son of George Q., who is studying medicine at the Jefferson school." Over the next few days they met and dined several times with Cannon and his wife, Ada.[110] Lillian Hamlin, plural wife of the recently deceased Apostle Abraham H. Cannon, wrote Susa Young Gates that after hearing Roberts and Pyper were in town, she planned to attend their services on January 24, and stated, "I never thought I would be so anxious to hear any of our elders speak as I am to hear Bro. Roberts."[111] While in Philadelphia, the three men wired their congratulations to Joseph L. Rawlins on his election to the US Senate.[112] Over the next few days they held two additional meetings, and braved the cold and stormy weather to visit the Catholic Basilica of Saints Peter and Paul.

---

108. Roberts to Mother, Jan. 25, 1897, box 4, fd. 7, Roberts Papers (UU).

109. Cannon (1870–1949) was the son of George Q. Cannon and his wife Eliza L. Tenney (1845–1908). Cannon returned to Utah after his graduation in 1898 and practiced medicine in Salt Lake City. He was also active in various church callings.

110. See Pyper Scrapbook, Jan. 24–25, 1896.

111. Lillian Hamlin to Susa Young Gates, Jan. 23, 1897, Gates Papers (CHL). Hamlin also indicated, "I don't know whether either of them know me, but I will take the risk."

112. "More Congratulations," *Salt Lake Herald*, Feb. 5, 1897, 6.

After the January 31 meeting, Elder Alonzo H. Parsons[113] and other leaders of the local Reorganized Church distributed notices of a forthcoming lecture on "Utah Latter Day Saintism, Commonly Called Mormonism, Exposed." The lecture was to be held on February 7 at 7:30 p.m. at the RLDS headquarters in Huntington Hall. The flyer extended a "cordial invitation to all … especially to B. H. Roberts and his co-laborers to be present." The meeting conflicted with Roberts's last meeting in Philadelphia, but it is unlikely they would have attended on a different night.[114]

On February 1, Roberts went to New York "to engage quarters for his party," and set them up temporarily in the Lincoln Hotel where Roberts had initially stayed in 1890 on his trip with John Morgan. He was met by mission president Samuel W. Richards,[115] and missionaries James H. Wilcox and David J. Watts. Wilcox noted that, like any tourists in the town, he and Roberts "wandered up & down Broadway looking at the windows full of finery … paying attention to books."[116]

Meanwhile, back in Philadelphia, Pyper reported that he and Midgley had "an excellent meeting on February 4, and that the "spirit was very much in evidence." Two days later they baptized Neils Elon Molden, his wife, Maria Jenette Molden, and her mother, Marian Randena Larsen, at "the Russian baths at 928 New Market Street." Pyper, who had never performed a baptism before, said that he felt "as if my ministry had commenced." Indeed, during the time the three men had been together, Roberts had paid particular attention to seeing that his colleagues felt fully involved, even though it was clear that he was the senior elder. He had matured greatly since his first days as a missionary, and clearly the experiences of the past decade—in the United States and England—had made him a confident, effective representative of Mormonism. Roberts delivered his

113. Parsons (1857–1933) was active as an RLDS writer and minister in a variety of places. His best-known work is *Parsons' Text Book* (Lamoni, IA: Herald Publishing, 1902). A significant part of the book deals with polygamy.

114. Pyper Scrapbook, Jan. 31, 1897.

115. Richards (1824–1909) converted to Mormonism in 1838 and came to Utah in 1849. He was president of the European Mission on two occasions, first from 1852 to 1854, and then from 1857 to 1858. He had six wives, but at this point only his second wife, Mary Ann Parker (1838–1914) was still living, and she accompanied him while he served as mission president, 1895–97.

116. Wilcox Journal, Feb. 2, 1897.

last lecture on the evening of February 6, on "The Second Coming of the Messiah, And The Events to Precede It," with Pyper noting: "We had a good audience and good attention and felt satisfied with our work."[117] Roberts and his colleagues left for New York City on the morning of February 8.

Pyper noted that they arrived "at the great city at about 12:30. Went immediately to our lodging.... Spent the day in getting baggage to our rooms and getting settled." On his previous visit Roberts had secured a furnished room at 153 E. 18th Street, which was a six story brownstone in a bustling neighborhood, close to Third Avenue near Union Square, and convenient to Hardman Hall. They were met by Wilcox and Watts who took them to the mission headquarters at 50 Concord Street, Brooklyn.[118] The Mormon presence in the area at that time was minimal, and was primarily centered in Brooklyn.[119]

For the next few days, Richards worked hard to gain press interest in Roberts' talks, especially in Brooklyn.[120] While visits by Utahns, especially those prominent in church, politics, and business, were fairly common in this period, Roberts's visit, based on his notoriety, would attract considerable attention.[121] The group, in the midst of "fierce snow storms," spent most of their first week in the city, in Pyper's words, "advertizing our meetings [and] getting the ear of the newspapers," while preparing for their "Sunday work." Additionally, Pyper noted that they had gone to the Aquarium and visited "the people at 50 Concord Street ... Miss Leah Dunford and Miss Donnette Smith ... [and] Henry Dinwoodey and Flod, the latter being sick at the Grand Hotel."[122]

The *New York Times* noted on the front page of the paper on

117. Pyper Scrapbook, Feb. 1–7, 1897.

118. Richards Journal, Feb. 9, 1897, in Samuel W. Richards Papers. Hereafter cited as Richards Journal.

119. For a brief overview see Tiffany, "Manhattan and the Mormons"; and Brooklyn District Historical Committee, *Zion in the Brooklyn District.*

120. Richards Journal, Feb. 9, 1897.

121. As Donnette Smith, daughter of Joseph F. Smith observed, "Miss Dunford and I go to ... Church to be in style, every Sunday, and lately we have met quite a number of Utah folks." Smith to Benjamin Cluff, Jan. 25, 1897, box 3, fd. 3, Cluff Presidential Papers.

122. Pyper referred to Henry Mills Dinwoodey (1867–1937) who was part of the important Salt Lake City furniture company. He married Florence Marion "Flod" Whitney (1866–1930) on September 21, 1897. She was the daughter of Horace and Helen Mar Kimball Whitney, and the brother of Orson F. Whitney. Pyper also noted

February 12 that "Mormon Church authorities have prepared for an evangelistic movement in this city and B. H. Roberts has been sent into the field" to "re-establish in the Eastern States the mission which flourished here about twenty years ago."[123] The *Times* covered Roberts's address on "The Relationship of Mormonism to Christianity," which he delivered in Hardman Hall on the snowy evening of February 14. Pyper noted that while there was "a good audience," it was "a very difficult task. The first row consisted of reporters and artists of the press who were dodging around and made it … unpleasant for us." But they did not get "the roasting by the press that we expected to get." Instead, while the press reports were "garbled," they were "not unfair as a whole."[124]

Beyond his actual speaking, Roberts and his associates were anxious to develop a relationship with the borough's major newspaper, the *Brooklyn Daily Eagle*. Brooklyn was a separate city from New York until unification in 1898, and one of the largest cities in the country in its own right. Indeed, the community saw itself as "Manhattan's competitor and, in some ways, its moral and cultural superior. It cultivated a quality of life that combined domestic virtues with the American nineteenth century belief in inevitable progress, and … self-confidence unified in … its seemingly inexorable expansion."[125] For Mormons, Brooklyn must have offered a better place to engage in the marketplace of ideas, despite the cost of halls, than perhaps New York City was.[126]

On Saturday, February 20, Roberts spoke at a church meeting in the afternoon, along with Pyper and Midgley, closing "the service with a powerful speech." Wilcox noted that "a number of non-Mormons" were present. That evening Roberts spoke "to a good house," at Hardman Hall, and was again joined by Pyper and Midgley as well as Watts and others. The *New York Tribune* reported his topic

that by then the weather was "now pleasant," but that the city had employed 25,000 "men to carry away the snow." Pyper Scrapbook, Feb. 13, 1897.

123. "A Mormon to Preach Here," *New York Times*, Feb. 12, 1897, 12; and "In The Religious Field," *Brooklyn Daily Eagle*, Feb. 13, 1897, 9. The *Salt Lake Herald* reprinted the full text of the *Times* article. See "Roberts in New York," *Salt Lake Herald*, Feb. 17, 1897, 6.

124. Pyper Scrapbook, Feb. 13–15, 1897. "The Mormon Doctrine," *New York Times*, Feb. 15, 1897, 10; "Mormon Elder's Lecture," *The Sun* (New York), Feb. 15, 1897, 3.

125. Schroth, *Eagle and Brooklyn*, xii.

126. On the paper and its link to the community see Schroth, *Eagle and Brooklyn*.

was "A Mormon View of the Gospel."[127] Wilcox stated that the "audience was most respectful and after the services the World and Herald correspondents spoke to Bro. Roberts."[128]

Roberts spoke again on the afternoon of Sunday, February 21, this time at the church's headquarters at 50 Concord Street. He gave a long explanation of the Mormon concept of the pre-existence. Such a doctrine, he said, was not new, but had existed though in a "distorted form" since antiquity. After reciting examples of Christ and several of his apostles on the subject, he concluded that "the scriptures teach us that not only did good spirits exist before they came here, but also the evil spirits and Lucifer himself. If Christ … lived in the spirit state, It is easy to believe in the light of revelation and holy writ that we did also. We all had the same origin. God is the common father."[129]

An interesting summary of their time in the city was compiled by the mission secretary, David J. Watts, at the conclusion of Roberts's visit. Watts said the group was "known throughout the east as the 'Mormon Evangelists,'" and over the course of two Sunday evenings they "held forth at the Hardman hall … besides taking part in our regular services at Brooklyn." Watts indicated that approximately three hundred people "who paid respectful attention" came to each of the New York meetings. At the first meeting

> Elder Roberts discoursed upon the relation of Mormonism to Christianity. The meeting was noticed and commented upon favorably by seven of the leading dailies, and that alone has accomplished an incalculable amount of good in awakening interest … and removing some of the prejudice which exists. … It is conservative to say that tens of thousands read the account of that meeting. … At the second meeting Elder Roberts' subject was "The Gospel of Christ," from a Mormon standpoint … but the opposing influence was already at work and several anti-Mormon articles appeared … which neutralized some of the good results expected.[130]

Wilcox wrote to his wife that he wished Roberts could have arranged for more meetings, "but the means they had for hiring halls

127. "Meetings and Entertainment," *New York Tribune*, Feb. 20, 1897, 12.
128. Wilcox Journal, Feb. 21, 1897; and Pyper Scrapbook, Feb. 20, 1897.
129. "Sermons in Brief Form," *Brooklyn Daily Eagle*, Mar. 1, 1897, 11.
130. Eastern States Mission, manuscript history, Mar. 2, 1897.

is exhausted. They have to pay $25 a night for Hardman and their expenses are heavy. They pay $9 a week for furnished rooms and board is extra."[131] Similarly, both David J. Watts and Wilcox had attempted to find suitable halls in Brooklyn, but found that they were too expensive.[132]

Roberts proved to be a novel figure not only in the New York papers, but throughout the country. The *New York World* wrote that Roberts, who had once been a blacksmith,

> may well be called a learned blacksmith. His diction is as pure as that of any teacher of the language, and he illustrates his pleasing phraseology with graceful gestures. The elder must have been a power at the forge. He is tall and strongly built—the frame of almost a giant. His years ... have brought him to the prime of physical well being. His voice fits the setting. It is virile and resonant. It is well controlled, with thunder for logic and softness for flights of word-painting and sentiment. Those who heard him last night agreed the he was a man of brains and judgement.[133]

Roberts met with photographer and antiquarian Augustus Le Plongeon,[134] whose interest in Mayan and Yucatan art, Eastern religion, and Freemasonry intersected with his interest in Mormonism. He had engaged in some correspondence with Roberts's mentor John Taylor in the 1880s. Not long after Roberts's visit, the *Deseret Evening News* noted that "to the Latter-day Saints, Dr. Le Plongeon's archeological labors are especially gratifying" because they seem to provide evidence in support of the Book of Mormon and other of Joseph Smith's teachings.[135]

As noted before, Roberts also visited with relatives of two LDS Church presidents—Donnette Smith,[136] daughter of Joseph F. Smith,

131. Wilcox Journal, Feb. 13, 1897.

132. Richards Journal, Feb. 15, 1897.

133. "He Ignores Polygamy," *New York World*, Feb. 22, 1897. Copy in Pyper Scrapbook.

134. LePlongeon (1825–1908) was a French-American photographer, amateur archaeologist, and author who studied pre-Columbian ruins.

135. "The Cradle of Civilization," *Deseret Evening News*, June 26, 1897, 5.

136. Smith (1872–1961), the daughter of Joseph F. Smith and Julina Lambson Smith, spent two years at Pratt. Her going to Pratt was important enough that Wilford Woodruff recorded it in his journal. See Woodruff, *Wilford Woodruff's Journal*, 9:388. She married Alonzo P. Kesler (1866–1918), who had succeeded Samuel Richards as Eastern States Mission president, on Dec. 26, 1900.

and Leah Dunford,[137] granddaughter of Brigham Young.[138] Both in their twenties, they were in New York studying at the Pratt Institute—Smith in teaching children and Dunford in domestic sciences and arts.[139] Roberts was smitten with Dunford. An article in *Ev'ry Month*, an influential journal edited by Theodore Dreiser, gives us a clue as to why that was the case:

> Miss Leah Dunford is a grand daughter of the renowned Mormon leader, Brigham Young, her mother, Mrs. Susa Young Gates, being one of the prophet's favorite children. Reared by a mother of pronounced literary ability, Miss Dunford has imbibed her advanced ideas. In person this young lady is the embodiment of fresh young womanhood, and is one of the best types of Mormondom. She possesses the superbly modeled figure, the abundant flaxen hair, and the brilliant complexion of Scandinavian women; she is a striking looking girl and would be noticeable anywhere for her beauty and grace. Endowed with brains, beauty and a defined social position in Salt Lake City, this young woman has nothing to desire. She intends, however, to employ her talent in teaching, being a firm believer in work for women.[140]

Roberts's attraction to Dunford tells us a great deal about him specifically, and gives us a glimpse into attitudes over plural marriage in the first few years after the Woodruff Manifesto—at least among the church's influential people—and is worth exploring.

However, Dunford had a prior relationship. While still in Utah, she had written to John A. Widtsoe, "I have always felt somehow that you liked me very well, perhaps more than any other young lady you knew; now I know that you <u>love</u> me. I can never doubt again; you will love me always, so long as I am worthy of your love, and I pray that I always shall be." She signed the letter "Your best girl, Leah."[141] Once back in Brooklyn, Dunford had reservations that she

137. Dunford (1874–1965) was the daughter of Susa Young Gates and Alma Dunford. She married future apostle John A. Widtsoe on June 1, 1898. She became prominent as an author, educator, and nutritionist. In addition to her studies at Pratt, she attended Harvard University in the summer of 1893, and also Brigham Young Academy, where she later became a teacher.

138. Richards Journal, Feb. 2, 1897.

139. See Leah Eudora Dunford, "A Visit to Pratt Institute," *Young Woman's Journal*, Mar. 1897, 249–59.

140. As quoted in "City and Neighborhood," *Salt Lake Tribune*, Aug. 8, 1897, 8.

141. Dunford to Widtsoe, Jan. 9, 1897, Widtsoe Family Papers (CHL).

shared with her mother: "Do you think that J cares for me or is he becoming indifferent?" Dunford told her mother, while she was sure Widtsoe's mother's opinion would not change, she admitted, "I am not quite so sure about him." Then she brought up an entirely new subject that would dominate their correspondence for several weeks:

> I must tell you about Bro. Roberts. Did I tell you the dream that Ann had about us? … All she remembers is that Bro. R took my hand, looked at it and caressed it & said how lovely & smooth it was and—that was all! Well, last Sunday we learned that Bro. Roberts was coming to NY to look for a hall etc. sometime during the coming week. We left many messages for him by Bro. Watts and Richards, not expecting to see him until they came for good. Last Tuesday, [February 2] one of the girls said that there were two gentlemen to see me. I had no idea who they could be but do you know it was Bro. Roberts in the flesh & Bro. Watts. He did hold my hand a good long time and seemed so pleased to see me. We talked for nearly an hour and a half and then I took them all through our Dept explaining every thing. Then we went down to see if we couldn't find Donnie as I knew she would feel hurt if they went off without speaking to her. Bro R was simply lovely. … I will tell you future developments.[142]

A week later, Dunford said that "Donnie and I had some callers. Bros Midgley, P[y]per, Roberts, Wilcox, Watts. They spent the evening and we had a jolly time—music etc. … They preach in NY tomorrow and tomorrow week. Donnie and I are going to take in a party of our schoolmates. We have each told all our teachers about it. We have advertized it as much as possible."[143]

The following week she attended Roberts's lecture and, as the evening was coming to a close, he asked Dunford and Smith to go to the "Art Gallery and other places with him" the next day. Dunford continued "I told him about my engagement … was sick about it." The next morning at 9:00, Smith and Dunford, accompanied by Roberts and Midgley, set out for the "Statue of Liberty as we had never been there. Talk about your delightful times! O dear it was lovely climbing those stairs with such company and I enjoyed every moment of it." From there they went to an art gallery and Roberts told Dunford "he would meet me after the opera & that we would

142. Dunford to Gates, Feb. 6, 1897, Gates Papers (CHL).
143. Dunford to Gates, Feb. 13, 1897.

go and have dinner and have a good visit together. He did meet me, we had a good dinner, and a perfectly lovely talk." Roberts spoke to Dunford in a way that made her think he had "a very exalted opinion of me."[144]

Dunford described Roberts's rhapsodic compliments: "How many times have you been told that you are beautiful?" Dunford replied that she had "never" been told she was beautiful, and "he didn't believe me of course till I told him equally as frankly that some few have accused me of being fine looking, distinguished and even handsome but never beautiful." Roberts did not miss his chance and replied that these previous suitors had "left … the proper adjective" for him, and that "it was the only one that described me." Dunford wrote that she "very meekly thanked him" and said that his sincerity was "without that false tone of empty, vapid flattery." Roberts added that, beyond her "angelic beauty," Dunford had "depth." She explained to her mother that she was not "annoyed" by any of this, because in addition to his frank praise of her appearance, while they ate dinner, there was "good serious talk which was the best part of it all." She "left him feeling richer in my spirit than before."[145]

The group of four continued to spend time together the next day visiting St Patrick's Cathedral in the morning. Roberts, with three wives already back in the West, told Dunford that if they continued to spend time together, "he would so begin to find me necessary to his happiness." Dunford was apparently stunned and "was mute," so Roberts, perhaps worried he had gone too far, asked if she "was offended." She replied "no because I enjoyed being there with him." To Dunford, at least, Roberts's meaning was clear. "I am led to believe that <u>if</u> there was no such thing as the manifesto and <u>if</u> I were not so in love with someone else, something might possibly happen." Roberts also told her that he was thinking of taking his families to Canada. She at least could not see a way forward to marriage, and so she felt that she had "gained a friend and I hope that I shall be able to keep him." She closed the news of this abrupt romance to her mother by begging her to keep it "confidential and

144. Dunford to Gates, Feb. 20, 1897.
145. Dunford to Gates.

that I trust you will keep it sacred to you" and to her mother's second husband, Jacob Gates, "only."[146]

If Dunford had closed the door to marriage, her mother tried hard to push it back open. Rumors of post-Manifesto plural marriages had swirled around Utah, and if Leah Dunford did not think a union with B. H. Roberts was possible, her mother knew better. Susa Young Gates, who had met John Widtsoe at Harvard and was the one who had initially pushed him to court Dunford, now said she "wouldn't give [up] BH [Roberts] for a regiment of J[ohn W[idtsoe]'s." Gates felt that "we can't decide the matter" just yet and begged her daughter to "think seriously before you decide to give BH the cold shoulder." She and Jacob Gates had discussed the matter, and both agreed that over time Dunford would "grow away from" Widtsoe because "narrow minds will dwarf you." But a marriage to Roberts would satisfy her "whole soul … in time & eternity with such a man for a leader and companion." Imagine, Gates asked her daughter, of the "children who come from a union with BH." Gates insisted she was not trying to "influence you one way or the other," but only wanted to remind her daughter that these "happenings are the vital turning points of your life."[147] A week later Gates wrote to Dunford and seemed to imply that she has accepted that Dunford would probably marry Widtsoe but remain friends with Roberts.[148]

Dunford responded more frankly this time, to put any talk of marriage to rest. Roberts "couldn't marry me if we both wanted to ever so much. Don't you know that? Then what would be the good of wasting my love and pining away for a man who can never be mine this side of eternity?" The two were still spending considerable time together, however. One night as it rained in New York City, Roberts commented that it "was too bad that it should be raining then of all times" and carried an umbrella." Dunford responded that "there was nothing unromantic about two being under an umbrella, that it was just the opposite and that we should not complain." She went on to tell Roberts of a "romantic experience" she had with Widtsoe "under an umbrella." If Roberts was jealous, he did not show it, and

146. Dunford to Gates.

147. Gates to Dunford, undated, Gates Papers (CHL).

148. Gates to Dunford, Mar. 5, 1897, Widtsoe Family Papers (CHL).

instead "laughed and said we could enjoy the romance but since the manifesto it was impossible to realize the other part of it." At the same time, she confided to her mother "But nevertheless, he is very fascinating to me and if—!"[149]

While she spent this time with Roberts, Dunford wrote a letter to Widtsoe, addressed to "My True Love John." In many ways it is a friendly, not passionate, letter. Indeed she refers to him as her "dear friend" Still she concludes: "Dear love. I love you so much that life is dearer & sweeter to me than I ever dreamed it would be." She thought of him "every morning, evening, night" and throughout the day." She knew "if we could only be together we could never be unhappy long," and signed it, "Your Faithful Sweetheart, Leah."[150] Dunford was enjoying the affections of two men. She wrote to her mother, asking her to "let me know what Bro. R says to you about me." Both mother and daughter continued to bemoan the existence of the Woodruff Manifesto. Dunford told her mother that "you and he could work together beautifully. Then if only it were not for the manifesto—!"This was a twist—was Dunford suggesting her mother as a plural wife for Roberts?

As Roberts prepared to leave for Chicago, he handed Dunford some shells in a handkerchief. She took the shells out and handed back the cloth "which was very dirty and uh, I was longing to wash," but told Roberts she wished she could keep it so "I might have some excuse for sending it to you." Roberts quickly put the handkerchief back in her hand, and she had to "send it to him, and thank him for the other favors." She worried that "his Dr" might see it instead of him, because "she may think it a little too profuse in its general tone."[151]

On March 15, after he had returned to Salt Lake City, Roberts wrote separate letters to both Gates and Dunford. He couched his words in the language of friendship and wrote almost as if he were a

149. Dunford to Gates, Mar. 7, 1897, Gates Papers (CHL). Leah Dunford seems to have understood and resented the way plural marriage affected women. At one point she told her mother, "Polygamy seems to make of women either angels or devils." See Dunford to Gates, Apr. 30, 1897, Gates Papers (CHL).

150. Dunford to Widtsoe, Mar. 13, 1897, Widtsoe Family Papers (CHL). The letter is written on Brigham Young Academy letterhead. It lists "Leah Eudora Dunford, Director, Dept of Domestic Science."

151. Dunford to Gates, Mar. 14, 1897, Gates Papers (CHL).

father figure: " You have many reasons dear madame to be proud of your daughter. I was proud of her, as a daughter of Utah, and would like to have introduced her to all New York and the whole world as a product of our dear old Mountain state, and of Mormonism." He said that he believed he and Dunford would "be friends firm and fast after this" and that "the grand passion we call love ends in friendship—permanent, endearing friendship." Still, he could not resist ending his letter with a plea to "pardon his allusions" while he praised Dunford's beauty: "Who can view the upturned nose and not admire? Or, curiously behold the smoothness of the skin, of beauty's cheek, nor feel the most can mean all grow old."[152] Gates forwarded the letter to Dunford. At the top of the first page, she wrote, "How superior to John's! Talk of poetry and passion. Yet how manly, dignified and controlled. You are a fortunate girl, Leah. At the very bottom, upside down, she wrote "I never mentioned your name in my letters to him."[153]

That same day Roberts wrote to "My Dear Sister Leah," responding to the letter with the handkerchief enclosed. He had "read [Dunford's letter] a number of times." He also sent her the handkerchief that had contained the sea shells so that "you may know it belongs to no one else. Tie our friendship with it."[154] Clearly reflecting his feelings, and possibly his ambivalence, he also wrote,

> You ask me if I remember the conversation of Saturday evening. Quite distinctly, and many other meetings and conversations we had during my sojourn in New York. Especially do I remember the parting at the hall after the last service was held and the half sickening loneliness that followed the parting with the firm friends I had found in that great city. If you remember I deplored the time we had lost by not meeting oftener where as well as not we could have done so; but where the regrets at parting came I tried to console myself with the reflection that perhaps had we been more together—I beg your pardon, I mean had I

152. Roberts to Gates, Mar. 15, 1897, Gates Papers (CHL).

153. Gates to Dunford, Mar. 22, 1897, Widtsoe Family Papers (CHL). "I enclose letter which I think will interest you. Please return BH's to me."

154. Roberts to Dunford, Mar. 15, 1897, Widtsoe Family Papers (CHL). He also explained that "I purchased a number of these at St. Louis. The merchant had a number of what he considered odd initialed ones and proposed to sell them cheap. I purchased half a dozen this evidently among them."

> been more in your company, the sadness of parting [would have] been still greater; for it is seldom that I ever experienced so much regret at a separation as that one.[155]

Roberts then turned more conversational, assuring Dunford he was "more than happy to learn that our work in New York and my conversations with you were a help to you in the matter of gaining you a firmer hold of our beautiful faith." He objected "against your use of the words 'ignorant girl' on describing yourself. You wrong yourself when you say that; and believe me when I tell you I find but few who have thought more or better than yourself on the subjects of religion." He hoped she would write him again, closed the letter with "most truly yours, your friend and brother, B. H. Roberts," then added a post script: "You ask me to forgive you for taking the liberty of writing to me: I will most heartily if you will repeat the offense. BHR."[156]

After that, the romance seems to have morphed into a genuine friendship, and there is only brief mention of Roberts between Gates and Dunford. Gates would write that she was "anxious to see" Roberts, but then later wrote that she did not see Roberts, or for that matter, Widtsoe, at general conference.[157] Finally on May 26, she notes: "Bro. R was here and spent Sunday with us; he says he received a lovely letter from you and he answered it, & you have not written again."[158] By then, Dunford and Donette Smith were making preparations to leave for Utah.[159] The interactions between Roberts, Gates, and Dunford would continue in a friendly manner until Leah was the only surviving member of the group.

Roberts had departed New York on the morning of February 22,[160] leaving Pyper and Midgley to work in Brooklyn.[161] Pyper noted it "was hard to part and break up our company after so much time together but it had to be."[162] Roberts arrived in Chicago the next day.

155. Roberts to Dunford, Mar. 15, 1897, Widtsoe Family Papers (CHL).

156. Roberts to Dunford.

157. Gates to Dunford, undated, ca. Mar. 1897, Widtsoe Family Papers (CHL).

158. Gates to Dunford, May 26, 1897, Widtsoe Family Papers (CHL).

159. "In the Social Realm," *Salt Lake Herald*, May 3, 1897, 8.

160. Richards Journal, Feb. 22, 1897. The ever-vigilant Samuel Richards noted that "Bro Watts prepared an article for the 'Eagle' of Elder Roberts's discourse at yesterday's meeting." It seems not to have been published.

161. Richards Journal, Feb. 22, 1897.

162. Pyper Scrapbook, Feb. 22, 1897.

On Sunday, February 28, he delivered two talks at meetings in Wicker Park Hall. The mission manuscript history noted that the audiences were "larger than usual" and included three local reporters.[163]

Despite the progress Roberts had made, there was suspicion in some press accounts. According to the *Chicago Chronicle*, the "Mormons have come to Chicago. They are here for converts and they are getting them." The paper warned readers that now that the Mormons "have pitched their tents … the residents of this city may as well make up their minds to take sides. They will have to be Mormon or anti-Mormons. … Once they get a foothold they are never driven out. And they have a foot hold here."[164] The *St. Louis Republic* observed that Mormonism's attraction was due to Chicago's easy divorce culture—why else would "that city's women be desirous for the marital peculiarities of orthodoxy in Salt Lake City." Women, mused the *Republic*, were apparently so desperate for the "marital stability" that was "impossible under Chicago methods," they would even turn to "a Mormon knot."[165]

The *Washington Times* felt that there were always enough people in big cities "who are dissatisfied with present conditions to make up anything new that is offered." It was a common argument: Only the ignorant and uneducated would flock to Mormonism. "Institute the queerest religion on earth" and "in less than a week, simply because there are an awful lot of people who do not know their own minds, and are willing to permit other people to tell them what to think." All it took was a "magnetic" man or woman and "with their aid … a sect will be founded."[166] Finally, a wire story circulated widely in many papers, often on the first page, suggested that the Mormon elders, "under the leadership of B. H. Roberts," planned to take a "colony of young people, many of them girls," to Salt Lake City in April.[167]

Instead of bringing a "colony of young" girls with him, Roberts

163. Northern States Mission Manuscript History, Feb. 23–28, 1897.

164. As reported in "For or Against," *Deseret Evening News*, Feb. 27, 1897, 4.

165. "Mormonism in Chicago," *St. Louis Republic*, Mar. 4, 1897, 6.

166. "Mormons In New York," *Washington Times*, Feb. 21, 1897, 18.

167. See for example "Mormons to Take Out Colony," *Independence (Kansas) Daily Reporter*, Mar. 3, 1897, 1; "Converts to Mormonism," *San Francisco Chronicle*, Mar. 3, 1897, 3; and "Abbreviated Telegrams," *Rock Island Argus*, Mar. 2, 1897, 1.

returned to Utah alone and met with the First Presidency on March 5, reporting "his labors as exceedingly agreeable to himself and the brethren who had been associated with him."[168]

168. Historian's Office, Journal History, Mar. 5, 1897, 2.

ELEVEN

THE CONGRESSIONAL CAMPAIGN OF 1898

Soon Roberts was back to his assignments as a member of the First Council of Seventy and the Young Men's Mutual Improvement Association (YMMIA) general board, often participating in events co-sponsored with the Young Ladies association (YLMIA). As part of his Seventies work, he and Kimball took the lead in urging the First Presidency to call Seventies on full-time proselytizing missions, rather than leaving that task to bishops and stake presidents. Roberts and Kimball were appointed by the First Council "to look after the missionary work to be inaugurated among the YMMIA." So they drafted a letter asking the stake young men's leaders to send in names of potential missionaries. The goal was to have these names approved by the organization's general board, and then send them "a regular call." The program began operation in December 1897, and the two men spent a great deal of time implementing the new approach.[1] On December 22, Kimball noted that "excellent results" were being realized in various places including Weber, Sanpete, Juab, and Utah Stakes.[2]

Roberts was made one of the original editors of a new periodical tied to the MIA, the *Improvement Era*.[3] The others were Joseph F. Smith as editor-in-chief and Heber J. Grant. From then on, the publication was an important outlet for Roberts's writings.[4]

On March 31, Roberts spoke to a large audience at the Assembly

1. See Kimball Journal, Oct. 14; Nov. 5 and 30; Dec. 2 and 21, 1897.

2. Kimball Journal, Dec. 22, 1897.

3. Roberts was involved in plans for the journal after he returned from the East. See Kimball Journal, June 23; July 7, 1897.

4. The *Lehi Banner* had reported that when he returned from his mission in December, Roberts would be called to head a new church publication. See "This, That and the Other," *Lehi Banner*, Dec. 8, 1896, 8.

Hall on the "Value of the Book of Mormon—Objections Considered and Answered" in which he responded to contemporary religious discourse. Too often, he said, modern critics sought to "tear down the Christian faith by picking flaws in the Bible." Recognizing that the "increase of scientific knowledge" had robbed the Bible of much of its historical value because while science had been expanding over the years, the Bible was still what it was "centuries ago," he argued that the Book of Mormon played an important role "in these latter days" by making clearer many subjects which the Bible "left doubtful and uncertain." Not only does the Book of Mormon add to the historical perspectives of the Bible, he concluded, but also "answers far better than can the agnostics and atheists these uncertainties … which the Eastern devotees of the so-called 'Higher Criticism' are hunting out and exhibiting to the people." In that spirit, Roberts concludes calling on all "thinking people" to see that value, and to regard the Book of Mormon increasingly "as an exposition of faith" for all Christians.[5]

In June, despite his partisan affiliation, Roberts was chosen to be part of the committee on arrangements for a forthcoming visit by Republican president William McKinley. With tongue in cheek, Roberts had commented in a Salt Lake Theater talk that he hoped the pioneer celebration would be worthy of the president, noting, "We may not have voted for him, but we can give him a warm and universal greeting."[6]

On July 20, Roberts participated at a big celebration in the Tabernacle featuring those who had arrived in Salt Lake Valley fifty years before. In lengthy remarks, Roberts expressed the gratitude of those who had come or were born "since your advent into the Salt Lake Valley," and who have benefitted from "the fruits of your labors." After recounting briefly the story of the expulsion from Missouri to Nauvoo, and the trek across the plains, Roberts told them,

> I doubt if you could have believed it had one of your number told you when you came here what a half century would result from your labors. Had one told of the railroads that would be built from ocean to ocean and … that you could travel to New York in less than four days, and to San Francisco in a day and a half; had he said … that you would harness

5. "Lecture By B. H. Roberts," *Salt Lake Tribune*, Apr. 1, 1897, 6.
6. "Reception to the President," *Daily Enquirer*, June 10, 1897, 4.

> the stream in Ogden Canyon and from it illuminate your city, deriving from it light and power; had he said that a noble temple of granite from foundation to capstone magnificent in its proportions would over look the city ... had he said [there would be] a mighty commonwealth, where Mormon, Jew and Gentile might dwell and enjoy the blessings guaranteed by the constitution and the will of the people; if you had been told these things I doubt your belief would have equaled the anticipation.[7]

Roberts praised these pioneers and said they were a "happy band" whose efforts had created a society where all enjoyed the "light and liberty planted her by you." Even though "your heads are mimicking the snow on the mountain peaks," and your steps "are feeble," Roberts told the group of veterans occupying the row in front of the pulpit, you are "immortal," and in the "meantime every hand will be stretched out to smooth your path."[8]

The fiftieth anniversary celebration itself was a grand affair with a parade that wound along Main Street, fireworks on Capitol Hill, baseball games at Fort Douglas, and bicycle races at Beck's Hot Springs. The *Salt Lake Herald* called the festivities some "of the finest ever witnessed in America."[9]

About this same time, Roberts attracted the attention of his former missionary acquaintance Nephi Y. Schofield, who was then a Fellow of the American Institute of Phrenology and a noted advocate of the nineteenth century's fascination with the pseudoscience.[10] Indeed, phrenology had roots in Mormonism extending to Joseph Smith's time.[11] Roberts became the thirteenth installment in a series of phrenological assessments Schofield published in the *Salt Lake Herald* of various church leaders and politicians, including Wilford Woodruff, Orlando W. Powers, Martha Hughes Cannon, Evan Stephens, and Warren Foster.[12] In assessing his friend, Schofield noted

7. "B. H. Roberts's Oration," *Salt Lake Herald*, July 21, 1897, 2.

8. "B. H. Roberts's Oration."

9. "This Is the Great Day," *Salt Lake Herald*, July 24, 1897, 1.

10. See Schofield, "Phrenological Society and Field Notes," and "American Institute of Phrenology." The journal noted that "the readers of the Salt Lake City 'Herald' are being favored with character sketches of the leaders of the city written by Nephi Y. Schofield, FAIP, and well done they are too."

11. See Bitton and Bunker, "Phrenology Among the Mormons."

12. N. Y. Schofield, "B. H. Roberts: A Phrenograph from Personal Examination," *Salt Lake Herald*, Apr. 11, 1897, 5. Hereafter cited as "Roberts: A Phrenograph."

Roberts's measurements: "head measures 24 inches in circumference, 15 inches from the orifice of one ear to the other over firmness," and "this the gentleman stands 5 feet 10 ½ inches high and weighs 190 pounds." Schofield did not hold back his hyperbole, writing that Roberts "has the physical organization of a Roman gladiator, and the mental caliber of a warrior and statesman combined." He called Roberts's "temperaments" as in such perfect balance "it is almost impossible to say which is in the ascendancy." Someone like Roberts could not be "a cipher." He determined that Roberts has to "be a power for good or evil, and wherever he may be he cannot fail to exert an influence that other swill feel and one that will command attention even if it does not win respect."[13]

Using the contours and measurements of Roberts's head, Schofield determined that if Roberts were ever "placed in the witness box the lawyers would find it exceedingly difficult to confuse him. He is not over-stocked with order … but … he will be watchful, practical, thorough, and able to display to the very best advantage the versatile talents of his mind." Turning to Roberts's personality, Schofield commented that "contrary to what many might suppose," Roberts would not be full of self-pride. This "bold and aggressive manner arises from the absence of fear," and it makes Roberts, Schofield continued, "not disposed to boast, nor does he crave authority." He found that Roberts was "contentious and benevolent, firm, thoughtful studious, keen, secretive, and remarkable active both in mind and body."

Schofield said that he was convinced his friend "will want and will demand a broad and liberal church in which to worship. There is not enough spirituality and reverence to attach him to any religious dogma, creed or faith unless it is well supported by reason. He is sure to reject any faith unless give a reason for entertaining it, and whatever partakes of bigotry or exclusiveness will be abhorrent to his soul." He concluded that Roberts was "an exceptional man" who possessed such an unusual amount of talents that he "could succeed in any direction or calling requiring literary ability or mechanical skill, and especially if it admitted ample physical exercise."[14]

As vacancies in the Quorum of the Twelve occurred, Roberts's

13. "Roberts: A Phrenograph."
14. "Roberts: A Phrenograph."

name was frequently mentioned as a possible replacement. Two such vacancies occurred in 1896 with the death of Abraham H. Cannon in July and the dropping of Moses Thatcher in November. As Anthon H. Lund[15] noted in April 1897, "Everybody wonders who the new apostles will be. This is a question which agitates the public mind very much. Some of the Democrats are afraid it will be B. H. Roberts and in that case they would say this was his reward for humbling himself. On the other hand if he is not called they will say it is because he cannot be controlled. So what ever is done carpers will find fault."[16] As it turned out, the two vacancies on the Twelve were not filled until October when Matthias F. Cowley and Abraham Owen Woodruff were sustained.

Roberts remained busy the next year, speaking at numerous engagements such as stake conferences, YMMIA meetings, education meetings, and events to raise funds for a national monument to honor the people killed in the sinking of the *Maine*. But in March 1898, the health of his twelve-year-old daughter, Lena, who suffered from heart ailments, worsened. When he heard the news, Roberts, who was attending the Bear Lake Stake conference in Paris, Idaho, one hundred miles north of the family home in Centerville, hastened to her side but arrived minutes after her death, leaving him devastated.[17] Her loss was especially painful because Roberts believed in promises he had given her in a patriarchal blessing that she would live to adulthood. Roberts seldom discussed the event publicly.[18] He told Susa Young Gates, who herself had lost several children

15. Lund (1844–1921) was born in Denmark, baptized in 1856, and immigrated to the United States in 1862. He settled in Sanpete County, where he married Sarah Ann Peterson (1853–1933) in 1870, under her condition that he never take a plural wife. He was called as an apostle in 1889, the only monogamist in the quorum at that time, and served until his death. Lund was a counselor in the First Presidency under Joseph F. Smith and Heber J. Grant. In addition, he served as president of the Scandinavian Mission, 1884–85, president of the Manti Temple, 1891–93, and president of the European Mission, 1893–96. Lund was Church Historian from 1900–1921, where he worked with Roberts.

16. Lund, *Danish Apostle*, 33.

17. Historian's Office, Journal History, Mar. 20, 1898, 4–5. See also "Centerville Chats," *Davis County Clipper*, Mar. 11, 1898, 1; and Apr. 1, 1898, 1. See also Madsen, *Defender of the Faith*, 280–81.

18. Georgia Roberts Livingston, "Life Story of Celia Dibble Roberts," 6–8. Copy in possession the author.

to disease and death, that "the absence of my little girl sometimes throws shadows across the brightest scenes."[19]

Though the trauma of Lena's death was still present, Roberts decided to make another run for Congress. He said very little in his autobiography about his decision, noting simply that considerable "political agitation was going on as to the forthcoming congressional election." The *Deseret News* reported that the "friends of B. H. Roberts, with every evidence and assurance of correctness," were asserting that he would become a candidate for Congress to succeed incumbent Representative William H. King, who, the paper believed, would not seek re-election. As early as June of that year Roberts had begun in earnest to secure the nomination,[20] taking the precaution of first gaining the blessings of church authorities.[21]

The *Salt Lake Tribune* reported that Roberts was a "puzzle" for many Democrats, and that he had engendered a great deal of curiosity because he had not been "active as an exponent of Democratic ideas for two years." Still, even those who had been critical of Roberts's action regarding the political manifesto "are more than willing now to forgive and forget." But he was "not taking the public into his confidences," and many Democrats were "unsure whether he aspired to the congressional seat." In a sort of back-handed compliment, the *Tribune* said Roberts was regarded by many as the "ablest Democrat in Utah who is a member of the dominant church."[22] Still, the question of who would be the Democratic candidate hung on the decision of incumbent William H. King, who had won the seat in 1896. Although still in his mid thirties, he had already achieved a great amount prior to his congressional election. Born in Fillmore in 1863, he had graduated from both the University of Deseret and Brigham Young Academy, served an LDS mission in Great Britain, 1880–82, and received a law degree from the University of Michigan, all before he was twenty-five.

19. Roberts to Gates, Sep. 30, 1898, Gates Papers (CHL).

20. Roberts, *Autobiography*, 199. See also "Mr. Roberts a Candidate," *Deseret News*, Aug. 15, 1898, 2; and "Roberts a Candidate," *Salt Lake Herald*, Aug. 15, 1898, 8.

21. Thomas G. Alexander suggests that this support, coupled with the fact that Woodruff, George Q. Cannon, and others, had limited the requirements of the Political Manifesto to "general authorities together with their approval of Roberts's candidacy … in 1898 is probably sufficient evidence that their motivation was religious not political." *Things in Heaven*, 317.

22. "Roberts Is a Puzzle," *Salt Lake Tribune*, Aug. 1, 1898, 8.

After that he had been elected Utah County Attorney, Provo City Attorney, and served three terms in the territorial legislature.

Finally, on August 16, the *Deseret News* reported that King had informed his supporters the night before that he would not be a candidate for Congress and instead would run for the US Senate.[23] The *Salt Lake Herald* conducted a revealing interview with an unnamed close friend of Roberts who was authorized to speak on his behalf, reporting that Roberts was "in the fight to stay till the finish." Roberts, this unnamed friend, continued, would "lend strength" to the Democrats and "would be a credit to the state" if elected. Remembering Roberts's previous campaign, the source continued that he was "entitled to the honor of the nomination" since "there has been no citizen who took a warmer interest in the organization of the party during the crucial formative period of both parties" in the state.[24]

The *Salt Lake Tribune* immediately turned its fire on Roberts's candidacy, claiming that anti-Roberts forces had neither "forgotten or forgiven" him for his earlier candidacy, and that they believed he had sought church approval to run, noting that "a growing tone of discord is beginning to manifest itself in the heretofore divine harmony of Democratic politics." His candidacy "threatens … to renew the old Thatcher–Roberts–church influence controversy."[25]

The paper constantly ran stories referring to the opposition within the party to Roberts, indicating that the question of his candidacy, and its negative consequences, was "uppermost" in the minds of many Democrats as they prepared to meet in their state nominating convention.[26] On September 8, a cartoon featured Roberts doing a "Triumphant War Dance" on top of King, suggesting that he put his own political agenda over that of the party even though King had opted out of the race of his own accord.[27] The paper also asserted that the majority of Roberts's opponents favored a strategy of "Anybody but Roberts." On the other hand, Roberts's supporters organized around "Nobody but Roberts," believing that

23. "King Not a Candidate," *Deseret News*, Aug. 16, 1898, 8.
24. "State Convention," *Salt Lake Herald*, Aug. 21, 1898, 8.
25. "Roberts Fight in Cache," *Salt Lake Tribune*, Sep. 1, 1898, 5.
26. See "The Anti-Roberts Fight," *Salt Lake Tribune*, Sep. 5, 1898, 8.
27. "Cartoon," *Salt Lake Tribune*, Sep. 8, 1898, 1.

Roberts's "political disabilities had lasted long enough."[28] For many Democrats the chief complaint against Roberts was his stand on suffrage, but for others it was his status as a polygamist. Throughout the month, the *Tribune* continued to fan the flames, asserting that a Roberts's nomination would hurt the Democratic Party—especially H. H. Rolapp's candidacy for Utah Supreme Court since he was also Mormon.[29]

Roberts faced other intra-party squabbles. In Cache County, local Democrats were divided into "pro-" and "anti-" Roberts factions, as evidenced by the fact that each faction was holding its own county conventions to choose delegates to the state convention. The *Salt Lake Tribune* said it "was the first split in the Democracy of Cache and … promises to be an impassable chasm."[30] At the heart of this division was Roberts's decision to sign the church's political manifesto, when Thatcher had refused to do so. The Cache County convention ended up sending a strong anti-Roberts delegation to the nominating convention, "as well as anti-Roberts nominees for the legislative ticket and county offices."[31] Similar anti-Roberts splits were found in other delegations, including Weber, Salt Lake, and to a lesser degree Davis, his home county.

All of this came to a head at the state Democratic convention. Roberts was nominated by James H. Moyle, who said that after some twenty years he well remembered a young man from the country then attending the University of Utah who was

> naturally rather silent, but dignified… His classmates soon discovered beneath that rough exterior those latent powers that were soon to mark him as one of natures favored sons. He may not be a Webster, Calhoun or Clay, and his oratory may not equal theirs, but his qualities of mind, his hours of study, his vigorous constitution … distinctly indicated the great career that would raise him from his lowly origin to the front ranks among men and the peer of any. … It was not long before his voice was heard in the cities and villages of the state and surrounding states, and his name for piety, for scholarly attainments,

28. "Roberts Fight in Cache," *Salt Lake Tribune*, Sep. 1, 1898, 5.
29. "Rolapp to Be Beaten," *Salt Lake Tribune*, Sep. 4, 1898, 5.
30. "Planning a Campaign," *Salt Lake Tribune*, Sep. 19, 1895, 8.
31. White, "Utah Sate Elections," 198.

> for oratory was well known ... [from] the class room to the public hall, the rostrum to the pulpit.[32]

Moyle noted that despite Roberts's religious calling, his "great ambition" was to "distinguish himself in his country's service," recalling that in 1892 Roberts "championed the cause of Democracy, acquiring the reputation of one of the most brilliant and powerful orators of the state." Then in the campaign of 1895, Moyle reminisced, Roberts became the "idol of Democracy" throughout the state. In his defeat, the people of Utah "did themselves an injustice" and now they should have the "privilege" of repairing it. Moyle called upon fellow delegates not to prejudice themselves against Roberts for being called in the service of his church in 1896, and thus dropping out of party politics for a time. "He comes before this convention ... free and prepared to stand for every principle of the party, as untrammeled as any delegate in this convention."[33]

At this point, while several names were mentioned, Fisher S. Harris was the most important alternative to Roberts. Though little remembered today, Harris, who was a few years younger than Roberts, was an active Democrat who had been talked about as a possible nominee for various offices since statehood. Born in Virginia, Harris had moved to Utah in the late 1880s, and worked for various Salt Lake hotels while also becoming involved in local politics. In later years he was a moving force behind the establishment of Salt Lake's Commercial Club and was its first secretary until his untimely death in 1909.[34] In that capacity, Harris served as executive secretary of the See America First League, engaging in a short lived campaign to promote tourism in the American West. The *Tribune* called Harris, who was then serving as a member of the State Board of Land Commissioners, "one of the most formidable of all the men seeking the [nomination]. He is the man always put to the fore at

32. "The Democratic Ticket Is Now Complete," *Salt Lake Herald*, Sep. 15, 1898, 3. On Moyle, see Moyle, *Mormon Democrat*. See also Hinckley, *James Henry Moyle*, 230–35.

33. "Varian Will Preside," *Salt Lake Tribune*, Sep. 14, 1895, 1.

34. Harris (1860–1909), who married Lillie May Pfoutz (1871–1939) in 1888, was the Democratic candidate for Utah secretary of state in 1900. See "Fisher S. Harris Claimed by Death," *Deseret News*, Nov. 8, 1909, 5. See also Warren Foster, "Letter to the Editor," *Truth*, Mar 7, 1908, 8–9.

Democratic gatherings when someone is required to fly oratorical darts toward the sky." [35]

Harris was nominated by William H. Dale[36] and seconded by state senator Martha Hughes Cannon. In her seconding speech, Cannon immediately alluded to Roberts's opposition to women's suffrage and said it "behooves us as delegates of an equal suffrage state to inquire into the soundness of a candidate on that question." She called out that women across the country had gathered in Washington, DC, to celebrate the fiftieth anniversary of the beginnings of the suffrage movement, and that "the western delegates pledged … that they would do all in their power to bring about national suffrage, and we say we would not be fulfilling this pledge unless we send a representative to congress that will see to that work for us"[37]

Cannon said her candidate was "as sound on the woman suffrage question as Susan B. Anthony herself."[38] Similarly, Ellen Jakeman[39] from Utah County, who served as the convention secretary, spoke against Roberts because of his "vigorous opposition" to women's suffrage, which was "loudly applauded by anti-Roberts delegates." Jakeman said the women of Utah County did not want his nomination and would not support him in the fall. Furthermore, she claimed that Roberts had stated in the constitutional convention that women's "sphere of usefulness" was in their homes. Jakeman, obviously referring to his plural marriages, wondered if "Roberts's own domestic duties were not sufficiently numerous and pressing to keep him at home. Don't insult us by nominating a man who is opposed to us and who we cannot support." As the *Utah County Democrat* observed, Jakeman's "very eloquent speech … almost stampeded the convention."[40]

35. "Roberts Is a Puzzle," *Salt Lake Tribune*, Aug. 1, 1898, 8.

36. Dale (1859–1933) married Kate Hurst (1865–1951) in 1885. They came to Utah in 1890 where he was active in business, banking, and insurance. Dale quickly became involved in Democratic politics, serving as a party officer; Salt Lake City Council member, 1895–97; and Salt Lake County Treasurer, 1900–02. He moved to Los Angeles in 1912.

37. "Roberts and Baskin," *Salt Lake Tribune*, Sep. 15, 1898, 5.

38. "Roberts and Baskin."

39. Jakeman (1859–1937) was born in Beaver. She was a journalist, typesetter, and author. In 1889 she assisted Susa Young Gates and Lucy B. Young in canvassing the state on behalf of the *Young Woman's Journal*. Her short stories and poetry appeared in several publications, including the *Juvenile Instructor* and the *Relief Society Magazine*. An ardent suffragist, she was elected as the first female Utah County Treasurer in 1896.

40. "Democracy," *Utah County Democrat*, Sep. 14, 1898, 1.

Finally the balloting commenced, and Roberts, who remained confident throughout the deliberations, won handily.[41] Out of 480 votes cast, Roberts received 264, Harris eight-one. The convention chose Robert N. Baskin,[42] a non-Mormon, over Mormon H. H. Rolapp as nominee for the Utah Supreme Court.[43] In the words of historian Jean Bickmore White, "There apparently was an understanding that one [Congress] would be given to a Mormon and the other [Supreme Court] to a non-Mormon."[44] Regardless, the choice of a polygamist and a non-Mormon, well-known for his stance against plural marriage, was an odd pairing.[45]

At the convention's evening session, Roberts thanked the delegates "with all the gratitude of my heart" for the honor they had bestowed, and pledged to be "worthy of your confidences, and to exert my best endeavors to win the election, and if we win to fill the post to the best of my ability and to bring to pass all things for the best interests of our state and the common country." He was aware of the opposition to his candidacy, especially over his support for suffrage: "I wish to state that it is part of my principles to acknowledge accomplished facts, and to acquiesce in the declarations of the majority, and when disturbing local questions are once settled it is bad politics and undemocratic to drag those questions at our heels. We are facing the rising not the setting sun." Moreover, he promised a campaign on the one "paramount

41. The *Tribune* quoted Roberts as saying that while accidents were "always apt to happen at political gatherings," he was "supremely confident" about prevailing. "I hold the trump cards," he told a *Tribune* reporter, "and I intend to play them." See "Varian Will Preside."

42. Baskin (1837–1918) came to Utah in 1865 on his way west and stayed, opening a law practice in Salt Lake City. Active in Liberal Party politics, he was an unsuccessful candidate for territorial delegate in 1876, but was elected Salt Lake City mayor in 1891, serving until 1895. He was elected to the Utah State Supreme Court in 1898 as a Democrat and served until 1905. The last two years he was chief justice.

43. Baskin's nomination is most interesting. As his biographer John Gary Maxwell notes, Baskin had a "legacy as the territory's foremost pugilist against polygamy and theocracy," and suggests it might have been uncomfortable for Baskin to face his good friend Charles Zane in the general elections. He also cites the *Tribune's* assertion after the election that Baskin had accepted the nomination as a quid pro quo for future support for a US Senate bid which the paper claimed would "round out his career in Utah." Regardless of his motivations, Baskin worked hard seeking to convince Utah Democrats to stand for Roberts. See Maxwell, *Robert Newton Baskin*, 281–83. See also "Baskin for Senate," *Salt Lake Tribune*, May 24, 1900, 8.

44. White, "Utah State Elections," 200.

45. Maxwell, *Robert Newton Baskin*, 283.

question" that "overpowers all others ... the opening of our mints for the free and unlimited coinage of silver with gold as primary money at the ratio of 16 to 1." He explained that "the Democratic party is loyal to the best interests of all the people—to the money of the people—constitutional money. It is my intention to see that the promises made by the Democratic party are faithfully kept."

The delegates identified three planks in their political platform: support for the principles of the national Democratic Party itself, the conduct of the war against Spain, and bimetallism. In the first plank, Utah Democrats declared their "steadfast devotion" to the "principles of liberty." Regarding the second, the platform called the war with Spain "necessary and inevitable if the Nation was to have any regard for the protection of its citizens." Despite the demand of the American people to avenge the "intolerable" actions of the Spanish, the platform stated, the McKinley Administration "hesitated ... in weakness" and failed its responsibility. Only after a combination of patriotic citizens and Democratic members of Congress, the platform asserted, did the administration respond.[46] Finally, on what Roberts called the "paramount" issue of bimetallism, the delegates asserted that the use of both gold and silver an "imperative necessity ... essential to the welfare and happiness of mankind."

But Roberts's opponents were predictably less interested in his positions on national questions and more interested in his church service and plural marriages. Roberts's "public and private life have been devoted to his creed almost exclusively," the *Tribune* editorialized, and it was his "reputation as a churchman that has given him his fame; all the symptoms point to the conclusion that it was his reputation as an extreme, indeed fanatical churchman, that made his nomination practically certain."[47] The paper asserted (without providing evidence) that "dozens" of prominent Democrats were upset by the manner of his nomination, and were seeking to defeat Roberts in the general election by failing to vote for him, believing that his candidacy was "inimical to the interests of the Democratic party."[48] The paper also printed a letter to the editor from an unnamed

46. A complete copy can be found in White, "Utah State Elections," 281–83.

47. "The Democratic Nominees," *Salt Lake Tribune*, Sep. 15, 1898, 4.

48. "Sore Over Roberts," *Salt Lake Tribune*, Sep. 16, 1898, 8.

"Radical Democrat," attacking the nominee on the issues of woman suffrage and the eight-hour day, which Roberts had opposed in the state constitutional convention. The writer said that the "toilers of the west" expected "something better from a man who had once been a toiler himself." But then the real issue rose to the surface. The correspondent said it was clear that the Roberts's nomination was "ordained by the high church authorities." Even if Roberts did win, the writer continued, "it is doubtful he could obtain his seat [because of his polygamous standing], then we should be left without representation in that house."[49]

George Q. Cannon noted that Judge George W. Bartch visited with him and Joseph F. Smith on September 21, telling them of the "danger we were in, in consequence of the antipathy to Brother Roberts's candidacy and the determination on the part of the Liberal Democrats to make war on the Mormons." Cannon arranged for Bartch to see Lorenzo Snow to whom he made "the same representation," and urged the church to take action.[50] J. Golden Kimball wrote that he met with LeGrand Young and Oscar Moyle in their law offices, "and we conversed for some time on the wisdom of B. H. Roberts being a candidate for congress. Bro Young seemed much concerned, believing it would bring trouble upon the L. D. Saints." Kimball felt that "if Roberts was not seated it would settle the question permanently that polygamous brethren and authorities of the church who are polygamous (And all of them that amount to much are) cannot go into the cesspool of politics, and leave their callings as servants of the living God." He believed that church leaders and members "have the right to run for any office" and that they are "among the most honest, efficient and wonderful men of the world." But he questioned "the wisdom of their doing so" because "politics is a filthy cesspool, and politicians are mud slingers, and they besmear anybody that intermingles with them."[51]

49. "A Disgusted Democrat," *Salt Lake Tribune*, Sep. 19, 1898, 8.

50. Cannon Journal, Sep. 22, 1898.

51. Earlier, Kimball had told Apostle Francis M. Lyman that he "had heard from Marshall Pratt that our enemies were determined to persecute and prosecute our polygamous Brethren that were living with their wives, and having children." Moreover, Young would repeat his concerns to Kimball on another occasion and it appears he had communicated them to Roberts. See Kimball Journal, Sep. 28; Sep. 30; and Oct. 21, 1898.

As this was taking place, the *Tribune* shifted its attack from Roberts the potential candidate to Roberts the nominee. In many ways the campaign against Roberts seemed to be personal, though the exact nature of that personal enmity was never clear.[52] Three days after Roberts nomination, *Tribune* editor C. C. Goodwin penned an editorial arguing that not only was Roberts unfit for office—his only previous experience was solely church related—but his election came only as a result of the efforts of apostle Heber J. Grant whom he labeled a "seat to seat canvasser" among the delegates. To elect Roberts would not only fly in the face of the time-honored tradition of separation of church and state, but would seriously compromise the assertion that the church was not dictating the state's political and economic circumstances. The eyes of the whole nation would be on Utah voters in November and on the candidate they chose. "From [your] vote the country will make new estimates of you; from it they will decide whether Utah is in fact a free American State or not."[53] The *Tribune* also printed a conversation between Roberts and a "prominent Democratic attorney" in Ogden. The gist of the article was that Roberts told the attorney that he would continue to live with his wives, have children, and keep the covenants he had made. According to the *Tribune*, the answers convinced the attorney he could not support him.[54] In a wry double entendre, they told the story of two friends talking and the one said to the other that Roberts was sure to win the three-way congressional race with a "plurality" of the vote. At that point a bystander observed: "Don't use that word plurality. It would be a fatal mistake!"[55]

While Roberts was being hammered in the pages of the *Tribune*

---

52. White, "Utah State Elections," 205.

53. See "It Rests With the People," *Salt Lake Tribune*, Sep. 17, 1898, 4. In response, the *Broad Ax* noted that while the *Tribune* felt it was "entirely wrong" for Grant to participate at the convention, it did not "condemn" the role played by Apostle John Henry Smith in "engineering the Republican County convention" or for nominating Emmeline B. Wells for the legislature. Moreover, the paper claimed there was a double standard which made it possible for Goodwin and Smith not to see "any impropriety in wallowing in the deep pool of politics ... but they think it is an outrage for any member of the Democratic party to criticize their actions or to become active participants in politics." See "The Ogden Democratic Convention," and "Hon. B. H. Roberts," *Broad Ax*, Oct. 1, 1898, 1.

54. "Living in Polygamy," *Salt Lake Tribune*, Sep. 23, 1898, 8.

55. "Supposed to Be Humorous," *Salt Lake Tribune*, Sep. 16, 1898, 8.

because of his religion, he was also attacked in other quarters because of his stand on suffrage, though ironically an old adversary came to his rescue. In early October, Martha Hughes Cannon said that Utah's women voters had come to see Roberts not as an opponent, but "as a St. Paul ... who would fight for the cause" and believed he would carry the "banner of woman suffrage right into the citadel of Washington." In response, Roberts asserted that since he was from an equal suffrage state, he would feel bound to represent the interests of his female constituents should the question "arise in congress."[56]

Many women were not convinced. Emmeline B. Wells wrote that the "women of the state generally" felt Roberts's nomination was "an <u>insult</u>." The day after he was nominated, a number of women, including some Democrats, sought Wells out for guidance on what action to take.[57] In her diary, Wells said it was "an outrageous thing for him to expect women's votes."[58] Wells, who was both a suffragist and a Republican, consulted new church president Lorenzo Snow and his counselor George Q. Cannon. She reported that the two were "opposed to Roberts's nomination" on various grounds and encouraged Wells to organize, either "privately or publicly," to defeat him. Armed with this shared opposition, Wells was determined to defeat Roberts.[59]

Roberts's Republican opponent, Alma Eldredge, was no stranger[60] as the two had served as members of the recent Utah constitutional convention,[61] and Roberts had visited and dined with him in

56. "It Was Democracy's Night," *Salt Lake Herald*, Oct. 5, 1898, 1. Earlier, Cannon had distanced herself from Jakeman, saying that she did not necessarily endorse her views when she had opposed Roberts's candidacy, but simply sought to make sure her sister delegate "be given time to speak." See "Political Notes," *Salt Lake Tribune*, Sep. 16, 1898, 8.

57. Madsen, *Advocate for Women*, 396.

58. See Wells Diary, Sep. 15, 1898. At the same time, Wells maintained cordial relations with Margaret, whom she referred to as Dr. M. C. Roberts. See Sep. 2, 1898, and Jan. 29, 1900.

59. Madsen, *Advocate for Women*, 396.

60. Eldredge (1841–1925) was born in Indiana where his family converted to Mormonism. He came to Utah in 1847 with his family in the Daniel Spencer Company. He was a farmer and merchant in Coalville, and active in politics. Eldredge served a mission to England, 1868–71, and was on the board of directors of the Coalville Cooperative Association. Eldredge was counselor in the Summit Stake presidency from 1877 to 1901.

61. See White, *Charter for Statehood*, 109.

Coalville where he was counselor to the Summit Stake president.[62] At fifty-six, Eldredge had a stronger political resume than did his forty-one-year-old opponent. Born in Indianapolis, Indiana, on October 13, 1841, he had served as Coalville mayor, Summit County sheriff, probate judge, county attorney, and a member of the Territorial Legislature in 1894. He had also been a member of two previous constitutional conventions, 1882 and 1887.

Eldredge began his campaign in earnest in mid-September, and was quoted in the *Salt Lake Tribune* that he was "encouraged by the outlook" of the contest, that "Democratic dissension" over Roberts improved greatly the chances "for Republican success."[63] Despite his political and governmental record, Eldredge clearly lacked both the name recognition and oratorical abilities of Roberts. And while he was a Mormon in good standing, his ecclesiastical office "was much lower in the hierarchy than that of Roberts," who, as a general authority, had spent many years "traveling throughout the state." Still, it "was by no means a foregone conclusion" that Roberts would be elected, and he faced a stiff challenge from his Republican opponent.[64]

The campaign further intensified when the Utah Populists entered the contest. Their candidate was Warren Foster, editor of the Populist paper *Living Issues* and a well-known Populist activist. At first, the *Salt Lake Tribune* seemed to regard Foster's nomination, and indeed the efforts of the Populists, with condescension.[65] The paper noted that the convention, which was held in GAR (Grand Army of the Republic) Hall, "would not have been overly crowded in a passenger elevator." Furthermore, at least one delegate had challenged Foster's credentials as a Populist, to which the nominee was forced to proclaim, lest there be the "slightest" doubt: "I am a Populist."[66] The *Tribune* changed its approach, however, when it was reported that Foster "intended to make his fight in the main against" Roberts because of his "open defiance of law" by living in polygamy.

62. Roberts, *History's Apprentice*, 206 (Nov. 8, 1890).

63. "Planning a Campaign," *Salt Lake Tribune*, Sep. 19, 1898, 8.

64. White, "Utah State Elections," 176.

65. The *Tribune* reported that Foster had only come to Utah in 1894. See "Sketches of the Nominees," *Salt Lake Tribune*, Sep. 16, 1898, 5.

66. "Ticket of the Populists," *Salt Lake Tribune*, Sep. 16, 1898, 1.

Foster also seemed to indicate if Roberts was elected, he would support efforts "not to seat him" in the new Congress.[67]

By October the campaign was beginning to heat up. Utah County Democrats provided an opportunity for Roberts "to start the political ball to rolling" in an address to voters on October 3.[68] A rally was held in the Opera House where Roberts spoke of the importance of the election beyond his own race. Particularly significant, he said, was electing a legislature because they would in turn choose the US senator. He also told listeners that while the war with Spain was not a political issue, the question of whether the U.S. would retain the territory it had conquered might emerge as one. Roberts focused most of his attention on the question of the importance of securing strong governmental support for silver. Only the Democrats, he proclaimed, would do what needed to be done on this crucial issue.[69]

The next day the *Salt Lake Tribune* covered the event by featuring a large cartoon on the front page showing Roberts speaking while in the background were two babies in a carriage. It was captioned: "While Roberts at Provo was trying to obliterate all issues but silver, Fisher Harris was soothing the twins."[70] The *Tribune* was referring to the twin girls born to Roberts's second wife, Celia, in August 1897. The day before the paper featured another cartoon showing Roberts with the twins on his shoulders, and a room full of cats, dogs, and children at his feet. The cartoon quoted Ellen Jakeman: "I consider that Mr. Roberts's domestic duties are wide enough to keep him at home."

But the matter was not confined solely to the *Tribune*. On October 28, George F. Gibbs,[71] an assistant secretary in the First

67. "Will Attack Roberts," *Salt Lake Tribune*, Sep. 18, 1898, 6.

68. "The Hon. B. H. Roberts," *Broad Ax,* Oct. 1, 1895. The paper reported that the "blacksmith orator" had selected Provo "as the most favorable point to begin the fall campaign." It assured its readers that Roberts would be the "principal orator on that occasion and all who attend can become familiar with the issues of the present campaign."

69. See "Provo," *Deseret News*, Oct. 4, 1898, 8; and "The State Campaign," *Deseret Evening News*, Oct. 4, 1898, 4. The *Broad Ax* took the occasion to re-establish its support for Roberts, saying that when he had run before, "he had no warmer or better supporter" than the paper. But when he got "entangled with the [political] manifesto" it "ceased in raising its voice" for Roberts. Today, the paper commented it was "willing to let bygones be bygones" and would "sink or swim with B. H. Roberts." See also "The Hon. B. H. Roberts," *Broad Ax* Oct. 1, 1898, 1.

70. *Salt Lake Tribune*, Oct. 5, 1898, 1.

71. Gibbs (1846–1924) was the son of English converts. He came to the United States

Presidency office, concluded a letter to Susa Young Gates dealing with other matters by asking: "Say, Sues, as you are a family woman imbued with public enterprise, can't you help look after Roberts's twins while he is engaged on the stump?"[72]

A few days later, Salt Lake County Democrats held a kick-off rally in the Salt Lake Theatre. Speakers included Joseph L. Rawlins, Moses Thatcher, Orlando W. Powers, Fisher Harris, D. O. Rideout, and, most significantly, Martha Hughes Cannon. All agreed that "silver was the chief issue of the campaign and that they would not permit their Republican opponents to divert them from it, and all pledged themselves to the success of the ticket from Congress to constable."[73]

While these Democrats were making their case in Salt Lake City, Roberts remained in Utah County, speaking at the Central Meeting House in Spanish Fork that same night. He made reference to female suffrage, saying that, even though he had opposed it at the constitutional convention, it had been decided. When a voice called out, "We won," Roberts commented, "That was not a female voice." As the audience laughed and bantered with him, he noted that he had never "raised my voice about it since, except to urge the women to exercise the means to vote. For me! If I can persuade them to do that. Let them give a manifestation of their intelligence by sustaining the Democratic Party."[74]

The political divisions of the state's newspapers in their reporting of the Roberts campaign was evident. For example, the Republican *Ogden Standard* reported on a Democratic rally, admitting that "while the crowd filling the Grand Opera House was admittedly large, it was anything but enthusiastic."[75] "After the crowd had left

---

in 1866. Gibbs served as the general conference recorder beginning in 1876, and acted as an assistant secretary to George Reynolds. He became secretary to the First Presidency in 1909 with the death of Reynolds, and served in that capacity until 1922.

72. George F. Gibbs to Gates, Oct. 4, 1898, Gates Papers (CHL).

73. "It Was a Democratic Night For Rejoicing," *Salt Lake Herald*, Oct. 5, 1898, 1–2. The *Tribune* had criticized Roberts for focusing all of his attention on the silver question to the exclusion of all other issues. The paper said a recent speech by the Democrat was a "dismal failure," because of his "dry silver logic." The issue of "the free coinage of silver was undisputed" by all concerned. See also "Roberts on the Issues," *Salt Lake Tribune*, Oct. 4, 1898, 1.

74. "Roberts's Reply to Mud-Slingers," *Salt Lake Herald*, Oct. 5, 1898, 8.

75. "The Political Pot Did Not Boil," *Ogden Standard*, Oct. 19, 1898, 2.

the building, a few of the leaders went out to lunch, and [when] last seen … Hon. B. H. Roberts … was walking all alone to his room at the Reed [Hotel]; no escort was to be found, but Judge Powers was up at the Weber Club enjoying an evening of refreshments."[76]

The *Salt Lake Herald*, on the other hand, reported on a meeting in Salt Lake City where the "house was filled" and the balconies were "thronged with enthusiastic people." When James H. Moyle introduced Roberts as a "man of energy," the candidate's name was greeted with "every demonstration of approval and it was several minutes ere he could proceed." Roberts concluded by exhorting to the cheering crowd that as the

> twentieth century begins to appear over the eastern horizon, in the skies you see a disposition to return towards plutocracy in this country, favored classes. You see a disposition to depart from the plain democratic principles of Americanism, and a love of plutocracy manifested on every hand, and now the time has come when the democracy in the American people should be appealed to, and again should be written on our banner: 'The sovereign people of America can be trusted with their own destiny.' And they can work out their destiny to a glorious consummation.[77]

By the middle of October, the *Salt Lake Tribune* ramped up its campaign to discredit Roberts, often using unidentified sources to weaken him. It claimed that state chairman James H. Moyle was "engaged in a desperate effort to woo back into the Democratic camp the large number of … deserters who refuse to support undesirable candidates." As the campaign intensified, the Democrats arranged for a special train "composed of two standard Pullman sleepers, a dining car, a day coach and a combination car" to spend three days touring the state with many prominent Democrats. The party hired a band to accompany the train, which was "decorated in the height of Democratic fashion, with roosters, silver dollars and the like."[78]

Soon an obvious attempt was made by Republicans and their supporters to turn voters against Roberts because of his plural

76. "Political Pot."

77. "Salt Lake County Democratic Hosts Give Roberts a Splendid Ovation," *Salt Lake Herald*, Oct. 23, 1898, 1.

78. *Deseret News*, Oct. 28, 1898, 8; Charles Ellis, "Notes on a Meeting," *Deseret News*, Nov. 5, 1898, 8.

marriages. The *Ogden Standard* labeled Roberts as "an open violator of the laws of the land." Not only does he "not deny the charge," the paper said, "he boasts of it." Will the women of Ogden and Weber County "endorse a criminal by your vote?" On the other hand, the paper called Eldredge "a moral man who has violated no statute" and "just as good a church man as Roberts." The paper called on women voters to vote for a "clean man and rebuke the unclean one."[79]

In October, the *St. Louis Post-Dispatch*, which had covered Roberts so closely two years before, commented that Roberts was "making a unique canvass for congress as a polygamist." The paper asserted that while Roberts was "nominally" the Democratic candidate, he has "chosen to stand upon the issue of polygamy" and intends to maintain his current marital status, if elected. Such a stance, asserted the *Post-Dispatch*, meant that Congress might "have to wrestle with the question of his eligibility, if elected. The paper concluded that opponents despaired of the chance of beating Roberts at the polls, so they were looking at efforts to exclude him. It is unclear who was providing this information to the *Post-Dispatch*, but much of it aligns with what was being said in the pages of the *Tribune*.

Perhaps the strongest attack on Roberts came from Utah governor Heber M. Wells, whose mother, Martha Givens Wells, was a sister-wife of Emeline B. Wells. The governor said he did not believe that Roberts had undergone a "complete change of heart" on the questions of protectionism and women's suffrage, despite his claims to the contrary. He called Roberts's candidacy a "mistake." Wells sharpened his critique and said, "The trouble with him is that he loves the sound of his own voice, not wisely, but too well." But primarily he attacked Roberts for running despite his plural marriages. He believed the Mormon Church was "not committed" to Roberts, and that a vote for the Democrat would "vindicate no principle, subserve no good or worthy purpose, but would be an utter disaster" because it would be an "open invitation" to Congress and the nation to "renew the warfare against the Mormon people which we all hoped and prayed was ended forever." In ominous terms, the Utah governor concluded that "I am unable to tell what Congress will do

79. "Grand and Glorious Republican Rally," *Ogden Standard*, Nov. 6, 1898, 1.

in the matter as to whether he will be seated or not, but I feel the agitation of the question will be a very great detriment to the state of Utah and to every interest of the people." Wells predicted that if Roberts won and there was a fight over his seat, "every financial interest here will suffer; every industrial enterprise of the state will be more or less retarded; the interests of the dominant church itself will be injured; and, the very class to which Mr. Roberts belongs will be placed in jeopardy."[80]

Roberts, who was deeply upset by Wells's comments, was "in a terrible state of mind" when he came into the First Council office. J. Golden Kimball recorded Roberts's outrage in his journal and wrote that "the Governor said that men violating the law, by living with their wives, cannot hold public office. Roberts called him a craven and a son of a bitch." Roberts was so agitated that Kimball felt that "the spirit" Roberts was manifesting "was from down below. The natural man prevailed. The spirit of God was not present. I felt badly about it."

The next day Kimball was so disturbed by Roberts, whose breath he said stank "strong with liquor of some kind," wrote, "I believe Roberts should be defeated. He is pompous, proud and defiant. I do not like his spirit." Roberts told Kimball he wanted to find the governor and "twist [his] nose and spit down his throat." He reiterated that "the spirit Roberts manifested was from hell. He was bitter and malicious."[81]

Republican candidate Eldredge brought his campaign to a close with a "large and enthusiastic rally held in the Nephi Tabernacle. The *Tribune* reported that prior to the speeches, "a large torchlight procession with over 200 torches led by the drum corp and shotgun brigade" filled the "principal streets" of the town, which were illuminated with bonfires. While Eldredge was speaking in Nephi, Roberts was closing out his campaign with a last-minute appearance in Coalville—his opponent's hometown. He admitted he was "wrong" on suffrage, "congratulated" those who had opposed him, and assured his listeners he supported it now. He did not convince everyone of his sincerity; Emmeline B. Wells wrote that she was "depressed and ill" that night over the prospect of Roberts being elected.[82]

80. "Roberts Must Be Beaten," *Salt Lake Tribune*, Nov. 5, 1898, 1.
81. Kimball Journal, Nov. 6, 1898.
82. Wells Diary, Nov. 8–9, 1898.

On election day, the *Deseret News* reported that the saloons were closed at midnight, according to law, not to open until 11:00 p.m. the following day, and the result has been "that the voting was proceeded with in noteworthy decorum with possibly an exception here or there." Bands were in evidence, and the city seemed to have taken on a "gala attire."[83] On the other hand, George Q. Cannon recorded, "I shall be glad when this is over. I have been very much displeased with election affairs before in this state, but never have been so thoroughly disgusted with them as I have this time."[84]

When the votes were counted, Roberts won a strong victory, garnering 35,296 votes to Eldredge's 29,631—a margin of 5,665 votes. The Populist, Foster, received approximately two thousand votes, mostly from Salt Lake and Weber Counties. Roberts had outpolled the other statewide Democratic candidate, Robert N. Baskin, by nearly seven hundred votes, though he too would be elected.[85] In the final tally, Roberts carried eighteen of Utah's twenty-seven counties, including major counties like Salt Lake,[86] Utah, Weber, and his home county of Davis (where he carried over 60 percent of the vote), while losing several other counties by small margins.[87] Emmeline B. Wells said that the Democrats were "jubilant and the entire party seems to be enjoying to the utmost the great victory," but that for her "it is a great disappointment … that Roberts was elected—it cannot but be detrimental in every way. My heart is very sad. I cannot understand how the women of the state can be so unscrupulous as to

83. "Magnetism at the Polls," *Deseret News*, Nov. 8, 1898, 1.

84. Cannon Journal, Nov. 8, 1898.

85. One of the most interesting ironies of the campaign concerns Baskin's previous relationship with Eldredge. Baskin had claimed that Eldredge and his brothers Edmund and Hyrum, along with several others, were guilty "beyond reasonable doubt" for the 1867 murders of Isaac Potter and Charles Wilson. The duo, "apostate Mormons with sullied records of arrest for theft," had been killed in Coalville. Yet, as Baskin's biographer John Gary Maxwell notes, "one searches in vain for evidence that Baskin told or reminded Roberts during the campaign" about his opponent's "alleged role in the crimes." See Maxwell, *Robert Newton Baskin*, 86, 284.

86. Roberts carried Salt Lake County with a plurality of 1,772 votes out of a total of 16,834 cast for the three congressional candidates. At the same time he polled fewer votes in the county than did Baskin. See "The Official Figures," *Salt Lake Herald*, Nov. 20, 1898, 8.

87. Interestingly, Apostle John Henry Smith simply noted in his diary, "The Democratic party have elected Representative, Judge, and Most of the Legislature." See Smith, *Church, State, and Politics*, 412.

vote for such a man."[88] Wells's biographer Carol Cornwall Madsen believes that, had Utah women either opposed Roberts or simply not voted, Roberts would probably have lost.[89]

The results were as disappointing to the *Salt Lake Tribune* as they were to Emmeline Wells. It editorialized that the disappointment lay in the fact "that a majority of the voters have declared that they … are determined to be a law unto themselves, and are willing to go on record as having deliberately entered into solemn covenants with the Congress and the President of the United States, with the intention all the time of breaking those covenants." The paper wondered how the country would respond and what they would "think of Utah as they read the verdict which the people rendered" in the election. The *Tribune* believed "it will be put down as an act of perfidy and dishonor without parallel in our country."[90]

The day after the election, the paper ran another cartoon depicting Roberts, accompanied by his children, gleefully dancing into the nation's capital, and embellished with a typical *Tribune* verse:

> Ha! Ha! Ha!
> There's my Pa,
> He'll Go to Washington
> But he won't take Ma.[91]

Despite that final shot, Roberts had "weathered all the attacks" and managed to satisfy a majority of the electorate "that he could represent their interests in the coming days."[92] But Roberts had little chance to savor his victory. Once the campaign was over, the attacks and vitriol generated by the *Tribune* would find resonance with a group of evangelical Protestants and others who sought to overthrow the will of the voters. A major storm loomed on the horizon for the Beehive State's new congressman.

---

88. Wells Diary, Nov. 10–11, 1898.
89. Madsen, *Advocate for Women*, 396–97.
90. "The Result in Utah," *Salt Lake Tribune*, Nov. 10, 1898, 4.
91. Cartoon, *Salt Lake Tribune*, Nov. 9, 1898, 1.
92. White, "Utah State Elections," 216.

TWELVE

A FORMIDABLE PROTEST, 1898–99

Article I, section 5 of the United States Constitution states that "each House [of Congress] shall be the judge of the elections, returns and qualifications of its own members." Until a lawsuit in 1969 clarified exactly what "qualifications" meant, both the House of Representatives and the United States Senate at times refused to seat members who had been elected by their constituents.[1] Most often it was Southerners during Reconstruction who were not seated, but high-ranking Mormons also came under scrutiny. Complicating matters, when Roberts was elected in November 1898, new congressmen were not seated until the next session began over a year later.[2]

The congressional election in Utah was hardly over before voices against seating Roberts were heard—both in Utah and around the nation. Indeed, the effort to unseat Roberts would last far longer than the campaign to elect him. As early as November 29, 1898, the *Salt Lake Herald* reported in a front-page story that a few Utahns who "were bitterly disappointed at Democratic success" had written to party leaders in Washington to suggest that Roberts be challenged.[3] Ten days later the *Ogden Standard* quoted two representatives from Missouri. Congressman James Cooney said that Roberts was "beyond doubt fairly elected," and would not vote to unseat him "if he had a thousand wives." On the other hand, his colleague Charles Pearce stated that while he was sure Roberts would be careful to not "openly practice polygamy in Washington," if he did so, it would

1. Powell v. McCormack, 395 US 486 (1969).

2. The Twentieth Amendment to the US Constitution, adopted in 1933, eliminated the lame duck period for presidents and congressmen.

3. "Some Utah Republicans Want Roberts Unseated," *Salt Lake Herald*, Nov. 19, 1898, 1. The paper believed such an effort would be unsuccessful because there was "no precedent whatsoever for contesting Roberts's election on the grounds suggested."

undoubtedly raise "the question of his eligibility." For its part, the paper editorialized that it believed that talk in Washington of Roberts being a "lawbreaker" was hypocritical, and that the many members of Congress who were clearly guilty of ethical and moral lapses should be the focus of concern, not the marital status of one member, if the goal was the "purification of congress." The *Standard* believed that Roberts "will take his seat; we believe he should take it. ... It is Utah's duty to stand by him and see him seated in congress."[4]

Roberts's Populist opponent Warren Foster had decided—despite some comments during the election itself—that he would not contest the election results. In a lengthy letter to the editor of the *Salt Lake Herald*, he said that part of his decision was logistical: to contest the results would take "work and lots of money"; and, as he noted, "The former I cannot do. And the latter I have not."[5] However, Foster was clear that his inability to contest the results should not be confused with his assent. He wrote that "statehood was granted Utah on the express condition that polygamous practices should cease." He insisted that "it has not ceased"—he may have been aware of the rumors throughout the state of new plural marriages after the 1890 Manifesto. Even so, he argued that "those having plural wives have continued to live with them, and Mr. Roberts is one of them." Roberts, he concluded, was in "open violation of that sacred compact, and for that reason, and for that alone, should be called to an accounting."[6]

Though Republican Party officials made it clear that they would not seek to contest Roberts's election, others were not willing to pull back. Only two weeks after the election, the *Tribune* reported on a communication it had received from "S. R." who noted that Roberts's friends believed that his position was "legally impregnable" because he had been duly elected, and at the very most had committed a misdemeanor. S. R. asked the *Tribune* if it believed such a

4. "Shall Roberts Take His Seat," *Ogden Standard*, Nov. 28, 1898, 2.

5. "Warren Foster Won't Contest," *Salt Lake Herald*, Dec. 18, 1898, 1. This letter was republished by the *Truth Seeker* shortly before Roberts's expulsion from Congress. Foster says that his views have not changed in the ensuing months and that he wanted "the Freethinkers of the world to know why I did not contest." See "The Views of Warren Foster," *Truth Seeker*, Jan. 13, 1900, 27.

6. "Warren Foster Won't Contest."

position were "tenable." The paper replied that it did not believe that a misdemeanor disenfranchised a person, but a felony did. The real issue, according to the paper, was that Roberts "was disenfranchised by an act of Congress and has never been pardoned." In that regard, noted the *Tribune*, if the matter came to Congress, the issue would be simple and straightforward: Was a "man who is an active, defiant polygamist" entitled to a seat even if "a majority of the votes of a sovereign state were cast for him." The House of Representatives, the paper stated, was the sole judge of its own members. That being the case, it was the *Tribune*'s belief that "if a contest is made, or a formidable protest is entered against his taking a seat in Congress, he will never be seated. We do not see how he can be seated, when the sentiment of the country on that subject is considered." The *Tribune* asserted that if he were seated, "we do not see why the Manifesto should not be withdrawn, for if the Congress of the United States representing the people, indorse polygamy, we do not see why there should be any inhibition of it in Utah.[7]

A popular campaign against Roberts's seating was mounting. On December 2, the local branch of the Women's Christian Temperance Union (WCTU) met to help "frame a protest ... against the seating of B. H. Roberts in the House of Representatives."[8] Two days later, the Salt Lake Ministerial Association[9] "most earnestly" called for the "people of the United States to join us in a strong protest to Congress against the admission of the member-elect from this state."[10] Their December meeting was attended by nearly two dozen clergy representing several Episcopal, Christian, Baptist, Congregational, Methodist, Presbyterian and African Methodist congregations in the city. Rev. W. M. Paden,[11] pastor of Salt Lake's First Presbyterian Church, said it "would be an outrage to have [Roberts] sit with the

7. "B. H. Roberts's Status," *Salt Lake Tribune*, Nov. 15, 1898, 1.

8. "Temperance Women Meet," *Salt Lake Tribune*, Dec. 3, 1898, 8.

9. The group contained ministers from Methodist, Baptist, Congregational, Presbyterian, Episcopal, and Lutheran congregations.

10. "Protest of Clergymen Against B. H. Roberts," *Salt Lake Herald*, Dec. 7, 1898, 1; and "Ministers Will Act," *Salt Lake Herald*, Dec. 6, 1898, 8.

11. Paden (1854–1931) was born in Pennsylvania. He came to Utah in 1897 and was associated with First Presbyterian Church until 1913. For additional information, see Baird, "Critique."

law-makers of this nation."[12] Those in attendance adopted a document, "Will the American People Allow a Polygamist to Sit in Congress?" which identified three basic reasons not to seat Roberts. First, Roberts was a high official of the Mormon Church, notorious for his defense of polygamy, who served a term in the state penitentiary for practicing it, and who, as recently as 1897, wrote an article in which he "affirmed polygamy in the most unmistakable terms," specifically denying that it was adultery. Second, there was "undisputed" evidence that Roberts had three wives—two living in Centerville, and one in Salt Lake. Finally, his seating in Congress would be in direct contradiction to the promises made by LDS officials to gain statehood.[13] These charges would be repeated nationwide throughout the remainder of the crusade against Roberts.[14]

Roberts's defenders fired back, and the *Broad Ax* took this group of ministers to task: "It is our opinion that they could accomplish a great deal more towards elevating the standard of morality if they would pass a resolution condemning the ministers of Wilmington, North Carolina, for assisting in helping to shoot down and murder innocent and law abiding black men, women and children." The *Ax* wanted to know what Roberts's practice of polygamy has "to do with the fact that no negro can enter a restaurant in this city?" The paper wrote that Paden knew little about "the habits and customs of the Mormon people" because he had "resided in this city less than two months." Paden, the paper concluded, was being used by more seasoned opponents of Mormonism "merely as a cat's paw." The paper applauded the stand of the "thorough scholar and honest steadfast Christian gentleman" Catholic Bishop Lawrence Scanlan who "held aloof and did not deem it wise for him to join with his orthodox brethren in waging warfare on Mr. Roberts and the Mormon people."[15]

An early effort against Roberts came from the Presbyterian

12. "Protest of Clergymen Against Roberts," *Salt Lake Herald*, Dec. 7, 1898, 1.

13. "Protest of Clergymen." See also "Because He Is a Mormon," *Ogden Standard*, Dec. 13, 1898, 6; B. H. Roberts, "Comment on Dr. Reiner's Letter," *Improvement Era*, May 1898, 471–82.

14. Roberts had served a term for unlawful cohabitation in the Utah Territorial prison from May 1 to September 10, 1889, and had paid a fine of $200. See Larson, *Prisoner for Polygamy*, 226.

15. "The Ministerial Association and B. H. Roberts," *Broad Ax*, Dec. 10, 1898, 4.

Church's Woman's Board of Home Missions, which issued the pamphlet *Reasons Why B H Roberts of Utah Should be Expelled from the House of Representatives*, and distributed it widely.[16] After outlining the various charges against Roberts, it accuses him of "tacitly" admitting he married Margaret Shipp "since Utah was admitted to statehood." This was an original claim, since most contemporaries agreed he had married her prior to 1895.[17]

The debate was not limited to Utah, and people throughout the country argued both for and against Roberts's seating. The *Springfield Republican* editorialized that Roberts was "not a willful violator of law" but a man "reared in the Mormon religion" who was finding it "difficult to readjust" to "new conditions." Roberts took "his duty toward the women he had married" seriously, and "men of his stamp are numerous among the older members" of the church. The paper felt that "the practical effects of making an issue" of Roberts's polygamy and his election were not worth the effort, and that polygamy would not survive for long in the face of hostile laws and public opinion. It was time, the *Republican* concluded, for "toleration of such cases as that of Mr. Roberts."[18]

The *Illinois Staats-Zeitung*, a German-language paper published in Chicago, came to the Roberts's defense, noting that he had remained an "honest Mormon" who was unwilling to "terminate the legal and family conditions existing between him and the different wives and children." Laws, the paper editorialized, cannot be made to "act backwards" nor should they interfere "in most sacred and by religion sanctioned conditions." The paper asked, "How many seats in Congress will stand empty if we apply the same measure to our colleagues and ourselves with which it is proposed to deal with Roberts?"[19]

The *San Francisco Chronicle* took the opposite view and wrote that the central issue was that Roberts was a "law breaker [who] ought not to be seated as a lawmaker." The paper based its case on a view that Roberts had not met the requirements of the pardons issued by Presidents Harrison and Cleveland. He flaunted the law by

16. "Roberts Disqualified," *New York Tribune*, Jan. 18, 1899, 7.

17. "Roberts Disqualified."

18. "The Polygamist Congressman," *Springfield (Massachusetts) Republican*, Nov. 24, 1898, 6

19. As cited in "Comment on Roberts," *Ogden Standard*, Dec. 28, 1898, 6.

continuing to live with his three wives, thus "whatever citizenship he might have claimed" was negated by his "imprisonment on a charge of polygamy several years ago." Roberts, they argued, was "no more of an American in the sense of legal citizenship than an unnaturalized foreigner or a convict who has served his time without getting a restoration of suffrage."[20]

In October 1899, a war broke out between the *Deseret News* and the *Tribune* over whether Roberts's second wife, Celia, had given birth to another child. Roberts's twin girls—Georgina and Joanna—were born on August 11, 1897, so it would be possible for Celia to have delivered another child. The *Tribune* asserted that "according to authoritative reports," Celia Dibble had given birth to a child on October 14, which "as yet had not been exposed to the common gaze." The *Tribune* was so confident of the birth of a new child that it informed its readers that the "arrival of the last babe, if it has arrived, was not unexpected. The approaching event has been known and talked of outside of Centerville." The *Tribune* reported that "three or four weeks ago, Celia Dibble retired to the obscurity of her home, and that Louisa Smith Roberts, the legal wife of the Congressman-elect, became an attendant in the household." Later it was rumored that "Dr. Maggie Shipp—number three in the Roberts list of spouses—paid a visit, probably professional, to the Dibble home."[21] The *Tribune* account received a quick denial in the *Deseret News* from the alleged mother, Celia, calling the account "false and malicious."[22] But the *Tribune* persisted, reporting that a Salt Lake resident who had gone to Centerville to investigate the circumstances "was received with demonstrations of marked hostility, and the willingness of the people there to have the matter fully investigated was shown, when it is said they gathered at the station and hurled stones at the gentleman as he was waiting for the train."[23] There is no evidence that Roberts and Celia had a child together in 1899, but another set of twins would be born to them in 1902.

In November 1899, the *Tribune* compiled Shipp's entries in local

20. "The Case of Polygamist Roberts," *San Francisco Chronicle*, Dec. 26, 1898, 6.
21. "Another Roberts Baby," *Salt Lake Tribune*, Oct. 17, 1899, 8.
22. "Will the Tribune Recant Now?" *Deseret News*, Oct. 18, 1899, 1.
23. As quoted in "How Do You Like it?" *Deseret News*, Oct. 19, 1899, 4.

city directories, noting that from 1891 through 1897, she was listed as living at three different Salt Lake addresses, and never with the same address as Milford B. Shipp. The *Tribune* stated that "in the spring of '97" she changed her last name in telephone directories, used Roberts when giving prescriptions to her patients, and asked "Dr. Luella Miles to change her name on the rolls of the medical society."[24] In "any state except Utah, the time that a woman takes a man's name would be fairly good evidence of the approximate date of marriage." If that rule were applied to Roberts, it would suggest that "he did not take his last plural until in the spring of 1897"—after the Manifesto. But even if Roberts had married Shipp "before the manifesto," the *Tribune* insisted he wouldn't be any less "blameworthy" because he had only recently been released from a term in the territorial penitentiary for unlawful cohabitation. He knew the law and the penalty.[25]

For Samuel E. Wishard, who had contended with Roberts in the past and now supervised the home missionary effort of the Presbyterian Church in Utah,[26] the Roberts case was not only an affront to social and moral mores, but also a direct attack on prevailing political values. However, Roberts also proved to be a wonderful organizing tool in the larger struggle against Mormonism: a means of raising funds throughout the nation in support of the work in Utah, "where Satan's Seat is."[27]

Despite all these efforts to prevent his seating, Roberts maintained an optimistic attitude. The *Iowa City Press-Citizen* published a drawing of Roberts's famous "tramp photo," noting that anyone who thought that Roberts might "give up the fight he is making to secure a seat in congress and resign" failed to understand the "character of the man." The paper then recounted the fearlessness of Roberts in retrieving the bodies of John Gibbs and William Berry after the Cane Creek Massacre. In both instances, the paper asserted, Roberts had "invaded the enemy's country" to obtain what was right.[28]

24. See "When She Took Roberts's Name," *Salt Lake Tribune*, Nov. 27, 1899, 5. Interestingly, US census records for 1900 and 1910 place the marriage as taking place in 1890.

25. "When She Took."

26. See "Wishard Takes the Field," *Salt Lake Herald*, Dec. 12, 1898, 5.

27. *96th Annual Report*, 32.

28. See "Roberts as A Tramp," *Iowa City Press-Citizen*, Mar. 13, 1899, 3.

Almost every paper in the nation ran a variety of articles dealing with the Roberts case, and those efforts were picked up by the Utah press.[29] On December 23, for example, the *New York Sun* reported on the various activities against Roberts and gave an overview of the potential approaches Congress might take with regard to his case.[30] The *Christian-Evangelist*, a St. Louis-based, Church of Christ-sponsored publication, reported on the Rev. William H. Bagby's actions against Roberts and called his petition "a strong presentation of a great moral issue."[31] Similar views were expressed by Presbyterian Rev. William Frost Bishop[32] of Liberty, Missouri, a noted minister and writer. In an article in the *Christian Observer*, Bishop argued that there had never been a church "calling itself Christian," which had ever tolerated polygamy, "a Christian government is bound to respect the conscientious conviction of its people" that polygamy is "pagan and obnoxious to Christian sentiment."[33]

Roberts responded to questions from a New York *Evening World* reporter in a lengthy written statement. He reassured that no plural marriages had been performed since the Manifesto, and he believed "the American people would not call on a man to cast off the wives … with whom he has lived nor to abandon his children."[34] He said he would defend himself if necessary, but he believed that "members of congress and the American people are more liberal, broad minded and generous than a few bigoted and contracted preachers of the Presbyterian church whose training, mode of life and trend

29. See "Opposition to Roberts Because He Is a Mormon," *Salt Lake Herald*, Dec. 13, 1898, 1; "Because He Is a Mormon," *Ogden Standard*, Dec. 13, 1890, 6.

30. "Editorial," *New York Sun*, Dec. 23, 1898, quoted in "Roberts the Mormon," *Ogden Standard*, Dec. 28, 1898, 7.

31. [No title], *Christian Evangelist*, Dec. 29, 1898, 810. The paper noted that it would be willing to print the entire document if space permitted to "arouse our readers to a sense of danger attending the seating of such a man in the highest legislative body of our country."

32. Bishop (1852–1913) served various congregations in Missouri, including in Liberty from 1891–1900. A native of Virginia, he attended schools there until he went to the University of Edinburgh, and later the University of Jena in Germany. In addition to his ministerial career he also taught school. He was a frequent contributor to the *Christian Observer,* which was published in Louisville.

33. "Will Roberts Be Seated," *Atlanta Constitution*, Feb. 19, 1899, 19.

34. As George Macdonald, a leader of the Free Thought movement, noted, the question being publicly debated was whether caring for plural wives "meant sleeping with them." See Macdonald, *Fifty Years of Free Thought*, 189.

of thought tend to unfit them for practical life." At the very most, Roberts said he felt that the only charge that could be leveled against him was that of unlawful cohabitation. "I am here," he noted, "and the courts are open. If anyone wants to test the point the way is clear." Roberts told the reporter he felt confident that there were no "legal obstacles" to prevent him from being seated, and that he had "the best legal advice obtainable." Roberts would later distance himself from these statements, but they seem consistent with his views of the time.[35]

Lorenzo Snow, newly ordained president of the church, also weighed in. He wired a signed statement to the New York *Evening World*. He "solemnly and emphatically" denied that the church was currently "encouraging or teaching polygamy." Since 1890, "polygamous marriages in the Mormon church have entirely ceased," and he was personally opposed to any change that would revive plural marriage, because such a move would be "contrary to the law." However, he also asserted that none of this had anything to do with Roberts's election to Congress, which "was an entirely secular affair." Snow insisted that the church had not orchestrated Roberts's election and that the "church and state in Utah are entirely distinct and separate." He also took pains to point out that "non-Mormons participated in [Roberts's] nomination in the regular convention of his party. Non-Mormons also aided in his election. Many Mormons, not being of his party, voted for his opponent." Roberts "was not a church candidate" because the "church has no candidate." This was, Snow said, a "purely political contest" that saw the election of "an American citizen, by American citizens."[36] Snow assured readers that, whether Roberts was seated or not, there would be no change in church policy toward plural marriage. "I am personally opposed to any such change," he asserted. "My associates in the leadership of the church unite with me in this determination." But there was still the question of men who had entered into the "sacred covenant" of polygamy before the Manifesto, and what they should do with their

35. "He Defends His Faith," *Waterloo Daily Reporter*, Dec. 29, 1898, 4. See also "Roberts Makes a Denial," *Ogden Standard*, Dec. 29, 1898, 2; "Anti-Roberts Methods Exposed by Mr. Roberts," *Salt Lake Herald*, Dec. 29, 1898, 1.

36. "Pres. Snow to New York World," *Salt Lake Herald*, Dec. 30, 1898, 1. See also "Denial of Polygamy," *San Francisco Chronicle*, Dec. 30, 1898, 3.

wives and children. Surely no one would want these men to do anything but "take care of them," "provide for them."[37]

William Igleheart, a correspondent from the *Louisville Courier-Journal,* came to Utah to look into Mormonism generally and the Roberts case specifically. Based on his personal acquaintance with him, the reporter noted that Roberts would be a "grave disappointment to anyone who expected to meet the typical Mormon elder as he appears in the magazines." He then sketched Roberts's previous career, mentioning his early education, missionary efforts in Tennessee, opposition to woman suffrage, 1895 race for Congress, and the difficulties he had gotten into with church officials. The reporter then provides a vivid sketch of Roberts the man, noting that he

> is a stalwart, broad-shouldered man ... with noticeable firmness of frame acquired when he learned his trade as a blacksmith. His ... hair which is almost curly frames a good forehead. His face is rather broad and the features have the ruggedness of one who has borne hardships. The eyes are gray, with an unexpected flash in them when he is pleased or angry; one who has seen him under the stress of strong emotions would call his temperament sanguine and perhaps accuse him of a tendency to hasty action in excitement. Even his enemies—and he has many—concede his leadership in the state as an orator. ... In conversation Mr. Roberts is earnest, his voice strikingly smooth and well modulated and might betray the boyhood spent in England, for no such smooth resonant tone ever had its early cultivation in the dry air of the mountains.[38]

Igleheart concluded that Roberts would be comfortable among the others in the halls of the US Congress.[39]

The *St. Louis Post Dispatch,* which had also covered Roberts a few years before, wrote that he was the "idol of the younger generation of Mormons," not because of his commitment to polygamy, but because of his courage in the recovery of Gibbs and Berry. The paper said that "photographs of Elder Roberts in the disguise [as a tramp]

37. "Pres. Snow to New York World." See also "Abandon Polygamy President Snow to Mormons," *New York Journal,* Jan. 9, 1900, 2.

38. William Igleheart, "Two Chiefs of the Mormons: Lorenzo Snow, B. H. Roberts," *Louisville Courier-Journal,* Jan. 8, 1899, III:3.

39. Igleheart.

he had to assume to do his work are for sale in every Mormon bookstore or picture store."[40]

One of the most interesting views of Roberts's election, and the voters who had elected him, came from Theodore Schroeder. Writing in the pages of *Lucifer's Lantern*—his occasionally published journal of all things Mormon—Schroeder said "that Gentiles did work and vote for him is true, but … they were confronted by a necessity of choosing between evils." The only gentile running—Warren Foster—was a "pronounced infidel and a Populist and had no chance of election," while the Republican nominee, Alma Eldredge, was "not in the least qualified for the position he was seeking," and possibly a Danite as well.[41] Why did so many "Gentiles" vote for Roberts? First, some may have realized that the spectacle of Roberts's seating would go before the nation—as it was then doing—and his expulsion would help bring an end to polygamy. Perhaps they felt that Roberts's election would ultimately "do the church more harm than good," and that if he retained his seat, he would be a "constant source of irritation" to the church due to ongoing bad publicity. Or perhaps their "zeal for the silver cause" had made them willing to forget questions of Roberts's sexual morality.

Roberts wrote a lengthy letter to his friend and colleague John M. Whitaker, who was out of the state on a mission in the East,[42] telling him that "assurances … from men in high standing and letters received from Washington go far toward convincing me that my enemies are helpless, and that we shall succeed beyond any question and carry out the will of the people of our sovereign state."[43] Roberts told Whitaker that he was going to keep out of "anything to do with the Senate contests" and to avoid campaigning or lobbying on behalf of any candidate. "My personal affairs are numerous enough, as you will see to keep me out of mischief. Indeed I sometimes feel that I would like to run away for a month or two and get rid of some

40. "Brigham H. Roberts, the Idol of the Mormons and the Reason of Their Adulation," *St. Louis Post-Dispatch*, July 9, 1899, 32.

41. Theodore Schroeder, "Roberts's Gentile Support: Was Alma Eldredge a Danite?" *Lucifer's Lantern*, Sep. 1899, 1123–26. While the article did not have an author listed, it was clearly Schroeder's work.

42. Whitaker served from December 1, 1897, until his release on January 25, 1900.

43. Roberts to Whitaker, Dec. 12, 1898, box 13, fd. 5., Whitaker Papers (UU).

of these constant cares. But in this world, we are tied to a stake and must remain on the ground where we are staked down."[44]

Whitaker wrote a letter to the editor of the *Boston Globe* and defended his friend, saying that Utahns had given a "vote of confidence" to Roberts personally, and it should not be construed as support for either extending plural marriage nor an endorsement of the church's involvement in politics or government. He also gave a ringing personal testimonial to Roberts's character as "a self-made man" who "rose from the humble trade of blacksmith." Because of his "native genius," Roberts had risen to "become a writer, a journalist, an orator, and an able and wise counselor." He told readers that his friend would "serve with fidelity to his constituency and aid in promoting the country's cause" and that Utah Mormons and gentiles "alike united in the election of a champion of freedom and justice."[45]

On January 19, Apostle Rudger Clawson reported that a letter was received from Southern States Mission president, Ben E. Rich, and that "prosecution was increasing in the South—due in measure to the Roberts case." Jens Peter Neilson, a missionary from Bluff, Utah, noted that "mobbing was increasing" and that two missionaries from San Juan Stake had been beaten.[46] On February 11, 1899, J. Urban Allred, then a missionary in Nashville, wrote that "the Nation is stirred to the center by the recent election of the polygamous Hon. B. H. Roberts." A few months later he recorded that he had engaged in a conversation with a noted Nashville judge, John W. Judd, who said that "the election of B. H. Roberts ... was an unrepairable injury to the State of Utah." In early December, Allred attended Nashville's First Presbyterian Church where the minister, Dr. James I. Vance,[47] said the efforts against Roberts were not "persecution" but rather "a righteous opposition to the cause of error." Allred recorded that the

44. Roberts to Whitaker.

45. John M. Whitaker, "Letter to the Editor," *Boston Globe*, Dec. 5, 1899, 3.

46. Carpenter, *Jens Peter Nielson*, 281. Even after Roberts's eventual expulsion, there were reports of violence toward missionaries. The *Truth Seeker*, for example, noted that in Concord, North Carolina, three missionaries "were whipped by a mob, then escorted to the edge of the county, where they were told not to return under penalty of death." See "News of the Week," *Truth Seeker*, June 30, 1900, 1.

47. Vance (1862–1939) came to First Presbyterian in 1895. In addition to his ministerial duties, he was a popular speaker and prolific writer.

ongoing discussion "demonstrated again the power of public sentiment. The name of Roberts is a common household word."[48]

That fall, Roberts's friend Whitaker wrote in his diary, "The Church and the Elders laboring here was bitterly attacked from every source especially by the churches and ministers thereof, and I met this challenge several times. The Eastern press is all against him."[49] But Whitaker also found that the case was helpful in bringing out an audience. When he was in Sanford, Maine, more than three hundred people turned out to one of his meetings, which, he felt, might be due, in part, to "the seating of B. H. Roberts and the exposure of Mormonism in the press [which] has aroused in many places a determination to find our truth."[50]

As the debate over his seating swirled around him, Roberts remained active in various ways. Along with William Spry and J. Golden Kimball, he chaired a committee to create a monument in memory of his late friend and mentor John Morgan.[51] Roberts and Kimball seemed to have patched up their differences caused by the election. Kimball says that the two "had a very enjoyable time together," and that they "sat by the fire and talked until midnight."[52] Roberts attended a First Council meeting on April 19, 1899, telling colleagues that President Snow had released him from his ecclesiastical duties so that he could focus on his activities as Representative-elect.[53] Roberts also reported that his monetary allowance would be stopped and that he would be relieved as editor of the *Improvement Era* beginning July 1.[54] In May he spoke to a joint conference of the Weber Stake Mutual Improvement Association (MIA) where he talked about the International Peace Conference then being held at the Hague. Roberts said

48. See "J. Urban Allred," Allred Family Histories, online as of this writing at https://sites.google.com/site/allredhistory/home.

49. Whitaker Diary, 423, 426, in Whitaker Papers (UU). Hereafter cited as Whitaker Diary.

50. Whitaker Diary, 455.

51. See Kimball Journal, Jan. 17, 1899. Kimball served as secretary/treasurer.

52. Kimball Journal, Jan. 7–8, 1899.

53. Kimball Journal, Apr. 19, 1899. Kimball said "in my opinion he has made a mistake. No man can be inactive in the Church and have much faith." A week later the two men met in a brief council meeting and Kimball wrote, "Conversed with B. H. Roberts over his political condition. I warned him not to become inactive as regards his spiritual labors." Kimball Journal, Apr. 26, 1899.

54. First Council of Seventy Minutes, Apr. 19, 1899, copy in possession of author.

he felt that young Mormons should be "profoundly informed concerning the issues of that conference" since they would soon inherit leadership. He provided a detailed overview of conditions in Europe, the size and extent of various armies, and the vast amount of money dedicated to military spending.[55]

Despite Lorenzo Snow's permission to relax his labors, Roberts maintained an active church schedule as summer approached. On June 7, Roberts, Kimball, Apostle John W. Taylor, and several others departed for a tour of the Mormon settlements in Canada. After he returned in early August, Roberts spoke to a "large audience" in the Salt Lake Tabernacle on "Thoughts on an Agnostic—Ingersoll." Roberts said that he partially agreed with Robert Ingersoll on one point—"that there is no such thing as a miracle," because a miracle "is something that is contrary to the laws of nature so far as we understand them, but therein lies the rub." Indeed, Roberts asserted, over the past "few years," humanity had learned to use its skill, intelligence, and technology to see natural law in a new way. As a result, he argued:

> Man has become almost the Lord of this earth; he has made the ocean, once an object of superstitious fear, his convenient highway; he has annihilated distance, and belted the earth with wires, over which his thoughts fly with the speed of lightning; and even the solid earth is no barrier, but he can transmit a message not only around it, but through it. And if man can do these things, is it not childish prattle to say that it was impossible for the Lord of life, the Creator of the universe, to increase the substance of a few loaves of bread or change the element of water into wine or even restore the dead man to life?[56]

It was vintage Roberts—taking on modernity head on, but answering it with fundamental religious precepts.

In September 1899 the *Salt Lake Tribune* quoted explosive comments purportedly made by Apostle Heber J. Grant. Grant said that because of his plural marriages, he was a "law-breaker," as were Orson F. Whitney and B. H. Roberts, and that because his wives "have brought me only daughters I propose to marry till I get wives who will bring me sons." Grant denied that he had ever made those

55. "Eloquence of B. H. Roberts," *Ogden Standard*, May 12, 1899, 5.
56. "Thought on an Agnostic," *Deseret Evening News*, Aug. 14, 1899, 8.

remarks in public or private "in writing or by word of mouth," and that the fact that he had not taken any new wives "since the manifesto was issued" was evidence of his lack of "intention on my part" to take other wives. The *Tribune* retorted that the remarks were made in the *Salt Lake Herald* office "in the presence" of Edwin A. McDaniel,[57] Alfales Young[58] and James H. Moyle, "all good democrats and two of whom at least will never deny it."[59]

"Polly Pry,"[60] the "sparkling correspondent of the *Denver Post*," came to Utah to look at various questions and—not surprisingly—spent time dealing with the Roberts case. She became convinced that there was "no doubt at all that Mr. Roberts was put up by the Mormon church, elected by order of the Mormon church, and is now being upheld by the Mormon church for the sole purpose of ascertaining the position the Government will take in regard to polygamists holding Government office." She wrote that if Roberts was seated because "Congress decides that a man's personal and private life has nothing to do with his political life," then the victory would not be Roberts's but the LDS Church's, and "there will be an end to even the transparent concealment of polygamy that exists today."[61]

Much of the opposition to Roberts coalesced around the idea that, if he were seated, it would be tantamount to Congress approving the practice of polygamy. In February, the Salt Lake Ministerial Association published a pamphlet, *Shall The American Congress Endorse Polygamy?* Soon the Women's Board of Home Missions of the Presbyterian Church sent a representative to Utah to gain information on the case and concluded that it would actively oppose

57. McDaniel (1856–1936) had managed the Utah Building at the Chicago World's Fair. A Democrat, he was secretary of the Utah Democratic State Committee in 1895 and attended the 1896 Democratic National Convention and the 1898 Utah Democratic convention. He was business manager of the *Salt Lake Herald* from 1895 to 1898. McDaniel started the *Salt Lake Journal*, an "independent Democratic paper," in May 1899, but it only lasted a month. He later moved to Los Molinos, California, where he was postmaster.

58. Young (1853–1920) was the son of Brigham Young and Eliza Burgess Young. He graduated from the University of Michigan in 1877 with a law degree. Despite that training, he worked primarily as a journalist for several papers. He was a longtime Democrat.

59. "That Awful Mouth Again," *Salt Lake Tribune*, Sep. 8, 1899, 4.

60. Pry was the pen name of Leonel Ross Campbell Anthony O'Bryan (1857–1938) who was a reporter for the *Denver Post* and social activist.

61. "Roberts's Election," *Salt Lake Tribune*, Sep. 19, 1899, 5.

Roberts's seating. Jeannette Fisk, president of the board, urged "every faithful Christian man and woman to send letters of protest" to Congress, and see to it that legislators were "snowed under" with the "demands of the people."[62] In San Francisco, the local Synodical Society held a mass meting to distribute anti-Roberts petitions and invited "women of all churches" to a nondenominational gathering.[63]

At its annual meeting in Cincinnati, the Woman's Home Missionary Society of the Methodist Episcopal Church passed a resolution opposing Roberts's seating. In January 1899, Elizabeth L. Rust, secretary of the Woman's Home Missionary Society's board of trustees, sent letters throughout the nation noting that they had spent over $80,000 since 1881 to "overthrow this iniquitous system and free our sisters from this iniquitous curse." The Maryland Section of the Methodist Woman's Foreign Missionary passed a resolution noting their "solemn protests" against Roberts, and pledged to "unite with all Christian women who may be engaged in organized efforts in this direction."[64] Similar efforts sprouted in the women's groups of several other denominations, especially the Baptists and Congregationalists.[65] The Congress of Mothers adopted a resolution stating that not just Roberts's seating, but indeed his very election, threatened "the sacred institution of monogamous marriage."[66]

In January, both branches of the Kansas legislature went on record with unanimous resolutions encouraging the Kansas delegation in Congress "to do all in its power to prevent Roberts's seating," stating that he was guilty of supporting "a worse crime than that of human slavery."[67] A similar action was taken by the North Carolina House of Representatives. Other legislative rebukes came from the Wisconsin State Senate and the Idaho House of Representatives.

Instrumental in these efforts was Helen "Nellie" M. Gould,[68] the

62. Mrs. Clinton B. [Jeannette] Fisk, "The Women's Home Missionary Society and Mormonism." *Northern Christian Advocate* (Syracuse, New York), Feb. 1, 1899, 5.

63. "Petitions Against Roberts," *San Francisco Call*, Jan. 19, 1899, 7.

64. "Women Oppose Roberts," *Brooklyn Daily Eagle*, Jan. 24, 1899, 3. See also "Protest Against Roberts," *Baltimore Sun*, Mar. 10, 1899, 10.

65. In addition to Riess, "Polygamy in the Nation's Capitol," this effort is explored in White, "Feminist Campaign for Exclusion," 46.

66. White.

67. "Kansas Wants Roberts Excluded," *New York Times*, Jan. 1, 1899.

68. Gould (1868–1938) had a long career as a philanthropist. She married Finley J.

wealthy daughter of Jay Gould,[69] who used her family's fortune to support a variety of Christian causes, and ultimately spearheaded the effort against Roberts.[70] Gould gave $6,000 to the League for Social Services to, in the words of the *New York Times*, "be used in the crusade against Mormonism." The league printed over a million pamphlets "aimed directly at Mormonism and Brigham H. Roberts."[71]

Gould followed the Roberts case closely. She also studied Mormonism carefully and came to believe that while Mormons used Christian terminology, they give it "an entirely different meaning." They "believe in a polygamous God, that Jesus Christ was a polygamist, and that plural marriage is a God-ordained law that must be obeyed in order to gain celestial glory." She commissioned the Gould family's private clipping service to scour the nation for all articles on Mormonism and Roberts. She also sought out former residents of Salt Lake City to discuss both the Roberts's election and the nature of Mormonism. She soon became "imbued with the conviction that he should not be allowed to take his seat." She enlisted not only on Christian congregations, but also the American Female Guardian Society, the YMCA, Salvation Army, Epworth League, and the WCTU, generating millions of signatures on petitions opposing Roberts.[72]

Gould was in attendance at a meeting held in Irvington, New

Shepard (1867–1942) in 1913. For more, see "Mrs. Finley J. Shepard Dies of a Stroke," *New York Times*, Dec. 21, 1938, 1. At the time of her marriage, Gould was reportedly worth $30 million. See "Miss Helen Gould Weds," *Ithaca Daily News*, Jan. 22, 1912, 1. See also Renehan, *Dark Genius of Wall Street*, 303–05.

69. Gould was well known in Utah because of his railroad empire that had economic ties to the state. See Grodinsky, *Jay Gould*, 354, 388–91. At his death in 1892, his fortune was listed in excess of $70 million, a figure worth well over $10 billion in 2020.

70. "News of the Week," *Truth Seeker*, Oct. 14, 1899, 645.

71. *New York Times*, Oct. 27, 1899. Another interesting viewpoint comes from the *Detroit Free Press*. The paper noted that Gould's effort in mobilizing such "tremendous opposition" to Roberts made it "extremely doubtful" that Roberts could be seated. At the same time, these efforts had led many to criticize a "compact" made by the McKinley administration with a "polygamous, slave holding sultan in the southernmost islands of the Philippines." Polygamy, the paper asserted, "did not comport" with American values anywhere, and this individual was "not entitled to any recognition" that we were not willing to extend to Roberts. See "Too Many Wives Here and There," *Detroit Free Press*, Oct. 29, 1899, 4.

72. I. D. Marshall, "Miss Gould's Fight Against Roberts," *Salt Lake Tribune*, Dec. 3, 1899, 9. Similar sentiments came from the New Jersey State Federation of Women's Clubs, which urged Roberts's expulsion. See "Jersey Women in Session," *New York Tribune*, May 12, 1899, 5.

York, her country home residence, on November 14, 1899. In many ways this meeting is typical of scores of similar meetings held throughout the country. The preparation had begun some three weeks before when Roberts's Utah antagonist W. M. Paden communicated with the local Presbyterian minister, Rev. John A. Ingham.[73] Paden wrote Ingham on October 21, 1899, making him aware of his time in Utah, and his findings on Roberts's marital situation. He alleged that the congressman-elect was tied to "at least" three women. While he does not elaborate on who those women were, Paden noted the evidence he has acquired would be "sufficient to convict him" on the charges. He also assured his ministerial colleague that he was "not known here as a Mormon-eater, but rather as one who is unready to go a bit further than is absolutely necessary in this matter of fighting polygamy." Paden promised to send Ingham proof of his assertions. After that correspondence Ingham was sympathetic to the arguments against Roberts. [74]

As a result, a large meeting, sponsored by a broad citizens committee, was held at Ingham's Irvington Presbyterian Church. The case against Roberts was made to a large crowd "notwithstanding that a heavy snowstorm was falling," Gould addressed the crowd, not from the platform but from the floor, "being too modest" to take a more prominent role.[75] Gould stated that her sources in Utah indicated that as recently as the general conference held the previous month that polygamy was a "sine qua non of attaining to the highest or celestial glory." Gould's main source was William R. Campbell,[76]

73. Ingham (1868–1944) served as pastor of the Irvington Presbyterian Church from 1894 until 1910.

74. Paden to Ingham, Oct. 21, 1899, as quoted in Baird, "Critique of Presbyterian Ministry," 72–73.

75. As one commentator noted: "Miss Gould's little talk at the Irvington meeting was her first experience so far as the public is aware, as a speaker before a mixed audience, and ... she spoke from the body of the house ... [which] detracted somewhat from the effectiveness of her remarks, but her voice was clear and distinct, her earnestness was decidedly apparent to all present. She could become a highly effective public speaker were she to consider it worth her while." I. D. Marshall, "Miss Gould's Fight Against Roberts," *Salt Lake Tribune*, Dec. 3, 1899, 9.

76. See "Mr. Campbell's Story," *Salt Lake Herald*, Oct. 17, 1899, 3. Campbell came to Utah in 1886 and was a well-known opponent of polygamy, occupying pastorates in Salt Lake City and Cache Valley. He was a close associate of Eugene Young. Campbell left Utah and the pulpit and was employed by New York Life Insurance Co. "Utahns in

a Presbyterian minister in Utah and editor of the *Kinsman,* which was described as "the special organ of the anti-Roberts campaign."[77] Gould quoted him as saying that Mormon women were

> taught that their only salvation is through their husbands. In the resurrection they can only be lifted from their graves and put into eternal life by their Mormon husbands who if they are displeased with them for any cause can threaten to leave them in their graves forever, so that they will not be able to see their children in the hereafter. Surely this is the worst sort of slavery for women. [78]

Gould concluded by calling on men and women throughout "these free United States" to "combine and do all in our power" to make sure that not only was Roberts "expelled from Congress, because he has three wives," but also to strike at the root of the matter by enacting "severe penalties for those who practice polygamy, and who inculcate it as a God-ordained law necessary in attaining the highest glory possible to man."[79]

Eugene Young, a grandson of Brigham Young who had left the church, attended the Irvington meeting, and became one of Gould's most "earnest allies" in her crusade.[80] If Roberts were seated, Young charged, the action would be hailed "throughout Utah as a manifestation of God's power turning the hearts of the nation toward Mormonism. It would carry gloom to the women of Utah, whose martyrdom has been too grievous already. It would serve a notice

---

the East," *Salt Lake Tribune*, Feb. 23, 1902, 17. Campbell spoke out on Mormonism as late as 1912, "Jamaica," *Brooklyn Chat*, Jan. 6, 1912, J-17.

77. "Change in Kinsman, Salt Lake Herald, December 2, 1899, 5. The journal said it was dedicated to the "expulsion of Roberts ... and securing a constitutional amendment prohibiting the practice of polygamy and polygamous cohabitation."

78. A copy of the remarks is found in the Helen M. Gould Shepard Papers, New York Historical Society, MSS 142, box 1, fd 2. Campbell said he had attended the most recent general conference where "Brother" George Q. Cannon "fully explained how some of the Saints had in the midst of great tribulation" obeyed the law of "Celestial Glory," a code by which he meant "plural marriage." Campbell's words only stoked Gould's antipathy to Mormonism.

79. Shepard Papers.

80. "No Roberts," *Salt Lake Tribune*, Dec. 3, 1899, 1. Young (1874–1939) was the fourth of five sons of Joseph A. Young and plural wife Clara Stenhouse. He was active as a journalist in New York, writing for both the *New York Times* and the *New York World*. See "E. J. Young Is Dead, Editor and Author," *New York Times*, Feb. 23, 1939, 23. Hereafter cited as "Young Obituary."

on the young men of Mormondom that their only hope of political advancement is through obedience to the priesthood." Moreover, he believed that this action would "embolden the Church leaders to bind their tyranny more securely on their followers, to reach out more aggressively in other states, and to plan for that national power which has been the ambition of Mormonism since the first 'prophet' Joseph Smith posed as a candidate for President of the United States."[81] Finally he warned that Roberts's success "will bring Mormonism, more aggressive than ever, to the doors of your homes. It will increase tenfold the activity of the missionaries, a detachment of whom are now making a house to house canvass."[82]

Despite this opposition, Roberts continued to be optimistic. He remained certain that he had not broken the law, except perhaps as a misdemeanor. He was open about his marriages, and he seemed to believe that his defense that he could not abandon his family was persuasive. So long as he did not enter into new plural marriages, Roberts failed to see what the problem was.[83]

Defenses of Roberts ranged from accusations of anti-Mormonism by ecclesiastical bodies to charges that opposition to polygamy, a dying practice, was misplaced given all the social ills in the world. Theodore W. Curtis, writing in the *Arena* as secretary of the Social Alliance, summed up much of the defense of Roberts in five basic points. First, demands for Roberts's exclusion were based on "vague implications" of morality because there was no evidence that Roberts or anyone else had contracted a plural marriage since statehood.[84] Second, Roberts's opponents came largely from "ecclesiastical bodies whose enmity pursued the Mormons long before polygamy was any part of their creed." Third, the definition and practice of marriage was "under the control of the several states," and Congress could only prohibit polygamy in all states through a constitutional amendment. Fourth, there were "practices more revolting to the moral sense and dangerous to the home than the offense charged against Utah's

81. "Women Everywhere Join the Fight," *New York Journal,* Dec. 21, 1899, 4.

82. "Women Everywhere."

83. As Jana Riess notes, "Public sentiment was a very different story, however, as Roberts was soon to discover." See Riess, Polygamy in the Nation's Capitol," 32–33.

84. As has been extensively documented, polygamy did continue after the 1890 Woodruff Manifesto, often in Canada and Mexico. See, for example, Hardy, *Solemn Covenant.*

representative." Finally, economic inequality and "the extremes of wealth and poverty ... are the greatest foe of morals and the home," and reduction of this inequality would result in the enhancement of "personal conduct and the suppression of crime." Curtis called the charges that Roberts was a "Mormon device for foisting polygamy on the nation ... baseless," and argued that Roberts was not attacked in his previous campaign for his multiple marriages; it was only when it appeared he would win on his second try that he was labeled a law breaker. Curtis argued that Roberts was nominated "because he was a good democrat, an able politician, a strong silver man, and a gifted orator. Both Gentiles and Mormons voted for him; many of the most prominent Mormons being arrayed against him."[85]

On the eve of the opening of Congress, liberal journalist Louis F. Post noted in *The Public* that it was not "possible" that Congress "will unseat Brigham H. Roberts, notwithstanding the clamor for it." The issues as stake were much greater "than that of Roberts's multitudinous family relations." If Congressmen took it upon themselves "to expel members for causes unrelated to their obligations as members" it would make elections moot, stripping the people of their right to elect representatives "in their respective districts."[86] Post went on to echo the *Springfield Republican* and argued that Roberts was a product of Mormonism who "grew up in a polygamous civilization." Men like Roberts and the church needed time as they underwent "transformation in the civilizing process."[87]

Support and opposition to Roberts made strange bedfellows. The Free-Thinker publication the *Truth Seeker* defended Roberts, arguing that "slavery, intemperance, polygamy—all of these and worse are firmly buttressed by the scriptures, and the Christian knows it. The attack upon Roberts is hypocritical and insincere. It is not he that should be unseated, but the book which has furnished wine to the toper, a master for the slave, and plural wives for the polygamist."[88]

---

85. "Open Letter of Social Alliance," *Boston Daily Globe*, Feb. 2, 1899, 4.

86. [Untitled], *The Public*, Nov. 25, 1889, 1.

87 *The Public*.

88. "Unseat the Book," *Truth Seeker*, Jan. 21, 1899, 36. Similar views may be found in letters to the editor published over the next few months. See particularly "The Godly Woman," *Truth Seeker*, Nov. 11, 1899, 711; and "A Poor Witness Against Polygamy," *Truth Seeker*, Nov. 25, 1899, 1.

At the April 1899 general conference, Apostle Joseph F. Smith assured those in attendance that the church was not responsible "for the actions of either of the political parties, in any sense, or form." If that "were the case," the Republicans and Democrats would cease "their quarreling and contending, and the bitterness and animosity toward one another would cease." The church would stop this partisan "wrangling," and the two parties would have "peace in their ranks." The fact that this has not happened, said Smith, is "proof positive" that the church has nothing to do with either party.[89]

The publicity surrounding the embattled Utahn caught the attention of Joseph Smith III, son of the martyred Mormon founder and president of the Reorganized Church (RLDS). Regardless of what happened to Roberts, he said, "the agitation caused by his election" had clarified the "main point" of the RLDS that polygamy was not a legitimate part of Mormonism. Smith's pronouncements set off widespread RLDS efforts against Roberts. The RLDS Church's 1900 general conference report noted that "many of the districts and branches of the Reorganization" had joined "almost all religious bodies" in protesting against Roberts's seating. As a result, the "press has given more attention to what they call 'Mormonism' within the last year than ever before, perhaps on account of the agitation occasioned by the election of Mr. B. H. Roberts." But the RLDS Church, the report said, had "not suffered materially therefrom, as the distinction has in many instances been clearly drawn, and it is quite well understood that the Reorganization is upon the side of respect for the law."[90]

In late November, Utah senator Joseph Rawlins publicly defended Roberts and noted that several LDS polygamists were holding "important Federal offices" in the state. None of this violated the compact, nor was it designed to "cram polygamy down the throat of the Nation or the State." He proclaimed that he would, "at the first opportunity," introduce a four-part resolution in the Senate, first, to call on the Senate's Committee on the Judiciary to examine to what extent polygamy was practiced in the United States; second, to ascertain whether polygamists have been elected in Utah,

89. "President Joseph F. Smith," *Conference Reports,* Apr. 1899, 41.

90. Reorganized Church of Jesus Christ of Latter Day Saints, "Minutes of General Conference, 1900," supplement to the *Saints Herald,* June 6, 1900, 229.

and if their election was "for the purpose of encouraging polygamy" or intended to violate of any compact between Utah and the nation; third, to assess whether polygamists had been appointed to office by the president and confirmed by the Senate; and finally, to propose "steps that should be taken or measures enacted" to prevent the practice of polygamy in the United States.[91]

In mid-November, The *Salt Lake Herald* reported on a meeting held in Rawlins's law office where James H. Moyle told those in attendance that he thought something should be done to "offset" the petitions that had been sent to Congress. But W. H. Dale said it was up to Roberts to take care of himself, and that while the Democratic Party "had nominated and elected" him for Congress, "its duty to him ended at that point." J. R. Letcher was "quite outspoken against Roberts, criticizing him for what he called bad faith and declaring that the congressman had "made a football out of the Democratic party as well as … his friends within the party." Ogden's Thomas D. Dee was "most emphatic" in expressing his opinion on the importance of majority rule, commenting that it was the "foundation stone of Democracy," and that as long as there was "in Utah one Democrat who thinks he knows more than two; as long as there are men who will not abide by the will of the majority; men who believe in the policy of rule or ruin, Democratic victories will do no good; the party will be crippled by the minority and it will be helpless."[92]

The *New York Times* reported that at a meeting of the Democratic State Committee held on December 2, party chair—and Roberts's attorney—James H. Moyle sought a statement of support for Roberts's right to be seated. It was a large meeting with some twenty-two in attendance—eight members of the executive committee and fourteen other prominent Democrats who were not members of the state committee but were in attendance by "special invitation."[93] After three

91. "Rawlins Defends Roberts," *New York Times*, Nov. 29, 1899, 8.

92. "Democratic Leaders Discuss Roberts Case," *Salt Lake Herald*, Nov. 19, 1899, 1; "Majority Must Rule," *Salt Lake Herald*, Nov. 20, 1899, 8. Moyle denied much of what the *New York Times* printed, specifically that he had called for counter petitions to be circulated. See "Democrats in Party Council," *Deseret News*, Nov. 20, 1899, 1. For a view on all of this from Roberts's antagonist William R. Campbell, see "The Political Aspects of Mormonism," copy in Mowry Scrapbook, 22–23.

93. The executive committee members present were: Moyle, O. W. Powers, F. S. Fernstrom, Sam King, Martha Hughes Cannon, Frank Y. Taylor, L. R. Martineau and R. C.

hours, the state party opted to stand by their embattled congressman, likely recognizing that any other course would prove disastrous. It was a contentious meeting that revealed the deep divisions in the party over the issue.

The Roberts case put Mormon women in a difficult position. Republican women like Emmeline B. Wells continued to oppose him at every turn,[94] while in the Democratic ranks, his old classmate Martha Hughes Cannon seems to have taken a lead role in making him more acceptable to women leaders within the party.

At the 1899 National Council of Women meeting, some delegates advocated that the group go on record as officially opposing Roberts as a way of demonstrating their commitment to the anti-polygamy cause, and as a measure of support for the many women's groups seeking to ban Roberts from Congress. Emmeline B. Wells, leading a ten-member delegation,[95] was in attendance and found herself caught between opposing the general authority Roberts or seeming to favor plural marriage by not supporting the resolution. In an attempt to chart a middle course, Wells proposed a compromise, known as the "majority resolution," which did not specifically mention Roberts, but simply called for all members of Congress to obey the law.[96]

At the same meeting, venerable feminist leader Susan B. Anthony asserted that it did not make sense to oppose Roberts simply because he had "violated the law of monogamy" when so many others in Congress had been guilty of the same behavior, "almost all men, as a general thing violate the sanctity of the home."[97] Anthony argued that it might be better to "enter into a crusade against the

---

Chambers. Those present by invitation were Fisher S. Harris, W. H. Dale, O. A. Smoot, Waldemar Van Cott, E. M. Conroy, J. R. Letcher, S. R. Thurman, Joseph M. Cohen, E. W. Wilson, W. H. King, H. P. Henderson, R. A. Deal, and John F. Howells. See "No Roberts."

94. See Madsen, *Advocate for Women*, 406–15.

95. For a list of the delegation, see [Susa Young Gates], "The Recent Triennial in Washington," *Young Woman's Journal*, May 1899, 195–215.

96. See Madsen, "Power of Combination." As Madsen notes, none of the Mormon women had supported Roberts's bid for Congress, but "all of them supported his constitutional right to take his seat" in the House of Representatives. Clearly the Roberts case was a difficult issue for Mormon feminists in terms of their efforts in the broader movement. On the other hand, the actions of the NCW turned some Mormon women away from the organization. Ultimately, however, church leaders supported the involvement of Wells and others in the council.

97. As quoted in "New Anti-Roberts Protest," *New York Times*, Nov. 19, 1899, 7.

licentiousness existing all around us," and simply let Congress deal with Roberts's fitness to serve.[98] Later she said she had

> more respect for the Mormon polygamist who follows the … teachings instilled into his very being, and all the traditions of his religious sect by marrying plural wives and openly supporting them and their children, than I have for the man who … gives his name and his support to one woman openly, while secretly desecrating their lives by living with other women. … By so doing he commits a crime not only against his lawful wife, but against the other women with whom he sins.

She called upon women to "require the same moral purity in men that men require in women," and if they did "society would soon undergo a revolution, a purification." Such a move, she said, would be "the surest blow aimed at polygamy," and nothing but "high moral teaching and its enforcement by our womanhood" will blot out both "polygamy in Utah and licentiousness in the East." The more Anthony tried to clarify her views, the less she seemed to be in sympathy with the growing movement opposing Roberts. Many papers agreed with Anthony's thoughts, including the *Sacramento Bee,* which observed that there were "many blacker stains on the United States than Mormonism." They pointed the finger east: "The Sodom of the United Sates is not Salt Lake, but rather New York." There, US citizens could find "wealthy society queens … who have shamelessly lived in adultery, and after they have been exposed have boldly wedded their paramours with the willing aid of ministers of a churches which professes to follow in the path blazed by Christ."[99]

By this time, the efforts to defeat Roberts had attracted the attention of William Randolph Hearst, the muckraking editor of the *New York Journal*[100] who created the National Anti-Polygamy League[101] to co-ordinate the anti-Roberts campaign.[102] It gained a membership

98. Harper, *Life and Work of Susan B. Anthony*, 3:1151–52.

99. As quoted in "The Sodom of the Country," *Deseret News*, Oct. 19, 1899, 4.

100. Moyer, "Dancing with the Devil," 84.

101. In April, the *San Diego Union* noted that Grace J. Cutler had contacted the paper to update its readers on the league's various and extensive activities. In response the paper noted that "decent people will of course hope that the house of representatives will have sufficient respect for itself to exclude the objectionable Mr. Roberts. At the same time the suggestion may be made that the best cause may sometimes be defeated by over zeal."

102. See "The Anti-Polygamy League," *Cambridge Tribune*, Jan. 21, 1899, 4.

of more than two thousand individuals, including religious figures, academics, and politicians. Beginning in December 1899, the Hearst paper featured a daily attack on Roberts. As Ben Proctor, Hearst's biographer, has written, because "circulation was all-important," the pages of the *Journal* sought to "entertain readers with intrigue and scandal," and, to many, the "titillating and ... outrageous story" about Roberts seemed perfect. The *Journal's* editors sent reporters throughout the country to interview and collect data, and dispatched Winifred Black to Utah to interview Roberts and his wives.[103]

James S. Clarkson, an important figure in Republican politics, business, and journalism, told Apostle John Henry Smith that the motivation for Hearst's effort was as much for money as morals. He reported that Philadelphia department store owner John Wanamaker had "made a bargain with the *Journal* to give it double the advertising that he gave to any other New York paper if it would [lead] the fight against Roberts." He was motivated to do this because there were "thousands of rich women in Philadelphia and New York" who would support Wanamaker's store while simultaneously opposing Roberts and the Mormon Church.[104]

The *Journal* asserted that President McKinley had "expressed his horror" at the possibility of a polygamist serving in Congress and was "preparing to defeat what he considers a desecration of the American home and an insult to American womanhood." As Jonathan Moyer reported, all of the members "of McKinley's church in Canton, Ohio, had signed the petition; surely a message to the president and the nation."[105] Hurst's *Journal* further contended that Congress "can refuse to seat any member for any reason" with a two-thirds vote. If they allowed this "brazen violator" to take his seat, "the responsibility" will be "theirs alone." Nevertheless, the paper called for a constitutional amendment outlawing polygamy, "intrusting

103. Proctor, *William Randolph Hearst*, 143–45. As part of the coverage, Black wrote a profile of Helen Gould whom she described as "simply an every day, matter-of-course, American woman" who was "trying to use the fortune her father left her to help." See Winifred Black, "Helen Gould: The Real American Girl," *New York Journal*, Dec. 4, 1898, 31.

104. Clarkson to John Henry Smith, Feb. 1, 1900, box 9, fd. 10, Smith Family Papers. Clarkson told Smith that Wanamaker "was among the first "to arouse the religious fanatics" to "begin the crusade" against Roberts and Mormonism. Clarkson also suggests that it had been Wanamaker's idea to enlist Helen Gould "to give the money to lead the crusade."

105. Moyer, "Dancing with the Devil," 205.

the work of 'suppressing' it to the Federal Courts."[106] The paper also featured a cartoon showing Roberts and three wives along with a Middle Eastern sultan in a fez, titled, "Is Constantinople moving to Washington?" with the caption, "Turkey is used to a polygamous lawmaker, but America doesn't like the innovation."[107]

By fall 1899, the press was reporting that it was likely Roberts would be sworn in, but there was no doubt his seating would be contested. Roberts left Utah on the evening of September 26 "to be gone a month or six weeks on business of a private nature."[108] The paper reported that Roberts planned to visit Chicago initially then go to Philadelphia, Boston, and New York prior to his arrival in Washington, where he "expects to find time to study some of the issues of the day and to inquire into some matters affecting his seat in congress." Roberts reportedly hoped then to return to Salt Lake prior to the city's municipal campaign, and return to Washington for the opening of congress. In his absence, "his private secretary George E. Hill, will be in communication with him."[109]

During this trip, Roberts said he was pursuing "purely private business," but press reports suggested that Roberts had left without advising his wives or closest political supporters of his whereabouts because he feared legal action against him.[110] The *Denver News* wrote that Roberts was "planning to secure some of the services of some of the greatest lawyers in the country to aid him in his fight for his seat in Congress." The paper reported "that Mr. Roberts is not of the same mind as he was early in the fight, when he announced that he would not bother about the matter at all, but would leave it entirely in the hands of his supporters in Utah."[111] When Roberts arrived in New York City, he soon faced "a veritable flood" of reporters. Edward H. Snow said that while most of the accounts were "lurid," the Brooklyn papers published some "very

106. "Let the Constitution Forbid Polygamy," *New York Journal,* Dec. 23, 1899, 6.

107. *New York Journal,* Dec. 23, 1899.

108. Roberts had spoken that afternoon at the Centerville Ward's meetings. See "Centerville Chats," *Davis County Clipper*, Sep. 29, 1899, 1.

109. "Mr. Roberts's Eastern Trip," *Salt Lake Herald*, Sep. 27, 1899, 5.

110. See "News of the Week," *Truth Seeker*, Oct. 21, 1899, 672.

111. As quoted in "Roberts Seeks Legal Help," *Salt Lake Tribune*, Oct. 18, 1899, 8.

fair articles." John M. Whitaker called Roberts "the most talked on man in the United States."[112]

One of Roberts's most important efforts to defend himself is an article he wrote for the *New York Times* in November 1899.[113] In addition to responding to the most frequent charges against him, he asserted that it was "extremely doubtful" that the House of Representatives had the power to either prevent a duly elected member from being seated or, once admitted, be expelled, especially since there had not been any charges of fraud in the election itself, nor had any challenge come from the opposing candidate. Though the precedents of the House were not "altogether harmonious on the subject of expulsion of members," the body had never expelled a member for "an alleged defect of moral character." As a result, he argued, the House risked the possibility of proceeding in a manner "utterly without precedent." While he realized the Constitution gave "each house" the power to determine its rules, he said the language of the document stated that the body could "punish its members for disorderly behavior." In his own case, he argued that disorderly behavior could not constitute "an alleged misdemeanor, which, if committed at all, was committed before the said member's election, was well known to his constituents, was charged against him during the campaign in which he was elected, and punishable under the laws of the State from which he comes." Continuing that many of those who were working against him were being "misled," he endeavored to take on some false assertions point by point.[114]

In the first place, he asserted, "no compact exists between the Mormon Church and the Government of the United States on the subject of polygamy." The only demand Congress put on Utah's Constitutional Convention was that "polygamous or plural marriages [were] forever prohibited," and the delegates responded by adopting that very language. Most importantly, he noted, the enabling act paving the way to statehood did not call for the dissolution of "existing"

112. Whitaker Diary, 494–96.

113. Brigham H. Roberts, "The Roberts Case in Congress," *New York Times*, Nov. 19, 1899, 23. At times Roberts's defense is written in the third person and at other times in first person. Moreover, it is written in the style of a legal brief. This account was picked up in both the *Deseret News* and *Salt Lake Tribune* as well. Hereafter cited at "Roberts Case."

114. "Roberts Case."

marital relationships, only prohibiting such marriages in the future. That, he stated, constituted the compact between "the United States and the people of Utah." That "compact has been kept on the part of the people of Utah. The people of my state are not covenant breakers, as her enemies charge." He wanted it clearly understood that there was "no attempt made to repeal or annul the parts of the Constitution prohibiting polygamous or plural marriages."[115]

Second, Roberts took on the repeated claim that he was "nominated and elected" by church influence. Such charges were false because the convention that nominated him was "conducted under the regulations usually governing such bodies," and the delegates included both Mormons and gentiles. While the church itself had nothing to do with the process, it was true that "Mormon Democratic friends" had worked for his nomination, while Mormon Republicans—many of whom were "high in the councils of the church"—had just as "earnestly sought by every honorable means in their power" to secure his defeat. He had carried "every non-Mormon stronghold in the State," while losing many "almost exclusively Mormon settlements" because the residents were predominately Republican. Thus, it was "not true that he was either nominated or elected by Mormon church influence."

Next, Roberts turned to the charges that he was "elected to crowd polygamy down the throats of the American Congress and people" to fulfill a prediction of Brigham Young. He wrote that as someone quite familiar with "all that Brigham Young ever said or wrote that is on record," he had never heard of such a prophecy either from Young or any of his contemporaries. Besides, such a charge made no sense. If a Socialist was elected from some district, he asked rhetorically, would the American Congress as a result endorse Socialism?

Finally, Roberts addressed the claim that Mormons, by discussing polygamy, were advocating polygamy, and as such were threatening the American home. Such charges undermined the constitutional freedoms of speech, he commented, and while that may have been acceptable in the decades between the "ninth and thirteenth" centuries, it most certainly does "not belong to the close of the nineteenth century."[116]

115. "Roberts Case."
116. "Roberts Case."

Roberts echoed others who said that the real danger to the American home "does not lurk in the sun-blessed valleys of Utah, filled with farming villages, where domestic peace and happiness rise every day to greet the morn and crown the hours with quiet joy." Loyal husbands and fathers who happened to be polygamists were not a danger. Rather, "within any thousand feet square [of New York City] may be found more that menaces the American home than ever existed, or I hope ever will exist in the State of Utah."[117]

In early November, Roberts wrote to Davis County Attorney William H. Streeper "in an effort to set at rest the rumors" then circulating in some New York papers that he was in the East "avoiding arrest."[118] Roberts was no doubt referring to the efforts of Charles Mostyn Owen, who in Senate testimony a few years later, said that in 1899 he went before County Attorney Streeper and "laid out an … affidavit … alleging that B. H. Roberts was guilty of adultery and also unlawful cohabitation." Owen's charges were based on the birth of the twins to Celia Dibble in 1897. He said that Streeper kept putting him off, and that after submitting several more affidavits "of a similar character [Streeper] absolutely failed to do anything." Owen also testified that he had brought similar charges to the Salt Lake County Attorney alleging that "Margaret C. Roberts was the plural wife" of Roberts "and that he was "unlawfully cohabiting with her." Owen said that after "great difficulty" was a warrant issued which led to legal action against Roberts a year later.[119]

Roberts assured Streeper that if he found it "necessary in order to discharge your official duties" to issue an arrest warrant, he would return to Utah at once.[120] He told the attorney that because his "home and fortune are permanently in Utah, there is no fear of my fleeing from justice, and no necessity for Utah officers of the law to get out extradition papers." In mid-November, a warrant was issued by Judge

117. "Roberts Case."

118. In his autobiography, Roberts noted that the Hearst papers "in New York and throughout the country thought it necessary to make special warfare upon me, and because I went east a few weeks before the assembling of Congress and resided in New York, they heralded me each day with special articles in their leading papers denouncing me as a fugitive from justice." See Roberts, *Autobiography*, 212.

119. See US Senate, Committee on Elections and Privileges, *Proceedings before the Committee*, 2:404, 412–13.

120. "Roberts Will Return," *Salt Lake Herald*, Nov. 3, 1899, 8.

Kroeger based on a "complaint of Charles M. Owen," charging Roberts with unlawful cohabitation with Louisa and Margaret during the period from June 1897 through July 1899. Owen said he would wait "until congress was about to convene" before deciding what action to recommend.[121] Roberts's secretary, George E. Hill, suggested his opponents had purposely brought these charges at a time when they knew full well that Roberts was out of town. County Attorney Graham F. Putnam admitted that Roberts could not be extradited on the charge.[122]

Roberts wrote his mother a letter from New York, labeling the attacks against him as "stage thunder." While his opponents "make considerable noise they will not be able to do much. This isn't much of a storm after all." He imputed their actions to the efforts of the devil whom he says is "always more noisy than dangerous."[123]

The storm would be much bigger than he thought.

---

121. "Warrant Is Out for B. H. Roberts," *Salt Lake Herald*, Nov. 12, 1899, 1; and "Warrant for Roberts," *Salt Lake Tribune*, Nov. 11, 1899, 8.

122. "Warrant Is Out for B. H. Roberts."

123. Roberts to My Dear Mother, Oct. 26, 1899, box 4, fd. 1, Roberts Papers (UU).

THIRTEEN

THE CONGRESSIONAL STORM

Roberts arrived in Washington on November 23, 1899, where he told a *Deseret News* reporter that he was not aware of any congressional challenge to him from being seated. Indeed, Representative George W. Comer of Indiana said that once the "fan fare" was over, Roberts would likely be seated because congressional Democrats would "never permit a free silver, anti-expansionist Democrat to be ousted."[1] However, the *Chicago Tribune* reported that "certain Republican leaders" had suggested that Roberts "could not hope to have a pleasant or very useful career as a public man in Washington. He would be ostracized socially and politically." He should be "allowed to take the oath, thus saving his personal rights and dignity, and then he should resign and permit" Utahns to send to Congress "a more acceptable man."[2]

Several other papers were reporting that "pressure was being brought to bear" by church leaders on Roberts to resign, fearing that his expulsion could "put the Mormon faith back at least a half century." Mormon leaders, the accounts stated, "are said to be ready to sacrifice Roberts."[3]

In early December, the *New York Journal* reported that former House Speaker and Treasury Secretary John G. Carlisle[4] was on his way to Washington in a "special car" to deliver petitions collected from the paper's campaign. It also noted that 22,000 members of the

1. As quoted in Haynes, "B. H. Roberts," 27–28.

2. As quoted in "To Step Out," *Salt Lake Tribune*, Nov. 11, 1899,1.

3. See "Want B. H. Roberts to Resign," *Arizona Daily Star*, Oct. 27, 1899, 1.

4. Carlisle (1834–1910) was a conservative Democrat from Kentucky who was active in state politics. He served as Speaker from 1883 to 1889; US senator, 1890–93; and secretary of the treasury, 1893–97. No friend of the Mormons, he would serve as counsel for those seeking to remove Reed Smoot from the Senate.

International Order of Good Templars had sent a communication "emphatically" protesting Roberts's seating. It also reported that the Arena Club of New Orleans[5] was sending "several thousand" signatures, and that the National Christian League for the Promotion of Social Purity[6] had pledged in excess of 13,000 signatures.[7] The next day, the paper proclaimed in bold headlines that "Many Millions Endorse the Journal's Fight Against Roberts."[8]

Roberts's antagonist Helen Gould donated a large collection of materials on Mormonism to the New York Public Library. Known as the Berrian Collection, it consisted of nearly five hundred volumes and pamphlets, including many rare early Mormon imprints, newspapers, and scrapbooks. Gould told the press she had decided to take this action because "people generally should become better informed on the subject of Mormonism in order to be on the guard against the Latter Day Saints."[9] But Roberts was not worried. He wrote to his mother that he had some "friends" in Washington when the "hour of trial comes," and assured her that "win or lose, I shall be alright still—and, by the way I am going to WIN!"[10]

Newspapers, as they had done for the past year, continued to

5. Organized in 1892, the club sought to "promote the cooperation of the sexes on lines of social and intellectual culture," and was dedicated to take "such private or public action as shall serve the interests" of both women and men. See Croly, *History of the Woman's Club*, 518–19.

6. Organized in 1886, and chartered by a special act of Congress in 1899, the league was headquartered in New York City and open to membership from any "Christian believer." According to its constitution, its goal was to "strive to elevate public opinion respecting the nature and claims of morality, with its equal obligation upon men and women, and to ... enlist and organize ... Christians in preventive, educational, reformatory, and legislative work in the interest of social purity." See Bliss, *Encyclopedia of Social Reform*, 914.

7. "Carlisle for Journal, Fights Roberts's Seating," *New York Journal*, Dec. 1, 1899, 4.

8. "Many Millions Endorse the Journal's Fight Against Roberts," *New York Journal*, Dec. 2, 1899, 1.

9. "Miss Gould Makes Gift to Library," *New York Journal*, Jan. 11, 1900, 1. The collection had been accumulated by Charles L. Woodward, a New York bookseller, and subsequently acquired by New York City merchant William Berrian. The *New York Times* called the collection "an important addition to the resources which that library can offer to the student of human errors." And, after lauding Gould's philanthropy, the paper editorialized that Gould's decision to "place this collection where it will become most accessible to scholars and students was a very wise one. Her choice of the New York Public Library was clearly the best that she could have made." See "Miss Gould's Gift to the Public Library," *New York Times*, Jan. 13, 1900, 22.

10. Roberts to "My Dear Mother," Dec. 1, 1899, box 3, fd. 13, Roberts Papers (UU). Interestingly, the letter is typed on House of Representatives letterhead.

publish signed and unsigned editorials both for and against Roberts. Nearly all for Roberts took pains to insist they did not approve of polygamy, but rather objected to the rank hypocrisy they smelled on adulterous politicians. Others continued to focus on constitutional questions and individual rights. The *Intermountain Catholic* published thoughts from Rt. Rev. Thomas H. Malone, of Denver, who said that "opposition to Roberts as far as we have been able to observe is not based on legal grounds" but rather on "antipathy" to his religious practices. Asserting that clearly Roberts met every constitutional requirement to his congressional seat, Malone concluded that "it matters not what the teachings and practices of the Mormon Church may be, the Constitution of the United States has affirmed that such practices shall not be made a test of eligibility of those who practice and profess them. This is the Roberts case as it stands stripped of all sentiment, hysteria and gush. If the religious test is to be applied to Roberts to whom will it be applied next?[11]

The *American Sentinel*, edited by Ellen G. White, and the official organ of the Seventh Day Adventist church, compared the crusade against polygamy to contemporary agitation "by thoughtful men in the Church and in the state" opposing "widespread" divorce. Because there was a "general moral" climate that allowed increasing divorce, how could that same popular opinion "be expected to be seriously concerned" over the spread "of what may be termed consecutive polygamy … which is unattended by divorce court scandals?"[12]

Corinne Stubbs Brown, a nationally known feminist who was the sister of Ogden activist Kate S. Hilliard, refused to support the petition against the seating of Roberts, attacking it as "sentimental twaddle." She asserted that "Congressman-elect Roberts supports his wives; he gives his children a name. There is a greater evil than this among our congressmen today. … There will be in Washington men who will fear Roberts for he is fearless and he has brains."[13]

George E. MacDonald, editor of the *Truth Seeker*, facetiously

11. Rt. Rev. Thomas H. Malone, "An Individual Opinion of the Legal Status of the Roberts Case," *Intermountain Catholic*, Dec. 9, 1899, 4.

12. "A National Anti-Polygamy Crusade," *American Sentinel*, Oct. 19, 1899, 643–44.

13. "Calls the Petition Twaddle," *New York Times*, Oct. 31, 1899. See also "Sister of Mrs. Kate Hilliard Dies in New York," *Ogden Standard*, Mar. 16, 1914, 8. Interestingly, Brown's remarks were also reprinted in the *Latter-Day Saint Southern Star*, Nov. 25, 1899, 416.

claimed that a resolution had been introduced into Congress calling for Roberts's expulsion and asked that any member "who had been faithful to three women or less cast the first vote in the affirmative," and that the chaplain "be allowed to come in on this deal." Macdonald claimed that as the chaplain and the members exited the chamber, "the gentleman from Utah made the point that there was no quorum."[14] A reader of the *Truth Seeker* from Nebraska shared a similar view. In a letter to the editor, he said that while he did "not approve of polygamy," he was more inclined to view with favor a man like Roberts who supported his wives "in season and out of season" than "the silk stocking Eastern congressman" A. Shaw with "his diamond bedecked mistress" who casts off the old wife "for a new one and never cares to what depths the old one sinks."[15]

Charles Ellis,[16] a non-Mormon Salt Lake City resident, wrote that the anti-Roberts crusade came from Evangelical churches because they sought "to save themselves against a more enticing faith than their own." Mormonism was running smoothly and growing fast without brimstone. Ellis believed that "if polygamy were permitted to die a natural death" then Evangelicals would not have a convenient foil in their quest for converts. The problem was not polygamy, Ellis wrote, "but envy and jealousy." The LDS Church had progressed much in the last half century. "Its missionaries are well dressed, and as a rule, fairly well educated. They are making converts fast. They stand upon the Bible and preach primitive Christianity as found in the New Testament." It was all of this that scared Evangelical churches, especially since Mormons no longer "preach nor practice polygamy at home or abroad. Right or wrong, they are creating a current that runs to the Mormon church with increasing volume and velocity."

The *Afro-American Advance* of Minneapolis, editorialized that the individuals in Washington who opposed seating Roberts "are

14. See "News of the Week," *Truth Seeker*, Nov. 18, 1899, 729.

15. Wm H. Crane, "Letter to the Editor," *Truth Seeker*, Apr. 21, 1900, 249.

16. Ellis (1839–1904) came to Utah in 1889. He was a writer and frequent lecturer in Salt Lake City, where he was known as a fair critic of Mormonism. Ellis was killed in an accidental fire, and even though he was a gentile, several Mormons, including Orson F. Whitney and George Albert Smith, spoke at his funeral. See "Charles Ellis Burned to Death," *Deseret Evening News*, Dec. 28, 1904, 10.

evidently without sin. It is better to be lawfully married to a dozen women than to secretly violate the much abused law—'Thou shalt not commit adultery.'"[17] A similar view came from the *Broad Ax*, "There are many greater criminals and scoundrels in the halls of congress than Brigham H. Roberts, and for one we would like to see him succeed in winning his fight."[18]

Finally there were the views of liberal thinker Moncure D. Conway who was then living in Paris. From that distance he felt a duty to warn Freethinkers who "are trying to deprive polygamists of their political rights that they are hounding on a mob of pious lynchers. … Polygamy is odious to Freethinkers, but Freethought is equally odious to the orthodox millions." Liberty, wrote Conway, "can be justly forfeited only by crime, not by immorality." No matter how despicable one might find polygamy, men were entitled to immorality. Bigamy was illegal because of deception against a second wife who might not know that a first wife exists. No law can exist "against immorality per se in states of social civilization."[19] Such diverse voices of support, however, were in a distinct minority.

House Republicans met informally on December 1 behind closed doors, and "after three hours of discussion" decided that Roberts "should not be sworn in or permitted to take a seat." The *New York Journal* said Rep. Robert Tayler (R-Ohio) was given the assignment to "spearhead the efforts" against Roberts.[20] The full House met on December 4, 1899, Roberts entering about 11:30 a.m. and immediately becoming "the cynosure of all eyes. He moved around the throng on the floor rather aimlessly. Just before the House convened he took the seat he had selected the previous day on the extreme right of the Democratic side in what is known as the 'Cherokee Strip.'"[21] The *New York Journal* reported that Roberts was busy all day "endeavoring to get united Democratic support, but … the Democrats will not act as a party."[22] A day later, the paper called Roberts a "burly

17. [Untitled], *Afro-American Advance*, Dec. 16, 1899, 2.

18. "Chips," *Broad Ax*, Dec. 16, 1899, 1.

19. As quoted in Macdonald, *Fifty Years of Freethought*, 189–90.

20. "House Republicans Decide to Hold Up Seating of Roberts," *New York Journal*, Dec. 2, 1899, 1.

21. "Roberts Fate in Committee Hands," *New York Times*, Dec. 6, 1899, 1.

22. "Journal's Petitions Will Rest Before the Speakers Bench," *New York Journal*, Dec. 4, 1899, 1. See also "Speaker Orders Roberts to Step Aside," *New York Journal*, Dec. 5,

and defiant man" who stood "truculently at ... the well of the House" before moving "to the rear of the chambers, unabashed with a touch of insolence in his demeanor."[23] According to *The Independent*,

> It was when the words, "Utah, Brigham H. Roberts," were called out by the Clerk that ears and eyes were strained from the galleries and the House became absolutely still. ... A criminal or a martyr will always attract attention, and in the opinion of nearly every one in the hall Mr. Roberts was neither one of them. I do not remember to have ever seen so large a proportion of ladies present. There was too, a goodly sprinkling of clergymen. ... Mr. Roberts had made his bed and must lie in it. Whether he shall have a seat and can sit in it depends upon whether he can prove he is not a polygamist. It is not alone Mr. Roberts, it is the State of Utah which is on trial.[24]

When Roberts's name was called by the clerk, Robert Tayler rose and introduced the mountain of petitions gathered throughout the nation that lay at the podium into the *Congressional Record*.[25] With obvious pride, the *New York Journal* commented that "nothing but a great moral impulse surging through the whole people could produce such results," and that the seven million petitions was double the standing armies of Europe and as many as the votes received by McKinley in 1896."[26] Tayler recommended that the matter be referred to a special committee of nine members. In the interim, he stated, it was his view that Roberts should not be "sworn in or permitted to occupy a seat."[27]

1899, 2. The paper said that Roberts would find no support among Southern representatives who were "arrayed against him as a solid phalanx" because of the "sad fate of the poor girls of the Southern states who have been induced to Utah by the hundreds since the war." The paper also raised the massacre of the Mormon missionaries at Cane Creek who "had been killed for leading women away from the home," forcing Roberts to "escape death at the hands of enraged Southerners" when he recovered their bodies.

23. "First Victory Won for American Womanhood," *New York Journal*, Dec. 5, 1899, 1. The paper said that some twenty thousand persons had tried to gain admission and those who had secured tickets "witnessed a remarkable scene."

24. "Our Washington Letter: Speaker Henderson and Mr. Roberts," *The Independent*, Dec. 10, 1899, 3356–58.

25. Moyer, "Dancing with the Devil," 207.

26. "Editorial," *New York Journal*, Dec. 4, 1899, 6. The paper was wrong on both counts: over seven million Americans had voted for McKinley and best estimates suggest European armies accounted for more than eight million.

27. US Congress, *Congressional Record*, 55th Cong., 1st sess., Dec. 4, 1899, 5. Hereafter cited as *Congressional Record*. While this was taking place, the New York City chapter

Democrats joined the protest as well. Rep. Thomas McRae (D-Arkansas) seconded Tayler's motion and called Roberts's election "an assault upon the American home, an effort to degrade American womanhood [which] would destroy the scared marriage system [uniting] one man to one woman."[28] McRae's remarks were met with applause. The vote on Tayler's resolution was postponed until the next day.[29] In the interim the *New York Journal* kept up the attack, saying that a poll of the House found no one willing to support the Utahn and proclaiming that the fight against Roberts was "manifestly won," that he was "doomed" because he was "an unrepentant, defiant criminal ... unfit to sit in the Congress."[30]

The next day, Tayler introduced the text of the proclamations of amnesty issued by Presidents Benjamin Harrison and Grover Cleveland pardoning those who had abstained from unlawful cohabitation since November 1, 1890, on the condition that they shall observe the laws of the United States henceforth (which Cleveland extended to January 4, 1893). Tayler's resolution also included the language of section eight of the Edmunds Act which stated that "no polygamist, bigamist or any person cohabiting with more than one woman, and no woman cohabiting shall be entitled to vote or eligible for appointment or election."[31]

Tayler stated that Roberts was convicted in February 1887 for unlawful cohabitation and pleaded guilty to that charge on April 29, 1889, whereupon he was sentenced to a term in the territorial penitentiary. Since Roberts had continued to live in polygamy, Tayler charged, he was not covered by either the Harrison or the Cleveland pardon. He asserted that Congress had the right to declare a member ineligible if it believed that a person was guilty of "crimes or offenses against civilization" and then recited a long list of times when Congress had denied seats to various people for various offenses. He told

of the Daughters of the American Revolution passed a resolution calling on members to preserve the "honor and integrity" of the House, and seek to "enact laws which shall prevent a polygamist from that body." See "New York City Chapter of D.A.R. to Oppose Roberts," *New York Journal*, Dec. 3, 1899, 45.

28. *Congressional Record*, Dec. 4, 1899, 5.

29. *Congressional Record*, 6.

30. "Journal Poll of the House Shows Roberts Doomed," *New York Journal*, Dec. 5, 1899, 2; and "Speakers Orders Roberts to Step Aside," *New York Journal*, Dec. 5, 1899, 2.

31. *Congressional Record*, Dec. 5, 1899, 39.

his colleagues, "What we do here we do before the open and gazing eyes of all the world, and we are at once dragged to the bar of history for our deeds.[32]

Roberts was nominally represented by Tennessee Democrat James Richardson, who introduced Roberts's certificate of election and said Roberts's "credentials are in due form" and come "with the same evidence of his right to a seat" as anyone else. Richardson also criticized Tayler's suggestion that Roberts was neither a naturalized American citizen nor a citizen of Utah—"he is in every respect eligible and he has complied with every constitutional requirement.[33] Richardson was hardly supportive of Roberts. He told his House colleagues that he was simply arguing the right of Roberts to be seated and sworn in to the House, but that if Roberts were "guilty of the offences charged against him he should not be allowed to retain his seat." Ironically, he quoted Senator George Edmunds, whose name adorned two anti-polygamy acts and who argued that the Constitution proscribes the necessary qualification to be a member of the House, and that body had no constitutional right to add others. Once someone is seated, however, the Constitution had provisions for the House to use against a member whom the House believed "ought not to continue therein."

At that point, Roberts rose and addressed his colleagues, proclaiming, "Under the shadow of the Constitution of the United States, I demand, both for myself and the people of my state, the protection that is due us." He then read from McCrary's *Laws of Elections*, which warned that an "evil disposed person" might use a challenge such as the one before the House as a way of "voiding the election results." He said there was no evidence of any criminal charge since the presidential amnesties, therefore, he was not guilty of any offense "that disqualifies me for the office to which I was elected." He also called the petitions into question, citing Grace J. Cutler, secretary of the National Anti-Polygamy League, who suggested that people seek the signatures of young people and

32. *Congressional Record*, 43.

33. *Congressional Record*, 43. A copy of the original certificate is found in Roberts Papers, box 2, fd. 15 (UU).

encouraged people to sign more than once. Roberts also offered evidence of his naturalization as a citizen.[34]

Roberts went on to quote at length from a letter from Robert N. Baskin which stated that Mormon polygamists "continue to hold important office under the appointment of McKinley. Yet, not a single word of objection to their continuance in office is heard from the Republican politicians who in this state are the most active in the effort to array public sentiment throughout the nation against seating Mr. Roberts."[35] Baskin specifically pointed to John G. Graham, who served as Provo postmaster, and to Orson Smith, who was postmaster of Logan. Baskin's strategy may have backfired; Graham's case came to the attention of President McKinley, who said he would not have appointed him had he been aware of the charges.[36]

Roberts finally stepped aside but indicated that he did not waive any of his rights[37] The *Congressional Record* shows that a vigorous debate ensued.[38] After several unsuccessful substitute amendments were offered, the House passed Tayler's resolution 304 yea, 32 nay and 18 not voting or abstaining.[39] Only one Republican, California Rep. Eugene Loud, opposed the resolution.[40] The House adjourned

34. *Congressional Record*, Dec. 5, 1899, 47. The original is found in Roberts Papers, box 2, fd. 13 (UU).

35. *Congressional Record*, 48–49.

36. See "McKinley Joins Journal Anti-Polygamy Crusade," *New York Journal*, Dec. 15, 1899, 1; "Journal Files on Roberts Consulted by the President," Dec. 15, 1899, 3; "McKinley Has Evidence Against Three Polygamists," Dec. 18, 1899, 4; and "President Gets Report on Alleged Polygamists," Dec. 19, 1899, 8.

37. *Congressional Record*, Dec. 4, 1899, 5. See also "Mr. Roberts Speaks In His Own Behalf," *Salt Lake Herald*, Jan. 6, 1900, 1; and "B. H. Roberts to the Committee," *Deseret Evening News*, Jan. 5, 1900, 1.

38. One of the most interesting attacks came from fellow Democrat John F. "Honey Fitz" Fitzgerald, grandfather and namesake of future US President John Fitzgerald Kennedy. The Massachusetts representative, who himself would later be removed from Congress, stated that Roberts's "criminal actions," not his religion, was the issue. Yet Fitzgerald also attacked the church's missionary system, saying it was a threat to liberty. *Congressional Record*, Dec. 5, 1899, 50.

39. Among those not voting was Idaho's at-large Representative Edgar Wilson, a Silver Republican, while Nevada's at-large Democratic Representative Francis Newland voted against the Tayler Resolution. Wilson had a large Mormon population in the state, and he sought not to alienate them with his vote. Wilson informed critics of his position that he believed the Richardson Resolution represented the "only proper, legal and constitutional method" for dealing with Roberts. See Edgar Wilson to "My Dear Sir," Feb. 1, 1899, box 2, fd. 3, DuBois Papers.

40. See "Roberts Fate in Committee's Hands."

after naming the members of the select committee, which consisted of nine members—six Republicans and three Democrats. The Republicans were Robert Tayler, who served as chair; Charles Landis, Indiana; Robert Morris, Minnesota; R. H. Freer, West Virginia; Smith McPherson, Iowa; and Charles Littlefield, Maine. The Democrats were David De Armond, Missouri; Samuel Lanham, Texas; and Robert Miers, Indiana.[41] That same evening, in celebratory fashion, Helen Gould attended a mass meeting in Tarrytown, New York, where she was lauded for her leadership in the fight against Roberts.[42]

Roberts responded to the committee, asserting that he was the victim of "sectarian hate" because he was a member "of an unpopular church." Benjamin T. Lloyd, a Salt Lake City investor in stocks, bonds, and mines, telegraphed him words of "congratulations on your peerless stand for constitutional liberty. ... The American people will never allow the fundamental pillars of their government to be torn down. The right of representation is inherent."[43]

As usual, Roberts's rhetoric was excellent, but he was not prepared for the halls of Congress. Congressional debate is governed by tradition, and deference to rules and courtesy is paramount. Roberts, as one historian has written, repeatedly "offended his colleagues by refusing to yield" his time to allow others to speak.[44] On the other hand, the *Boston Globe* noted that even those who opposed Roberts "most warmly" must admit that he is a "plucky and persistent fighter."[45]

On December 13, the committee met to hear witnesses. Roberts sat at the foot of the committee table and was joined by "the Rev. Dr. [Thomas] Iliff, Mr. [A. Theodore] Schroeder[46] and others—here to direct the case against Roberts." Iliff had run in to Roberts while

---

41. For a useful summary of the background of the members of the committee, see Moyer, "Dancing with the Devil," 212–13. At the same time, John G. Day of Malvern, Iowa, wrote to Roberts that in November 1899 McPherson had "publically declared himself in favor of unseating you," and that had he promised to do all in his power to stop the Utahn. See Day to Roberts, Dec. 9, 1899, fd. 684, Roberts Collection. Day's relationship to Roberts is unclear.

42. "Anti-Roberts Mass Meeting," *New York Times*, Dec. 6, 1899, 2.

43. Lloyd to Roberts, Telegram, Dec. 8, 1899, fd. 684, Roberts Collection.

44. Moyer, "Dancing with the Devil," 210. See also "Roberts Argues His Case," *New York Times*, Jan. 6, 1900.

45. As quoted in (Cleveland) *Plain Dealer*, Dec. 11, 1899, 4.

46. "Roberts Asks Open Hearings," *New York Times* Dec. 9, 1899, 3.

doing ecclesiastical work in Utah and had pledged that if Roberts "attempts to enter the halls of congress I will be heard in every state of the Union."[47] Schroeder, whose role in the proceedings was to "examine witnesses," was eventually paid $1,000 by Josiah Strong "in recognition for your essential services in the Roberts case."[48]

The first witness was Charles Mostyn Owen who told the committee that Dr. Margaret Shipp Roberts was listed in the Salt Lake City directories as "Dr. Margaret C. Roberts," and that the "general reputation" in Salt Lake was that Margaret and B. H. "maintained the relationship of husband and wife."[49] During Roberts's cross-examination, he got Owen to admit that his accusations were not based on personal knowledge, but Roberts failed to have Owen's testimony stricken from the record.

US Army Captain Elias H Parsons testified that during an 1896 stay in Salt Lake City someone had asked him to call Dr. Shipp's residence, and a man answered who identified himself as B. H. Roberts. Roberts indicated he would seek to have Parsons's testimony stricken because it was "irrelevant."[50] The next witness, Arthur McEwen, a reporter for the *Philadelphia North American*, testified that in a recent interview Roberts had spoken of his "wives" and indicated that his obligations toward them had been "incurred prior to the enactment of the polygamy law."[51] Rev. Iliff testified that the "general reputation" in Utah was that Celia Dibble Roberts was the "plural wife of B. H. Roberts." The *Times* notes that in cross examination Roberts sought "to show that Dr. Iliff was hostile to the Mormons ... stating that his hostility was to the polygamous feature of Mormonism."

The final witness was Rev. George W. Martin, a Presbyterian minister then living in Manti, Utah. Martin testified as to the

47. Gillilan, *Thomas C. Iliff*, 67–68.

48. See Josiah Strong to Schroeder, Dec. 13, 15, 1899, and Feb. 15, 1900, Schroeder Collection. See also Brudnoy, "Of Saints and Sinners," 274–75.

49. "Roberts Again on Trial," *New York Times*, Dec. 14, 1899, 5.

50. "Roberts Again on Trial."

51. McEwen was no stranger to the Mormons or those who opposed them. In the 1870s, he had been a journalist on the staff of the Virginia City, Nevada, *Chronicle* where he was associated with C. C. Goodwin. See "Arthur McEwen," *New York Times*, May 2, 1907. See also Bloom, "Edwin A Van Valkenburg." Bloom notes that Mc Ewen had joined the *Philadelphia North American* in 1899 and brought a "West Coast breeziness" to the paper.

"polygamous status" of both Celia A. Dibble and Margaret Shipp Roberts, saying he had seen "statements to this effect in the Salt Lake City newspapers." The status of Roberts as a polygamist was "a matter of common repute" in Utah, as was the fact that "twins were born to Celia Dibble Roberts." In cross-examination, Martin admitted that his views were not based on personal knowledge but solely on statements in the press. With that, the committee adjourned.[52]

On December 19, several witnesses appeared before the committee to discuss Roberts's marital arrangements. The basic point was (1) to confirm his marriages to Louisa and Celia, (2) establish that he had children by these two women, and (3) to identify Margaret Shipp as someone Roberts referred to as his wife. The *Journal* reported "Roberts's defiant spirit weakened when he cast his eyes over the committee room and saw the witnesses ... who he has known personally for years."[53]

Dr. Luella Miles, a physician practicing in Salt Lake City, testified that on April 12, 1897, she had called on Shipp who instructed her to refer to her as "Dr. Roberts," indicating that she had been married to B. H. Roberts for seven years.[54] Rev. S. E. Wishard told the committee that in September 1897 he had met the couple in Manti, Utah, and that Roberts had introduced Shipp to him as "my wife, Mrs. Roberts." Similarly, Maria McDougall testified that on July 22, 1898, she had been on board a train with Roberts, who consistently referred to Margaret as either his wife or Mrs. Roberts.[55] Edwin McDaniel, a former colleague of Roberts at the *Herald*, testified that in 1896 Roberts had told him that he had "three families and was raising children by two of them."[56]

Finally, there was the testimony of Thomas J. Brandon who had known both Roberts and Louisa for more than twenty years. As postmaster, he had been asked by Celia to keep her mail separate

52. "Roberts Again on Trial."

53. "Roberts's Last Hope Gone; Adverse Report Certain," *New York Journal*, Dec. 20, 1899, 1.

54. "The Mormons Brood," *Altoona Mirror*, Dec. 20, 1899, 3.

55. "Said Roberts Drew a Salary," (Cleveland) *Plain Dealer*, Dec. 20, 1899, 2. See also *Boston Herald*, Dec. 20, 1899, 7, where Wishard noted that he had subsequently asked Shipp if the young lady accompanying Roberts to Washington "was her daughter and she answered in the negative."

56. "Roberts's Last Hope Gone."

from Louisa's. He also testified that he had gone to Luna's funeral and that her headstone identified her as the daughter of "B. H. And Celia Roberts."[57] Roberts cross-examined him and "tried to diminish" his strength as a government witness by getting him to admit that he had been "at school for considerable periods" and was thus not always present in the area, and that he had been "fined twice for minor assaults."[58] Concluding that the evidence in the case was already sufficiently strong, the committee decided not to hold additional hearings in Utah.

Though the committee did conduct rigorous hearings, their examination was completed so quickly that it seemed to have reached a conclusion at the beginning rather than the end of the deliberations.[59] But Roberts's performance in the committee was uneven as well. Throughout the proceedings, he did not introduce evidence and seemed to believe that deflecting the accusations would lead to sympathetic acceptance of his innocence. His cross-examination of some witnesses, for example, was odd. While he got them to admit that they had no direct evidence that he was a polygamist, Roberts himself had made his loyalty as a husband of plural wives a cornerstone of his public relations campaign the previous year. Instead of raising issues of constitutionality, his adherence to the law, and his rights under the presidential proclamations pardoning polygamists, Roberts responded evasively. What is more, he probably did not help his case by serving as his own counsel.[60]

Doubtless anticipating support from home during this time, Roberts found an editorial in the *Deseret News* disheartening. Titled "The Way to Do It," part of it focused on the polygamy issue explicitly and Roberts implicitly:

> The changed conditions in Utah and the peculiar situation in which a portion of its older citizens are placed—ought to be viewed with due regard to the best interests of the State, and with as little hardship as possible to the individuals who are the most directly affected by these circumstances. But the willful violation of existing laws must in the

57. "Roberts's Last Hope Gone."
58. "The Mormon Brood," (Cumberland, MD) *Evening Times*, Dec. 20, 1899, 1.
59. Moyer, "Dancing with the Devil," 214.
60. See Haynes, "B. H. Roberts," 37; and Moyer.

> nature of things bring trouble upon flagrant transgressors, and at least they will be placed at a great disadvantage. ... Good citizenship requires desire and intent to live within the laws and to yield some private interest for the public welfare.[61]

In a letter to *News* editor Charles W. Penrose, Roberts stated that when he saw the editorial it made him "sick from my head to my feet," and believed that the paper had "failed him." He called the editorial an "abject surrender to all the *[Salt Lake] Tribune* has stood for and is humiliation at the foot of an arrogant, insolent and contemptible foe." He asked Penrose, "Can it be that peace has become so dear to us that it is to be purchased at the price of laying down low in the dust at the feet of those whom we should, figuratively speaking, clutch by the throat and hurl out of our pathway." "I am going to win," Roberts wrote, "though everybody in Utah has given up the matter."[62]

At the same time, there was occasionally a moment of levity in the proceedings. On New Year's Day, 1900, the *Salt Lake Herald* ran a humorous feature supposedly capturing prominent Utahns' resolutions for the coming year. Two of them especially bear on the Roberts case, and give some sense of the level of frustration, and perhaps weariness, of the long dragged out episode. According to the paper, E. W. Wilson resolved the he would *not* put Roberts's name in nomination in the future "unless requested by the unified voice of Heber J. Grant and P. H. Lannan." At the same time, the *Herald* wryly commented that Utah's Republican secretary of state, James T. Hammond, whose office was in charge of elections in the state, had resolved that he would "not be withheld" from seeking Roberts's congressional seat at some future date, "providing of course, that I can present to Congress a certificate of election."[63]

As he awaited the committee's decision, Roberts wrote to his mother that he believed the "majority report ... will favor my being sworn in." He assumed that the report would be accepted and that there would

61. "The Way to Do It," *Deseret News*, Jan. 1, 1900, 5.

62. Roberts to Penrose, Jan. 9, 1900, Box 4, fd. 12, Kenney Collection.

63. "Make Good Resolves," *Salt Lake Herald*, Jan. 1, 1900, 8. Despite these "resolutions," machinations had already begun to find a replacement. See "Is Glassman a Candidate for Congress?," *Ogden Standard*, Jan. 1, 1900, 5.

not be the needed two-thirds vote to expel him. At the same time, he chided his "strange lot of relatives," who had not sent "one word of encouragement" during his hearings. Many Mormons had grown discomfited by the attention given to Roberts's quest for his seat.[64]

At the same time, Roberts's zeal was making it difficult for some to support his case. Among them was Representative Edgar Wilson of Idaho, who sought to avoid antagonizing local Mormons while not alienating others in the state who opposed Roberts. As he told Idaho senator Fred T. DuBois, "I have had several talks with Roberts since you left here. He has, as you know, made it very hard for those who are disposed to support him and his position." Roberts may not have realized that some shrewd politicking might have won him supporters. Wilson continued, "I have not fully made up my mind, and am anxious to see and read the report of the Committee. I tried very hard to get Roberts to make a clear statement of his case on the merits."[65]

LDS Church leaders were becoming increasingly apprehensive about how the fight against Roberts would affect the church. On December 13, Seymour B. Young met with Lorenzo Snow and "entered ... into a most confidential conversation regarding Bro. Roberts & his going to Congress."[66] A meeting was held in the president's office on December 29, 1899, specifically to discuss possible efforts to "disenfranchise all the Mormons." Apostle Anthon H. Lund recorded that some believed "there is a plan on foot to take the franchise away from the Latter-day Saints for 30 years." Lund worried "that the Republicans feel that they have been deceived in thinking that we were inclined to that party and then turned Democrats."[67]

Clearly there was a sense that the Roberts episode had changed things dramatically. Young suggested that in the face of the Democratic dominance of the state politically at that time, Republicans might be placated if a Republican replaced Roberts and Heber Wells became senator. "Let these men go to Washington," George

64. B H Roberts to "My Dear Mother," January 11, 1900, Box 8, folder 13, Roberts Papers (UU).

65. Edgar Wilson to Fred T. DuBois, Jan. 11, 1900, box 2, fd. 2, DuBois Papers.

66. Seymour Young Journal, Dec. 13, 1899. Young asked Snow if the church could provide Roberts with $200 to defray his expenses. He reported that Snow concurred.

67. Lund, *Danish Apostle*, 63–64.

Q. Cannon argued, "and keep in touch with the party, and they could remove many prejudices and do us a world of good."[68]

William M. McCarty,[69] who was the federal judge in Utah's 6th judicial district, wrote to John Henry Smith that it was "now conceded by all parties that the present representative of this state will be denied his seat in Congress." McCarty told Smith he was "apprehensive" that a constitutional amendment would "be adopted and the US Courts given jurisdiction of certain public offenses, local in nature." McCarty blamed the editorial stance of the *Deseret News* as the "cause of so much anxiety and apprehension in the East." In his view, the paper had "done all in its power" to make Roberts "a church candidate."

Apostle Smith received similar views from Washington, DC, attorney Louis T. Michener,[70] who said the "condition of affairs in Mormondom is misunderstood by the general public partially because they are misrepresented by the principal papers in Salt Lake City, especially the *Deseret News*." Michener encouraged Smith to work to change that with regard to the *Deseret News* while admitting that "nothing can be done about the Tribune."[71]

Roberts's old antagonist Emmeline B. Wells noted that his actions were making "his case more and more hopeless."[72] The *Provo Enquirer*, a Mormon-owned paper, criticized Roberts's performance in the hearings, which it said had not been "frank or courageous." The paper predicted that "the course he has pursued has alienated many of his warmest friends, and he will return home a political outcast."[73] In response, the *Ogden Standard* said that while Roberts could have made a "stronger plea for his rights," talk of him being a political outcast was "nonsense." At the same time, while Roberts had made many

68. Cannon Journal, Dec. 30, 1899.

69. McCarty (1859–1918) was born in Alpine, Utah, and attended Brigham Young Academy, 1881–82. McCarty served in the 6th district as a Republican from 1895 to 1902. He later served on the Utah Supreme Court from 1903 until his death. He was Chief Justice, 1906–08 and 1912–15.

70. Michener (1848–1928) was a prominent Republican and friend and political advisor to Benjamin Harrison. He managed Harrison's campaign in 1888 and 1892. Michener also served as Indiana Attorney General, 1886–90.

71. L. T. Michener to John Henry Smith, box 9, fd. 7, Smith Family Papers.

72. Wells Diary, Jan. 11, 1890. See also January 25, 1900, where Wells notes, "News from congress—all against Roberts being admitted."

73. As quoted in "Roberts's Mistakes," *Ogden Semi-Weekly Standard*, Jan. 2, 1900, 1.

mistakes, "he has been deserted by the Democratic party of his state and left alone to battle against all kinds of prejudice and cunning and taunting trickery on the part of his persecutors." If only the Democrats had "given him the support which was his by right, a different story could be told today and Roberts might be occupying the seat which unconstitutional means have prevented him from taking."[74]

Meanwhile, the hearings continued. When the reports were eventually issued, the outlook was grim for Roberts. The majority report called for his immediate expulsion; the minority report urged Congress to seat Roberts—then expel him.[75] The majority argued there were three "distinct" grounds for disqualifying Roberts. First, they asserted that Roberts had violated the Edmunds Act. Second, they argued that Roberts was guilty of "notorious and defiant violation of the law of the land, of the decisions of the Supreme Court, and of the proclamations of the President, holding himself above the law and not amenable to it." Finally, they held that Roberts's election as representative was an "explicit and offensive violation of the understanding by which Utah was admitted as a state." The supporters of the majority report argued that to exclude him was "entirely in accord with principle, authority and legislative precedent, and not antagonistic to any legislative action which the House of Representatives has ever taken."[76]

On the other hand, the minority did not believe Roberts was disqualified under the Edmunds Act nor that he had violated a compact with the federal government established under the enabling act. The minority held that they believed that Roberts had the "legal, constitutional, right to be sworn in as a member, but the facts are such that we further believe the House, in the exercise of its discretion, is not only justified, but required by every proper consideration involved, to expel him promptly after he becomes a member."[77]

74. "Roberts's Mistakes."

75. There was bipartisan support for the minority position since Littlefield was a Republican and De Armond a Democrat.

76. US House of Representatives, *History and Legal Digest of all the Contested Elections*, 583–84. Hereafter cited as *Digest of Contested Elections*. For a broad discussion of the constitutional issues raised, see Gordon, *Mormon Question*. See also "B. H. Roberts," *Ogden Standard*, Nov. 29, 1899, 1, which captures the views of some members of Congress.

77. *Digest of Contested Elections*, 592, 594, 595.

After considering other business, Tayler requested ninety minutes for Roberts to address the House. Drawing upon his reputation as the "Blacksmith Orator," Roberts defended himself on constitutional grounds, summarized the history of polygamy in the Bible, traced the outlines of Mormon polygamy and its repudiation of it, and defended the legitimacy of his election. He told the members of Congress that he believed he was before them because the voters of Utah wanted him—even in light of his marital status—because they knew who he was and what he had done. As a result, the voters of Utah were the best judges of his fitness because they "knew of his struggles from boyhood; knew how he came of an obscure family, without prestige, without property, himself bareheaded and barefooted when he came into the state; of his boyhood home that never consisted of more than two small log rooms." The voters of Utah were his people, and they knew how he persisted to give himself an education, and how "he earned by the sweat of his brow the bread that he ate … until his anvil was left behind and he found his way into the forum of the people, becoming the editor of newspapers and of magazines."[78]

Roberts assured the House, as he had told them in December, that "I am not here begging the question; I am not here asking for favors; I am not here on my own behalf, but on behalf of my people, to demand for myself and for them our constitutional rights."[79] Then he turned personal, noting that some of the papers discussing the case (no doubt referring largely to Hearst's *New York Journal*) had called for the Congress to shame Roberts and send him back to his people. He addressed the Speaker directly, and proclaimed that he thanked God that the power to

> brand me with shame is something quite beyond the power of this House, great as that power is. The power to brand with shame rests with each man and nowhere else. The Almighty God has conferred it upon no one else. I have lived up to this day in all good conscience in harmony with the moral teachings of the community in which I was reared and am sensible of no act of shame in my life. Brand me with shame! Why if

78. *Congressional Record*, Jan. 23, 1900, 1104.
79. *Congressional Record*.

> you finally determine either to exclude or expel me, I shall leave this august chamber with head held erect and brow undaunted and walk God's earth as the angels walk the clouds, with no sense of shame upon me. And if in response to the sectarian clamor that has been invoked against [me] you violate the Constitution of your country, either in excluding or expelling me, all the shame that there is in this case will be left behind me and rest with this House.[80]

Those words ended Roberts's defense. Some audience members applauded; others hissed.

The next day, Representative Miers, one of two Democrats on the special committee to support the majority report, said the committee agreed on the basic facts of the case: Roberts was a practicing polygamist, he was convicted under the Edmunds and Edmunds–Tucker Acts, and he had served a sentence for those violations. As a result, Miers observed, "the gentleman is not entitled to remain as a member of the House. It is now a question of procedure. The majority of [the] committee says it is legal, it is constitutional, it is orderly to … exclude him without the administration of the oath. The minority says he should not be excluded; that the constitution requires that the oath should be administered, and after the oath has been administered he should be excluded."[81] Regardless, B. H. Roberts was not going to serve his term as a member of the House of Representatives.

The issue finally came to a vote on January 25, 1900. The minority resolution was offered, and the vote was 81 aye, 244 nay, and 29 not voting. The majority resolution was offered, and it passed 268 to 50, with 36 not voting.[82] The record notes that the results were met with "loud applause."[83] The long, rancorous crusade had reached its conclusion: Roberts's seat was declared vacant.[84] Vociferous Roberts

80. *Congressional Record.*

81. *Congressional Record,* Jan. 24, 1900, 1137.

82. Republicans were almost unanimous in their voting, with only seven out of 175 members voting to seat Roberts. Democrats were more divided "but even those who had voted to seat Roberts had already announced their intention to expel him." Some Republicans did sympathize with Roberts though they were not willing to challenge their party leaders. See Moyer, "Dancing with the Devil," 229, quoting an article from the Jan. 26, 1900, issue of the *New York Journal.*

83. *Congressional Record,* Jan. 25, 1900, 1217.

84. *Digest of Contested Elections,* 582. See also US Congress, *Report of the Special*

critic Josiah Strong said the vote "that a polygamist was unfit to sit in Congress is a triumph of decency, a triumph of the people, a triumph of Modern and Christian Civilization."[85]

Roberts issued a lengthy statement to the press,[86] telling them he had been elected "by the substantial plurality of 5,665 votes" and was excluded by an "unconstitutional and unprecedented" process. He said he had "contended for my rights and the rights of my constituents single-handed and alone to the best of my ability, but have been overwhelmed by force of numbers." Roberts also told the press that he had received an anonymous letter signed "Republican Friend," on House letterhead, which said, "I regret that I am not at liberty to vote as my conscience dictates on this question for reasons which you full understand. President McKinley and Speaker Henderson have made the support of the Tayler resolution the test of Republican orthodoxy, and I am obliged to wear the Yoke." Roberts told the press that the expulsion would not "ruin him," and that he faced the future "with a light heart and a determination to succeed." He also assured the press that he would not stand for re-election.[87] In Utah, Seymour B. Young noted that Roberts had already written to church transportation agent William Spence "for transportation home."[88]

Thomas Price Wells, a Democrat in the US House of Representatives from Texas,[89] introduced a resolution that was referred to the rules committee. It affirmed opposition to polygamy but commended "Roberts for his manly course in refusing to abandon his plural wives and their children, and it is the opinion of this house that if all the members of congress who are guilty of violation of the moral code of the character charged against … Roberts, would vote to seat [him] there would not be found a corporals guard opposed

Committee. For a good overview, see also "Roberts Retires Thursday," *Salt Lake Tribune*, Jan. 21, 1900, 1.

85. Josiah Strong, "A Notable Triumph," *Social Service*, Jan. 1900, 2.

86. See "Will Retire to Private Life," *Salt Lake Herald*, Jan. 26, 1900, 1; "Roberts Is Kicked Out," *Salt Lake Tribune*, Jan. 26, 1900, 1; and "Roberts's Salary and Mileage," *Washington County News*, Feb. 10, 1900, 2.

87. "Roberts Makes Statement," *Salt Lake Tribune*, Jan. 26, 1900, 2.

88. Young Journal, Jan. 25, 1900.

89. Wells (1873–1951) represented District 8, Bells, Grayson County, Texas. A banker and farmer, he served from 1899 to 1903.

to the same."[90] Later that year, one of Roberts's longtime allies, *The Broad Ax,* commented that "at the instigation of women throughout the country," Congress had "violated and trampled under foot every known precedent and law governing it in order to prevent the oath of office" being administered to a duly elected member.[91]

A few days after the vote, more than eighty-one representatives confided to the *New York Times* that Littlefield's proposition that Roberts be seated and then expelled now seemed to them the right method of dealing with the Mormon question, but "carried on by the tide of public opinion, they had voted with Tayler."[92] It was too late for Roberts and, either way, he would not have served in Congress.

Roberts says very little in his autobiography concerning the campaign against him. He singled out the Hearst press for finding it "necessary to make special warfare" against him on a daily basis. But he also noted that it was not a "one-sided battle" because a number of "prominent and influential persons and dignified papers" had expressed support for him personally and opposition to the "violations of constitutional rights." In words that called up memories of the violence of Tennessee, he wrote his old friend Bernard Moses, "It is a case of the success of popular clamor against that which is right and just. But I have the satisfaction in this instance of standing for what is right, and though unable to resist the force of mob law, I have the superior satisfaction of knowing that I stood for what was right, true, and manly."[93]

Roberts also took parental pride in the fact that Adah had accompanied him and had attracted favorable attention. The *Jefferson (Iowa) Bee*, for example, wrote that Roberts has "had the assistance, counsel and filial support of his daughter, a very pre-possessing young woman, who … may be seen making suggestions as to the best mode of procedure."[94] The *Boston Post* published an extensive

90. "Texans Are in Sympathy with Mr. Roberts's Course," *Salt Lake Herald*, Jan. 26, 1900, 1.

91. "The Women's National Federation and Mrs. Ruffin," *Broad Ax*, June 16, 1900, 1.

92. Moyer, "Dancing with the Devil," 231.

93. Roberts to Bernard Moses, undated, Jan. 1900, Moses Papers.

94. "Dewey Is All Right," *Jefferson Bee*, Jan. 25, 1899, 1.

article on Adah in early December,[95] referring to her as "tall and straight and hazel-eyed … and she is proud as she is fair and humble as she is proud, and altogether as sweet and lovely as she is versatile." The paper stated that while the twenty-year-old Adah had the "charm of youth," she appeared "somewhat older." Upon stating that she was never happier than when busy, the reporter asked if all the women of Utah were "so ambitious to be useful?" Adah replied, "The women of Utah are just like the women of any other place, which means paradoxically, they are unlike any other women and unlike each other. Did you ever find two women alike?" She explained that Utah women were not the exotic species the reporters seemed to envision: "You Eastern people amuse me greatly. Why should you think Mormon women unlike Catholic or Methodist or Episcopalian women? Mormonism is a religion. Can a difference in creed make a vast difference in kind?"[96]

After deflecting questions about plural marriage and Roberts's other wives, she indicated that her current status assisting her father resembled her activities as his secretary during the campaign itself. Adah stated that she thought she could be useful to her father because she understood "his temperament and ways so well that we have always gotten along splendidly together. We are great chums you know." She defended her father and, according to the paper, "rose to her full height of five feet nine" and stated that a "sense of injustice within me rises when I think of the unkind and inhuman treatment he has received. … I cannot respect judgement which is based on a misunderstanding of facts. … Nor can I regard it seriously enough to be angered by it."[97]

Looking back on the events some three decades later, Roberts observed that his case had furnished the "Christian" ministry an opportunity to air their anti-Mormon prejudices and proclaim their "great holiness and impeccability in relation to loyalty to monogamous marriage, etc., and each sought to proclaim his own sanctity by throwing stones at the member from Utah. Writers for the press

95. "Miss Roberts Talks on Father's Position," *Boston Post,* Dec. 4, 1899, 5. Hereafter cited as "Miss Roberts Talks."

96. "Miss Roberts Talks."

97. "Miss Roberts Talks."

availed themselves of like opportunities both for themselves and their own people, especially those of the sensational order."[98]

Historian Jonathan Moyer concludes that the fight over Roberts "marked the beginning of a new series of problems" for the LDS Church that would have profound effect in the first decade of the twentieth century. Roberts's election, writes Moyers, "touched off animosity in the nation's newspapers and churches. It exacerbated tensions in the South, leading to beatings and deaths of Mormons there. Congress was not content with excluding the Mormons; it continued to debate a constitutional amendment against polygamy." Moreover, Roberts's denial of his seat set the stage a few years later for Apostle Reed Smoot, newly chosen senator from Utah, to face a similar battle. Although Smoot was not a polygamist, the hearings over his seat would bring to the surface all the unresolved issues from the fight over Roberts's seat. The LDS Church would have to chart a new course, including the issuance of a second manifesto that paved the way for church discipline, including excommunication, for those who entered into new plural marriages.[99]

Joseph F. Smith, who was both a friend and an occasional critic of Roberts, wrote his son Joseph R. Smith that "I think Congress will oust Hon. B. H. Roberts. But if so, it will be a blot upon the House of Representatives and the nation. I'll venture to guess there is not another man in Congress save it be [Utah Senator Joseph] Rawlins, who is as clean and free from taint of crime as he. If ousted it will be by the force of sectarian cant and hypocrisy, simon pure!"[100]

Some twenty-five years after he was denied his seat in Congress, Roberts confided to a group of Eastern States' missionaries that he "would have loved to be in Congress, representing our people, using the talent and strength God has given me, to promote and maintain peace," and to make it possible for all to have an "opportunity

98. Roberts, *Autobiography*, 218. Some years later Roberts blamed much of his defeat on a combination of "long-haired" ministers and "short-haired" women activists. The remark has an implicit accusation of homosexuality. See Roberts, *Recent Discussions*, 35. At the same time, the *Truth Seeker* observed that it was "over sexed" women who "trouble themselves about the domestic affairs of Congressman Roberts." See "Observations," *Truth Seeker*, Nov. 4, 1899, 696.

99. Moyer, "Dancing with the Devil," 240–41.

100. Smith and Kenney, *From Prophet to Son*, 65.

to enjoy the benefits of citizenship."[101] A similar story was told by Henry D. Taylor, an Eastern States missionary and future LDS general authority, who spent several months with Roberts in 1926 as the mission secretary. In his autobiography, Taylor said that for Roberts, the denial of his seat in Congress was one of the "most bitter and disappointing frustrations" in his life. "As we were talking about this one day, he [Roberts] remarked, 'Brother Taylor, when I think about that event, even though it was years ago, it is like pouring salt in a fresh wound.'"[102]

On January 25, 1900, freshly ousted from Congress, B. H. Roberts, just two months shy of his forty-third birthday, stood at a crucial turning point in his public life.[103]

101. As quoted in Madsen, *Defender of the Faith*, 269.

102. Taylor, *Autobiography of Henry Dixon Taylor*, 73.

103. For a good contemporary overview of the case, see Adolph Bierck Jr., "The Case of B. H. Roberts," *Truth Seeker*, Jan. 6, 1900, 6–7.

FOURTEEN

FINDING A NEW PLACE, 1900-10

The day after the vote, Roberts began to adjust to his new reality. That evening he made his way to the Lafayette Theater to watch the play *Becky Sharp*.[1] Roberts had the opportunity to witness "the morality of those who voted him out of congress" while watching the performance. He "occupied a balcony seat and was in full view of an immense audience. ... There was a bustle and stir of whispering comments as he came in." Walking back to his hotel from the theater, Roberts told a reporter:

> I have been under a heavy strain for some time now, but now that it is over I feel very comfortable, for I have the approval of my own conscience which is worth more to me than all the seats in congress. This is not the first fight I have ever had and I expect it will not be the last. When I was a younger man I had delusions common to youth that the men who make our laws held sacred the Constitution, but I found that the Constitution, like the party platform may be used to subserve the purpose of those having the power to establish their influence.[2]

Contrary to what Roberts said publicly, John Henry Smith noted that he had called upon Roberts, saying that the two men had "quite a lengthy talk,' and that while Roberts was "somewhat depressed in spirits," he was bearing up "in a reasonably good way."[3]

Toward the end of January 1900, as he made plans to return home, Roberts made a formal request to the House Sergeant at Arms for $2,000 in salary and mileage owed him to cover the time between his arrival in Washington and his expulsion. Though the request was

1. The play, written by Langdon Mitchell, was based on William Thackery's novel, *Vanity Fair*.

2. "Roberts Favors R. W. Young," *Salt Lake Herald*, Jan. 26, 1900, 1.

3. Smith, *Church, State, and Politics*, 444.

initially refused,[4] Roberts would eventually receive the money, but not until late July, which was unfortunate because over the course of the next few months, he found himself in serious financial difficulty.[5] J. Golden Kimball records in his journal that the First Council of Seventy had appropriated $200 "while contesting his seat in Congress," because the quorum concluded Roberts had "fought a Church fight."[6] As Roberts left Washington, one paper noted that a "large trunk packed with dashed hopes has been checked from Washington to Salt Lake City, and B. H. Roberts holds the check."[7] But he kept up a positive public image. The *Washington Post* commented that "if Brigham H. Roberts is at all disconsolate over the vote of the house he does not betray it in his attire or by his conduct. On the contrary he seems gleeful." Roberts had met "two newspaper men … in patent leather shoes and a full dress suit." Roberts assured the reporters, "I return to the west, but my face will still be toward the rising sun."[8]

En route, Roberts and his daughter Adah stopped in Chicago on January 31 where they stayed over night. Met by the press, he told them that he was not sure of his "future line of action," but that he intended to consult with his attorney to see if his "case could be brought to the U.S. Supreme Court for review."[9] Roberts recounted his history of religious persecution, telling reporters, "I have been mobbed in the streets of London, and I have been mobbed in some of the Southern cities, but I never expected to be mobbed in the halls of Congress, for I have been little else than a victim of mob law there." Still, he believed that "the Constitution of the United States has been injured more seriously than I have been."[10]

The Constitution was not the only casualty. The national budget had also sustained a few nicks and bruises: the clerk of the House of Representatives stated that the government had spent $1,675 to

4. "Congressional," *Greenfield (Massachusetts) Daily Recorder Gazette*, Feb. 3, 1900, 1. Accounts of this request were picked up by many papers around the country. See also "Is Shut Out," *Salt Lake Tribune*, Jan. 30, 1900, 1.

5. "Ex-Congressman B. H. Roberts Gets $2000 from Treasury," *Salt Lake Herald*, Aug. 3, 1900, 8. See also Historian's Office, Journal History, May 13, 1900.

6. Kimball Journal, Aug. 8, 1900.

7. [No title], *Portsmouth Herald*, Jan. 29, 1900, 4.

8. As reported in "Mr. Roberts Is Coming Home," *Salt Lake Herald*, Jan. 30, 1900, 1.

9. "B. H. Roberts in Town," *Chicago Daily Tribune*, Feb. 1, 1900, 1.

10. "B. H. Roberts in Town."

expel Roberts, primarily in transportation of witnesses, witness fees, and secretarial expenses.[11]

Roberts arrived in Salt Lake City by train on the afternoon of February 3, 1900. Adah accompanied him as far as Centerville where the *Deseret News* reported, "The man or woman who imagines that Mr. Roberts has been worn out or become disheartened under the tremendous mental and physical strain that has been upon him during the past few weeks, is very much mistaken." Far from being fatigued, Roberts looked strong and healthy, and "where discouragement might have been written, the cheerfulness and satisfaction that comes from duty well done, clearly display themselves; and behind it all are well defined signs of a determination that knows no surrender even in defeat."[12]

The *Salt Lake Tribune* refused to let up on Roberts, referring to him as the "Congressman Eject,"[13] and noted that while dressed in "the height of fashion," he returned "unheralded and alone."[14] Roberts had "absolutely nothing to say" to the *Salt Lake Tribune*," as he avoided a cab "but instead chose a … plebian, ramshackle old street car that … caters to the hotels and other trade." The *Tribune* made sure that its readers knew that there had been "no public demonstration yet at Centerville in honor of Roberts,"[15] but that upon his return home, there was one more surprise for him. He was "courteously presented" with a warrant for his arrest[16] initiated by Charles Mostyn

11. "What Roberts Rejection Cost," *Salt Lake Tribune*, Feb. 5, 1901, 4.

12. "Roberts Returns from Washington," *Deseret Evening News*, Feb. 3, 1900, 1.

13. "The Congressman Eject," *Salt Lake Tribune*, Feb. 6, 1900, 4. Later, the paper reported on a local high school minstrel show featuring jokes at Roberts's expense. One went: "Say, do you know why you oughtn't ever to play poker with Mr. Roberts? No, why not? Because he would be sure to pull on you three of a kind and one pair," in a reference to Roberts's wives and sets of twins. The paper reported that audience "broke into a storm of applause." See "Amusements," *Salt Lake Tribune*, Feb. 17, 1900, 3.

14. "Roberts at His Firesides," *Salt Lake Tribune*, Feb. 4, 1900, 1. The paper refers to Roberts's twin daughters with Celia, Georgiana and Joanna, born in 1897, and who had become a campaign issue in 1898. The *Tribune* featured a front-page cartoon with the twins running toward their father while in the background a man held a "Warrant for Unlawful Cohabitation." Another set of twins, David and Lawrence, would be born to the couple in 1902.

15. "Roberts's Quiet Day," *Salt Lake Tribune*, Feb. 5, 1900, 8.

16. Interestingly, he was arrested by Salt Lake County sheriff John Howells who had attended the December meeting to discuss Roberts's fate.

Owen on the charge of "unlawful cohabitation with Dr. Maggie C. Shipp-Roberts." He was released on his own recognizance.

Two days later, Roberts conferred with the First Presidency and Matthias F. Cowley. Counselor George Q. Cannon noted that in the long conversation, Roberts sought to explain "the course he had taken" during the hearings in Washington. Roberts was "especially desirous" to justify his strategy of calling attention to the fact that the McKinley Administration "had appointed polygamists in Utah to office." Cannon told him "plainly" that "President McKinley had shown a willingness to appoint our people to office, and I thought it came with a very bad grace from one of us to turn on the opposition against him." Roberts disagreed, saying that these appointments were well known before he had said anything. Cannon still felt that his tactic had "given our opponents weapons to use against us." But Cannon admitted that Roberts had found himself in "a very difficult position ... and that a great deal could be pardoned in a man who was in such a close place ... and he had my sympathy."[17]

While Roberts was speaking with the First Presidency, James H. Moyle represented him in Judge Gustave Kroeger's[18] court, pleading him not guilty to charges of unlawful cohabitation and paying a $300 bond. The *Deseret News* reported that the arraignment "consumed but ninety seconds."[19]

Soon, attention turned to electing Roberts's successor at a special election in April. The likely Democratic candidates were former Representative William H. King and David C. Dunbar.[20] Roberts favored Dunbar, possibly still seeing King as a more formidable adversary should Roberts think about returning to the political arena.

17. Cannon Journal, Feb. 6, 1900.

18. Kroeger (1865–1936) was born in Germany, came to the United States in 1881, and became a citizen in 1887. A Democrat and lawyer, he served as justice of the peace for the fifth precinct. Kroeger moved to Boise in 1904 and practiced law there until his death.

19. "Roberts Arraigned," *Deseret News*, Feb. 5, 1900, 1.

20. Dunbar (1858–1938) was a classmate of Roberts and graduated in the same class from the University of Deseret in 1878. He worked for the *Salt Lake Herald* and served as Salt Lake County Clerk, 1896–1902. At one point, he broke with Democrats and briefly supported the anti-Smoot American Party. He was later appointed Internal Revenue Collector for Utah by President Woodrow Wilson in 1919. Three years later, he was an unsuccessful candidate for Congress. See also "Ex-Utah Political Chief, David C. Dunbar, Dies," *Salt Lake Tribune*, Nov. 21, 1938, 18.

The *Salt Lake Tribune*, in a typical flight of literary excess, said that Roberts was "flooding the state" with letters of support, and would have "writer's cramp" except that he was "assisted by a corps of stenographers and typewriters."[21]

A nominating convention—convened to choose a candidate for Congress, draft a state party platform, and select delegates to the Democratic national convention—was held in Salt Lake City on March 1. Roberts was a delegate from Davis County. King's name was put in nomination as was Dunbar's. Roberts rose to second Dunbar's nomination and was "loudly cheered" as he assured the delegates that with Dunbar at the head "the Democratic Party of this state will march to a triumphant victory in the election only thirty days hence."[22] But when the votes were cast, King won easily with 338.5 votes to Dunbar's 175.5. But Roberts worked for King's election anyway. He wrote to his friend Bernard Moses, "I take to the stump next week for ten days or more. I look for a close election. After that I do no know what I shall turn my attention to; it will be a case of 'statesman out of a job,' but not for long, as I am sure to find an opening somewhere in this busy work, and if nothing else presents itself can always buy a bottle of ink, pen and paper and go to work."[23] There is a sense of gloom in Roberts's letter that likely reflects his feeling that he has lost his place of prominence. This seems confirmed by an article in the *Tribune* announcing that George E. Hill, whom they described as the "late private secretary to ex-Congressman Roberts," would soon be leaving for Rigby, Idaho, to practice law and operate a farm that he owned.[24]

Despite his diminished status, on March 12 Roberts returned to the political battles, delivering "his first speech of the campaign" to a Democratic group at Springville. Roberts stated that after a quarter century of Republican rule, the nation was near bankruptcy. He accused the McKinley administration of pursuing and supporting wars of aggression. The *Salt Lake Herald* reported he was "vehement" in

21. "Roberts's Billet-Doux," *Salt Lake Tribune*, February 17, 1900, 8. A *billet doux* is a love letter.

22. "King Wins on First Ballot," *Salt Lake Herald*, Mar. 2, 1900, 1.

23. Roberts to Moses, Mar. 6, 1900, Moses Papers.

24. "Political Notes," *Salt Lake Tribune*, Mar. 17, 1900, 8.

his attacks on imperialism.[25] King won handily in the special election on April 2, defeating Republican James T. Hammond to serve out the rest of Roberts's term.

Soon Roberts's attention was being diverted to legal matters. On March 5, he was charged in Third District Court with unlawful cohabitation. The prosecution, which was represented by assistant county attorney Ray Van Cott,[26] alleged that the "offense was committed on July 1, 1898, and at divers times, and continually between said date and July 1, 1899." The complaint, which was brought by Charles Mostyn Owen, claimed that this offense had occurred between Roberts and Dr. Margaret Shipp while Roberts was legally married to Louisa Roberts.[27]

One paper reported that there was an "unusually large" attendance at Roberts's trial five weeks later, noting that "groups of ladies were among the first arrivals." Also present was Charles Mostyn Owen who sat at the press table. Once a jury was seated, the county attorney stated that "the whole case would be submitted on agreed statements of fact" and that "neither side would present witnesses." As part of the charges, the date for the offense was moved back to 1897 based on the fact that after that date Margaret had gone by the name of Dr. Margaret C. Roberts, not Shipp. In the formal charges, reference was made to testimony given in the congressional hearings. Dr. Luella P. Miles,[28] for example, had stated that while visiting with Shipp, Roberts had entered the house without knocking. J. R. Letcher noted that he had found Roberts in bed at Shipp's residence, recuperating from an operation, and that he had introduced him to her as his wife. Letcher said on other occasions the two had appeared in public as man and wife.[29]

As the trial resumed on April 29, Putnam argued that the evidence presented by the state led "irresistibly" to the conclusion that

25. "B. H. Roberts Speaks," *Salt Lake Herald*, Mar. 13, 1900, 2.

26. Van Cott (1869–1944) graduated from the University of Deseret in 1891 and Cornell Law School in 1895. He served as assistant county attorney for four years. Van Cott was an active Democrat throughout his career.

27. "Roberts Information Filed," *Salt Lake Herald*, Mar. 6, 1900, 5.

28. Miles (1860–1930) was a well-known physician and surgeon in Salt Lake City. She became the first president of the Woman's Medical Society of Utah in 1910. She split her time between Utah and California.

29. Historian's Office, Journal History, Apr. 30, 1900, 4.

the defendant's relationship with Shipp was as charged. Moreover, he argued, it was clear by many actions that Roberts was intent on proclaiming to the world that he was living in a polygamous relationship in violation of the law, and that he intended to continue to live in violation of the law. Moyle countered that "the defendant and Dr. Roberts" had been seen together during the time in question only "a few times, and not long intervals, and the association between them had not been shown to be such as existed between man and wife." Moyle reminded the jurors that the word "cohabit" meant "living and associating together."[30]

The jurors deliberated for seventeen hours over two days. As they returned to the court, the *Deseret* News described them as looking "pretty well fagged out." Jury foreman, Joseph Knight, stated that they had not reached a verdict, and that there was no possibility of doing so. Apparently a six to two vote had maintained throughout the deliberations, with the minority for acquittal. After the dismissal, most of the jurors were reluctant to talk, but some suggested that the fact that the case was based on an "agreed statement of facts" made it difficult for them to sort matters out.[31]

On June 18, county attorney Putnam noted that the trial would continue, but it would not proceed "on an agreed statement of facts," and issued subpoenas for several people, including Shipp herself, Hiram B. Clawson, his wife Margaret J. Clawson,[32] and several others close to Shipp who would be called as witnesses for the state.[33]

When the trial recommenced on June 21, Putnam immediately went into a private conference with Moyle. When court resumed, Moyle dropped a bombshell, telling Judge Norrell that Roberts "would offer no resistance to a verdict of guilty." Moyle's strategy was for his client to consent to the charge so that he could appeal the case to the Utah Supreme Court on the grounds that "evidence was only admissible as to acts committed in the county in which the

30. "Jury Fails to Agree in the Roberts Case," *Deseret Evening News*, May 1, 1900, 1.

31. "Jury Fails to Agree in Roberts Case."

32. Clawson (1826–1912) was active in church, business, and theatrical circles, serving as manager of the Salt Lake Theater. Clawson married four wives, including two of Brigham Young's daughters. He served as bishop of the Twelfth Ward from 1884 until 1902.

33. "Trial of B. H. Roberts," *Deseret Evening News*, June 18, 1900, 2.

alleged offense was committed."[34] Since Margaret resided in Salt Lake County, and Louisa in Davis, Moyle believed this technicality would result in a dismissal of the charges. The jury retired to deliberate at 11:25 a.m., and by 11:40 a.m. returned and stated they found Roberts guilty of unlawful cohabitation. Sentencing was to be pronounced on June 23.[35]

During sentencing, Moyle told the court that his intention was to save the state the expense of a full trial. He also indicated that Roberts's marriage had taken place prior to the Manifesto, and felt that it was "unclear" if the ruling would stand "for the reason that it covered a period of time in 1897 during which … there was no law against unlawful cohabitation." Judge Norrell admitted he too had doubts "on that point of law," and believed "it should be passed upon by the Supreme Court." Moyle told the court that he believed Roberts had been punished enough. Roberts "was one of the most honorable and respected citizens of the state. He had never shown a disposition to willfully disobey the laws of the land." County attorney Putnam agreed that Roberts had "practically admitted his guilt," but thought "he should be made an example of."

Norrell sentenced Roberts to a fine of $150 and a term of 150 days in the county jail. He also ordered a stay of thirty days.[36] Soon, the case went to the Utah Supreme Court, where, after many months of legal maneuvering, on May 13, 1901, the court ruled that there was insufficient evidence to convict Roberts.[37] Ultimately the case was dropped at the request of the Salt Lake County district attorney on November 25, 1901.[38] This action effectively put an end to legal attempts to discredit Roberts over polygamy. After that, "Mr. and Mrs. B. H. Roberts" are mentioned as attending various social, civic,

34. "Roberts Found Guilty," *Salt Lake Tribune*, June 22, 1900, 8.

35. "Roberts Found Guilty." The event was reported outside of Utah as well. For example, see "News of the Week," *Truth Seeker*, June 30, 1900, 1.

36. "Court Declines to Exact a Promise," *Deseret Evening News*, June 23, 1900, 2.

37. "End of the Roberts Case," *Salt Lake Tribune*, May 14, 1901, 5. The court used the case of John G. Graham as their legal precedent. In that case, the court held that "there was a fatal defect in the information that did not allege that the offense was committed" in more than one county. See also "Loses His Homestead," *Salt Lake Herald*, Feb. 13, 1901, 5.

38. See "B. H. Roberts Case Dismissed." *Deseret Evening News*, Nov. 25, 1901, 5; and "End of Roberts Case," *Salt Lake Herald*, Nov. 24, 1901, 5.

and church functions. While Shipp is rarely mentioned specifically, she is clearly the wife in question. Finally, Roberts could move on from being a lightning rod of politics and polygamy.

On May 16, 1900, Lorenzo Snow and George Q. Cannon met to discuss the "employment of B. H. Roberts as editor of the proposed history of the Church." At that time he was being paid $1,200 annually for his service on the First Council of Seventy. Roberts had proposed a sum of $2,500 to undertake the project, but both Snow and Cannon believed "that this was too much," because they were seeking an editor, not an author, and they did not believe it required full-time work.[39] But first they asked the aging George Q. Cannon how he felt about taking the position. He said if that "was the mind of President Snow" he had no alternative but to "place himself in their service,"[40] but Cannon died in April 1901 with little done on the project. A month later, the First Presidency hired Roberts to edit the history under the supervision of Church Historian Anthon H. Lund.[41] Snow told Lund "that the work shall be made the leading matter in Bro. Roberts's labors and be pushed as fast as possible and that his other appointments in the Priesthood shall be made subject to the interests of that work."[42] Over the next few years, Lund and Roberts worked closely on the preparation of the history and other projects in the Historian's Office.[43]

Roberts also began to work closely with J. Golden Kimball, who had been selected a few months before to serve as the secretary of the First Council of Seventy. The pair frequently fulfilled assignments together and cooperated on council business. But on other occasions the two clashed, in what seems to be, at times, a divided

39. Cannon Journal, May 16, 1900.

40. Cannon did maintain an interest in the project and told the First Presidency on October 24, 1900, that he was "now in a position to turn my attention to this work." He also noted that after some conversation it was decided to "call it the History of the Church." He said he wanted to be "very particular in the supervision of the work, as it is the feeling of all the brethren that they would like me to do so, because they seem to have confidence in my judgment and in my familiarity to do the work something like justice." Cannon Journal, Oct. 24, 1900.

41. On Lund's appointment and the situation in the Historian's Office, see Cannon Journal, July 20, 25–26, 1900.

42. First Council of Seventy Minutes, June 5, 1901.

43. Horne, *Life of Orson F. Whitney*, 230.

and contentious quorum[44]—sometimes over differences of opinion on the Council or the Young Men's Mutual Improvement Association (YMMIA) general board on which they both served, and sometimes over money since both men were constantly seeking additional sources of income.[45]

Roberts remained heavily invested in politics. He felt that Utah was "certain to go Democratic by a large majority," and the *Salt Lake Herald* reported that he would soon "take the stump for the Democratic ticket."[46] Indeed, Roberts spoke at a large campaign rally in Salt Lake City on October 27, 1900. He stood and received a "magnificent ovation" as he launched it to what would be a nearly two-hour speech. He singled out the Republicans saying that their "adoption of the so called protection policy ... was a wide departure from the proper sphere of government as outlined by Jefferson." The policy was designed to create monopolies, lower wages, and increase corporate profits. Corporations, Roberts asserted, had no souls—and trusts, which are simply combinations of corporations, are "doubly soulless." "What matters to them being soulless? They have no love of country, no interest in humanity further than to fleece and enslave" American workers and consumers.[47]

Roberts then commented on the recent war with Spain, which he said was originally conceived as a war for humanity, seeking the enlargement of liberty for the Philippine people. Yet, once the war was concluded, he argued, the United States used its power to oppose indigenous nationalist forces in an effort to deny them the right of self-government. He felt that such a policy was in direct contradiction to the American constitutional view that governments derive their just powers from the consent of the governed. Roberts called on listeners to reject the "imperialistic tendencies" of the Republican Party by voting for William Jennings Bryan and the entire Democratic ticket.

Despite many instances of this fervent rhetoric, when the votes were counted, the Democrats suffered a major loss. King lost narrowly

44. Kimball Journal, June 27, 1900.

45. Kimball Journal, Aug. 29, 1900.

46. "B. H. Roberts at Home," *Salt Lake Herald*, Oct. 18, 1900, 3.

47. "Democrats Have Big Parade and Hear B. H. Roberts Speak," *Salt Lake Herald*, Oct. 28, 1900, 3.

to George Sutherland[48] by a vote of 46,180 to 45,939. Roberts's friend and attorney James H. Moyle fell short in his effort to defeat incumbent governor Heber M. Wells. The state legislature shifted from Democratic to Republican control, where Thomas Kearns defeated Alfred McCune for US Senator. Moreover, presidential candidate William Jennings Bryan lost Utah narrowly with 45,006 votes to William McKinley's 47,139. As one scholar has observed, the party split from these defeats—which had begun in 1898–99 over Roberts's election and expulsion, and the inability of the Democrats to elect a United States Senator—was "so deep that the party … had effectively destroyed its own political power."[49] This was all the more remarkable because a generation of Mormons had had an affection for the Democratic Party since much anti-Mormon legislation, both successful and not, had been passed by Republican-controlled congresses, signed by Republican presidents, and used as a rallying cry by Republican candidates as early as 1856.[50] Moreover, it was under Democrat Grover Cleveland that the process for statehood had begun.

These defeats ushered in a new era of political domination for Utah Republicans. By May 1902, Joseph F. Smith—one of the main builders of the Utah Republican Party—was president of the LDS Church. Over the course of the next few years, assisted by several allies, most notably apostle and future senator Reed Smoot—and, for a time, William Spry[51]—control of state and federal offices was in

48. Sutherland (1862–1942) was born in England and came to Utah in 1863 with his parents who were converts to Mormonism. The family broke with the church, and Sutherland was never baptized. He attended Brigham Young Academy and the University of Michigan where he obtained a law degree. He practiced law in Provo and Salt Lake City, and was an unsuccessful candidate for Provo mayor as a Liberal. Soon after that, he helped organize the Utah Republican Party and launched a successful political career. His record included service in the Utah State Senate, the US House of Representatives, the US Senate, president of the American Bar Association, and associate justice of the US Supreme Court.

49. Craner, "Influence of the LDS Church," iv, 90. As Craner notes, the Democrats "had shown they were capable of winning elections, but they were so badly divided they were incapable of uniting and solving the day-to-day problems of government."

50. That year, the Republican platform had campaigned against the "twin relics" of barbarism—slavery and polygamy. For more on the anti-Mormon bills, see Larson, *Outline History*, 198–201, and Gordon, *Mormon Question*.

51. Spry (1864–1929) was a leading figure in the Utah Republican Party. Born in England, he came to Utah in 1875. In 1894 he began his political career serving as Tooele County Tax Collector, then in the Utah House of Representatives, 1903–05. He was

Republican hands. In addition, a "loosely-knit" organization known as "The Federal Bunch" (the title given to it by its foes) controlled party machinery and the elections themselves.[52]

On Memorial Day, Sunday, May 30, 1901, Roberts participated at the dedicatory service of the John Morgan monument. The *Deseret Evening News* noted that "hundreds of the relatives and friends of the deceased and scores of strangers," were present for the service. J. Golden Kimball, who had worked so long and hard on the project, joined Roberts and gave the opening prayer. Roberts recounted the efforts to build the monument, which included the support of seventy current and former missionaries in the Southern States Mission. After outlining aspects of Morgan's life, Roberts noted that his friend and mentor "was pre-eminently a missionary and drew all men to him by the kindness of his own great soul. He had one quality above most men, that is that he loved without limit his fellow men." Morgan, Roberts said, had done much in "the short period of fifty-two" years he lived. He was also "successful as a colonizer and educator" and "a member of the General Sunday School board and rendered valuable service in that capacity."[53] However, according to Kimball, "not one of the apostles put in an appearance, although they were invited. Morgan's first wife failed to come as she is not feeling kindly towards the erecting of the monument."[54]

In April 1901 Roberts accepted a position as an insurance solicitor with the Mutual Life Insurance Company of New York,[55] starting him into a career in finance. A year later Roberts became president of the Union Savings and Investment Company[56] and

---

president of the Utah State Land Board from 1905 until 1909. Spry was elected governor in 1908 and served until 1917. During his second term he was involved in the controversial execution of union songwriter Joe Hill. Spry was defeated in a bid for a third term in 1916, and lost a race for Congress in 1918. In 1921, President Warren G. Harding appointed him head of the General Land Office, and he held the post until his death.

52. At other times the group was called simply "The Smoot Gang." See Craner, "Influence of the LDS Church," iv, 96–109.

53. "Monument to Late John Morgan," *Deseret Evening News*, May 30, 1901, 1.

54. Kimball Journal, May 30, 1901.

55. "Personal Mention," *Salt Lake Tribune*, Apr. 6, 1901, 8. This may have happened because Roberts's colleague on the First Council of Seventy, Rulon S. Wells, was the company manager.

56. "Union Savings and Investment Co.," *Salt Lake Herald*, Mar. 25, 1902, 5. See also "Union Savings and Trust, Articles of Incorporation, #3477, Salt Lake County Archives.

was prominently featured in news articles and ads touting the company's prospects.[57] The company boasted "agents in every town of Utah," and "one of the safest and best methods of investment to the public." The company was also involved in home building throughout the state.[58]

After some charges of serious mismanagement, the company was reorganized, and David J. Williams, Union Savings' vice president, asserted that the company was "perfectly solvent," but that "from now on a new administration will be in the saddle, and President Roberts will be better paid and have more to do with the management of affairs."[59] Roberts remained in this role for at least seven years, though the company was troubled at various times by additional charges of mismanagement—its officers accused of "buying cheap real estate and unloading it upon the association at extravagant prices."[60] In November 1905, Seymour B. Young discussed Roberts's business ties with George Reynolds. Young brought Roberts's connections with the company to the attention of the First Council of Seventy presidency who discussed "the advisability of asking Bro [Roberts] to sever his connection with the Union Savings … viewing it as we do as a base concern."[61] But it is unclear if such advice was offered, and if it was, when Roberts followed their directive.[62] Ultimately, the company ceased doing business in April 1916.[63]

While occupied in business matters, and perhaps reflecting the

57. See "The Union Savings and Investment Company," *Deseret News*, Mar. 24, 1902, 2; and "Advertizement," *Deseret Evening News*, Dec. 17, 1904, 89, which paints a glowing account of the company's success, noting, "What BETTER investment could you make?" The ad also indicates the company had over $144,000 in assets at that point, more than twice what they had held the year before.

58. "The Union Savings and Investment Co.," *Truth*, May 26, 1906, 10; and "Many New Homes For Salt Lakers," *Salt Lake Tribune*, May 22, 1905, 17.

59. "In a Good Condition," *Eastern Utah Advocate*, Aug. 17, 1905, 8; and "Statement Is Issued," *Salt Lake Telegram*, Aug. 8, 1905, 1.

60. "Would Have Been Like Equitable," *Salt Lake Tribune*, Aug. 6, 1905, 8. See also "Snow Quits Company," *Salt Lake Herald*, Aug. 9, 1905, 5.

61. Seymour B. Young Journal, Nov. 28, 1905, in Young Papers.

62. Incorporation records suggest he was president continuously from 1902 to 1908. Other sources suggest he continued beyond that. See *Business Directory of Salt Lake City* (Salt Lake City: n. p., 1910), 123.

63. A letter from David Mattson, Utah secretary of state, to Thomas Homer, Salt Lake County Clerk, April 6, 1916, stated that the company's right to do business was "cancelled," and its charter was "revoked."

many things going on in his public and professional life, his drinking again became an issue. During the 1898 campaign, J. Golden Kimball had made reference to smelling liquor on Roberts's breath,[64] and Roberts's use of alcohol continued to impact his associations, especially with other church leaders. In 1901 Roberts confessed to the First Council "as to his violation of the word of wisdom." His struggles would continue in the next few years. After the council had "a heart to heart" talk with him in 1906, Roberts traveled to Los Angeles for treatment.[65] In 1908, Seymour B. Young wrote that council members "have had to take up a labor with" Roberts because he "has been many times much the worse for liquor."[66]

Despite these difficulties, Roberts continued in his various church, community, and political efforts. In September 1901, notwithstanding his personal partisan affiliation, Roberts joined with other Americans in lamenting the assassination of President William McKinley. He told a memorial congregation in the tabernacle that they joined all citizens in "standing in the shadow of a great national tragedy." There was "no excuse" for this violence he said, and cautioned that at times like this there were "no political partisans ... and no sectarians." The president, he said, was a self-made man who had been slain in "the full vigor of his manhood, and at the height of his glorious career."[67]

Two new Roberts books, *The Rise and Fall of Nauvoo* and the *Missouri Persecutions,* were published and widely advertised. But some colleagues were annoyed that the books had taken him away from his ecclesiastical duties. According to J. Golden Kimball, on December 18, 1901, President Joseph W. McMurrin[68] took "Bro. Roberts to task for not doing his part in filling appointments. A very plain talk was

64. Alcohol and its dangers had long been a concern for Kimball. While on his mission he had written in a notebook: "Whiskey is good in its own place, there is nothing like whiskey for preserving a man when he is dead. But it is one of the worst things in the world for preserving a man when he is living. If you want to keep a man dead keep him in whiskey. If you want to kill a living man put whiskey into him." See Kimball Notebook, 1884, vol. 1, 118, in Kimball Journals.

65. Young Journal, Jan. 6 and 10, 1906.

66. See Quinn, "The Seventy," in *Extensions of Power*, 145–46, 687–88; and Seymour B. Young, 1908 Notebook, undated, copy in author's possession.

67. "B. H. Roberts's Eloquent Tribute," *Deseret Evening News*, Sep. 16, 1901, 2.

68. McMurrin (1858–1932) served as a member of the First Council from 1898 until his death. He was ordained to that office while serving a mission in England. Roberts and McMurrin had a complicated relationship on the First Council; sometimes

indulged in by … Roberts, McMurrin, Kimball, also by Bro. Young." Roberts explained that his work on the "History of the Church" with Apostle Lund took him away from other responsibilities because it was too difficult to stop in the middle of the work and then return to it to "gather together his information again." Kimball wrote that the meeting ended amicably: "While Bro Roberts's feelings were hurt, it will result in doing good."[69] However, Roberts only became more involved in church history. In 1902 he was appointed an Assistant Church Historian, a task he relished and filled until his death.

On August 18, 1902, a set of twin boys was born to Roberts's second wife Celia Dibble. The *Richmond [Utah] Dispatch* reported that the twins "are strong and healthy, weighing nine pounds each. Roberts has not named them yet, but it is intimated he will have them christened Andrew Jackson and Thomas Jefferson Roberts. Mr. Roberts is very happy and proud over this added pair of obstacles to a successful campaign for a seat in the House of Representatives."[70]

Roberts was not especially active in the 1902 campaign. William H. King was nominated for Congress and was soundly defeated in November by the Federal Bunch candidate, Joseph Howell.[71] The Utah Legislature was overwhelmingly Republican by this time. Roberts did continue to speak both in church and political circles after the election. One of his most interesting talks came at general conference in April 1903 when he dealt with the subject of Mormons and labor. In the past, he noted, most young men, if they felt constrained by where they were living, "could remove a few miles where lands could be obtained, and out of these lands make themselves homes and … furnish themselves with employment." But, as "our communities increase in number and our centers of population become more and more crowded," many young men will turn their attention to the acquiring of a skill in some kind of useful labor."

---

they were allies, sometimes not. His grandson Sterling W. McMurrin was an important Mormon intellectual and Roberts scholar.

69. Kimball Journal, Dec. 18, 1901.

70. "New Roberts Set of Twins," *Richmond Dispatch*, Aug. 26, 1902, 1.

71. Howell (1857–1918) lived in Wellsville where he taught school and was mayor, 1882–84. He also served in the Territorial House of Representatives from 1886 to 1892, and as a regent of the University of Utah, 1896–1900. He was active in business and banking as well as politics. A close ally of Reed Smoot and an integral member of the Federal Bunch, Howell served in the US House of Representatives from 1903 until 1917.

Inevitably such decisions will raise the question of joining labor unions. He continued:

> This is an age of organization both of capitalists and labor. The hosts of men that are engaged in the several trades have found it necessary in some way or other to protect themselves, that they may command a reasonable price for that labor. In other words, they have combined to control wages just as far as it is possible to control them. It is beyond question that these organizations in some cases become oppressive and work great mischief. They feel power and forget right. But something had to be done in order to make it possible for labor to hold its own against the growing force and greed and power of combined capital.

As a result, Roberts stated, no matter what concerns we might have about the possible downsides of labor unions, "organization and union on the part of labor became an absolute necessity to the working masses." Roberts admitted that he did not intend his remarks to be a definitive statement on the question, but rather to encourage the "wise men in Israel" to keep the young men of the church in mind "as they enter into mechanical arts and trades as the means of sustaining themselves by their labor."[72] Historian Ethan R. Yorgason writes that Roberts "increasingly stuck out as the exception to the majority of church leaders who easily accommodated capitalism."[73] Roberts also seemed in consonance with YMMIA manuals of the time, which he likely authored, in part, that discussed both the rights of capital and the right of wage labor to expect fair and equal treatment.[74]

Roberts was becoming less interested in the day-to-day activities of the First Council of Seventy. Based on J. Golden Kimball's observations, Roberts had begun finding the work of the First Council tedious, especially in light of his experiences in building the church in the East and in the political realm. Kimball described a "noticeable change" in his friend saying that he was "wondrous, charitable and believes in patiently letting things drift along and not try to reach too high a state of perfection all at once. To me it is a bad

72. "Elder B. H. Roberts," *Conference Reports*, Apr. 1903, 12–13.

73. Yorgason, *Transformation of Mormon Culture*, 89. See also McCormick and Sillito, *History of Utah Radicalism*, especially chapters 12 and 13.

74. Yorgason, *Transformation of Mormon Culture*, 207. See particularly the YMMIA manuals from 1910–11 to 1914–15.

indication on his part. He despises small things, & dislikes detail work."[75] Roberts's visits to local quorums were some of the lowest of any of the Seven Presidents,[76] and he increasingly either did not attend the meetings, came late, or left early.[77] At one meeting, Seymour B. Young wrote that "after transacting the usual amount of business, Bro Roberts was asked if he could not find time to devote a little more time to his Seventies duties. He said no and seemed offended that such a question should be asked."[78] At times, his colleagues seemed to get on his nerves and he would ask to be excused from discussions, leaving the work to be done by others.

In 1902, Apostle Reed Smoot was elected by the legislature to the US Senate, and, as with Roberts four years before, he was immediately challenged. The *Memphis Commercial Appeal* wryly observed, "Now that the Republicans have elected a Mormon Apostle Smoot to the United States Senate we shall see whether they are as dreadfully shocked as they were when the Democrats elected Brigham H. Roberts to the House of Representatives."[79]

Roberts responded to the attacks by noting that Smoot was much like himself when he was elected: possessed of the necessary constitutional qualifications, fairly elected, and in violation of no state or federal laws. And even though Smoot, being a Republican, was "a representative of a school of politics with which I have no sympathy ... he is undoubtedly the choice of the people of Utah ... and ... has a right to his seat."[80]

Smoot was unlike Roberts, however, in one essential way: he was not a polygamist. Smoot, also unlike Roberts, was allowed to take his seat with the understanding that the Senate's Committee on Elections and Privileges would hold hearings to assess his fitness. In the wake of that action, a coalition similar to the one that had challenged Roberts began to develop. At first, Smoot's opponents charged that

75. Kimball Journal, July 25, 1900.

76. Kimball Journal, Feb. 17, 1904.

77. Kimball Journal, Nov. 16, and Dec. 21, 1904; and Mar. 22, 1905.

78. Young Journal, Dec. 18, 1901, in Young Papers.

79. As quoted in "Clippings of Current Comment," *Brooklyn Daily Eagle*, Nov. 11, 1902, 4.

80. "B. H. Roberts Says Senator Smoot's Enemies Can Now Only Curse and Cry," *Salt Lake Telegram*, June 3, 1903, 3.

he was a polygamist—an accusation they knew to be false.[81] After that charge was dismissed, Smoot's adversaries "narrowed to the charge that he could not in good conscience hold the dual positions of apostle and senator."[82] The committee, which included Roberts's old antagonist Robert W. Tayler, who had moved from the House to the Senate, held hearings that investigated charges of ongoing plural marriages and brought in Joseph F. Smith and other church leaders, including Roberts, to testify.[83]

Roberts took the stand on April 20, 1904, and was interrogated by Senator Tayler who, as a congressman, had chaired the committee that had investigated him. The aim of Tayler's questioning was to ascertain whether Utah politics was under LDS Church control. Tayler asked Roberts to describe the differences he had with church authorities over his 1895 race. Roberts responded:

> Previous to my becoming a candidate for member of the constitutional convention, there had been some unpleasantness arisen about men in high church standing having anything to do in politics, and the presidency of the church at that time decided that members of the quorum of apostles, members of my own council, the presidents of the seventy, and the presidents of stakes, bishops of the wards, would better stay out of politics, and to that I consented or agreed. But during my brief absence from the State in the Fall of 1894 I was nominated by our county convention to be a member of the constitutional convention, and on my return, being informed of the nomination, in conversation with some friends I stated that it was a nomination I could not accept.[84]

But then he was informed that things had "somewhat changed," and, after consultation with church authorities, concluded that he could run. Tayler pressed him on exactly whom he consulted: a member of the First Presidency? Roberts was evasive, simply agreeing that it

81. Still, the charge of having more than one wife was picked up around the county. The *Decatur [Il] Herald,* for example, noted "Smoot will rhyme admirably with shoot, and that is where the Mormon aspirant for the senatorship should get it if he should presume to attempt to enter the upper branch of congress. Reed Smoot should be permitted to remain at home with his numerous wives and study the fate of Brigham H. Roberts." See [Untitled], *Decatur Herald,* Nov. 21, 1902, 4.

82. Craner, "Influence of the LDS Church," 20.

83. For more on the Smoot hearings, see Flake, *Politics of American Religious Identity.*

84. Paulos, *Mormon Church on Trial,* 214.

was someone "superior in authority." (Roberts later admitted it was indeed a member of the First Presidency, Joseph F. Smith.) Then Roberts told how Joseph F. Smith's "oracle" comment at general conference affected both his and Moses Thatcher's campaigns.[85]

Once that line of questioning was finished, Smoot's co-counsel, Waldemar Van Cott, asked Roberts to review the chronology of the political manifesto, and particularly to address how any "points of conflict" between Roberts and the church were "fixed up and settled." Roberts stated that he had at first opposed the political manifesto because he believed the church leaders were seeking to bring their influence to bear on who would be nominated for political office. But in "the course of several meetings with them for the purpose of discussing these matters, however, they satisfied me that it was not their intention to control the politics of the State, but they sought only the management of their own in ecclesiastical affairs." Roberts testified that with this clarification, he "joined with them in signing the rule that hereafter men should not accept positions of any kind that would take them from performance of their ecclesiastical duties without the consent of the superiors." Roberts finally concluded "that one is not entitled to seek political preferment until he first obtains a leave of absence or is excused from his official duties."[86]

Then the interrogation turned to the nature of the marriage ceremony as it was performed in the temple and its similarity with that performed previously in the Endowment House. Roberts carefully told the committee he did not "feel at liberty" to discuss these matters, but it was his belief that there was nothing in the ceremonies performed in either the Endowment House or the temple that "in any way binds you to disobey the laws of the land or make any arrangement against the government, or its officers … or anything contrary to the discharge of all the duties of a good citizen."[87] Committee members had become interested in LDS temple ceremonies and the so-called "Oath of Vengeance," a brief part of the ceremony

85. Paulos, 215–18.
86. Paulos, 224, 228.
87. Paulos, 232.

when participants covenanted to pray to "avenge the blood of the prophets" upon the United States.[88]

With his part in the hearing concluded, Roberts left Washington, DC, on April 26 and arrived back in Salt Lake City on May 8. He noted that "he could have returned sooner, but Bro. Franklin S. Richards," a church attorney, asked that Roberts remain and assist him in "counseling and advising some of the witness who were to come before … the committee."[89]

Two years later, on June 11, 1906, the committee passed a majority report saying that they were convinced that "political affairs of the state of Utah" were under the control of the Mormon hierarchy and that Smoot was "not entitled to a seat in the Senate.[90] Despite this action, Smoot had become acquainted with President Theodore Roosevelt, who believed in Smoot's personal integrity and "quietly" made his influence felt.[91] Ultimately, the Senate voted 42 to 28, with 20 not voting, to seat Smoot. He remained a senator until Democrats swept into power on a tide of anti-Herbert Hoover anger in the election of 1932.

When 1904 rolled around, Roberts took an active role in the state convention, nominating party officers and selecting delegates to the national convention. He sat on the stand and promoted the candidacy of David H. Peery,[92] who was ultimately chosen. Roberts was also pulling for his friend James H. Moyle, who was a candidate for governor. Moyle won on the first ballot by a landslide. The Democrats nominated Alton B. Parker as their candidate to face Theodore Roosevelt and held an enthusiastic rally in downtown Salt Lake.[93] By that fall, Roberts was campaigning in various places throughout

88. For more, see Buerger, *Mysteries of Godliness*, 175–79.

89. First Council of Seventy Minutes, May 11, 1904.

90. Craner, "Influence of the LDS Church," 23–24.

91. For an early assessment, see Ivins, "Theodore Roosevelt and Reed Smoot." See also Theodore Roosevelt, "Mr. Roosevelt to the Mormons," *Colliers Weekly*, Apr. 15, 1911, 28–36.

92. David Henry Peery (1866–1907) was the son of Utah pioneer D. H. Peery and inherited much of his business interests after his father's death in 1901. He was Ogden Police and Fire Commissioner, and served a term in the Utah State Senate, 1899–1901. A single, wealthy stockbroker and business entrepreneur, he died in Los Angeles. Roberts spoke at his funeral at Peery's request. See "Impressive Funeral Services Over D. H. Peery," *Ogden Standard*, Dec. 13, 1907, 3.

93. "Parker Pleases Utah Democrats," *Salt Lake Tribune*, July 10, 1904, 3.

the state. Seymour B. Young wrote that Roberts was "out on the stump for the Democratic party & telling the Saints & all the people what a sweet clean pure man Judge O. W. Powers is and how proper it is for the Saints to send him to Congress."[94] In his standard stump speech for Moyle and Orlando W. Powers, with whom he had occasionally been at odds, Roberts asserted that "the material and social interests" of the people of Utah were at stake in the election. Only with a strong Democratic victory, he said, would Utah—and the nation—prosper.[95] He brought his efforts to a conclusion with a rousing appearance in Ogden on election eve. When the votes were counted, however, the Democrats suffered a major defeat. Roosevelt defeated Democratic nominee Alton B. Parker 62,446 to 33,413; Moyle lost to Republican John C. Cutler 50,837 to 38,047; and Powers was overwhelmingly defeated by Joseph Howell 57,432 to 37,445. The Democrats found themselves with small memberships in both the state house and senate, which meant the election of Republican George Sutherland as US senator.

Roberts noted in a letter to Heber J. Grant that he believed it was "within the possibility of things that the Democrats by their failure at the election have missed a disastrous victory such as under which they suffered in 1892, and that the party in power may reap the disaster of their own policies. Ah well we shall see." Roberts assured Grant that he was not "much troubled from the results either in the nation or our own state. The importance of political elections grows less as I increase in my certainty that for the most part the general trend of things will not be very much affected by them." He told Grant that part of his disinterest stemmed from the fact that he was "absorbed" in the work of the Historian's Office and that "I feel well in my labors and have great joy therein." He was also happily engaged in the work of his ministry, noting, "The truth of this great work which grows in force upon my mind as the years go by notwithstanding the fact that for many years now it has been an actual certainty to my consciousness."[96]

But soon Roberts was back to speaking on politics, this time

94. Young Journal, Sep. 23, 1904.

95. "B. H. Roberts on the Stump," *Salt Lake Tribune*, Oct. 21, 1904, 4.

96. Roberts to Grant, Nov. 15, 1904, box 4, fd. 12, Kenney Collection.

navigating a complicated relationship with socialism when he spoke to the Utah Federation of Labor in May 1906. He began by arguing that socialism did not really liberate workers, but rather took away their liberties. In his view, he stated, socialism meant "a general condition of equality to be brought about and enforced by law." He noted that the supposed curse that "man shall earn his bread by the sweat of his brow was really a blessing in disguise" because all great nations relied on individual "industry and work" to maintain their greatness. Roberts said he recognized that there were "economic evils" which required a remedy, especially the "unequal distribution of the products of labor and capital," but "exact equality was a thing impossible with human nature." He asserted that he believed competition was key to bringing about a more equal society, arguing that when you took away competition, you removed "man's incentive to excel" which would "result in man failing to bring out that which is best in him." At the same time, calls by socialists to "remove from the mind of man the haunting fear of privation for himself and those dependent on him" were counterproductive because removing that fear would result in a diminished incentive on the part of workers to produce. Roberts concluded that despite his objections to socialism, he was "strongly in favor of labor organizations and unions" which had "accomplished great good for the laboring class in the past and would continue to do so in the future."[97]

Roberts, was concerned that some—both Mormon and gentile—sought to link Mormonism and socialism together in a positive light. On one occasion he told a "large audience" in the Ogden Tabernacle that "there could be no equality of men" in human society, and denied that there was any scriptural passage that would support otherwise. He said that he was opposed "to a more equal distribution" of the important things in society, and stated that equality would come "in the world hereafter." He argued that only through Mormonism could the goals of socialism be achieved—the essential elements being cooperation, human dignity, and the voluntary

97. The paper noted, "That the audience was not made up entirely of those who believe in socialism was clear from the applause which greeted several of the keenest thrusts at the doctrine." See "Opposes Socialism as Taught; Roberts Talks," *Salt Lake Telegram*, May 7, 1906, 3.

consecration of property to a larger community. In support of his position, he referred to Doctrine and Covenants 49:20, which states, "But it is not given that one man should possess that which is above another, wherefore the world lieth in sin." Roberts also suggested that Doctrine and Covenants 51 implied that all would be treated equally "according to his family, according to his circumstances and his wants and needs."[98]

Despite these criticisms of socialism, Roberts's opponents—especially Reed Smoot—asserted that Roberts's support for some progressive reforms constituted ipso facto support for socialism itself. The senator saw support for his assertions in sections that Roberts proposed for church manuals on the question of public utilities, which Smoot believed "were in favor of Government ownership and in some cases Socialistic."[99]

On the eve of the election, October 12, 1906, Roberts and George Albert Smith were given a special assignment[100] by the First Presidency "to pay a visit to the Churches comprised in the Eastern and Southern States missions."[101] The First Presidency was seeking more favorable publicity in the midst of on-going attacks over plural marriage and the effects of the Reed Smoot case.

Smith, Roberts, and John G. McQuarrie,[102] president of the Eastern States Mission, met in Chicago on October 19 to begin their several-month tour.[103] In many ways, the experience stood in marked contrast to Roberts's earlier tours through those areas, especially his time as a missionary. Gone were the days of laborious advertising, small meetings, and antagonistic audiences. Part of this probably had to do with the growth of the church over the previous twenty years, but part of it also had to do with Roberts's notoriety. Just about every newspaper account remarked on his ejection from

98. See Roberts's notes on socialism in fd. 495, Roberts Collection.

99. Smoot, *In the World*, 116.

100. George Albert Smith, Diary, Oct. 11, 1906, in Smith Family Papers. Hereafter cited as Smith Diary.

101. First Presidency to George Albert Smith, Oct. 12, 1906, box 38, fd. 18, Smith Family Papers.

102. McQuarrie (1867–1962) was called to the Eastern States Mission in August 1900 and succeeded Edward H. Snow as president in February 1901, serving in that capacity until July 1908.

103. Smith Diary, Oct. 18, 1906.

Congress, the Smoot hearings (which were still ongoing), and (often to Roberts's approval) the details of Mormonism. Though the group encountered some suspicion in Fairmont, West Virginia, where the city clerk told them that they "would not be tolerated in the city," Smith noted that after spending some time in conversation with him he "left feeling sure I had removed some prejudice."[104] While in Washington, DC, they visited the White House where they met President Theodore Roosevelt.

Roberts spoke at a New York dinner meeting of the Sunrise Club—a religious Free-Thought group—on "Some Contributions of Mormonism to Modern Religious Thought." Those contributions included, first, a distinctive American volume of scripture; second, a doctrine of continuous revelation; third, a belief in the existence of God "as completely as at any time in history," and a belief in the imminence of God's return; fourth, a commitment to proclaiming a "universal" reign of law in harmony with the laws of science; and, finally, a doctrine of salvation that was based on humans attaining increasing knowledge as they went through life. Roberts emphasized the Mormon belief that it was "impossible to be saved in ignorance."[105] The *New York Times* reported that there were some two hundred in attendance, and the discussion afterward included "both friends and opponents of Mormonism," among them "agnostics, Socialists, free thinkers … and the representatives of all shades of religious belief."[106] The event made an impression on George Albert Smith who recorded in his diary, "After a forty minute talk discussion followed and the variety of ideas advanced was quite a surprise to me. The most of those present were agnostics and [they] ridiculed our belief in revelation. The discussion lasted until nearly twelve o'clock being participated in by quite a number."[107]

After touring the northern states, Roberts and Smith moved south, stopping in Kentucky, Tennessee, Virginia, South Carolina, Florida, Alabama, Mississippi, and Louisiana.[108] It was here that

104. Smith Diary, Oct. 26, 27, 1906.

105. B. H. Roberts, "Some Contributions of Mormonism to Modern Religious Thought," *Liahona: The Elder's Journal*, July 22, 1913, 49–55, 57–58.

106. "Roberts at Mormon Dinner," *New York Times*, Nov. 20, 1906.

107. Smith Diary, Nov. 19, 1906.

108. See Southern States Manuscript History, Nov. 27–Dec. 21, 1906.

Roberts's racial views were heard publicly. Foremost, he assured Southerners that the Mormons were not promoting racial integration: "It is a commandment of God with us that there should be no amalgamation between the white race and the black, and that each race should be taught to preserve itself from such amalgamation. The heaviest church disabilities would result from the contraction of such views."[109] Roberts made similar statements in South Carolina, declaring to the *Charleston News and Courier* that the Mormons teach separation of the races as a commandment of God. "No negro is permitted to enter the priesthood of the Church and there are few negro members although the church does not withhold its benefits from them." Roberts's views "on the negro question," the paper reported, "came from his religious faith, and they are common among the Mormons of the West."[110]

Roberts first came into contact with African Americans on his mission. But his views on race, and more specifically the LDS priesthood ban on blacks, can be traced to an article he wrote in the *Contributor* in April 1885.[111] It relies heavily on verses in the Pearl of Great Price,[112] which had been canonized five years earlier, elevating it to the same status in the eyes of Latter-day Saints as the Bible, the Book of Mormon, and the Doctrine and Covenants.[113] In discussing those who had been valiant in the pre-existence and those who had followed Lucifer, he drew attention to some who "were so indifferent in their support of the righteous cause of our redeemer, that they forfeited privileges and powers granted to those who were valiant for God and correct principle."[114] Roberts identified one such group as the descendants of Ham who had married Egyptus, a descendant of Cain who had killed his brother and thus was cursed with a mark, which Roberts believed, based on the Pearl of Great Price, was a

109. See "Mormons Will Help," *Indianapolis News*, Dec. 5, 1906, 16; "Mormons Hit Race Mixture," *Des Moines Register*, Dec. 6, 1906, 8; "Mormons to Settle the Race Problem," *Keowee [SC] Courier*, Dec. 19, 1906, 6; and "Brigham H. Roberts on the Race Problem," *Deseret News*, Dec. 6, 1906, 8.

110. "Mormons Meet in Columbia," *Charleston News and Courier*, Dec. 17, 1906, 1.

111. See Harris and Bringhurst, *Mormon Church and Blacks*, 48–50.

112. See Abr. 1:26–27

113. B. H. Roberts, "To The Youth of Israel," *Contributor*, May 1885, 295–99.

114. "To The Youth," 297.

dark skin.[115] As a result, he believed the black race consisted of those spirits who, while they may not have rebelled against God, were "not valiant in the great rebellion in heaven," and who, through "their indifference or lack of integrity to righteousness, rendered themselves unworthy of the priesthood and its powers and hence it is withheld from them to this day."[116]

Roberts went on to say that in the contemporary world, some individuals were "more faithful, noble and intelligent than others." By implication, those who were none of these things possessed a black skin. In a January 27, 1895, talk given in the Salt Lake Tabernacle, Roberts notes that though "the negro race" is blessed with the "privileges of the gospel," they "cannot receive … the rights of the Holy Priesthood."[117] Roberts also amplified his views in his book *Seventy's Course in Theology*. In a special lesson entitled "The Law of the Lord in Ancient and Modern Revelation Applied to the American Negro Race Problem," he quoted Southern apologist William Benjamin Smith[118] that "the Negro is markedly inferior to the Caucasian," asserting that in that sense, the "commingling" of the two races "must only lower the higher."[119] Roberts was also drawing upon views held by his mentor, deceased LDS president John Taylor. Indeed, as Newell Bringhurst writes, toward the end of the nineteenth century "a number of church periodicals … were quoting chapter and verse from the Pearl of Great Price in upholding the inferior place of black people within Mormonism." Such a view was endorsed by a 1912 First Presidency response to the question of priesthood denial to blacks based on this scripture, and the idea had become "well established" as a "foundation of church policy."[120]

---

115. See Gen. 9:18–27.

116. "To the Youth," 297. For a useful overview, see Harris, "Mormonism's Problematic Racial Past;" and Reeve, *Religion of a Different Color*.

117. "What is Man," *Deseret Weekly*, Mar. 16, 1895, 387.

118. Smith (1850–1934) was a white supremacist and professor of mathematics at Tulane University. Roberts drew upon Smith's book *The Color Line: A Brief in Behalf of the Unborn* (New York: McClure, Phillips & Co, 1905), 12.

119. Roberts, *Seventy's Course in Theology*, 163–66. Roberts also referenced a US history text by Confederate vice president Alexander Stephens. This is yet one more suggestion that Roberts was sympathetic to a southern states' rights view of race.

120. Bringhurst, *Saints, Slaves, and Blacks*, 150–51. See also Bush, "Mormonism's Negro Doctrine," 11–68; and Caldwell, "Moral and Religious Aspects." Caldwell is one

To the *Times-Union,* Roberts said that the "amalgamation" of the white and African race by "marriage or promiscuity" was "unthinkable"; he argued that the line of "separation" would not be served with "the dream of social equality of these races, entertained by some very good and very much mistaken humanitarians." Such views, he said, should be abandoned, and he placed himself squarely in the attitudes of most white southern segregationists:

> The African race in America owes something—yes, very much—to the white race. His condition here is much improved over that of his race in the Congo … or other parts of Africa. If he would have those advantages continue for himself and his posterity he must consent to such relationships between himself and that white race which alone are tolerable—complete separation of the races sexually and socially.[121]

After holding well-attended segregated public meetings in Jacksonville, Florida, where Roberts paid "an eloquent tribute" to Southern customs, The *Jacksonville Metropolis* assured readers that the Mormons "regard the negro race as forbidden. No negro can rise in the Mormon church, nor can he affiliate with the Mormons. The church has set its fiat against social or other equality."[122] This assessment likely came from Roberts's remarks or in interviews with reporters.

On December 23, Roberts's party arrived in New Orleans where George Albert Smith noted that they intended "to spend a couple days resting and looking around." On Christmas Eve, Smith and Roberts "left at night for the land of Utah." They "had traveled 10,500 miles" since leaving Salt Lake City in October.[123]

Roberts arrived home from his extended trip on December 31, 1906, reporting that he found "the conditions of the various missions visited" to be "in excellent condition."[124] Smith concurred, noting

---

of the first to suggest that "an analysis of Latter-day Saint scripture indicates that this doctrine is not explicit but inferred."

121. "Mormon Elder Discusses Smoot," *Pensacola Journal*, Dec. 23, 1906, 2:11.

122. "A Mormon Church in Florida," *Ocala Banner*, Dec. 28, 1906, 8.

123. Smith Diary, Dec. 20–28, 1906. They traveled on the Texas Pacific train line through Pueblo, Colorado. It appears that Roberts may have stayed in Colorado for a few days since he arrived later in the month than did Smith.

124. "B. H. Roberts Returns," *Salt Lake Telegram*, Jan. 1, 1907, 2. Many national newspapers covered various aspects of Smith and Roberts's efforts, especially in the South. See "Personal Points," *Cleveland Plain Dealer*, Dec. 31, 1906, 4.

that "the work was prospering"; that the world was gradually accepting Mormonism; and that "the time was never more propitious for the spreading of the gospel."[125] The two men submitted a ten-page report on their activities to church leaders, suggesting that "owing to the peculiar conditions prevailing there past and present," the church should avoid active proselytizing in Washington, DC—probably referring to the Reed Smoot hearings. Beyond that, they focused on what they believed were the prevailing weaknesses of missionaries in the field, including a "woeful lack in training in what we would call good manners." They stated that the church needed to improve "missionary classes in our academies and universities, as also … in our quorums." For Roberts, that meant a reexamination of the work of the various seventies quorums throughout the church.[126]

Over the next few years Roberts sought to strengthen the ties between the First Council and the individual quorums. In 1910, for example, Roberts and his colleagues visited all 164 local seventies units, and he pledged that thenceforth "one of the council expected to visit every quorum in the church each year."[127] Roberts could be a tough taskmaster at these visits. He told the members of the Eighty-Seventh Quorum of Seventy in Plain City, Utah, that he was dismayed that only some 3,800 of the 9,000 seventies in the church were then serving full-time missions. He reminded those in the quorum that "the office of a Seventy was not to honor man but to honor God and his work," and believed members of the various quorums should "be true to their colleagues and give their service whenever asked to do so."[128]

125. "Joseph F. Smith Defies Enemies," *Salt Lake Tribune*, Dec. 31, 1906, 1.

126. George Albert Smith and B. H. Roberts to the First Presidency, undated report, ca. Jan. 1907, box 28, fd. 18, Smith Family Papers.

127. See Roberts's remarks in Plain City Ward Quorum of Seventy Minutes, Nov. 20, 1910, and Dec. 16, 1911.

128. Plain City Ward, Dec. 16, 1911.

FIFTEEN

POLITICAL STATESMAN

Roberts's days of making any significant waves nationally were largely over. The press and various ecclesiastical and women's groups would continue to hold him up as the public face of polygamy. But mostly he made his political acumen useful in various ways locally. For example, in April 1907, he played an important role in mediating a street-car strike in Salt Lake City. Roberts had been involved in settling a work stoppage the year before,[1] and was "trusted" by the workers to do so again. Using the Kenyon Hotel on Main Street as his base of operations, Roberts shuttled between meeting with the union representatives and their company counterparts.[2] Finally, after an all-day session, an agreement was reached near midnight that provided for a two-year contract covering the motormen, conductors, and barn men. Motormen and conductors received a twenty-five-cent raise on May 1, with a thirty-cent raise scheduled for a year later. The barn men obtained an across-the-board 10 percent increase. The decision was announced to a "delighted crowd of car men" early in the morning. Union leaders and rank-and-file alike praised Roberts for his "earnest and efficient efforts" and for his role on both occasions in bringing about a settlement.[3] Roberts's colleague in the Historian's Office, Anthon H. Lund, concluded that

1. "Officers Announced by Street Car Men at Reception Given Pratt," *Salt Lake Telegram*, June 25, 1906, 3.

2. "Street Railway Statement Ready," *Salt Lake Telegram*, May 2, 1907, 8.

3. See "Carmen's Strike Over: Both Sides Are Well Pleased," *Salt Lake Telegram*, Apr. 30, 1907, 1; "Peace Arranged by B. H. Roberts," *Deseret Evening News*, Apr. 30, 1907, 5; and "Union Men Denounce Organ of Church and Commend the Police," *Salt Lake Telegram*, May 1, 1907, 3. The *Salt Lake Telegram*, however, saw Roberts's role differently, claiming he "did not fix the terms, he was but a messenger." See "Who Settled the Strike?" *Salt Lake Telegram*, May 1, 1907, 12.

Roberts had "done well in [reconciling] the parties."[4] Later that year, Roberts would also play a role in helping to end a strike between the International Brotherhood of Electrical Workers and the Independent Telephone Company.[5]

However, Roberts's political leanings also stirred up controversy in the upper ranks of church leadership where he clashed with Republicans generally and Reed Smoot particularly. Always a controversial figure, Smoot had attracted the enmity of several politically active Mormon Democrats such as Heber J. Grant and James H. Moyle. Some resented the powerful machine Smoot had created; others felt there was too much involvement by the hierarchy in Smoot's ascendancy; some saw him as a direct obstacle to their own political ambitions. Roberts seemed to have been especially critical of Smoot. Smoot's biographer, Milton R. Merrill, writes that Roberts was jealous of an "average man like Reed Smoot," while Roberts himself was a "brilliant orator" and "great performer on the stump." Roberts would sometimes burst out in criticism of Smoot, and while these attacks "were made in the heat of battle," Merrill is correct that they also represented Roberts's true feelings.[6]

During the 1908 campaign, Roberts expressed his views on Smoot to Richard R. Lyman[7] in a letter that became public. Roberts wrote to Lyman that he believed Smoot possessed none of the abilities and qualities that should distinguish a leader at his level politically, "since within his party alone there are at least 500 men in the state, any one of whom would discharge the duties in an equally acceptable manner, and some of them both with greater credit and advantage to the state, and without perpetuating the old antagonisms and exciting new ones."[8]

The letter offended many of Roberts's colleagues in LDS leadership and reignited many of the problem's leaders had had with

4. Lund, *Danish Apostle,* 363. In the original, Lund used the phrase "reconciliating."

5. "No Change in Bell Strike," *Ogden Standard-Examiner,* Oct. 22, 1907, 8.

6. Merrill, *Reed Smoot,* 109–10.

7. Lyman (1870–1963) was a professor of engineering at the University of Utah. He served as vice chair of the Utah State Roads Commission, 1909–18. Lyman became a member of the Quorum of the Twelve Apostles in 1918 and served until his excommunication in 1943.

8. Roberts to Lyman, Mar. 3, 1908, quoted in "Roberts Is Opposing Smoot," *Ogden Standard,* May 7, 1908. See also Merrill, *Reed Smoot,* 120.

Roberts in the past. On May 6, the First Presidency and the Twelve discussed Roberts's views at their weekly meeting. All of the men were there except Rudger Clawson, Charles Penrose, and Smoot himself. The letter by Roberts "was read which seems to place him in a more dangerous place. It is an attack on Reed Smoot."[9]

Anthon H. Lund wrote that it was clear that Roberts was "down upon Smoot, he slurs him as an apostle and as a senator. He predicts this state will go out of our hands in ten years and then makes the plea: Shall we make it an anti-Mormon state as well as a non-Mormon state?"[10] Later in the month J. Golden Kimball noted that "much time [was] spent" at the meeting of the First Quorum of Seventy in the temple discussing Roberts's "political position."[11]

Roberts also raised the ire of Presiding Bishop Charles W. Nibley, who told him, "Reed Smoot has more practical business sense in his head and will accomplish more practical results in one year than B. H. Roberts could accomplish if he lived a hundred years." Cautioning Roberts that he was "on dangerous ground," Nibley warned him that in his criticism he risked lending "aid and comfort to the enemies of Christ."[12]

The *Richfield Reaper* weighed in on the controversy as well, saying that a "careful reading" of the letter paints Roberts as a "petty, jealous, peanut politician," not as the intellectual he was claimed to be by his admirers. The paper asserted that Roberts demonstrated the weakness of his argument that the senate and the apostleship are "too much for anyone man to do justice to" when one considers that "Mr. Roberts was much in favor of the election of Moses Thatcher to the senate of the United States and Mr. Thatcher was an apostle of the dominant church."[13] Roberts was not formally censured for his letter.

Smoot was not the only political issue facing Roberts and the Democrats. At its convention in Logan on September 22, the party nominated a slate of candidates, including Jesse Knight for governor and Roberts's friend and colleague Lyman R. Martineau for

9. Smith, *Church, State, and Politics*, 601.

10. Lund, *Danish Apostle*, 380.

11. Kimball Journal, May 20, May 21, 1908.

12. Nibley to Roberts, June 10, 1908, box 4, fd. 12, Kenney Collection. Roberts forwarded a copy of the letter to the First Presidency.

13. "That Roberts Letter," *Richfield Reaper*, May 14, 1908, 2.

Congress. Though Knight declined the nomination, delegates nominated him anyway by acclamation.[14]

Not long after that, Knight's son, J. William Knight,[15] a staunch Democrat and active Mormon, became the party's gubernatorial standard bearer. Roberts was instrumental in making that shift. "The sounds of a battle royal every day," Roberts proclaimed, "come over the Wasatch hills," and the Republican Party is in "full retreat." Even if that were not the case, Roberts argued, and the Democrats faced certain defeat, they could not "stand idle" in opposing the Republican Party for its myriad of failures, especially in the economy.

Despite Roberts's best efforts during the campaign season, however, Utah Democrats again suffered a major defeat in 1908. Republicans swept the state legislature—with a total of only two Democrats elected to the sixty-one-member state house and senate—while losing Knight's race for the governorship to William Spry by a margin of nearly ten thousand votes. At the same time, Roberts's friend Lyman Martineau lost his race for US House to incumbent Joseph Howell by double that number. Roberts's political hero William Jennings Bryan lost his third presidential bid and was defeated in Utah by William Howard Taft by nearly twenty thousand votes. Soon the Republican legislature would send Smoot back to Washington as well.

Roberts and all Democrats lost an important ally when the *Salt Lake Herald* was sold to the *Intermountain Republican*.[16] More personally, Roberts lost his good friend and political ally Moses Thatcher who died on August 21, 1909. The funeral was held in the Logan Tabernacle on August 26, where, in the words of John Henry Smith, "the building was filled to suffocation." The *Salt Lake Telegram* estimated the attendance in the thousands.[17] The Oregon Short Line railroad put two extra cars on the route north just to

14. "Record Breaking Convention Nominates Jesse Knight After Great Demonstration," *Salt Lake Herald*, Sep. 23, 1908, 1; "Jesse Knight Expresses Regret at Being Unable to Accept Honor," *Salt Lake Herald*, Sep. 23, 1908, 6.

15. Knight (1874–1956) graduated from Brigham Young University in 1894. He became a counselor in the Utah Stake presidency just prior to his nomination. He later served in the Utah State Senate, 1919–21, and supported the League of Nations.

16. Craner, "Influence of the LDS Church," 92.

17. "Thousands at Funeral of Thatcher," *Salt Lake Telegram*, Aug. 27, 1909, 6. Interestingly, the paper does not make mention of Roberts's remarks.

accommodate the many people attending.[18] Among the mourners were Representative Joseph Howell, former governor John C. Cutler, a number of LDS general authorities, several political friends, and many residents of Cache Valley.[19] While Smith and Newell W. Kimball[20] of the Cache Stake presidency offered brief remarks, Roberts was the main speaker. Obviously, because of what the church authorities had done to Thatcher, this was a sensitive assignment.

The *Salt Lake Tribune* said that there "was a strong note of defiance in Roberts's voice and his frame trembled" as he addressed the crowd. Roberts "shouted at the top of his voice" to the congregation that

> you cannot rob him of what he has done. What if he did make mistakes? All human beings make them, but in comparison with the brilliancy of his record for the Church, his mistakes slip into insignificance. He bore witness of the truth by suffering. In the days of his sorrow and trouble men set a price upon his membership in the Church and he paid it. And what a price it was too. He … remained true to the end. Who shall decry him? No man can question Moses Thatcher's faith in Mormonism. … He was a leader whom the people would follow for they had confidence in him. … Moses Thatcher's life was constant admonition for better living and thousands are better for his having been. God will judge by the heart alone, and Moses Thatcher's heart was right. I say peace to his ashes; his soul cannot die.[21]

As Utah elections swung more solidly Republican, national attention focused on the Beehive State. The firm Mormon–Republican alliance, the *St. Louis Post-Dispatch* argued, was demonstrated in the way that Roberts had been treated in Congress as opposed to Smoot. In the former case, Republican opposition was almost unanimous, with but one Republican voting for Roberts, while Republicans "nine years later, were all but solid for Smoot." No doubt, the paper

18. "Many People Attend Funeral," *Salt Lake Herald*, Aug. 27, 1909, 3.

19. The funeral for federal marshal Benjamin B. Heywood was held on the same day in Salt Lake City. No doubt many political friends of Thatcher had to choose which funeral to attend. See "Last Rites Paid to Ben B. Heywood," *Salt Lake Telegram*, Aug. 27, 1909, 5.

20. Kimball (1853–1931) was the son of Heber C. Kimball, and lived his entire life in Logan. He was a businessman and member of the Logan Commercial Boosters Club. A Democrat, he was a Logan City councilman in 1886 and 1894–96; mayor from 1896 to 1897; and a Cache County commissioner.

21. "Last Rites Over Moses Thatcher," *Salt Lake Tribune*, Aug. 27, 1909, 1.

editorialized, Smoot's unwavering support for tariffs played a role. But there was more to the Republican acceptance of once-criticized "Mormon morals" than that, since nothing had been revealed "to show that what was said of the Mormons when Roberts was on trial was not true when Smoot was under fire." After the Roberts debacle, the *Dispatch* editorialized, when Smoot was elected, the church moved from "an indefinite, incoherent state of homogeneity to a definite coherent belief that they had enough votes in Utah, Wyoming and Idaho to keep the Republicans on their side forever." The LDS Church had become well versed in politics and "sophisticated." Now, "they have learned that the way to the Republican heart is through the ballot box."[22]

Over more than thirty years, Roberts and Smoot would always hold each other at arm's length, particularly in terms of politics—but the antipathy spilled over to church issues as well. When Smoot was sustained as an apostle in April 1900, Roberts "did not give his hand at first" to sustain him. Anthon H. Lund recorded that while there was "general satisfaction" concerning the call," Roberts "explained he had heard that Bro. Smoot ... said 'I do not believe in sending a man to congress who is all wind.' Bro. Roberts thought this meant him, while Bro. Smoot referred to W[illiam] H. King."[23] One senses that the two men—despite some times of common labor—were simply fated to misunderstand each other. A good example can be found when Smoot notes in his diary that at general conference in October 1909 Roberts "occupied most of the time and spoke of the faults and shortcomings of the Prophet Joseph [Smith] and others and the necessity of keeping sacred an agreement etc. His whole remarks had behind them a spirit of fault finding but many of the things he said of and in themselves were fine." But Roberts's words earned him "a rebuke" by Joseph F. Smith, and many "people wondered what he was driving at."[24]

Indeed, Smith stated that he felt it was his "duty" to caution the brethren to avoid casting judgment on the church, its members, or its leaders, and on their "shortcomings, faults and failings." He said that

22. "Sophisticated Mormons," *St. Louis Post-Dispatch*, Sep. 26, 1909, 12.
23. Lund, *Danish Apostle*, 81.
24. Smoot, *In the World*, 35.

judgments on the "supposed defects of the Prophet Joseph Smith or Brigham Young, or any other of the leaders of the Church," was reserved to God. He cautioned the congregation that "when the Lord wants to reveal something new to us, He knows the channel through which to reveal it … through the proper channels of the Priesthood. Don't forget that!"[25] Smith and Roberts had a long history—as was the case with Smoot—of having periods of antagonism and divisions of opinion. Rudger Clawson, for example, records in his diary of conflicts between the two men over the question of card playing. At a July 9, 1903, meeting of the First Presidency and the Twelve, Smith said he disagreed with those who held that there was nothing "wicked in a game of cards," and called it a "waste of time" and a practice that might "easily lead to evil." Smith referred obliquely to Roberts who he said "advocated it as a means of keeping his children at home." Two weeks later, Roberts again returned to the subject and stated that, despite believing card playing was an "innocent amusement," he had decided to accept Smith's view of the matter.[26]

What neither Smoot nor Smith seemed to understand about Roberts's conference address was that he—while cautioning that he did not lay claim to the title—was speaking in his role as a historian, and using historical events to make a larger point—namely, that while God had given them "a system of truth that constitutes the Gospel of Jesus Christ," a system which was "invulnerable" and "perfect," but which sometimes also exhibited examples of "fanaticism … narrowness and bigotry." Roberts warned the congregation that it was a "dangerous thing for a people to feel they are the especial favorites of heaven and that God has marked them off from the rest of mankind by giving them a special mission, and exalts them by making them the repository of His law, of His truth, and the executors of his Will in the earth." He reminded listeners that, at times in the LDS past, "some of our brethren, under the sense of being the chosen of God, gave way to fanatical expressions of boastfulness [which] angered the people by whom they were surrounded."[27]

Roberts continued that he understood that this behavior in no

25. "President Joseph F. Smith," *Conference Reports*, Oct. 1909, 124–25.
26. See Clawson, *Ministry of Meetings*, 640, 649.
27. "Elder Brigham H. Roberts," *Conference Reports*, Oct. 1909, 103.

way justified the outrages committed against the Saints. Still, he maintained that clearly "over zeal, fanaticism and unwisdom" were at the heart of the of the "disaster that befell our community in Missouri." Such a view, he said, was supported by passages in the Doctrine and Covenants. Moreover, he turned to the same scriptural source to suggest that Joseph Smith had "made his mistakes and was several times reproved of the Lord." Roberts assured conference goers that "that there is no desire in my heart to assume any function that does not properly belong to my ministry." He concluded that he had "the fullest confidence that whatever may be erratic or sporadically wrong among us will be corrected; and the presiding brethren will find me, heart and hand, with them in maintaining the honor and glory of this great empire of the Christ."[28]

His remarks, which do not seem to have been published in the local papers, touched off a firestorm. Orson F. Whitney indicated that Roberts's remarks, while "eloquent," were "not imbued with the Spirit of the Lord. It caused sorrow to his friends and doubtless gave aid and comfort to the enemy." Whitney felt that the remarks "did not sit well with the Brethren," including himself. A week later, Roberts went to the First Presidency and said if his remarks had been "radically wrong" he would let it be left out of the *Conference Report*.[29] According to Lund, President Joseph F. Smith asked Roberts to submit his remarks to Lund, "and what I suggested would meet his mind." Lund told Roberts to "make what changes he desired and we would go over it together." Whitney does not mention the two men meeting to go over the remarks. Thus, we must assume that the published *Conference Reports* version was accepted by all parties.[30]

Not long after this, Roberts took a break from political and philosophical battles when his mother died in January 1910. The *Deseret News* noted that Ann Everington Roberts Woolley was especially tied to the young people through the Sunday School and the Primary. The paper called her "a woman of strong personality, gentle in demeanor, refined and intelligent. She wielded a powerful influence in her family up to the last … and … took a lively interest in the affairs

28. "Elder Brigham H. Roberts," 108.
29. Horne, *Life of Orson F. Whitney*, 294–95, Lund, *Danish Apostle*, 405.
30. Lund, *Danish Apostle*, 405.

of the community in which she lived."[31] Roberts and his mother were close, and he was devastated. He wrote to his friend Isaac Russell, "My mother died in my arms on the 11th ult., and we buried her a few days later. She reached the ripe age of 83 years and ... retained all her faculties to the last and could wait upon herself within a day or two of her demise. I could not wish either for her or myself a happier ending of Life's fitful dreams; but the departure of one so beloved as she was leaves something of sadness with us who remain."[32]

Part of the loss, as Roberts complained to Russell, was the lack of a close relationship. He told his friend that one of the things "from which I suffer greatly is a lack of sympathetic companionship. Mormon officialdom is strangely dumb to me. ... More and more, administrative affairs seem to concentrate into the hands of a few, and it is difficult to form an opinion as to what are really the trend of affairs." He told Russell that he was "resolved to turn philosopher and say 'this too shall pass away;'" but also admitted he would be "sorry to lose interest in the things to which I have devoted a life of service."[33]

On the political front, he hoped that things were beginning to change for the Democrats. There was more party unity. A strong leadership group of Roberts, James H. Moyle, William H. King, and others emerged, which, while not always united on every issue, was united in its opposition to Smoot and the Federal Bunch. But lacking a senatorial election or that of governor and state officers, the 1910 election was somewhat low key. "The Fall political campaign is upon us," Roberts wrote again to Russell, "and while the whole country is a blaze with splendid insurgency within the Republican party we haven't [seen efforts] in Utah in that party to throw off the shackles of stand-patism reinforced as it is by Smoot." He admitted that he was growing "pessimistic" regarding the slow pace of change. "The betterment forces move so slowly in Utah." He lamented that ousting incumbents is "so difficult," and that "our own people are not quickly responsive to appeals made to them. They are so accustomed to being led and to their leaders." Roberts worried that young people were leaving Mormonism: "Here and there, are dropping

31. "B. H. Roberts's Mother Dies at Bountiful," *Deseret News*, Jan. 2, 1910, 5.

32. Roberts to Russell, Feb. 10, 1910, box 7, fd. 9, Russell Papers.

33. Roberts to Russell.

from the ranks of our church some of the brightest intellects and best souls that we have. Not openly and defiantly but just quietly dropping out—losing interest and patience and faith." Roberts himself seemed unhappy, and wrote his friend that "the situation to me is only tolerable because I have an abiding faith in the higher and deeper principles of Philosophic Mormonism with which I am interested myself and which the errors … and sometimes the stupid inefficiency of Church officialdom cannot effect."[34]

In September, the state Democratic convention met in Provo and nominated Ferdinand Ericksen,[35] former Mt. Pleasant mayor and judge of the seventh district court, for Congress, and Democratic stalwart C. C. Richards for the state supreme court. The Democrats passed a progressive state platform advocating statewide alcohol prohibition, direct primaries, direct election of US senators, and the initiative referendum and recall.[36] Roberts appears not to have attended the convention, and may have been somewhat disengaged. Clearly he disagreed with the party stance on statewide prohibition, noting he did not have "confidence in the effectiveness of such legislation," though he admitted that public opinion in the state demanded it.[37]

After pleas from others, he became more involved. Roberts wrote to "My Dear Moyle" that "You win your case. Responding to your requests and what you say is a wide-spread demand that I should take part in the campaign I have concluded to say that you can make appeals to me throughout the remainder of the canvas and I will do all in my power to help your cause." Roberts then reviewed the leading Republicans saying "our Senior Senator" is lost in the "cold bleak Alps" of the tariff; the "little piping voice of St. George Sutherland

34. Roberts to Russell, Sep. 9, 1910, box 4, fd. 15, Kenney Collection

35. Ericksen (1863–1927) was raised and educated in Sanpete County, and later attended the University of Michigan law school. A "staunch Democrat," Ericksen practiced law in Mt. Pleasant, and served as Sanpete County attorney and treasurer as well as mayor of Mt. Pleasant. After his defeat for congress, he moved to Salt Lake City where he practiced law and was general counsel for the Utah Fuel Company. See "Ericksen Rites to Be Saturday," *Salt Lake Telegram*, Apr. 21, 1927, 5; and *History of the Bench*, 133.

36. "Utah Democrats Declare for Statewide Prohibition," *Salt Lake Herald*, Sep. 16, 1910, 1.

37. *B. H. Roberts Discusses the Republican Deal with the Liquor Dealers*, broadside addressed to James H. Moyle, Oct. 21, 1910.

has grown so faint that we can hear him no more. I feel he is lost;" I have long wondered what has become of our Solid and Sole Representative, Joseph Howell"; while Nephi Morris, the "white plumed Knight of Prohibition is stricken and his voice is no longer heard in the land." He concluded his letter: "So Mr. Chairman make me all the appointments you can and I am yours to the end of the campaign."[38]

Much of Roberts's criticism of Republicans centered on prohibition, alleging, according to Smoot's diary, that they "were guilty of a deal with the liquor interests."[39] On November 6, 1910, Smoot recorded that Roberts had "made an attack on me in the Salt Lake Theater" which Smoot believed "pleased the Tribune immensely." Smoot concluded that it was his view that Roberts was "a very contemptible man and dishonest in his life and utterances." Smoot noted that he had been told by Moyle that Roberts "had challenged me to debate the contents of an editorial appearing in the Herald Republican." Smoot responded to Moyle that he had "paid no attention to the personal attacks of B H Roberts in the past, and saw no reason to change that course in the future."[40]

As always, Roberts's political involvement led to charges that his views were at variance with those of most of his ecclesiastical colleagues. Anthon H. Lund and Roberts both attended a Young Men's Meeting where Roberts presided and, according to Lund, "sought to make himself affable." Lund wrote, "If I had taken a stand as he has I should feel I had disgraced my priesthood and hurt my church. I am sorry that he has so little control over his feelings and feels so vindictive toward Senator Smoot."[41]

With Roberts's help, Ferdinand Ericksen campaigned vigorously on the Democratic ticket, predicting a "tremendous victory." As Ericksen told one audience: "There seems to be a strong determination of the people to break the power of the Federal Bunch. Until … that gang is broken we cannot hope for peace in Utah."[42] When the votes were counted, however, Joseph Howell was easily re-elected over Er-

38. Roberts to Moyle, Oct. 29, 1910, box 4, fd. 15, Kenney Collection.

39. Smoot, *In the World*, 77.

40. Smoot, 76–77.

41. Lund, *Danish Apostle*, 444.

42. "Ericksen Hopeful of Big Democratic Victory," *Salt Lake Telegram*, Oct. 24, 1910, 6.

icksen, and Democrat C. C. Richards lost to Republican Daniel N. Straup.[43] Beyond the votes themselves, it is interesting that while Roberts could be strident and personal in his campaign utterances, he could also reach out to his opponents. While he would never be more than civil to Smoot, he and Nephi L. Morris did reach a friendly understanding. Morris said that despite "the differences which unhappily arose between us in the campaign," he strongly disapproved of the way Roberts had been treated by Smoot, the *Herald Republican*, and others "in branding you as a liar." Roberts replied, saying, "I have never received a communication which brought to me greater delight or established profound respect and admiration for a brother than did your letter speaking out in such an unexpected manner for truth and honor among men." Roberts asked Morris to forgive him if he had offended him in any way, while members of "opposing parties … hereafter let us be brothers indeed."[44]

As for Roberts's relationship with Joseph F. Smith, however, it seemed Smith had run out of patience with Roberts's outspokenness. Roberts wrote to Isaac Russell, "I am aware of a coldness on the part of the President, an aloofness and lack of cordiality on his part, but we meet occasionally and transact such business as our official relations make necessary, beyond that we have no commerce. … I respect the President for his many sterling qualities, and sympathize with him because of the many perplexing problems he has inherited from previous administrations." Roberts went on to say he would help Smith "if he could," but not by "abject surrender to his policies largely the outgrowth … in many instances, of his misconceptions and prejudices."[45]

James H. Moyle indicates that the Democratic Party was at a low ebb after the 1910 election. Because the Republicans had become so dominant and Democratic "success was so completely lost," a majority of party leaders, including Roberts and O. W. Powers,

---

43. Straup (1862–1945) was born in Indiana, and came to Utah in 1890 and formed a law practice with Orlando W. Powers. Straup served on the Utah Supreme Court, 1905–17, and 1922–35. On three occasions he was chief justice: 1908–10, 1915–17, and 1933–35.

44. See Morris to Roberts, Nov. 4, 1910; and, Roberts to Morris, Nov. 15, 1910, box 4, fd. 15, Kenney Collection.

45. Roberts to Russell, Feb. 13, 1911, box 7, fd. 9, Russell Papers.

"urged the disbanding of the party as a protest against the baneful influence which had so much to do with our repeated defeats." The *Salt Lake Tribune* reported that twenty-five leaders had met in Moyle's office to consider closing the party headquarters.[46] Those at the meeting were "outraged at the methods resorted to by the church Republicans in order to accomplish the downfall of the Democrats at the polls." The *Tribune* (always a partisan source in such matters) continued, some

> of those at the meeting favored abandoning the fight until such times as the church should cease to dabble in politics. They recognized the futility of trying to win in the face of ecclesiastical opposition and favored retirement. Others said the Democrats were in the position of being condemned if they did out a ticket in the field and eternally damned if they did not. Among a large portion of the small portion of Democrats left in the party there is a growing sentiment against making the pretense of a fight against the ... church Republicans.[47]

Moyle "vigorously opposed" this move, and the others "dropped their opposition" when he agreed to serve as party chair. This debate represented one of the few times Roberts and Moyle were on opposite sides in party matters.[48]

In addition to his political work, much of Roberts's activity during this period centered on the ongoing *History of the Church* publication and his work for the Mutual Improvement Association (MIA). In March he represented the MIA general board and was the "principle speaker" at the Cache Stake MIA conference held in the Logan Tabernacle.[49] In August Roberts participated in what the *Evening Standard* called "the most successful tri-stake Young Men's and Young Ladies associations ever attended in the county." The meetings, which brought together the Weber, North Weber, and Ogden Stakes, drew an "exceptionally large audience" from Weber County.

46. "Democrats Are in a Quandary," *Salt Lake Tribune*, Nov. 13, 1910, 32. There was "a great deal of talk" among Logan Democrats who felt it futile to make any local campaigns "until such time as conditions are more favorable to Democratic success." See "Democratic Party Much Dissatisfied," *Deseret News*, Nov. 11, 1910, 9; and "Charge Church Influence," *Evening Standard*, Nov. 16, 1910, 4.

47. "Democrats Are in a Quandary."

48. See Sessions, *View of James Henry Moyle*, 125–26.

49. "B H Roberts to Lecture M.I.A. Conference," *Logan Republican*, Mar. 16, 1912, 4.

But politics was never far from his mind, and it appeared that things were getting better for the Democrats. Roberts looked forward to 1912 as a good Democratic year, especially as it became apparent that the Republican ranks would be split between President William Howard Taft and Taft's former ally, Theodore Roosevelt. Roberts asserted that his position was "stronger than before with the fair minded Mormons. I have greater influence than for a number of years." He pointed to the fact that he had delivered the annual memorial address to the Elks Association, and had appeared at the Commercial Club where he "discussed ... what steps were necessary to bring about better understanding and better conditions."[50] On August 1, 1912, Roberts was chosen as the temporary chair of the Democratic state nominating convention to be held later that month.[51] He was also part of a forty-three-member committee "entrusted with the work of compiling data for campaign literature and resolutions for submission to the state convention.[52] The *Salt Lake Telegram* reported that after being introduced by Judge Samuel R. Thurman, "Mr. Roberts advanced to the front of the stage [where] he was greeted with applause which lasted for over two minutes before he was able to commence his speech." The convention passed a detailed platform and nominated John F. Tolton[53] for governor, Tillman D. Johnson and Mathonihah Thomas[54] for Congress (whom Roberts nominated), a full slate of state officers, and presidential electors.[55]

50. Roberts to Russell, Feb. 13, 1911.

51. "Democrats Getting Busy," *Evening Standard*, Aug. 2, 1912, 1; and "Report of Permanent Organization Committee," *Salt Lake Telegram*, Aug. 30, 1912, 1.

52. "Democrats Prepare for Big Campaign," *Salt Lake Tribune*, Aug. 2, 1912, 14.

53. Tolton (1861–1950) was born in Ephraim to British convert parents, and lived his life in Beaver. After attending Brigham Young Academy, 1882–83, he served a mission in Great Britain, 1884–85. He was active in business, politics, and church life. He served a term in the territorial house, and several terms in the Utah State House of Representatives where he was speaker from 1917 to 1919. He was president of the Beaver Stake at the time of his nomination for governor, serving from 1908 to 1916.

54. Thomas (1872–1931) was born in Wales and came to Utah in 1878. After graduation from the University of Michigan Law School in 1900, he practiced law in Salt Lake City. He was a member of the Salt Lake City School Board, 1904–13, and the Board of Trustees of the Utah Agricultural College, 1909–13. He ran again for congress in 1920 but was defeated by E. O. Leatherwood. A few years later he and his wife moved to Southern California.

55. See "J. F. Tolton of Beaver Nominated for Governor by Democrats," *Salt Lake Telegram*, Aug. 30, 1912, 1; and "Utah Democrats Name Ogden Man," *Evening Standard*, Aug. 30, 1912, 1.

What is also clear is that Roberts was increasingly attracted to the candidacy of Woodrow Wilson, a "conservative" progressive, and a states-right Democrat. At the convention he defended Wilson against some critics saying the nominee had "a keen grasp of the problems of his age," and a logical program "for solving these problems. Roberts's admiration of Wilson and his political philosophy would remain for the rest of his life.[56]

Not long after that, at the LDS Church's October 1912 general conference, Roberts made a provocative statement about the relationship between the church and politics. He told the congregation that "so far as … absolute and positive essentials are concerned," he believed the church stood on "very firm and solid ground." These essentials were: "the knowledge of God's existence; the great fact of human redemption; the blessing of the atonement and the resurrection; and, the concept of obedience to the laws and ordinances of the gospel." But in the "sphere of civil government," Roberts admonished his listeners that "one man's judgement may be as good as another's." This was one reason why he valued the Book of Mormon so much, which taught, time and again, that "while governments derive their just powers from the consent of the governed, there goes with that awful, moral responsibility direct to God, of every man and woman participating as sovereign in a free government that obtains in such [a] country." He asserted that "upon this principle," God had inspired the Founding Fathers to lay the "corner stones" of the Republic. Thus "let us not think because we believe in the great truth that the Constitution … was the product of divine inspiration, that new conditions and a constantly changing status would not warrant, from time to time, changes in the fundamental law of the land."[57]

The *Eastern Utah Advocate* reported that "a tense expectancy seemed to pervade the auditorium" after Roberts finished speaking.[58] Church president Joseph F. Smith (a Republican) rose and, clearly referring to Roberts, stated, "I think that … all men should … seek God for guidance [rather] than the … harangues of polit-

56. See "Democrats Name J. F. Tolton for Governor," *Salt Lake Tribune*, Aug. 30, 1912, 1.

57. "Elder Brigham H. Roberts," *Conference Reports*, Oct. 1912, 30–34.

58. "Inferentially Rebukes," *Eastern Utah Advocate*, Oct. 10, 1912, 2.

ical leaders."[59] The paper went on to say that Roberts's "eloquent pleas for personal liberty of church members in all things pertaining to civil government and political issues" was challenged by "every speaker save one" in the conference, though the dissenting voice was not identified.[60]

A few weeks later, Roberts spoke in the Ogden Theater, suggesting that "those in Utah who have espoused the cause of Progressivism … are to be congratulated and encouraged, for they are fighting for principle rather than the emoluments of office." He contrasted President Taft, who believed that "the constitution is a thing to be used only when it serves the purposes of the … commercial and industrial … [interests] of the country," with the Democrats, who believed the Constitution "was made for the good of the people." Both Democrats and Progressives "believe that the people should rule and that political graft and evil doing should be done away with. Both Democrats and Progressives believe … that political bossism should not prevail and that the government should be brought nearer to the people."

On November 2, Roberts and others took part in a "Wilson Day" rally in the Salt Lake Theater similar to what was taking place around the country to support candidate Woodrow Wilson. Roberts spent much of his time attacking Reed Smoot who had said that Wilson was "not much of a business man." Roberts said that Smoot seemed not to "take into account executive ability, intelligence and other qualifications" that enabled him to be a governor and president of Princeton. Moreover, he lauded Wilson for favoring "education for all and in more rights, better conditions and so on for workingmen."[61]

When the votes were counted in November, Taft—who clearly had the backing of Smoot, Joseph F. Smith, and others—won the Beehive State with 42,013 votes to Wilson's 36,579 and Roosevelt's 24,179.[62] Wilson, however, won the race nationally, and, in addition

59. "President Joseph F. Smith," *Conference Reports*, 41–42. Reed Smoot recorded that Roberts's remarks were "no doubt intended as an answer to the opening speech of Pres Smith and his [Improvement] Era article. Just before the close of the meeting Pres Smith referred to it and then punctured it completely." Smoot, *In the World*, 165.

60. "Must Take Counsel," *Eastern Utah Advocate*, Oct. 10, 1912, 2.

61. "Democrats Gather at Last Meeting," *Salt Lake Herald*, Nov. 3, 1912, 1.

62. Walker, "Taft Victory."

to Utah, Taft only carried Vermont. In Utah's statewide elections, the Democrats again came up short. Spry and Howell were both re-elected. Because Utah had gained a second congressional seat, Republicans sent Jacob Johnson[63] to Washington. Once again, the legislature was overwhelmingly dominated by Republicans. But there was one bright spot for Roberts's party. A 1914 constitutional amendment mandated that senators be elected directly rather than by the legislature. For the first time, Smoot would truly have to face the voters. Another bright spot may have surrounded Roberts's son Ben, a newspaper reporter who was emerging as a leading young Democratic activist. As a result of Wilson's victory, young Roberts was named for a federal patronage position as surveyor of customs with an annual salary of $1,500.

But Roberts's taste for debate was far from sated. For some time he had engaged in an on-going dialogue with Episcopal Bishop Franklin Spencer Spalding on the historicity of the Book of Abraham. Spalding had been in Utah since 1905 and had taken great interest in Mormonism—its theology and its people. As a result, he had written a number of tracts gently challenging Mormon beliefs and practices.[64] In 1912, Spalding wrote *Joseph Smith Jr., as a Translator*[65] in which he stated that if the "Book of Mormon is true, it is, next to the Bible, the most important book in the world." He then quoted Roberts as saying "the Book of Mormon must admit to every test ... it must submit to every analysis and examination. It must submit to historical tests, to the tests of archeological research, and also to the higher criticism."[66]

---

63. Johnson (1847–1925) was born in Denmark and came to the United States in 1854. He lived in Ogden until 1863, then moved to California. He returned to Utah and settled in Spring City in 1872 where he practiced law. A lawyer, Johnson served as US District Attorney, 1880–88; a member of the Utah Commission, 1881–93; Sanpete probate judge, 1888–90; Sanpete prosecuting attorney, 1892–94; in the Utah Territorial House, 1893–95; and seventh district judge, 1896–1905. An active Republican, he served the one term in Congress but was not nominated for a second term.

64. See Sillito and Bradley, "Franklin Spencer Spalding."

65. Spalding, *Joseph Smith as Translator.*

66. Spalding, 11–12. Roberts's revised remarks were published as "Higher Criticism and the Book of Mormon," *Improvement Era*, June 1911, 645–77, and July 1911, 774–87. The article in question is Jones, *Bible and the Book of Mormon*. Jones, like his mentor Spalding, whom he succeeded as bishop, was also interested in Mormonism. See also Jones, *Points of Contact.*

Spalding took up Roberts's challenge, focusing on Joseph Smith's translation of the Book of Abraham papyri as a test case for the Book of Mormon's correctness. Relying on the assistance of several Egyptologists, Spalding concluded that Smith's translating abilities were faulty, and if the Book of Abraham was not translated correctly, neither was the Book of Mormon.

Roberts responded to Spalding with "A Plea in Bar of Final Conclusions," published, along with several other responses, in the *Improvement Era*.[67] He argued that the "inspiration" of the translation was the most important aspect of both the Book of Abraham and the Book of Mormon. "I believe in the translations Joseph Smith has given to the world—confessedly not by scholarship but by inspiration, by his own spirit being quickened by contact with god's spirit—that in those translations are truths that are part of a mighty system of truth, the like of which is not found elsewhere among men." Roberts believed that God's "system of truth ... will receive, ere the end, a splendid vindication both as a system and in all its parts."[68]

In January 1913, Roberts joined with several other local religious figures to oppose a "suggestion made by Judge Thomas Marioneaux that condemned persons be allowed to poison themselves" rather than face hanging or execution by firing squad. Many called this "permissive suicide." Roberts told the *Salt Lake Tribune* that he opposed such a step, labeling it "one of the most barbarous methods for any civilized land to adopt. If the state concludes a life should be taken the state should take it." He said the judge's suggestion "would lead to disastrous consequences," labeled it "the sin of suicide" and "self murder," and argued that "sacredness of human life should be maintained." Roberts said that he supported the Mormon belief in the biblical admonition "that whosoever committeth murder his blood shall be shed."[69]

As in the past, Roberts remained interested in business opportunities. In March 1913 he became one of the directors of the Modern

67. B. H. Roberts, "A Plea in Bar of Final Conclusions," *Improvement Era*, Feb. 1913, 309–25.

68. Roberts, "A Plea," 325.

69. "Clergymen Oppose Permissive Suicide," *Salt Lake Tribune*, Jan. 20, 1913, 12.

Stenographic Institute, which was incorporated in Salt Lake County on December 26, 1912.[70] Other directors included Utah governor William Spry; railroad executive Hezekiah Edgar Van Housen; Orson F. Whitney; Joseph W. Neville,[71] the husband of Margaret's daughter Milfordetta, who also served as president; and Byron Spry, the governors nephew, who served as the vice president. With local pride, the *Davis County Clipper* reported that the "primary object of this institution is to teach 'Modern' short hand typewriting by mail or class lesson or partially by both. It is also anticipated that sometime in the future all branches will be taught similar to the big correspondence schools of the east with this distinction that this will be a western institution."[72] Roberts apparently ended his relationship with the school during the war, and its charter was revoked on September 10, 1919.[73]

By then, Roberts's finances seemed to have stabilized. Like all members of the First Quorum of Seventy, he received an allowance of $1,200 annually during the 1890s.[74] Moreover, Roberts averaged between $3,000 and $4,200 per year.[75] This is borne out by the amount of tithing Roberts paid during the same period. Occasionally his tithing figure goes up—dramatically in 1915 and 1919–20, for example. There is no way of knowing the reasons for this, but it might be the result of book royalties, military pay, or other outside income and investments. On two occasions—1918 and 1922—it dropped

---

70. Modern Stenographic Institute, Articles of Incorporation, #6540, Dec. 26, 1912, Salt Lake County Archives. The institute was a member of the National Education Association.

71. Neville (1875–1946) married Milfordetta "Detta" Shipp (1874–1964) on August 9, 1899. A seventy, after their marriage he was set apart on November 28, 1900, by Roberts for a mission to the Northern States. He returned on June 12, 1902. After leaving the institute, Neville worked for many years as a clerk on the Los Angeles and Salt Lake City Railroad.

72. "Centerville Chat," *Davis County Clipper*, Jan. 10, 1913, 1.

73. See Harden Bennion to J. H. Clark, Sep. 10, 1919; and Modern Stenographic Institute Articles of Incorporation, both in Salt Lake County Archives. See also "By the Governor of the State of Utah: A Proclamation," *Salt Lake Tribune*, Mar. 25, 1919, 5. Apparently the company was in arrears for taxes and penalties, amounting to $16.50, which were due on November 15, 1918.

74. Quinn, *Wealth and Corporate Power*, 10.

75. Quinn, 13.

somewhat.[76] What is clear is that he was never financially comfortable, and was constantly open to additional sources of income.

Roberts's activities during 1913 stayed local and focused on education. He delivered the baccalaureate sermon to the University of Utah graduating class where he argued that joy came primarily "through a sense of growth and enlargement. Progress is joy. Give a man … growth and whatever his station he will have joy. Through all the ages … the upward movement of God's great work is progress."[77]

In July, Roberts spoke in the Salt Lake Tabernacle to an audience of some 5,500, many of whom were delegates to the National Education Association conference on the topic of "Mormonism and Education." He told them that educational effort in Utah began with the settlement in Nauvoo, came west as the Saints crossed the plains, and was found in the books the emigrants carried with them which led to the opening of a territorial library by 1850. Roberts then discussed the development over time of "a very acceptable public school system," and the creation, decline, and rebuilding of the University of Deseret into the University of Utah. By statehood, he said, public education included both Mormon and gentile, and he lauded the role "our non-Mormon friends" have played in creating a strong school system. At the current time, he said, Mormons support their own denominational school system while "doing their share maintaining the public schools through the payment of taxes."[78] In a similar vein, Roberts spoke in the Tabernacle in September on the growing tendency of modern thought to bolster LDS tenets. He argued that "great and profound thinkers were coming to look upon the fundamental principles with which religion deals," in much the same way as had Joseph Smith. Chief among these, he said, was the Mormon view of the continuance of human personality after death, and quoted "from eminent philosophers and … others in an effort to show that the belief in such a personality was becoming more popular."[79]

76. Quinn, 168–71.

77. See "Commencement Week Exercises," *Daily Utah Chronicle*, May 29, 1913, 1; "B. H. Roberts Tells University Graduates to Hold High Ideals," *Salt Lake Telegram*, June 2, 1913, 3; and "High Aim Theme of Talk to Graduates," *Salt Lake Tribune*, June 2, 1913, 14.

78. "Mormon Pioneers in School Progress," *Salt Lake Tribune*, July 7, 1913, 14.

79. "B. H. Roberts Gives Doctrinal Sermon," *Salt Lake Tribune*, Sep. 15, 1913, 12.

In September Roberts, along with the community itself, was shocked to learn that his old adversary—and friend—Bishop Franklin Spencer Spalding had been killed in an automobile accident.[80] Roberts attended funeral services for Spalding held at St. Mark's Cathedral two days later, along with former governor Heber M. Wells, former chief justice Charles H. Zane, and as the *Salt Lake Telegram* reported, "many other men distinguished in the life of the city and state."[81] Spalding's body was taken to Denver for burial shortly thereafter. A memorial service was held in the Salt Lake Theater on November 1, 1914. Roberts, one of the speakers, lauded Spalding as "a most honorable opponent," and said that in his death "all Utah, Mormon and Episcopalians, all manner of men in fact, had suffered a real loss." He eulogized Spalding as one who had

> dedicated his life and his energies to the betterment of mankind, irrespective of their condition or beliefs. His religion knew no petty limitations born of creed or class. Bishop Spalding was intellectually honest, a quality as big and precious as it is rare. He was tolerant of the views of others, always a student of the problems of life, a worker, a reformer, a leader and an idealist whose idealism, though as high as the stars, nevertheless had a direct and personal communication with the everyday affairs of life. His death has left us with broken harmonies.

Roberts's remarks are interesting in light, as we have seen, of his own development as a progressive reformer. Spalding was a well-known socialist—a fact Roberts does not mention though was undoubtedly aware of. While Roberts rejected that philosophy, it and broader progressive impulses were in the air and, apparently, they were affecting him as much as others both within the church and outside.[82]

Roberts was particularly involved in the 1914 election when his good friend James Moyle ran against incumbent Senator Reed

80. "Episcopal Bishop Killed," *Salt Lake Telegram*, Sep. 26, 1914, 10. Spalding was hit and killed as he crossed South Temple near Firth East. Ironically, the car that hit him was driven by Adrienne King, the seventeen- year-old daughter of Roberts's Democratic colleague, former congressman William H. King. See "Death of Bishop Spalding," *Daily Utah Chronicle*, Sep. 28, 1914, 2.

81. "Spalding Funeral Held," *Salt Lake Telegram*, Sep. 28, 1914, 14

82. "Glowing Tributes Paid to Bishop Spalding's Memory," *Salt Lake Tribune*, Nov. 2, 1914, 12; and "Loving Tribute is Paid to Spalding," *Salt Lake Telegram*, Nov. 2, 1914, 5.

Smoot.[83] The race represented the first time that Smoot faced voters directly, and Roberts and the Democrats were optimistic about their chances. Taking comfort from the fact that Wilson had run second in Utah in 1912, and that the Progressives officially were allies, the Democrats campaigned under the slogan "A vote for Moyle is a Vote for Wilson."[84] Smoot and the Republicans took a similar tack and sought to make the election not so much a referendum on Smoot, but to focus the race on national Democratic policies. Roberts was dismayed when Smoot defeated Moyle, 56,281 to 52,050. But things were changing. In the off-year election, while Joseph Howell was re-elected to congress, a non-Mormon Democratic political newcomer, James H. Mays,[85] was elected to the first of his three terms in the House of Representatives, defeating incumbent Jacob Johnson. Mays won as the nominee of both the Democratic and Progressive Parties, a combination that portended for good things for the Democrats of Utah.

The Democrats had, at times, an uneasy alliance with the Progressive Party—the remnants of the Bull Moose crusade of 1912.[86] Also during this period there were two cliques within the Democratic Party itself vying for influence. One consisted of Roberts, Moyle, and Simon Bamberger, and they "were variously opposed by William H. King, his brother Samuel A. King, Chauncey P. Overfield,[87]

83. See for example, "B. H. Roberts Speaks at Rally in Provo," *Deseret Evening News*, Oct. 31, 1914, 8.

84. The total vote for Wilson and Roosevelt in Utah in 1912 was 60,753. Taft, even with the support of church president Joseph F. Smith, polled 42,100.

85. Mays (1868–1926) was born in Tennessee. He graduated from the University of Michigan in 1895, and from the University of Michigan Law School in 1896. He came to Utah in 1902 and practiced law as well as was engaged in business. He served three terms in the US House of Representatives (1915–21) but did not seek re-election in 1920. After leaving Congress, he moved to Wendell, Idaho, where he was a rancher.

86. Stauffer, "Utah Politics," xi.

87. Overfield (1872–1958) was born in Brooklyn, New York, and came to Utah in 1896 for health reasons. He was owner of the Overfield Investment Company and active in the Episcopal Church, serving as a vestryman at St. Marks from 1906 to 1936. He was active in the Democratic Party, serving as a party officer, treasurer, and delegate to the 1912 Democratic National Convention. He broke with the Democrats and supported his friend Charles Evans Hughes as the Republican candidate for president in 1916. After that, he affiliated with the Republicans and was an unsuccessful candidate for state senate in 1930.

and William R. Wallace."[88] But in many ways these cliques were reconciled with the actions of the 1916 Democratic convention.

In 1915 Simon Bamberger, a wealthy Jewish state senator, let it be known that he was "available" for the nomination for US Senate in 1916. While Bamberger was known as a strong financial backer of the Utah Democrats, as Frank T. Morn has noted, he lacked experience with "matters outside of Utah's political world." So he set out on a visit to the Eastern states and then to Cuba to broaden his education, ultimately deciding not to run for Senate, realizing that he would be a much stronger candidate for governor, especially since William King was thinking of running for the Senate. The duo would make for "a more balanced ticket."[89]

In 1916, King was nominated for the US Senate to run against incumbent Senator George Sutherland. The Democrats re-nominated James H. Mays for Congress in the second district, and chose a Mormon, Milton H. Welling,[90] to run for an open seat in the first district since Joseph Howell had decided not to seek another term. The party selected a docket that included several candidates who had been nominated by the Progressive Party. It was, to use Roberts's phrase, a "well balanced ticket," featuring both Mormons and non-Mormons, as well as progressives and conservatives.

While nominating Bamberger for governor, Roberts called for an end to the political split in Utah, saying it was an "anomalous condition" which exists in Utah and no where else. As he argued,

> we have thought we must name candidates because they are Mormon or non-Mormon, instead of upon the basis of American citizenship, and their fitness and capacity for the service. Thus the "unwritten law" in Utah in relation to political preferment is that the governor must invariably be a Mormon; the United States senators for the state shall be one "Mormon" and one "Gentile," and a like division shall obtain as to

88. Stauffer, "Utah Politics," 86.

89. Morn, "Simon Bamberger," 112–14.

90. Welling (1876–1947) was born in Farmington and a graduate of the University of Utah. An active Mormon and a Democrat, he served as president of the Malad Stake, 1902–08. He was elected to the Utah House of Representatives from 1911 until 1915. After he was elected to the US House in 1916 and 1918, he was defeated in a bid for US senator in 1920. Eight years later, Welling was elected Utah secretary of state, serving until 1937. Welling was Bear River Stake president at the time of his first election to Congress.

> the congressmen; and the division in a general way is to continue down the line as to the rest of the ticket.[91]

Roberts called for smashing this 'absurd political practice,' which he labeled "utterly un-American," and instead hold candidates to a simple standard—citizenship and competence. Bamberger, he argued, met those qualifications and would usher a new day into Utah politics, establishing a "new precedent" which would never return to "plague us."[92]

The speech would stand out in the minds of those who heard it. More than a half century later, Herbert B. Maw, a delegate to his first state Democratic Convention and a future governor, remembered Roberts as "a good Democrat and a powerful speaker. He put Bamberger into office." Maw recalled that he did not think Bamberger, as a Jew, had "a chance," but "after that speech I tell you he went in overwhelmingly." A few years later, Maw and Roberts, whom he had never met, would serve together as LDS chaplains.[93]

Bamberger faced three formidable candidates—long-time party activist Alfred W. McCune,[94] and two future apostles, Stephen L. Richards[95] and Joseph F. Merrill.[96] But Bamberger came within twenty-one votes of being nominated on the first ballot, and then received the nomination on the second with one hundred votes to

91. Democratic Party of Utah, *Proceedings of the Democratic Convention*, 19–21, hereafter cited as *Proceedings*. See also Barlow, "Election of 1916."

92. *Proceedings*, 19–21.

93. Maw Interview, 23.

94. McCune (1849–1927) was born in India, where his father was a British soldier. Beginning in the mid-1870s, McCune, who had moved to Nephi, became involved in railroad building, mining and other business ventures, and was one of Utah's wealthiest men. As a prominent Democrat he was associated with many important business and political figures, especially Heber J. Grant. He was an unsuccessful candidate for US Senate in a chaotic legislative contest in 1899. He sought the seat again in 1901 but was again unsuccessful. McCune was a candidate for the Democratic nomination for Governor in 1916, but lost to Roberts's choice, Simon Bamberger. He died in Cannes, France, while on an overseas tour, but was buried in Nephi.

95. Richards (1879–1959) was a lawyer and faculty member at the University of Utah. An active Mormon, he served as a member of the Sunday School general board. Richards became a member of the Quorum of the Twelve Apostles in 1917, serving until his death.

96. Merrill (1868–1952) was head of the College of Engineering at the University of Utah. An active Mormon, he would later serve as Church Commissioner of Education, and as a member of the Quorum of the Twelve, 1931 until his death.

spare.[97] Roberts's oratory had carried the day.[98] Bamberger told the delegates that he had not told Roberts what to say, but his words had lifted him up and "I thought I was among the angels and I have hardly come to earth yet."[99] He told fellow Democrats that he was confident in victory, and promised them that "If we lose, I'll walk back to the Wyoming line where I came into Utah years ago."[100]

Roberts also took an active role in championing President Wilson's re-election. In September, for example, he chaired a meeting that attracted five thousand people to the Auditorium on Richards Street, with another two thousand outside, in support of Wilson's re-election. The main speaker was former US secretary of state, and many-time presidential candidate, William Jennings Bryan. Roberts spent two hours "on the issues of the campaign in the interests of President Wilson and the Democratic party in general."[101]

Roberts continued his pro-Wilson efforts that fall. A series of meetings, dubbed "Woodrow Wilson Day," were held throughout the state on October 28 featuring prominent Democratic speakers and "a message from the president." Roberts joined Simon Bamberger as the "chief attractions" in headlining the Ogden meeting, which had been preceded by a "parade and other demonstrations."[102] On his speech notes, Roberts wrote a reminder to "state a personal note for the re-election of Wilson."[103]

When the votes were counted in November, it was a Democratic sweep in Utah. President Wilson received 84,501 votes, defeating Republican Charles Evans Hughes who polled 54,340. William H. King defeated incumbent Senator George Sutherland 80,895 to 56,862, and Simon Bamberger garnered 55 percent of the vote for governor with 78,502, while Republican Nephi L. Morris's 59,522

97. "Ballots For Governor," *Salt Lake Tribune*, Aug. 19, 1916, 1.

98. Interestingly, Roberts did not include a discussion of these events in his autobiography, nor is there much discussion of this in Truman Madsen's *Defender of the Faith*.

99. See B. H. Roberts, "Remarks," in *Proceedings*, 20. For an overview of the campaign itself, see Hainsworth, "Utah State Elections."

100. "Bamberger Chosen for Governor," *Salt Lake Tribune*, Aug. 19, 1916, 1.

101. Roberts's efforts were covered in Bryan's newspaper. See "Mr. Bryan Campaigns for Wilson," *The Commoner*, Oct. 1, 1916, 22–23.

102. See "Will Sound Praises of Woodrow Wilson," *Salt Lake Tribune*, Oct. 28, 1916, 5; and "Bourbons to Hold Wilson Day Rally," *Salt Lake Telegram*, Oct. 28, 1916, 2.

103. See fd. 526, Roberts Collection.

votes represented 42 percent. Both James H. Mays and Milton H. Welling won as well. Most of the Democrats benefitted from running jointly with the Progressives.

The election was, as historian Kenneth Stauffer writes, more "than a Democratic victory." The state of Utah, and the rest of the country, had come to see local politics controlled by Senator Reed Smoot and the LDS Church. The win, then, "was somewhat of a revolution," concludes Stauffer. The *Salt Lake Tribune* called Smoot the "self-appointed director" of the state. Bamberger, the state's first—and, as of this writing, only—Jewish governor, said that "the Mormon Church is no longer endeavoring to control politics in the state and is now a denomination just as any other church."[104]

Another historian, Brad E. Hainsworth, writes that in the 1916 election it "was the healing influence of a mild German-born Jew" who "ended, for a while at least, the schism between Mormon and non-Mormon in Utah politics."[105] Indeed, Welling, who was elected to the first of his two terms in Congress that year, would later recall that he had "achieved without preparation or planning what Powers, Roberts, Moyle and dozens of others had fought for and died with broken hearts trying to get."[106]

But while Roberts savored a vicarious political victory, war clouds across the Atlantic Ocean would soon bring conflict to the United States, directly affecting his life.

---

104. Stauffer, "Utah Politics," 189–90. The *Salt Lake Herald* took a different view, saying that the reason Wilson carried the state, which assisted the Democrats, was because "the peace craze swept Utah on election day as the silver craze swept it twenty years ago." Moreover, the paper noted that the election results should not be seen as repudiation of Reed Smoot, since he had not been an issue in either Idaho or Wyoming, both of which went for Wilson. See "As to Results in Utah," *Salt Lake Herald*, Nov. 10, 1916, 4.

105. Hainsworth, "Utah State Elections," 45.

106. Stauffer, "Utah Politics," 191.

SIXTEEN

WAR, PEACE, AND THE LEAGUE OF NATIONS, 1917–21

Roberts's support for Simon Bamberger's gubernatorial nomination and election was rewarded quickly. In one of his first official acts as governor, Bamberger appointed his friend as a member of the State Board of Equalization, replacing Harden Bennion, who had become Utah's Secretary of State. The *Salt Lake Telegram* reported that the position carried a "salary of $1500 a year" and editorialized that the appointment "of a man as capable as is Mr. Roberts" signified that Bamberger wanted "the best Utah brains working on the difficult question of what to do with Utah's taxation system."[1] Indeed, Bamberger faced a $500,000 budget deficit as he took office, and among other things advocated "a more equitable taxing schedule," focusing on raising taxes on corporations.

But very soon World War I started to encroach on the lives of Utahns. On March 24, 1917, Governor Bamberger issued a proclamation calling for "all able bodied men of the commonwealth, not exempted by law, and of military age," to voluntarily enlist in the Utah National Guard.[2] The war, which began in Europe in 1914, impacted Americans from a distance, even as the nation tried to avoid direct involvement.[3]

Roberts had long been watching the unfolding war in Europe,

---

1. "B. H. Roberts Is Made Member of Equalizing Body by New Executive," *Salt Lake Telegram*, Jan. 2, 1917, 9.

2. See T. DeWitt Foster, "Governor in Demand for Guard Recruits," and "Here's Proclamation," *Salt Lake Telegram*, Mar. 25, 1917, 1. This chapter draws heavily on Roberts, *Legacy*. Also useful is E. W. Crocker, *History of the 145th*.

3. For accessible single-volume histories of the war, see Keegan, *First World War*, and Tuchman, *Guns of August*.

commenting that it was a war that "might have been avoided if the people of the different nations had lived according to the commandments of God.[4] That fall he toured the Pacific Northwest and a reporter for the Portland *Oregonian* asked if Roberts thought "peace would come soon?" Roberts not only said, "I fear not," he went on to explain that, "radical" as it may sound, he hoped the war would not end abruptly. "If there should be a sudden cessation of the hostilities now there would still be in the hearts of those battling a hatred that would rankle until there was another outbreak. It will only be when they have satisfied the madness that the thing will be fought out and the final baptism of blood will have cleansed from their hearts and minds the desire for battle."[5] Saying that while the causes of the war were "complex," he listed Russian expansionism, the "jealousy and mistrust" between Germans and the "Slavic race," and the Franco–German antagonism that had existed since the 1870s as at the root of the conflict.[6] Pride, power, revenge, and nationalism let nations of the world "forget justice."

Roberts believed that Joseph Smith had prophesied the first world war in an 1832 revelation (D&C 87) when he predicted that the "day will come when war will be poured out on all nations." Roberts said the world was now witnessing various nations allying with each other, "now in this interest, now in that interest, for the purpose of maintaining in the language of the times, the 'balance of power' among the nations in Europe."[7] Roberts was appalled by the willingness of both sides to invest millions of men and large amounts of money to the "awful spectacle" of war. "Notwithstanding treaty and counter-treaty, plot and counter-plot, all of it, if we believe the utterances of these great combinations of nations is in the interest of peace." Roberts was cynical of these professed claims of wanting peace, and he believed, because of Smith's prophecy, that it could not come. "The cry is 'Peace, Peace,' … and yet there is no peace; and

4. "B H Roberts Heard by Large Audiences on Sunday," *Ogden Standard*, Aug. 10, 1914, 5.

5. "Mormon Chief on Visit," *Oregonian*, Sep. 8, 1915, 4; and "Mormon Official Will Speak," *Oregonian*, Sep. 8, 1915, 5.

6. B. H. Roberts, "A Mormon View of the World War of 1914," *Liahona*, Oct. 20, 1914, 257–64.

7. Roberts, 258.

God has decreed in this wonderful prediction of his servant [Joseph Smith] ... that not withstanding all the treaties of these nations "War Shall be Poured out upon all nations." Devastation seemed inescapable as Roberts identified "a war spirit that is rampant in the midst of nations."[8]

Early in the war, he supported America's "strict neutrality." Roberts said he hoped that the United States, through the efforts of President Woodrow Wilson, could offer "the embattled nations of Europe her ... good offices to bring to pass an understanding among the nations now at war and establish the peace." But how did Mormonism stand in relation to the slaughter overseas? In one speech, Roberts focused on Doctrine and Covenants sections 45, 98, and 105:39, which calls on the Latter-day Saints to become "an ensign of peace unto the ends of the earth."

> I believe that we ... certainly do hold a relationship to these great calamities. We hold, for instance, the relationship of a fore-knowledge of them for God has not permitted this calamity to come upon the inhabitants of the earth without warning. ... One other relationship we stand in ... is the relationship based on hope, upon the assurance that notwithstanding the greatness and fierceness of this cataclysmic war that ... there is the promise of the coming of God's kingdom. ... The revelations of God in these last days are replete with promises that after the world conflict, there shall come world peace, and the earth shall rest.[9]

He said he hoped that "the Latter-day Saints ... will be numbered among those who engage" in the work of participating "with other neutral nations and with the belligerent nations, in seeking to establish the world permanent peace." He felt that there "will doubtless be constituted a league of nations that will in a way, establish an empire of humanity ... that the intensity of national feeling shall not be again permitted to disturb the peace of the world."[10]

But soon, the United States stood on the brink of entering the fight. Although Woodrow Wilson ran in 1916 against joining the war, the sinking of US ships by Germany interwove with other issues to draw America closer to the conflict. On March 26, 1917,

8. Roberts, 259.
9. "Elder Brigham H. Roberts," *Conference Reports*, Oct. 1916, 140–43.
10. "Elder Roberts," 143–44.

Roberts was one of many prominent speakers at a mass meeting with a crowd estimated at ten thousand, with almost every seat in the Salt Lake Tabernacle filled. The *Salt Lake Tribune* noted that "practically every organization in Salt Lake, including the commercial bodies, religious, military and civic were represented, and the people of the city turned out in masse."[11]

Those in attendance passed a resolution saying that while "every honorable effort has been made conscientiously to keep this country out of war," it was time for "all patriotic Americans to take a stand with the republic and the flag and the president." Roberts joined with allies like Bamberger and Senator William H. King, and adversaries like Reed Smoot, in this statement of support. Like King, Roberts believed that at this juncture "the people are united—they are one behind the president. We are no longer Republicans or Democrats."[12]

At the meeting, Roberts announced his intention to join up. He said that though he was barred "by age limits from the ranks," he was "not barred as being a chaplain."[13] *Goodwin's Weekly* noted that "no one was in the least surprised that [Roberts] should desire, in spite of his advanced years, to don the khaki and accompany the boys. … That was truly typical of the man." The report announced that "every citizen of the state rejoiced" in Roberts's decision because it "made it easier" if the boys had to leave.[14]

The next evening, Roberts was the "principal speaker" in a similar rally held in the Ogden Tabernacle. The *Deseret Evening News* reported that the tabernacle "was much too small to accommodate the great concourse of people who gather to give expression to the fact that the citizens of Ogden will stand with the president in this hour of national danger."[15] Roberts told the boisterous crowd, "Our rights

11. "Utah Pledges Loyal Defense of Nation's Honor and Flag," *Salt Lake Tribune*, Mar. 27, 1917, 1.

12. "Loyal Utah Speaks: Stands Behind President in Present Crisis," *Deseret Evening News*, Mar. 27, 1917, 1.

13. General Order #28, in National Guard, *Official Scrapbook of the 145th Field Artillery*. Hereafter cited as *Official Scrapbook*. On March 28, 1917, Roberts was "appointed Major and assigned to duty as Chaplain on the Governor's Staff."

14. "The Spectator," *Goodwin's Weekly*, Feb. 23, 1918, 5.

15. "B H Roberts Says He Will Go to the Trenches with the Boys," *Deseret Evening News*, Mar. 28, 1917, 11. In addition to Roberts, the other speakers included judge John Murphy; Civil War veteran M. M. Clothier; Reverend Carver; and Roberts's Democratic

and privileges, the freedom of the seas to which we are entitled, both by international and common law have been transgressed and American lives have been sacrificed as a result of a disrespect of American neutrality.[16] The Ogden *Standard*, rhapsodized that Roberts "like [a] revolutionary preacher ... threw aside the robe of his sacred calling, and stood revealed as a warrior, as a field leader of God's people in the battle for human rights. ... One must see him, must follow closely his sledge-hammer logic, his crushing sarcasm, his soul-stirring appeals, to appreciate the power of his speech."[17]

Roberts's motivations both for his strong support of American involvement in the war and his willingness to enlist in the Utah National Guard are not discussed in his edited autobiography. Truman Madsen speculates that Roberts came to the conclusion that "the war symbolized a worldwide failure of churches and their leaders," and he held out the hope that a united effort in support of the war might "help break down the unnecessary divisions" within Christianity. While this is clearly an Anglo-centric viewpoint, it seems to make sense in light of Roberts's general attitudes. Madsen speculated that another "strong motivation to serve in the army was to actively demonstrate that the charges waged against him during his congressional battle that 'his life has been one of disloyalty' were unjust."[18]

On April 15, Roberts addressed Utah National Guard troops at religious services held in the Ogden Tabernacle. The troops gathered first at the armory, and then marched in a body to the Sunday afternoon meeting itself. With a number of religious, educational, and governmental officials on the stand behind him, Roberts—using as his text Exodus 15:3 that the "Lord is a Man of War"—told the congregation that "righteous wars were sanctioned by the Divine Creator," and that "retaliation against German aggression on the high seas was worthy of the same sanction." He spoke at length of his pride in his new association with the National Guard, and said

political ally C. C. Richards. Among the musical presentations was thirteen-year-old Loring Nichols, who would achieve fame in a few years as jazz artist "Red" Nichols.

16. "Prominent Men Offer Services to National Guard," *Ogden Examiner*, Mar. 28, 1917, 1.

17. "Intense Patriotism in Ogden," *Ogden Standard*, Mar. 28, 1917, 1.

18. Madsen, *Defender of the Faith*, 304.

directly to the uniformed men seated in front of him: "In this relationship I bid you hail and welcome. I hope our brotherhood may grow hard and fast together, and I will consecrate my life to your service when we are called into the conflict now at hand."[19]

Roberts was an enthusiastic part of efforts to recruit for the National Guard. On May 5, he spoke at a massive recruiting rally which brought some five thousand people to the *Salt Lake Tribune* building. He also spoke at a large meeting in the Salt Lake Theater. Roberts told the gathering that the "most serious business from now on must be the prosecution of the war to a successful conclusion." He criticized as a "disgrace" those men who avoided enlistment to wait for their chances in the draft itself.[20]

In July, Roberts resigned as a member of the State Board of Equalization to accept his appointment as regimental chaplain of the 145th Field Artillery.[21] Eventually he would drop the honorific title of major, which had been bestowed by Governor Bamberger, when he was appointed a first lieutenant.[22] On August 26, Roberts told a congregation in the Salt Lake Tabernacle that at times there are conflicts in which "God himself takes part," and he believed that this war was one of them. He proclaimed that the "great purpose is that it shall be the end of all war, and as the thunder of cannons is silenced, I hope we shall hear the Angels sing." Roberts also endorsed

19. "War Sanctioned by the Scriptures Says Major Roberts in Tabernacle," *Ogden Standard*, Apr. 16, 1917, 12. Interestingly, other churches in Ogden seemed not to address the war, although that same evening the sermon at Ogden's First Presbyterian Church was on "Pacifism and the Present War." While there is no account of what was said, it appears that the question revolved around whether accepting pacifism would bring the country "respect and honor" at a time of war. See "Pacifism to Be Sermon Sunday," *Ogden Standard*, Apr. 14, 1917, 11.

20. See "To Hold Mast Meeting in Liberty's Cause," *Salt Lake Tribune*, June 25, 1917, 12; and, "Appeal to Patriotism Is Followed by Enlistments," *Salt Lake Tribune*, June 27, 1917, 18.

21. "B. H. Roberts to Quit to Serve at the Front," *Salt Lake Tribune*, July 24, 1917, 4. He was replaced on the board by George Romney Jr. (1864–1943), a Democrat, active Mormon, and prominent Smithfield, Cache County, resident. Romney had previously served as a member of the Utah Legislature, and as secretary-treasurer of the Municipal League of Utah. He moved to Burley, Idaho, in 1922 and at the time of his death, he was serving his fifth term as a member of the Burley City Council. See "Ex-Utah Lawmaker Dies at 78 in Burley, Idaho," *Salt Lake Telegram* Mar. 15, 1943, 15.

22. "Confirmation of Army Appointments," *Ogden Standard*, Sep. 3, 1917, 8.

a growing movement to establish "a league of free nations to guard against the arrogant dominating influences of imperial autocracy."[23]

Because he had strongly attacked the Kaiser and imperial Germany—its militarism, and foreign policy goals—Roberts apparently attracted the criticism of some Utahns of German heritage.[24] Roberts responded in a talk advertised as "The Duty of the German Citizen in the Present War Crisis" at sacrament services in Salt Lake's Cannon Ward on Sunday, September 30, 1917. In return for the freedoms America offered, Roberts stated, individuals "must absolutely foreswear allegiance to native country." Roberts told listeners that he had "no unkind word or thought against alien citizens," and said he was not singling out Germans, that his remarks were "applicable to all natives of foreign countries." As a result, so that there be no possible misunderstanding, Roberts said he had changed the title of his remarks to "The Duty of Alien Citizens in the War Crisis." Roberts's choice of the term "alien citizens" is interesting, implying that he meant "hyphenated" citizens who still clung to an affinity for their homeland as opposed to non-citizens.[25] He said that "German-American citizens as a whole are loyal and true American citizens, but those who are disloyal and give aid to the enemy are traitors and will be dealt with under the stern regulations of war." Now that the U.S. had entered the war, "This is no time to further treasonable spirits and give them the rights of citizenship while they seek to undermine the government and hamper it in its defense of itself and its citizens."[26]

While working with his guard unit, Roberts dedicated much of his time to looking out for the temporal well-being of his troops. In July 1917, for example, he appealed to Jesse Knight and his son J. Will to donate $1,000 to purchase baseball equipment. The money would "provide a complete baseball outfit," consisting of a dozen uniforms, bats, balls "and other paraphernalia required for the national

23. "Says God Takes Part in Certain Great Conflicts," *Deseret Evening News*, Aug. 27, 1917, 5.

24. For an overview, see Allan Kent Powell, "'Our Cradles Were in Germany': Utah's German–American Community in World War I," in Powell, *Utah and the Great War*, 205–25.

25. "B. H. Roberts Is Quite Outspoken," *Ogden Standard*, Sep. 10, 1917, 10.

26. "Roberts Replies to Critics," *Salt Lake Tribune*, Sep. 10, 1917, 16.

pastime" for each of the six companies.[27] Roberts also obtained "a complete moving picture outfit" along with a "programme of the latest features in 'movies' each night."[28]

Because of his age, Roberts would not be assigned to active duty. But, intent on being with his boys "all the way to the front," he appealed to the war department for "active status as a chaplain." His request was rejected. Roberts wanted the assignment badly enough that he reached out to the one person who could help him: Reed Smoot. He telegraphed the senator, saying, "You must get me in." Smoot replied that Roberts would have to travel to Louisville, Kentucky, to Camp Zachary Taylor for academic and physical tests. Roberts readily agreed, "to the chagrin of his family, and perhaps the army," as Madsen wrote.[29]

Roberts's regiment arrived at Camp Kearny in San Diego "in fine shape" on October 13, 1917.[30] While there, Roberts "held weekly sacrament service for the Latter-day Saints, and nondenominational services for the whole regiment. ... He was tireless in daily counseling interviews with soldiers and distributed fifteen hundred khaki editions of the bible" supplied by the Mutual Improvement Association.[31]

In November, Roberts joined with Colonel Richard W. Young to urge Utahns to financially back the efforts of the Soldiers Welfare Work Fund, administered through the YMCA. Roberts sent a telegram, saying that at Camp Kearny the facilities sponsored by this organization had made "for straight, clean manhood living" and that "Utah should do her whole duty" in supporting such activities. Roberts sought to help his men understand that while war was necessary,

27. "Utah Batteries to Be Fully Equipped with Outfits for Baseball," *Salt Lake Tribune*, July 26, 1917, 10; and "Knights Make Donation for the Purchase of Uniforms," *Eureka Reporter*, Aug. 3, 1917, 3.

28. "Movies Provided For Utah Artillerymen," *Salt Lake Tribune*, Sep. 6, 1917, 5.

29. Madsen, *Defender of the Faith*, 302. See also "Mormon Trains as Chaplain in Army," (Mount Vernon, OH) *Democratic Banner*, June 14, 1918, 1, which noted, "Chaplain Roberts is the only Mormon at the school." Reed Smoot's assistance put a temporary end to Roberts's and Smoot's ongoing disagreements, which would flare up again after the war.

30. *Official Scrapbook*.

31. Madsen, *Defender of the Faith*, 304–05.

it was important "to live above the moral barbarism of the battlefield and not lose their sense of the sacred."[32]

Late one evening, toward the end of December, Roberts penned a most interesting letter explaining his decision to enter military service. The letter was addressed to his two eldest sons—Louisa's Ben, and Celia's Harold—and written from Camp Kearny. Roberts told his sons that as the heads of the respective families, if he did not "come out of this war alive," he wanted them to be aware of what motivated him to join in the fight. He assured them he was not worried that his death might cut off "a very few years of my earthly existence." Roberts believed "in the absolute righteousness" of the war, which he called both "necessary as well as ... just." He told his sons that he firmly believed the United States needed to fight "to maintain our rights ... protect the liberties of our people," and to guarantee the "respect, security and honor of our country." Because modern democracy had its roots in the founding of the United States, he believed it was "fitting" that our nation should "enter into the war on the side of the free nations ... battling for the freedom of all nations." He also told his sons that he hoped and believed that the war "was a war against war itself," and peace would last "for a thousand years at least." Inherent in that desire was his view that the United States should play a role in the post-war world of establishing "peace for the world." These sentiments reflected a consistently Wilsonian approach.[33]

In February 1918, according to the Utah press, Roberts, under "the influence of the martial muse," composed a "stirring ode" which could be sung to the tune of "Maryland, My Maryland." Titled "Nativeland, My Nativeland," the last stanza reads:

I hear the distant thunder hum,
Nativeland, my Nativeland!
The old bugle, fife and drum,
Nativeland, My Nativeland!
Join thou the great heroic throng,

32. "Col. R. W. Young and Lieut. B. H. Roberts Indorse Movement," *Deseret Evening News*, Nov. 10, 1917, 2.

33. B. H. Roberts, "My Reasons for Enlistment," typescript, Dec. 20, 1917, box 9, fd. 11, Roberts Papers (UU).

That stalks with Liberty along,
And sing thy dauntless slogan song
Nativeland, My Nativeland![34]

Roberts was soon given the title of "Our Fighting Chaplain." People in Utah were delighted by his service. The *Manti Messenger* editorialized:

> We are glad that B. H. Roberts is with the Utah boys. We are reminded of an incident in one of the darkest days of our civil war. Frederick Douglass was expressing his despair for the future of his race to a great colored audience when Sojourner Truth rose and stretching out her long thin hand cried out "Frederick, is God Dead!" What Sojourner Truth was to her people, B. H. Roberts will always be to the boys of the 145th. And they will doubtless face conditions when they will need his faith.[35]

Clare H. Oliphant[36] of Orangeville in Emery County wrote to his local paper that "one thing to be specially thankful for and that is that we have a man of the type of Chaplain B. H. Roberts to give his whole time and talent to the spiritual and moral side of the soldier, and he is doing a great work here." Roberts acted "as a father to the boys, especially those from Utah who seek him" and gave them "a spiritual feast every Sunday morning at 10:20."[37]

In that spirit, Roberts said that the "healthy and stalwart" Utah men "have a reputation for orderliness," have the fewest arrests by military police, and "are well liked … because of their good conduct," though he spoke out on the character of all the troops he was overseeing, not just the Utahns. He defended them as being better

---

34. For a complete version, see "B. H. Roberts Writes a War Poem For the Soldiers," *Ogden Standard*, Feb. 20, 1918, 2; and "The Spectator," *Goodwin's Weekly*, Feb. 23, 1918, 5. A "corrected copy" of the song, dated October 19, 1926, in Roberts's hand, can be found in box 9, folder 10, Roberts Papers (UU). Roberts noted that he first wrote the song "in the Spring of 1917," when the U.S. entered the war, and that the line "Join then the great, heroic throng," referred to the Allied Powers arrayed against Germany. This information discredits the newspaper accounts as to time and place of its authorship, but seems more accurate in terms of its intent.

35. "Sojourner Truth and B. H. Roberts," *Manti Messenger*, Dec. 21, 1917, 10.

36. Oliphant (1888–1983) was a farmer living in Orangeville when he entered the military. He served in the army from October 1917 until January 1919, all stateside.

37. "With the Colors," *Emery County Progress*, Jan. 5, 1918, 1. Oliphant noted that the LDS troops were also able to attend service in the "very beautiful" chapel in San Diego where "one gets the same feeling of mingling with brother and sister which one feels at home."

"morally, physically and spiritually than the young man at home," and said that concerns for their welfare by the "home folks" were unfounded. Roberts said the government had "taken every precaution to safeguard its soldiers. The world has never before seen the like of it, and a new national character will spring from it."[38]

Ever the historian, Roberts completed seven volumes of scrapbooks documenting the activities of the 145th, containing clippings, photographs, names of the officers and men in the regiment, and a brief history of the unit itself.[39]

In April 1918, while still stationed at Camp Kearny, Roberts was ordered to Camp Taylor in Louisville to finally undertake the strenuous training required to hold formal military rank. Roberts passed through Salt Lake City on his way east during general conference, but was under strict orders to remain on board the train. Once at Camp Taylor, his life shifted to a world of drills, obstacle courses, marches, marksmanship tests, and cavalry training, all done alongside younger men.[40]

When given an opportunity to be exempted from the daily strenuous sit-up exercises, Roberts told his trainers, "No sir, I came here to take the full course." He successfully passed the challenge "to the surprise and sometimes envy of other chaplaincy candidates" and returned to Camp Kearny, admitting that it "was the most strenuous and anxious six weeks within my experience."[41] Upon his return to Kearny in early June, he wrote to Celia that because some of the unit had left and the camp was deserted, he felt the first "twinges of homesickness," and yet he was unhappy because he had thought by this time he would be in France "in the thick of the war," and that he hoped that day might "come soon."[42]

That wish would begin to be fulfilled in July when the bulk of the regiment left for New York, passing through Salt Lake City on their way east. Upon their arrival, Roberts had arranged for the regiment's

38. "B. H. Roberts Says Evangelism Is Overdone," *Salt Lake Herald*, June 30, 1918, 8.

39. "State's Archives to Have Addition," *Salt Lake Tribune*, Aug. 15, 1918, 14. In addition, there are several scrapbooks concerning World War I and the role of the 145th contained in folders 680–83, Roberts Collection (CHL).

40. Madsen, *Defender of the Faith*, 306.

41. As quoted in Madsen, 307.

42. Roberts to Celia, June 7, 1918, quoted in Madsen, *Defender of the Faith*, 306–07.

band to play on the front lawn of the Beehive House for President Joseph F. Smith, who gave the men "a kindly reception" and reminisced about his past association with Roberts. When inside the house itself, Smith told his former occasional religious and political adversary that there was "no rot of bitterness" toward him, and Roberts admitted that this example of "personal peacemaking" was important to him as he embarked for the uncertainty of the battlefield.[43] The troops moved on until they arrived in New York. After two months there, the regiment boarded the three-thousand-passenger troop ship *Scotian*, joining thirteen other troop ships, and embarked on the dangerous two-week crossing to England, docking at Liverpool on September 5, 1918. Roberts was met by European Mission president, Apostle George F. Richards, and addressed the Saints at a special sacrament meeting. According to the *Millennial Star,* Roberts referred to Doctrine and Covenants 87:3, which stated that the time would come when Great Britain would find it necessary to "call upon other nations to defend themselves against other nations." This prophecy had come true, he said, pointing out that until a few years ago, Britain had gloried in its "splendid isolation," but the efforts of the Central Powers had brought them into an alliance with France and Russia to thwart the opening of the "flood gates of armed conflict" that had opened against them. Roberts assured the Liverpool Saints, and by extension all of England, that the United States would make sure "no matter at what cost" that Germany and its allies would not win their war of aggression.[44] Three weeks later, the regiment moved across the English Channel to France and was stationed at Camp DeSouge, approximately seventy-five miles from the battlefront.

Finally, after delays only someone with military experience can appreciate, the regiment was ordered to the front on November 9. But the order was quickly rescinded as armistice talks began. Two days later—at the eleventh hour of the eleventh day of the eleventh month—an armistice was signed and the war was over. The 145th had not seen hostile military action. Roberts lamented that while that "was not our fortune," he was pleased "to know it was

43. Madsen, 308.

44. Historian's Office, Journal History, Sep. 5, 1918, 4.

not our fault."[45] In the next few weeks, however, the regiment engaged another deadly enemy—the Spanish flu—which eventually took fourteen lives from the 145th. Illness would kill more American soldiers in World War I than combat. As chaplain, Roberts was involved with the care of the sick and the disposition of effects of the dead, including writing letters to their families. Roberts comforted these families, telling them that their fallen loved ones had

> made just as complete a sacrifice of their lives to their country as any who have fallen … in the battle line. They … faced a condition as deadly to them as charging through bursting shells, or the patter of machine guns or rifle bullets. The miasma of the dread disease proved for them as deadly as the poisonous German gas waves of shells, and their restless suffering from fever tortured bodies and congested lungs was as pitiful as any death from wounds of bayonet thrusts or shrapnel rents. The heroism of the soldier consists in the fact that he offers his life to his country … whatever fate may befall him. It is not his prerogative to choose his place in the line of battle, or to say when or how or where or in what manner he may fall, if fall he must. He does his part when in response to his country's call for service says "Here I am, send me."[46]

Soldiers were grateful for Roberts's service. A letter from Walter Burdette[47] was published in the *Deseret Evening News*: "Think of holding a sacrament service away over here in France. … We are certainly blessed in having a man like B. H. Roberts with us."[48] Edwin K. Slack[49] from Toquerville in Washington County wrote, "So, you see mother, we are still at home as far as religious services go."[50] *Goodwin's Weekly* reported that Roberts was "immensely popular with the boys."[51] Indeed, Roberts developed a high level of camaraderie with the men that would last throughout the rest of his life.

---

45. Madsen, *Defender of the Faith*, 311.

46. "Utah Heroes Are Accorded High Praise," *Deseret News*, Feb. 13, 1919, 6.

47. Burdette (1893–1963) was a member of Headquarters Company of the 145th Field Artillery. He served in the army from August 1917 until January 1919, all stateside. Burdette went on to work as a letter carrier for the postal service.

48. "Utah Soldier Is Much Impressed With Work of Regimental Chaplain," *Deseret Evening News*, Nov. 5, 1918, 6.

49. Slack (1895–1996) served with the 145th until the unit returned to Utah. After returning to Toquerville he continued farming and later worked for the Union Pacific railroad and the US Soil Service.

50. "Will See It Through," *Washington County News*, Nov. 7, 1918, 1.

51. "The Spectator," *Goodwin's Weekly*, Feb. 23, 1918, 5.

The regiment left Bordeaux, France, on December 14, 1918, and arrived in New York on January 4, 1919. A few days later, after a triumphal tour through Salt Lake City, Ogden, and Logan, the unit was formally "mustered out."[52] Roberts spoke on several occasions. A. J. Hansen, one of the soldiers of the 145th, later recalled Roberts's talk in Logan: "It was like a father ripened in years and wisdom, speaking to his own sons. And every word found its way to the hearts of his hearers who took at attention. The overwhelming applause at the end of his talk spoke louder than words of the love and esteem that the boys of the 145th held for their chaplain."[53]

In assessing the impact of the war on Roberts, nephew David W. Smith noted that while he still found him "a man of reserve" he was "much warmer than before." Truman Madsen agrees, concluding that because Roberts had spent so much time with the sick and dying, and many men who were full of "doubts and dreads" about the war, his ecclesiastical calling and humanity had been increased.[54] At the same time, Roberts seems to have taken a measure of pride in the irony of his service in the war. As he later told his friend Bernard Moses: "While the government rejected me as a representative in Congress, they did accept my service as a chaplain in the war and I had the joy of serving overseas. You see I was trying to get even with Uncle Sam for turning me out of Congress."[55] On November 11, 1920, Roberts's service was officially recognized with a certificate from the State of Utah.[56]

In February 1919, Roberts told LDS Church Historian Anthon H. Lund that he had been asked by Governor Bamberger to serve as Utah's official historian, but he "declined the appointment as he did not want to be confined to the detail work which this office would require."[57] In March, Roberts was in Richfield, Utah, where he spoke at a memorial service for Leo Jensen, a local boy killed in the war. After his tribute to the fallen, Roberts called President Wilson the

52. For a good overview, see Roberts, "Utah National Guard."

53. Undated and unidentified clipping in Mowry Scrapbook, 127.

54. Madsen, *Defender of the Faith*, 305.

55. Roberts to Bernard Moses, June 24, 1925, Moses Papers.

56. "Act of Legislature March 20 1919, Certificate," given to Roberts. Copy in Mowry Scrapbook, 60.

57. Lund, *Danish Apostle*, 729.

"first citizen of the world," and called on the US Senate to ratify the League of Nations. According to the *Richfield Reaper,* Roberts saw "in the peace conference and the proposed league of nations the beginning of the millennium when weapons of war will be turned into the implements of the husbandman."[58]

Roberts continued to promote the league when, a short time later, he became involved as a member of the Speakers and Information Committee of the League to Enforce Peace.[59] A Utah branch of the group was organized in 1916, and after the war expanded its efforts "in favor of a league of nations to establish peace based on liberty, justice and the orderly progressive development of the world."[60] The league had sponsored several appearances in Utah by ex-President William Howard Taft the previous month.

Roberts had previously spoken out on the issue at a Sunday tabernacle service, saying that those who opposed the League of Nations were wrong when they asserted that U.S. entry into such a group would be contrary to George Washington's "warning against European entanglements." This was "good advice" in the 1790s when America was "isolated and the Atlantic Ocean presented an obstacle to travel that meant something." Under contemporary circumstances, however, the nation was "related to other nations and concerned with world policies that it becomes an absolute demand that we aid in dispensing universal justice and in guaranteeing freedom for all peoples." Roberts said that those who saw American entry into the league as meaning "the surrender of U.S. Sovereignty" were also wrong. If the league "called for the complete surrender of the sovereignty of the United States none of us would be in favor of it." But times had changed, and "in the world today there can be no absolutely sovereign nation. Such a nation would have to live entirely to itself and independent of the laws of nations. With

58. "Lieut. Roberts Will Speak Here," *Richfield Reaper*, Mar. 15, 1919, 1. Roberts also spoke at similar services in Salina and Monroe. "Chaplain Roberts Delivers Discourse," *Richfield Reaper*, Mar. 22, 1919, 1.

59. Haddock (1877–1931) came to Utah with his parents in 1879. Active in education and various business pursuits, he served as a missionary to Great Britain, and for a time was associate editor of the *Millennial Star*. Haddock was also an author. See "Former Utah Realtor Dies," *Salt Lake Tribune*, Oct. 18, 1931, 12b.

60. See "Peace League Gives Outline of Motives," *Salt Lake Telegram*, Jan. 31, 1916, 5; and "Resignations Accepted By League," *Salt Lake Telegram*, Aug. 29, 1919, 20.

every treaty the United States [makes] sovereignty is surrendered."[61] Roberts also compared this with the "individual states" which gave up some of their sovereignty to join the Union, but "the gains far outweighed these concessions."

While Roberts was speaking out in favor of the League, several of his ecclesiastical colleagues were expressing similar views. At the October 1919 general conference, for example, supportive statements were given by Charles W. Penrose, Anthony W. Ivins, Richard W. Young, and others.[62] As Reed Smoot's biographer, Milton R. Merrill, observed, that fall's conference constituted a "League of Nations rally."[63] Public opinion, as well as most Utah newspapers, were supportive of the idea in 1919.

The League of Nations' most forceful opponent was J. Reuben Clark, a respected lawyer, who saw in the league a threat to American sovereignty,[64] though the league seemed to have the support of church president Heber J. Grant, both the *Salt Lake Tribune* and the *Deseret News*, and other important public opinion makers. As historian James B. Allen has observed, Clark "boldly stumped the state of Utah" in an effort to defeat the potential league.[65]

Clark came to Salt Lake City to deliver a major address to a packed tabernacle, speaking for more than two hours to an audience that featured both supporters and opponents of the league.[66] Though eloquent, Clark's views were in many ways the "standard fare" of those throughout the country who emphasized a loss of sovereignty and an "invitation to European meddling" in American affairs.[67]

While most of the audience seems to have been moved by Clark's oratory, Roberts was not. He "sprang to his feet with his own message" and let the audience know that he would challenge and refute

---

61. "B. H. Roberts Scores League Opponents," *Salt Lake Tribune*, Mar. 10, 1919, 16.

62. See *Conference Reports*, Apr. 1919.

63. Merrill, *Reed Smoot*, 325.

64. For an overview of Clark's views, see a special issue of *BYU Studies* 13 (Spring 1973).

65. Allen, "J. Reuben Clark Jr.," 347–48. As Allen notes, Clark's "fight against the League of Nations was only the beginning of over four decades of struggle against what he considered to be the withering away of certain fundamental American traditions."

66. See "Clark Sees Calamity in League," *Salt Lake Tribune*, Sep. 4, 1919, 1.

67. Fox, *J. Reuben Clark*, 295.

every one of Clark's assertions in future lectures.[68] Indeed, after Clark's tabernacle remarks, the *Salt Lake Tribune* announced that Roberts would "answer" Clark at a mass meeting to be held Monday, September 8, 1919. Many prominent Utahns were on the stand during the address, including Governor Bamberger, several LDS apostles, Anthon H. Lund, Andrew Jenson, and General Richard W. Young.[69] Roberts spoke for over two hours.[70]

Opponents of the league represented an interesting combination of political interests. The Utah Federation of Labor, which was then in one of its more radical phases, "emphatically" opposed the league, calling it "simply ... one big union of the world's capitalists."[71] Strong opposition also came from Roberts's friends in the streetcar men's union. However, in October, Anthony W. Ivins wrote to Utah Congressman Milton H. Welling that "since our recent conference there remains no doubt that our church ... [is] not opposed to the League of Nations."[72]

Roberts became the most outspoken proponent of the league in church leadership, and spent the next few weeks, in the words of James Allen, as a "sort of traveling spokesman in favor of the League," while Clark opposed him.[73] Roberts traveled to Tooele—Clark's home territory—Logan, Ogden, and Salt Lake City. Clark responded in kind. By this time, Utah support for the League of Nations ran along party lines, and the issue grew heated.[74]

Remarks Roberts made in Ogden countered a central issue for Mormon opponents of the league, when he wondered why the League of Nations could not be divinely inspired. "Major Clark, Bishop C. W. Nibley, and Senator Reed Smoot admitted that the Constitution of the United States is inspired. I can't understand their refusal to admit that the league of nations is also inspired." Why could not God, Roberts asked, "understanding the longings of

68. Fox; and "Clark Sees Calamity in League."

69. "Roberts Replies to Major Clark," *Salt Lake Tribune*, Sep. 9, 1919, 1.

70. Lund, *Danish Apostle*, 719.

71. "League Is Opposed by Utah Labor Federation," *Salt Lake Tribune*, Sep. 12, 1919, 20.

72. Ivins to Welling, Oct. 13, 1919, box 1, Welling Papers.

73. Allen, "Personal Faith and Public Policy," 81–83.

74. Fox, *J. Reuben Clark*, 295.

the men at the peace conference," similarly inspire "them to draft the covenant of the league of nations?"[75]

In the midst of the efforts surrounding the League of Nations, Roberts received a bittersweet letter from Utah Representative Milton H. Welling about an "incident" which had occurred on the floor of the House and which was "reminiscent of your short and rather turbulent career as a representative." This involved the question of whether socialist Victor Berger should be seated. Welling noted that the Roberts precedent was "frequently referred to in the debate, justifying the right of the House to take the action that was at hand." Welling told Roberts that he would be "glad to know that no unkind word, so far as the Roberts case was concerned, was spoken," and assured him that "if any word was said regarding your worthiness to a seat in congress," he would have told the House of the "character of service that you had given to your Country from that day to the present time; and especially during the war." Welling said he could not "refrain from saying to you here, however, that I regard your unselfish and patriotic devotion to the boys of our State during the War as one of the highest points of a lifetime devoted to unselfish public service."[76]

In August 1919, Bamberger decided not to seek a second term for governor. Invigorated by Democratic success in 1916 and 1918, his wartime service, and his commitment to the League of Nations, Roberts's political juices were flowing. According to Reed Smoot, Roberts requested permission from the First Presidency and Quorum of the Twelve to become a candidate, but Heber J. Grant, Charles W. Penrose, Stephen L. Richards, and Anthony W. Ivins—all Democrats—thought such a candidacy was "very unwise." Still, as Smoot admits, Roberts was told that he was free to make the race.[77] On August 2, 1920, Roberts announced in an interview with Sherman S. Smith[78] that he was "an active candidate" for governor.

75. "Tabernacle Crowded When B. H. Roberts Replies to Clark on the League of Nations," *Ogden Standard*, Sep. 17, 1919, 5.

76. Milton H. Welling to Roberts, Dec. 10, 1919, box 1, fd. 4, Welling Papers.

77. Smoot, *In the World*, 451.

78. Sherman Sylvor Smith (1854–1931) was active in Democratic Party affairs. Earlier Smith had been a Populist and spoken against Roberts. See "Weber County 'Insurgents,'" *Salt Lake Herald*, Oct. 6, 1896, 1.

As part of a western swing, Franklin D. Roosevelt, vice presidential nominee, arrived in Salt Lake City on August 26, speaking to some six hundred Denver & Rio Grande railroad workers at lunchtime, and then sped off to speak to the local Kiwanis Club and huddle with Democratic Party officials in the Hotel Newhouse.[79] That evening he spoke in the tabernacle. The vice presidential nominee told the audience of ten thousand that within sixty days of presidential candidate James M. Cox's inauguration, the peace treaty and the League of Nations would be enacted into law. Roosevelt said the American people would "declare themselves so un-mistakenly for the league of nations as to make impossible a repetition of the horrors of 1914."[80]

Two days after Roosevelt's visit, Roberts "announced his withdrawal" from the race for governor, saying that he was doing so as a way "putting the party before himself." He had no doubt that he could have "won the nomination," but had come to the conclusion that in the general election it would be alleged that "the interest of the dominant church would require the defeat of the candidate for governor on the Democratic ticket" and he was "most anxious to keep [that issue] out of our Utah politics" especially since it would draw attention away from what he considered the most important issue: entrance into the League of Nations. It was imperative that Utahns elect a senator "who will be for the ratification of the treaty, including the league of nations covenant, without stultifying reservations, and will stand out in bold relief, and I am unwilling to be the occasion of jeopardizing exclusive consideration of that issue." Part of the reasoning behind the decision may have been health related. Anthon H. Lund recorded in his diary that Roberts "asked me if he could take a vacation for a couple of weeks to California. I told him that a man whose brain machinery was always running at full speed ought to take a rest."[81] Instead, Roberts pledged that the party "may

79. Roosevelt was running with Democratic presidential nominee James M. Cox, governor of Ohio. Roosevelt was in Utah one year before he would contract polio in August 1921 and be confined to a wheelchair.

80. See "Candidate Roosevelt Talks to Rail Workers of Labor and Its Wage," *Salt Lake Telegram*, Aug. 26, 1920, 1; and "Ten Thousand Listen to Franklin Roosevelt," *Salt Lake Telegram*, Aug. 27, 1920, 20.

81. Lund, *Danish Apostle*, 777.

rely upon my services in the present campaign to the full extent of my humble abilities."[82] Roberts began a statewide tour in the middle of October on behalf of both the Democratic candidates and the League of Nations—and against Reed Smoot.[83]

One of the most interesting of Roberts's appearances occurred at a Democratic rally held at Ogden's Orpheum Theater on October 25,[84] attended by over 1,500 people. "Why are any of you opposed to the league of nations?" Roberts asked. "What has come over you? Is it because the league has become a party issue and you are better partisans than you are humanitarians?" He criticized Smoot for an article in a Universal Press Service interview on August 19, 1920, in which he declared that league membership was in opposition to Mormon Church doctrine. He also examined the league itself, its covenants, and the "sacrifices made by the United States and other allied nations," commenting that the seeds for the league were in the teachings of Isaiah as much as in the minds of Wilson and the other Allied leaders. Rising to the occasion—at times forceful, at others colloquial—he shouted, "In the name of God, what has come over you to give up the teachings of your religion to run after the shadows of Republican propaganda?" Roberts, although he had not seen combat, remembered his time in the war. "You withdraw from the league and I tell you as coming from one who has smelled the battlefields of France that you will betray the blood of the 81,000 men who paid the supreme sacrifice." Voters risked doing that very thing "if you do not vote right on this great issue which is soon to be presented to you in that great referendum on November 2."[85]

Roberts said Americans would feel differently if they had suffered

82. "B. H. Roberts Quits the Race for Governor," *Salt Lake Telegram*, Aug. 28, 1920, 1.

83. Smoot recorded that in a regular meeting of the First Presidency and Quorum of the Twelve held on October 14, 1920, that Roberts's "attacks and false statements made against me were brought up by Pres Grant. … As usual Bro Ivins jumped in the breach for Roberts. I stated I wanted no attention paid to them. I had never done so in the past and never expected to in the future." A few days later, Smoot recorded that he had attended an "old folks" rally in Preston, Idaho, where he was requested to answer a "tirade" Roberts had made against him in that city "a few days previous." Smoot replied, "I told them I would not do so. I never mention his name in Public." See Smoot, *In the World*, 458, 460.

84. "B. H. Roberts Speaks Tonight," *Ogden Standard Examiner*, Oct. 25, 1920, 9.

85. "B. H. Roberts Raps Smoot," *Ogden Standard-Examiner*, Oct. 26, 1920, 18. See also "Roberts Speaks of Smoot and Church," *Salt Lake Telegram*, Oct. 26, 1920, 5.

as much as had citizens in the other Allied countries. "If the United States had suffered nine million casualties which would have been in the same proportion to that of France, and a coterie of senators in the congress of the United States would have entered into a round robin to prevent us putting a stop to war forever, what would you do about it?" Despite his tone, Roberts assured the paper's readers that "I don't want to use harsh words" and said he was restraining himself from saying "what I really wanted" to make everyone "sit up and take notice." He had "brought" voters "to the edge and now it's up to you to jump over."[86]

Roberts also called for disarmament. "Why the deuce do you [ranchers] dehorn your cattle?" It was to "take away the disposition to hook each other." Similarly, he asserted, it was time to take away "the disposition of nations to hook each other by reducing armaments. Take away from them these infernal establishments of militarism and you take away the dreams of conquest over other nations." According to the account in the *Standard-Examiner*, while "an attempt was made to heckle the veteran speaker," his critics were unsuccessful, and their charges lost in a "storm of applause" from the supportive audience.[87] Energized by Roberts's efforts, Ogden Democrats intensified their efforts in the final days of the campaign.[88]

In the end, however, Utah voters followed national trends and handed the Cox/Roosevelt ticket a crushing defeat. In local races, Smoot defeated Milton Welling, 82,566 to 56,862, and Republican gubernatorial candidate Charles R. Mabey[89] defeated Democrat Thomas N. Taylor by a similar margin of 81,550 to 54,914. Democrats also lost the two congressional races, with Republican Don B.

---

86. "Roberts Raps Smoot."

87. "Roberts Raps Smoot."

88. "Cottage Meetings of Democrats Arranged," *Ogden Standard Examiner*, Oct. 27, 1920, 16.

89. Mabey (1877–1959) lived in Bountiful, where he held office as a justice of the peace, city councilor, and mayor. Mabey graduated from the University of Utah in 1896. After service in the Spanish–American War, he filled a mission to Germany from 1900 to 1903. A businessman and banker, Mabey was a Republican member of the Utah House of Representatives from 1913 to 1915. He returned to military service with the 145th Artillery during World War I. He was elected governor in 1920, defeated for re-election, and served until 1925. After leaving office, he was head of the Bountiful State Bank and was a member of the general board of the Young Men's Mutual Improvement Association.

Colton defeating Democrat James W. Funk, 41,749 to 27,074; while E. O. Leatherwood defeated Mathonihah Thomas by a margin of 39,235 to 28,021. These totals indicate that most Utahns voted a straight Republican ticket, and apparently most of them disagreed with Roberts on the importance of American participation in the League of Nations. Indeed, Smoot confided in his diary that Salt Lake City's streets were "wild with excitement," and, as the results became clear, noted "A great day for America. The American people have declared unmistakably they want nothing of the Wilson League of Nations and … I have received a great vindication in [my] position taken on the League of Nations."[90]

Scholars agree that the League of Nations was, in the words of Brad E. Hainsworth, "the paramount issue in the Utah political campaign of 1920," and that Smoot's reelection was "synonymous with the question of the league to Utahns." Similarly, Geraldine Thorup Kline argues that Roberts suffered a significant defeat because he had tied himself so directly to it, and more broadly to Wilson himself. Without clear support from the church, Utah voters concluded that a vote for Harding and Smoot meant opposition to the league, while a vote for Cox and the Democrats "meant the United States would in all likelihood enter the League."[91]

Despite their victories in 1916–18, after November 1920, Roberts and his Utah Democratic colleagues, with some exceptions, were entering upon a period of diminished political success. But for Roberts himself, though deeply stung by the victory of Smoot and the defeat of the League, another important challenge was on the horizon.[92]

---

90. Smoot, *In the World*, 459–60.

91. Hainsworth, "Utah State Elections," 70, 76; and Kline, "Public Opinion," 53.

92. For more on this aspect of Roberts's views, see John Sillito, "Drawing the Sword of War Against War: B. H. Roberts, World War I, and the Quest for Peace," *Utah Historical Quarterly* 87 (Spring 2019): 100–115.

SEVENTEEN

EASTERN STATES PRESIDENCY, 1921-26

With the coming of the New Year, Roberts, though his interests were as broad as they had ever been, began to look inward at the trajectory of his life, and became more nostalgic and introspective. Along with his current activities—church assignments and events connected to his chaplaincy—he also spent an increasing part of his time reflecting on his life experiences. While participating in a quarterly conference in the Curlew Stake, "for a brief period he was reminiscent," recalling that after his first mission "he was broke, he said, and took the first employment offering which happened to be shearing sheep."[1] At other ward and stake conferences he stressed repentance and forgiveness. The death of his friend and colleague in the Historian's Office, Anthon H. Lund, led him to observe that he believed "the best possible commentary on any system of religion" was to live a "blameless life … in so far as it is given to mortal man to live a blameless life." Lund, he said, embodied that quality among others.[2] Finally, in this vein, Roberts spoke at the dedication of the monument to the Mormon pioneers at the mouth of Emigration Canyon in Salt Lake City. One wonders if Roberts reflected on his own travel down that canyon as a boy of nine.[3]

In 1921, Roberts also turned his attention to a question that had occupied his thoughts for a half century. As more and more questions arose surrounding the ancient historicity of the Book of Mormon, Roberts was asked to write something in its defense. He produced two essays: "Book of Mormon Difficulties" and "A Book

1. "Curlew Stake Holds Conference," *Box Elder News*, May 17, 1921, 3.
2. Roberts, "Remarks."
3. "Dedicate Monument to Pioneer's Entry," *Ogden Standard-Examiner*, July 26, 1921, 3.

of Mormon Study." He submitted the first manuscript to the Quorum of the Twelve in January 1922, and in it he questioned several aspects of the Mormon scripture, including the numerous languages that had evolved among Native Americans, the lack of archeological evidence for the book's civilizations, and the "mention of domestic animals, iron steel, wheat, barley and wheeled vehicles." The second essay, which apparently was not presented to church leaders at this point,[4] discussed parallels between the Book of Mormon and Ethan Smith's *View of the Hebrews* (1823), and "internal inconsistencies" within the Book of Mormon itself.[5] Roberts told church authorities that he was "absolutely convinced" that such inconsistencies could be problematic in the future, and that it was important to address them honestly and directly. He told church president Heber J. Grant, "Maintenance of the truth of the Book of Mormon is absolutely essential to the integrity of the whole Mormon movement, for it is inconceivable that the Book of Mormon should be untrue in its origin and character and the Church of Jesus Christ of Latter-day Saints to be a true church."[6] Roberts's studies would prove to be controversial within the ranks of the general authorities who would debate the assertions for several years thereafter.[7] What is more, Roberts's own beliefs, and what he really thought about Book of Mormon historicity, continue to be debated.[8]

In March 1922, Roberts may have inadvertently set a new course for the next few years of his life when he spoke in Ogden at the quarterly conference of the North Weber Stake. He voiced stinging criticism of the church's missionary system, calling it the "weakest link in the church, and that which gives it the least honor." Roberts said he wished the church would send "men of experience rather than the 'stammering, tongue-tied ignorant boys' to preach

4. It appears this study was completed in 1923, after Roberts had been called to serve as president of the Eastern States Mission.

5. Bergera, "Editor's Afterword," in Roberts, *Autobiography*, 254. For more on *View of the Hebrews* and claims that it influenced Joseph Smith, see Brigham D. Madsen, introduction to Roberts, *Studies of the Book of Mormon.*

6. Bergera, "Editor's Afterword," 255.

7. Never published in his lifetime, the manuscript was later published first by Jerald and Sandra Tanner, and then as Roberts, *Studies of the Book of Mormon*, edited by Brigham Madsen.

8. See, for example, Montez, "Secret Mormon Meetings."

the gospel to the nations." He admitted that Mormon missionaries "were the finest young men in the world," and while not lacking in moral quality or spirituality, they needed proper guidance, training, and experience. As he viewed it, "You can say what you like about the spirit of God coming to the aid of these young men, but even God must have a fitting instrument to use and through which to express himself." Even God could not rely on "a young man who is limited in his capacity to express the truth." Roberts also lamented how missionaries behaved when they returned. "Many of the young elders upon their return from their missions lapse into the lawless element, indulge in cigarette smoking and card playing. This is because they left their homes before their characters were crystalized and are not strong enough to withstand the old temptations."[9] He blamed the failure of the missionary system on the Seventies for not providing this experience and guidance.[10]

That year, Roberts may have been ramping up for another political race. He was selected as a member of the twenty-five-member advisory committee of the Democratic Party's state central committee,[11] and spoke throughout the state on political questions. But on May 10, 1922, he was called by Heber J. Grant to replace George W. McCune[12] as president of the Eastern States Mission.[13] Grant said that Roberts had performed "one of the greatest missions in the Church in the Southern States," and "displayed much bravery in the risk of even his own life" in recovering the bodies of the martyred elders, Gibbs and Berry. Grant also stated that Roberts had proven

9. "Missionary System of LDS Church Criticized by Roberts," *Standard-Examiner*, Mar. 13, 1922, 10.

10. Roberts's remarks seemed to have been taken seriously by the North Weber Stake leaders. A few weeks later he returned to Ogden where he added new members to the reorganized fifty-third and fifty-fourth quorums of Seventy. See "Seventies Gain Members Here," *Standard-Examiner*, Apr. 24, 1922, 12.

11. "Ogden Democrats on Committees," *Ogden Standard-Examiner*, Apr. 8, 1921, 3.

12. McCune (1872–1963) was active in Ogden church, civic, and business affairs. He served a mission to England from 1896 to 1898 and was president of the Eastern States Mission, 1919–22. After his return he moved to Southern California where he was Los Angeles Stake president, 1923–27, and Hollywood Stake president, 1927–31.

13. On April 30, Reed Smoot wrote without comment that McCune had told him "Roberts was to be President of the Eastern States Mission," and that McCune would serve as president of the soon-to-be created Los Angeles Stake. See also Smoot, *In the World*, 501.

over the years in many places to be an "extraordinary missionary."[14] In a letter dated May 29, the First Presidency indicated they wanted Roberts to leave "immediately," while McCune was still at mission headquarters, to take "charge and oversight" of the mission.[15]

Roberts wrote in his autobiography that the First Presidency initially had proposed several potential avenues for him to be of service, including presiding over a domestic mission or even "taking editorial charge of the *Deseret News*." Roberts said he finally selected the Eastern States Mission because it was the "most populous mission in the United States and comprised at that time eleven states within its boundary, including the industrial section of the American Union and its population exceeding thirty-three millions of people—truly a noble field." Roberts was also pulled by the LDS history within the mission: "the birthplace of the prophet … the early scenes of the prophet's life, the first vision, and the coming forth of the Book of Mormon. … These many adventures of the prophet would endear this section of the country to my mind and heart."[16]

The choice to appoint Roberts baffled a few people. J. Reuben Clark, Roberts's adversary in the League of Nations fight, was "stunned." Clark wrote to Heber J. Grant on May 24, 1922, that he was concerned because of the bad publicity that had come to the church as a result of Roberts's expulsion from Congress. He told Grant that he could understand the appointment if their goal was to "induce persecution for the sake of the increased solidarity which would follow." He also worried that Roberts's presence would "impact the church's credit and business ties with non-Mormon bankers, particularly in the Northeast." Grant replied on June 8, agreeing "that Roberts might stir up controversy," but he also thought Clark was "perhaps a little over exercised about the matter."[17] But George McCune, the outgoing mission president, also wrote to Grant with concerns. Even friends like Roberts's Democratic colleague Milton H. Welling "wondered a little bit about Bro. Roberts being sent

14. "B. H. Roberts Will Be Eastern States Mission President," *Deseret News*, May 10, 1922, 1.

15. First Presidency to Roberts, May 29, 1922, box 10, fd. 11, Roberts Papers (UU).

16. Roberts, *Autobiography*, 231.

17. Quinn, *Elder Statesman*, 39, 446; and Quinn, *J. Reuben Clark*, 35. Apparently Reed Smoot had similar reservations about such a selection. See Smoot, *In the World*, 501.

to New York," because of "his enemies both in church and state." Among these enemies, Welling identified particularly Reed Smoot. As he told McCune, "Bro. Smoot will always be a figure in affairs connected with that mission and I suspect, with good reason, your successor will be less likely to consult him than you have been."[18] Roberts's good friend William H. Smart wrote expressing his "pleasure at his having been called."[19]

At the time Roberts was assigned, the Eastern States Mission, and its approximately 140 missionaries, included New York, Pennsylvania, and New England. Roberts suggested that the mission should also include West Virginia, Maryland, and the District of Columbia. These suggestions were accepted. Upon Roberts's arrival, the Eastern States Mission had some thirty-two million residents.[20]

Accompanied by his twenty-five-year-old daughter Georgia,[21] one of the twins born right before the 1898 congressional campaign, Roberts left Salt Lake City in early June 1922.[22] Once he arrived at the mission home in Brooklyn, he began to get acquainted with the staff and the area.[23] Initially none of Roberts's wives accompanied him east. Margaret was involved in a number of social activities at home including various clubs like the Friendship Circle, where she served as a member of the program committee. Many prominent women, including general authority wives, were also members. De-

18. Welling to McCune, June 22, 1922, McCune Papers.

19. Smart Diary, May 20, 1922.

20. Madsen, *Defender of the Faith*, 315–16. At the time, the states comprising the mission consisted of one fourth of the states of the Union, 6 percent of the land, and some 30 percent of the population. The largest state in the mission was New York, with a population of just over ten million, while the smallest, Delaware, had a population of a little fewer than a quarter million. By contrast, the population of Utah at the time was fewer than ninety thousand.

21. Roberts's daughter was born Georgiana, and by this time she was using Georgia. Like her father, she was set apart by Charles W. Penrose on May 29, 1922. She would stay for a few months as a missionary herself, spending part of her time in Albany, New York, before being released in September 1922. See Adele Howells, "Utah News from Gotham," *Deseret News*, July 22, 1923, 1–2.

22. See First Presidency to McCune, May 29, 1922, McCune Papers. Church leaders—Grant, Charles W. Nibley and Anthony W. Ivins—assured McCune that "your labors have met with our hearty approval."

23. Adele Howells, "Utah News in Gotham," *Deseret News*, July 1, 1922, 1. The ties between Utahns, especially Latter-day Saints, and New York City were strong enough to make such a column newsworthy. A similar column, "Utahns in New York," by Elsie Greene, ran in the *Salt Lake Telegram*.

spite earlier difficulties, she remained an active member of the Utah Federation of Women's Clubs, and was appointed by that group to assist the Utah Public Health Association.[24] Consequently, for a period of time, Georgia assisted Roberts.[25]

The mission home, a two-story brick structure with a large ground floor study, was located at 233 Gates Avenue in Brooklyn.[26] Close by was the Brooklyn LDS chapel. After a few weeks, Roberts presided over a "farewell party" for McCune which featured games, refreshments, and an "entertaining program" for the "thirty-six guests who had gathered from Brooklyn and New York."[27] With that, Roberts was officially in charge.

Because of the geographical size of the mission, Roberts spent a considerable amount of time traveling, and he acknowledged in a letter to his family in Utah that keeping up with his responsibilities was "rather strenuous for an old man."[28] He had turned sixty-five in March. One of his missionaries, Elton Taylor, wrote his mother: "President Roberts said he could take all the LDS missionaries in the world today and easily lose them in the Eastern States Mission."[29]

Roberts received some important assistance when LeRoi Snow, son of LDS president Lorenzo Snow and Roberts's colleague from the Young Men's Mutual Improvement Association (YMMIA), was appointed to serve as mission secretary. Snow's wife, Burma, would serve as matron of the mission home.[30] The mission home was a center of activity of all kinds for Mormons and Utahns visiting New

24. "Program for Promotion of Health Outlined," *Deseret News*, Oct. 4, 1921, 9.

25. Once she did arrive in the mission, Margaret Shipp Roberts took her role as "Mission Mother" seriously and frequently traveled with Roberts to his assignments. Interestingly, she also took to referring to herself as M. C. Roberts, dropping her ex-husband's last name.

26. For a good overview, see Brooklyn District History Committee, *Zion in the Brooklyn District*, 13–14. In an ironic twist, one of Roberts's most vociferous critics, Mary E. James, had lived with her family for many years at 250 Gates Avenue, across the street from the mission home and the chapel. See "Editorial Notes," *Home Mission Monthly*, Oct. 1916, 289, which noted, "Surely no encroachment of Mormonism could touch our hearts more closely than this." Neither Mary nor her husband were alive at the time of the chapel's construction.

27. Adele Howells, "Utahns in Gotham," *Deseret News*, July 1, 1922, 3.

28. As quoted in Madsen, *Defender of the Faith*, 319.

29. Taylor to Mother, Feb. 6, 1923, box 1, fd. 5, Elton L. Taylor Papers.

30. Eastern State Mission Manuscript History, Nov. 20, 1922. Snow (1876–1962) married Maud Mary Ford (1875–1962) in 1900, had a daughter, and divorced in 1909.

York. In July, for example, Roberts performed the marriage of Glen Croft and William W. Horsley, former University of Utah students on their way to Boston where the groom was attending Harvard medical school.[31]

Georgia, who by then was then serving in Binghamton, New York, wrote to her father on July 27, 1922, about difficult experiences with some local ministers. Roberts complimented her on the way she had dealt with the situation and noted, "But the experience of Dad is that ministers are a rather hard 'bunch' to deal with in the matter of conversion, because all their interests stand out against any change, since it affects their occupation. However, once in a while, we do get one, and you may have the joy yet." He told her he was glad she was "getting a little real missionary experience … because it will be a means of your finding the Lord more completely than you have ever done before." He said to be "sure to remember me to Mother … and say to her that I am sure both of us have a right to be proud of our daughter's missionary record." He signed it, "Your president and father."[32]

During his first summer as mission president, Roberts spoke at several meetings in Philadelphia.[33] The next month he attended a conference at the Joseph Smith farm in Royalton, Vermont.[34] By September, he wrote to Apostle George Albert Smith that he had conducted "successful conferences" in western Pennsylvania and Portland, Maine, and that things "are beginning to speed up a bit in our mission and I truly hope for a continuation of it."[35] That fall, Roberts spoke at a meeting held at, but not sponsored by, the Society for Ethical Culture. His topic was "Why Mormonism."[36] The

---

He married Burma Celia Thompson (1892–1976) in Thatcher, Arizona, on May 16, 1912. They served in the mission from 1922 until their release on May 20, 1924.

31. "Salt Lake Society," *Ogden Standard-Examiner*, July 3, 1922, 4; and "Society," *Deseret News*, July 26, 1922, 3. The couple settled in Lovell, Wyoming, where he was a surgeon and she was his nurse. Croft's father, also a physician, was the longtime president of the Big Horn Stake, which may have been the connection to Roberts.

32. Roberts to Georgia, Sep. 7, 1922, Mowry Scrapbook, 79.

33. "Latter Day Saints Meet," *Philadelphia Inquirer*, June 26, 1922, 6; and Adele Howells, "Utah News in Gotham," *Deseret News*, July 8, 1922, 1–2.

34. Adele Howells, "Utah News from Gotham," *Deseret News*, Aug. 5, 1922, 5.

35. Roberts to Smith, Sep. 8, 1922, box 49, fd. 22, Smith Family Papers.

36. See "Religious Notices," *New York Times*, Nov. 4, 1922, 2; Nov. 8, 1922, 15; and Elsie Green, "Utahns in New York," *Salt Lake Telegram*, Nov. 12, 1922,

Brooklyn Daily Eagle said Roberts challenged "anyone who scorned the Mormon faith" to find a more powerful scripture than the Book of Mormon. He said that Mormonism best answers the questions "What does this whole thing mean? Why is this old earth spinning about?" Roberts concluded with

> three reasons why Mormonism is the great religion of the Western hemisphere. It is to establish among men a knowledge and a right conception of God, to bring a right knowledge to men of the purpose of the creation of the world and man, and to introduce the new and lasting dispensation of Christ. … I am sorry that the age has departed so far from the idea of a Christ without all the attributes of a human being. I do not like to think of a Christ without love and passion, love of good and a hatred of evil. Let me believe in Christ who gave us such a strong revelation of love and hatred of evil and corruption.[37]

Roberts used these public talks as both a missionary tool and as a way of presenting a positive image to the general public, and he was constantly publishing notices of his talks in the local press. Sometimes they would be in the form of short announcements along with those of other religious groups. On other occasions, he took out good-sized ads in the paper, often including his photograph.[38] His efforts bore fruit. As missionary Stanley McAllister noted, frequently "crowds gathered in the Chapel and it was impossible to get seats unless you were there an hour before the service."[39] However, as one of his missionaries put it, "Baptisms were few and far between throughout our mission at that time."[40]

In September, as he prepared to return to Salt Lake City to attend general conference, Roberts sent a circular letter to his missionaries, calling attention to several important issues. One was the Word of Wisdom, noting it went "without saying that Elders in the mission are required to keep the word of wisdom in all aspects; and there is to be no plea of avoidance about it." Saying that deception

37. "'Why Mormonism' Answered by Elder," *Brooklyn Daily Eagle*, Nov. 11, 1922, 3.

38. For examples of these ads, see *Brooklyn Daily Eagle*, May 31, 1924, 7; Aug. 29, 1925, 8; and Dec. 19, 1925, 6.

39. McAllister to Truman Madsen, Dec. 22, 1969, copy in New York Stake History Archives.

40. See Chipman, "Highlights from My Life," 19, fd. 2, Chipman Papers. Hereafter cited as Chipman, "Highlights from My Life."

would lead to destruction, he asked the missionaries to "unite with me in being true to this instruction." Possibly he had his own struggles with alcohol in mind. Roberts also counseled that "every effort should be made to secure the privilege of holding street meetings ... we ought not be backward in insisting upon a proper recognition of our right of freedom of speech and assembly." At the same time he counseled the missionaries to "strictly observe" any laws or ordinances governing such activities.[41]

In February 1923, he sent out another circular letter saying that he was concerned that "inefficient and slothful tracting in large part is the cause of our failure to sell Books of Mormon and other literature; for by thorough and vigorous tracting we create an interest in our literature which in turn creates the demand for it, which leads to the sales of it to investigators of our message." In his view, tracting—going door-to-door—within the mission had "been wholly promiscuous and desultory," with each missionary making his or her own decisions on how best to tract. He prepared "a series of new tracts under the general heading 'God Hath Spoken'"; and instituted a systematic method of distributing the tracts in sequence. He made sure local members had copies of the materials as well as the missionaries so that they could "become fellow laborers with us in the work." He urged his missionaries to take this new approach "seriously," and said its success or failure rested in their hands.

Roberts gave specific instructions to the missionaries to "impart life and vigor in every part of the work." He emphasized ongoing tracting, more time spent in the field making individual contacts, stressed the significance of the Book of Mormon as not only representing "the glory of God" but also the means for the "salvation of souls," and urged the sister missionaries, since they could not "participate in the adventurous campaign of the country work," to seek to "keep the local campfires of the work burning brightly." His slogan was "Let there be no *dawdling* nor any form of *listlessness*, no idleness. May God sharply reprove you if there is idleness. Work, then, work—hunt for souls that they may be put in the way of salvation."[42] He encouraged missionaries to "fear not the faces of men," and, on

41. Undated circular letter, ca. Sep. 1922, fd. 357, Roberts Collection (CHL).

42. Roberts to Eastern States Missionaries, May 19, 1923, in Lundquist Scrapbook.

a more mundane note, to gain the necessary funds for their work locally, cautioning them not to "telegraph for money—unless there is *dire* and *absolute necessity for it.*"[43]

On March 13, 1923, Roberts marked his sixty-sixth birthday with cards and other tributes from missionaries and friends from home. One came from his old colleague George D. Pyper. Recalling their "labors of 1896 and 1897," and the "kaleidoscopic trip" to Kansas City, St. Louis, Pittsburgh, Philadelphia, and New York, he wrote he could "never forget the choice moments spent with you on that mission and even though your remark 'I'd rather sleep with a wet dog than a man,' has come down in history, nevertheless my years rooming with you has nothing but pleasant memories." Pyper told him he was glad that Roberts was again laboring in the East.[44]

That spring, Roberts began a concerted effort to promote what he called the "summer campaign" of 1923. On March 14, O. Ragnar Linde,[45] who was then working in the mission home, wrote that Roberts brought the group together at a 10:00 a.m. meeting where he "outlined very extensively the summer campaign and his new tracts."[46] The *Brooklyn Daily Eagle* reported that Roberts had announced that he would send 150 missionaries in "house to house canvasses to show the Mormon church to be whiter than it has been painted." It quoted LeRoi C. Snow that the purpose of the "campaign will be chiefly that of clearing up certain misapprehensions in the non-Mormon mind, especially as to polygamy."[47]

The summer campaign was just the warm-up act, however. Roberts wrote to his friend Isaac Russell about the main event. "This coming summer, starting perhaps about the 15th of May, which is an important anniversary of an event in our church history, I am expecting to start all our Elders, about one hundred and thirty in

43. Lundquist Scrapbook, July 5, 1923. At the same time, in a letter dated October 29, 1923, Roberts discouraged the "increasing habit among the missionaries of borrowing one from another" and encouraged them never to borrow funds from local church members.

44. Pyper to Roberts, Mar. 7, 1923, box 2, fd. 12, Roberts Collection (BYU).

45. Linde (1900–92) was born in Sweden, came to the United States in 1908, and was baptized two years later. He was set apart on December 5, 1922, by Joseph Fielding Smith, and was released on February 26, 1925.

46. Linde Journal, Mar. 14, 1923, box 1, fd. 1, Linde Papers.

47. "Mormon Church Plans Drive Here to Get Converts," *Brooklyn Daily Eagle*, Mar. 31, 1923, 18.

number, on a summer campaign, or hike, into the country districts preaching without purse or scrip … being, if my plans do not miscarry, a somewhat great adventurous undertaking with a climax at the Hill Cumorah on September 23."[48] Roberts told his friend that he believed "these plans would win us some publicity, if handled right, with the New York papers," and wished that Russell were "in New York at the proper time to help us out." He also suggested the possibility of filming some of the events at Cumorah "if we had someone to handle it."[49] Russell responded with "greetings and congratulations on your great 'hiking' plan," but did not take up the hint to assist.[50]

The fall of 1923 brought Roberts's long-planned Hill Cumorah effort to fruition.[51] It was held to celebrate the one hundredth anniversary of the appearance of the Angel Moroni to Joseph Smith on September 21, 1823. It would prove to be a major event in Roberts's ministry and public career. The *Binghamton Press and Sun Bulletin* reported on a group of six missionaries who "started in Boston, covered 500 miles … traveling on foot." They held "Street Meetings" along the way "in Lowell, Worcester, Springfield, Pittsfield, Albany and Schenectady."[52] And finally, "through the kindness of motorists arrived in Syracuse" on September 19.

Elton R. Taylor, one of the missionaries, records his journey in more detail:

> We were instructed that we were to walk to Palmyra … which was to take us a period of six weeks. We were not to be a day early or a day late. We were to arrive at Palmyra [on] September 21, 1923. We had an unusual garb for missionaries that we wore, consisting of Khaki britches, leather puttees, a suit coat, and straw hat. Across our coat was a pennant which had picture of the Hill Cumorah and the words "Cumorah—1823–1923." This pennant created considerable interest and opened up opportunities to explain what we were doing and carry on gospel conversations. We

48. Roberts to Russell, Mar. 21, 1923, box 7, fd. 11, Russell Papers.
49. Roberts to Russell.
50. Russell to Roberts, Apr. 6, 1923.
51. For an overview, see Neilson and Teuscher, "Pilgrimage to Palmyra."
52. "Susquehanna Expects Mormon Delegation" *Binghamton Press and Sun Bulletin*, Sep. 20, 1923, 13.

carried an umbrella, along with a fiber suitcase in which we carried our tracts and books, our shaving kit and toilet materials.[53]

While on the trek, the elders had forwarding addresses "where our tracts and literature were sent to us, where we spent the weekend. We rented a room where we slept, did our laundry ... and then struck out again Monday morning." Taylor recalled that, when possible, the missionaries contacted the police chief of "the town or city in which we stayed, and after receiving permission held a street meeting on Saturday night." The missionaries would seek out other Mormons, and "if there were any Saints in the area, we held cottage meetings and meetings in rented halls. We crisscrossed over much of western Pennsylvania and western New York. I carried a little walking pedometer in my pocket and it registered something over 1500 miles by foot in six weeks' time."[54]

Before the opening of the conference, the *Rochester Democrat and Chronicle* estimated that six hundred were expected to attend, including church authorities.[55] Among the dignitaries at the conference were Heber J. Grant; his wife, Augusta Winters Grant;[56] Joseph Fielding Smith; Helen Woodruff;[57] and June Woodruff.[58] This group left Salt Lake City on September 18 and arrived in Chicago on September 20.[59] They were joined there by Rudger Clawson; his wife, Lydia Spencer Clawson;[60] Northern States Mission president John H. Taylor;[61] his wife, Rachel

---

53. See Taylor Oral History, and Taylor, *As I Remember*.

54. Taylor, *As I Remember*.

55. "Mormons Plan Centennial at Palmyra Farm," *Rochester Democrat and Chronicle*, Sep. 18, 1923, 4.

56. Grant (1856–1952) was a school teacher when she became the first plural wife of Heber J. Grant on May 26, 1884. By 1923 she was Grant's only living wife.

57. Woodruff (1901–90) was the daughter of Abraham O. Woodruff and Helen M. Winters Woodruff. Orphaned as a child after her parents died of smallpox, she lived with Heber J. Grant and his wife Augusta Winters Grant until her marriage to Alexander Pyper Anderson (1893–1984) in 1924.

58. Woodruff (1902–95) was also the orphaned daughter of Abraham O. and Helen M. Woodruff. She married Isaac M. Stewart (1904–90) in 1927, who served as president of the Tabernacle Choir, 1962–75.

59. Eastern States Mission Minutes, Sep. 18, 1923.

60. Lydia Spencer Clawson (1860–1941) married Rudger Clawson on March 29, 1883, in the Endowment House. She was the first of Clawson's plural wives.

61. Taylor (1875–1946), a grandson of John Taylor, was a missionary to England from 1896 to 1898. A dentist by profession, he served on the YMMIA general board and

Grant Taylor;[62] and their daughter Lucy Taylor.[63] From there the party arrived in Palmyra on September 21 where they were met by Apostle James E. Talmage. But "on their arrival they found President B H Roberts … quite ill and confined to his bed."[64] The *Rochester Democrat Chronicle* reported on the opening day that the rain "failed to dampen the ardor of the disciples, and that "hotels in the vicinity are overflowing."[65]

Taylor's walking missionary group arrived at Manchester, New York, "where we spent the night. From Manchester, we walked up the road, passing the Hill Cumorah, into Rochester, where we went to the Joseph Smith Farm." It was there they spied a large tent "on the lawn and cots" where the female missionaries would sleep. The men slept in an "old barn … across the street from the Smith Home." The meetings went on for a week "in this tent where events were depicted and talks given under the direction of President Roberts." Taylor said that the elders "washed and shaved in the brook at the rear of the barn. At that time of the year the water was really cold."[66]

On September 22, the *Rochester Democrat and Chronicle* reported that "Mormonism today entered into its second century accompanied by the military blare of a bugle and the prayers of nearly 500 disciples." Purple, gold, and blue Cumorah banners were raised with the red white and blue "each signifying a never-ending struggle for liberty of thought." There was a "light rainfall with a gloomy haze that threatened hourly" turning the conference in to a "veritable city of tents." Roberts felt well enough to attend and speak on "the wonderful scenes that had taken place on and near this place a hundred years ago." That evening Jesina Allred,[67] a nineteen-year-old missionary

as the church's commissioner for scouting. Taylor was president of the Northern States Mission from 1923 to 1928.

62. Rachel Grant Taylor (1878–1969) was the oldest child of Heber J. Grant and Lucy Stringham Grant. She married John H. Taylor on September 20, 1899.

63. Lucy Taylor (1900–1978) was active in the YMMIA and served as second counselor in the auxiliary from 1944 to 1948 to her aunt, Lucy Grant Cannon.

64. Eastern States Mission Minutes, Sep. 21, 1923.

65. "Mormons Meet for Centennial at Sacred Hill," *Rochester Democrat and Chronicle*, Sep. 22, 1923, 3.

66. Taylor Oral History, 43.

67. Allred (1902–1962) was living in Raymond, Alberta when she was set apart for her mission on January 31, 1922 by Melvin J. Ballard. She returned on October 2, 1924. Despite what the paper indicated, she was baptized on May 7, 1910.

from Alberta, Canada, "delivered an eloquent address." The newspaper noted that Allred was raised on a farm and "converted to the Mormon faith when she was fifteen years old and is steadily proving herself to be one of the most successful missionaries of the church."[68]

On September 23, a "brilliant sunrise playing over the crest of Mount Cumorah greeted the 500 followers of the Mormon faith as they arose this morning. … The sunshine poured enthusiasm into the hearts of those present, coming as it did after two rainy, desolated days, and many for the first time … were permitted to view Western New York at its best."[69] The Canandaigua New York *Daily Messenger* said that "one of the most impressive of the day's events was the singing on the hilltop led by Elder LeRoi C. Snow. Missionary Marie [Mary LaReal generally called LaReal] Jones[70] was the principal speaker on 'Christ's visit to the American continent.'"[71]

One account in the *Rochester Herald* particularly delighted Roberts. The presentations at the conference constituted "the very basis of Mormon theology and belief." As a result, "The speakers at the conference told the story with the simplicity and directness of a Norse saga … and when a speaker dramatically pointed to the earth and mentioned that upon that spot some of the epic events might have taken place, there was a decided thrill to being there."[72] Roberts wrote to Celia that this account "by a non-Mormon newspaper justified the entire effort."[73]

On the final day of the conference, September 23, 1923, the Saints met in the Sacred Grove at 10:00 a.m. for Sunday services. Roberts, feeling better, conducted and gave the invocation. He quoted William Cullen Bryant that "the groves were God's first Temples."

68. "Mormons Open New Century of Their Faith," *Rochester Democrat and Chronicle*, Sep. 23, 1923, 1.

69. "Mormons Near Final Session of Centennial," *Democrat and Chronicle*, Sep. 24, 1923, 2.

70. Jones (1892–1993) was educated in Provo city schools and attended the University of Utah and Brigham Young University. She taught at Spanish Fork High School. Jones was set apart on July 25, 1922, by George Albert Smith. She returned on October 9, 1924.

71. Clarke, "Short History of Mary LaReal Jones Mitchell." Copy in author's possession. Madsen states that Jones read a paper prepared by Roberts himself. See Madsen, *Defender of the Faith*, 322.

72. "A Newspaper Writer's Impression of the Cumorah Conference," *Rochester Herald*, Sep. 23, 1923. Typescript copy in Lundquist Scrapbook.

73. As quoted in Madsen, *Defender of the Faith*, 321.

Joseph Smith understood this, he told the congregation, and "came to this grove, as to a solemn temple, to submit his mind and will to God." Taylor remembered that when those in attendance entered the Sacred Grove they "felt that we were truly on hallowed ground." At 2:00 p.m., a public meeting was held at which the "Hosanna Shout" was led by LeRoi Snow. That evening at 7:00 at another public gathering a number of LDS general authorities spoke. With that, the historic meeting closed and participants left the next day.[74] The *Daily Messenger* reported that the missionaries "departed rejoicing in the glorious spiritual feast they had been privileged to attend. Much good was accomplished, prejudice was removed and the truth received a firmer hold in the land where the Lord first revealed it in this dispensation of the fullness of times."[75] As Taylor remembered, "At the end of the conference we were happy that we were able to go back home by train to Pittsburgh, which was our headquarters, instead of having to retrace our steps by foot."[76]

By all accounts, the conference was a success, but it came at a great cost to Roberts. While he dismissed his ill health as "just a cold," and soldiered on as best he could, a local physician examined him and diagnosed him with diabetes. Though ordered to his bed by the physician, Roberts persisted in completing his various assignments as much as possible. Heber J. Grant, however, demanded that he return to Salt Lake City, and so he "walked weakly to the automobile that was to take me to Buffalo and thence to continue the journey westward." Roberts had intended to make the journey alone, but at the direction of Grant "one of the returning elders was detailed to be my companion." Roberts later learned that one of the "Twelve present remarked, though not within my hearing—it was afterwards related to me—'There goes the last of Elder Roberts, he will not recover.'"[77] Roberts arrived in Salt Lake City on September 28, where Dr. Charles F. Wilcox met him and administered insulin. He remained in Utah until mid-October.[78] The *Salt Lake Telegram*

74. Eastern States Mission Minutes, Sep. 24, 1923.

75. "Mormon Services Are Concluded, Canandaigua, New York," *Daily Messenger*, Sep. 24, 1923, 3.

76. Taylor Oral History. See also Taylor, *As I Remember*, 6–8.

77. Roberts, *Autobiography*, 233.

78. Madsen, *Defender of the Faith*, 322–23.

reported that Roberts "was somewhat improved but still very weak," and was confined to his home.[79] Other press reports continued to say that Roberts was seriously ill.[80] He remained bedfast in Centerville for several weeks. He later wrote: "In the days that followed, the loving care and rest afforded me by my family was sweet. I was grateful for the relaxation and sense of security which all accorded me. Gradually I began to be restored to normal conditions except that I appeared emaciated and weak. In the course of a few weeks, however, I mustered the strength and courage to return to my field of labor as if there had been no break in my general health."[81]

For a man of normally vigorous health, this must have been a difficult ordeal, and his illness marked the beginning of a long, slow decline over the next decade of his life. While his activities were in no way stopped by these health challenges, they were certainly affected by them. He wrote that "I am reminded occasionally that I am walking something of a tight rope and I need to keep myself carefully balanced or else it means falling off for there is quite a bit I should like to do before it happens. Among these is the publication of my Americana history of the Church. If I fail to accomplish that, the major fact of my life I feel will be left done."[82]

President Grant extolled Roberts in a general conference address, telling the congregation that "a very remarkable conference" commemorating the one hundredth anniversary of "Joseph Smith's first view of the plates from which the Book of Mormon was translated" was held over the course of three days, and as a result a "rich outpouring of the Spirit of the living God was experienced." Grant expressed his gratitude to Roberts particularly "for arranging that conference, for I am free to confess, that in the multitude of duties and responsibilities resting upon me I might have neglected" it. Roberts, on the other hand, "did not allow it to pass without a very splendid conference." Everyone "who attended," Grant believed, "will look back to with that same pleasure and joy and satisfaction

79. "Brigham H. Roberts Arrives from East," *Salt Lake Telegram*, Sep. 29, 1923, 7.
80. "B. H. Roberts Seriously Ill," *Duchesne Courier*, Sep. 28, 1923, 1.
81. See Madsen, *Defender of the Faith*, 323; and Roberts, *Autobiography*, 233.
82. Roberts to Smith, Dec. 31, 1925, box 57, fd. 15, Smith Family Papers.

from which we look back upon the dedication of our temples, and the passing of other milestones … in the history of this Church."[83]

Roberts also attended the conference and spoke about the "Summer Campaign" and the "Cumorah Conference," and the spirit that was there. He said that the Eastern States Mission was located in the "most densely populated territory within the United States, and while there were only 5,000 members within the mission boundaries, and another 140 or so missionaries, the "workers of this thin, long line are extremely faithful and devoted to the work in which they are engaged."[84] A year later in another conference address, Roberts pointed with pride to the creation of new chapels in Baltimore, Maryland,[85] and Fairmont and Charleston, West Virginia. He told listeners that the total cost of these chapels was $54,000, and that fully one third of the amount needed for the West Virginia buildings had been raised "by the Saints and their friends" in the local area. Roberts also illustrated his talk with a detailed statistical report of just the first eight months of the year. Based on the figures available to him, he told the congregation that 902 meetings had been held, 18,924 hours had been spent in tracting, another 8,443 hours had been devoted to gospel study, 43,105 tracts had been distributed, and 197 copies of the Book of Mormon had been sold. Still, he stated, despite this "great volume of missionary activity," the chances of gaining converts remained difficult, and only thirty individuals had been baptized during that same period.[86]

After the October 1923 general conference, Roberts returned to his duties, and Margaret went with him to Brooklyn.[87] It turned out that Roberts's earlier criticisms of the missionary program were not just hot air. Roberts streamlined expectations by requiring missionaries to work in pairs, and by creating formal lessons for the missionaries to teach. Roberts's methods were later adopted by the

83. "President Heber J. Grant," *Conference Reports*, Oct. 1923, 4–5.

84. "Elder Brigham H. Roberts, *Conference Reports*, Oct. 1923, 88–92.

85. See "B. H. Roberts to Speak Here," *Baltimore Sun*, Dec. 14, 1924, 14.

86. "Elder Brigham H. Roberts," *Conference Reports*, Oct. 1924, 60–61.

87. Madsen reports that Celia's health made it impossible for her to travel, and she was disappointed that she could not accompany her ailing husband east. Madsen, *Defender of the Faith*, 323. See also "First Woman Doctor in Utah Retires," *Salt Lake Tribune*, Apr. 13, 1919, 7.

church and used in missions throughout the world. As one historian writes, Roberts "honed proselyting skills to a near science."[88]

Roberts was concerned that prior to his arrival, the missionaries were basically left to devise their own proselytizing approach. As missionary John K. Edmunds,[89] who left right before Roberts took over, said, "there weren't many suggestions from our mission in those days as to how you went about your teaching." The missionaries were encouraged to "hold cottage meetings" and "street meetings." But no "formal plan" existed for how to organize or hold those meetings. There were "no printed lessons at all, and no outline to follow."[90]

According to the recollections of one of his sister missionaries, VaLois South (later Chipman),[91] Roberts was "shocked at the lack of basic gospel knowledge of missionaries coming into the field. He had gone out as a youth into the mission field with a better knowledge of the Gospel than most modern missionaries had when they came home." He also felt the missionaries lacked a sense of historical context in terms of the growth and development of the church itself.[92]

So Roberts decided to give his missionaries the tools to be more successful. He began on an annual basis to "have all the new missionaries come to mission headquarters" where they spent a week for "intensive training." At the time, no missionary school or training center existed in the church. According to Henry D. Taylor, who attended, "The classes taught by President Roberts were instructive and inspiring." The missionaries were divided by groups named after LDS terms. Taylor "was in the 'Liahona Group.'" Taylor remembered it as "a week never to be forgotten."[93]

---

88. Tiffany, "B. H. Roberts," 13.

89. Edmunds (1900–89) was set apart by Melvin J. Ballard on September 9, 1919. He returned on April 5, 1922. After his mission service, Edmunds went to Northwestern Law School and settled in Chicago where he practiced law and was involved with various church assignments.

90. Edmunds Interview.

91. South (1906–2003) was set apart for her mission on March 3, 1925, by David O. McKay. She was released on March 29, 1927. South married W. Paul Chipman (1908–67) on March 21, 1941. She would work as a secretary to James E. Talmage and J. Reuben Clark.

92. See Chipman Oral History, 7, in Chipman Papers; and Chipman, "Highlights from My Life," 19.

93. Taylor, *Autobiography*, 67.

VaLois South Chipman later recalled that Roberts would teach the "gospel doctrine and public speaking classes, our top tracting missionaries taught door to door tracting, and … prominent former Utahns taught the other classes—dress and speech, budgeting, and Sister Roberts … gave us a course in health, diet etc." Missionaries were "expected to study in the evenings, but had Saturdays off and were expected to use that day to attend "culturally uplifting entertainment." The missionaries would often attend the opera and visit museums. South called the schools a "rich experience," and noted that she returned to her mission assignment "more deeply converted, committed and consecrated."[94]

In his autobiography, Roberts pointed to this effort as one of the most important activities under his direction. In order to bring a large number of missionaries together for the instruction while not "discontinuing the active work … in the respective conferences,"[95] he would bring in about one-third of the missionaries at a time, some fifty or so, on a weekly basis over a four-week period. The missionaries were lodged in private homes in the vicinity, which both lowered the costs to them and increased their contact with residents. Because he was cognizant of the visibility of the missionaries in this area, Roberts believed that "the deportment of the missionaries won the respect of these neighborhoods to the Mormon people and their faith." Some of the people living near the LDS chapel "would come to the services and at times materially increased the attendance … and throughout … these mission students won golden opinion for the church they represented."[96]

Roberts's training schools were held on five separate occasions: one in 1924, two in 1925, and one in both 1926 and 1927. One missionary, Milford I. Gardner,[97] of Star Valley, Wyoming, told his local paper that the school under the direction of the "beloved" Roberts was an essential part of his ability to conduct his missionary work.

94. Chipman, "Highlights from My Life," 7–9, 20.

95. Roberts, *Autobiography*, 234.

96. Roberts, 234–35.

97. Gardner (1902–92) lived in Afton, Wyoming, when he was set apart for his mission on June 3, 1924, by George Albert Smith. He returned on July 16, 1926. In later years, Gardner was a plumbing and heating contractor in Afton, where he was active in church and scouting.

Its purpose, he said, was so "that we might overcome some of the difficult problems that confront us in getting our message to the people in the east."[98] Ezra C. Lundahl[99] wrote his wife, Leatha, that he had just completed the missionary school, noting "we have the most wonderful talks from President Roberts … it just thrills me through and through. Oh but he is a wonderful man, he sure does have the spirit of the Lord with him. I … would rather hear him preach than any one on earth."[100] VaLois South Chipman remembered in her autobiography: "President Roberts was considered one of the greatest missionaries, orators and authors of this dispensation. … He penetrated my very being with his teachings and sermons."[101]

Despite these messages of support, Roberts recalled later that some of the visiting authorities of the church to the mission were "inclined to criticize this increasing [of] the efficiency of the missionaries, holding that it scarcely justified the withdrawal for so many missionaries from the respective fields of labor." To Roberts, however, this only reinforced the need for the schools because these skeptics "either did not sufficiently realize how needed the instructions were which were imparted through the school" or were unaware of the lasting "background created for those who attended the school." Roberts was comforted knowing that the missionaries themselves "were fully persuaded of the high value of these schools and quite generally rated them as the most profitable and interesting period of their mission experience."[102]

Even one of Roberts longtime critics, Reed Smoot, admitted that Roberts's progressive approach had brought "splendid results."[103] At the same time, as Elton L. Taylor[104] remembered, "President Roberts

98. Milford I. Gardner, "Missionary Letter," *Star Valley Independent*, Jan. 30, 1925, 1.

99. Lundahl (1900–1995) was set apart on November 11, 1924, by Joseph M. Smith, and returned on October 20, 1926. After his mission, he was active in church and business affairs in Logan.

100. Lundahl to "My Dearest Leatha," Jan. 22, 1925, Lundahl Collection.

101. Chipman, "Highlights from My Life," 18.

102. Roberts, *Autobiography*, 236. Madsen, *Defender of the Faith*, 319–20.

103. Smoot, *In the World*, 593.

104. Taylor (1900–92) was set apart for his mission on January 16, 1923, by George F. Richards, and returned on May 20, 1925. After his service in the Eastern States, Taylor settled in Price where he was active in business, civic, and church affairs including a seventeen-year stint as Carbon County Stake president.

was of the old school, and he still believed in doing country work, proselytizing without purse and scrip."[105] He also drew on his many years of missionary experience to assist those under his charge as they faced hostility. VaLois South Chipman recalled that Roberts gave instruction on how to counter charges of polygamy. "Ask them if they expect to get to the bosom of Abraham when they die, and if they know their bible they will say 'yes.' Then remind them that to get there they will have to go through one of the gates of the twelve sons of Jacob—all of whom were born in polygamy." South said she used this technique successfully.[106]

The mission had a large number of female missionaries, and believing they were an asset, Roberts and Margaret cultivated and mentored them.[107] At the same time, he was also a man of his times and, as he told Henry D. Taylor, was "of the opinion that the relation between the sisters should be more in the nature of a partnership than senior and junior companions."[108] Roberts constantly challenged missionaries to do their utmost to build the church membership. During the last six months of 1926, for example, he sponsored a Book of Mormon sales contest, which helped sell more than three thousand copies of the book.[109]

However, Roberts could be hard on missionaries as well. One historian has written that Roberts "was known to stall letters from home, delay monthly checks to 'test their faith,' and lecture parents who sent more support than the allotted $40 per month."[110] But Stanley McAllister noted that mostly Roberts was "tender and sympathetic to his missionaries."[111] On one occasion a meeting was held to consider the case of a missionary who "had transgressed morally."

105. Taylor Oral History, July 19, 1981.

106. Chipman, "Highlights from My Life," 20.

107. Margaret took the title "Mission Mother" literally. And Roberts seems to have as well. On January 26, 1926, for example, he wrote to Henry D. Taylor, instructing him to "tell Sister Skolfield it is too early for her to be cutting her wisdom teeth, and she can well afford to postpone all that until at least the close of her mission." See Roberts to Taylor, Jan. 26, 1926, Taylor Correspondence.

108. Roberts to Taylor, Feb. 24, 1926, Taylor Correspondence.

109. See box 2, fd. 12, Roberts Collection (BYU). The winner in the women's category was Zina Kunz, who sold thirty-seven copies.

110. Tiffany, "B. H. Roberts," 13.

111. Tiffany. McAllister noted that at the same time "members of the Brooklyn Branch were put off by Roberts's lack of warmth and personal interaction."

After serious discussion of the individual, who was a "bright, talented, young elder with great promise," the missionary was excommunicated and sent home. Henry D. Taylor wrote, "After all the others had left, I was alone with the president in his office. He then broke down and wept bitterly. Many had the opinion that he was a stern and hard man, but he could be so tender and considerate."[112]

On another occasion, Roberts demonstrated his fondness for his missionaries and they for him by noting that the elders and sisters had remembered his birthday. As he got ready to leave for general conference, he told them that he appreciated "your kind greetings to me on the late anniversary of my birthday. Every kind expression and every wish for many happy returns of this anniversary, and more especially your strong pledge of support in our missionary undertakings, and your approval of our plans, greatly moved me, and increased all the more my desires for the success of those plans which have been laid." Roberts told the missionaries he also appreciated the beautiful gift they had given him "in the form of a fine, gold mounted, ebony cane." He admitted to not being "fond of a cane," but this one would always remind him of "the birthday celebration [which] will be long remembered by me.[113]

Despite his occasional sternness, Roberts had developed a good rapport with his missionaries. Ezra C. Lundahl wrote to his wife that on a forthcoming Saturday night Roberts was "going to have us over to his home and we are going to have a real party." Lundahl and several of his companions proposed a skit for entertainment that was a spoof on Roberts and his missionary schools. Lundahl was assigned the role of the mission president, but told his wife he was not concerned because "President Roberts is the best sport in the world when it comes to having a good time."[114] In the years ahead, Roberts's missionaries would form their own group that continued to meet until 1982, when it dissolved, as the last chair, Milo S. Marsden, put it "due to the ravages of time."[115]

---

112. Taylor, *Autobiography*, 72.

113. Roberts, "To The Missionaries of the Eastern Sates Mission," undated, in Roberts Letters to Missionaries.

114. Lundahl to Letha, Jan. 23, 1925, Lundahl Collection.

115. See fd. 2, Chipman Papers. The group had sixty-five dollars remaining in their treasury, which they donated to the Primary Children's Hospital.

At the same time, Roberts struggled with his longtime lack of personal funds. In March 1925, his daughter Georgia apparently sent him a check for some money she owed him. Roberts told his daughter, "I am very sorry that my financial conditions will not permit me cancelling the check and sending it back to you, thus making you a present of the amount, but my financial matters, as you know, with me are too scrimp to allow me to be doing generous things, and this is the chief source of all my sorrows."[116] Roberts did however send a check to cover "the amount of interest on the little loan, as I did not intend that you should pay me interest." Roberts also expresses his "displeasure" for not writing Georgia sooner, and comments in a telling way that

> as you know, my correspondence in the mission field and with the parents of missionaries, and the church officials at Salt Lake, in addition to 140 missionaries wears me right out. In the matter of correspondence this is something that comes every day, until it nearly wears the soul out of me out. Then, too, I have adopted the practice when writing to my own people to do it by my own hand and this makes the task all the more difficult, and so for one cause and another I have managed to keep excusing myself from month to month until I am heartily ashamed.[117]

Roberts did not mean that he wrote personal letters in long hand, but rather that he typed them himself, which means that he frequently had to correct and make additions to them in his own hand. He assured Georgia that she "left a splendid tradition in the mission field" during her short tenure, and that the work "has developed quite nicely in Binghamton, and is constantly increasing in importance. We have two lady missionaries there now and two Elders, with an increasing number of friends and investigators."[118]

---

116. This would continue for the rest of his life. At his death, his estate was probated at a value of $348, one of the lowest of any general authorities. In 2010 dollars that would be approximately $5,846. As of 2021, perhaps $7,000. See Quinn, *Wealth & Corporate Power*, 176.

117. Roberts to Georgia, Mar. 21, 1925, 149, Mowry Scrapbook. Georgia was living in St. George at the time, and he remembered having "been in St. George a number of times, but stayed such a little while there, and it was so long ago, that I doubt if I have many acquaintances there who would remember me, but I have always admired the little temple city set down there like a jewel in the midst of the red mesas, and surely it is one of the most picturesque cities."

118. Roberts to Georgia.

In addition to running the mission, Roberts was still involved with the activities of the First Council of Seventy, and he became the senior president in 1924. As a result of both callings, he returned to Salt Lake City regularly, especially during April and October general conferences. Clearly this was a demanding, but fulfilling, time in Roberts's life. And while he had to remain somewhat politically neutral, he and Margaret attended the 1924 Democratic National Convention in Madison Square Garden.[119]

Although Roberts lived with Margaret as if they were a monogamous couple, he was still a polygamist. His first wife, Louisa, died on May 17, 1923, at age sixty-eight.[120] Roberts had been in Salt Lake City the previous month to attend general conference, and wanted to return for the funeral, accompanied by Margaret. He wired Louisa's family and asked them to postpone the funeral for his arrival, but, according to family biographer Richard Roberts, the "resentment and misunderstanding" between Roberts and Louisa's family was so great that a telegram was sent telling him "essentially … don't bother," and he arrived after the services.[121] Her funeral was held in the Centerville First Ward, and among the speakers were J. Golden Kimball, Seymour B. Young, and John M. Whitaker. The *Davis County Clipper* mentioned that there "was a very large attendance and numerous beautiful floral offerings at the services.[122] Newspaper accounts of the funeral were somewhat minimal in nature, however, especially considering that Louisa was married to a general authority. Not long after the funeral, an advertisement in the *Davis County Clipper* offered that Roberts's "attractive" Centerville

---

119. "Utah Standard Waves Protest at Convention," *Salt Lake Telegram*, June 26, 1924. This incarnation of Madison Square Garden was demolished two years later. Most Utah delegates supported New York governor Al Smith for the nomination.

120. "Mrs. B. H. Roberts Called by Death," *Davis County Clipper*, May 18, 1923, 1. The paper noted that all of her children "were at her bedside when she died."

121. Richard Roberts notes that his father, Harold D. Roberts, told him that "B. H. stayed until the next Sunday meeting … held in the Centerville Ward, and … tried to explain why he had missed the funeral and made some expressions of regret, and love for [Celia] and their family." See Roberts, *History of the B. H. Roberts Family*, 126.

122. See "Mrs B H Roberts Called by Death,"; "Centerville Chats," *Davis County Clipper*, May 25, 1923, 1; "Services Are Held for Mrs. Roberts in Centerville Ward," *Salt Lake Tribune*, May 22, 1923; and "Last Respects Paid to Mrs. Sarah L. S. Roberts," *Deseret News*, May 22, 1923.

home of "8 rooms and one and a half acres of ground ... on the Salt Lake-Ogden highway" was for sale.[123]

Relations between Roberts and his first two families worsened in November 1923 when he took out a marriage license in Chicago so that he could marry Margaret in a civil ceremony. No doubt Roberts hoped this action might escape public scrutiny, but the event was mentioned not only in local newspapers, but also in the *New York Times* and *San Francisco Chronicle*.[124] The Ogden *Standard-Examiner* commented that the marriage was "understood" locally as an effort to "legalize a church polygamous ceremony performed with Mrs. Margaret C. Shipp years ago."[125] On the other hand, this action, which seemed to be just one more slight, led Celia's oldest son, Harold Dibble Roberts, to tell his own son that it "had made a bastard out of him."[126] No doubt critics like J. Reuben Clark would have seen this decision as further evidence of how unsuited Roberts was for his post.

Two and a half years after their civil marriage, in early March 1926, Margaret accompanied Roberts to a conference in West Virginia, and, after having a dream "that her time was near," contracted a cold and a deep cough. Her medical training convinced her that the situation was serious. The couple returned quickly to Brooklyn where the doctor diagnosed her with acute pneumonia and recommended hospitalization, but they returned to the mission home instead. Her condition worsened, and early on March 13, a rotation of Roberts and three sister missionaries—Elizabeth

123. "For Sale," *Davis County Clipper*, Aug. 31, 1923, 4. In April 1926 the paper reported that Arthur Pettit had purchased the north half of the lot and was planning on building "a house and a garage on the same." See "Centerville Chats," *Davis County* Clipper, Apr. 16, 1926, 1.

124. "B. H. Roberts to Wed Again," *New York Times*, Nov. 10, 1923, 2; "Mormon Chief and His Plural Wife Wed Anew," *San Francisco Chronicle*, Nov. 15, 1923, 9. According to the *San Francisco Chronicle*, Roberts said that he had "contracted three marriages" prior to the 1890 Manifesto, and Louisa's death left him "free to marry Dr. Shipp, the second of his polygamous wives. The third woman [Celia] to whom Roberts married is an invalid living at Centerville, a suburb of Salt Lake City."

125. "Chicago Marriage License Granted to B. H. Roberts," *Standard-Examiner*, Nov. 10, 1923, 3.

126. Roberts, *History of the B. H. Roberts Families*, 146.

Skolfield,[127] Elsie Cook,[128] and Luella Benson Owen[129]—watched over her. Skolfield sought out Roberts at 6:30 a.m. and told him that Maggie, age seventy-six, had died.[130] Roberts told Skofield that "he knew [Margaret] was going to die and she knew she was; they had talked about it several weeks before. But he didn't think it would come so soon."[131] He said that her life was

> one of mingled great joys and great and deep sorrow ... every experience that can come to mortals came to her, and in acutest forms. She well earned the rest, which I am sure is hers, and great peace. In this hour I shall not think of what I have lost, but I remember God's goodness to me in giving me such a companion, for more than thirty-six years. She has been friend, pal, and sweetheart-wife all for me. Surely God was good to me when he brought us together. I shall never fail in my gratitude for her and her sweet, pure love.[132]

Roberts arrived with Margaret's body at the Salt Lake City train depot on the morning of March 17. He was greeted by a "delegation

---

127. Skolfield (1902–79) was born in Denver and living in Salt Lake City when she was set apart for her mission by Richard R. Lyman on July 7, 1924. She returned on September 30, 1926. Skolfield had only recently been appointed to serve "in the office of President of the Relief Society and recorder of the mission," replacing Luella Benson Owen. See Roberts to Henry D. Taylor, Feb. 24, 1926, Taylor Correspondence. See also "Relief Society Convenes Sunday," *Standard-Examiner*, February 25, 1928, 8.

128. Cook (1901–73) was set apart for her mission on April 9, 1925, by Rulon S. Wells, and returned on October 3, 1927. She was the longtime secretary for Roberts. After his death, she continued to work for the LDS Church as a stenographer. Cook later became a secretary for US Senator Elbert D. Thomas (D-UT).

129. Owen (1902–67) attended Utah State Agricultural College, and was living in Wellsville when she was called on her mission on November 20, 1923. She was set apart by George F. Richards. Owen returned on March 13, 1926. In 1936, she moved to Brigham City where she was active in her ward and as a member of Beta Sigma Phi sorority, the women's Soroptimist society, and the Business and Professional Women's Association. She was the Box Elder County Deputy Clerk for over seventeen years prior to her death.

130. Eastern States Mission Manuscript History, Mar. 13, 1926. The mission records also say the cause of death was acute pneumonia. This diagnosis is confirmed in a death certificate issued when her body was returned to Utah for burial. See Margaret Curtis Roberts, cn 5995, "New York, New York City Municipal Deaths, 1795–1949"; and "Salt Lake County, Register of Deaths, 1849–1949," #W503, Mar. 17, 1926, both available through familysearch.org.

131. Madsen, *Defender of the Faith*, 332.

132. Madsen. Interestingly, Roberts placed the date for the beginning of their relationship as 1890.

of general authorities … and a large number of friends."[133] A viewing was held that day from 11:15 to 11:45 a.m. before the funeral at noon. The *Deseret News* editorialized that those "who know her best speak of her as a soul of unusual worth, a woman whose life is rare among God's noblest creatures. She was … unafraid of standing for her convictions, but she welcomed and embraced ideas advanced her by others. … She was highly intellectual and a mate fit for the man she honored with her love and devotion."[134] Speakers at the funeral included President Heber J. Grant, along with George Albert Smith, George F. Richards, and Orson F. Whitney of the Quorum of the Twelve, and Rulon S. Wells from the First Council of Seventy. In addition, apostles Charles W. Nibley, Rudger Clawson, and Richard R. Lyman attended.[135]

Roberts asked for, and received, permission to be excused from the April general conference that year because he "desired to avoid the hundreds who might bring up my recent bereavement." On April 1, Roberts told the Seventies, "I need not mention the experience of Sister Roberts [who] had the most beautiful experience in all her life while in Brooklyn. It was a very joyful time for her in the mission field, and I am very grateful to the Lord that we had that experience together and I am grateful to the Lord for giving me such a companion for over 35 years. It has been a blessing and salvation to me."[136] If Roberts was being literal in his use of "over thirty-five years," then he set his marriage date somewhere near 1891.

Margaret's death saddened the Eastern States missionaries as well. Henry D. Taylor wrote, "Frequent visits to the mission headquarters for tracts and other supplies provided opportunity for contact with

133. "Funeral Is Held for Dr. Roberts," *Deseret News*, Mar. 17, 1926, 4.

134. "Dr. Margaret Roberts to Be Buried March 17," *Deseret News*, Mar. 15, 1926, 1.

135. Roberts's last wife still living, Celia, did not die until nearly three years after Roberts's own passing. Her services were held at the Centerville First Ward where the speakers were Heber J. Grant, Richard R. Lyman, and John H. Taylor. "Funeral Services Held Tuesday for Mrs. Celia Roberts," *Davis County Clipper*, Mar. 27, 1936, 1. When Roberts himself died, the death certificate listed Celia as his widow, and the information for the certificate was provided by her son, Harold D. Roberts. Similarly, when Celia died, she was listed as the widow of Brigham Henry Roberts, again with the information provided by Harold. Copy of originals in author's possession. For an overview of Roberts's home life, see Madsen, *Defender of the Faith*, 273–85; and Roberts, *History of the B. H. Roberts Family*.

136. First Council of Seventy Minutes, Apr. 1, 1926.

President and Sister Roberts." At Christmas missionaries and members were invited to the mission home for "singing and storytelling." It was a family atmosphere, and her death put a damper on that. Taylor remembered that "Sister Roberts … proudly bore the title of 'Doctor.' She was a very cultured, refined woman with a deep sense of spirituality." Margaret taught the missionaries cleanliness, and one of the elders joked "it took him five minutes in which to bathe and another 15 minutes in which to scrub the tub so that it would meet sister Roberts's standards and requirements." Taylor recalled the Robertses sitting in the mission home reading, discussing scriptures, and talking. "With her passing, President Roberts evidenced a spirit of loneliness and seemed to lean more and more on the mission home staff for companionship. He made us feel that we were his family."[137] Truman Madsen interviewed and corresponded with some of the missionaries who served under Roberts, and he reported that "missionaries heard Roberts later say she had the most brilliant mind he had ever encountered in a woman."[138]

In September 1926, Roberts oversaw the purchase of the Peter Whitmer Farm in Fayette, New York, where Joseph Smith and Oliver Cowdery had completed their translation of the Book of Mormon.[139] It was an important highlight as his mission began to wind down, as the last few months of his tenure proved to be increasingly difficult. He refused an offer from his daughter Georgia to return and assist him. His approach to the supervision of the mission had changed, delegating an increasing amount of work to secretaries and assistants, reducing the number of meetings, and withdrawing "at all hours to his den or to the New York Public Library to read, write and take notes." This change in behavior bothered some of the missionaries and members of the Brooklyn congregation who found him cold, unreachable, and eager to retire quickly from ward meetings. Roberts, affected by Margaret's passing, was also absorbed in his writing. He later admitted that, in fact, he had changed, and asked his fellow members to forgive him for appearing to be indif-

137. Taylor, *Autobiography*, 69.

138. Madsen, *Truman G. Madsen Story*, 329.

139. "Mormon Church Buys Historic Whitmer Farm," *Salt Lake Tribune*, Sep. 28, 1926, 24.

ferent but that he felt he "had little time for play … or to cultivate friendships." He was writing "every free minute" because he felt his own mortality, and believed he had "much to do before I die."[140] As he recounted in a letter to his daughter Georgia, he had

> written thirteen tracts[141] while serving as mission president, and during that time there has been reprinted my little work on The Gospel and re-printed another edition of the Outlines of Ecclesiastical History, also the second volume of my New Witnesses, all of which have required revision by me and quite a bit of proof reading. This in addition to the administrative affairs of the Mission and I have held five Mission Schools, which is also work above that which is done by Mission Presidents of other Missions—and this has greatly added to my responsibilities and labor. I sometimes think that mere administrative work, if I confined myself to that, would not be so laborious, but with these other things added, together with the creeping of old age, makes the work much more strenuous and leaves less time for … leisurely pursuits which sometimes I think I would like to indulge in; a genteel sort of way in the closing years of my life, and now I have a sense of neglecting a number of tasks that I had projected for myself in old age, but maybe this is more important, who knows?[142]

Roberts also admitted to his daughter that, as he looked back, he regretted his "separation from the family," and said it had become clear to him that his family needed him much more than the time he had actually spent with them. "Our separation from each other cannot help but result in something of sadness, and yet I do not see how it could have been otherwise seeing that my life's work has become what it is."[143]

Roberts was released from his mission at the April 1927 general

---

140. Madsen, *Defender of the Faith*, 334.

141. Roberts's leather-bound copy of twelve of his tracts is still extant at the CHL. These are: "On Tracting"; "The Lord Has Spoken," numbers 1–5; "Why Mormonism," numbers 1–4; "The Lord's Day"; and "Mormonism: Its Origin and History." See Roberts, *Gospel Tracts*. A thirteenth is apparently "The Second Coming of the Messiah and Events to Precede It," which is not included. Finally, a much larger work published during that time is Roberts, *Mormonism: The Relation of the Church*.

142. Roberts to Georgia Roberts, Mar. 9, 1927, box 2, fd. 2, Roberts Collection (BYU). See also copy of the same letter in Mowry Scrapbook, 32. He signed it, "Lovingly, Father."

143. Roberts to Georgia.

conference.[144] The *Ogden Standard Examiner* reported that Roberts's "advanced years is given as the reason for his retirement."[145] In his conference address, Roberts expressed "gratitude" for the "opportunity of laboring" in the Eastern States Mission. He said his tenure was a time of "great joy," especially because of "the esteem and friendship of the five hundred young people with whom I have come in contact since I began my labors."[146] Calling the Eastern States "one of the noblest missions in the world," he confessed that while he accepted his release, it was with "some degree of personal sadness." He mentioned the growth in terms of buildings he had supervised, and called his missionary schools one of the "outstanding features" of his administration.[147]

Roberts wrote to his surviving wife, Celia, that he would not remain at general conference "as it is constant torture to have one's wounds opened afresh by nearly every one who meets you." He had no intention of seeing her before he left. "I find it necessary to see as few people as possible and so I am going to say good bye to you by this note … before starting East."[148] Roberts had received permission from Heber J. Grant and the First Presidency for a six-month leave of absence to stay in New York to work on his literary efforts.

Upon his return to Brooklyn he wrote a circular letter to his missionaries, speaking highly of the new mission president, Henry H. Rolapp, who he said had been successful in a number of church callings, and believed his successor would be "a competent, earnest administrator" of mission affairs. Roberts admitted to leaving with

144. In a report to the First Council of Seventy on April 7, Roberts noted that on April 1 he had been "called into the President's Office and received the information of my release and the appointment of Brother Henry H. Rolapp." See First Council of Seventy Minutes, Apr. 7, 1927.

145. "Church Grows, Mormons Told at Conference," *Ogden Standard-Examiner*, Apr. 4, 1927, 1.

146. Later his missionaries formed the "B. H. Roberts–Eastern States Mission" group with the goal to "foster good fellowship and social contact for those who had served missions, were a spouse or resident of some ward or branch in the mission" from 1921 to 1927. The group remained active into the 1950s. A copy of the roster and constitution is found in box 2, fd. 12, Roberts Collection (BYU).

147. "Elder Brigham H. Roberts," *Conference Reports*, Apr. 1927, 33–34. Among them are "Why Mormonism," "The Lord Hath Spoken," and "The Spirit and Power in Which the Gospel Should Prevail."

148. Madsen, *Defender of the Faith*, 332–33.

"mingled feelings of both satisfaction and regret. … Satisfaction that the work has prospered measurable well during the years that I have been in charge of it, and regret that I must sever relationships that have become very dear to me." But still, he encouraged the missionaries to guard against any "slackening of your efforts in the continuation of the work."

> Brethren and Sisters, work I pray you, and let not any idle disposition be manifested in your labors. Remember that I have so often told you that the success of your mission depends upon YOU and upon your doing every day's work faithfully and well. Most earnestly do I pray that the Lord will bless you and continue to inspire you with renewing and enlarging testimonies of the truth of God's Latter-day Work, and through this combination of help from the Lord coupled with your own efforts, the happy result of success in your Mission be attained.

He signed this farewell letter "Always and Lovingly, Your Brother in the New and Everlasting Covenant, B. H. Roberts."[149]

149. Roberts, undated circular letter, ca. Apr. 1927, in Roberts Letters to Missionaries.

EIGHTEEN

THE FINAL YEARS

For the next several months, Roberts dedicated his energies to a major book he called "The Truth, The Way, The Life."[1] He moved from Brooklyn into the Morningside Heights section of New York, living in the fashionable Hendrick Hudson apartments[2] on Riverside Drive where he could be closer to Columbia University and the New York Public Library. He was up early to write drafts, had a solid breakfast and a brisk walk, and then met Elsie Cook to dictate for several hours. He worked there for several months before returning to Utah in the fall of 1927. Back home, he renewed his activities "in connection with the First Council of the Seventy."[3] He also returned to his job as an Assistant Church Historian under Apostle Joseph Fielding Smith.[4] Roberts envisioned the book as a course of study for the Seventies, into which he hoped "to incorporate within its pages a full harvest of all that I have thought, and felt and written through nearly fifty years of my ministry." The six months granted to him by the First Presidency were not wasted, he assured his colleagues, and he had dictated "the rough draft of this book, and the last few months have been revising and directing the re-writing of it. ... I am informed by the Deseret News Press ... that they could produce such a work once the manuscript is in their hands in the course of four or five weeks."[5] A month later Roberts told his fellow seventies that "he had finished" the book, "paid the stenographer and

1. For an overview, see Stan Larson, introduction to Roberts, *The Truth, The Way, The Life.* The First Presidency also "authorized his hiring a stenographer."

2. Built in 1907, the apartments featured a café, barbershop, and billiard parlor.

3. Roberts, *Autobiography*, 237.

4. According to the mission history, Cook was "honorably released" on April 29, 1927. See Eastern States Mission Manuscript History, Apr. 29, 1927.

5. First Council of Seventy Minutes, Sep. 20, 1928.

delivered it" to Apostle Rudger Clawson "to deliver it to the Twelve, with the memorandum that the Deseret News can print the Manuscript within thirty days after its delivery."[6]

In 1928, Democratic Party officials called on Roberts once more. They told him that several states in the West had requested that Roberts campaign in behalf of presidential candidate Alfred E. Smith,[7] who was being criticized because of his Catholicism. Roberts gave a lecture on "Why Utah Voters Should and Would Vote for Al Smith," which was, according to the *Park Record,* a "challenge to the hideous monster of religious prejudice was hurled to the high and low of the state of Utah."[8] The *Vernal Express* noted that "the grey haired old warrior who knows so much about being the object of religious bigotry sounded anew the battle cry," and Roberts promised that if anyone raised the question of Smith's religion, he "would be the first to rush to the battle line and with every energy at his commandment crush such spirit until it was dead."[9] On October 15, Roberts spoke on "Al Smith and the Constitution," which was broadcast over KSL's radio station,[10] and then toured throughout Wyoming and Idaho in Smith's support. Roberts, born before the Civil War, lived to travel in automobiles, hear voices out of radios, and watch flickering images on movie screens.

In an effusive letter, Utah governor Dern wrote to Roberts that if the Democrats were to be "successful at the polls ten days hence it will owe much to your convincing eloquence." Dern told Roberts that he was swamped with news of Roberts's eloquence and "powers of analysis and of persuasion." Dern asked Roberts to visit Weber County where Democrats felt "neglected in that you have not appeared before them." Dern believed that if Roberts were to appear there, it "would mean the changing of many hundreds of votes now committed to the other party."[11]

---

6. First Council, Oct. 25, 1928.

7. "Many Requests Received for Utah Campaign Speaker," *Salt Lake Tribune*, Sep. 28, 1928, 7.

8. "For Our Democratic Readers," *Park Record*, Sep. 21, 1928, 4.

9. "B. H. Roberts Stamps Heel to Religious Prejudice and Strongly Endorses Smith," *Vernal Express,* Oct. 5, 1928, 8.

10. "Plans Complete for Robinson," *Ogden Standard-Examiner*, Oct. 14, 1928, 7.

11. Dern to Roberts, Oct. 26, 1928, box 8, fd. 40, Roberts Papers (UU).

However, while Roberts's friend William H. King won re-election to the Senate, the national Democratic ticket fared poorly in Utah that fall. Herbert Hoover defeated Al Smith in the state 94,688 to 80,897, and swept to victory across the country and into the White House.

Roberts continued to broadcast over KSL, delivering a series of weekly sermons discussing "The Falling Away" from March 10 to June 30, 1929. In these radio talks he sought to explain both how Christianity had not only lost its original authority and how the Christian [LDS] Church had been "re-established" in the "Dispensation of the Fullness of Time." These sermons were collected into the volume *The Falling Away: Or The World's Loss of the Christian Religion and Church.*[12]

Then, in 1930, Roberts compiled one of the most significant of all of his historical narratives, known as the multi-volume *Comprehensive History*. Roberts had originally published the history serially between 1909 and 1915 in *Americana* magazine. He then suggested a chronological history of the LDS Church as a member of the Church's Centennial Committee as early as 1928. Compiling and editing these earlier articles was a major commitment of time and effort, and he cut back on some of his speaking engagements and First Council duties. He dragooned family members into engaging in "typing, proof reading and checking footnotes."[13] Despite his infirmities, Roberts worked late into the night and on Sundays to move the project along. He recognized his obsession, telling his former missionary Elizabeth Skolfield Hinckley that he had very few social diversions: "I have well-nigh ceased to be a family man; I live and work alone, am cross as a bear, speak shortly, cuss, usually under my breath, but sometimes it escapes into audibility, to my shame. I am irritable, disappointed, unapproachable, impatient—especially with stupidity of which the world is full."[14] Roberts's break-neck schedule and his irritability may have been evidence of his advancing diabetes. Roberts might have been so driven because he felt that the *Comprehensive History* was his magnum opus.[15] During the writing process, Roberts, seventy-three when the

12. Roberts, *Falling Away*.
13. Madsen, *Defender of the Faith*, 359.
14. As quoted in Madsen.
15. Madsen.

history was published, realized that he was describing events in which he himself had participated. As an older man, he had that sense of déjà vu that he had lived history, perhaps even was history.

> I feel that I am a little associated with the pioneers of Utah, for as a boy I marched beside our ox teams every foot of the way from the Missouri river to these mountain valleys, to this city. I felt the restraining influence of the Church's hand upon me in the wayward days of my boyhood; and as I passed into manhood, a deep conviction of the teachings lay hold of my heart. I spent the best days of my life as her representative abroad and in the United States, in the midst of persecution and mob violence. I passed through all these experiences.[16]

Generally he chronicled these events without mentioning his name, or, as in the case of the congressional fight against him, using the third person. Ultimately, he completed the six-volume work, and it was a major addition to Mormon historiography. He told Bernard Moses that the history was "regarded by my associates as the masterpiece of my life's work."[17] He was working on other writing projects as well, including contributions to the "Church News" section of the *Deseret News*.

More events occurred, beyond writing about himself in history books, to remind Roberts of his age. During this same period, a number of Roberts's family passed away. In February 1930, his sister Anna Willey died. According to the recollections of Elden M. Stephenson, a great grandson, near the end of Roberts's speech at her funeral, he "leaned over to look into the face of his sister, to speak directly to her, though she had passed on. He told her that when she gets to the other side to tell their father that all is well here and that his temple work is done."[18]

In late July Roberts returned east to participate in the church's centennial observations at Palmyra, New York. Roberts gave an evening lecture on church history[19] and joined with a thousand par-

16. Undated notes, fd. 534, Roberts Collection (CHL).

17. Roberts to Moses, Nov. 23, 1931, Moses Papers.

18. Eldon M. Stephensen to Truman Madsen, Oct. 20, 1970, box 6, fd. 9, Roberts Collection (BYU).

19. Henry E. Mitchell, "Mormon Missionaries Tell of Activities at Palmyra Celebration of Centennial," *Rochester Democrat and Chronicle*, July 26, 1930, 4; and "Mormons Open Centennial Celebration Program with Rites Near Palmyra Today," *Rochester Democrat and Chronicle*, July 24, 1930, 9.

ticipants in services held in the Sacred Grove. A missionary named James Ercil Henrie[20] reported back to his hometown of Panguitch, Utah, that "at the [Sunday] afternoon session, Brother Roberts gave the crowning address of the conference, his subject being 'What Hath God Wrought.'" Roberts ended his "very touching sermon in the Sacred Grove" with a prayer to God "in thanks for this great work restored." Henrie said that Roberts's "white hair and wonderful kind face grown old in the service of the church, presented a picture that one could never forget."[21]

That fall, Roberts found himself on a list of the greatest living Utahns. The idea behind this ranking began with the *Salt Lake Telegram*, which received an "amazing response" when it was put to a popular vote. Some 5,500 votes were ultimately cast for 565 different individuals. Unable to narrow the large selection, the list was divided into two groups. On the first was Reed Smoot, Maude Adams, George H. Dern, Heber J. Grant, Cyrus E. Dallin, Anthony W. Ivins, J. Reuben Clark, Elmer I. Goshen, William H. King and Elbert D. Thomas.[22] The second list included George Sutherland, Evan Stephens, Nathaniel Baldwin, Roberts, James E. Talmage, Emma Lucy Gates Bowen, Harvey Fletcher, Ralph Chamberlin, John Held Jr., and Mahonri Young. Roberts must have been miffed that two political opponents—Smoot and Clark—along with his ally William H. King were in the first list. On the other hand, Roberts was ahead of several of his general authority colleagues including John A. Widtsoe, Charles W. Nibley, Orson F. Whitney, Levi Edgar Young, and Richard R. Lyman, all who ranked below him on third, fourth and fifth ranking lists.[23]

Throughout the remainder of the year, Roberts spoke at many events throughout Utah, including the Nebo Stake conference in Payson, the Kolob Stake conference in Springville, and two special services celebrating the Armistice—leading a parade in Ogden and

20. Henrie (1907–93) was living in Panguitch, Utah, when he was set apart on November 27, 1928, by Melvin J. Ballard. He returned on December 19, 1930.

21. "Interesting Missionary Letter," *Garfield County News*, Sep. 12, 1930, 1.

22. "Ten Greatest Living Utahns Announced," *Salt Lake Telegram*, Oct. 26, 1930, 3.

23. "Second List of Greatest Living Utahns," *Salt Lake Telegram*, Oct. 26, 1930, 3; and "The Third Ten," *Salt Lake Telegram*, Oct. 26, 1930, 3.

dedicating the city's new municipal stadium.[24] As 1931 began, Roberts spoke at the Alpine Stake's quarterly conference in American Fork, at BYU's Leadership Week, at the annual meeting of the Utah Academy of Arts and Letters, at the annual meeting of the Utah State Press Association,[25] and finally at the Juab Stake quarterly conference held at the Nephi Tabernacle.[26] Sadly, almost a year to the day after the death of his sister Annie, Roberts had to speak at the funeral of his sister Mary, who had accompanied him across the plains.[27]

In April 1931, Roberts's physicians informed him that the diabetes had progressed to the point that he likely faced the amputation of one or both feet. As one of his missionaries recalled, "Roberts was a proud man, very distinguished looking, and he once told us missionaries he would rather be dead than be a cripple."[28] He was now seventy-four years old, worn out physically, and the medical personnel worried about the effect of the surgery on their patient. After having part of his right foot removed Roberts seemed to be recovering well, however. He asked for the manuscript of volume seven of his earlier history of Joseph Smith, planning to dictate articles and correspondence to Elsie Cook, but then Roberts spiraled in to a deep depression. This was an almost overwhelming episode of a lifetime of struggling with what Roberts called the "black dog." His suffering also included intense headaches that had plagued him off and on for most of his life, and for which he had turned to alcohol for relief. On top of that, his old friend Orson F. Whitney died.[29] Roberts, depressed and devastated, wrote a note and pinned it to

24. "Ogden to Join in Observing Anniversary of War's End," *Standard-Examiner*, Nov. 10, 1930, 1.

25. "Publishers of Utah Hold Annual Meeting," *Times-Independent*, Jan. 29, 1931, 1.

26. "Stake Conference Was Held in Nephi," *Times-News*, Mar. 12, 1931, 1.

27. See "Mrs. Anna Willey, Sister of B. H. Roberts Died Last Sunday," *Davis County Clipper*, Feb. 14, 1930, 1; and "Mrs. Mary H. Day, Sister of B. H. Roberts Died at Her Home," *Davis County Clipper*, Feb. 20, 1931, 1.

28. Chipman Oral History, in Chipman Papers.

29. Despite Roberts's physical and emotional state, some newspapers reported that he might be a likely successor to Whitney. As one paper noted, Roberts had been mentioned for "more than a generation" to be elevated to the Twelve because "for many years [he] has been the most militant of all church leaders and ... is the most distinguished orator in the church and next to Reed Smoot ... the most active churchman in the field of politics." See "Mormons Will Name Apostle," (Wikes-Barre, PA) *Evening Standard*, Sep. 21, 1931, 2.

his door: "*Absolutely* no visitors, B. H. Roberts."[30] In May, the *Ogden Standard Examiner* had reported that three Mormon leaders were ill and that Roberts's condition was the "most serious."[31] But, through a combination of his doctor's efforts and support from friends and family members, Roberts mustered up the will to gradually recover. He was released from the hospital on May 23, and spent the next few months convalescing. Later, he admitted that the "ordeal" had brought him "deep down into the shadows of another world. In fact I feel as if I … passed through the experience of death, and am now trying to adjust myself to a new phrase of experience."[32]

In a major address in the Salt Lake Tabernacle, Roberts reflected on his brush with mortality, remarking that if there has

> been any purpose in bringing me back to activity, any remnant of duty, or anything I can do for the cause of God, before passing on, I announce myself as being very willing to undertake it, if God will lead me to it; for I confess before you all that without him man can do nothing. We are utterly dependent upon him, and the presence of his spirit, to achieve the things he would have men do. … If there is any unfinished business in my life that I can attend to, beginning now, I declare that I am most willing to undertake it.[33]

Indeed, he took up his speaking engagements once again in the ecclesiastical, civic, military, and political spheres.

Roberts was cheered with that year's election results in Utah, which brought about a solid victory for the Democrats, with Franklin D. Roosevelt garnering 116,750 votes to the incumbent Hoover's, 84,795. In the race for United States senator, Roberts's old antagonist Reed Smoot was defeated by New Deal Democrat Elbert D. Thomas,[34] 116,909 to 86,066.

Howard R. Driggs wrote to Roberts encouraging him to write an autobiography. Roberts told Driggs that he was not sure if he had the energy to undertake the task. More importantly he told Driggs,

30. Madsen, *Defender of the Faith*, 371.

31. "Three Church Leaders Ill," *Ogden Standard Examiner*, May 1, 1931, 13.

32. I rely on the work of Truman Madsen for this overview, since he had access to materials (including interviews of associates of Roberts) I have not. See Madsen, *Defender of the Faith*, 371–73.

33. Published as Roberts, "Mission of the Church."

34. Thomas (1883–1953) served as US senator from Utah, 1933–51.

"There seems to loom large so many more important things that I feel I ought to give attention to them first." He also told Driggs that "I have succeeded in making progress enough to get away from the hospital, and … am told that I have every hope of recovery which may continue my life for a number of years, and I hope I shall be able to make some contribution to our general cause that may be helpful, otherwise I can see no reason why my life has been preserved.[35]

Though Roberts said he was not sure if he had the energy to undertake such a task, according to Gary Bergera, Roberts began the "bittersweet task" of producing drafts and collecting his notes sometime in late 1932 and into 1933.[36] While Roberts omitted much—both personal and professional—the autobiography is an important source for understanding Roberts's life and career. The autobiography comes in two versions: the first is a 473-page double-spaced narrative which was typed by his secretary Elsie Cook; the second is a 237-page single-spaced copy produced later by his daughter Georgia Roberts Livingston.[37] The work itself would not be published until some sixty years after his death.

In early August, Roberts was present at a "prettily appointed" sixty-ninth birthday party for Celia held in Centerville, which brought his family together. Along with several of his children—Harold, Hazel, Lawrence, David, Georgia, Naola, and Luna—Roberts and the other guests, joined Celia at a "long table [which] held as a centerpiece a mound of pink and green sweet peas."[38] Perhaps it was an effort to heal the wounds that existed between him and the family.

Though Roberts's health was again flagging, he undertook an assignment to represent the church at the forthcoming meetings of the World Fellowship of Faiths to be held in Chicago.[39] The gathering was organized by Charles Weller, who had created the League of Neighbors in 1918, and Das Gupta, organizer of the Union of

35. Roberts to Driggs, June 12, 1931, box 10, fd. 109, Driggs Collection.

36. Gary James Bergera, introduction to Roberts, *Autobiography*, xv.

37. Both versions are housed at Special Collections, Marriott Library, University of Utah. Moreover, each version was used by Gary Bergera in producing the *Autobiography of B. H. Roberts*.

38. "Centerville," *Davis County Clipper*, Aug. 11, 1933, 4.

39. "Impressive Meeting to Launch Meeting of World Faiths," *Chicago Daily News*, Aug. 26, 1933, 8.

East and West in America, who had merged their organizations and began to bring various religious faith traditions together in Chicago. The meetings attracted a number of reformers and religious figure, including Margaret Sanger, Wisconsin governor Phil LaFollette, Bishop William Montgomery Brown, Mary Church Terrell, Charlotte Perkins Gilman, Muriel Lester, and Rev. Frederick V. Fisher.[40]

Roberts left Salt Lake City by train on the evening of August 24, arriving in Chicago on August 26, where he "was met at the railroad station by the Mission President [George S. Romney] and the secretary."[41] The *Chicago Daily News* noted Roberts's arrival and compared the World Fellowship of Faiths to the Parliament of World Religions.[42] When the meeting opened, Fellowship officials made specific reference to Roberts's treatment at the hands of the World Parliament of Religion organizers forty years before in the same city. According to Romney, "President Roberts was honored, it seems to me, more than any other of the distinguished people who spoke."[43] Roberts later told Josiah E. Hickman[44] that he had "received very much better treatment at the hands of the ... World Fellowship of Faiths" than he had at the parliament.[45]

In his first address, Roberts noted that he believed whereas the Parliament of World Religions had been "a parade of rival religions," the present conference was built on the idea of all people of faith uniting to solve the "urgent problems" impeding world progress. Roberts said he believed nothing constituted a greater threat to human progress than "the possibility of international war, which threatens "the very existence of civilization." He built upon scriptural injunctions, both traditional Christian and Mormon, to

40. See "Religious Groups Open Parliament, *New York Times*, June 19, 1933, 17; and "Problems for the Fellowship of Faith at Chicago," *Literary Digest*, July 8, 1933, 21.

41. Northern States Mission Manuscript History, Aug. 26, 1933.

42. "Impressive Meeting to Launch Meeting of World Faiths," *Chicago Daily News*, Aug. 26, 1933, 8.

43. "Elder George S. Romney," *Conference Reports*, Oct. 1933, 40. Romney said this treatment was "indicative of a change in public opinion" toward the church.

44. Hickman (1862–1937) spent most of his life as an educator in LDS schools. He obtained degrees from the University of Michigan and Columbia in 1907. He wrote many articles on LDS topics and was the author of *The Romance of the Book of Mormon* (Salt Lake City: Deseret News Press, 1937).

45. Roberts to J. E. Hickman, Sep. 8, 1933, Roberts Papers (CHL).

demonstrate God's injunctions to renounce war and proclaim peace. Such a policy, he said, had become even more urgent as a result of the "dreadfulness" of the last war.[46]

In his second address, the "Economics of the New Age," Roberts outlined what he believed would constitute the "New Age" in human civilization. First, he states, such a new age "will ultimately come to recognize God as the owner of the whole earth, and as a "concomitant of this will run the conception that all that man can possess of God's earth and its wealth, will be a stewardship held in trust ... for the benefit of others as well as for the temporary possessor." In that way, "the economics of the New Age will require the consecration of the surplus property of these holdings" to the community as a whole, administered by "the wisest, most efficient and experienced" leaders that community can produce—an idea with roots in the early Mormon communitarian ethos.[47]

John K. Edmunds later recalled that Roberts told him he "had been waiting forty years to deliver this talk." Then Edmunds recalled with a chuckle about the time he and his fiancée were driving Roberts

> to his hotel one night from the mission home during the fair. He had just that day been to the booth [in the Hall of Religion] and listened to our presentation. I took occasion to ask him how he felt about the work at that booth, our display, and the lecture. I felt very surprised at the quick answer that he gave. He said, in almost a disgusted voice ... "Sunday School stuff! Why doesn't the church come out and talk religion at these places and tell the people that God has spoken again from the heavens, that He reestablished His church, called a prophet, and had him ordained, and that revelation is continuous in the church. They ought to get down to the meat of it, rather than this Sunday School stuff." That was his reaction to a program that we thought was pretty good.[48]

Earlier in the summer Roberts had spoken at the funeral of his former missionary colleague Adelbert Cazier. The two had made a pact while in the Southern States that whichever one of them survived would preach at the other's funeral sermon. After the services he joined the Cazier family for refreshments, reached for the needle

46. Roberts, "Standard of Peace."
47. Roberts, "Standard of Peace."
48. Edmunds Interview, 241–42.

for his insulin shot, and discovered it was not there. As a result he suffered a "down spell" over the next few days, demonstrating how serious his diabetes had become.[49]

Despite these health concerns, Roberts kept up a full schedule. Utah was in the middle of a campaign to determine whether it would support or repeal prohibition. Heber J. Grant, a longstanding foe of alcohol, opposed any effort to weaken prohibition arguing that the Word of Wisdom was for the temporal salvation of all people. Roberts, however, had a different view. When asked by Apostle Rudger Clawson to address a forthcoming meeting on the relationship of prohibition to the Word of Wisdom, Roberts replied that Clawson's request exceeded the bounds of propriety because it sought to extend church influence over a political matter: "There is no connection between state prohibition and the Word of Wisdom," he said. "State prohibition is based on compulsion as all human-made laws must be, while the Word of Wisdom is just what its name implies, namely a Word of Counsel from the Lord as to what is good for all his saints, but it is not given by way of 'compulsion,' or 'constraint;' and certainly des not rest upon physical force as state prohibition does and must do if it continues."[50]

In mid-September 1933, Roberts, accompanied by Elsie Cook, joined a delegation to survey "the living conditions of the miners, activity of strike organizations, and reputed disturbances" which had occurred during a recent strike in Carbon County sponsored by the National Miners Union (NMU).[51] His group, which included several Utah leftists and progressives,[52] had a lot to tell the press when they returned, reporting that "100 armed special deputies" had been used against the strikers, and eighteen men were held incommunicado for six days, unaware of the charges against them and without warrants. They concluded that "individual liberties constitutionally

49. Madsen, *Defender of the Faith*, 377.

50. Roberts to Rudger Clawson, Sep. 20, 1933, Clawson Papers.

51. "Salt Lake Group Studies Strike Area Conditions," *Salt Lake Tribune*, Sep. 19, 1933, 3. For an overview of the strike, see Papanikolas, "Unionism, Communism and the Great Depression."

52. Among them were Warwick C. Lamoreaux, Wilford Owen Woodruff, Murray E. King, Alfred Sorensen, and Belle Taub, a New York organizer for the International Defense League.

guaranteed [were] being violated by Carbon county officials" and that they planned to make "a formal protest" to Governor Henry H. Blood after they had finished collecting all the "necessary facts."[53] In response, local law enforcement officials in Carbon County accused the delegation of being biased, interviewing only the prisoners and strike sympathizers and not government officials.

Roberts was also pushing another project along, a special "Seventies Convention" to be held during the October general conference sessions. Three days after his return from Carbon County, Roberts announced that the First Council of Seventy strongly supported a recent church decision that the second Sunday of each month be known as "Seventies Sunday." He would never get the chance to move it forward.

On September 17, 1933, Roberts spoke at a friend's funeral where future apostle Hugh B. Brown noted that he thought Roberts appeared ill and lacked his usual vigor. As he finished his remarks, Roberts looked over the heads of the congregation and said, "So long, Jack. I'll be seeing you in a few days."[54] Roberts continued to ail.

After "several days of illness," he was taken to the LDS Hospital on Wednesday morning, September 27. He went immediately to intensive care, seemed to rally, then turned to a nurse and reportedly said: "You had better give me my coat. I am not going to stay here in bed. I have stayed long enough."[55] They were his last words. Within minutes he slipped into a coma. He had several visitors, among them Heber J. Grant who tearfully said to Roberts's son, "Oh Harold, what will I do without him."[56] According to his secretary, Elsie Cook, "When I came back I looked at him and said 'You don't feel so good,' and he didn't say a word but he looked sort of strange." Cook called the nurse who "immediately called the doctor. … I went to the phone and called Ben Roberts and told him his father was dying. He

53. "Carbon County Lawlessness," *Deseret News*, Sep. 22, 1933, 4.

54. Madsen, *Defender of the Faith*, 379.

55. Madsen, 381.

56. Elsie Cook told Truman Madsen that during Roberts's last few days, Heber J. Grant "was so wonderful during all that time and so understanding. He really was his best friend." Madsen, 383.

came immediately and stood at the foot of the bed. … I think I just went back to the office and cried."[57]

Roberts's pulse gradually faded and, with "a number of family … at his bedside," he died that afternoon.[58] According to his death certificate, Roberts died of diabetes mellitus and diabetic endarteritis, an inflaming of the arterial lining. A contributing factor was listed as dysentery, which had lasted for five days.[59] His daughter Adah Roberts Naylor wrote of his final days:

> He had recently returned from Chicago … . He seemed in fairly good condition on his return, but he went immediately into the Southern part of the state where there was a coal strike on, as arbitrator for the miners. A hard trip and a difficult task. On his return he was a bit upset and very weary and was confined to his room for a day or two—tho there seemed nothing alarming about his condition until Wednesday morning when a physician was called and he was taken to the hospital for treatment. … He soon sank into unconsciousness and passed away the afternoon of that day.[60]

In its coverage, the *Deseret News* mentioned all three of Roberts's wives as well as the surviving children by each wife. The paper editorialized that because of his "fearlessness and his staunch defense of the principles of the gospel, President Roberts has won many outsiders to friendship for the Church," and that for those who knew him, his "stalwart, princely figure" would be missed [61] The paper added that Roberts was "active to the very end—actually working against time knowing that there were many things yet that

57. Cook makes no mention of his supposed last remarks. See Madsen; and Cook to Truman Madsen, undated, Aiwohi Papers.

58. Madsen, *Defender of the Faith*, 382. Roberts's death was not only reported in the Utah press, but a United Press report was carried widely in newspapers throughout the country, including the *New York Times*. There is some difference of opinion over the time of Roberts's death. The newspapers, relying on the death certificate, list the time as 4:20 p.m. On the other hand, Elsie Cook suggests it came just after 1:00 p.m. See Cook to Madsen.

59. For a copy of the death certificate, see Series 81448, Department of Health, Office of Vital Records and Statistics Death certificates, Utah State Archives.

60. Adah Roberts Naylor to Bernard Moses, Oct. 15, 1933, Moses Papers. For letters of condolences to another daughter, see Mowry Scrapbook.

61. "B. H. Roberts's Funeral Sunday," *Deseret News*, Sep. 28, 1933, 1. The paper also included a sidebar dealing with Roberts's retrieval of the bodies of Gibbs and Berry.

he wished to accomplish."[62] The church's First Presidency issued a formal statement on Roberts's death that captured his life and message. One of the most heartfelt tributes came from his old friend, and occasional adversary, J. Golden Kimball. No doubt returning in his mind to the days of danger they had experienced in the South, Kimball said: "I have been associated with President Roberts for the last 50 years. During that time we counseled together and our friendship was continuous." Kimball remembered that Roberts always searched for the truth with a "humble pride in overcoming and solving the great problems that defy us unless guided by the Holy Ghost." He eulogized him as "a masterful and a great leader with faith and the courage to his convictions. He had an abiding faith in God and humanity and was a man able to deliver Christ's message to God's children."[63]

Kimball missed his friend and further expanded on his feelings a few days later at general conference.

> I never felt more lonely or helpless, in a way, than I do now. Brother Roberts has been my mentor; he has been my teacher; he has been my chronicler. I was relieved of reading the great histories. I didn't have to read a whole library searching for information. What did I have to do. When anything troubled me about the history of the Church or scriptures, I went to Brother Roberts. He had the most wonderful mind and memory of any human being I have known, right up to the very last. A great light has gone out in my life.[64]

A similar tribute came from William H. Smart. Noting that Roberts was one "of our leading writers and speakers," and recounting their experiences at the time of his congressional challenge, Smart commented, "I admired him for his faith, works, intelligence

62. "President Brigham H. Roberts," *Deseret News*, Sep. 28, 1933, 4. See also the sidebar on Cane Creek, "Roberts's Rescue of Elders' Bodies Reveals Courage," *Deseret News*, Sep. 28, 1933, 2.

63. "Noted Leader of LDS Dies," *Salt Lake Telegram*, Sep. 28, 1933, 1.

64. "Elder J. Golden Kimball," *Conference Reports*, Oct. 1933, 43. Kimball went on to say that as much as he honored and respected Roberts, he had never "felt inferior to him in his presence," and while he recognized that his friend had "greater intellect, greater intelligence," he had gifts that were equal. As he said: "I have preached by his side many times, and after he got through preaching, I reached those that he missed. He often said in the south 'our love is akin to that of David and Jonathan.'" Kimball would die five years later in an automobile accident.

and integrity. In many respects he impressed me as a great character. I am touched deeply by his passing."[65] At the same time, Roberts's death reminded many Utahns of his service in World War I. Frank Francis, writing in the *Ogden Standard-Examiner*, recalled that Roberts's "death brings back to mind he day in 1919 when the 145th regiment marched up twenty-fifth street to the martial music of the bands." With people displaying "war helmets, guns and uniforms," the whole episode "was one to thrill the beholder." Roberts was at the "top of the parade … head held high, step elastic. White were his locks, but his spirit was that of youth. Never did a man look more heroic or more fit to head a home coming of soldier boys than did B. H. Roberts on that occasion. He radiant patriotism and soul found expression in pride of service for those he loved."[66]

Other remembrances of Roberts can be found in newspapers around the nation, For example, the San Luis Obispo, California *Daily Telegram* reported that "Roberts died Wednesday night, but almost as death laid still his towering frame the liberalism and courage characteristic of him prevailed." Even as he was sick and ailing, he "invaded Carbon county less than a week ago as a representative of the Civil Liberties Union to demand fair play and justice for striking coal miners who, incidentally, are not Mormons."[67]

Another interesting remembrance can be found in a Welsh-oriented paper, the *Druid,* published in Pittsburgh. Reporter John James wrote that Roberts was "extremely proud of his Welsh ancestry," and that he often attended and spoke at Welsh Mormon meetings throughout the state. Roberts was, James wrote, "As an orator he had few equals in the West. … He was a man of striking appearance, and commanded the respect of all with whom he came into contact. While a strong and able advocate of the faith of his church, he was most tolerant and considerate of the opinions and beliefs of others." James remembered Roberts as a tireless advocate for "the laboring man," and also reported on Roberts's visit to the

65. Smart Diary, Sep. 28, 1933.

66. Frank Francis, "News and View," *Ogden Standard-Examiner*, Sep. 28, 1933, 1. Francis called Roberts "warm in his personal likes and gracious in his public contacts."

67. "'Grand Old Man' of Mormon Utah Dead," *Daily Telegram*, Sep. 29, 1929, 2.

coal strike. "The working classes, regardless of their religious or political affiliations, had the utmost confidence in him.[68]

Roberts's funeral, which was organized by President Heber J. Grant with the assistance of Roberts's secretary Elsie Cook,[69] was held in the Salt Lake Tabernacle on Sunday, October 1, at 2:00 p.m. The services were carried over the radio.[70] Several thousand people "stood in silent worshipful tribute to a modern day leader of Israel as his flag-draped coffin entered and exited" the building.[71] Prior to the services, people had come "from long distances" to stand near the casket "just as they were accustomed to gather to hear him in his prime expound the principles which he had championed from his youth."[72] Inside, several thousand people—estimates vary—were in attendance; there was a profusion of floral offerings, which stood out against the stand that was draped in white; and six military associates, all of whom had served in the 145th Artillery, in full uniform, were designated as pall bearers.[73] It must have seemed odd to those who knew him that after his decades of almost peripatetic activity, the man, in the words of his friend Anthon H. Lund, "whose brain machinery was always running at full speed," lay still and quiet.[74] After the opening hymn, "When First the Light of Truth" concluded, Roberts's longtime friend George D. Pyper offered "an eulogistic invocation, in which he outlined the many excellent attributes of the departed."[75]

After a rendition of "Abide with Me," Rulon S. Wells, of the First

---

68. John James, "Noted Utah Writer Is Called by Death," *Druid,* Nov. 1, 1933, 8. See also a much earlier mention of Roberts's ties to Wales in an interview with James in "Mormons and the Welsh," *Scranton Republican*, Apr. 16, 1897, 6. James stated Roberts had ties to Pembrokeshire, North Wales.

69. Cook to Madsen.

70. William H. Smart noted, "Listened to funeral services of Pres. B. H. Roberts in Salt Lake Tabernacle. ... I was a great admirer of him, was touched by his death and in services & appreciated much being privileged to be at [the] event even by radio." Smart Diary, Oct. 1, 1933.

71. "President Roberts Honored by Vast Throng at Funeral," *Deseret News*, Oct. 2, 1933, 1.

72. See "Thousands Pay Homage to Roberts," [Logan] *Herald-Journal*, Oct. 2, 1933, 1; and "Rights Include High Tribute," *Ogden Standard Examiner*, Oct. 2, 1933, 2.

73. They were Maj. W. G. Williams, Col. LeRoy Bourne, Col. Curtis Y. Clawson, Maj. Willard Christopherson, Maj. Clarence Hawkins, and his political ally Maj. C. Clarence Neslen. See "President Roberts Honored."

74. Lund, *Danish Apostle*, 776.

75. "Thousands Pay Homage."

Council of Seventy, spoke. Roberts "wore out his body" in service to the church and God, he said. He found no pleasure unless he was "up to his ears in work. He has gone to a well-earned rest though not a cessation of activity. Not by any means would B. H. Roberts be happy idle. He is a Seventy and where he is now there is much missionary work to do."[76] Wells went on to say that no one had contributed more to church literature than Roberts, that his works "would live after him," because there "was something about his style of writing that went right to the heart of the reader."[77]

Alvin Keddington sang "The Soldier's Farewell," and Clarence Neslen, who had succeeded Roberts as chaplain of the 145th Artillery, spoke, saying that "although his voice and pen are stilled, he still lives in our hearts." Roberts "was not a one-sided man. He developed his body, his mind, and his soul. While his heart was ever ... in advancing the interests of his church, he never neglected his civil duties, never failed in his duty to his country." Neslen then captured Roberts's impact as chaplain when he was the

> spiritual counselor of 1500 young men from all walks of life—Mormon, Jew, Gentile and others—unto whose lives had never entered thoughts of God and Godliness. To him, however, all these men were drawn. His tolerance and understanding enabled him to reach into their hearts. At this time more than 60 years of age, nevertheless the boy in the man still lived. Young soldiers marveled at his sprightly step and martial bearing. In the saddle he was as much at ease as a cowboy. A sparkling sense of humor and the sympathy, kindness and dignity of a respected father, was his way with these young men. It was through him that many lads who long since lost touch with their homes were reunited with them. Many an unbeliever, fearing to face the great adventure spiritually alone, gained fresh courage as this man of God cleared the way for them.[78]

The concluding speaker was Heber J. Grant, who said the "great

---

76. "President Roberts Honored," and "Thousands Pay Last Respects," *Salt Lake Telegram*, Oct. 2, 1933, 7.

77. "Thousands Pay Homage."

78. "Throng Pays Respect to Church Head," *Salt Lake Tribune*, Oct. 2, 1933, 14. Similar sentiments were expressed in an editorial in the *Ogden Standard Examiner*, calling Roberts a "source of great comfort to the boys who regarded him as a father administering to their well being." See "Death of B. H. Roberts," *Ogden Standard Examiner*, Sep. 28, 1933, 4.

audience" in the tabernacle bore "witness to the esteem and affection the people held for President Roberts." Grant spoke at length about his interactions with Roberts over a half century, saying he had "experienced no greater pleasure than when associated with President Roberts." He spoke of Roberts as "the chief defender of the faith … [with] the great ability … to defend the truth." Grant rejoiced "in the wonderful faith of President Roberts, and in his knowledge of the faith and courage to defend it. He was a champion of right. There was no doubt in his mind that Joseph Smith was a prophet of God and that the revelations of the Doctrine and Covenants were given of God to Joseph Smith." It was in that faith and in that testimony that "President Roberts not only brought many souls to a knowledge of the Gospel," and, Grant believed, his writings and works would continue to "bring many to a knowledge of the Gospel after he has been dead for many years." Grant wished that more in the world had "just such a faith in Jesus Christ … as possessed by President Roberts. I rejoice in his great accomplishments."[79]

The services concluded with the Tabernacle Choir singing "Rest, Rest, on the Hillside Rest," and a benediction from Apostle Joseph Fielding Smith, Roberts's associate in the Church Historian's Office. From there, a funeral procession with upwards of seventy automobiles bore Roberts's body to the Centerville cemetery[80] where, with many of his colleagues from the 145th in attendance, he was buried in a military ceremony.[81]

With that, the long, complicated, often controversial and challenging, yet fulfilling, mortal journey of Brigham Henry Roberts, from immigrant lad to man of prominence, ended.

79. "President Roberts Honored."

80. According to the account of the funeral in the *Salt Lake Tribune* quoted above, Grant announced that J. Golden Kimball was "confined to his home by illness." This conflicts with the apocryphal story that Kimball was at the burial and, noting the sparseness of the cemetery, commented that it was "a hell of a place to put one of the Lord's anointed!" Another version has it that Kimball said "a hell of a place to bury a churchman and statesman." It is possible that Kimball said this at a later date, possibly when a headstone was erected with the support of Roberts's former missionaries.

81. "President Roberts Honored."

EPILOGUE

For many people, over many years, B. H. Roberts became the intellectual face of Mormonism. He was indefatigable in his speaking, preaching, and prose, and he consistently sought to meld his advocacy of Mormonism with his commitment to public life. In the years after his death his stature would continue to grow, though there were times when he seemed forgotten.

Immediately after his death, his surviving wife, Celia, and her family received several letters of condolence that conveyed the respect held for Roberts. In early November 1933 Heber J. Grant wrote, "My dear friends, I wish you to know that I deeply sympathize with you in the separation from your beloved husband and father. His life of devotion to the truth must certainly be a source of consolation to you all." Grant also sent "books not flowers" on such occasions, but did not indicate which volume he had sent.[1] Around that same time, Apostle Richard R. Lyman replied to a letter from Celia telling her that it brought "a long line of memories." Lyman reminded her that Roberts and he were "close and intimate friends," and predicted that "Roberts will grow greater and richer with time." He shared a story from Alice Reynolds, who told Lyman that as a child listening to Roberts, she "came under the spell of his great personality."[2] A few years later Lyman would join Heber J. Grant and others as speakers at Celia's funeral.[3]

In light of such an outpouring, the family continued to seek ways to keep Roberts's memory alive.[4] The summer after he died the

1. Heber J. Grant to the Family of Elder B. H. Roberts, Nov. 1, 1933, Mowry Scrapbook, 157.

2. Richard R. Lyman to Celia Roberts, Nov. 2, 1933, Mowry Scrapbook, 159.

3. "Funeral Services Held for Mrs. Celia Roberts," (Layton, UT) *Weekly News-Express*, Mar. 26, 1936, 1.

4. Most of this activity came from Celia Roberts's family. Over the years there was tension between the children of Roberts's first wife, Louisa, and Celia's family. His

fiftieth anniversary of the Cane Creek Massacre was commemorated with a monument in Tennessee.[5] Four months later on November 10, 1934, sixteen years after the armistice, his family donated an oil painting by Lewis A. Ramsey titled *Somewhere in France* to the state of Utah. The painting, with Roberts as the central figure, came "from an enlarged photo of a battalion of the 145th field artillery while engaged in a prayer." The painting had been commissioned by the family a few weeks before his death.[6]

But in addition to his family, perhaps those who missed Roberts the most were the missionaries who had served under him in the Eastern States. These individuals kept in touch with each other as a result of serving under "President Roberts." A group of them met at an Eastern States missionary reunion at 8:30 p.m., Saturday, April 7, 1934, at the roof garden of the Hotel Utah across the street from Temple Square. According to press accounts, "The missionaries who served under the late President B. H. Roberts are to furnish the program and will be the special guests of honor."[7] Roberts was the glue that held many of those former missionaries together, and reading their letters, diaries, reminiscences, and other accounts, one senses how strongly these men and women felt about Roberts—as a mentor and as a friend. The April 1934 gathering would prove to be a catalyst for future actions.

In a letter to the Roberts family in May 1935, the newly formed "B. H. Roberts Missionary Committee" told them that a memorial to "our President" would be erected on June 8, 1935. The "dark academy granite" included the inscription "churchman-soldier-statesman," which the former missionaries wrote to the family, "Represents his life's service to God, to country, and to the people." The committee was

grandson through Celia, Richard Roberts, said that "there were certainly some hard feelings," and the "separation of families became quite distinct." At the root of the difficulties, Richard Roberts believed, was that Celia had never had a civil marriage ceremony with Roberts, while both Louisa and Margaret had. See Roberts Oral History.

5. "Milo L. Jones Describes Visit to Spot Where Utah Missionaries Were Killed," *Ogden Standard-Examiner,* July 8, 1934, 7

6. "Family Presents Valued Painting of Army Chaplain," *Salt Lake Tribune*, Nov. 11, 1934, B1. See also, "Roberts Family Presents Wartime Painting to State," *Salt Lake Telegram*, Nov. 10, 1934, 9.

7. "Eastern States," *Deseret News,* Apr. 7, 1934, 16; and [Untitled], *Mt. Pleasant Pyramid*, Mar. 30, 1934, 3.

led by Roberts's secretary, Elsie Cook, who served as chair, with former missionaries Leland G. Larsen, treasurer, and Rose Dalton Hardy, Valois South (later Chipman), Fred L. Markham, and Corom B. Holt as committee members.[8] At 6:00 p.m. on Saturday, June 8, 1935, a sunset graveside service was held in the Centerville cemetery to unveil the monument. The gathering included an invocation by Edward Eliason and remarks by J. Golden Kimball.[9] The rest of the program featured other speakers, a poetry reading, and a musical performance by six missionaries who had served under Roberts. Clarence J. Hawkins, who served in World War I as band master of the 145th Field Artillery, led a brass quartet. The Roberts family offered the committee "sincere appreciation of your thoughtfulness."[10]

This group, later renamed the "B. H. Roberts Group—Eastern States Mission," would continue to meet for a number of years until it disbanded in the early 1980s. Its purpose, according to its constitution, was to promote the "development and renewal of acquaintances with individuals who served in a common cause under B. H. Roberts." The group pledged to meet annually during the October LDS general conference, and invited to join those who had both lived and served in the Eastern States Mission from 1921 to 1927, as well as their spouses.[11] On October 2, 1980, a final banquet was held at the Lion House. Two years later, in September 1982, according to Valois South Chipman and Milo S. Marsden, the group dissolved "due to the ravages of time," and donated the balance in its bank account—sixty five dollars—to Primary Children's Hospital.[12] Those who served under Roberts frequently mentioned their association with him in their life histories, and some missionaries recalled meeting their spouses on the mission.[13] One couple who met while

8. See box 10, fd. 14, Roberts Papers (UU).

9. "Missionaries Will See Grave Memorial," *Salt Lake Telegram*, June 1, 1935, 11; and "LDS Missionaries Will Be Honored at Memorial Ceremony," *Salt Lake Tribune*, June 8, 1935, 7.

10. Box 10, fd. 14, Roberts Papers (UU).

11. B. H. Roberts Group, *Constitution and Membership*.

12. Box 1, fd. 2, Chipman Papers. At the time Marsden, an attorney who had served under Roberts in 1925–27, was the last chair.

13. For example, see Milford I. Gardner, obituary, *Star Valley Independent*, Apr. 6, 1992; Alda Fugal Gardner, obituary, *Star-Valley Independent*, Nov. 9, 1985; and Mary Edna Brown Allen, biography, at orsonprattbrown.org.

serving as missionaries under Roberts was Mary Edna Brown and Harold Tranter Allen. The two married after they returned home. Years later, the first of their four sons, James B. Allen, would serve as an Assistant Church Historian under Leonard Arrington.

Many of the female missionaries, including Elsie Cook, were also members of Estalami—a portmanteau of Eastern States Lady Missionaries.[14] The first chapter was organized in Ogden in 1923[15] while Roberts was still mission president, then a second chapter emerged in Salt Lake City in May 1929.[16] While the largest membership in the group was centered in Salt Lake City, there were members throughout the state. Missionary organizations were common in Utah, "but the Estalami society differs in that it is an organization of only women from a certain mission."[17] For many years the group met monthly, often to hear from recently returned missionaries, and also came together for an annual banquet held during the church's April general conference. One missionary remembered that "it gave us an opportunity to continue our church activity." The women organized a chorus and participated in different ward worship services.[18] They held an annual banquet that became the society's major event but, like the other Roberts missionary group, by the 1990s "age had taken its toll!"[19] Roberts probably never met with the group itself, though he interacted with individual members such as Elsie Cook and others.

In the decade after Roberts's death, a number of memorials were held in his honor. To commemorate his eightieth birthday, for example, the LDS Centennial Society sponsored a Saturday social gathering in the Belvedere Hotel with speakers Heber J. Grant, J.

---

14. At various time it was referred to as either a society or a club. See Estalami Society Record Books.

15. See "Estalami Society Entertainment," *Ogden Standard-Examiner*, Mar. 16, 1924, 21; "Estalami Group Plans Silver Jubilee Program," *Ogden Standard Examiner*, Sep. 19, 1948, 14; and "Reunion Dated by Mission Society," *Ogden Standard Examiner*, Sep. 22, 1948, B-1.

16. "Honor for Missionaries," *Salt Lake Tribune*, May 23, 1929, 3.

17. "Annual Banquet Held by Estalami Society," *Salt Lake Telegram*, Apr. 8, 1939, 3.

18. Ethel Lenzi Sonntag, "A Personal History," 1978. Copy in author's possession.

19. Robert J. Williams, "Thirty Plus Years of ESTALAMI Reunions," *Deseret News*, Sep. 29, 2013.

Golden Kimball, and George D. Pyper, "followed by dancing."[20] One group of people that attended this gathering had been formed in 1930, solely for the purpose to study Roberts's *Comprehensive History of the Church*.[21] Similar study groups would meet for another twenty years.[22]

Other recollections of Roberts in later years surrounded his service as a military chaplain. On the twentieth anniversary of the American entry into World War I, one columnist recalled:

> I remember some of the boys of yesterday who marched along Twenty-fifth street when the 145th returned home from overseas. ... When the survivors came home there was great rejoicing. At the head ... was B. H. Roberts, chaplain, marching proudly—a most heroic figure. ... No army ever assembled had finer manhood, filled with the spirit of victory. ... They have aged now that ... they hear echoes of the war drums beating in distant lands. They still have enough of youth left so that if their country needed them they would be a mighty force to sustain the prestige of the nation.[23]

It is a sentiment Roberts would have shared.

Roberts's prodigious output of books and articles allowed him to remain visible in the public eye. At the time of his death, nearly all of his book-length studies had been published, and many of them stayed in print well into the 1970s.[24] One exception was the *Last Seven Discourses*, a compilation of several of Roberts's speeches delivered shortly before his death, including his remarks at the World Fellowship of Faith.[25] The volume, edited by Elsie Cook, was published in 1948.[26]

---

20. In addition to Woodruff, other members of the committee included Alan G. Wood, Orson Rega Card, Matthew Cowley, Virginia Freeze Barker, Mary G. Judd, and Elizabeth O. McKay Hill.

21. Mowry Scrapbook, 6; "LDS Groups Plan S.L. Meet for March 13," *Salt Lake Tribune*, Mar. 5, 1937, 9; and "Centennial Societies to Pay Honor to Historian," *Deseret News*, Mar. 13, 1937, 11.

22. See "Friends Continue to Fete Popular Leader," *Salt Lake Tribune*, Mar. 16, 1941, 2e; and "Study Group Hears Dr. Virginia Cutler," *South East Independent*, Jan. 10, 1957, 5.

23. Frank Francis, "News and Views," *Ogden Standard-Examiner*, Mar. 31, 1937, 1.

24. This does not include his study *The Truth, The Way, The Life*.

25. Roberts, *Discourses*.

26. "Discourses of B. H. Roberts," *Deseret News*, Mar. 20, 1948, 8.

Over the years, several individuals who went on to church leadership had been influenced by Roberts. One was future apostle and First Presidency counselor Hugh B. Brown. When Brown came to Salt Lake City in the 1920s to practice law, he recalled that Roberts, Heber J. Grant, Anthony W. Ivins, and others told him "at different times and separately that if I wanted to belong to a party that represented the common people I should become a Democrat." On the other hand, they indicated that if his intention was to "be popular and … be in touch with the wealth of the nation, I should become a Republican." When Grant switched allegiances during the New Deal he encouraged Brown to follow his lead, but Brown remained a Democrat. Roberts had a profound impact on Brown. As he recalled, while Roberts was "sometimes out of harmony with many of the other brethren," he was willing to "stand up for what he believed in and suffer for it." Brown, who "knew him well," thought Roberts "was the greatest defender of the church we had had up to that time."[27]

Another individual influenced by Roberts was Henry D. Taylor whose long church career concluded with service as an Assistant to the Quorum of the Twelve. Taylor served under Roberts in the Eastern States Mission and described him as "an extremely impressive and distinguished figure, very well built, with broad shoulders, fine silvery white hair and a close cropped mustache. He carried a cane which he used as a walking stick, and this added to his dignity. When he felt that he was right, he was absolutely fearless in defending his position." Roberts, Taylor thought, was "very meticulous, careful and exacting." Taylor also remembered Roberts's speaking style and sermons in much the same way as others had. Roberts was "forceful, dramatic and convincing." He would start slow, "in a low, very deliberate manner." As he would continue, "his voice would rise" and he would begin to gesticulate. One time, as Roberts grew increasingly animated, "his upper dentures came dislodged and flew into the air. He caught them expertly in mid-air, replaced them

27. Firmage, *Abundant Life*, 16–18. Brown's biographers, Eugene Campbell and Richard Poll, quote him as saying that Roberts was a "wonderful man … a very powerful speaker, a powerful man." See Campbell and Poll, *Hugh B. Brown*, 104–06.

quickly, and in an unruffled manner proceeded on with his sermon with but a scarce pause."[28]

In the mid-1960s Roberts's expulsion from Congress was reexamined in the light of another congressional challenge—the seating of controversial Harlem congressman Adam Clayton Powell. Noting that the House of Representatives had not refused to seat a duly elected member in more than a half century, journalist James J. Kilpatrick suggested the body should be "reminded" of the Roberts case. Kirkpatrick then gave an overview of Roberts, his marital situation, the charges against him, the "astonishing seven million persons from throughout the country" who had signed petitions against him, and the action taken to deny him his seat.[29] In Powell's case, like Roberts, he was expelled, but unlike Roberts, he ran in a special election and returned to Congress. A few years later the US Supreme Court ruled that the House had acted unconstitutionally when it excluded Powell. The opinion, written by Chief Justice Earl Warren, argued that while the Constitution gave the legislative branches the power to judge the "qualifications of its own members," since Powell had met the constitutional requirements of holding his office, and because he had been duly elected to that office, "the House was without power to exclude him from its membership." Anyone who understood the circumstances of Roberts's case must have found the decision ironic.[30]

As those who knew Roberts personally aged, many sought tangible ways of remembering him. In 1965 his daughter Georgia Roberts Mowry donated a bust of Roberts sculpted by Mahonri Young to the BYU library "where it would be assured permanent preservation." Library director and historian, S. Lyman Tyler, was

28. Taylor, *Autobiography of Henry Dixon Taylor*, 78. This story may be apocryphal, since former Utah governor Calvin L. Rampton, who knew Roberts in his youth, told me the same story but remembered it as occurring in Davis County.

29. James J. Kilpatrick, "Obstacles Faced by House in Disciplining Re. Powell," *Los Angeles Times*, Dec. 13, 1966, 4. More than twenty years later, conservative columnist Cal Thomas, in the midst of a congressional ethics crisis surrounding personal behavior, recalled the Roberts hearings. In his view, the "debate over Roberts left no question about the linkage between public and private morality in the minds of House members in those days." Cal Thomas, "House Should Police Its Own Home," *New York Daily News*, Oct. 9, 1989, 10.

30. Powell v. McCormack, 395 U.S. 486 (1969).

instrumental in obtaining the bust.[31] In addition, Roberts's extensive papers, including his library of nearly 1,400 volumes of books, pamphlets, and periodicals, were, and still are, held by the LDS Church History Library. Other important collections can be found at the University of Utah and Brigham Young University libraries. Still, as memories faded, traces of Roberts faded as well. His home on Main Street in Centerville, which was built for his first wife Louisa, was torn down in December 1972.[32]

As the one hundredth anniversary of Roberts's birth approached in 1957, scholars began to turn their attention on his career. The first examination came with Davis Bitton's study, "The B. H. Roberts Case of 1898–1900," published in the *Utah Historical Quarterly*.[33] Between then and his own death fifty years later, Bitton examined other aspects of Roberts's career, philosophy, and writings.[34] In 1966 Robert H. Malan's study, *B. H. Roberts: A Biography*, was published by Deseret Book.[35] A more valuable examination came in 1980 with Truman Madsen's *Defender of the Faith: The Life of B. H. Roberts*.[36] Madsen's study was the most significant of its time. As I explain in the introduction, Madsen's biography is not without its faults, but it includes details not available elsewhere, and Madsen had access to sources that previous and subsequent biographers have not. In addition to Madsen and others' books, a number of theses and dissertations explored various aspects of Roberts's life and thought.

Another sign of interest in Roberts occurred in 1967, when the Deseret Club of Princeton University[37] reissued his *Joseph Smith the Prophet–Teacher: A Discourse*, which had first been published in

31. "University Gets Bust of Noted LDS Historian," *Daily Herald*, May 27, 1965, 16A.

32. LeAnn Blodget, "Tearing Down," *Davis County Clipper*, Dec. 29, 1972, 25.

33. Bitton, "B. H. Roberts Case," 27–46.

34. For example, see Bitton, "B. H. Roberts as Historian"; and Bitton, "B. H. Roberts at the World Parliament of Religions."

35. Malan, *B. H. Roberts*.

36. Madsen, *Defender of the Faith*. Madsen's biography went through several printings.

37. The group was organized in 1960 for LDS undergraduates, and was associated with "other College Deseret Clubs." See "Mormon Group Organizes Here," *Daily Princetonian*, Apr. 8, 1960, 4. The Deseret Clubs were first organized at UCLA in 1931 to foster "gospel instruction and social activities among Latter-day Saint students," and spread to other institutions over the years. The clubs were discontinued in 1971 when the Latter-day Saints Student Association was created. See John P. Livingstone, "Deseret Clubs," in Garr, Cannon, and Cowan, *Encyclopedia of Latter-day Saint History*, 289–90.

1908. Ads appeared in both the *Salt Lake Tribune* and the University of Utah's *Daily Chronicle* touting the new edition of a "heretofore rare book," which constituted an "important but little known philosophical treatise on Mormon Theology."[38] The reprint contained an introduction by Sterling W. McMurrin, who would play a major role in keeping Roberts's name alive, lamenting that Roberts had become, since his death in 1933, "a much-neglected figure in the Church." McMurrin believed that Roberts had once been "the most interesting and exciting and stimulating person in [LDS Church] leadership, its most prolific writer, its chief theologian and historian, and its most capable defender." But over three decades later, Roberts, McMurrin mourned, was "scarcely known to large segments of the Church. He has been eclipsed by a deluge of writers of varying but lesser talent, many of whom lack even the grace to acknowledge their indebtedness to him." McMurrin believed that there was a "resurgence of interest" in Roberts.[39] That resurgence paralleled a growing scholarly assessment of Mormonism, including the creation of *Dialogue: A Journal of Mormon Thought*.[40]

Another group, the B. H. Roberts Society, was organized in 1980. Its initial statement of purpose said it was formed "to generate open inquiry and discourse concerning the fundamental issues of the human experience." Initially the group envisioned lectures, forums, debates, and publications. A number of Mormon intellectuals formed the leadership of the group, and they continued to craft its mission. A January 1983 press release described the society as "dedicated to the study of timely issues in Mormonism," seeking "diverse experiences and opinions," and "espous[ing] no particular point of view."[41]

The Roberts Society held an initial forum on August 21, 1980. It was chaired by Allen Roberts and featured Truman Madsen speaking

38. See *Salt Lake Tribune*, July 16, 1967, 12W; and *Utah Daily Chronicle*, Nov. 1, 1967, 6.

39. Sterling W. McMurrin, "Introduction—Brigham H. Roberts: Notes on a Mormon Philosopher–Historian," in Roberts, *Joseph Smith*, iv, reprint edition.

40. The advertisement in the University of Utah paper ran across from a half-page ad for *Dialogue*, featuring a quote from Michigan Governor George W. Romney calling on Latter-day Saints to honor their "teachings and scriptures to be their brothers keepers" in turbulent times. Romney was then a candidate for the Republican Party nomination for US president. See also Bitton, "B. H. Roberts as Historian."

41. Fd. 1, B. H. Roberts Society Records.

on "B. H. Roberts, Individual Responsibility, and the 13th Article of Faith." It was held at the Social Hall at This Is the Place Heritage Park, with Davis Bitton and Anne G. Osborn responding to Madsen.[42] The event attracted an overflow crowd; Leonard Arrington estimated that the hall itself held three hundred and "there must have been at least one hundred standing in the halls."[43] The event set the pattern for the future. Despite its original ambitious goals, the society primarily sponsored public presentations. Over the years, under its sponsorship, there were panels on a wide range of topics including the institutional church and impact on members, faithful history, media, sexuality, nuclear disarmament, Mormon/non-Mormon relations, and church and politics.[44] In 1994, an important presentation dealt with the extent of anti-Mormon discrimination at the University of Utah. The panel, which attracted coverage by the Associated Press, featured panelists Lynne Kanavel Whitesides, Robert Goldberg, Susan Staker, and William Mulder It followed a previous discussion of academic freedom issues at Brigham Young University.[45]

Still, despite providing previous assurances that the LDS Church had no objection to the group, the society was viewed warily by some members of the church hierarchy. In 1987 the Roberts Society sought to use the Assembly Hall on Temple Square for its meetings, but the request was denied.[46] Money to support the lectures was always an issue. In March 1983 the group announced an annual fundraising lecture with "a voluntary contribution … requested from every person attending." Held at Highland High School in Salt Lake City, the topic was excommunication and featured Lester Bush, Douglas Alder, and J. Bonner Ritchie.[47] Many who attended society panels still remember the "B. H. Roberts top hat," rented from Salt Lake Costume, which was passed around at events for contributions, with a suggested

42. "B. H. Roberts Society Organized," *Daily Herald*, Aug. 20, 1980, 42.

43. Arrington, *Confessions of a Mormon Historian*, 3:106–07, 288. Arrington served as a member of the group's steering committee.

44. Fd. 6, B. H. Roberts Society Records.

45. See "University Organizes Panel to Address Anti-Mormonism," *Casper Star-Tribune*, May 10, 1994, 13; and "Panelists Discuss Discrimination against LDS," *Casper Star-Tribune*, May 14, 1994, 13.

46. See Ardean Watts to Presiding Bishop, Apr. 9, 1987, and Ronald D. John to Watts, May 7, 1987, fd. 3, B. H. Roberts Society Records.

47. "B. H. Roberts Meeting Told," *Daily Herald*, Mar. 23, 1983, 33.

donation of four dollars.[48] For a time, the group prospered, but by the mid-1990s most of the original members had left. Their energy left with them and the society slowly exited from the scene. During its heyday, however, it was yet one more example of the Mormon intellectual ferment of the times, something Roberts would have celebrated.

During the 1980s and 1990s, collections of Roberts's papers, and the materials of others who knew and worked with him, were donated to various repositories. Significant holdings came to the Church History Library. A major collection of Roberts's correspondence and subject files joined Roberts's personal library. Unfortunately, as of this writing a portion of those materials is still restricted to scholarly use. Even more significant was the donation of personal papers and manuscripts to the University of Utah's Marriott Library.[49] There is also a significant collection of Roberts material at BYU, some of which came from Truman Madsen. My own research files and the original manuscript of this work have been donated to Weber State University's Stewart Library Special Collections, which houses my papers.

Additional books and articles appeared beginning in the 1990s. Important studies included Roberts's autobiography edited by Gary James Bergera,[50] a B. H. Roberts family history written by his grandson Richard C. Roberts,[51] and my own edited collection of several of Roberts's diaries.[52] Other studies examined Roberts's views on scripture and theology, such as Brigham Madsen's *Studies of the Book of Mormon*[53] and *The Essential B. H. Roberts*.[54] Perhaps most significant

48. Fd. 6, B. H. Roberts Society Records. See also "Calendar," *Salt Lake Tribune*, May 12, 1995, E15.

49. Several family members of Roberts's oldest son, Benjamin E. Roberts, enabled the transfer of a large Roberts collection to the University of Utah between 1981 and 1991. The family also provided funds to assist in processing the collection, making it available for research. Edwin B. Firmage donated a copy of the manuscript "The Truth, The Way, The Life," kept by his grandfather Hugh B. Brown, to the university. See Cooley, "B. H. Roberts Papers"; and Thom Roberts, "Foreword," in Roberts, *The Truth, The Way, The Life*, ix, edited by Larson.

50. Roberts, *Autobiography*.

51. Roberts, *History of the B. H. Roberts Family*.

52. Roberts, *History's Apprentice*.

53. Roberts, *Studies of the Book of Mormon*, edited by Madsen. For a contemporary account of the issues raised by the publication of Madsen's book and events surrounding it, see Ron Bitton, "B. H. Roberts Book Stirs Controversy," *Sunstone*, Dec. 1985, 36–39.

54. Roberts, *Essential B. H. Roberts*.

was the emergence of two separate volumes of Roberts's controversial theological treatise, *The Truth, the Way, The Life*.[55] The work itself had existed in manuscript form and was known among some in the thriving community of scholars and amateurs dedicated to Mormon studies. Moreover, the story of Roberts's unsuccessful efforts in the face of opposition to see it published was also known.[56] Still, its publication was a major event in the years since Roberts's death.

Each of the two volumes contained Roberts's manuscript and individual essays by a number of scholars, along with various appended materials. In his foreword to Stan Larson's edition, Leonard Arrington noted that Roberts considered the manuscript "to be the most important work he had written. While people may differ with him on that judgement, this ambitious treatise deserves to be published."[57] Sterling McMurrin provided a thoughtful analysis of the manuscript, calling it "a summary of [Roberts's] theological work, setting forth in considerable detail, and often with extensive commentaries, his understanding of the basic doctrines of the LDS church." McMurrin was not without criticism of the shortcomings and limitations of Roberts's views and analysis,[58] but he still believed that while he was not "a major historian or theologian of the first order ... within the limits of the intellectual life of the Mormon people, he was preeminent as both."[59] McMurrin returned to his common theme: "for far too many years the name of B. H. Roberts has been in eclipse in the LDS church." He hoped that the publication of this volume would "help to bring that important name to the full attention of a generation that is seriously inquiring into the nature and meaning of Mormonism."[60]

By contrast, Davis Bitton argued in John Welch's edition of *The Truth, The Way, The Life* that Roberts was one of the few "larger than life" general authorities over the years who were "especially noticed

55. See Roberts, *The Truth, The Way, The Life*, one edition edited by Stan Larson, another edited by John W. Welch. Hereafter each volume is cited by its editor.

56. For a good overview, see Allen, "Story of *The Truth, The Way, The Life*." The essay was also reprinted in the Welch edition of *The Truth, The Way, The Life*.

57. Arrington, "Foreword," in Larson, xi–xii.

58. See, for example, Larson, xxii–xxv.

59. McMurrin, in Larson, xiii.

60. McMurrin, xxiv–xxv.

while alive and expansively remembered in subsequent generations." While acknowledging that the book has "serious limitations," Bitton placed Roberts in the context of other intellectuals of his time and said the book was "on the same plane as those few other works considered to be classic statements of Mormon belief at the end of the Church's first century."[61]

Most who commented on *The Truth, The Way, The Life* admitted that the book was the product of an amateur, and that many of its ideas were antiquated by the 1990s. But while Bitton echoed some of Arrington's concerns, Bitton was more acerbic. His comments were critical enough that he felt the need to defend himself against those who might accuse him of "heartless criticism."[62] Clearly Roberts, who was controversial and problematic for many during his lifetime, remains so for some to this day.

Still more of Roberts's work was printed after his death. Lynn Pulsipher published two volumes of "scrapbooks" that brought together articles from a variety of church publications and newspapers. He produced a compilation titled *A New Witness for God*, consisting of a series of articles first published when Roberts was on a mission to England to avoid arrest for unlawful cohabitation. Pulsipher also reprinted one of Roberts's lesser-known works of fiction, *Corianton*.[63] Brian H. Stuy compiled a limited printing of *Essays in Defense of the Faith: Being a Collection of Writings and Sermons by Elder B. H. Roberts, President of the First Quorum of the Seventy*. Stuy was also one of the first to bring out a limited run of *Excerpts from The Truth, The Way, The Life: An Elementary Treatise of Theology*.[64] Simultaneously, a number of independent publishers produced their own editions of Roberts's work, many of which had been out of print for some time. While this was taking place, major LDS publishers, including Bookcraft and Deseret Book, kept several key titles in print, including *The Life of John Taylor*, *Outlines of Ecclesiastical History*, and Roberts's multi-volume histories of the church.

In part because of his writing, people remember Roberts as a

61. Davis Bitton, "A Masterwork of Mormon Theology?" in Welch, 561–67.
62. Bitton, 566.
63. Roberts, *Scrapbook*; Roberts, *New Witness for God*; and Roberts, *Corianton*.
64. Roberts, *Excerpts from The Truth, The Way, The Life*.

speaker, an intellectual, and as a historian, and each of these three roles offers a window into who he was. Roberts enjoyed the clash of ideas, and the give and take of debate—both political and theological. Both his contemporaries and those who have studied his speaking style have felt that Roberts was exceptional on the public platform. Roberts believed in appealing "to the intellect rather than emotions." One student of his speaking style, Ralph Pace, described Roberts as a "man of keen intellect with an enthusiasm for knowledge" who "felt that oratory was an art." Roberts was "energetic, dramatic, eloquent, logical," and clearly "one of the most outstanding and conscientious advocates of the Mormon faith and of truth and justice in general."[65]

Another historian of Roberts's rhetorical style, Eric Stephan, interviewed several individuals who remembered hearing Roberts speak. Roberts was always "well groomed, alert, and cultured." Most people remembered Roberts's tendency to rely on quotations to make his points. Roberts's talks were "always polished and very consistently sustained with proper quotations." They also tended to be long; Roberts would frequently ask for his listeners' indulgence as he carefully developed his ideas, which he arranged "in a long, neat row" as he "established a sincere relationship with his audience." He facilitated understanding by always "select[ing] words that were readily comprehended" by his audience. Roberts put a great deal of effort and preparation into his speeches because he possessed "a mind capable of storing vast amounts of knowledge." He rarely used notes even for long speeches. Octavo Holmgren Weiler remembered when Roberts paid a visit to her mission in West Virginia: "Without any visible preparation, he could speak at the drop of a hat. And he gave long discourses too!"[66]

Roberts's friend and colleague George D. Pyper recalled that he "was called and probably was a natural-born orator, yet his superior ability was acquired by hard study and ceaseless preparation." Pyper remembered that "I could never arise in the morning early enough

65. Pace, "Study of the Speaking of B. H. Roberts," 4, 24, 27, 182–83.

66. Stephan, "B. H. Roberts: A Rhetorical Study," 80–81, 146, 159, 192, 266–67. A contemporary of Roberts noted, "His exordium has been criticized as somewhat lengthy, but the peroration was always clear and convincing." See A. J. Hansen, "B. H. Roberts, in Memoriam," (Logan) *Herald Journal*, Sep. 30, 1933, 2.

to find him in bed. He was usually under a lamp or at a window at daybreak, studying."[67] Another contemporary and friend, Josiah E. Hickman, lamented Roberts's passing as "the dimming of one of the greatest lights that has ever cast its rays amidst this people." So powerful and logical was Roberts in marshaling "facts and polemics" in his public speaking, Hickman argued, that "his hearers felt that they saw the destructive effects of a cyclone." Hickman had heard some of the great orators of America and Europe, but felt that Roberts stood alone in his skill. He remembered that "as an orator he swept his audience along with him like an ocean wave before the storm," and when the combination of his thoughts, "forceful language," logic, and "charming and power-impelling voice" came together, it "became a contagion with his audience."[68]

In the view of Sterling McMurrin, who heard him in person, Roberts became "the most powerful orator in the Mormon Church—in the days when authentic oratory counted for something, before television, before general conference speakers began to read their prepared sermons from prompters while appearing to speak extemporaneously. In those days, for a Mormon to read a sermon in church or even to use notes was a clear indication of a lack of the spirit." At the same time, McMurrin asserted, "No one had a greater impact on [a] congregation than B H Roberts." Drawing upon his own memory, he noted that he well remembered

> one of Roberts's visits to the old Adams Ward in Los Angeles, where I lived during my early years. Microphones had just come into the churches, and although our ward didn't need one, we had to keep up with fashion. Roberts was using a cane, and he would wander away from the pulpit. After the bishop had brought him back to the mike three or four times, Roberts swung his cane at the mike with great force, shouting 'Damn that damn thing—we've even got one now in the tabernacle.' He missed the microphone but left a deep dent in the pulpit. For years afterward members would point out the place where the great man had landed his cane.[69]

---

67. As quoted in Lundwall, *Assorted Gems*, 63–64.

68. J. E. Hickman, "B. H. Roberts—In Memoriam," (Logan) *Herald Journal*, Sep. 30, 1933, 2.

69. McMurrin, "Remembering B. H. Roberts," 74–75.

Finally, in an account of his own approach, Roberts said he believed that oratorical success "depended very largely upon one's ability to think continuously and systematically while on his feet in the presence of an audience." Roberts also felt that "the chief cause of failure in public speaking arises, I believe, from a lack of complete knowledge of the subject." Regardless of a speaker's "natural or acquired knowledge," Roberts argued, with imperfect knowledge a speaker will "soon fall into confusion, thence into incoherency, and by these steps meet failure."[70] Roberts, writing these remarks for an LDS audience, also reminded readers that a successful speaker needed to rely on "the aid of God's spirit," along with the "presence and power of the Holy Ghost." In the realm of public speaking, he concluded, "as in all things it will be found that the works of God; or those which he inspires, far outshine the works of man."[71]

Roberts is also remembered as a Mormon intellectual. As early as 1969, in a lengthy essay on the Mormon intellectual tradition, Leonard Arrington asked some fifty prominent Latter-day Saints to identify the "most important intellectuals in Mormon history." Roberts ranked first in that survey.[72] Stan Larson conducted a similar survey in 1993; once again Roberts was first. Larson concluded, "What the present survey demonstrates is that sixty years after his death, B. H. Roberts remains the foremost intellectual in Mormonism."[73] More recently, a 2011 article in the *Deseret News* listed Roberts as number one of the top ten intellectuals in the LDS Church's history. Among those he outdistanced were Joseph Smith and Roberts's own intellectual inspiration, Orson Pratt.[74]

In considering Roberts's role as an intellectual, Arrington regarded him as an "enthusiastic and optimistic" advocate of the movement in the last decades of the nineteenth century for Mormons to attend schools in the East, then return home "full of new ideas and anxious to share them with their fellow Saints." Roberts's own formal education was limited to two years at the University of Deseret, but he was a lifelong learner who "became a voracious

70. B. H. Roberts, "Public Speaking," *Contributor*, Oct. 1891, 458.

71. Roberts, 458–60.

72. Arrington, "Intellectual Tradition."

73. Larson, "Intellectuals in Mormon History," 189.

74. Hal Boyd, "Top 10 LDS 'Intellectuals,'" *Deseret News*, June 10, 2011.

reader, devouring considerable quantities of history, science, philosophy and religion." Arrington believed Roberts was committed to Latter-day Saints taking the advantages "of educational opportunities to advance the cause of God" and that he "saw the hand of God" in the "scientific and artistic advance of civilization."[75]

Roberts introduced large numbers of Latter-day Saints to several other public intellectuals. He more broadly introduced many Mormons, and even many Americans, to a whole range of political and theological ideas. After his election and subsequent expulsion from Congress, Roberts may well have been the best-known Latter-day Saint in America. Newspapers throughout the country followed both the case and Roberts in close detail. Even after his expulsion, Roberts continued to be a frequently quoted individual as he traveled to wards and stakes, attended missionary conferences in the Eastern States, and spoke from the political stage in Utah and neighboring states. While much of what he argued was based on his LDS views, he also spoke out on government, constitutional protections, and political issues of the day. Newspaper accounts of his travels are replete with language suggesting to readers that a B. H. Roberts talk—both religious and secular—would be full of solid reasoning and thoughtful analysis, while ably delivered. Roberts acted as what we might call today a public intellectual: a well-known, intelligent individual who has become visible to specialized audiences, as well as the general public, for a willingness to comment on current affairs and whose views command respect.

Throughout the church, local leaders and rank-and-file members thought of him as a friend, and they looked forward to his periodic visits to their communities. At the same time, a good example of the respect with which Roberts was held, even by those who disagreed with him, can be found in his relationship with Utah's Episcopal Bishop Franklin Spencer Spalding, a frequent critic of Mormonism. While Roberts challenged Spalding's views on several questions, and Spalding reciprocated, the two men could also "agree to disagree agreeably and had a warm personal relationship," which apparently included one of them occasionally attending the other's public

75. Arrington, *Faith and Intellect*, 83–116.

addresses.[76] This friendship would remain until Spalding's untimely death on September 25, 1914. In a memorial service held in Salt Lake City in November 1914, Roberts discussed their relationship and their many discussions on theology, noting that the city and state "are the poorer because of his leaving in the morning of his usefulness."[77] Roberts also said that "all creeds have lost by his death," and that Spalding's "religion knew no petty limitations of creed or class," and that he was "a most honorable opponent never stooping to subterfuge in a controversy."[78] Spalding's respect for Roberts seemed mutual. At one point, while in the midst of an exchange over theology, he noted that although he disagreed with Roberts on "many matters of theological belief," he still maintained "perfect confidence in his honesty and sincerity."[79] Such an assessment reflects the view held by many of Roberts himself over the years.

Finally, there is the more familiar role that Roberts played in Mormon historiography. While over the years professional LDS historians have judged Roberts's historical writing and methodology as mixed, he remained influential among believing Latter-day Saints. Because his books remained in print and readily available for so long, his are among the first history books a faithful Mormon might have bought. Roberts, according to Leonard Arrington and Davis Bitton, significantly influenced "the way most Latter-day Saints thought about their history."[80]

Through Roberts's missionary labors, he emerged as a unique and important voice within Mormonism, and along the way he "picked up more than a little journalistic experience" writing for publications such as the *Millennial Star* and the *Salt Lake Herald*. It was journalism that led Roberts to publish two of his earliest books: *The Missouri Persecutions* and *The Rise and Fall of Nauvoo*. These, along with the publication of the *Life of John Taylor*, in turn led to his employment in 1902 as an Assistant Church Historian. It was then that Roberts began the work that would eventually be published as

76. For more, see Sillito and Bradley, "Franklin Spencer Spalding"; and Keller, "Episcopalian Bishop Franklin S. Spalding."

77. "Many Tributes to Bishop Spalding," *Deseret Evening News*, Nov. 2, 1914, 5.

78. "Loving Tribute Is Paid to Spalding," *Salt Lake Telegram*, Nov. 2, 1914, 5.

79. Keller, "Episcopalian Bishop Franklin S. Spalding," 244.

80. Bitton and Arrington, *Mormons and Their Historians*, 69.

the multi-volume compilation, *History of the Church of Jesus Christ of Latter-day Saints*. Roberts pulled together various versions of Joseph Smith's writings, which had been published previously, and made the work "more readily accessible for historians and general readers."[81]

Roberts was not a meticulous fact checker and, because of his editorial approach, which often failed to compare earlier versions with his manuscript, the *History of the Church* "perpetuated many of the original publication errors." At the same time Roberts also "made additional unacknowledged changes, hundreds of them," which proved problematic. Despite the many flaws in the seven volumes, Roberts's work remained a key source for historians of Mormonism until one hundred years later, when the original Smith history was published online by the LDS Church History Library. Roberts, according to Arrington and Bitton, "also made extensive use of primary sources," even though much of that primary record was "so poorly organized" in the Historian's Office that it was "virtually inaccessible."[82]

Roberts's later *Comprehensive History of the Church*, first published in the *Americana* magazine, introduced wider audiences to Mormon history. It too became a common resource for faithful Latter-day Saints, lining the bookshelves of homes and LDS ward libraries around the United States and beyond. His biography of John Taylor remained one of only a handful published on the third LDS Church president for nearly a century, ensuring that readers interested in Taylor's life would inevitably turn to Roberts. Roberts's historical writing, for all its flaws, has perhaps influenced how Latter-day Saints think about their past more than almost any other writer.

Sterling McMurrin, however, believed that Roberts's "most important lasting contribution to Mormonism is not his work as a historian but rather as a theologian." It was McMurrin who summarized Roberts better than anyone else who has studied his life. He wrote in deeply personal terms: "I never missed an opportunity to attend a lecture or sermon by Roberts. I had several conversations with him and, of course, read most of his books. He was the church's most prolific writer." But even McMurrin recognized that while Roberts was "a quite remarkable person" who was a "success in

81. Bitton and Arrington, 74–75.
82. Bitton and Arrington, 76.

his public life," he was "something less than admirable in his family life." Roberts was a direct writer, McMurrin said, and it was always clear what Roberts was "driving at." Perhaps McMurrin said it best when he acknowledged that Roberts was respected, but "I cannot say that he was loved. He wasn't the lovable type."[83]

Roberts was not the lovable type. But there was something in his manner, as a man who lived his life in the public arena, that perpetually draws the Mormon gaze. In a church that values obedience and conformity, a man who was rebuked by church leaders for his obstinacy more than once remains respected and admired. His books are still read, his sermons are still quoted, and his intellectuality is held up as a positive example to emulate. Roberts may not have been loved, but he will not be forgotten.

The prominent American historian Eric Foner was asked once what he had learned as his study of Reconstruction had proceeded over the years. To paraphrase, he said that the fate of all historians was that no book was the final word. They expected that their work would be challenged, and eventually superseded, by the work of others. As he observed, "I have simply written the latest word, not the last word." Indeed.

83. McMurrin, "Remembering B. H. Roberts," 73–76.

PHOTOGRAPHS

The iconic image of Roberts disguised as a tramp in order to retrieve the bodies of murdered missionaries William S. Berry and John Gibbs. Roberts noted the image was made in "a colored man's" photograph gallery so that he could show his family "the outfit in which I made the trip." It was widely reprinted in Utah, and Roberts kept a copy in his office until his death.

John H. Morgan was a major in influence on Roberts. He attended Morgan's Commercial College, served under him in the Southern States Mission, and was his colleague in the First Council of Seventy.

Bernard Moses, a Jewish merchant in Chattanooga, loaned the money to purchase caskets and ship the bodies of Berry and Gibbs to Utah. Moses and Roberts would remain friends for the rest of their lives.

Roberts and J. Golden Kimball were colleagues in the Southern States mission and later in the First Council of Seventy. At times their friendship was strained by politics and Roberts' drinking. Still, at the time of his death he called Roberts his friend and teacher, and said that a "great light" had gone out of his life.

Roberts at the time he fled to England to escape prosecution for unlawful cohabitation.

Roberts as he looked during the congressional races of 1895 and 1898.

Emmeline B. Wells was a critic and would not support Roberts. She called his nomination an insult to Utah women, and was "depressed and ill" when Roberts was elected in 1898. Wells questioned in her diary how Utah women could be so "unscrupulous as to vote for such a man."

Martha Hughes Cannon was a college classmate and critic of Roberts because of his stand on woman suffrage. She would later support his congressional candidacies.

Helen M. Gould, the wealthy daughter of Jay Gould, was the main source of funding for the efforts to make sure that Roberts would not be seated in congress. An outspoken opponent of polygamy, she told reporters that she believed it would be "sad indeed to see a man who stands for the Oriental Harem seated among our lawmakers."

George D. Pyper

Melvin J. Ballard

Edward P. Midgley

The First Presidency sent Roberts on a mission to the major cities of the Midwest and East in 1896-1897. He was accompanied initially by George D. Pyper, Melvin J. Ballard, and later Edward P. Midgley.

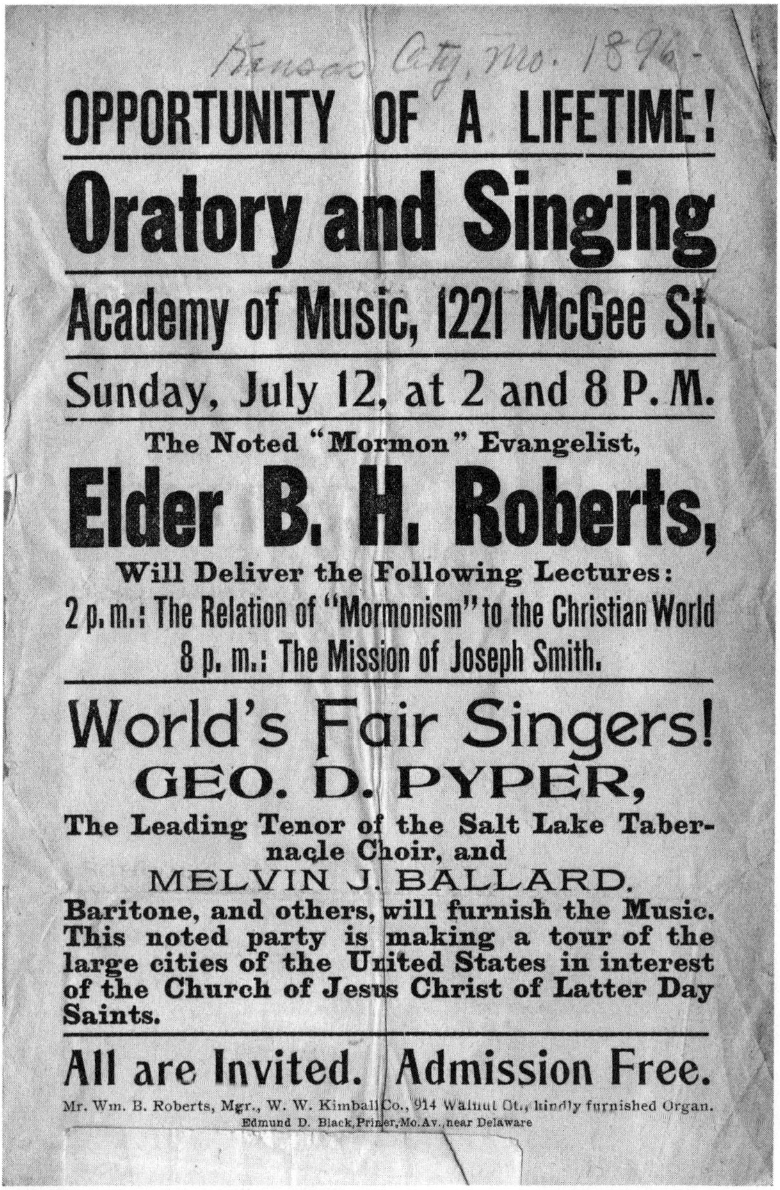

Kansas City, Mo. 1896-

OPPORTUNITY OF A LIFETIME!

Oratory and Singing

Academy of Music, 1221 McGee St.

Sunday, July 12, at 2 and 8 P. M.

The Noted "Mormon" Evangelist,

Elder B. H. Roberts,

Will Deliver the Following Lectures:

2 p. m.: The Relation of "Mormonism" to the Christian World
8 p. m.: The Mission of Joseph Smith.

World's Fair Singers!

GEO. D. PYPER,

The Leading Tenor of the Salt Lake Tabernacle Choir, and

MELVIN J. BALLARD.

Baritone, and others, will furnish the Music. This noted party is making a tour of the large cities of the United States in interest of the Church of Jesus Christ of Latter Day Saints.

All are Invited. Admission Free.

Mr. Wm. B. Roberts, Mgr., W. W. Kimball Co., 914 Walnut St., kindly furnished Organ.
Edmund D. Black, Printer, Mo. Av., near Delaware

One of some 25,000 handbills advertising the groups appearance at the Academy of Music in Kansas City, Missouri. Despite their efforts the meeting was poorly attended and the hall was expensive to rent.

While on this mission he met Leah Dunford, the flirtatious 23 year-old daughter of Susa Young Gates, who was attending Pratt Institute. Roberts was clearly smitten, and confided to Leah that he was thinking of moving to Canada where he could take another wife. Once returning to Utah, however, nothing more was said of the episode, and Dunford married future Apostle John A. Widtsoe in 1898.

Roberts accompanied Apostle George Albert Smith on another special assignment from the First Presidency to the Eastern and Southern states in 1906. In the wake of the Reed Smoot case, they assured non-Mormons that the church had abandoned polygamy, was loyal to America, and believed in the "complete separation of the races sexually and socially."

By the first two decades of the twentieth century, Roberts settled into his role as a Democratic elder statesman, historian and writer. In this photo he looks like the epitome of a solid and successful citizen.

Once America entered World War I, Roberts sought and received an appointment as a chaplain, serving with the 145th artillery in France. After his wartime service however, he would become a staunch advocate of the League of Nations and world peace. *Utah State Historical Society*

To the consternation of J. Reuben Clark and others, Roberts was called to serve as president of the Eastern States Mission in 1922. It proved to be one of his most important, and rewarding, church assignments.

Roberts traveled widely throughout the mission. Here he is in Portland, Maine, looking as much like a prominent attorney or physician as much as a church leader. *Marriott Library Special Collections, University of Utah*

Despite his rigorous standards for his mission, Roberts also like to enjoy his time in the east along with his missionaries. Here he is at the seashore looking relaxed if still somewhat formal. It is unclear what he holds in his gloved hands. *Marriott Library Special Collections, University of Utah*

In Summer 1923, he organized a major event in Palmyra, New York to celebrate the appearance of the Angel Moroni to Joseph Smith. Over 150 missionaries trekked from all points of the mission to meet President Heber J. Grant and other church leaders at the Hill Cumorah. Here are four of those missionaries en route.

Even though he was not always at his best, Roberts enjoyed his time with his missionaries. Here he stands with Mary Edna Brown on his right, and Harold Tranter Allen at his left. The two married in June 1925, and fifty years later their son James B. Allen would, like Roberts, become an assistant Church Historian.
James B. Allen

Despite the event's success, Roberts himself became very ill, was diagnosed with diabetes, and forced to return to Utah for medical attention. It marked the beginning of several bouts of ill health that Roberts would experience in the last decade of his life. He seems haggard in this photo.

Closing her medical practice and traveling to the mission home in Brooklyn with her husband, his third wife, Margaret was a great comfort to Roberts.

Elsie Cook

Elizabeth Skolfield*

Luella Benson Owen

When Margaret became ill, she was attended to by Elsie Cook, Elizabeth Skolfield (Hinckley), and Luella Benson Owen (MacFarlane) who stayed beside her until she died on March 13, 1926—Roberts's sixty-ninth birthday. Elsie Cook was very close to Roberts, assisting him with his literary efforts after his release, and working as his secretary back in Utah. * *Gene Hinckley Bennion*

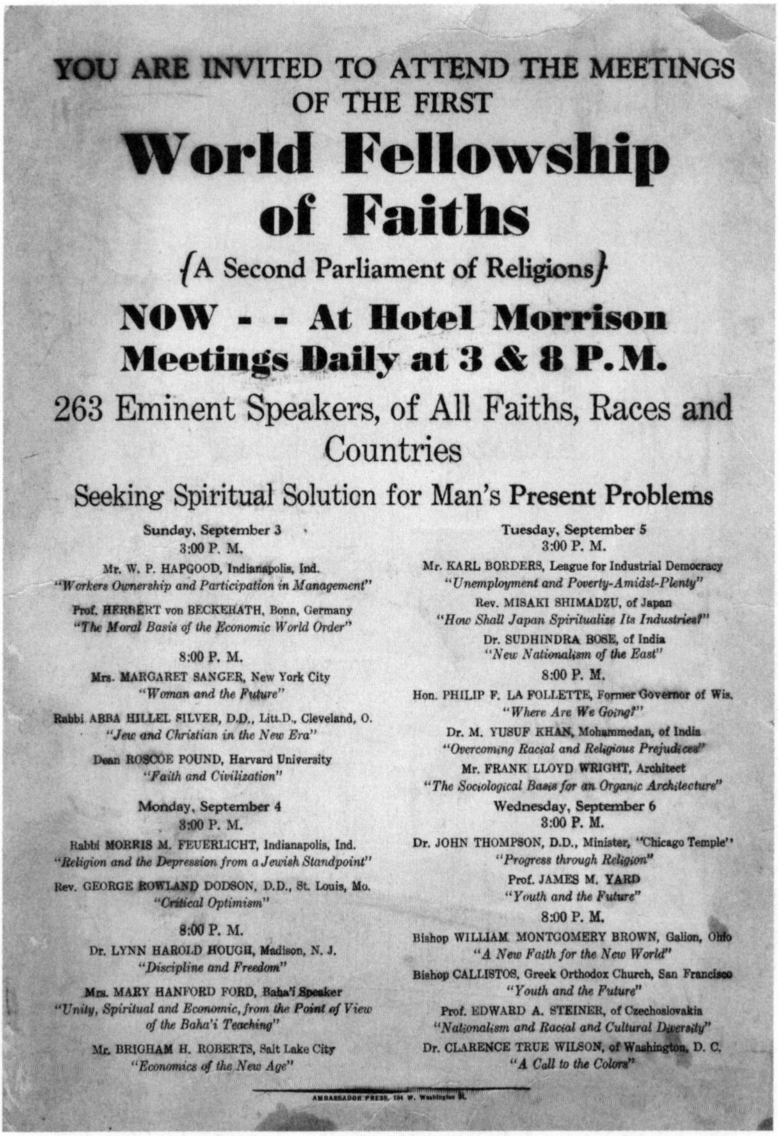

YOU ARE INVITED TO ATTEND THE MEETINGS OF THE FIRST

World Fellowship of Faiths

(A Second Parliament of Religions)

NOW - - At Hotel Morrison

Meetings Daily at 3 & 8 P.M.

263 Eminent Speakers, of All Faiths, Races and Countries

Seeking Spiritual Solution for Man's **Present Problems**

Sunday, September 3
3:00 P. M.

Mr. W. P. HAPGOOD, Indianapolis, Ind.
"Workers Ownership and Participation in Management"

Prof. HERBERT von BECKERATH, Bonn, Germany
"The Moral Basis of the Economic World Order"

8:00 P. M.

Mrs. MARGARET SANGER, New York City
"Woman and the Future"

Rabbi ABBA HILLEL SILVER, D.D., Litt.D., Cleveland, O.
"Jew and Christian in the New Era"

Dean ROSCOE POUND, Harvard University
"Faith and Civilization"

Monday, September 4
3:00 P. M.

Rabbi MORRIS M. FEUERLICHT, Indianapolis, Ind.
"Religion and the Depression from a Jewish Standpoint"

Rev. GEORGE ROWLAND DODSON, D.D., St. Louis, Mo.
"Critical Optimism"

8:00 P. M.

Dr. LYNN HAROLD HOUGH, Madison, N. J.
"Discipline and Freedom"

Mrs. MARY HANFORD FORD, Baha'i Speaker
"Unity, Spiritual and Economic, from the Point of View of the Baha'i Teaching"

Mr. BRIGHAM H. ROBERTS, Salt Lake City
"Economics of the New Age"

Tuesday, September 5
3:00 P. M.

Mr. KARL BORDERS, League for Industrial Democracy
"Unemployment and Poverty-Amidst-Plenty"

Rev. MISAKI SHIMADZU, of Japan
"How Shall Japan Spiritualize Its Industries?"

Dr. SUDHINDRA BOSE, of India
"New Nationalism of the East"

8:00 P. M.

Hon. PHILIP F. LA FOLLETTE, Former Governor of Wis.
"Where Are We Going?"

Dr. M. YUSUF KHAN, Mohammedan, of India
"Overcoming Racial and Religious Prejudices"

Mr. FRANK LLOYD WRIGHT, Architect
"The Sociological Basis for an Organic Architecture"

Wednesday, September 6
3:00 P. M.

Dr. JOHN THOMPSON, D.D., Minister, "Chicago Temple"
"Progress through Religion"

Prof. JAMES M. YARD
"Youth and the Future"

8:00 P. M.

Bishop WILLIAM MONTGOMERY BROWN, Galion, Ohio
"A New Faith for the New World"

Bishop CALLISTOS, Greek Orthodox Church, San Francisco
"Youth and the Future"

Prof. EDWARD A. STEINER, of Czechoslovakia
"Nationalism and Racial and Cultural Diversity"

Dr. CLARENCE TRUE WILSON, of Washington, D. C.
"A Call to the Colors"

AMBASSADOR PRESS, 184 W. Washington St.

In September 1933, Roberts, though still in poor health, represented the church at the World Fellowship of Faiths meeting in Chicago. Here he is listed as lecturing on the "Economics of the New Age." It was one of his last public events before his death on the afternoon of September 27. Upon his death, Elsie Cook, who was with him at the end, would lead the efforts to plan his funeral.

Roberts toward the end of his productive life.

At his death, Heber J. Grant tearfully said to Roberts' son: "Oh, Harold, What will I do without him?"

A typical cartoon of the time, *San Francisco Examiner*, Jan. 18, 1900, 1.

BIBLIOGRAPHY

96th Annual Report of the Board of Home Missions of the Presbyterian Church of the United States. New York: Presbyterian Building, 1898.

Aiwohi, Elsie Cook. Papers MS 3790, CHL.

Alexander, Thomas G. "Charles S. Zane: Apostle of the New Era." *Utah Historical Quarterly* 34, no. 4 (Fall 1966): 289–314.

———. *Edward Hunter Snow: Pioneer, Educator, Statesman*. Norman, OK: Arthur H. Clark, 2012.

———. *Mormonism in Transition: A History of the Latter-day Saints, 1890–1930*. Urbana: University of Illinois Press, 1986.

———. "The Odyssey of a Latter-day Prophet: Wilford Woodruff and the Manifesto of 1890." In Baugh and Black, *Banner of the Gospel*, 277–325.

———. *Things in Heaven and Earth: The Life and Times of Wilford Woodruff, a Mormon Prophet*. Salt Lake City: Signature Books, 1991.

Allen, James B. "J. Reuben Clark, Jr., on American Sovereignty and International Organizations." *BYU Studies* 13, no. 3 (1973): 347–72.

———. "Personal Faith and Public Policy: Some Timely Observations on the League of Nations Controversy in Utah." *BYU Studies* 14, no. 1 (1973): 77–98.

———. "The Story of *The Truth, The Way, The Life*." *BYU Studies* 33, no. 4 (1993): 690–741.

———, and Glen M. Leonard. *The Story of the Latter-day Saints*. Salt Lake City: Deseret Book, 1976.

———, Ronald K. Esplin, and David J. Whittaker. *Men With a Mission, 1837–1841: The Quorum of the Twelve Apostles in the British Isles*. Salt Lake City: Deseret Book, 1992.

Alter, J. Cecil. *Early Utah Journalism*. Salt Lake City: Utah State Historical Society, 1938.

"An Address: The Church of Jesus Christ of Latter-day Saints to the World." *Improvement Era*, May 1907, 481–95.

Anderson, Carleton Q., Betty Shawcroft, and Robert Compton, eds. *The Mormons: One Hundred Years in the San Luis Valley of Colorado, 1883–1983*. N.p.: LaJara Stake, 1984.

Arrington, Leonard J. *Confessions of a Mormon Historian: The Diaries of Leonard J. Arrington, 1971–1997*. Edited by Gary James Bergera. 3 vols. Salt Lake City: Signature Books, 2018.

———. *Faith and Intellect: The Lives and Contributions of Latter-day Saint Thinkers*. Edited by Gary James Bergera. Salt Lake City: Signature Books, 2019.

———. "The Intellectual Tradition of the Latter-day Saints." *Dialogue: A Journal of Mormon Thought* 4, no. 1 (Spring 1969): 13–26.

Ashton, Wendell J. *Voice in the West: Biography of A Pioneer Newspaper*. New York: Duell, Sloan, and Pierce, 1950.

Badger, Rodney J. *Liahona and Iron Rod: The Biography of Carl A. and Rose J. Badger*. Bountiful: Family History Publishers, 1986.

Baird, Edwin. *Autobiography and World War I Journal*. N.p.: by the author, ca. 2005.

———. *Life of James Hyrum Baird, 1848–1891*. N.p.: Baird Family Association, 1972.

Baird, Frederick, Gilbert Cooper, and James Hyrum Baird, comps. *Remembrances and Biography of James Hyrum Baird, 1848–1919, and His Wives and Children*. N.p.: Baird Genealogical Association, 2012.

Baird, Paul Jesse. "A Critique of Presbyterian Ministry in the Great Basin, Particularly as Seen through the Life and Ministry of William Mitchell Paden." PhD diss., San Francisco Theological Seminary, 1977.

Baker, Shane A. "Illness and Mortality in Nineteenth Century Mormon Immigration." *Mormon Historical Studies* 2, no. 2 (Fall 2001): 77–90.

Ballard, Melvin J. Scrapbooks, MSS 8064, BYU.

Ballard, Melvin R. *Melvin J. Ballard: Crusader for Righteousness*. Salt Lake City: Bookcraft, 1966.

Barlow, Tiffnie J. "The Election of 1916: Simon Bamberger's Amazing Race." Master's thesis, University of Utah, 2002.

Barrows, John Henry. *The World's Parliament of Religion*. 2 vols. Chicago: Parliament Publishers, 1893.

Bartholomew, George M. Diary, Oct. 1880–Nov. 1882. MS 2761, CHL.

Bartholomew, Rebecca. *Audacious Women: Early British Mormon Immigrants*. Salt Lake City: Signature Books, 1995.

Bashore, Melvin T. "Life Behind Bars: Mormon Cohabs in the 1880s." *Utah Historical Quarterly* 47, no. 1 (Winter 1979): 22–41.

———, and Fred E. Woods. "Consigned to a Distant Place." *South Dakota History* 27 (Spring–Summer 1997): 21–36.

Bates, Irene. "William Smith, 1811–93: Problematic Patriarch." *Dialogue: A Journal of Mormon Thought* 16, no. 2 (Summer 1983): 11–23.

Baugh, Alexander L., and Susan Easton Black, eds. *Banner of the Gospel: Wilford Woodruff*. Provo: BYU Religious Studies Center, 2010.

Bean, Willard. Collection, 1916–49. MS 5617, CHL.

Beesley, Alvin A. Journals, 1894–96. MS 12716, CHL.

Belnap Family. Papers Collection, 1829–1971. MS 916, CHL.

Belnap, Hyrum. Papers, 1879–1936. MS 2905, CHL.

Berry Family. Autobiographies and Biographies, ca. 2004. MS 19140, CHL.

Berry, William S. Journal, Apr.–Aug. 1884. Typescript, MS 12045, CHL.

B. H. Roberts Group—Eastern States Missionaries, 1921–27. *Constitution and Membership*. Salt Lake City: B. H. Roberts Group, 1947.

B. H. Roberts Society. Records, 1980–1995. Accn 0764, UU.

Bird, Twila. A *Century of Saints: A Front Range History of the Church of Jesus Christ of Latter-day Saints*. Englewood, CO: R&M Color Graphics, 1997.

Bitton, Davis. "B. H. Roberts as Historian." *Dialogue: A Journal of Mormon Thought* 3, no. 4 (Winter 1968): 25–44.

———. "B. H. Roberts at the World Parliament of Religion 1893, Chicago." *Sunstone*, Jan.–Feb. 1982, 46–51.

———. "The B. H. Roberts Case of 1898–1900." *Utah Historical Quarterly* 25, no. 1 (Jan. 1957): 27–46.

———. *George Q. Cannon: A Biography*. Salt Lake City: Deseret Book, 1999.

———, and Leonard J. Arrington. *Mormons and Their Historians*. Salt Lake City: University of Utah Press, 1988.

———, and Gary L. Bunker. "Phrenology Among the Mormons." *Dialogue: A Journal of Mormon Thought* 9, no. 1 (Spring 1974): 42–61.

Bliss, William D. P. *The Encyclopedia of Social Reform*. New York: Funk & Wagnalls, 1897.

Bloom, Robert L. "Edwin A Van Valkenburg and the Philadelphia North American, 1899–1924." *Pennsylvania History* 21 (Apr. 1954): 109–27.

Bloxham, V. Ben, James R. Moss, and Larry C. Porter, eds. *Truth Will Prevail: The Rise of the Church of Jesus Christ of Latter-day Saints in the British Isles, 1837–1987*. Salt Lake City: Deseret Book, 1987.

Bonney, Charles C. "The Genesis of the World Religion Conference of 1893." *New Church Review* 1 (Jan. 1894): 73–100.

Bowman, Matthew. *The Urban Pulpit: New York City and the Fate of Liberal Evangelism*. New York: Oxford University Press, 2014.

Brackenridge, R. Douglas. "'About the Worst Man in Utah:' William R. Campbell and the Crusade Against Brigham H. Roberts, 1898–1900." *Journal of Mormon History* 39, no. 1 (Winter 2013): 69–157.

Bradford, Roderick. *D. M. Bennett: The Truth Seeker*. Amherst, NY: Prometheus Books, 2006.

Bradley, Martha Sonntag, and Mary Brown Firmage Woodward. *Four Zinas: A Study of Mothers and Daughters on the Western Frontier*. Salt Lake City: Signature Books, 2000.

Bringhurst, Newell G. "The Private vs. The Public David O. McKay." *Dialogue: A Journal of Mormon Thought* 31, no. 3 (Fall 1998): 11–34.

———. *Saints, Slaves, and Blacks: The Changing Place of Black People within Mormonism*. Westport CT: Greenwood, 1981.

———, and Frederick S. Buchanan. "The Forgotten Odyssey of Obadiah H. Riggs, Early Pioneer for Education Reform." *Utah Historical Quarterly* 66, no. 1 (Winter 1998): 48–64.

British Mission. British Mission Manuscript History and Historical Reports, 1841–1971. LR 1140 2, CHL.

Brooklyn District Historical Committee. *Zion in the Brooklyn District: One Heart Many Voices*. Brooklyn: Brooklyn, New York, District of the Church of Jesus Christ of Latter-day Saints, 1997.

Brudnoy, David. "A Decade in Zion: Theodore Schroeder's Initial Assault on the Mormons." *Historian* 37 (Feb. 1975): 241–56.

_____. "Of Sinners and Saints: Theodore Schroeder, Brigham Roberts, and Reed Smoot." *Journal of Church and State* 14 (Spring 1972): 261–78.

Buerger, David John. "The Adam–God Doctrine." *Dialogue: A Journal of Mormon Thought* 15, no. 1 (Spring 1982): 14–58.

———. *The Mysteries of Godliness: A History of Mormon Temple Worship.* 2nd ed. Salt Lake City: Signature Books, 2002.

Buice, David. "'All Alone and None to Cheer Me': The Southern States Missionary Diaries of J. Golden Kimball." *Dialogue: A Journal of Mormon Thought* 24, no. 1 (Spring 1991): 35–54.

———. "Chattanooga's *Southern Star*: Mormon Window on the South." *BYU Studies* 28, no. 2 (Spring 1988): 5–15.

Burrows, Edwin G., and Mike Wallace. *Gotham: A History of New York City to 1898.* New York: Oxford University Press, 1998.

Bush, Lester E. Jr. "Mormonism's Negro Doctrine: An Historical Overview." *Dialogue: A Journal of Mormon Thought* 8, no. 1 (Spring 1973): 11–68.

Bushman, Richard Lyman. *Joseph Smith: Rough Stone Rolling.* New York: Knopf, 2005.

Butt, William F. Papers, 1881–1940. MSS 1397, BYU.

———. Diaries, 1880–1897. MS 4778, CHL.

Caldwell, Gaylon L. "Moral and Religious Aspects of the Status of the Negro in Utah." *Western Humanities Review* 13 (Winter 1959): 102–06.

Campbell, Eugene, and Richard D. Poll. *Hugh B. Brown: His Life and Thought.* Salt Lake City: Bookcraft, 1975.

Cannon, Abraham H. *Candid Insights of A Mormon Apostle: The Diaries of Abraham H. Cannon.* Edited by Edward Leo Lyman. Salt Lake City: Signature Books, 2010.

Cannon, George Q. The Journal of George Q. Cannon, 1849–1901. Typescript online at churchhistorianspress.org/george-q-cannon. Originals in CHL.

Cannon, Kenneth L., II. "Isaac Russell: Mormon Muckraker and Secret Defender of the Church." *Journal of Mormon History* 39, no. 4 (Fall 2013): 44–98.

———. "The Modern Mormon Kingdom: Frank J. Cannon's National Campaign Against Mormonism, 1910–1918." *Journal of Mormon History* 37, no. 4 (Fall 2011): 60–114.

Carpenter, David S. *Jens Peter Nielson: Bishop of Bluff.* Provo: BYU Studies, 2003.

Carter, Kate B. *Our Pioneer Heritage.* 20 vols. Salt Lake City: Daughters of Utah Pioneers, 1958–77.

Centerville, Utah, Centennial Book Committee. *Centerville, Utah: Our American Hometown*. Bountiful, UT: Carr Printing, 2015.

Chamberlin, Ralph V. *Memories of John R. Park*. Salt Lake City: Deseret News Press, 1949.

———. *The University of Utah: A History of Its First Hundred Years, 1850–1950*. Salt Lake City: University of Utah, 1960.

Chattanooga Directory. 1883–84. Chattanooga: Cotton Belt Publishing Company, 1883, 1884.

Chipman, VaLois South Papers, 1925–80. ACCN 1323, UU.

Chipman, William H. Notebook, 1866. MS 915, CHL.

Church of Jesus Christ of Latter-day Saints. *Declaration and Defense: The Church of Jesus Christ of Latter-day Saints to the World*. Salt Lake City: Church of Jesus Christ of Latter-day Saints, 1907.

Clark, Caroline Hopkins. Diary, 1866. Film Utah 101 #10, Special Collections, Merrill–Cazier Library, Utah State University.

———. "Liverpool to Utah in 1866." In Holmes, *Covered Wagon Women*.

Clark, James R., comp. *Messages of the First Presidency*. 6 vols. Salt Lake City: Bookcraft, 1965–75.

Clarke, Cathy Ann. "A Short History of Mary LaReal Jones Mitchell." Copy in author's possession.

Clawson, Rudger. *A Ministry of Meetings: The Apostolic Diaries of Rudger Clawson*. Edited by Stan Larson. Salt Lake City: Signature Books, 1993.

———. Papers, 1870–1943. MS 0481, UU.

———. *Prisoner for Polygamy: The Memoirs and Letters of Rudger Clawson at the Utah Territorial Prison, 1884–1887*. Edited by Stan Larson. Urbana: University of Illinois Press, 1993.

Cluff, Benjamin. Presidential Papers. In Office of the President Correspondence. UA 1093, BYU.

Collier, Maurine R., comp. *Mission Journals of James Roskelley*. N.p.: by the author, 1983.

Conference Reports of the Church of Jesus Christ of Latter-day Saints. 1897–present. Bi-annual report containing speeches delivered at the church's semi-annual general conference. Salt Lake City: Church of Jesus Christ of Latter-day Saints.

Cooley, Everett L. "The B. H. Roberts Papers at the University of Utah." *Dialogue: A Journal of Mormon Thought* 26, no. 3 (Fall 1993):190–92.

Craner, Darwin Kay. "The Influence of the LDS Church in Utah Politics, 1902–16." Master's thesis, University of Utah, 1969.

Cripps, John W. Family Papers. Copy in author's possession.

Crocker, E. W. *History of the 145th Field Artillery Regiment of the Utah National Guard.* Provo: Grant Stevenson, 1968.

Croly, Jennie J. *The History of the Woman's Club Movement in America.* New York: Henry G. Allen, 1898.

Crookston, Douglas O., ed. *Henry Ballard: The Story of a Courageous Pioneer.* Layton, UT: by the editor, ca. 1994.

Crow, Bruce. *A Land of Strangers: Cane Creek Tennessee's Massacre and Its Tragic Effects on the People Who Lived There.* Lewisburg, TN: AMH Press, 2013.

Curtis, Donald R. *"And Should We Die:" The Cane County Mormon Massacre.* Bandenburg, KY: Bearhead Publishers, 2011.

Daughters of Utah Pioneers. *Museum Memories.* 9 vols. Salt Lake City: Daughters of Utah Pioneers, 2009–17.

Davis, Paul S. "Biography of James Jarvis Chandler." Master's thesis, Utah State University, 2000.

Davis Stake. Young Men's Mutual Improvement Association Minutes and Records, 1879–82. LR 2160 16, CHL.

Democratic Party of Utah. *Proceedings of the Democratic Convention Held at Ogden, Utah, August 18, 1916.* Salt Lake City: Century Printing, 1916.

Denbaugh, Edwin L., and William duBarry. *William H. Webb: Shipbuilder.* Glen Cove, NY: Webb Institute of Naval Architecture, 1989.

Derr, Jill Mulvay, Carol Cornwall Madsen, Kate Holbrook, and Matthew J. Grow. *First Fifty Years of Relief Society.* Salt Lake City: Church Historians Press, 2016.

Derr, Jill Mulvay, Janath Russell Cannon, and Maureen Ursenbach Beecher. *Women of Covenant: The Story of Relief Society.* Salt Lake City: Deseret Book, 1992.

Dilley, James W. *History of the Scofield Mine Disaster.* Provo: Skelton Publishing Co., 1900.

Done, Willard. Journal, Mar. 1893–Mar. 1903. MS 19454, CHL.

Drake, James. *A Historical Sketch of Wilson County, Tennessee: From Its First Settlement to the Present Time*. Tavel, Eastman, & Howell, 1879.

Driggs, Howard R. Collection. Ms 120, Barbara A. Matheson Special Collections, Gerald R. Sherratt Library, Southern Utah University.

DuBois, Fred T. Papers, 1868–1930. MC 004, Special Collections, Eli M. Oboler Library, Idaho State University.

Dunford, Leah Eudora. "A Visit to Pratt Institute." *Young Woman's Journal*, Mar. 1897, 249–59.

Eastern States Mission. Conference Papers, 1923. LR 2475 39, CHL.

_____. Manuscript History and Historical Reports, 1830–1977. LR 2475 2, CHL.

Edmunds, John K. Interview with Gordon Irving, Salt Lake City, 1979–1980. OH 624, 519.

"Elder Roberts Issues a Challenge." *Millennial Star*, Nov. 20, 1893, 760–62; Nov. 27, 1893, 776–78; and, Dec. 4, 1893, 785–86.

Eldredge, Alma. Diaries, 1869–1924. MS 1618, CHL.

_____. Reminiscences and Diaries, 1869–98. MS 14865, CHL.

Embry, Jessie L. *Spiritualized Recreation: Mormon All-Church Athletic Tournaments and Dance Festivals*. Provo: BYU and Charles Redd Center, 2008.

Entz, Gary R. "The Bickertonites: Schism and Reunion in a Restoration Church, 1880–1905." *Journal of Mormon History* 32, no. 3 (Fall 2006): 1–44.

———. "The Mormon Origins of St. John, Kansas. Kansas." *History* 24 (Summer 2001): 98–117.

Estalami Society. Record Books, 1929–92. MS 2908, CHL.

Fairbanks, John B. Diaries, 1877–1914. MSS 140, BYU.

Firmage, Edwin B., ed. *An Abundant Life: The Memoirs of Hugh B. Brown*. 2nd ed. Salt Lake City: Signature Books, 1999.

First Council of Seventy. Minutes. Copy in author's possession.

First Presidency. Correspondence, John Taylor, 1877–1887. CR 1 180, CHL

_____. Missionary Calls and Recommendations, 1877–1918. CR 1 168, CHL.

Fish, Stanley L., Bradley J. Kramer, and William Budge Wallis. *History of the Mormon Church in Cincinnati, 1830–1985*. Cincinnati: Cincinnati Ohio and Cincinnati Ohio North Stakes, 1997.

Hedges, Andrew, and Richard Neitzel Holzapfel. *Within These Prison Walls: Lorenzo Snow's Record Book, 1886–1897*. Salt Lake City: Deseret Book, 2010.

Hillam, Ray C., Charles D. Tate Jr., and Laura Wadley. *J. Reuben Clark Jr., Diplomat and Statesman*. Provo: BYU Press, 1973.

Hinckley, Bryant S. *Sermons and Missionary Service of Melvin Joseph Ballard*. Salt Lake City: Deseret Book, 1949.

Hinckley, Gordon B. *James Henry Moyle: The Story of a Distinguished American and an Honored Churchman*. Salt Lake City: Deseret Book, 1951.

Historian's Office. Journal History of the Church, 1830–2008. CR 100 137. Church History Library, Salt Lake City. Daily scrapbook; entries primarily contain newspaper clippings and typed extracts from other sources.

History of the Bench and Bar of Utah. Salt Lake City: Interstate Press Association, 1913.

History of Western Iowa. Sioux City: Western Publishing Co., 1882.

Holley, Val. *Frank J. Cannon: Saint, Senator, Scoundrel*. Salt Lake City: University of Utah Press, 2020.

Holmes, Kenneth L. ed. *Covered Wagon Women*. Vol. 9, *Diaries and Letters From the Western Trails, 1864–66*. Lincoln and London: University of Nebraska Press, 1990.

Horne, Dennis B. *Latter Leaves in the Life of Lorenzo Snow*. Springville, UT: CFI, 2012.

———. *The Life of Orson F. Whitney: Historian, Poet, Apostle*. Springville, UT: CFI, 2004.

Howard, Susan W. "William Jarman: The Anti-Mormon Apostle of the British Isles." *Journal of Mormon History* 43, no. 1 (Jan. 2017): 59–86.

Hulmston, John K. "Mormon Immigration in the 1860s: The Story of the Church Trains." *Utah Historical Quarterly* 58, no. 1 (Winter 1990): 32–48.

International Society Daughters of Utah Pioneers. *Pioneer Women of Faith and Fortitude*. Salt Lake City: Daughters of Utah Pioneers, 1998.

Iverson, Joan Smyth. *The Anti-Polygamy Controversy in U. S. Women's Movements, 1880–1925*. New York: Garland, 1977

Ivins, Anthony W. *Cowboy Apostle: The Diaries of Anthony W. Ivins, 1875–1932*. Edited by Elizabeth Oberdick Anderson. Salt Lake City: Signature Books, 2013.

Ivins, Stanley S. "Theodore Roosevelt and Reed Smoot." *Western Political Quarterly* 4 (Sep. 1951): 440–53.

Jackson, John William. Diaries, 1880–85. MS 309, CHL.

Jacoby, Susan. *Freethinkers: A History of American Secularism*. New York: Metropolitan Books, 2004.

Jardine, Winnifred C. *The Life of Joseph Morrell: February 11, 1856–May 30, 1905*. Logan: by the author, 1989.

Jarman, William. *Uncle Sam's Abscess: Or Hell Upon Earth*. Exeter, England: H. Leduc, 1884.

Jennings, Priscilla P. "Dr. Margaret Curtis Shipp Roberts." In Carter, *Our Pioneer Heritage*, 6:373–77.

Jenson, Andrew. *Church Chronology*. 2nd ed. Salt Lake City: Deseret News Press, 1899.

———. *Encyclopedic History of the Church of Jesus Christ of Latter–day Saints*. Salt Lake City: Deseret News Publishing, 1941.

———. *Latter-day Saint Biographical Encyclopedia*. 4 vols. Salt Lake City: Andrew Jenson Historical Co., 1901–36.

Jeppson, Joseph H. "The Secularization of the University of Utah to 1920." PhD diss., University of California–Berkeley, 1973.

Jones, Paul. *The Bible and the Book of Mormon: Some Suggestive Points from Modern Bible Study*. Logan: n.p., 1911.

———. *Points of Contact: A Consideration for Dissatisfied Latter-day Saints*. Salt Lake City: Arrow Press, ca. 1915.

Jones, William H. Reminiscences, 1885. MS 5407, CHL.

Keegan, John. *The First World War*. New York: Vintage, 2000.

Keller, Roger. "Episcopalian Bishop Franklin S. Spalding and the Mormons." *Utah Historical Quarterly* 69, no. 3 (Summer 2001): 241–44.

Kelly, Charles. *The Outlaw Trail: The Story of Butch Cassidy and the "Wild Bunch."* New York: Bonanza Books, 1959.

Kenney, Scott G. Collection, 1820–1984. MS 0587, UU.

Kesler, Donnette S. *Reminiscences*. Salt Lake City: A. P. Kesler Family, 1952.

Kimball, J. Golden. Journals, 1883–1908. MS 1354, CHL.

Kimball, Richard Ian. "Muscular Mormonism." *International Journal of the History of Sport* 25 (Apr. 2008): 549–78.

Kline, Geraldine Thorup. "Public Opinion in Metropolitan Utah and the League of Nations, 1918–1920." Master's thesis, University of Utah, 1965.

Larsen, Kent S. "The Life of Thomas Kearns." Master's thesis, University of Utah, 1964.

Larson, Gustive O. *Outline History of Utah and the Mormons*. Salt Lake City: Deseret Book, 1958.

Larson, Stan. "Intellectuals in Mormon History: An Update." *Dialogue: A Journal of Mormon Thought* 26, no. 3 (Fall 1993): 187–89.

Launius, Roger. *Joseph Smith III: Pragmatic Prophet*. Urbana: University of Illinois, 1998.

Law, Vernon D. "Some Things About Vernon Deem Law." Undated typescript in possession of author.

Lieber, Constance L., and John Sillito, eds. *Letters From Exile: The Correspondence of Martha Hughes Cannon and Angus M. Cannon, 1886–1888*. Salt Lake City: Signature Books in association with Smith Research Associates, 1989.

Linam, Alisha M. "'Our Sorrows They've Seen:' The Tennessee Mormon Massacre." Master's thesis, Middle Tennessee State University, 2013.

Linde, O. Ragnar. Papers, 1921–66. ACCN 1462, UU.

Livingston, Georgia Roberts "Life Story of Celia Dibble Roberts." Typescript in possession of author.

Ludlow, Daniel H., ed. *Encyclopedia of Mormonism*. 4 vols. New York: Macmillan, 1992.

Lund, Anthon H. *Danish Apostle: The Diaries of Anthon H. Lund, 1890–1921*. Edited by John P. Hatch. Salt Lake City: Signature Books, 2006.

Lundahl, Ezra C. Letters, Nov. 1924–Sep. 1926. MS 19581, CHL.

Lundquist, Roland C. Missionary Scrapbook, 1922–24. MS 20677, CHL.

Lundwall, N. B., comp. *Assorted Gems of Priceless Value*. Salt Lake City: Bookcraft, 1944.

Lyman, Edward Leo. "The Alienation of an Apostle from His Quorum: The Moses Thatcher Case." *Dialogue: A Journal of Mormon Thought* 18, no. 2 (Summer 1985): 67–91.

———. *Finally Statehood! Utah's Struggle, 1849–1896*. Salt Lake City: Signature Books, 2019.

———. "Isaac Trumbo and the Politics of Utah Statehood." *Utah Historical Quarterly* 41, no. 2 (Spring 1971): 128–49.

———. *Political Deliverance: The Mormon Quest for Utah Statehood*. Urbana: University of Illinois, 1986.

McAllister, G. Stanley. Papers, 1920–2006. ACCN 1398, UU.

McCormick, John S., and John R. Sillito, "Henry W. Lawrence: A Lifetime in Dissent." In *Differing Visions: Dissenters in Mormon History*, edited by Roger Launius and Linda Thatcher, 220–40. Urbana: University of Illinois, 1994.

———. *A History of Utah Radicalism: Startling, Socialistic and Decidedly Revolutionary*. Logan: Utah State University, 2011.

McCune, George W. Papers, 1896–1952. MS 6156, CHL.

Macdonald, George E. *Fifty Years of Free Thought*. Vol. 2. New York: Truth Seeker, 1929.

McMurrin, Sterling M. "Remembering B. H. Roberts." *Dialogue: A Journal of Mormon Thought* 26, no. 3 (Fall 1993): 73–76.

Madsen, Barnard N. *The Truman G. Madsen Story: A Life of Study and Faith*. Salt Lake City: Deseret Book, 2016.

Madsen, Carol Cornwall. *An Advocate for Women: The Public Life of Emmeline B. Wells*. Provo: BYU Studies, 2006.

———. *Emmeline B. Wells: An Intimate History*. Salt Lake City: University of Utah, 2017.

———. "The Power of Combination: Emmeline B. Wells and the National and International Councils of Women." *BYU Studies* 33, no. 4 (1993): 646–73.

Madsen, Truman G. "B. H. Roberts and the Book of Mormon." *BYU Studies* 19, no. 4 (1979): 427–45.

———. *B. H. Roberts, His Final Decade: Statements about the Book of Mormon*. Provo: Foundation for Ancient Research and Mormon Studies, 1985.

———. *Defender of the Faith: The B. H. Roberts Story*. Salt Lake City: Bookcraft, 1980.

Maher, Richard. *For God and Country: Memorable Stories From the Lives of Mormon Chaplains*. Bountiful: Horizon, 1976.

Malan, Robert H. *B. H. Roberts: A Biography*. Salt Lake City: Deseret Book, 1966.

Malmquist, O. N. *The First 100 Years: A History of the Salt Lake Tribune, 1871–1971.* Salt Lake City: Utah State Historical Society, 1971.

Mason, Patrick Q. *The Mormon Menace: Violence and Anti-Mormonism in the Post-Bellum South.* New York: Oxford University Press, 2011.

Maw, Herbert B. Interviewed by John R. Sillito, 1975. OH 447, CHL.

Maxwell, John Gary. *Robert Newton Baskin and the Making of Modern Utah.* Norman, OK: Arthur H. Clark Co., 2013.

Merrill, Milton R. *Reed Smoot: Apostle in Politics.* Logan: Utah State University Press and Department of Political Science, 1990.

Mikkelsen, D. Craig. "The Politics of B. H. Roberts." *Dialogue: A Journal of Mormon Thought* 9, no. 2 (Summer 1974): 25–43.

Milewski, Melissa Lambert. *Before the Manifesto: The Life Writings of Mary Lois Walker Morris.* Logan: Utah State University, 2007.

Missionary Department. Missionary Registers, 1860–1959. CR 301 22, CHL.

Missionary Reports, 1831–1900. MS 6104, CHL.

Moffitt, John Clifton. *History of Public Education in Utah.* Salt Lake City: Deseret News Press, 1946.

Montez, Shannon Caldwell. "The Secret Mormon Meetings of 1922." Master's thesis, University of Nevada, Reno, 2019.

Morgan Commercial College. Collection. MSS C 360, UDSH.

Morgan, John Hamilton. Papers, 1845–1986. ACCN 1465, UU.

Morgan John, and B. H. Roberts. *To The Presidents of Conferences and Traveling Elders in the Southern States.* Chattanooga: Southern States Mission, 1884.

Morgan's Commercial College: The Pioneer College of the Rocky Mountains. Salt Lake City: Telegraph Book and Job Printing, 1869.

Morn, Frank T. "Simon Bamberger: A Jew in a Mormon Commonwealth." Master's thesis, Brigham Young University, 1966.

Morrell, Joseph. Correspondence, 1883–1906. MS 30, CHL.

———. Letters Received, 1883–1906. MS 1218, BYU.

Moses, Bernard. Papers, 1899–1950. Mss SC 904, BYU.

Mowry, Georgiana R. Scrapbook, ca. 1897–1933. MS 30037, CHL.

Moyer, Jonathan H. "Dancing With The Devil: The Making of the Mormon–Republican Pact." PhD diss., University of Utah, 2009.

Moyle, James Henry. *Mormon Democrat: The Religious and Political Memoirs of James Henry Moyle*. Edited by Gene A. Sessions. Salt Lake City: Signature Books, 1998.

Murray, Louis Paul. "The Life of Brigadier General Richard W. Young." Master's thesis, University of Utah, 1959.

Mutual Improvement League. *Constitution and By Laws of the Mutual Improvement League*. Salt Lake City: Magazine Printing, 1896.

National Guard. *Official Scrapbook of the 145th Field Artillery, 1st Utah, Compiled by the Statistical Section of the Regiment*. Series 10339, Utah State Archives.

Naylor, Adah Roberts. "An Immigrant Mother and her Son." *Relief Society Magazine*, Jan. 1934, 3–8.

Neilson, Patricia Ward. *A History of Joel Ricks Jr.* N.p.: by the author, 2003.

Neilson, Reid L. *Exhibiting Mormonism: The Latter-day Saints and the Chicago World's Fair*. New York: Oxford University Press, 2011.

———. "Mormonism's Blacksmith Orator: B. H. Roberts at the Chicago World's Fair Parliament of Religion." *Mormon Historical Studies* 12, no. 1 (Spring 2011): 53–84.

———, and Carson V. Teuscher. "Pilgrimage to Palmyra: President B. H. Roberts and the Eastern States Mission's 1923 Commemoration of Cumorah." *BYU Studies* 58, no. 2 (2019): 4–43.

———, and Fred Woods, eds. *Go Ye Unto All the World: The Growth and Development of Mormon Missionary Work*. Provo: Religious Studies Center, 2012.

Nichols, Jeffrey. *Prostitution, Polygamy, and Power: Salt Lake City, 1849–1918*. Urbana: University of Illinois Press, 2002.

Nicholson, John. *The Tennessee Massacre and its Causes: Or the Utah Conspiracy*. Salt Lake City: Juvenile Instructor, 1884.

Northern States Mission. History of the Northern States Mission. In Northern States Mission General Minutes, 1875–1930. LR 6227 11, CHL.

———. Manuscript History and Historical Reports, 1831–32, 1875–1977. LR 6227 2, CHL.

Official Reports of the Proceedings and Debates of the Convention Assembled at Salt Lake City on the 4th Day of March 1895, to Adopt a Constitution for the State of Utah. 2 vols. Salt Lake City: Star Printing, 1898.

Pace, Ralph Wayne. "A Study of the Speaking of B. H. Roberts, Utah's Blacksmith Orator." Master's thesis, Brigham Young University, 1957.

Palmer, William M. Diaries, 1880–87. MS 9463, CHL.

Palmer, William R. "Early Day Trading With the Nevada Mining Camps." *Utah Historical Quarterly* 26, no. 4 (Oct. 1958) 353–68.

Papanikolas, Helen Z. "Unionism, Communism, and the Great Depression: The Carbon County Strike of 1933." *Utah Historical Quarterly* 41, no. 3 (Summer 1973): 254–300.

Parrish, Alan K. *John A. Widtsoe: A Biography*. Salt Lake City: Deseret Book, 2003.

Parrish, Mahala S., and John F. Parrish. *A History of William Reed Smith and His Families*. Los Angeles: n.p., 1953.

Partridge, Edward Jr. Diaries, 1854–99. MS 0628, UU.

A Patchwork History of Hickman County. N.p.: Hickman County Historical, 1984.

Paul, Charles Randall. *Converting the Saints: A Study of Religious Rivalry in America*. Salt Lake City: Greg Kofford Books, 2018.

Paulos, Michael Harold. *The Mormon Church on Trial: Transcripts of the Reed Smoot Hearings*. Salt Lake City: Signature Books, 2008.

Pierce, Realto E. *History of Clayton County, Iowa*. Chicago: Robert O. Law, 1916.

Plain City Ward. Eighty-Seventh Quorum of Seventy Minutes, 1885–1912. LR 6982 21, CHL.

Powell, Allan Kent. "Tragedy At Scofield." *Utah Historical Quarterly* 41, no. 2 (Spring 1973): 182–94.

———. *Utah and the Great War: The Beehive State and the World War I Experience*. Salt Lake City: Utah State Historical Society/University of Utah Press, 2016.

Powell, John. "A Summary of the Religious Side of My Life." MS 4675 1, CHL.

Proctor, Ben. *William Randolph Hearst: The Early Years, 1863–1910*. Indianapolis: Indiana University Press, 1998.

Putney, Clifford. *Muscular Christianity: Manhood and Sports in Protestant America, 1880–1920*. Cambridge: Harvard University Press, 2001.

Pyper, George D. Papers, 1834–1975. MS 0001, UU

Quinn, D. Michael. *Elder Statesman: A Biography of J. Reuben Clark*. Salt Lake City: Signature Books, 2002.

———. *J. Reuben Clark: The Church Years*. Provo: BYU, 1983.

———. *The Mormon Hierarchy: Extensions of Power*. Salt Lake City: Signature Books in association with Smith Research Associates, 1997.

———. *The Mormon Hierarchy: Wealth and Corporate Power*. Salt Lake City: Signature Books, 2017.

Radke-Moss, Andrea. "'Truly Her Soul Rejoiced in Helping the Helpless': Emily Sophia Tanner Richards (1850–1929)." In *Women of Faith in the Latter Days*, vol. 3, edited by Richard E. Turley Jr. and Brittany A. Chapman, 131–43. Salt Lake City: Deseret Book, 2014.

———. "Mormon Women, Suffrage, and Citizenship at the 1893 Chicago World's Fair." In *Gendering The Fair: Histories of Women and Gender at World's Fairs*, edited by T. J. Boisseau and Abigail M. Markwyn, 97–112. Urbana: University of Illinois Press, 2010.

———. "Polygamy and Women's Rights: 19th Century Mormon Female Activism." In *The Persistence of Polygamy: From Joseph Smith's Martyrdom To the First Manifesto, 1844–1890*, edited by Newell G. Bringhurst and Craig L. Foster, 263–97. Independence, MO: John Whitmer Books, 2013.

Reeve, W. Paul. *Religion of a Different Color: Race and the Mormon Struggle for Whiteness*. New York: Oxford University Press, 2015.

Renehan, Edward J., Jr. *Dark Genius of Wall Street: The Misunderstood Life of Jay Gould, King of the Robber Barons*. New York: Basic Books, 2005.

Rich, Emily A. Diary. In Dr. Edward I. and Emily Almira Cozzens Rich Diaries. MS 74, Special Collections, Stewart Library, Weber State University.

Richards, Claude. *J. Golden Kimball: The Story of a Unique Personality*. Salt Lake City: Bookcraft, 1966.

Richards, Kent F. *A Family of Faith: An Intimate View of Church History through the Journals of Three Generations of Apostles, Willard Richards, Franklin D. Richards, George F. Richards*. Salt Lake City: Deseret Book, 2013.

Richards, Samuel W. Papers, 1839–1909. MS 1841, CHL.

Richardson, Arthur. *The Life and Ministry of John Morgan*. Salt Lake City: N. G. Morgan, 1965.

Ricketts, Jeremy R. "The Tennessee 1884 Mormon Massacre and the Cane County Vigilante Movement." *Tennessee Historical Quarterly* 67 (Fall 2008): 208–35.

Riess, Jana. "Polygamy in the Nation's Capital: Protestant Women and the 1899 Campaign Against B. H. Roberts." In *Mormonism and American Politics*, edited by Randall Balmer and Jana Riess. New York: Columbia University Press, 2016.

Roberts, B. H. *The Autobiography of B. H. Roberts.* Edited by Gary James Bergera. Salt Lake City: Signature Books, 1990.

———. "Celestial Marriage and the Acts of Congress." Series of articles in the *Contributor*, Nov. 1884, 50–54; Dec. 1884, 107–11; Jan. 1885, 134–39; Feb. 1884, 168–72; Mar. 1885, 205–210; and Apr. 1885, 252–56.

———. Collection, 1870–1927. MSS 1430, BYU.

———. Collection, 1883–1933. MS 1278, CHL.

———. *A Comprehensive History of the Church of Jesus Christ of Latter-day Saints: Century I.* 6 vols. Salt Lake City: Deseret News Press, 1930.

———. *Corianton: A Nephite Story.* N.p.: Lynn Pulsipher, 2011.

———. *Defense of the Faith and the Saints.* 2 vols. Salt Lake City: Deseret News Press, 1907–12.

———. *Discourses of B. H. Roberts of the First Council of the Seventy.* Salt Lake City: Deseret Book, 1948.

———. *The Essential B. H. Roberts.* Edited by Brigham D. Madsen. Salt Lake City: Signature Books, 1999.

———. *Excerpts from The Truth, The Way, The Life: An Elementary Treatise on Theology*. Edited by Brian H. Stuy. N.p.: privately printed, 1975.

———. *The Falling Away: Or the World's Loss of the Christian Religion and Church.* Salt Lake City: Deseret Book, 1931.

———. *The Gospel: An Exposition of its First Principles.* Salt Lake City: The Contributor Company, 1888.

———. *Gospel Tracts.* N.p.: by the author. M208 R643g, CHL.

———. *History's Apprentice: The Diaries of B. H. Roberts, 1880–1898.* Edited by John Sillito. Salt Lake City: Signature Books, 2004.

———. *Joseph Smith, The Prophet Teacher: A Discourse.* Salt Lake City: Deseret News, 1908. Reprint edition by Deseret Club of Princeton University, 1967.

———. Letter to Eva Lewis, June 21, 1924. MS 6978, CHL.

———. Letters to Missionaries, ca. 1922–27. MS 25752, CHL.

———. *The Life of John Taylor*. Salt Lake City: George Q. Cannon and Sons, 1892.

———. "The Mission of the Church of the New Dispensation." In *Last Seven Discourses of B. H. Roberts*, 11–30. Salt Lake City: Deseret Book, 1948.

———. *Mormonism: The Relation of the Church to Christian Sects, Origin and History of 'Mormonism,' Doctrines of the Church, Church Organization, Present Status*. Independence, MO: Zion's Printing and Publishing, 1927.

———. *A New Witness for God*. Provo: Publisher's Press, 1986.

———. *New Witnesses for God*. 3 vols. Salt Lake City: Deseret News Press, 1906–09.

———. *Outlines of Ecclesiastical History*. Salt Lake City: George Q. Cannon & Sons, 1893.

———. Papers, 1825–1976. MS 0106, UU.

———. Papers, 1880–1965. MS 2729, CHL.

———. Papers, 1888–1920. MSS SC 1922, BYU.

———. *Recent Discussions of Mormon Affairs*. 1907. Reprint, London: Forgotten Books, 1913.

———. "Remarks." In *In Memoriam: Anthon Henrik Lund*, edited by J. M. Sjodahl, 28–32. Salt Lake City: n.p., 1921.

———. Scrapbook, 1896–98. MS 8616, CHL.

———. *A Scrap Book*. Compiled by Lynn Pulsipher. 2 vols. Provo: Pulsipher Publications, 1989–91.

———. *The Seventy's Course in Theology*. 5 vols. Salt Lake City: Deseret News, 1907–12.

———. "The Standard of Peace." In *World Fellowship: Addresses and Messages by Leading Spokesmen of all Faiths Races and Countries*, edited by Charles Frederick Weller, 871–79. New York: Liveright Publishing, 1935.

———. *Studies of the Book of Mormon*. Edited by Brigham D. Madsen. Urbana: University of Illinois Press, 1985. 2nd edition Salt Lake City: Signature Books, 1992.

———. "To the Youth of Israel." *Contributor*, May 1885, 295–99.

———. *The Truth, The Way, The Life, an Elementary Treatise on Theology: The Masterwork of B. H. Roberts*. Edited by Stan Larson. San Francisco: Smith Research Associates, 1994.

———. *The Truth, The Way, The Life: An Elementary Treatise on Theology*. Edited by John W. Welch. Provo: *BYU Studies*, 1994. Revised and expanded, 1996.

Roberts, Richard C. *A History of the B. H. Roberts Family*. Salt Lake City: Eborn Books, 2009.

———. *Legacy: The History of the Utah National Guard.* Salt Lake City: National Guard Association of Utah, 2003.

———. An Oral History. Interview by Sydnee Gale, Mar. 5, 1971. Oral History Program, University Archives, Stewart Library, Weber State University.

———. "The Utah National Guard in the Great War, 1917–18. *Utah Historical Quarterly* 58, no. 4 (Fall 1990): 312–33.

Robison, Willis E. Journals, 1882–84. MSS 1591, BYU.

Roderick, Judith Ann. "A Historical Study of the Congressional Career of John T. Caine." Master's thesis, Brigham Young University, 1959.

Roskelley, James. Collection, 1856–1919. MS 7390, CHL.

Royal Commission on Labor. *Digest of the Evidence taken Before Group B of the Royal Commission of Labour*. London: Her Majesty's Stationery Office, 1892.

———. *Minutes of Evidence with Appendices Taken before Group B, Agricultural, Docks, Wharves and Shipping*. London: Her Majesty's Stationery Office, 1892.

Russell, Geneva Bean. "Biography of Leo Albert Bean." Copy in author's possession.

Russell, Isaac. Papers, 1898–1927. M444, Special Collections, Stanford University Libraries.

Russell, William D. "King James Strang: Joseph Smith's Successor." In Sillito and Staker, *Mormon Mavericks*, 131–58.

Salt Lake Ministerial Association. *Shall The American Congress Endorse Polygamy?* Salt Lake City: The Association, 1899.

Schofield, Nephi Young. "The American Institute of Phrenology." *Phrenological Journal and Science of Health* 103, no. 3 (Mar. 1897): 144.

———. Autobiographical Reminiscence. Typescript, online at www.familysearch.org.

———. "Phrenological Society and Field Notes." *Phrenological Journal and Science of Health* 103, no. 1 (Jan. 1897): 49.

Schroeder, A. Theodore. "The Mormon Breach of Faith." *Arena* 23 (February 1900): 113–20.

———. Collection, 1845–1901. MS 9391, CHL.

Schroth, Raymond A, S.J. *The Eagle and Brooklyn: A Community Newspaper, 1841–1955.* Westport, CT: Greenwood, 1974.

Seager, Richard Hughes. *The Dawn of Religious Pluralism: Voices From the World's Parliament of Religion, 1893.* LaSalle, IL: Open Court, 1993.

———. *The World's Parliament of Religions: The East/West Encounter, 1893.* Indianapolis: Indiana University Press, 1995.

Seegmiller, Janet Burton. *"Be Kind to the Poor": The Life Story of Robert Taylor Burton.* N.p.: Robert Taylor Burton Family Association, 1988.

Seferovich, Heather M. "History of the LDS Southern States Mission, 1875–1896." Master's thesis, Brigham Young University, 1996.

———. "Hospitality and Hostility: Missionary Work in the American South, 1875–98." In Neilson and Woods, *Go Ye Unto All the World*, 317–40.

Sessions, Gene A. *Biographies and Reminiscences from the James Henry Moyle Collection.* Salt Lake City: n.p., 1974.

———. "Myth, Murder and Mormonism in the South." *South Atlantic Quarterly* 75 (Spring 1976): 212–25.

———. *A View of James Henry Moyle: His Diaries and Letters.* Salt Lake City: n.p., 1974.

Shepard, Helen M. Gould. Papers. MS 1422, New York Historical Society.

Shirts, Kathryn H. "The Role of Susa Young Gates and Leah Dunford Widtsoe in the Development of the Priesthood/Motherhood Model." *Journal of Mormon History* 44, no. 2 (Apr. 2018): 104–39.

Sillito, John R. "'Drawing the Sword of War Against War': B. H. Roberts, World War I, and the Quest for Peace." *Utah Historical Quarterly* 87, no. 2 (Spring 2019): 100–15.

______. "Franklin Spencer Spalding on Mormonism: A Documentary Approach. *Sunstone*, July–Aug. 1979, 33–35.

———. "'The Goliath of Their Cause': The B. H. Roberts and William Jarman Debates in England, 1887–88. *Journal of Mormon History* 43, no. 1 (Jan. 2017): 87–110.

______. "Shaping Mormonism's Public Image and Building the Faith: B. H. Roberts's Mission to the Midwest, 1896." *Journal of Mormon History* 45, no. 1 (Jan. 2019): 53–85.

———, and Martha Bradley. "Franklin Spencer Spalding: An Episcopal Observer of Mormonism." *Historical Magazine of the Protestant Episcopal Church* 54 (Dec. 1985): 339–49.

———, and Susan Staker, eds. *Mormon Mavericks: Essays on Dissenters.* Salt Lake City: Signature Books, 2002.

Smart, William B. *Mormonism's Last Colonizer: The Life and Times of William H. Smart.* Logan: Utah State *University Press,* 2008.

Smart, William Henry. Diaries, 1898–1937. MS 85, CHL.

Smith, Ethan. *View of the Hebrews.* Reprint of the 1825 2nd ed. Provo: Brigham Young University Religious Studies Center, 1996.

Smith, George Albert, Family. Papers, 1731–1969. MS 0036, UU.

Smith, John Henry. *Church, State, and Politics: The Diaries of John Henry Smith.* Edited by Jean Bickmore White. Salt Lake City: Signature Books, 1990.

Smith, Joseph F. Papers, 1854–1918. MS 1325, CHL.

Smith, Hyrum M., III, and Scott G. Kenney. *From Prophet to Son: Advice of Joseph F. Smith to His Missionary Sons.* Salt Lake City: Deseret Book, 1981.

Smith, Konden Rich. "Appropriating the Secular: Mormonism and the World's Columbian Exposition of 1893." *Journal of Mormon History* 34, no. 2 (Fall 2008) 153–80.

———. "Mormons and the World's Fair 1893: A Study of Religious and Cultural Agency." PhD diss., Arizona State University, 2012.

Smoot, Reed. *In The World: The Diaries of Reed Smoot.* Edited by Harvard S. Heath. Salt Lake City: Signature Books, 1997.

Snodgrass, Judith. *Presenting Japanese Buddhism to the West: Orientalism, Occidentalism and the Columbian Exposition.* Chapel Hill: University of North Carolina, 2003.

Snow, Alice Northrup, and Harry Nicholas Snow. *The Story of Helen Gould.* New York: Revell, 1938.

Snow, R. J. "The American Party in Utah: A Study of Political Party Struggles During The Early Years of Statehood." Master's thesis, University of Utah, 1964.

Snow, William. Journal, 1899–1901. MS 27683, CHL.

Sonne, Conway B. *Saints on the Seas: A Maritime History of the Mormon Migration, 1830–1890.* Salt Lake City: University of Utah, 1983.

Southern States Mission. Manuscript History and Historical Reports, 1832–1978. LR 8557 2, CHL.

———. Telegrams, 1884. LR 8557 35, CHL.

Spalding, Franklin S. *Joseph Smith as a Translator*. Salt Lake City: Arrow Press, 1912.

Speek, Vickie Cleverley. *"God Has Made Us a Kingdom": James Strang and the Midwest Mormons*. Salt Lake City: Signature Books, 2006.

Spencer, Samuel G. "Some Reminiscences." In Rudger Clawson, Papers, 1870–1943, box 16, fd. 18, MS 0481, UU.

Stauffer, Kenneth G. "Utah Politics, 1912–1918." Master's thesis, University of Utah, 1972.

St. Louis Branch. Minutes, 1896–1910. LR 7783 25, CHL.

Stephan, Eric George. "B. H. Roberts: A Rhetorical Study." PhD diss., University of Utah, 1966.

Stewart, James G. Memorandum, 1885. M544, Western History Collection, Denver Public Library.

Stone, Daniel P. *William Bickerton: Forgotten Latter Day Prophet*. Salt Lake City: Signature Books, 2018.

Stovall, Mary E. "Orthodoxy Vs. Conformity: The Mormon Experience in Tennessee and Mississippi, 1875–1905." History 747, Seminar Paper. University of Chicago, 1976.

Stuy, Brian H. *Collected Discourses*. 5 vols. Burbank, CA: BHS Publishers, 1987–92.

Sweeney, Michael S. "Julius F. Taylor and the Broad Ax of Salt Lake City." *Utah Historical Quarterly* 77, no. 3 (Summer 2009): 204–21.

Tanner, Nathan Jr. Diaries, 1884–1886. MS 1664, CHL.

Tanner, Nathan C. Collection, 1853–2008. MS 23785, CHL.

Taylor, Elton J. *As I Remember: Events in My Life*. Provo: n.p., 1984.

———. Oral History. Interviewed by Sandra Skousen. Orem Utah, Lake View Stake Oral History Program. MS 2735 #421, 1981, CHL

———. Papers, ca. 1920s–ca. 1970s. ACCN 1360, UU

Taylor, Henry D. *Autobiography of Henry Dixon Taylor*. Provo: BYU Press, 1980.

———. Correspondence, 1925–27. MS 6814, CHL.

Taylor, John. Collection, 1829–94. MS 1346, CHL.

Taylor, Levi J. Papers, 1868–1935. MSS 2200, BYU.

Taylor, P.A.M. *Expectations Westward: The Mormons and The Emigration of Their British Converts in the 19th Century*. Edinburgh and London: Oliver & Boyd, 1965.

Teasdale, George. Papers, 1770–1984. MS 678, UU.

———. Papers, 1853–1906. MS 13496, CHL.

Thatcher, Linda. "Ruth May Fox: Forgotten Suffragist." *Utah Historical Quarterly* 49, no. 3 (Summer 1981): 239–53.

Thompson, Harold M. "An Account of the Gibbs and Berry Massacre, Or The Tennessee Massacre." Copy in author's possession.

Tiffany, Scott D. "B. H. Roberts: Father of Modern Missionary Work." *New York LDS Historian* 4 (Spring 2001): 13.

———, ed. *City Saints: Mormons in the New York Metropolis*. New York: New York Stake LDS History committee, 2004.

———. "Manhattan and the Mormons, 1890–1933." *New York LDS Historian* 4 (Spring 2001): 1–2, 15–16.

Trustee In Trust. Tennessee Martyrs Fund Donations, 1884. CR 5 28, CHL.

Tuchman, Barbara W. *The Guns of August: The Outbreak of World War I*. New York: Random House, 1962.

US Congress. *Congressional Record*. 55th Cong., 1st sess., 1899–1900. Vol. 33. Washington, DC: Government Printing Office, 1900.

———. *Report of the Special Committee on the Case of B. H. Roberts*. H.R. 85, to accompany H.R. 107, 56th Cong., 1st sess., part 2. Washington, D.C., Government Printing Office, 1900.

US House of Representatives. *A History and Legal Digest of all the Contested Elections in the House of Representatives of the United States from the First to the 56th Congress, 1789–1901*. Washington: Government Printing Office, 1901.

US Senate, Committee on Privileges and Elections. *Proceedings before the Committee on Privileges and Elections of the United States Senate: In the Matter of the Protests Against the Right of Hon. Reed Smoot, a Senator from the State of Utah, to Hold His Seat*. 4 vols. Washington: Government Printing Office, 1904–06.

Utah Commission. Election Returns Register. Series 396, Utah State Archives.

———. Minute Book G. Series 1126, Utah State Archives.

———. *Report of the Utah Commission to the Secretary of Interior, 1895.* Washington: Government Printing Office, 1895.

Van Orden, Bruce A. *Prisoner For Conscience Sake: The Life of George Reynolds*. Salt Lake City: Deseret Book, 1992.

Van Wagonen, Lola. *Sister Wives and Suffragists: Polygamy and the Politics of Woman Suffrage, 1870–1896.* Provo: BYU Studies, 2003.

Van Wagoner, Richard S., and Mary Van Wagoner. "Arthur Pratt: Utah Lawman." *Utah Historical Quarterly* 55, no. 1 (Winter 1987): 22–35.

Volker, Jacob A. "The Kaysville Cooperative Mercantile Institution." Senior history project, Weber State University, 2012.

Young, Ann Eliza Webb. *Wife Number 19: Or the Story of a Life in Bondage, Being a Complete Expose of Mormonism, and Revealing the Sorrows, Sacrifices and Sufferings of Women in Polygamy*. Hartford: Dustin, Gilman, 1875.

Walker, Don D. "The Taft Victory in Utah in 1912." *Utah Historical Quarterly* 32, no. 2 (Spring, 1964): 44–56.

Walker, Kyle R. *William B. Smith: In the Shadow of a Prophet*. Salt Lake City: Greg Kofford Books, 2015.

———. "William B. Smith and 'The Josephites.'" *Journal of Mormon History* 40, no. 4 (Fall 2014): 73–129.

Walker, Ronald W. "B. H. Roberts and the Woodruff Manifesto." *BYU Studies* 22, no. 3 (1982): 363–66.

———. "A Mormon 'Widow' in Colorado: The Exile of Emily Wells Grant." *BYU Studies* 43, no. 1 (2004): 175–93.

———., Richard E. Turley Jr., and Glen M. Leonard. *Massacre at Mountain Meadows*. Oxford University Press, 2008.

Welling, Milton Holmes. Papers, 1910–1920. ACCN 2302, UU.

Wells, Emmeline B. Diaries. MSS 510, BYU. Transcripts available under MSS 1407, BYU.

Whitaker, John Mills. Papers, 1847–1963. MS 0002, UU.

———. Papers, ca. 1884–1927. MS 2777, CHL.

White, Jean Bickmore. *Charter for Statehood: The Story of Utah's State Constitution*. Salt Lake City: University of Utah Press, 1996.

———. "Utah State Elections, 1895–1899." PhD diss., University of Utah, 1968.

———. "Woman's Place is in the Constitution: The Struggle for Equal Rights in Utah in 1895." *Utah Historical Quarterly* 42, no. 4 (Fall 1974): 344–69.

White, Richard. *The Republic for Which It Stands: The United States during Reconstruction and the Gilded Age, 1865–1896.* New York: Oxford University Press, 2017.

White, William Griffin, Jr., "The Feminist Campaign for the Exclusion of Brigham Henry Roberts from the Fifty-Sixth Congress." *Journal of the West* 17 (Jan. 1978): 45–52.

Whitney, Orson F. *Speeches of Hon. O. F. Whitney In Support of Woman Suffrage Delivered in the Constitutional Convention of Utah, March 30th, April 2nd and April 5th 1895.* Salt Lake City: Utah Woman Suffrage Association, 1895.

Widtsoe Family. Papers, 1824–1953. MS 5417, CHL.

———. Papers, 1866–1966. MSS B 92, UDSH.

Wilcox, James H. Journals, 1897–1936. MS 22772, CHL.

Wingfield, Marshall. "Tennessee's Mormon Massacre." *Tennessee Historical Quarterly* 17 (1958): 19–36.

Woodruff, Wilford. *Waiting For World's End: The Diaries of Wilford Woodruff.* Edited by Susan Staker. Salt Lake City: Signature Books, 1993.

Woodruff, Wilford. *Wilford Woodruff's Journals.* Edited by Scott G. Kenney. 9 vols. Midvale, UT: Signature Books, 1983–85.

Yorgason, Ethan R. *Transformation of the Mormon Culture Region.* Urbana: University of Illinois Press, 2003.

Young, Brenda Dustin. *Seth Dustin: Mormon Pioneer—Man of God.* Meridian, ID: B. D. Young, 2010.

Young, Seymour B. Papers, 1857–1924. MS 1345, CHL.

INDEX

C

N

S

ABOUT THE AUTHOR

John Sillito is professor emeritus at Weber State University (Ogden, UT). He earned bachelor's and master's degrees in history at the University of Utah. His edited collection, *History's Apprentice: The Diaries of B.H. Roberts, 1880–1898*, won the Mormon History Association's best documentary book award in 2005. He is the co-author of *A History of Utah Radicalism: Startling Socialistic and Decidedly Revolutionary*, and co-edited *Letters from Exile: The Correspondence of Martha Hughes Cannon and Angus M. Cannon, 1886–1888.*